THE FASHIONING OF ANGELS

THE FASHIONING OF ANGELS

PARTNERSHIP AS SPIRITUAL PRACTICE

STEPHEN LARSEN AND ROBIN LARSEN

Chrysalis Books

West Chester, Pennsylvania

Library of Congress Cataloging-in-Publication Data
Larsen, Robin.
The fashioning of angels : partnership as spiritual practice / Robin Larsen, Stephen Larsen.
p.   cm.
Includes bibliographical references and index.
ISBN 0–87785–390–8
1. Spiritual life. 2. Interpersonal relations—Religious aspects. 3. Man–woman relationships—Religious aspects.
I. Larsen, Stephen. II. Title
BL626.33. L37 2000
158.2–dc21   99–087311

Edited by Mary Lou Bertucci
Cover design by Caroline Kline
Interior design by OX + Company, Haddonfield, New Jersey
Set in Goudy by Sans Serif, Inc., Saline, Michigan
Printed in the United States of America.

Acknowledgments
"Questions about Angels," page xiv, from *Questions About Angels* by
Billy Collins, ©1991. Reprinted by permission of the University of Pittsburgh Press.
"Magic Words," page 29, from *Magic Words*, copyright © 1968, 1967
by Edward Field. Reprinted by permission of Harcourt, Inc.
"Come into Animal Presence," page 37, by Denise Levertov, from *Poems 1960–1967*,
copyright ©1961 by Denise Levertov. Reprinted by permission of New Directions Publishing Corp.
"On the Other Side," page 53, from *The Collected Poems, 1931–1987* by Czeslaw Milosz and
translated by Robert Haas. Copyright © 1988 by Czeslaw Milosz Royalties, Inc.
Reprinted by permission of HarperCollins Publishers, Inc.
Excerpts from poetry of Ramprasad, pages 174 and 175, from Lex Hixon, *Mother of the Universe:
Visions of the Goddess and Tantric Hymns of Enlightenment* (Wheaton, Ill.: Quest Books, 1994).
Reprinted by permission of the Theosophical Publishing House.
Material from recordings of Joseph Campbell's lectures, used throughout chapter nine,
courtesy of the Joseph Campbell Foundation, San Anselmo, California (www.jcf.org).

Chrysalis Books is an imprint of the Swedenborg Foundation, Inc. For more information, contact:
Chrysalis Books
Swedenborg Foundation Publishers
320 N. Church Street
West Chester, Pennsylvania 19380
(610) 430-3222
Or
http://www.swedenborg.com

CONTENTS

Part Two

LITTLE PEOPLE, GHOSTS, AND DAEMONS

Contents

Contents

ILLUSTRATIONS

Cover illustration: Edward Burne-Jones, *The Days of Creation: The Sixth Day.* Courtesy of the Fogg Art Museum, Harvard University Art Museums, Bequest of Grenville L. Winthrop. Photo Credit: Rick Stafford. Image Copyright: ©President and Fellows of Harvard College, Harvard University.

Chapter 1: "*Anima Mundi.*" Alchemical image by M. Merian (from Robert Fludd, *Utriusque Cosmi Historiam* . . . , Oppenheim, 1610). Soul of the world connecting natural to divine through the terrestrial and celestial spheres.

Chapter 2: The Lady of the Beasts. ©1995 by Hrana Janto. Reproduced by permission of artist. The paleolithic mother of "all our relations."

Chapter 3: Psyche and her sisters. Jean de Bosschère, 1923 (Apuleius, *Golden Ass,* William Adlington trans. (16c), London: John Lane, The Bodley Head, Ltd., 1923. From the collection of Robin and Stephen Larsen.

Chapter 4: The Nixie of the Millpond. H. F. Ford, 1894 (Andrew Lang, *The Yellow Fairy Book* [New York: Dover, 1894, 1966]). The *anima* often appears as a numinous sprite or nixie; her imagery includes seduction and allurement, but she connects us with the watery abyss of the psyche.

Chapter 5: Vision of the Empyrean. (Paul) Gustave Doré (illustration for Dante's *Divine Comedy, Paradiso,* 1861). Dante and Beatrice behold the celestial mandala of union.

Chapter 6: Deliver Us from Evil. John Flaxman, relief plaque. Property of Glencairn Museum, Academy of the New Church, Bryn Athyn, Pennsylvania. Photo credit: Robin Larsen. Angelodaemonic and daemongelic energies struggle for the soul.

Chapter 7: Lha-Mo, fierce black goddess of Tibet. Photo credit: Robin Larsen. In Mani Rimdu, Sherpa Buddhist masked dance *(Cham)* performed by *lhamas* at Thami Monastery, Solo Khumbu, Nepal, May 1976. Across a spectrum of world religions, "demonic" figures are often transmuted into defenders of the faith, like these "Eight Terrible Ones."

Chapter 8: Knights in combat. Howard Pyle, *The Story of King Arthur and His Knights,* 1903. Knights meet in combat, while Merlin, the Wisdom Principle, looks on.

Chapter 9: Sir Gawain meets another beautiful lady. Howard Pyle, *The Story of King Arthur and His Knights,* 1903.

Chapter 10: Kissing.©1983 by Alex Gray. Reprinted by permission of artist.

Epilogue: Shiva Ardhanari. Shiva and Parvati in divine union. Shrine in sculpted relief, Elephanta Cave Temple, Bombay harbor, India. Photo by Stephen and Robin Larsen, 1976.

Appendix: Portal: Alembic I. Personal shrine. Assemblage, Robin Larsen, 1984.

FOREWORD

Jean Houston

In Plato's *Symposium*, Aristophanes, the most comic of the participants, tells the most tragic of tales. He says that human beings originally consisted of two persons in one body, with two heads and four arms and legs.

These beings were shaped like a ball, and, in their completeness and satisfaction, they rolled along in ecstasy, ready and able to do almost anything. The Titans, fearful of the enormous power available to these extraordinary double beings, forced Zeus to split them in half, thus diminishing both their powers and their happiness. It is said that we spend our lives yearning to find our other half.

This tragic-comic tale shows the twinned but divided self to be a major source of the sorrow and the yearning that haunts the human condition. The yearning, however, is also the impetus that drives us in our journey toward wholeness.

In this profound and original book, Stephen and Robin Larsen describe a new natural philosophy based on loving partnership as the creative force of evolution. Their own marriage of over thirty-five years has been exemplary of the hope that is held in Plato's allegory: two souls who have rediscovered each other and, through hard work, much searching, and rich intimacy, have created enterprises of mind and spirit as potent as they are therapeutic. Together, they have taken depth soundings of culture and consciousness, established a center for symbolic studies, written books, created art works, treated patients, taught college, traveled widely, and mentored many. They have not bored God! In fact, they have done what Swedenborg said was possible: the fashioning of an angel out of two lovers in consonance. And this particular Angel, Robin-Stephen, pours forth intellectual and spiritual matter that expands the horizon of the possible as it extends the boundary of the heart.

In their intense conversations, we see that these are beloveds who have struck gold in each other's soul. With their great friend Joseph Campbell as catalyst and Emanuel Swedenborg as principal guide, Carl Jung as provocateur and Rainer Maria Rilke as poetic muse, they explore the vast terrain of partnership, creating in the process new maps of the psyche, a cosmology that includes all our relations and relationships in both the visible and the invisible worlds. They show how the evolutionary lure of becoming finds renewed expression in the rising archetype of the Beloved of the Soul. Whether it be numinous borderline persons or the family dog, the folk of the air or the man on the street, the Beloved is always the potential of any relationship.

The great desire for the Beloved of the Soul, while always present, moves to the foreground when civilizations undergo whole-system transitions. Such eras are also marked by the rise of mystery religions, with their emphasis on dramatic inward journeys and the ecstasy of union with the archetypal Beloved, which provide people with a sense of a deeper identity and belonging. Thus, we find the rise of the Egyptian and Eleusinian mysteries in ancient times, as well as the great rituals of the sacred marriage in Sumer, and the rise of spiritualism, theosophy, and secret societies coinciding with the Industrial Revolution.

Today, we are undergoing a profound transition, moving from a cosmopolitan to a planetary culture. We are attending a wake for ways of being that have been ours for hundreds, even thousands of years. At the same time, our cultures, beliefs, and practices intertwine one with the other. Increasingly, I sense a new cultural music coming into time. A welter of multiple meters and offbeat phrasing, it is a coding of creativity and imagination, a counterpoint of styles of knowing and being. As cultures come together and exchange their essences, they join in a cadence of awakening through partnership, a new idiom of consciousness and connection that is exhilarating and revolutionary. This rhythm carries us from the ballads of local concerns to the concerto of a larger ecology of being. Thus, we are experiencing a revolution in relationships between men and women. We are revising our notions of family and community. Through the Internet and other technologies, the World Mind is taking a walk with itself. We are living in times in which it appears that the world is trying to coalesce into a new and higher unity for which we are unprepared.

The Larsens would say that the only preparatory force that is emotionally powerful enough to call us to reeducate ourselves for sacred stewardship is communion and partnership with the Beloved. It is an impetus to all our evolutionary striving. Its basis in the human soul is very deep, for it is the memory of a union that fails to go away, a union that can only be partially explained and mirrored through human loving or partnership. Consider the transformative power of earthly love, which can and does evoke in us the divine response: unconditional acceptance and forgiveness, deep and unspoken communion and communication, the ecstasies of Eros and the fires of union, a wavetide of giving and receiving so abundant that it seems drawn from the very ocean of abundance itself, the living together of all life's dramas. Taken seriously, spiritual partnership hones us into our many-dimensional selves, rich in stories, loved and loving, in transit from where who we are to who we are becoming—which is why the Larsens give so much expression to the mythic basis of partnership with the beloved. Myths themselves are cosmic codings as well as the DNA of the human psyche, the source patterns originating in the ground of our being. They offer us patterns to instruct us, warn us, and lure us onto a greater journey. They are mysterious agents that never were in time and space but, nevertheless, are always happening to give us the key to our personal and historical existence.

My own work, like that of Stephen and Robin Larsen, has shown that myths are modules of collective intelligence, open-ended blueprints of the journey that is ours. Whereas most creatures come in hardwired with instincts that guide their life stages, we arrive with nothing like their instinctual advantages, but have to keep on a strenuous learning curve to make it through life's many mazes. Over many years, I have guided thousands of research subjects and seminar participants into their own inner space and listened as they described what they found there: adventures of the soul so grand, so mythic, and yet so filled with universal themes, that I can readily testify to the existence of a collective pool of myth and archetype residing in each human being as part of their natural equipment. It would seem that myth and archetype hold a kind of meta-instinctual code, giving us guidance and impetus as they illumine our transitions.

In the great myths of love and loss, such as Isis and Osiris, Psyche and Eros, Tristan and Isolde, we learn about the pathos and passion that perpetually confounds and regenerates the relationship between the sexes. In the life story of the Persian mystic and teacher Jalaluddin Rumi, we explore the exquisite rapture that comes of awareness of the divinity within another. The Christ story teaches us to love our neighbor as ourselves, while Buddha's deeds show us compassion as the highest expression of human relationship.

When we come to appreciate the forms of these stories of love and partnership—or better still, as in the Larsen's work and their ritual-creating counterparts in indigenous cultures, when we enact them outwardly in song, drama, and active process or in inward imaginal spaces as the reader is invited to do—we begin to look at ourselves and at others in ways that exceed our local knowings, our limited history. Having assumed the ancient stories and their persona, having walked in the shoes of folk who lived at their edges, we inherit a cache of experience that illumines and fortifies our own. This book is a veritable cornucopia of such tellings and shows us how the mysteries of love and partnership can bring forth the fashioning of angels.

There is a delightful story, said to be true, about an unexpected glory that such partnership produces. A young man in northern India went on retreat with a master of Bhakti yoga (the yoga of love and devotion). The master told the young man to go into a secluded room and just think about love for a while.

After a few minutes, the young man came out and sheepishly told the master that he couldn't concentrate because he was worrying about the precious little bull he was raising and for whom he cared so much. The master told him that his concern was wonderful, for it had brought him an object of meditation.

"Go back in the room and meditate on how much you love your little bull," said the master.

The young man did as he was told. Hours went by, and the young man did not emerge from the room. A whole day and night passed, and still he stayed there. After another day and night had elapsed, the master peeked into the room and saw the young man sitting there, lost in meditation, a beatific smile on his face.

"Why don't you come out and have something to eat," he inquired.

"Oh, I cannot, Master," said the young man, beaming with happiness. "My horns are too large to fit through the door."

Of all the questions you might want to ask
about angels, the only one you ever hear
is how many can dance on the head of a pin.

No curiosity about how they pass the eternal time
besides circling the Throne chanting in Latin
or delivering a crust of bread to a hermit on earth
or guiding a boy and girl across a rickety wooden bridge.

Do they fly through God's body and come out singing?
Do they swing like children from the hinges
of the spirit world saying their names backwards and forwards
Do they sit alone in little gardens changing colors?

What about their sleeping habits, the fabric of their robes,
their diet of unfiltered divine light?
What goes on inside their luminous heads? Is there a wall
these tall presences can look over and see hell?

If an angel fell off a cloud would he leave a hole
in a river and would the hole float along endlessly
filled with the silent letters of every angelic word?

If an angel delivered the mail would he arrive
in a blinding rush of wings or would he just assume
the appearance of the regular mailman and
whistle up the driveway reading the postcards?

No, the medieval theologians control the court.
The only question you ever hear is about
the little dance floor on the head of a pin
where halos are meant to converge and drift invisibly.

It is designed to make us think in millions,
billions, to make us run out of numbers and collapse
into infinity, but perhaps the answer is simply one:
one female angel dancing alone in her stocking feet,
a small jazz combo working in the background.

She sways like a branch in the wind, her beautiful
eyes closed, and the tall thin bassist leans over
to glance at his watch because she has been dancing
forever, and now it is very late, even for musicians.

Billy Collins, *"Questions about Angels"*[1]

SWEDENBORG'S ANGEL

To undertake this book together in the thirty-fifth year of our own relationship would seem to have symbolic implications. We realized that we have spent the great majority of our mature lives together and must have learned something in the process; however, we are also appalled at what we have yet to learn and are painfully aware that in this field, perhaps above all others, there are no simple answers. What a perfect project, full of insoluble paradoxes. It is perhaps all too much like those koans that the Zen masters lay on their disciples—to evoke their awakened minds or to drive them mad in the process.

We knew that such a project could put a couple to the test indeed. Writing about complex and volatile things could "sow the storm," as a professional couple, friends of ours writing just such a book, found out. As they researched the mythologies of gender misunderstandings and spousal abuse, they were forced to confront the same elements in their own relationship. The strife intensified, and their marriage fell apart. After all, the gods and goddesses are as famous for their enmities as for their divine affiliations.

As a loving couple in our fifties, we were, our friends told us, "an endangered species," skating on the culturally thin ice of a world in transition. Families and styles of relationship seem in the current world to be changing at an unprecedented rate, and we know that not only a century but a millennium is about to end. "Things fall apart," said the poet Yeats, in *The Second Coming*, one of the most quoted apocalyptic poems of our time, "the center cannot hold. . ."

We are both fairly complex people, and quite different from each other. Sometimes we would joke—in the later, more reflective stages that follow our arguments—that we had just enacted the Civil War (Robin is from South Carolina, Stephen from New York). And the history books tell us that Vikings (Stephen is of Norwegian background) and Celts (Robin is Welsh and Irish) didn't always get along—though they do produce beautiful children. Traveling together in Ireland and seeing the ubiquitous tall stone towers, Stephen had an insight:

"Didn't my ancestors used to chase your ancestors up into those things?"

"Yes," said Robin, "and we poured horrible things down on you as you tried to get in at us!"

Like it or not, we carry our ancestors and our cultures within us.

But as we meditated on our theme, with all its paradoxes, an unquenchable excitement began to build. This is the piece of work for our time! Our world is so divided, fragmented, wounded—precisely by the kind of divisions we encounter in our own relationship, our own biological and cultural genealogies, our own version of the gender wars. If we can bring these antipathies, these opposites, together in love, we are accomplishing a major healing work for our time, our culture, and our world. Isn't this the reason, we thought (thinking mythologically), why the love story is central to all our dramas? Novels and movies alike resolve adventures, ordeals, estrangements by what the hermeticists and the medieval alchemists called the *hieros gamos*, the sacred marriage. The loving and finally united couple walk, in full symbolic splendor, into the sunset, beneath the rainbow, or into the fairytale castle or the cottage with the white picket fence, the eternal setting in which their love will flourish eternally. Our exile from paradise ends in homecoming at last.

Human beings do not reproduce by loving ourselves—that is, by biological self-fertilization—but by making love to another. Nor, it seems, is it good for us to mate with our closest kin. Our mate should be someone from a different gene pool—along with which come, perforce, the very differences we encountered in our own relationship. We carry on the species by mating with someone sufficiently different on the biological level, but along with the "deal" come social, psychological, and even spiritual differences. "As above, so below," said the alchemists. We grow as a species, emotionally and psychologically, by uniting in love that which originally was unrelated. It is never easy, but it can be extraordinarily rewarding, to bring together differences in love.

Stephen has been a practicing psychotherapist for thirty years and brings to this book an appraisal of the extraordinary painfulness that can arise around family problems: abuses, verbal, physical, and sexual; addictions and compulsions; conflict and estrangement. Robin, as a director of programs for youth, regularly works with adolescents wounded in parental crossfire. We have co-led many workshops for couples, facilitating their working-through of conflicts using dreams and "personal mythology" techniques. Both of us were students of the eminent mythologist Joseph Campbell, and he imbued us with respect for the wisdom of the species embedded among the world's mythologies. When gods and goddesses relate—or fail to relate— they do it divinely or grandly. It is clear that their stories magnify and underline the human condition.

Wherever possible, in the chapters that follow, we have inserted a myth, folk or fairytale to emphasize the issue we are addressing. Not only are they often wiser than the academic studies, but such "materials," as Campbell called them, nestle more easily into the mind and lodge more comfortably in the soul, helping you, the reader, both understand and remember them. Joseph always emphasized that relationship of any kind, especially marriage between two creative individuals, is "hard work." But he also added that it is the most rewarding kind of soul-work, and its challenges and rewards lead us to the pinnacle of human evolution. We therefore make frequent reference to Campbell's ideas and to his wonderful interpretations of love stories down through the ages. Further, with the unique perspective bestowed on us as his authorized biographers, we are able to make observations on how well Campbell did at that "hard work," trying to live out the principles that he taught.[2]

Researching mythologies for love stories can be a fascinating endeavor, and indeed every major mythology captures some important dimension of the love story: Isis and Osiris, Innanna and Dumuzi, Krishna and Radha on the divine side; Antony and Cleopatra, Paolo and Francesca, Romeo and Juliet on the human—or those remarkable unions of divine with human epitomized in the fable of Eros and Psyche found in Apuleius' *The Golden Ass*, or Zeus's longing for Leda or Semele. Each of these myths offers commentary on psychological and social levels: the delights and horrors of incest, the obsession of love, the love rescue. The love of gods and goddesses for humans is "eternity in love with the productions of time," as Campbell used to say, as is the inverse, the always ecstatic, but not infrequently fatal love of human for divine beings, humans with immortal longings. This is a subject to which we devote some time.

There is a popular literature emerging, certainly in America, but also in the rest of the world, that looks to ancient wisdom—the realm of mythology—to solve the riddles of everyday life. The best of these approaches open myths delicately, like a flower, attending to the intricate complexity and details of the inner parts and respectful of nature's design. The worst approach pries nature open roughly, as if merely to find something to justify what one thinks already—ethologists who use crude anthropomorphism or mechanistic metaphor to understand biology, or eighteenth century ethnographers who scorned and patronized the very cultures they were investigating. (There are reductive psychological approaches that treat the myth as illustrative of this-or-that infantile drama, or, read sociologically, as merely a demonstration of male dominance or the gender wars.) These approaches seem to understand that myths contain wisdom but assume naïvely that they know better than the myths themselves. Kerényi says of science that "explained the drink in the cup to us so well that we knew all about it beforehand, far better than the good old drinkers,"[3] and he asks if any authentic enjoyment of mythology is still possible, given this reductionism.

Joseph Campbell, more than any other scholar of the twentieth century, always insisted that you had to train a mind in the art of paradox to read a multiform, polyvalent image, bursting redundantly with meaning. One should also be attentive to one's own states and feelings while "opening" the myth, because the symbolic dimension tickles, moves, and sometimes vexes us within.[4] Mythological fundamentalism is always a danger, and the type of fanaticism that is particularly perilous is monotheistic; and here we are not talking merely about Islamic holy wars and Moral Majority intolerance of diversity—although those certainly wreak their share of world mischief. There are subtler dogmas that emerge unnoticed from our secret fears and desires, our paranoias and cynicisms: the world is a pretty bleak place; people are out to get you; the universe is random, chaotic and uncaring (the scientific fundamentalism). Most important, Campbell said, for anyone who ventures into the understanding of mythology—or religion—is to not get attached to simplistic or unidimensional representations of ultimate meaning. The transcendent source of all meaning itself is beyond all categories of meaning: "the tongue has not soiled it" in the elegant Sanskritic rendition; or "the Tao that can be spoken of is not the Tao," in Lao Tzu's words.

When we bring up myths in the chapters that follow, then, and bask in their wisdom, we hope the reader will join us in treating myths as any skilled analyst treats a dream—to open delicately its subtle layers of wisdom, an exquisite, living, piece of nature; leave yourself open to reflect on the stories and go beyond the interpretations we are choosing to work with in the book. They are only our linear models that come to us as we work with the themes that emerge in our study. Make no mistake: The stories do contain powerful messages, sometimes even polemical ones; but the mindfulness that such contemplation invites is a holistic process, as the hologram embedded in the myth touches your holographic mind.

Campbell and the myths clued us to the spiritual dimension of the partner relationship, but we were still looking for one central metaphor through which to develop a model for spiritual partnership in our time. Then we remembered Swedenborg's angel.

Emanuel Swedenborg was an eighteenth-century Swedish nobleman and public servant who sat on the Swedish Board of Mines for many years. His scientific and technical knowledge was vast, and he published many technical papers on physics, astronomy, chemistry, metallurgy, anatomy, and psychology. After a spiritual crisis at the age of fifty-five, Swedenborg directed his attention entirely to spiritual matters, turning out many volumes based on revelations that came to him in a visionary meditative state and also while reading and contemplating the scriptures. Swedenborg should be credited with the development of the first "transpersonal" or spiritually based psychology. Though he remained a bachelor to the end of his days, Swedenborg also had some profound insights into the nature of human relationship, especially a spiritual psychology of relationship, which he outlined in his book *Conjugial Love*.

The idea is as follows: a human man and woman are intended, by the divine principle in the universe, to find, come together, and to complement each other. All human beings are, for Swedenborg, recipients of a divine influx that divides into two streams of vital energy he calls "goodness" and "truth": goodness or divine love flows into the human will or receptacle of love; truth, into the understanding or intellectual mind. Women and men are differently disposed in their reception of this *influx*. Women receive into and manifest love from their external self, while their internal receives truth, which becomes a kind of deep inner wisdom. Men are complementary, showing understanding or intellectual orientation externally but holding a deep affection within. His loving interior and wise exterior match her wise interior and loving exterior. When the dynamisms are interlaced in harmony, all heaven breaks loose; spiritual and physical natures unite in the couple, and blessings are bestowed on every side. (Mythologically, paradise is regained, and a loving couple stands once again in the garden of delights.)

Swedenborg claimed to witness intimately what happens to human beings in the after-death state. Throughout your life, you may have considered yourself to be only a biological or a social creature; but, in fact, you were a spiritual being all along. Your spirit dwells, unconsciously as it were, in a spiritual dimension at the same time as your physical body moves and exists in the three-dimensional world. When the physical body "falls away," you become entirely spirit. Now, your history of affections, your "bliss-body" becomes like a wind that carries the spirit to destinations in a multitiered dimension. ("Above" and "below" the world of spirits opens into the vastness of the heavens and hells that Swedenborg wrote about in such detail in his work *Heaven and Hell*.)

Each soul now gravitates toward what it loves the most. Lovers, separated at death but now carried on that wind, are reunited. The processes of growing and learning together begun on earth continue in the world of spirits. Swedenborg's model not only peoples heaven with such loving couples, but also offers hope for those who feel that they are still wrestling with their differences, even in the last phase of life. The spirits travel and move together because they choose to be together, and Swedenborg says that to his own spiritually awakened eyes or to those of other spirits, the lovers are perceived as one luminous being, a single being with two aspects. An angel is in the process of being formed, as two natures, originally different, mingle their bodies of desire and bliss. That most fragile, mortal-seeming of things—a human relationship—is in the process of giving birth to an immortal being.

For Swedenborg, heaven and hell are not end destinations to which we are sent by a divine judge; only metaphorically are they "places" in the spiritual "landscape" to which one's own desires carry one. (But our minds are strongly conditioned, as Immanuel Kant first postulated, by the categories of existence in the physical world.) "Places" are really more like spiritual "conditions." Those who enjoy sharing love with others affiliate—with the immediate valency of spiritual dynamics—with others of like mind. Heavenly "communities" are formed by those whose main business is love. But most importantly for those still living earthly lives, we are preparing for that outcome at this very moment by, as Campbell said, "following our bliss." We are in heaven or hell right now, but our attention, as consciousness psychologists have suggested, inclines us to focus on the "three-dimensional world"—the one materialists seem to feel is the only one there is.

Swedenborg's idea is exciting for many reasons. On the mythical level, it offers an exquisite resolution to what we will refer to as "the great dissociation"—our original fall from harmony with the divine oneness—and the beginning of our internal splitting. It is there in the story in Plato's *Symposium* (told by Jean Houston in her foreword) and in the famous biblical story of the expulsion from the garden (as well as other versions explored in this book).

Swedenborg's account of the fashioning of an angel details both the joys and the complexities of the bringing together of the halves. It is a process both physically and psychologically challenging but, in potential, exquisitely rewarding. Unlike the simplistic or romantic love story, with the stroll into the sunset, it is a never-ending story that goes on as love finds new ways of expressing itself and as the couple wrestles with the differences and complexities that seem endlessly to surface from the depths of the human psyche. Another way of saying it is that Swedenborg's account takes up where the stroll into the sunset leaves off!

What is most exciting for those interested in the spiritual dimensions of partnership is that we don't have to "make" our relationships somehow spiritual.

Swedenborg says that they are spiritual by their very nature and from their inception. What we call physical love is just an enjoyable and compelling entrée, arranged by divine providence, to introduce us to an eternity of creative relating, eventuating in the creation of an immortal spiritual being. "Love for many and with many is a natural love," says Swedenborg in *Conjugial Love*, section 48, "for it is in common with beasts and birds, and these are natural; while conjugial love is a spiritual love and peculiar and proper to men, because men were created and are therefore born to become spiritual. For which reason so far as a man becomes spiritual he puts off the love of the sex and puts on conjugial love."[5]

In this book, we will follow this idea closely, finding the physical, emotional, psychological and spiritual intertwined at every level of the human relational process. What is wonderful about Swedenborg's angel is that it is neither a simplistic Disney-World mockup nor a medieval scenario of angels circling the divine throne, chanting in Latin. What he covers in his quaint-sounding term "conjugial" is nothing less than a developmental psychology of spiritual relationship.

Because Swedenborg believed that creation was seamless and symbolically interconnected, he offers a model of a kind of "love ladder" of creation that reaches from the warm, earthy grottoes of animal love to the celestial heights of angel-making. It is a truly Buddhist concept that regards creation holistically, not moralistically. Harsh dualistic judgments delivered against the material reality of vegetative and animal life are bypassed in the service of seeing through the universe as transparent metaphor of itself. A cosmic mirror, it echoes and speaks of itself at every level.[6] That is why the songs of birds and bees may excite the sonnets of Shakespeare. The natural supports the spiritual, which becomes the gateway to the celestial, true mystical immersion in the source and union with the divine beloved. But more than mere support, the natural is the developmental precursor of the spiritual in the same way that crude nutrients and amino acids become complex human neurotransmitters—and ultimately refined human thought.

As a psychotherapist, Stephen has come to believe that, invariably, the most complex psychological and maturational challenges that people meet in their lifetimes are occasioned by relationship problems and crises. (For many men, it is the *only* thing that brings them into therapy and psychological self-examination.) But these experiences also clearly offer the greatest opportunities for spiritual growth that a person can encounter in this lifetime. We start in the clay, in the mire, of our sexual attractions—which may be superficially erotic, improper, pornographic, or even sadomasochistic. We love, Swedenborg said, the many—hence, conflict, choice, pain; or as Campbell often quoted the sequence: "desire—fulfillment—regret!"

Our first intoxication with the real meaning of Swedenborg's angel led us into feeling that we were on the track of the major spiritual development of the twenty-first century and that this was the very piece missing from the spectrum of world spiritual practices. Could an image like this heal the gender wars, heal broken families? Could it help to heal the world?

But we also knew that such exalted mythogems must encounter limitation, human unconsciousness, and inertia. The image seemed at once unattainable and fraught with failure for modern people; where was its dark or shadow side? Couldn't that which blesses also curse? That which heals also wound? What about the dae-monic side of the angelic, so visible in modern life, through marital and sexual abuse, neglect and inertia? We saw that there was a *daemongelic* dynamism as well as an *angelodaemonic*: How is it that some of the best intentions drown in failure and acrimony? (This would be movement in the daemongelic direction.) Or can health be constructed out of the rejected, neglected material of our pathologies? (This would be the angelodaemonic direction, toward spiritual evolution.)

We will return to this provocative and central image of Swedenborg's angel throughout the book. In exploring it, we have come to feel that, if it should prove a luminous-enough image, it would not be diminished by an excursion to the shadow side to see it in full contrast. Thus, our storytelling leads off with myths of alienation and dissociation and moves cautiously toward the light through the shadow lands. Exploring mythic love stories down through the ages, we looked to tragedy and unsuccessful outcomes, which, truth be told, far outnumber the blessed instances. We took stock of the awful modern demographics on divorce, single-par-ent families, and familial violence and abuse of all kinds and found the sober side of our initial excitement. How do you heal a wound as big as the world? (Please note, dear reader, that—so often having no answers—we will merely ask a question. We ask that question not just to invite you to join the fraternity of the perplexed, but to invite you to grapple deeply and meaningfully with the same paradoxes we have faced.) With many of these riddles, the answer may only be answered by individu-als living them out with integrity in their personal lives.

More heartening has been the growing literature of men's and women's movements because it seems that, by better understanding ourselves and our own genders, we can understand the other. In both of these movements, we have seen women and men willing to look at the shadow sides of their own gender identities and still work through the dark places to recover self-esteem and the light of com-passion to shine on others' journeys. Both of us explored individually, whether as participants or leaders of men's and women's retreats—sometimes bringing men and women together at the end of several days of segregated questing for very powerful meetings and integrations. We could discern their degree of empowerment by the ceremony, kindness, and attentiveness shown by each group to the other. When we are truly lodged in our own power, we do not seek dominion, "power-over" as some theorists have called it, but "inner empowerment."

Along the path of researching this book, we have found much cause for hope, as well as the persistence of old bad habits of misunderstanding between our genders. The topic is vast enough to let us know that we are far from having all the answers, and we encourage each of our readers who is in a relationship to take our research and observations to a new level of expression and discovery. We hope that you will learn from us, but reach beyond us to new levels of sublimity in this po-tentially sublime realm. Whether you are in a traditional male/female or some other relationship with an emotionally significant other, we believe the essential principles hold.

Our discussion throughout this book weaves together three topics very alive in the current cultural imagination: angels, spiritual practices, and human re-lationships. We believe the unique virtue of our treatment is the synthesizing and intertwining of these areas. To the somewhat ethereal popular literature on angels, we try to make a start at answering Billy Collins' challenge: what do angels do when they are not occupying two-dimensional silhouettes in the popular mind? What is their history, their genealogy? How might such immortal beings be hatched? Where is the shadow as well as the light in their genesis? What zones of experience have they passed through to make them such faultless guides on the journey through life?

And for people who have thought that the categories of spiritual practice and relationship were mutually irreconcilable pursuits, here is a synthesizing paradigm, one that shows how deeply embedded in the actual is the highest and truest spiritual potential. We feel that, by the time you have read us through and tried some of the exercises at the end of the book—our "couples koans"—you will agree with us that personal relationship, especially that between a man and a woman, provides the most challenging obstacle course in all of the inventories of trials of the soul, but also that, with skillful engagement and attuned learning all the way along the line, it can be converted to a dance floor: graceful encounter superceding effortful grappling.

We felt that this book must itself model, to a certain extent, what we are talking about—how this idiosyncratic couple creates something together, something useful for others. You will find, therefore, many of our own dialogues throughout, as well as those of other people we have interviewed—creative people sharing a life, people who are succeeding in relationship and those who have failed. The dialogues are found at the end of each chapter, with chapter 10 being devoted solely to interviews. Some of our respondents had the graciousness to be identified as themselves, and we are delighted that they will be credited with their own words in our book, so that it is also their book. Others, especially those dealing with very sensitive material or those who felt that it would be otherwise uncomfortable to be identified, have lent us their words and insights, and we will refer to them by a fictitious first name: "Thomas, currently in a separation and probably divorce, shared that he had never enjoyed an actual friendship with his wife." In some cases, Stephen has used stories derived from his psychotherapy practice. Where specific information has been used, he has obtained permission from his clients to "tell their stories." In other cases, a typical or general scenario has been made from a composite of such stories. These instances will usually be indicated in the text: "In a typical situation encountered by many men, Tom felt disempowered by a talented woman. . . ." Ultimately, men and women learn from the experiences of other men and women in the face of their destinies and the twists of fate.

We began to find some of the themes and images that offer to lead to the long road to healing that we are going to share with you herein. So expect lots of storytelling and mythmaking, along with the sociocultural, psychological, and psychotherapeutic observations. All are brought together to empower and embolden you to find a spiritual dimension to your own relationships.

We interviewed many couples on subjects related to relationship, such as the idea of "soul mates," styles of working things through, parallel or joint creative lives. We tried to tap into their wisdom, their love, and found it excited our own. We went pretty deep with some of these, interviewing people who are, we feel, among the most exciting couples of our time: Jungian analysts Barry Ulanov and Anne Belford Ulanov, artists Alex and Allyson Grey, healer Ron Lavin and filmmaker Penny Price, and others. The four-way conversations that unfolded sometimes verged on the visionary, the paradoxical, the hilarious. Angels like angels, and that is why couples like to invite each other over to have a drink, play cards, or whatever. But we ourselves prefer metaphysical pajama parties, or a foursome at a little café right by the cathedral with a bottle of wine. *In vino veritas.* When we live in an open and free space with each other, we can communicate across worlds and gender boundaries, and vex and empower the creative muse.

We hope you will find some of these as exciting as we do. We found as we did these dialogues that they brought up the very stuff they were about—we had to work many issues through and, in wrestling with them, educate ourselves and each other. Ultimately, we found working on this book not only to enhance our communication skills, but to deepen our understanding and love.

If the text is not otherwise marked, it is "our" voice. Where there is a good reason to have a discussion about something or where we have felt the subject invited a man/woman in dialogue, or that the reader might like to hear what each of us has to say on a subject, we set the discussion apart that way, indicating which of us is speaking.

For us, this process has had aspects of a mid-life adventure, spanning the ages of both our innocence and our experience and calling us to quest together, consciously, for some truths about the nature of human relationship. We invite you to join us in the hope that our quest for wisdom might cast helpful light on your own, and we invite you to share the outrageous hope that our deepest obsessions might help illuminate our path to spiritual awakening, and bless and empower our earthly delights.

Part One

ALL MY RELATIONS

Angels are baffled when they hear that there actually are people who ascribe everything to nature and nothing to the Divine, people who believe that their bodies, where so many heavenly marvels are assembled, are just put together out of natural elements. . . .Yet if only they could raise their minds a bit, they would see that things like this are from the Divine, not from nature, that nature was created simply to clothe the spiritual, to act as its correspondent, and to give it presence in the lowest realm of the overall design. Angels compare people like this to Owls, who see in the dark, but not in the light.

Emanuel Swedenborg, *Heaven and Hell* 457

THE WEB OF LIFE

Visualize the great Web of Life: all things living, coexisting, loving, begetting, relating, failing to relate, struggling, fighting, experiencing victory, knowing defeat, dying in one another's arms. From a droplet of water where protozoans slide past and engulf each other, engage in meiosis and mitosis, squirm and wriggle in and out of each other's lives, to the Permian seas where life begets and eats life endlessly, certain life forms emerge to become dominant. But by a quirk of nature or an ingenious design of the divine spirit, no thing may ever become wholly independent of others. "Never imagine," says the old Zulu storyteller, "that the Lion hates the gazelle upon which it springs, oh no, it loves the gazelle." Interdependency is the name of Nature's game. Human beings are the inheritors of this dance, Darwin's dance of survival and dominance, yes, but also the dance of interdependency. The DNA of our genetic material is imprinted with its ancient dramas: love and competition, struggle and union, birth and death.

As our essence forms in our mothers' wombs, we have the experience of unity. "Oceanic unity," Freud called it, floating on the warm, friendly fluids of the Great Mother, nourished, cared for. The transpersonal psychologist Stanislav Grof describes this as "Basic Perinatal Matrix I (BPM I), the "undisturbed intrauterine environment" that symbolic psychologies equate with paradise. Then the birth that is about to happen announces itself—through subtle hormonal messengers, amniotic portents. Something momentous looms! What is it? There is a rumbling, a churning, the discordant notes of the apocalypse. During this second perinatal matrix (BPM II), all anxiety, all paranoia, all intimations of something momentous, good or evil about to break upon us are formed.[1] Then comes perinatal matrix three, the wild volcanic expulsion down the birth canal. Expulsion from the garden is now enacted; primordial union with the mother is lost. Attached to BPM III are all acts of violence, reform, transformation. There is a great eruption and a new condition is obtained—the experience of being born (BPM IV), paradise regained.

Now we are separate, mother and I; we may nestle, nuzzle or nurse, but sometimes we regard each other across an empty space, two "skin-encapsulated egos" as Alan Watts was fond of saying. I scan her face and read her body language to see if she loves me—above all else, this is the important thing! Crucial imprints may occur in the very first few minutes of life; and if the mother is allowed to have eye and body contact with the infant and her attitude is nurturing, they are bonded—and for the most part the new little being will become lively, emotionally healthy, and interactive with other children and adults. Studies show that children deprived of this initial contact, however, may become despondent, self-absorbed, unrelated. During the first months of life, institutionalized children who are fed, sheltered, and diapered, but lack that personal contact, still "fail to thrive"; they are underweight, less strong, poorly coordinated. Sometimes, they die of no apparent cause at all.

When our own daughter Gwyneth was born (twenty-one years before the writing of this book), we knew, on a theoretical but not practical level, how important eye contact was. Robin was in her thirties and had a blood-sugar problem; Gwyneth was full term indeed—nine pounds, eight ounces—and it was hard for her to come out. The labor was in its tenth hour. Our obstetrician had a charming way about him (he too, was exhausted; it was the wee hours): He took Stephen aside and said, "The fetal heartbeat is being affected. You have five minutes to decide if we cut your wife (do a Caesarian section)." It felt like Sophie's choice.[2] As Stephen remembers that time:

> Robin looked very tired; I told her of the decision imminently facing us. As our eyes met, I saw exhaustion in hers, she saw the torture in mine over such a choice. We had already named our child, had talked about her as if she were already born, a knowable, lovable child. "I'm afraid Gwyneth is being hurt," she said. I knew the decision we both had to make, even as I knew Robin's courageous heart. I was not allowed in the operation room itself but was allowed to see them right afterwards. Gwyneth's eyes were wide open, and she met mine, then Robin's. As we sat together in the hospital room, it seemed all we could do was look into each other's eyes. When Gwyneth came home with us, her crib was under a Tibetan guardian mask with tusks and bulging eyes (some might call it daemonic, but when you come to understand its role in the religion, it is seen as an elemental energy in the service of the dharma). From the first, Gwyneth looked directly into the face of the mask as if it were a living person. Totally unafraid, she met those fierce eyes, gurgled and chirped at the mask happily, every day; it became her own guardian spirit, and companion.

Because Gwyneth had received a primary positive imprint, all her other relationships seem to have followed suit; she has wonderful and abundant close friendships. Relationship begins with separation. Once together; now apart. But there must be something of the original oceanic oneness about our relationship— unconditional love that bears all the vicissitudes of life. It is a wonderful and terrible thing, this unconditional love. We can't do without it, but if we get too much of it—at least at the wrong stages—it leads to "spoiling." Jungian analyst Erich Neumann says that, at a certain point in the child's development, separation from the mother and independence must be achieved. If it is not, the loving, nurturing mother now becomes a devouring mother, a dragon of holding-on, that must be slain by the young hero if he is to take the adventure of life.[3]

"Indissociation" from the original oneness is a perilous thing. On the positive side, we are still connected to the Great Mother, and all that lives is "our relation," as the Native Americans say. This is what Stephen has called "mythic identity," the matrix of all mystical experience in the psychological sense. But the negative aspect of this condition is truly terrifying: we fail to distinguish between others and ourselves and act as if "autistic"—or "egocentric" in the Piagetian sense. I may become a terrorist or dictator, and condemn people to death because I don't like them (especially if I am psychologically stuck at perinatal matrix III). I may become paranoid and think they're all after me (matrix II). Or, ultimately, I may believe other people are all really just extensions of myself and have no separate reality (Matrix I). In this way, primordial patterns of relatedness—whether we call them "family drama" in the Freudian sense, find the archetypal "little people" of Jung, or explore their origins in primate behavior—show us our behavioral tendencies. Mythic identity, indissociation, will play a role throughout this book; for a frozen or regressive version of it characterizes all kinds of failures to relate.

Suffice it to say, however, that there is strong evidence, from psychoanalyst Alice Miller and others, that children who were nourished both emotionally and physically during those vulnerable first years do not so readily become the dictators.[4] It is the ones who are neglected and abused who seem to perpetrate infantile tantrums that involve millions and try to drown the world in blood. Thus, dismemberments in the family lead to dismemberments within people and in the body politic and the public theater, where they, in turn, shape the myths that emerge, consciously or unconsciously, and become the dreams of whole cultures.

We begin now with dissociations and myths that address them, both old and emerging ones. These involve gender and our mythologies of both nature and the supernatural. We then peek up and down the ray of creation for answers and for allies, guides, and teachers: the relationship first to nature and animals (our "natural relations"); and next to those bright figures with which we people our metaphoric skies and heavens, the angels of our title, and all the inhabitants of the spirit realms, as we can discern them in glimpses through the portals and by way of those strange "psychic telescopes" we call visionaries. In both of these "vertical domains," however (people "above" the animals, angels and gods "above" humans), the goal is still relationship. We leave for the second and the last parts of the book the horizontal relations, between people, focusing primarily on men and women, and the images and myths that are interwoven around them.

Anima Mundi

CHAPTER ONE

THE
GREAT DISSOCIATION

The old petrifying mother is like a great lizard lounging in the depths of the unconscious. She wants nothing to change. If the feisty ego attempts to accomplish anything, one flash of her tongue disposes of the childish rebel. Her consort, the rigid authoritarian father, passes the laws that maintain her inertia. Together they rule with an iron fist in a velvet glove. Mother becomes Mother Church, Mother Welfare State, Mother University, the beloved Alma Mater, defended by father who becomes Father Hierarchy, Father Law, Father Status Quo. We unconsciously introject the power inherent in these archetypal figures which, in the absence of the individuation process, remain intact at an infantile level. So long as they remain intact, uninterrupted by the consciousness that can disempower them, the inner dictators enslave more cruelly than the outer.

Marion Woodman, *The Ravaged Bridegroom*[1]

DRAGONSLAYING

MANY OF THE WORLD'S COSMOLOGIES and mythic cycles begin with a paradisal condition of unity which is somehow broken, either by human action or that of a god or gods in response to human violations. Sexuality is inevitably mixed in somehow, as is pride, knowing or trying to know too much. In this way begins our human descent, in prolonged process ever since, a kind of free fall into fallibility, with sin, mortality, and sexuality all tangled together in the package.

The biblical version is the main "creation story" people in the West have heard—although there are hundreds of others worldwide. In the famous sequence, clearly belonging to *illo tempore*, the "once upon a time" that characterizes all myths of origin, the Lord God creates Adam from the dust of the earth, then creates a beautiful garden—"Eastward in Eden," with four rivers flowing out of it and over all the earth, then all the animals. Then he "brought them to the man to see what he would call them." God tells Adam (but not Eve) that he may eat of every tree except that of "the tree of the knowledge of good and evil, . . . for in the day that you eat of it you shall die" (Genesis 2:16–17).[2] Afterwards, "the Lord God caused a deep sleep to fall upon the man . . . ; then he took one of his ribs . . ." and from it made a woman. Adam said, "This at last is bone of my bones and flesh of my flesh; this one shall be called Woman, for out of Man this one was taken" (Genesis 2:21–23).

("Funny," say the feminist scholars, "it's usually the other way 'round; all the men I know were taken out of women. That story must have been invented by a man.")

Adam and Eve are naked but do not know it, so innocent are they in the dawn of creation. Then the serpent, "more crafty than any other wild animal that the Lord God had made," speaks to Eve about the dietary prohibition, and contradicts God (even though the text says the serpent is his creation): "You will not die; for God knows that when you eat of it your eyes will be opened, and you will be like God, knowing good and evil" (Genesis 3:4–5). The text, in fact, gives truth to the serpent and God the lie, for the couple does not die "but the eyes of both were opened, and they knew that they were naked; they sewed fig leaves together and made loincloths for themselves" (Genesis 3:7).

The Lord God seems to have been absent for most of this, but then guilt enters history, along with self-consciousness, for the first couple hides when God enters the garden. Then emerged the first recorded instance of "buck-passing": when God confronts the man, Adam blames "the woman whom you gave to be with me," while Eve, in turn, says "the serpent tricked me, and I ate" (Genesis 3:12–13).

The Lord treats all the miscreants harshly. The serpent now must crawl on his belly (presumably having legs before this), and enmity is put between the creature and the seed of the woman. To the woman, he says, "I will greatly increase your pangs in childbearing; in pain you shall bring forth children, yet your desire shall be for your husband, and he shall rule over you" (Genesis 3:16), thus condemning future generations of women to painful childbirth—until Lamaze and le Boyer came along. God curses the ground Adam walks on and says, "Thorns and thistles it shall bring forth for you; and you shall eat the plants of the field. By the sweat of your face you shall eat bread until you return to the ground, for out of it you were taken; you are dust, and to dust you shall return" (Genesis 3:18–19).[3] (Both authors remember, as children, rankling at this prohibition. Why did God wish us to remain in childish ignorance?)

In this story, humanity is depicted as disobedient—like bad children—to divine law (which is irrefutably good) and of wanting to know too much: That is to say they desire the God-like "knowledge of good and evil."

In the symbolic interpretation, the affiliation between Eve and the serpent implies a secret identity. "Eve," therefore, becomes the primordial reptilian, a crushing, swallowing, instinctual being that won't let go of things, as well as a restless instinctive energy that does not respect "rules." A little further on in this book we will see how this negative depiction of the feminine has persisted for two thousand years and allowed cruelly dissociated attitudes and acts against women to be justified.

The early Greek creation story made popular by Plato, already referred to in the introduction, also focuses on the pride or hubris of protohumankind, but is less gender-skewed. The primordial human form is depicted as unimaginably powerful and complete (those beings with four arms and legs and two heads that Zeus split into two halves with his lightning bolt). Thus, each human being, we are told, is a partial creature, longing for its counterpart: the ones that were originally androgynous, for their male or female complementary half (the great majority); the ones originally all male, for other males; and all female, for other females. So, we wander the world looking for a significant other, who was united with us *in illo tempore*, that time before time began. Myths usually explain something psychological, and it is evident that we are being reminded both of our incompleteness and of our semidivine potential.

The Greek myth regards the masculine and feminine powers as equal. One is not "better" than the other. It seems also to allow for the presence of gay men and women in the natural order, by placing the origins of sexual proclivity since "the dawn of time." Although it speaks of human fragmentation, it also implies a power so available to the "complete" humanity that it somehow imperils established divinity. This is potent stuff.

The Dogon people of Africa tell us that the human soul is double, both masculine and feminine. In the beginning, most births were like this; but as we proceeded in generations farther from the first people, twin births became rare. So Nommo, the water spirit, who is him/herself a twin-being, created for humans the twin-soul: at birth, a child must be placed on the earth, face down, its arms and legs spread out, over a drawing of the twin shadows that Nommo has made for it. The female shadow is drawn first, then the male shadow. By this act, the child claims its full soul. Because of this, girls and boys until puberty are both male and female; the purpose of the rites of puberty is to make the boy completely a man, the girl completely a woman, so that they can procreate.[4]

A number of stories from the different culture regions of India describe how the primal One became Two, then out of the passion of their lovemaking gave life to all beings. Here is one from the Brihadaranyaka Upanishad:

> In the beginning was Atman (Self) alone, in the shape of a person. He, looking round, saw nothing but his Self. He first said, "This is I"; therefore he became "I" by name. . . . He feared, and therefore anyone who is lonely fears. He thought, "As there is nothing but myself, why should I fear?" Then his fear passed away. . . But he felt no delight. Therefore a man who is lonely feels no delight. He wished for a second. He was as large as man and wife together. He then made this, his Self, to fall in two, *(pat)* and thence arose husband *(pat)* and wife *(patni)*. Therefore [he] said, "We two are thus (each of us) like half a shell." Therefore the void which was there is filled by the wife. He embraced her and men were born. She thought, "How can he embrace me after having produced me from himself? I shall hide myself." She then became a cow, the other became a bull and embraced her, and hence cows were born. The one became a mare, and the other a stallion, the one a female ass, and the other a male ass. He embraced her, and hence one-hoofed animals were born. The one became a

she-goat the other a he-goat; the one became a ewe, the other a ram. He embraced her and embracing each other through the whole of creation they produced all kinds of animals and beings.[5]

Notice that the original being, Atman, does not make the woman. Atman, as large as both man and wife, divides himself into the two. Like the split descendants of the Greek original creature, each of us is "half a shell." Then the fun begins, the shape-shifting chase throughout the unfolding universe and down through time, of which we can sing the echoes in so many folk songs from virtually every part of the globe: "If all the young men/were hares on the mountain/Then all the young women/a-hunting would go. . . ."

In the biblical version, the mood is less playful, and the element of sin comes into the picture. This sin seems to lie in breaking God's commandments and seeking to "know too much." The mix also includes Eve's penchant for, or secret identity with, serpents, Adam's forgetfulness and suggestibility, and the "shame" that comes with knowledge—consciousness of nakedness and of one's sexuality. The expulsion from the garden is immediately followed by the first murder, the fratricide of Abel by Cain, as if to show how truly far we had fallen. Taken literally, the myth disempowers just about everybody except God, who remains righteously wrathful, waiting for the next time to "smite" his miscreant children. The opportunity does not seem long in coming, with the human misbehavior that occasions the "Great Flood" and God's visitation of *logophrenia* (a dissociation of language) on the builders of the Tower of Babel. (Pride—or spiritual aspiration—did indeed seem to afflict the architects of the Middle East, as the remains of many ziggurats and pyramids attest.)

In another highly gender-polarized Middle-Eastern version of the great dissociation, we have the Babylonian account of Tiamat and Marduk. Tiamat is a great, abundant, overflowing Earth Mother, symbol of the old matriarchal order. In her negative inflection, she is depicted as a monstrous sea dragon. Her consort is Apsu, Ocean; their rule is a timeless period of paradisal but undifferentiated chaos. Among Tiamat's numerous children are the gods, who decided they must bring order to the universe. Apsu, annoyed by his restless children, tries to kill them, and war begins. Tiamat hesitates, unwilling to kill her offspring; so Apsu alone falls to the younger gods and is destroyed by their leader, Ea, Earthwater. Then, Tiamat, that great old dragon mother of the primal abyss, is moved at last to war. One by one, the host of the gods falls back. None of them can stand against Tiamat, but they pool their energy into Marduk:

> His body was beautiful; when he raised his eyes great lights flared; his stride was majestic. . . .
>
> His limbs were immaculate, the making a fearful mystery beyond comprehension; with four eyes for limitless sight, and four ears hearing all; when his lips moved a tongue of fire burst out. Titanic limbs, standing so high he over-topped the tallest god; he was strong and he wore the glory of ten, and their lightnings played round him. . . .
>
> [His father, Ea, cried out in his joy:] "My son, my son, son of the sun, and heaven's sun!"[6]

Marduk, the young, son of Ea, is a newcomer to the company of the gods. He offers to be their champion if he is given power equal to that of the other gods. The council of the gods agrees, and Marduk becomes their overlord against the vast sea dragon Tiamat. Meanwhile, Tiamat has married Kingu, chief of her army, and has strengthened her numbers by giving birth to monstrous beings—venomous serpents, "the howling storm," the "man-scorpion."[7] She is more powerful than ever. The new chieftain of the gods must be invincible.

To test his acquisition of power, the gods place a garment before Marduk; by the power of his words alone, he causes it to be annihilated, then causes it to re-exist. Thus powerful, and armed with the bow of the rainbow, with the lightning, and with a net filled by the four winds, Marduk goes forth, riding the tempest, to battle with Tiamat and her host.[8]

The decisive turn comes with Marduk's magical net and his mastery of the winds; he catches Tiamat in the net and orders the winds into her, so that the dragon inflates, as it were. He then shoots an arrow down her gullet and into her heart, dispatching the great beast.

Marduk now takes possession of the tablets of destiny from Kingu, Tiamat's consort, thus becoming the most powerful entity in the universe. He sets about ordering the universe, using the dismembered parts of the giantess Tiamat:

> Splitting Tiamat's body in two, he raised half to form the heavens and placed the other half opposite Ea's dwelling place to form the earth. He created the stars and constellations, the planets, the order of succession of the calendar. Under Marduk's directon, Ea then took the blood of the executed Kingu and made men to be the servants of the gods. As their last and greatest work, the grateful gods, now organized and each with his work to do, built a capital city for their chief.[9]

The Babylonian myth is yet another version of the great dissociation, but also the tale of how the world as we know it came into being. Mythologist Robert Graves has pointed out in many of his works how stories of both fights and marriages among the goddesses and gods are often transformed accounts of the collision of religions—the patriarchal religion of the warrior Aryans, (Danaans, Ionians and Dorians in the Aegean) as well as here, and considerably earlier, the Babylonians —showing the supplanting of the religion of the Great Mother by a Sky God (Zeus, Marduk, Indra, Jehovah).

Looked at in this way, the myth provides a graphic account of the values of the matriarchy yielding to the patriarchy.[10] Tiamat as dragon is depicted as holding—after the acquisitive fashion of dragons—all the riches and potentials of the world. The "new world order" needs these things to build its cities, its civilizations. In the slaying of the dragon and the apportionment of her parts, we are instructed, symbolically, about this process.

First, the net of Marduk: it is the web of logic and communication, the Cartesian grid that immobilizes the Great Mother. Then, he blows wind (who can doubt the possession of this power by the patriarchy, who has heard a political filibuster or legal rant in the courtroom). After that, the phallically pointed arrow is driven deep inside, wounding her great archaic heart. Next comes the sword (traditionally a male weapon) that cuts things into little pieces: separating, discriminating, analyzing. And at last, in all fairness, come the great acts of construction and making a world, with its cities (the emerging hieratic city-states of the Middle East that surely represent the cradle of civilization). It is said that this tale, the Enuma Elish, was recited and enacted every New Year, in Babylon. It was a reminder to the world's first urbanites of how their novel milieu, the city, came into being:

> This is Babylon,
> "dear city of god"
> your beloved home!
> The length and breadth
> are yours, possess it,
> enjoy it, it is your own.[11]

Marduk must show his mastery of language by using it magically (making the garment disappear with a word, then reappear). He is armed with lightning (the suddenness and explosiveness of men?), the celestial hero's spear to wield against primordial darkness and abyssal murk.

> Thus Marduk, as god of the planet Jupiter, lighting the night, became equivalent to Sin, the moon god. Through his consort Sarpanitum [one of those goddesses annexed to the god realm], Marduk was father of Nebo, the culture god, inventor of writing and herald of the gods, and originally the god of Borsippa, which became a suburb of metropolitan Babylon as that great city expanded.[12]

Well, there we have it: a tale that implies we could blame (or credit) the following activities on men: words, wind, lightning (boys who love things that flash and go bang!), also ritual murder, abstraction, analysis, dissection, classification, but also cities, building, social differentiation, arts, culture, writing.

That would seem to leave everything not covered in the foregoing inventory to women; and so it appears, at least on the mythological level—namely, birthing, growing, fecundity, nurturance, waiting, healing, bonding, putting things in context, relating, educating. These patriarchal versions always seem unaware of women's part in the creation of culture and the arts: the domestication of animals and the cultivation of seeding plants; the demarcation of time (the earliest calendrical notations are periods of twenty-eight-day cycles: male scholars, who ruled the field until recently, have assumed, of course, that these were left by a man noting the moon's cycles. Why a man?); the origination of pottery and weaving (who does the housework while the men are out hunting and fighting?); the beginnings of literature and music (who sings and tells tales to children—only men?)—nothing more substantive than assumption has attributed these to men rather than women. Why is it that women sometimes feel men are so preoccupied with their important work of running the world that they are missing some of the details?

It is important to read a myth both for what it tells us about the people who made it—our relations—and for what it therefore tells us about ourselves. We learn about what we can be from the great web of tales, surviving in both words and images, that we have woven throughout time around our whole world. To this end, it can be helpful to pose one mythic system in a mirroring relationship to another: god-worldview facing goddess-worldview.

As we now know, the citizens of the city of Babylon were not, in fact, the first urban people. Agrarian communities had begun to cluster around towns at least as early as 6400 B.C.E. (Çatal Hüyük in central Anatolia). Their predecessors were living in agricultural communities as early as nine- to ten-thousand years ago; and the complex symbolic alphabet that they inherited from their forebears is to be found engraved on cavern walls, on stone and bone artifacts, as far back as twenty-five-thousand years ago. The religious focus in these communities was on the divine as feminine, manifesting through a variety of goddess images of significantly distinct character (not simply one "Great Mother"); careful study of the prolific symbolic remains of these people, in pottery and sculpture, shows us a religious life considerably more subtle than the simpleminded "fertility worship" hitherto rather casually ascribed to all goddess cultures (perhaps by scholars impatient to get on to the examination of the more important eras when the burials of warrior kings were the cultural preoccupation?). Archeological evidence is also growing that these farming cities were primarily peaceful: they have left no signs of warrior classes or of warfare as a major occupation; weapons are few among their many implements; they only began to surround their cities with walls after the raiding nomads entered their region (from the Volga River basin) from around the fourth to the third millennium before the present era. While it is clear that women occupied positions of respect and authority in religion and government, there is also no indication that men were devalued or regarded as subservient. Gimbutas, in the introduction to *Language of the Goddess*, makes use of Riane Eisler's term *gylany*, meaning an egalitarian system that is nonmatriarchal and nonpatriarchal, although it may have elements of matrilineal inheritance (a system that has left its remnants in systems of inheritance worldwide). As revealed through the painstaking detective work of archeomythology, "Old Europe and Anatolia, as well as Minoan Crete, were a gylany," Gimbutas tells us, "non-violent, earth-centered," and preserving in the evocative remnants of their cultures, our "true European heritage."[13]

Joseph Campbell, in his foreword to Gimbutas' work, says, "The message here is of an actual age of harmony and peace in accord with the creative energies of nature which for a spell of some four thousand prehistoric years anteceded the five thousand of what James Joyce has termed the 'nightmare' (of contending tribal and national interests) from which it is now certainly time for this planet to wake."[14]

The Marduk/Tiamat story is probably older than the versions of the great Earth Mothers Gaia and Rhea that appear in Hesiod's *Theogony*, but very similar in that the goddess represents the old order, while the new gods of the patriarchy are presented as those who will undo the old order and usher in the new. We return to masculine and feminine mythologies many times throughout this treatment, always being sure to disentangle them from literal equation with male and female human beings, and yet eager to see how the bright images of mythology hypnotize and fascinate us, ever and again.

——————————— A ZULU CREATION MYTH ———————————

A ZULU MYTH TOLD BY THE GREAT STORYTELLER Vusumazulu Credo Mutwa shows us this theme of the great dissociation with a more hopeful inflection, one that offers a healing path not only for the genders but for the separate races of intelligent beings—both on and off this world.

At the dawn of time, there was a great battle between the men and women on a world adjacent to this one, called "the Red Sand World." (It certainly sounds like Mars and is consistent with that planet's mythological energy of war and strife.) Men and women lived as separate races on that world, only coming together ritually and periodically for procreation—a wild, violent mating. At other times, men and women lived far apart, were hostile to each other, and even would hunt down each other for sport. The Red Sand World was cruelly divided along gender lines.

A male hero, the brave Moromudzi, and an equally courageous female, Banu Kiranmireva, disrupted the status quo by falling in love. After they met in a mating ritual, each could not forget the other, unheard of on the Red Sand World. The love of the couple was so great that it further polarized their divided people.

Moromudzi and Kiranmireva were joined by other men and women who wanted to try intergender relationships. But fanatics from both "races," who could not image a world without war, denounced the rapprochement. So the hero and heroine, with their followers, left the Red Sand World in a dragon-shaped starship.

After a long journey, they came to the Dog Star, called in Zulu, Peri Orifici Orimbisi (Sirius). They saw the star with its strange white-dwarf companion—a collapsed star circling around a healthy one (also known to the Dogon of Central Africa), and around it were habitable planets. They chose one of these, a blue globe they called the "Water World."[15] There they were greeted by friendly and intelligent amphibious beings named Nommo, whose wise king was also named "Nommo." (This being is featured in the Dogon mythology of Central Africa, as well, and pictures of a similar being are found in ancient Babylonian reliefs.) The human exiles lived for a while in happy coexistence with the amphibians on beautiful archipelagoes in the vast sea of the Water World.

But violent tendencies surfaced again in some of the humans; they killed, and it was said, ate, one of the intelligent Nommo beings. At this outrage, the formerly peaceful Nommo would have killed all the humans in retribution; but the wise king took pity and asked his two sons, Wowane and Mpanku, to return the humans to the Red Sand World. Now these boys, like the cosmic twins of many mythologies, were beings of supernatural power. They journeyed into the voids of interstellar space and stole the egg of the Firebird, a fearsome cosmic creature who lived in the black spaces between the stars. Then they blew out the contents of the egg and made it into a hollow vessel for the human creatures for the long voyage across interstellar space to the world from which they had come. The twins returned to Water World "rolling" the empty egg through space; the humans were put in, and the twins began to "roll" it toward the solar system of the Red Sand World.

When they approached the Red Sand World, a horrendous, echoing cry broke through the universe: it was the Firebird, realizing that its egg had been desecrated and stolen. Wowane and Mpanku faltered in their attention, as the cosmic monster soared toward them through the interstellar spaces. They overshot the Red

Sand World, approaching a blue-green globe closer to the sun; but the Firebird was overtaking them now. . . .

> Wowane saw its approach and said to Mpanku, "My brother, you must get away; you must dive into the sea far below. Then you will be safe." And Mpanku dived down. But the bird caught Wowane and took him away. And it tied him to a great big stone . . . a standing stone, and then slowly it ripped his guts out, while he was tied to the stone. It tore out his liver, his heart, and everything else, telling him that he would scream for many thousands of years, because he had robbed her of her egg. Even to this day, when a person does something and is punished out of all proportion to the crime, we say that "He has stolen the egg of the Firebird."[16]

Why is this myth so familiar? It is not unlike the fire-theft by Prometheus for humankind, and his punishment by great Zeus. One of the twins—Wowane—was hung up like Odin, like Christ, for being humanity's benefactor.

Mpanku and the egg fell to Earth—for our own blue-green globe it was—landing in the sea; but the egg was going so fast that it burrowed further into the Earth before coming to rest. The people crawled out safely underground, eventually emerging from one of the fissures in the earth still sacred to the Zulus as the origin place of humankind. Mpanku (a demigod) labored mightily to retrieve the egg. Then he put it into space not far from the blue-green world, where it circles to this day "and that is why the moon resembles a great pockmarked egg," says Mutwa (with his deep, rich storyteller's inflection).

Mpanku liked the ocean, after all, did he not come from a water world? And since his mission was fulfilled and his brother gone, he dived into the deep blue depths. Later, it is said, he fell in love with and married a mermaid and had many children—the dolphins. And that is why dolphins are warm-blooded and so familiar-seeming. Baba Mutwa says,

> We believe that dolphins are people and they are able to talk to us. This is why Zulu people call dolphins Hlengeto, which means "the one who saves." We believe that these creatures are so good-hearted that if you fall into the sea they will rescue you and bring you back to land.[17]

And so it seems to be: dolphins, of all creatures of land or sea, betraying a human-like or even higher intelligence, altruism, and a playful sense of humor. Dolphins offer us a paradigm of what a truly interspecies relationship could be (if we ourselves were able to rise to the occasion).

A more complete version of this story is told in *Song of the Stars*, although when Stephen asked Credo Mutwa, he assured us that the complete story in its oral form takes two-to-three months to tell. An unusual account, even in the galaxy of creation cosmologies, the Zulu story is still another version of what we are calling "the great dissociation," which begins with the fallen, separated status already present among humanity. And here, as in other traditions, the hero-progenitors of humankind are great reconcilers and communicators, not to mention starry adventurers.

Myths always address psychological truths as well as narrative histories, and the Zulu myth addresses the question of why men and women, to this day, still squabble so easily and are often more comfortable in the presence of their own genders. The Zulu myth also deals with the question of why men and women seem to speak two different languages—they were different races and cultures originally. (This is a theme that has gotten much attention recently among social scientists, and we return to it throughout the book.)

But the Zulu tale also sets forth another theme we wish to return to later: the real heroes are the men and women who learn to talk to each other and even enact the first mythical love story, the prototype of what happens in a thousand novels and movie theaters all over the world, where the pivotal piece remains the reconciliation of that which has become, somehow, sundered or divided. We joke about the obligatory "they lived happily ever after," or "they walked hand and hand into the sunset"; but this is the precise mythogem that is required: it hints at "the great reconciliation," not only between the genders but between all the forces and elements that have been fragmented.

Ever since the great dissociation, things have been in a state of cold war. There is a mythic implication, then, in the foundations of the world, that the division in sexuality is connected to a more fundamental dissociation. The first time that Joseph Campbell attended the elite Eranos conference of European scholars, he heard the renowned Japanese scholar D.T. Suzuki describe the great dissociation this way: Suzuki was asked by another participant what he thought of Western religion, particularly the Judeo-Christian tradition. "Hm, let's see," replied the diminutive and puckish Suzuki, rubbing his hips for emphasis: "Man against God, God against Man; Man against Nature, Nature against Man; God against Nature, Nature against God, very funny religion!"[18]

Now, for the sake of the subject of this book, we might add, apropos of the Zulu myth, "man against woman, woman against man," the same theme as in the Genesis story. This is how the mythic theme of our dissociation emerges, through a filter, a tincture, that is sexually polarized.

Could we begin to look at this mythic dissociation from a different angle? We wonder: are these cosmogonies not merely indictments of human fallibility, sexuality, sinfulness, and violence; but also hints about our potential for healing and redemption as a species? Isn't love right there from the beginning? And we want so much to get it back! But we keep getting it wrong. We get it wrong when we allow separatism, violence, hatred, exploitation to supervene. Yet in the very dissociation, a message has been hidden, like the Tibetan *termas*, scriptures that have been hidden by the wise until the most auspicious time arises for them to be found. We are still learning to read the message; and this book is an attempt at decipherment, as well as an encouragement to delay no longer in seeking the reconciliation depicted in the Zulu myth. The healing of the world begins and ends in love. It is *the* love story itself that leads us to the *hieros gamos*, the sacred marriage, and a reuniting that is the crown of the human experience.

The corollary, then, is that a healing that affects the war-torn zone of gender also affects all the other wounds and splits, the schizophrenias of our souls. When a man and a woman come together in love, it is as if a sacrament were being celebrated on a battlefield; a ray of hope arises, and a blessing is given. Thus, the love story is basic to all reconciliations, all comings together, and is featured in most mythologies. As an archetype, it wields uncanny, perennial power.

Another aspect of this Zulu myth is the relatedness of the two races: the humans and the Nommo. The Nommo, a wise and altruistic, as well as magically powerful species, are clearly more advanced than forgetful, bloodthirsty *Homo sapiens*. Amazingly creative, clever, and adaptable—humankind, sadly, shows its lack of wisdom; an adolescent species, raiding the cupboard, trampling the garden, and peeing in the water. The Nommo figure also appears as Oannes, a Babylonian demigod who is a benevolent instructor and culture-bringer for humankind. Oannes is depicted with a fish's tail, emerging from the water. If the origins of all life do indeed lie in the sea, this figure emerges as a mythic bridge between that briny original oneness and the independence and mobility of land creatures. He is the wisdom of the primordial abyss, even older than that much maligned reptile, the serpent.

——————————— ANGELS AND ALIENS ———————————

CREDO MUTWA TOLD STEPHEN during the writing of *Song of the Stars* that many races from the stars are watching this planet Earth (probably, he said, about twenty-one, with specific agendas). But that we are under "an interstellar quarantine." No one is to speak to us or open overt communication. It would be too confusing to our hysterical, reactive species. While we continue to be confused and murderous, all we see are strange craft and hear tales of visitations and abductions. The "Song of the Stars," an ancient melody interwoven through the galaxies, is not yet heard on Earth:

> The great Nommo told our people that we must get rid of war, of hunger and disease. If we could do this, then people would again be able to visit the twelve beautiful worlds, which used to be visited by human beings. Then Nommo explained that the gods used to have a chain which connected all the worlds together; and that one day people could climb up and down this chain, to visit any world they chose, and truly, not just in dreams.[19]

In this regard, it seems that, when we are ready for a relationship, whether between the races of men and women or humans and star-beings, the relationship will arise. Keith Thompson shows an equivalency to the mythologies of angels and aliens.[20] His thesis is that celestial presences are in contact with human beings. In a prescientific culture era, they were thought of as angels, in postscience times (and science fiction) as aliens. What the mythologies clearly have in common is that something magical appears in the skies, something not of this world. There is a luminosity and a suddenness about these phosphorescent apparitions, still alive and lively in the cracks between the worlds. Suffice it to say that, in contemporary popular folklore, accounts both of angels and aliens intervening in people's lives are widespread enough to make us realize that scientific fundamentalism has not shackled the mythic imagination. Thompson quotes R. J. Stewart's *Creation Myths*, in which he defines a myth as "a story embodying and declaring a pattern of relationship between humanity, other forms of life, and the environment."[21]

Years ago, Steven Spielberg captured the public imagination with this mythogem. In his movie, *E.T.*, children (*Homo sapiens* still open to wonder) meet an extraterrestrial being (E.T.) and become wonderful friends. The relationship clearly transcends xenophobia or the "alienness" of the star being. Both E.T. and the human children are shown as capable of relatedness, empathy and love, and this is what brings them together. In this positive gloss, it is the presence of these connecting qualities, combined with the "otherness" of the alien, that makes the connection so poignant. It is an affirmation with which both William Blake and the Lakota shaman Black Elk would have agreed: "Everything that lives is holy!"

Xenophobia probably does come from our more ancient roots, as animals and human infants and children all seem to fear and reject strangers. And both equine and ungulate herds reject outsiders of their own species, and primate groups do the same thing.[22] But the vastness of the universe now known to science gives xenophobia a scale and grandeur never heretofore possible. *E.T.* gets our attention because it shows love and empathy to be not smaller than this newly emerging grand vista of existence.

John Mack in *Passport to the Cosmos* says,

> It seems as if transdimensional or inter-species relationship is itself a fundamental part of this whole process. . . . A deep familiarity and sense of meaningful connection develops between the experiencer and one or more of the beings, which can reach heights of love so profound as to be felt to be incompatible with earthly love. . . . The beings appear to be greatly interested in our physicality and emotionality, seeming, as is said of angels, to envy our embodiment. They are enthralled with sexuality, maternal love, and other expressions of sensuality or dense physicality, as if this were a new or lost possibility for them.[23]

This idea of relatedness across species, now spanning galactic voids, appearing in science fiction, films, and all the anomalous "abduction" and "close encounter" scenarios, certainly deserves to be identified as a modern mythogem. It is not unlike the magical human-animal bonds that are so pivotal in fairy tales or human-spirit bonds that are so pivotal to shamanism and to the mythologies of the otherworldly. Also common in fairytale and folklore are the stories of abduction into the "hollow hills," beneath an enchanted lake, or into some other variant of the fairy realm, where time obeys a different rhythm that than of day and night beneath our familiar sun: Such tales do bear an uncanny kinship with these alien abduction stories, so that, whatever else may be happening, we can certainly know that there is a timelessness about the theme, as well as a current urgency.

Credo Mutwa says, in an essay on "fear" in *Song of the Stars*,

> Today there are people who walk about in this world fearing other people;
> a man of one race is conditioned to fear people of another race. In fact,
> this is the deadliest, most devastating fear that we human beings have got

to face: Our fear of our own brothers, our fear of our own sisters. How can one overcome this fear? As I have said to you, the more unfounded a fear is, the deeper the roots and the deeper its intensity often is.

First you must ask yourself, why do I fear those people? What do I know about them that I have got to fear? Face your fear, look at it in the face as a lover looks into the face of a lover. What have I got to fear? If I am black, what have I got to fear from the whites? If I am white, what have I got to fear from the blacks? If I am Caucasian or Aryan, what do I have to fear from the Jews? Or if I am a Jew, what do I have to fear from the Gentiles? You will find on facing your fear squarely that your fear is based not on what you know about those people, but on what you do not know about those people. And once you make it a point to know more about those people, then you will overcome your fear.[24]

Thus, a very human prescription for prejudice and xenophobia from a Zulu wise man, who certainly, under the years of vicious apartheid he endured, had adequate cause to see and feel the effects of racial prejudice. Yet he seems to hold no rancor. It is a gnostic path he recommends. Through knowledge (same root as the word *gnosis*), understanding, and empathy, we enter the condition of another and are reconciled to brother- and sisterhood. *Song of the Stars* ends with an appeal to humanity to awaken that reminds us of the high poetry of Black Elk, his Native American counterpart and spiritual brother:

Take these teachings: that we are all brothers and sisters; the children of one father and mother; that all human beings are interconnected; that we share many thoughts and feelings that we imagine about the world, about the future, about each other; and that the images and dreams we hold in our minds and hearts do matter. Treat children and animals with kindness, and pass this wisdom on to the generations to come, and I assure you that there will come a time when our grandchildren, or our great-great-grandchildren will live in a world of beauty and harmony. And they will hear a far-off music, a beautiful cosmic music, that will lift them beyond all fear, all suffering and limitation, into a universal brotherhood, beyond this little world and its fearful dreams. That music will draw closer and yet closer with its message of hope and becoming. That music is the Song of the Stars. Indaba.[25]

AUTHORITY AND IDENTITY

BUT WHAT OF THIS INERT DRAGON that Marion Woodman depicts, in her quote that stands at the beginning of this chapter? What of the forces of massive inertia and corrupt authority that maintain the status quo? And what of its presence in psychology as well as in the world?

After the attempted genocides of World War II, this same issue began to be addressed by social scientists worldwide. The most famous were the Frankel-Brunswick, Adorno, et alia, studies on "the authoritarian personality." The compelling question for psychology and sociology was, "What are the ways in which people become unconscious puppets of authority?" These were followed by the Milgram studies in which an authority figure posing as the psychological experimenter ordered subjects in a learning experiment to give a full range of electric shocks to "learners" who weren't "getting it" and who made lots of mistakes.[26] (These were actually stooges of Milgram, not receiving actual shocks; but they moaned and screamed as if they were.) It was, unfortunately, a very small minority of students who turned to the experimenter and said, "You know, I don't care what results you're after, I don't approve of hurting people for a silly old experiment—here's your money back!" About seventy-five percent of the subjects obeyed the authority figure unquestioningly, just as did the SS and SA men when Hitler sent out his extermination orders.

If we are not introduced into the idea of making our own choices and bearing the consequences of those choices, if we are not able to understand ourselves as autonomous choice-making entities, then it is very easy for us simply to knuckle under to authority, not because it is just, not because it partakes of universal ethical principles or spiritual values, or even supports the social well-being of the group, but simply because it is authority.

And this is what was being questioned in the 1950s and still must be questioned today, with genocide, totalitarianism, and mindless prejudice still very present dangers to the entire world. How do we grow people who have these "universal ethical principles," who won't simply do what unjust authority figures tell them to do? And how do we form models of partnership and marriage that support each individual's personal ethical integrity? This last question becomes especially significant when we extend our investigation of relationship to authority into the area of traditional models of marriage: here we most often find that the man is made entirely responsible for ethical decisions and the woman is required, by the very language of the marriage vow, to obey, whatever his position. As we know all too well from the debris of broken covenants in our time, this can pose an insoluble dilemma to people of conscience.

In the cognitive studies by Lawrence Kohlberg, conducted on the subjects of the Milgram experiment, it was found that many of the ones who resisted authority had formed something like universal or permanent human values of respect, understanding and tolerance toward other human beings, and simply were offended or repulsed when someone—no matter how authoritative—ordered them to do something inconsistent with these deep values. The other participants were still at the developmentally primitive stage that a parent induces in a child, when the child asks "why?" and the parent says, "Because I told you so!"[27]

Jean Piaget traced the stages of mental development which lead toward adulthood. In the early phases of socialization, children need to take into themselves "schemata" that have to do with obedience to authority and social rules.[28] In the simplistic mythologies of younger children, then, parents enjoy a godlike power and respect. Nor can one stand to be separated from them, especially the mother, in the early years. Gradually, with "fully operational" thinking, a critical sense of evaluation and perspective-taking emerges, in which the parents now may be (and usually are) criticized: falling from divinity to something so "uncool" and embarrassing as to be dissociated from at all costs—and over just a few years in the early teens.

In *The Eden Project*, James Hollis begins by saying, "Every relationship begins with a separation, and ends in separation."[29] The first separation is the child from the cosmos and from the mother. There can be, in fact, no relationship until there is a separation, until there is an acknowledgment that this other to whom we are relating is a separate being, a full being, recognized as another person. In a family where the mother has not adequately understood that her children are separate human beings, not just extensions of herself, she's going to be overprotective, over-controlling. She will think for them and fail to give them appropriate experiences in thinking for themselves, or of taking their own risks, making their own mistakes.

Fathers are, of course, in no way immune from the same problem. There are families where the father believes that everybody else in the family is just an appendage of himself. With the best of intentions, he is still probably going to be over-controlling; and he may be unnecessarily harsh in his discipline. Because, after all, any failure to do what Father would have done is seen as a disobedience. Father knows best. Even if the child or the wife is simply doing what is natural to them as an individual and is not necessarily threatening, fighting, or disobeying him, it is still seen as a disobedience and a threat, simply because it is different from what the patriarch himself would have done. Therefore, the unruliness of the event is "in the eye of the beholder," a reminder that the father is not really fully in control of his environment, because this part of his environment is not behaving properly.

The most distressing aspect of this situation for the male in a patriarchal era is that because he is strong and dominant, he thinks of his wife and his children as simply "his." Therefore, he can abuse them. This belief is socially supported in many male-dominant societies; and, until recently, it was often the case in these societies that, if the wife or the child went against the paterfamilias, he could even kill one of them, as long as he could cite a "good reason" and rally the rest of society around him. If the society is unconscious of its patriarchal bias, it sets up men ill-equipped for such a powerful role to become oppressors of women. If the normative social pattern encourages indissociation, a "mythic identity," an adult egocentricity, can be released that is bound to be destructive; as we know, "if power corrupts, absolute power corrupts absolutely." The father comes to be a tyrant without even realizing it: there is no difference between his children and himself. They are, in effect, in him, in his sphere of influence, and therefore have no separate identity.

If instead of irresponsible dictators, would-be failed demigods, we agree to be human, we can model successes and failures, and acknowledge our own anxieties and our own mistakes to our children; thereby allowing them to learn to do the same. When we model tolerance toward children, they will model it toward themselves, and one day to their own children. The parent who is unable to pass through the developmental stages of emancipation with his or her own child has the more serious problem, and one that will surely be imprinted upon that child. The young have to experience being acknowleged and respected as a self, and then they will evolve into a more authentic selfhood.

─────────── STEPHEN AND ROBIN IN DIALOGUE ───────────

Robin: Gwyneth [our daughter] has said to us that one of the sadnesses of her child-hood was being the baby. Sometimes, in a very active, lively, talkative family, she was not able to get in a word. She felt very much the littlest, felt she might not be heard as quickly as everybody else. As she grew older, she learned how to get those words in, and became a very well-spoken person, and expressed this need. But even so, I think there were times that, because she was a beautiful little girl, it was all too easy for me, as a mother, to want to keep her as this beautiful "little girl."

Stephen: Weren't you one yourself?

Robin: I remember my own struggles with my mother about this, her wanting to keep me just as "her little girl." I, however, was determined to become a very differ-ent creature: to become independent, to be an artist, a scholar, on my own!

With Gwyneth, I had, very consciously, to make myself aware that she was a growing person, with her own inner darkness, and that she had to go into that darkness to be a full person. We had some interesting conversations, when she was quite small, about dreams she had that were very disturbing.

I had to make myself not brush them away, and not say, "It's okay; it's only a dream. Don't think about it," but say instead, "Let's look at this," recognizing "this" as a legitimate, deepening, soul-growing darkness in my daughter, who is a full human being. It was going to be necessary for her to go through that darkness in order to become the person she was becoming.

Stephen: There was a story you told me once, about how, when you were growing up, your parents really showed you that you weren't just their property.

Robin: There were a number of times like that, and they were very important for me. This particular story occurred when I had just graduated from brownie to girl scout.

Our girl scout troop called a meeting, with mothers and daughters; but my dad came with me instead. We sat there through most of the evening, hear-ing all the mothers talk: they said, "My daughter is never going to do this," and "My daughter should do that." Even the more moderate among them said, "Well, we allow a little freedom, and just that amount of freedom, but we insist on this and that." Constantly we heard, "My child will never . . ." or "This is what my child is allowed." Most of the parents were really urging other parents to be firmer and more controlling, so that they all could be controlling together and be consistent.

Today, looking back, I can understand that it was a really good thing for par-ents to come together and lay down consistant guidelines for children in a close community like that. But as I sat there listening, I felt very separate from it; I knew that I lived in a family where it just wasn't done that way.

Then there was a point in the meeting when everyone had spoken; all the while, my father had just sat there quietly, and nobody had even looked at him: It was just such an anomaly to have a man there. Then my father finally spoke up. He was a poet as well as an attorney. He had a gentle, but attention-getting manner. He gave them this beautifully eloquent speech about parenting and responsibility, but remembering the importance of preserving and nurturing the independence and the dignity of your child. I wish I had his exact words. He was addressing the most repressive of the parents, a woman of very little thoughtfulness at all, who kept saying loudly, "My daughter this and that." But what he said that seemed to shock was something like this: "We don't own our children, they are loaned to us by the universe; they come through us. But they are full human beings. They are given into our care as helpless babies; and it's important for us to raise them to the point where they begin to be able to move around separately from us. And then we need to encourage them to grow as independent beings. And everything that we teach them, and every way we direct them, is toward that end. We need to help them become fully independent, thoughtful, self-determined human beings, who can then live in a free society and make intelligent decisions and not be controlling bullies of other people. We need to grow people," he said, "who will pass this on, to everybody around them, and to the next generations—this sense of responsibility and freedom and independence and thoughtfulness."

It was a beautiful moment for me, because I knew that he wasn't just talking. Not only was he capable of thinking those thoughts in the 1950s, but he had really tried hard, and was always trying, to live them. It was something my parents checked themselves against constantly; and when they faltered in it, they checked each other, and they came back to me and we talked about it. I was very blessed in my parents.

Stephen: I believe that I was very much a wanted child. My mother had lost children, I think four miscarriages or stillbirths before I was born. I was very much loved, given that unconditional, positive regard that small children need so much.

There was one time as a young therapist, I had empathically relived with my client—himself a wounded, talented therapist—the brutalities of his immigrant working-class upbringing, constant fighting, alcoholism, abuse, and abandonment. After the session, sitting alone in my Kingston basement office, I suddenly realized how truly blessed was the island of my childhood, and immediately called my parents to tell them so. It was fairly late in the evening, and they were surprised at the call. When I heard the familiar voice of my father on the phone, I became speechless, and realized that I was weeping profoundly. When I finally could talk, I just stumbled over my words, thanked them, told them I loved them, and hung up.

Robin: I think I remember that time: your relationship to your father was getting better all the time.

Stephen: My problems with my father had begun to emerge as I hit older childhood, and then went into puberty and the teenage years. He was a kind and good man, had gone through his own life tribulations and transitions, and I think that those had matured him an enormous amount.

After a kind of religious crisis he went through when I was very small, he would often quote from the Bible, or speak about God and God's wishes for the world and for us in our unique little family. Somehow there was the feeling there that God was in his heaven and my father, well, right next door to him.

I suppose at an earlier Piagetian stage of development, where we tend to worship our parents uncritically, that was fine. But when you begin to develop your own way of thinking, and your own will and volition—well, then I found I was constantly coming up against his authority. And there was no brooking his authority: Behind him stood "the Big Man." He became somewhat of an object of fear to me.

Robin: He used corporal punishment?

Stephen: Oh yes, and it's been very useful for me, in this regard, to read Alice Miller's work, because there was very much that dimension in his punishment.[30] He was fairly liberal with physical punishment, which always included, for serious offenses, the strap.

Even the taking off of the belt in an ominous way became for me threatening, in the way of Pavlovian conditioning. I can remember shaking with fear when I heard his heavy footstep in the house unexpectedly. (I'd probably be down in the basement, very likely doing something I wasn't supposed to be doing with the tools and the workbench. I was forever doing that.)

If I, in any way, as I faced these beltings, questioned the necessity of the procedure, he would remind me with grave looks that he himself had been subject to the "cat of nine tails" by his own father (I almost threw up when I first saw one of these diabolical devices in a museum, with its lead balls on leather thongs). So all I could think, as he laid on, quite thoroughly, was that I was really pretty fortunate that I hadn't been exposed to his own fate: The belt was a pretty benign thing by comparison to "the cat," and he was actually doing me a favor.

Nonetheless, his presence did become fearful to me, and I can remember possibly the first time that I, with my peers in a kind of primitive encounter group, expressed being angry with my father and the way he treated me.

By the time I was in the military, I had developed a kind of almost unthinking deference to authority, along with a kind of inner rebellion, which I believe in a certain way has plagued me and haunted me to this day. No unthinking organization man or unthinking follower, I find myself despising those who are. I kick at the traces, and that itself is a problem. In other words, in this mix, I'm sensitized to authority structures, and particularly toward males in authority roles.

I would say that those experiences left me with that complex, and I've had to work and struggle with that element, in relationship, ever since. Do I have no authority or all authority? I'm never sure whether I'm powerless in a situation; and if I feel I am, then I sometimes exert autocratic power, and so overdo it.

My father was very much enamored of the "training" model, and he felt that we were "well-trained boys," for the most part. (But he didn't see all the various ways in which we disobeyed when we were out of his sight.) That can lead, in a child, to a kind of split personality, because you may be beautifully obedient and tractable-seeming in one situation, and a real hellion and hell-raiser and oppositional-defiant in others—especially when certain "buttons" have been pushed.

Robin: Hearing you talk, Stephen, I'm struck by the difference in the kind of things that I was scolded or punished for at home, as opposed to the kinds of things that I was very much punished for when I was in the other two households where I spent my younger years, when my dad was away in World War II, and in the years right after when all our families were going through the post-war changes.

At home, most of the struggles were to get me to do something, like my homework, behave in school, or eat properly, or—this would be a little later on—dress up and be a nice young lady, and keep clean, and that kind of thing. Later it became a struggle between my mother and me about what she thought a young lady should look like, with makeup and paraphernalia. It was mostly the things that they were trying to get me to do that were good for me, socialization things. But I was a fairly wild young scamp, and I think identified with a wild horse rather than with a little girl.

I was told, and made to feel, even when I was quite little, that my parents both felt that I had basically good judgment, that I would make sensible decisions. I was not told that if I ran into the road, I would be spanked. It was more that I was expected to stop, and look and think, and be cautious about cars in the road; that I was expected to be sensible.

So I was given a good deal of freedom to go where I pleased and to move around quite freely. If I came back late, the interaction was more like, "It was thoughtless of you to not let us know where you were," rather than simply, "Come home on time, no matter what." They would ask, "What did happen? Please explain this . . ." rather than immediately punishing me. That made me not want to make them suffer and worry about where I was. I felt that they really did suffer if I wandered off somewhere and didn't come back in time.

I think that my mother was very aware that being overprotective and clutching was not a good way to teach a child to look and be careful, to think for herself and take care of herself. That kind of open discussion in the home really was important for me, and I'm seeing that the notion was of "education" as opposed to "training." Also, my mother believed strongly that to hit a child was extremely serious, not the way to teach them anything. This was a very important thing in our household; it made us quite different from our neighbors. My mother was a professional educator who was very dedicated to her work.

My parents were flexible and imaginative. I might be told, with complete certainty by my dad, and with absolutely no sense of wishy-washiness or hesitation, that something I had done was dangerous and foolish, and that I was not to do it again. But there was always the sense that, when he said something with that kind of firmness, I wouldn't go against him. His respect mattered to me. I didn't want him to think that I was foolhardy and would just do something dangerous without thinking about it. Part of that was that he also had a sense of humor, and that he was understanding.

It was also important for me that he could admit that he did dangerous and silly things when he was a kid, and that he understood the lure of them. What he was saying was not, "I'm the adult; I possess you; what I'm saying is absolutely right;" but "Look, I've lived longer than you; I've seen a lot; I've learned since I was a kid your age; I know what can happen to you because I've been through some of this myself." He never said, "Because I told you so," he never said, "Don't talk back," he never said, "Don't question me." There were a few times when he said, "Don't question me now; I'll explain later." And he did.

25.

As a child I observed that many adults would quickly say "No!" because they just didn't want kids to be jumping and running too many ways at once, and being too out of control. I never felt that with my parents. I felt if they said no, there was a reason.

When it came time to parent our own children, I think, I hope, these various models having worked on me, I was able to choose my own, more balanced response.

Stephen: As I grew older, as the older child (my brother was four years younger), I did fight it out with my parents. I think it's painful, but in retrospect probably healthy. I was able to come to some kind of reckoning with authority. My father was very outraged because the battles were pretty fierce sometimes.

As I look back now, in retrospect, when I became a young adult, and I had my own profession, was starting to raise a family of my own, I became very good friends with my father. My brother, who never did struggle through those emancipation issues as much as I did, really never did develop that mature, good relationship with my father. He always seemed to have, even as a thirty- and forty-year-old man, rebellious and even vengeful ways of getting back at our parents, particularly our father. I think that those phases of conflict and parental readiness for them are extremely important.

In regard to corporal punishment, there was a very telling moment with raising our own son. Merlin was about seven or eight years old, and there hadn't been any corporal punishment in our family; but an occasion came up, where it seemed he deserved a spanking. He had been disobedient, and I began to spank him with my hand; but he just kind of looked at me, a meeting of the eyes; and it just didn't feel right. Yes, he had been a disobedient child, and he was "my" child. But he was also a being of equivalent complexity and dignity to myself. I would also be hitting the adult within the child, and replicating what had been done to me.

I remain grateful to that something that stopped me. Subsequently it was easy to find ways of discipline that were more educational or psychological. With our daughter, Gwyneth, there was no need for punishment of any kind, nor even disciplinary action. She was such an obviously sensitive child that a disapproving glance was plenty for her. Both of these children now seem, in young adulthood, to be very inner directed, autonomous, and healthy in that way. At least they don't seem to have the same kind of authority problems I did.

In studying partnership as a spiritual practice, there can be no question but that our early experiences predispose us to our later ones. In both of our cases, we were very fortunate. We had uncommonly loving and devoted parents, who tended to support each other. Your father, Robin, was not only supportive, but respectful, teaching you to respect yourself and, by extension, others. The critical issue here seems to be the willingness of the adult to listen, and not just pay lip service to, but really understand what the child or youngster is saying, is all about.

If you are listened to on a deep level that reinforces your depth and invites you to find yourself at the same level at which you were heard and respected, then you will be able to be a genuine listener for others.

What was successfully modeled for you, Robin, but less so for me, was the empowerment of coming into one's own selfhood through being trusted. This seems to produce the highest and most ethical of adaptations to life and gives the young person the confidence to experiment, to try and fail, and evaluate his or her own performance without anxiety or self-abuse.

The Lady of the Beasts
by Hrana Janto

Chapter Two

THE SOUL OF
HUMAN-ANIMAL RELATIONS

In the very earliest time,
when both people and animals lived on earth,
a person could become an animal if he wanted to
and an animal could become a human being.
Sometimes they were people
and sometimes animals
and there was no difference.
All spoke the same language.
That was the time when words were like magic.
The human mind had mysterious powers.
A word spoken by chance
might have strange consequences.
It would suddenly come alive
and what people wanted to happen could happen—
all you had to do was say it.
Nobody can explain this:
that's the way it was.

"Magic Words," an Inuit song[1]

HEALING RELATIONS

ENTER A NATIVE AMERICAN SWEAT LODGE, one of the ancient ways, and hear the animals proclaimed as our brothers and sisters. *"Aho Mitoquiye Oyasin!"* goes the invocation: "blessings to all my relations." The living tradition called by Swedenborg "the Most Ancient Church" is characterized by animism, the belief that all nature is alive and aware, and shamanism, permeated by spirits who might be accessible to communication. Everything is alive, everything has a spirit, everything is worthy of our respect. In that distant time when this "Most Ancient Church" was everywhere on the earth, Swedenborg said, people knew, felt, and thought intuitively. Outer language might not even have been developed yet, but we talked to our "relations" mind to mind.

The prayers of the shaman in the sweat lodge or in the pipe ceremony address the "four-leggeds," the creeping things or snake nation, and the "wingeds," the many species of birds of the air, each one of which may be deemed to carry a different message of *Wakan Tanka*, the Great Spirit, or *Tonkoshola*, the "grandfathers." Black Elk, a little nine-year-old Sioux (Lakota) boy, witnessing the attempted genocide of his own people in his lifetime, fell ill with what was later recognized as a shaman-sickness. In visions, he was taken to a tipi lined with living animals—like the paleolithic caves of the Dordogne, where the "herds of eternity" are spread across the walls and vaulted ceilings in the "Sistine Chapel of the Paleolithic era." But these animals, the "essences of animals," were already present in the genesis of creation. What an ancient lineage!

In Black Elk's great vision, he was brought into a rainbow lodge in the sky with six old men—"old like hills, like stars." One of them addressed him, gently: "His voice was very kind, but I shook all over with fear now, for I knew that these were not old men, but the Powers of the World."[2] In his vision, Black Elk was shown that there is no essential difference between people and animals: all are "relations," as the Inuit shaman song says.

Perhaps the innate rapport many children have for animals (and animals, for children) points back to this ancient mentality. We have all seen instances of dogs' being protective of—or saving—helpless babies, with almost human concern; and we have all seen normally fierce or reactive dogs being enormously tolerant of the antics of small children. When human beings treat animals kindly, the favor is always returned.

There should be such a rapport between children and animals, then, when the psychological atmosphere is healthy. Children gravitate toward stuffed animal toys. They long for and preoccupy themselves with pets of all kinds, furry, finny or feathery. Children's literature of all genres is filled with talking ducks, mice, dogs. In the Children's Apperception Test, psychologist Henry A. Murray substituted animals for the humans—including children—shown in the "typical situation" pictures used in the adult test. The reason? Children can project more easily into animals in these situations (being "potty-trained" or rebuked for misbehavior.) For children, the world of adults and adult human situations is incomprehensible and frightening, and even other children may be challenging. But cast the same events with animals as characters, and the tender psyche empathizes and resonates with the meanings and interpretations that help the psychologist understand the child.

This is the reason reports that children who kill their peers start with animal torture are so disturbing. Cruelty to animals should be noticed by parents and significant others as the first warning sign that the connection with "all our relations" is broken. In effect, the later transformations are just predictable developmental outcomes of a tear in the web of life and in the psyche. While it is normal for small children to need instruction in gentleness (as in how to pick up—or not pick up—a cat), empathy seems to develop naturally, for the most part. But those children who can inflict needless suffering, even on insects (boys who pull the wings off flies, for example) are becoming capable of hurting other children, themselves, and adults. They should be identified early and exposed to very skillfully designed and subtle educational and therapeutic remediation.

Swedenborg says animals represent "the affections." Someone who hurts animals, then, has deeply hurt or wounded feelings somewhere inside. The causes include overt physical, sexual, emotional abuse, inconsistency of response to the child—hysterical or violent outbursts—and psychological torture, in which the child is made to feel worthless or defective. In addition to these causal factors, there is also a category of "sins by omission," in families where children are simply left to fend for themselves—eating junk food from the convenience store and watching mindless entertainment too often characterized by the cruelty and violence found everywhere on television (*Beavis and Butthead* mirrors this adolescent world all too cogently). Here, children, unprotected by the "second womb" of a loving and engaged family, are direct victims of the "wasteland" mythology that is pandemic in our contemporary world. And we see what happens to the "affections," the animals of the soul, when nothing means anything anymore.

Samuel Ross is a distinguished philanthropist who set up a working therapeutic and educational community called "Green Chimneys,"[3] a place where wounded children come in contact with wounded animals. Youth-at-risk from a wide variety of abusive or unsupportive backgrounds encounter and care for eagles with one wing, damaged in the Valdez oil spill; Andean condors who have recovered from illness, elderly horses, cattle, pygmy sheep and goats, and many other creatures injured and cast off by our careless society. It is an amazing thing to see the young urban people in contact with these animals and to experience the palpable atmosphere of affection. The healing for both is undeniable.

Hospitals and homes for the elderly are using pet-therapists, mainly dogs and cats brought in for contact or petting, but sometimes more unusual animals like wolves or birds. At Stone Mountain Farm, our own Center for Symbolic Studies has been bringing together youth-at-risk with animals both tame and wild for a number of years; our Wildlife Educator, licensed falconer Judith Havrilla, may bring an owl, a civet cat, or some other fascinating creature to meet young and adult participants in our programs. We have also hosted, for several years, a program of gardening for developmentally disabled adults, conceived and directed by occupational therapist Al Havrilla, Judith's husband. In 1999, we added horseback riding to their activities: contact with these large, loving animals has a visible effect on the participants' self-esteem and vitality. What at first was only understood intuitively—and regarded with some suspicion by the scientifically minded—has now proven itself, both scientifically and practically: relating to animals is good for people.

————————— ANIMALS OF THE SOUL —————————

MARIE-LOUISE VON FRANZ, THAT EXTRAORDINARY WISEWOMAN and member of C. G. Jung's inner circle of analysts, was especially known for her interpretation of fairytales. For von Franz, fairytales are always telling us about one person—the self—although they might dress it in the beliefs and folk wisdom of many different periods and peoples. In her lectures and writings, she has given us guidelines on how to learn from these enduring yet constantly evolving collective fantasies.[4] Von Franz herself modeled meticulous scholarship, patient attention to the tiniest details, and a disciplined willingness to hold both knowledge and intellect in check while simply waiting and listening—like a cat at a mouse hole (an image she used to describe this process). She gave a great deal of attention to the many kinds of animals in fairytales and to their meanings for the human psyche in its process of individuation. The authors were privileged to hear her speak about fairytales on several occasions, and remember in particular her emphasis on the importance of the guiding or *helpful animal*. While the underlying structures of fairytales can be diagramed (and von Franz has left us some excellent diagrams), they are by no means simple or predictable. They are as numerous and varied as the peoples who have created, modified, and passed them on through time.

"I was fascinated by the idea of finding some generally human code, simple, but beyond national and individual differentiations," von Franz says in one published talk. "I have to confess that I have not found a standard basic rule, or rather, I have found it and I have not found it, for there is always a contradiction!"[5] She goes on to say that she can tell us stories where it is plain that we must resist, or even fight back vigorously, against evil; we must be honest, not tell lies, not dissemble; we must even kill, sometimes for no apparent or humanly justifiable reason. But for each of these examples there are just as many stories that warn us not to confront evil but to run away; or not to react to violence with more violence, but to restrain our tendency to fight back. And there are stories in which the hero or heroine prevails by trickery, deceit, or outright lying. Fairytales, von Franz always reminds us, are the people's stories, carrying the impressions of many cultures—but they speak to individuals. There is one constant, and it is found in the realm of the animal:

> The one exception to the rule of contradictions, however, seems to be that one must never hurt the helpful animal in fairy tales. I have found a few cases where disobedience leads to trouble, but in the long run does not lead to disaster; you may temporarily disobey the advice of the helpful fox or wolf or cat. But if basically you go against it, if you do not listen to the helpful animal or bird, or whatever it is, if any animal gives you advice and you don't follow it, then you are finished. In the hundreds and hundreds of stories that is the one rule which seems to have no exception. . . . This would mean that obedience to one's most basic inner being, one's instinctual inner being, is the one thing which is more essential than anything else. In all nations and all fairy tale material I have never found a different statement.[6]

Von Franz's words are the distillation of a long life of listening to the outpourings of the human psyche and of years of study of the dreams and fantasies of human culture: myths, folklore, and fairytales. We believe she is speakiing to us as individuals, but the message is equally applicable to us as a collective in our time, very much what the elders and shamans of indigenous peoples are saying: listen to the animals. In the case of von Franz, these are the animals within us, the magical creatures that animate our inner world of soul. The messages they bring us are about feeling, intuition, and the creative, fully energized life.

For the early Christian fathers, it was very important to de-spiritualize animals; pagan divinities were closely associated with animals, often had the forms of animals, and were worshiped in those forms. Animal and divine, like animal and human in our Inuit poem, were not separated. But Christians—and Jews and Muslims—were careful to establish that separation. Their god did not wear the face or walk in the body of a beast; his home was not here on earth, nor, by the time of the Council of Nicea, was it to be found everywhere in the hearts of men and women (untutored by bishops), but in heaven and its church. This was a part of that great dissociation: by it, a terrible wound was given to the world of nature, of animals and plants, and of human instinctual depths.

Yet this separation from the animal world has not always been the rule in Christianity. The tradition has been enriched by the persistence of both an esoteric nature mysticism and a more common sort of everyday pantheism that seems as simply acceptable to many ordinary Christians as it is execrable to theologians. And most people do talk to their pets and their houseplants, by such simple acts maintaining an ancient and necessary connection to nature.

In the hymns of the poet-monks of the early Celtic church, we find a faith informed by God's immanence in nature. To Saints Patrick, Columba, and Adomnan are attributed songs of praise to a God who is revealed in sunlight, flowing water, birdsong, flower, and leaf. Christopher Bamford quotes Saint Patrick at Tara: "Our God is the God . . . of Heaven and Earth, of sea and river, of sun and moon and stars, of the lofty mountain and the lowly valley. . . . He has put springs in the dry land and has set stars to minister to the greater lights."[7] Bamford goes on to assert that Patrick's Christianity was one still in touch with ancient nature-worship:

> Everywhere in Celtic Ireland we will find a holy intimacy of human, natural and divine . . . an abandonment to spiritual work and simultaneously a cultivation of the earth. There is at once a unique passion for the wild and elemental . . . coupled with a gentle human love for all creation, fellow creatures all with God.[8]

Saint Kieran is said to have lived alone in the wilderness, his congregation made up entirely of wild animals. Among these were a once-fierce boar, a doe, and a wolf, all of whom became Christian monks and served the saint meekly. However, one of these monks, a fox, was not entirely sincere in his piety and lusted after flesh—so he stole and ate the saint's brogues (sandals). But the saint forgave him, the fox repented, did penance, and became—we are told—"as righteous as were all the rest."[9] Kieran, of course, is not unique to Christian tradition; more recently, Saint Francis of Assisi preached to beasts and birds and renewed this ancient message of kinship.

Writing and teaching in Alexandria in the second century C.E., Adamantius Origen may not have thought of himself as a lover of nature, but he was aware of the presence of nature within the human psyche. He described "a second little world" inside us, where we are to "Understand that thou hast within thyself flocks of cattle . . . flocks of sheep and flocks of goats. . . . Understand that the birds of the sky are also within thee."[10]

Swedenborg also experienced the complexity of the worlds within and the multiplicity of their "inhabitedness." His work amplifies the significance, to a degree of detail and subtlety found nowhere else in the literature of the visionary tradition, of each kind of creature we encounter on our inward journey. Trained in the physical sciences, Swedenborg worked in them for many years before his exploration of the spiritual worlds began. We see the meticulousness of the trained field scientist and taxonomist in his descriptions of life beyond the bounds of body and of the ways in which spirit and body interact:

> In general, the land animals correspond to affections. . . . Specifically, cows and calves correspond to affections of the natural mind, sheep and lambs to affections of the spiritual mind. The various kinds of winged creatures, on the other hand, correspond to intellectual elements in the one mind or the other. . . .
>
> The reason that animals, genus by genus and species by species, are affections, is that they are alive. For nothing possesses life except out of affection and according to affection. This is why every animal has innate knowledge in keeping with the affection of his life.
>
> *Heaven and Hell* 110

Animals connect us with our life: this is what we find, again and again, as we work with fantasies, dreams, active imagination, and spontaneous visions of contemporary people. We have already mentioned von Franz's work; we will talk more later about Jung's "little people" of the psyche; and we will touch upon the work of other present-day healers like Marion Woodman and Anne Belford Ulanov, who are exploring the ethology of the inner world.

The words of Origen and Swedenborg also remind us of the many shamans of both North and South America, who tell us that we are accompanied by spirit animals who protect and guide us, and who bear witness to our native powers of vision and healing as these develop during our life. At one time, we may walk in company with a spirit bear; at another, we may have a cat, a fox, a hawk—sometimes one, sometimes several, spirit creatures can be seen by those with a shaman's sight.

This ancient tradition of "totem" animals informs the psychotherapeutic work of Stephen Gallegos, who teaches contemporary urban people to identify their interior animals, to locate them in the body, and to enter into ongoing healing dialogues or conferences with them.[11] In keeping with Swedenborg's observations about the correspondence of animals to the affections, Gallegos's work is powerfully affective. Gallegos guides the subject deeply into her or his own body, to a specific part through a specific animal, the layer—say, the "root-base" chakra—where a specific animal dwells. Root bases do well with reptiles: tortoises, serpents (the kundalini herself), but also elephants, patient hippos, and workhorses. If you have a skylark or a butterfly in this position, there might be problems, the same as if you had a hippopotamus obscuring the vision of "the third eye" (*ajña* chakra). The important thing in Gallegos' work is to have a dialogue with the animals, or even a parliament, in which you bring them together to powwow about the state of the chakras—hence, the personality and the whole living organism.

Swedenborg, also, was concerned that spirits and certain spiritual experiences should be understood as communicating through specific areas of the body:

> I have also been taught that it is not just one community [of spiritual beings] that flows into a given organ or member but many, and that there are many individuals in each community. . . .
>
> The particular viscera and members, or motor and sensory organs, are responsive to communities in heaven.

Arcana Coelestia 2628[12]

In *The Mythic Imagination*, Stephen has recounted numerous dreams from his collection of many hundreds, in which contemporary people have received initiatory summons to soul-growth from numinous animals.[13] Even as we write this book, such dreams continue to come to our attention. One spoke powerfully to a young man seeking to recover his relationship to his own deeper nature. He is a serious woodsman and wilderness guide, who receives nourishment when he spends time in the woods. He dreamed:

> I am in a spacious, sub-alpine meadow. I can feel there are large trees around, rather than the scrubby small ones that mark the high altitudes. It is a beautiful day and the air is clear in the mountains. I am leading a group of people, less than a dozen, all interested in what I am saying; I am feeling rather full of myself. All of a sudden my attention is drawn upward. A bald eagle and a raven are in combat. But as I watch their interaction, it seems more like an amazing dance, with ritualized rules, than a combat to the death. Their dance is charging the air above the meadow with power, with electricity. I can feel it in the marrow of my bones. I awaken with my heart beating fast, and the feeling that I have witnessed a mystery.

This mystery is to be experienced in nature. It calls us both out of ourselves and back into ourselves. The spirit-birds carry us beyond the world into the greater realm of spirit; but they also lend us their far-sight, as Native American shamans remind us, so that we can see our place in the vast and intricate matrix of spiritual nature.

One troubling element we encounter in fairytales and folklore, and sometimes in dreams, is that of the sacrifice of the magic animal. At a time when we are attempting to reforge our broken bond with the natural world, we do not need to carry on disproportionate notions of human importance: we are increasingly aware that, if we continue to sacrifice the natural world to our concepts of reason and spirit, we will soon have no viable earth left for our home. What, then, can be the truth behind such paradoxical images?

First, a caution: traditional stories come from many sources, and no one simple cause, origin, or intent can be found for them. Fairytales, for example, probably derive from all of the different sources various folklorists have suggested: some carry remnants of ancient myths; others may have grown up around actual events, people, or specific geographical features; some may spring from the imagination of a gifted storyteller or from one individual's dream or vision; others preserve elements from long-lost rituals. All of these elements have co-mingled over generations of tale-swapping, even crossing oceans so that similar stories or fragments appear in Brazil, China, France, and South Africa. When we work psychologically with animals, as we meet them in dreams, in the sacred stories of shamanic people, and in fairytales of all traditions, we need to remember that we are evoking vital forms in our own deep psyche: these are divine, not mortal creatures, not human even when they shapeshift into a human form. They come to us bringing the gifts of ensoulment and the call to individuation. It is because they are not meant to be bound in a human relationship that the magical animal must often die in these human soul-stories. In Native American stories, again and again Bear-woman's Bear-husband must die, so that she can return to the human tribe with her gifts of healing and life-renewal.[14] In the European fairytale of the Cat-Princess, she must become fully human so that she can be a complete, mortal mate to the king's son, and the kingdom of the psyche can become whole: that is, with masculine and feminine, "king" and "queen," in their proper places, ruling together, informed by their secret, shared initiation in the magical realm of cats and fairies.

ANIMAL PRESENCE

EVEN AS THE CENTER OF THE WORLD IS EVERYWHERE (as Black Elk has reminded us), so each of us is the center of the world—but only so long as we accept the full responsibility of that position: responsibility to be *responsive* to each other's center of the world. We must learn to open the eyes of the heart, to look out into the living matrix of which we are one part, one center, and recognize the luminous eyes that look back at us: They are the eyes of other soul-full persons, some humans of other ages, other sexes, other races; but many more look back at us from faces of other species, furred, feathered, finned, or the even more *other* faces of the "creeping nations."

We are part of the matrix, the web, or net of the mother. Animals, like siblings in a family where one member is out of control and violent, suffer from our acts of unconnectedness. They remind us that we are part of the whole, of the family of "all our relations." Shamanic cultures are bearers of this ancient sense of relatedness; the shaman is both the mediator between the human community and the world of spirit, and the connecting link with the world of animals. Indeed, as we have seen, in shamanic traditions, the realms of spirits and animals are intricately embedded one within the other, so that usually no clear boundary can be detected.

We have talked about dreams and traditional stories. In everyday life, too, animals come to us as teachers. They teach us to pay attention to small things, to take a moment to be gentle and attentive to another living creature. They teach us to listen to messages that are not loud and obvious: messages from the earth and from within ourselves where we, too, are still part of nature.

Since the latter part of the last century, we have been witness, increasingly, to the voices of native peoples compelled to speak out, each from the wisdom of their own tradition, but all cautioning against the "developed world's" disregard of the natural world. High in the Andes of Colombia, the Kogi people had kept their existence a secret, never revealing themselves to outsiders. Their elders are individuals selected in childhood, raised in darkness and solitude, carefully trained to see with eyes of the spirit. In the early 1990s, these isolated visionaries, disturbed by the messages of disharmony, illness, and death coming to them from the plants and animals of their mountain home, sent word out into the world that they, too, must now speak. Alan Herrera, of the BBC, responded to their invitation and took a video crew into the remote Andes to record their urgent message to the technological nations. This remarkable meeting of worlds is recorded in the BBC video *Elder Brother Speaks*.[15] The gist of the message is the same one coming to us from our own personal dreams and encoded in fairytales as old as our psyches: Younger brother—or sister— has forgotten that we are all relations, living in one house.

Animals do mirror back to us the depths of our own ancient souls, but they also meet us in the everyday, as individual creatures. We need to recognize and respect them as themselves, both for the good and growth of our own souls, for the safety and salvation of the earth we share, and *for their own sakes*. They are our teachers, guides, and companions—and they are themselves. They may not, ultimately, need us, but we need them very much.

Who are they, then, these other creatures? Who lives behind the eyes of our dog, our cat, our horse, our canary, our goldfish? When they are not being archetypes, symbols, psychopomps, who are they?

Perhaps only they can tell us. Perhaps we can never really know. But we can teach ourselves to ask the question over and over and to listen with open heart for whatever answer may come. Sister snake, brother raven, grandmother bear, grandfather salmon—who are you?

Denise Levertov reminds us that animals are not only our stories about them: "Come into animal presence," she says, for "No man is so guileless as the serpent." Their very nature invites us into the presence of that once familiar mystery:

> . . . What is this joy, that no animal
> falters, but knows what it must do?
> that the snake has no blemish,
> that the rabbit inspects his strange surroundings
> in white star-silence? The llama
> rests in dignity, the armadillo
> has some intention to pursue in the palm-forest.
> Those who were sacred have remained so,
> holiness does not dissolve, it is a presence
> of bronze, only the sight that saw it
> faltered and turned from it.
> An old joy returns in holy presence.[16]

The relationship of humans with animals is as old as our race. This is an idiotically simple statement; but let us re-examine it, remembering that many humans now think it is a relationship we can live without. As human partners must at times, we look back over the years we have spent together, asking ourselves if we each can live without the other, so let us briefly look back on the prehistory of our relationship with animals.

Richard Leakey, son of Louis and Mary Leakey whose discoveries in the Olduvai Gorge in Tanzania, East Africa, have restructured our thinking about human evolution, asks a poignant question at the inception of his examination of human evolution, in his book *Origins:* "Why is it that humanity seems determined to spiral ever faster towards self-made destruction?" Citing the studies of aggression by Raymond Dart and Konrad Lorenz, and the popularization of the "aggressionist" theory by Robert Ardrey, Leakey lays the groundwork for his thoughtful examination of the origins of human culture:

> The idea was proposed that man is unswervingly aggressive. . . . And the notion is elaborated with the suggestion that at some point in our evolutionary history we gave up being vegetarian ape-like creatures and became killers. . . . It makes a good, gripping story. More important, it absolves society from attempting to rectify the evil in the world. But it is fiction—dangerous fiction.[17]

Leakey traces the human journey out of Africa from the earliest appearance of crude tools through the crucial development of the ability to transport things: food, then water, later fire, and, finally, ideas. The ability to carry water, Leakey says, freed *Homo erectus* (many times great-grandmother "Lucy," three million years ago, was of this kind) to travel long distances through unknown territory and to migrate. The ability to transport ideas allowed separate groups to exchange, cross-fertilize, and invent culture. These early hominid were primarily gatherers—eaters, among many other things, of insects, which may have been a major factor in refining their thumb-to-forefinger dexterity. As they added meat to their diet—perhaps increasingly as they moved northward—they also became increasingly effective at cooperative efforts. Here is where Leakey's interpretation of human prehistory departs from the aggressionists:

> A serious biological interpretation of these facts does not lead to the conclusion that because once the whole of the human race indulged in hunting as part of its way of life, killing is in our genes. Indeed, we argue that the opposite is true, that humans could not have evolved in the remarkable way in which we undoubtedly have unless our ancestors were strongly cooperative creatures. . . . Meat-eating was important in propelling our ancestors along the road to humanity, but only as part of a package of socially-oriented changes involving the gathering of plant foods and sharing the spoils.[18]

Leakey proposes that the seeds of historical aggression and war are to be found in the transition to agriculture and the acquisition of possessions. He points out that the lives of hunter-gatherers, in fact, generally lack the sustained periods of unoccupied time necessary for organized warfare, while farming communities have such periods after the harvests are gathered in, which were when many historic warrior societies engaged in attacks on their neighbors. Farmers also accumulate possessions, which need protection. While these two observations remain essentially true, they have been amplified and refined by the work of archeologist Marija Gimbutas.[19]

In her extensive examination of the artifacts and iconography of neolithic Anatolia, Gimbutas has created the most complete catalogue yet made of primeval images of the goddess in her many emanations: bird goddesses of several specific types, pig goddess, lion goddess—each with its particular province and aspect. But nowhere among the richness of images and artifacts does one find evidence of warfare: these early farmers, for thousands of years, made few if any weapons and saw no need to enclose their towns with walls. Women, who were significant in the providing of food, were evidently highly regarded among them. They were a peaceful people, as Joseph Campbell emphasized in his later lectures.[20]

It was later, around three to two thousand years before the common era, when nomadic herders and warriors moved into the Near Eastern world, that warfare became a frequent, organized and increasingly large-scale event in human life. These were peoples who combined the warrior mystique of the hunter with the *ownership* of domestic animals. Men, the primary providers of food in a society which glorified the hunter even if the herds provided the greater body of meat, also *owned* women. Those warrior people, who added the horse and bronze weapons to their possessions, became virtually invincible. They invented war as the profession of a ruling class.

The human habit of aggression, Leakey suggests, is no more than ten thousand years old (and Gimbutas's work cuts that period down by one-third): thus, it is not a part of our primal equipment. Further, in examining the evidence of several million years of early hominids, he sees our dominant characteristics as the ability to cooperate, along with innate flexibility and adaptiveness. Violence against one's own kind and intemperate violence against other species, Leakey maintains, are not natural elements in the makeup of any animal predator or omnivorous primate; nor can it be of human beings. That would be counterrevolutionary. It occurs as a reaction to environmental and social factors, and is subject to change when those factors change. In animals, such violence is usually short lived, a response to an extremely unbalanced environment—years of unusual cold, floods, or drought, or severe overcrowding in a restricted environment, or unaccustomed pressure from an increase of human neighbors, for instance.

It is here that we return to our discussion of human relationship with animals and with all of nature. It is we who have created—out of our cleverness and ability to work together—an overcrowded, unbalanced environment and a species at war with itself. If we are going to use our formidable skills to heal ourselves and our wounded world, we need healthy models to guide us. We do have them: the evidence is that for millions of years we lived lightly on this earth, in harmony with our animal kin and neighbors. As gatherers and hunters, we respected the plants and animals who sustained us.

Joseph Campbell suggests, in his lectures on the paleolithic beginnings of art and religion, that it was in the stress of the paradox of living by death that our ancestors faced the first ethical and spiritual crisis.[21] Because they were *related* to the animals they hunted—that is, they structured their entire community life around a respectful and intimate connection with the animals—they found it necessary to examine, to seek meaning in, and ultimately to spiritualize through ritual and art the act of killing the animal. Its death was a magical and sacred event: Death brought life to the people. The people made a compact with the animals, with the spirit- or master-animal of each species, promising to celebrate the animal and perform rites for its proper return to the world of spirit and its eventual rebirth into the world of nature. We know these ancient stories and rites from those contemporary indigenous people who continue to live "in a sacred way."

One such story is that of the young woman who made a marriage with the buffalo-spirit and returned to her people bearing the dance of healing and renewal for both tribes, buffalo and human. A related story is that of White Buffalo Calf Woman, who first appeared to two men of the Lakota nation; she was a beautiful young woman, dressed in white buffalo skins and wearing a bundle on her back. One man knew her immediately for a spirit-being and greeted her respectfully; the other man looked upon her with lust. A cloud billowed around the lustful man briefly, then blew away; when it was gone, nothing was left of the man but a heap of bones and maggots. His blindness to the spirit brought him death. But White Buffalo Calf Woman had come to bring new life. She sent the first man ahead to tell his people of her coming; they prepared a large tipi in which she established herself. She brought the Sacred Pipe to them and lived among them for a time, teaching them the tribe's songs and rituals. She told them that, when they prayed with the Sacred Pipe, they would be praying with all living creatures on earth, with the four winds and with the earth itself. When she left to return to her own kind, she showed herself in the form of a white buffalo calf.

In our time, the ritual of the Sacred Pipe is again coming to the fore as peoples of all nations sit in council circle together, praying for peace. Those who honor the traditional ways of native people in North America celebrate the birth of the rare white buffalo cow-calf—named Miracle—on a Wisconsin farm in 1994. Such a birth, it was prophesied, signals a time of change and a possibility of the severed nations coming together in harmony.

In acknowledging our vital contract with the animals, Joseph Campbell has said, we find one of the main foci for the beginning of art and religion. The earliest animal images made by human hands, which have been recovered to date, are probably the little engravings on bone, horn, and stone of reindeer and other prey animals from about 150,000 years ago; the artists were Neanderthals. They buried their dead with flowers of healing herbs and honored the cave lion's bones with ochre painting.

For over a hundred-thousand years, the Cro-Magnon people, who succeeded the Neanderthals in Europe, continued to record in art, engraved, sculpted, and painted their celebration of the pact of renewal with the animals. Between forty- and twenty-thousand years ago in France and Spain, the Cro-Magnon left to us, their descendants, a large number of extraordinary shrines to this "Most Ancient Church," as Swedenborg called it.[22] The best known, of course, is the extensive cavern of Lascaux, in the Dordogne region. Called the "Sistine Chapel of the Paleolithic," its art, now meticulously examined by several generations of art historians, is regarded with veneration for the aesthetic perfection it displays. Recognition of the high degree of cultural evolution that must have preceded this outpouring of excellence has transformed our estimation of our ancestors. Lascaux is likened by Campbell more to a "cathedral" than a "chapel." "No crude anthropological theory of 'primitive magic' suffices," he says, "to explain its extraordinary beauty, the aesthetics of its organization, or the magnificence of its forms."[23]

> As in Chartres Cathedral the mystery of the hidden history of this universe is revealed through the imagery of an anthropomorphic pantheon, so here, in these temple caves, the same mystery is made known through animal forms that are at once in movement and at rest. These forms are magical: midway, as it were, between the living species of the hunting plains and the universal ground of night, out of which the animals come, back into which they return, and which is the very substance of these caves.[24]

"For these herds," Campbell says in another place, "are the herds, not of time, but of eternity."[25] And among the primitive hunters who painted them were, very likely, "cosmically initiated" individuals, shamans and elders whose fully human minds and subtly articulated sensibilities (certainly far more so than any city-dweller's) were directed toward eternal questions of mortality and renewal, and perhaps of transcendence. When our forebears went down into the womb of earth, they found there a portal opening out upon the stars in the heavens: as below, so above. It is important to remind ourselves that the mystery to which the animal-guides direct us is not a little or lesser mystery: it is the Great Mystery. We can reach it by passing through the sun door of the ascetics, or we can pass into it through the starlit darkness of a mare's eyes.

About fifteen thousand years later than the paintings at Lascaux, not far away in the French Pyrenees, in the cavern to be named "Les Trois Frères" after its twentieth-century discoverers, another group of hunters created enduring and inspiring art. Their intention was certainly to inspire awe, even fear, and to instill in those who viewed their art a profound sense of respect for the hidden world of power within the natural world. Early twentieth-century visitors to the cave describe crawling for extended periods through damp, slick passages where they sometimes had to cling desperately to the rock to keep from sliding off a ledge, frequently bumping their heads on the ceiling, sometimes so constricted they could hardly pass their shoulders through, all the while pushing oil lamps before them in the suffocating darkness. The reward for this effort is a vision of the "herds of eternity" engraved, with taut, energetic strokes and contours, on the central sanctuary wall of Les Trois Frères. There, a complex montage of many species—horses, lions, bison, reindeer, and others—swirls around the central figure, a dancing biped apparently clothed in a buffalo hide and head, who reminds us forcefully of a buffalo dancer of the North American plains, playing the instrument that preceded the weapon—the musical bow. On an opposite wall, fifteen feet above the floor in a "vaulted" niche, facing the great wall of animals, is the lone, eerie figure known as the "sorcerer" of Les Trois Frères.

Is he a shaman, masked, entranced, dancing his healing vision? Is he the Master Animal, stag-antlered, owl-eyed, wolf-pelted, prancing among his earthly emanations, the bison, caribou, and horse-herds of old Eurasia? Is he the god himself, consort to the great-bellied Mother of Creatures, leading the multiformed

Milky Way of star-beasts across the heavens? Is he an ancient magic mirror, showing us the image of our own three-million-year-old soul? Campbell comments:

> In such a context, the hunter and the hunted beast—in ritual terms, the priest and his sacrifice—would have to have been experienced in some psychological dimension as one and the same—even as the mixed form of the presiding presence of the Sanctuary, the semihuman, semianimal, dancing Animal master, already suggests. The beast to be slaughtered is interpreted as a willing victim, or rather, as a knowing participant in a covenanted sacred act wherein the mystery of life, which lives on life, is comprehended in its celebration. And the essential effect of all this upon the young boys who were to be turned by the rites of this sacred place into initiated hunters would have consisted, finally, in the opening of their minds to such an experience of the secondary nature of the passing forms of time that they should become capable of expressing reverence for life in the act of taking it.[26]

But in our time it is common to kill without reverence, to commit sacrifice without meaning, without reference beyond our little moment to the Great Mystery. We have broken faith. We countenance the continued violation in every part of the globe—of preserves and wild lands that are the only refuge left to many species; the daily torment of animals in laboratories, sacrificed to projects that are trivial or contrived to keep funds flowing; immoderate and often illegal hunting of endangered species; toxic wastes in air, water, and earth.

Surely by now we all know the list of betrayals. Many of us are actively engaged in addressing several of these or related problems. We have hope that a generation of children raised with more awareness of the urgency of earth's plight—our plight—will turn the tide. We work hard to prepare the ground for their work, knowing the time is short.

But as we work for the future, we need to remember the past. We made promises to the animals and to the plants, to the whole spirited world of the natural powers: we promised to remember, to listen, and to sing the songs and dance the stories they teach us. If we can learn to do this again, it may be that, as we continue the hard work of saving the world, our souls will feel more alive, our hearts more hopeful. A Pawnee chief, Letakots-Lesa, early in the twentieth century, spoke with knowledge of these hundred-thousand-year-old mysteries as they were practiced in his day, as they are still, in ours:

> When a man sought to know how he should live, he went into solitude and cried until in vision some animal brought wisdom to him. It was Tirawa, in truth, who sent his message through the animal. He never spoke to man himself, but gave his command to beast or bird, and this one came to some chosen man and taught him holy things. Thus were the sacred songs and ceremonial dances given the Pawnees through the animals.
>
> So it was in the beginning.[27]

———————— AMBASSADORS OF NATURE————————

WHILE WE WERE WORKING ON THIS BOOK, a friend arranged for us to meet Dr. Jane Goodall, the famous field ethologist, at the University of Western Connecticut. A rare opportunity, with about thirty others present—mostly professors, biologists of different sorts, and ecologists—it also proved to be a very intense and moving encounter. Dr. Goodall opened with a story.

There is a growing movement among zoos and animal parks to abandon the small steel and concrete cages in which many animals are confined and to put them in more lifelike and natural-seeming habitats. Jojo was an older male chimpanzee who had spent most of his life being gaped at by the public in a small cage. Now he was released onto an island with other chimpanzees, surrounded by a moat separating them from the public (chimpanzees being notoriously poor swimmers). A tough, younger male came forth and challenged Jojo, whose earlier solitary life had unsuited him temperamentally for such an experience. Panicking, Jojo jumped a barrier and landed in the water-filled moat.

Well, swimming lessons had not been included in Jojo's early education either, so down he went. A visitor to the zoo, a man standing watching with his family, started to go to Jojo's rescue. He was immediately shouted at to stay back by the chimpanzee handler and other zoo people, who knew how dangerous 130-pound male chimpanzees are. On the other bank was the macho male group of chimpanzees, all worked up. It was a compelling existential dilemma; but the man, while his family and the zoo staff gaped in horror, dove into the moat!

The man had to go under the water to retrieve Jojo. When he brought the unconscious chimpanzee to the surface, he tried to push him up the sloping concrete bank, where the other males were screaming and menacing. The handlers and the family were screaming at him to come back. Jojo was still unconscious and threatening to slide back into the water.

The man literally carried Jojo up the bank, and the three male chimpanzees drew back. Finally, Jojo coughed up water, came back to himself, and weakly crawled to safety.

The man swam to safety himself, back to his astonished family. The handlers explained that the reason they were so anxious was that chimpanzees are very afraid of strange humans, ones they do not know, and could easily have attacked.

The handlers asked, "Why didn't you come back? What stopped you? You could have been killed!"

The man shrugged his shoulders and said, "I looked into his [Jojo's] eyes, and they were like the eyes of a person, any person, and they were saying, 'Help me! You are the only one who can help me,' and I couldn't do anything else!"

The story was gripping for us because we had heard Joseph Campbell dozens of times tell a story of a comparable altruistic event that took place on the mountainous Hana Highway on Oahu, Hawaii:

A man, for reasons known to himself alone, was about to jump off the high cliff. An off-duty policeman saw and rushed to save him—as it turned out, at peril to his own life. The situation was precarious for a while, the policeman himself in danger of going over with the man. But at last he brought them both to safety.

Then Campbell would ask the compelling question: Why should it be that a man, at risk to his own life, can so participate in the predicament of another, personally unknown to him?

The question was asked in the context of the German philosopher Arthur Schopenhauer's work; in framing it, Campbell would weave in the Upanishads, Kantian ethics, Inuit (Eskimo) metaphysics, and even knightly honor as an inflection of the hero journey. But the answer to which he homed, like the moth to the flame, was the one that Schopenhauer himself had drawn from Eastern metaphysics: *Tat tvam asi*: "Thou art that:" "I and thou are one." It was a compelling excursus and always brought people a little closer to that insight.

At the Goodall symposium were several professional wildlife rehabilitators. Their stories of extraordinary "I–thou" exchanges with animals seemed to support the point Goodall and Campbell had presented. Profound rapport can occur between human beings and animals, when humans are in an attuned state of consciousness.

But then several biologists grew stern and lofty: "These personal stories are well and good," they said (a wee bit condescendingly) to the animal rehabilitators, "But aren't you being, er, a little 'anthropomorphizing' and sentimental? The real thing to focus on for science is the study of species, not individuals. Besides, these animals, like Jojo, were almost impossible to return to their natural environments." (And lastly:) "You might be doing more harm than good!"

The room was somewhat jarred by the cynical perspective, but the response from Goodall, and most of the people who worked one-on-one with the animals, was passionate. They spoke of the undeniable communications that had taken place between themselves and the animals and how important this was for the world *itself* to feel and know: we have to return, they were saying in effect, to that time the Inuit poem speaks of, when humans and animals could communicate.

Stephen offered that, from a psychological perspective, these interspecies relationships were precisely attempts to bridge the barrier of anthropomorphism and move more to an apprehension like that proposed by Arne Ness in Deep Ecology, the nonanthropocentric view. Weren't these animals ambassadors from the rest of nature to our estranged "human island"?

Dr. Goodall sparked with the comparison. "Yes, yes, that's it!" she said, "I call them my 'Ambassadors,' and I believe that this work of human beings' really encountering the animals is one of the most important things I'm doing—along with lots of other people. It's bridging the gap with the other species, realizing that we are all relations. I think of my chimpanzees as ambassadors to the world, and they take to the role very well."

─────── STEPHEN AND ROBIN IN DIALOGUE ───────

Stephen: Jane Goodall certainly seemed to have no trouble with the idea that an altruistic act is an altruistic act, whether directed to a human or an animal; it is an equivalent thing. Campbell's point was that such acts occurring spontaneously say something about the nature of the universe. They erupt from that deep mystical level and can clearly be seen to cross species boundaries. The man who saved Jojo would have been much more comprehensible to most folk if it were a human child that was saved. He would have been a less ambiguous hero, for some of them.

Robin: Because the victim, the object of the saving, was furry should make no difference. It is the impulse itself we marvel at and how it erupts from the psyche of healthy human beings (just as its opposite, the wish to hurt animals, erupts from underlying pathology).

I think Dr. Goodall needs to be credited with taking the I–thou relationship (of Martin Buber, the theologian) into interspecies communication and, in doing this, opening up a whole realm of study. The idea is most recently found in the work of Penelope Smith and others, where they are really seeing that the best mediums of communication with animals may not be language, but gestural and facial, and often intuitive or telepathic.[28]

Stephen: There are acts of spontaneous altruism noted in the developmental psychology literature, in children as young as under two years of age: one child's giving a rattle to another crying child or trying to warn it away from something dangerous. That suggests that the root of altruism is innate, just as Swedenborg says, but that to the impulse must be grafted environmental echo and support.

But what I marvel at, in the story of Jojo's rescue, was that man's ability to resist authority. Those guys in uniforms were yelling at him, the chimpanzees (furry authorities, I guess) were screaming at him to ward him off; and still the spontaneous impulse broke through. That's heroism in my definition: the ability to stand by your deepest impulse, against distraction.

Robin: So much work has been done in the last thirty years, and interestingly quite a bit of it by women, about communicating with animals: I think of the people who have done the field and lab work with gorillas—in communication, using sign language—and the families of the researchers who have taken them into their homes.

I am thinking also of Hope Ryden's work, studying wild horses. She observed all sorts of social subtleties and individual differences in the structure of the social order in wild-horse herds; and now field researchers have confirmed that such "cultures" are quite different in different parts of the western United States, in different environments.[29]

Ryden noticed what the academic observers hadn't: horses have a matriarch, the old mare who leads the herd. Horsemen in many places did know this, but it hasn't been well understood generally before her work. Women have been doing a lot of going out and living with the animals, and so really coming to know them in their context: Penny Patterson with gorillas, Jane Goodall with chimpanzees.

I told Dr. Goodall this today, and it felt good to pass it on to her, because she really understood it: Joseph Campbell would say at different times that there were two images that to him signified that we were at the threshold of an immense evolution in consciousness, a whole new phase of "what it is to be human." One was the image of our planet as a beautiful blue globe, hanging there in space (as seen from the Apollo spacecraft). To know that we all live on that globe together, that's our world—seeing it all at once—we may be able to feel we are looking into the face of Gaia, the Great Mother. The second was the image—and I can clearly remember Joe's slide—of Jane Gooddall holding a chimpanzee, as a mother holds a child, and the eyes of the human and the eyes of the chimpanzee are both intelligent, and both filled with love.

That's the experience that you, Stephen, have been talking about that breaks through this wall we have around us. It's the wall between men and women, between adults and children; the wall between races and classes and professions and nations of people; the wall between people and animals, people and plants; between people and all the living life of the planet, including the very rocks and soil, and the sun's fire bubbling within; and the sun itself. Because we are part of all that, and whoever told us that it's not alive?

Stephen: That's what Jung meant when he said the *anima* and the *animus* both have theriomorphic aspects, animal-shaped forms. The soul is made up of animals, just as Swedenborg said; they are our animated feelings, our affections, our warm mammalian (and dark reptilian) brains. Jung found that his women patients experienced the animus as collectives of animals, herds of horses, flocks of birds, but also collectives of men marching, male humans in groups.

Robin: I'm fascinated by that idea, that the animus appears as an animal, because as I have been reading for this book, I find that the most thoughtful women writing about gender psychology all acknowledge that the animal figure is extremely important and powerful in the woman's psyche. It often carries this soul-growth and vitalizing power that the anima carries for the man. There's something really there, really important, in these figures of stags with luminous eyes, wolves, unicorns, dragons.

Susun Weed says that a dragon is a group of menstruating women, working in their full blood power, together. I think that's a very interesting notion. I think it's probably part of the picture, and maybe a significant part of it.[30]

But a dragon is also an untamable, elemental, enormous power; probably primally that very first uncoiling burst of light that created the universe, with its endless little nubs of more universes spinning off. I think of galaxies and atoms—the "chaos" images we see in computer simulations are also essentially dragon images—from that first energy. And these things seem, somehow, to be deeply embedded in the woman's process of self-recognition and rebirth. The intensity and the profundity of these images are important for a woman. They might even have to do with the way many women have felt out of place in the male-defined social order: That is, woman have not been identified as "powerful," yet when these images are spontaneously engaged, power surges up within us. There doesn't seem to be much you can do, there's no place for this kind of image in anybody's structured society. What do you do with a dragon in the depths of your psyche?

Stephen: Whew! What do you do? Men's dragons are more on the surface, or out in the world, grumbling along the highways or flying through the skies; or in owning things, in the acquisition of baubles—including women sometimes—and in fire-breathing tirades directed at whomever.

Robin: Well, maybe the dragons can find a way to mate. I think traditionally they do it in the upper airs—in the sky! And Chinese dragons are far more benevolent than the ones in the western hemisphere; they bring good fortune and bestow magical gifts. Perhaps our dragons could learn from them.

Stephen: We keep coming back to the beautiful symmetry of Swedenborg's model of the psyche. If my inner dragon can meet yours. . . . In fact, if the soul is a menagerie, when mine meets yours, there is bound to be squawking and snapping; a couple produces a kind of Noah's Ark of the mind. I think of Stephen Gallegos' "parliaments," where he brings all the animals together. Two people can do this together, even meeting each other's animals and getting to know them.

Robin: Maybe that's why some imaginative renditions of angels have eyes and wings and hands everywhere: it's the soul-menagerie that is being glimpsed.

Stephen: I'm thinking of ways in which attitudes about animals have really divided people, perhaps just as seriously as religious issues. There's the story that Elizabeth Kübler-Ross told at the International Transpersonal meeting in Davos, Switzerland. When she was growing up, her family had a very large, tame rabbit that she loved. Her father, to punish her, or maybe, "to grow her up" ("for her own good," as Alice Miller has it), made her carry her pet to the butcher, watch while it was killed and dismembered; and then bring the parts back and join the family meal when it was eaten.

Robin: I recall that it left her sick to her stomach, and very, very angry.

Stephen: At the time we heard the story, we were only a few miles from where Kübler-Ross had grown up and initiated her postwar bicycle trips as a teenager, to see the reality of the death camps. Having read Alice Miller, I find the scenario with her father horrible but believable. It did not, however, have its desired effect. It traumatized her, estranged her from her father, and yet set her on a lonely path filled with compassion for the dying. You see, young Elizabeth's father killed not only the physical pet, but her childish projections of soul into and around the animal, and he did wrenching violence to those soul-parts of his daughter in his "lesson."

There was another event, from my therapeutic practice. A sensitive, literary woman in her late thirties, whom we shall call "Laura," had come for counseling. Her husband was a race-car driver, woodsman, and hunter. Married young, they had raised two children together, who were now young adults becoming independent. The woman thought that she had loved her husband, but wasn't so sure any more. The critical incident had involved a bear.

For Laura, the natural setting they lived in was a temple; that was what she loved about their rural life, while her husband reveled in the hunting and fishing exploits—and talking about them, usually with other men. One day, a visitor came to their back yard; it was a young, glossy black bear. It probably weighed only about two-hundred-fifty pounds and was a little lean from the winter's long hibernation.

Laura's husband went in for his gun. She tried to stop him and begged for the bear's life. "He's like a visitor; he doesn't mean any harm. It's not like going out to hunt him; let him be!" She tried everything, but he, silently and implacably, just went outside and shot the bear dead.

The woman had been distraught ever since and hadn't slept with her husband; and the gap between them just seemed to be widening and widening.

Robin: The man was probably coming from his own deep instinctive wildness: "No one tells me what to do! I'm the primeval hunter. The bear comes into my yard, my territory; I kill the bear, and that's what I can understand!"

There was a part of his wife that probably really loved him for his wildness; but when that part is running automatically, will not stop, will not listen to the woman at all, that's bad. There needs to be a dialogue. Sometimes it is time to kill: "The children have to be fed; how do we feed them? We have to go on, you know!" But it's important, then, to say to the bear, while you kill compassionately and cleanly, "You would eat me to feed your children; I'm going to eat you to feed mine," or if it's to a deer, "I'm taking your life; my life is not better than yours but I'm doing this, this is nature, this is the way we live; but I honor you."

When the masculine is no longer listening to the feminine, and the masculine thinks it doesn't have to listen because it's got all the power, then there's a problem. That leaves no place for the woman to continue in the "relationship" which is *no* relationship.

Stephen: The story seems paradigmatic of masculine and feminine styles of relationship to nature, to the world of instinct, and to the animal. It probably touches back to that original world of the hunters and gatherers, and thus touches on shamanism.

In the olden times, it is believed among many indigenous peoples, before the days of rifles, there was an unspoken covenant between the animal and the hunter that the animal in some way offered itself to the hunter, came to be slain in that way. Hunting was thus a kind of mystical seeking of the animal, who was, in turn, a willing victim, who freely offered itself. When the tool of slaying was a spear or a boomerang or a bow and arrow, you were in the immediate vicinity of the creature and could feel its soul. There was a chance for eye contact, a chance to feel that deeper level of the spiritual compact between you.

Now this was one of the things that came up as firearms were introduced into the world of the Inuit. The tryst or the covenant with the animal was no longer possible for two reasons. First was the greater striking-distance and relative infallibility of the gun; but the second was much more dangerous: there was a kind of spiritual dyslexia or agnosia going on in which the ancient compact had been forgotten. Something sacred and elemental in the relationship sense was lost, and that was the double whammy—both the animal *and* the magical worldview of the interaction and symbiosis of nature with spirit itself was destroyed.

Robin: I liked very much what you said in the Goodall symposium when you talked about the spiritual and the natural, the organic, that they are the same thing, not separate. In that moment I saw Jane Goodall smile, a very small smile that seemed to come from deep inside her. It seemed she was nodding when you said that, and she was very glad to hear it being acknowledged.

Stephen: It was based on the real inner meaning of Swedenborg's "correspondences" and the "discrete degrees" of creation. I had a wonderful tutor, Paul Hartley, who explained all this to me at about the age of ten. The divine source radiates out in the form of inexhaustible love and wisdom; along the way there are "stepdowns" in the ladder of creation, called "discrete degrees." Divine energy goes out from the source successively (and this is not so different from the "ladder" of Dionysius the Areopagite) to the "celestial angels" (in three degrees) and the "spiritual angels" (in three degrees); then through the vast labyrinthine "world of spirits," into human experience as psychospiritual; and then into the animal realm and vegetable realms, and the world of nature, the biological side of the human. At the age of ten I was a little overwhelmed with all this angelic lore, but the net effect was a glimpse of a multifoliate tapestry of creation that is this universe. It is a seamless whole, a truth recognized by the animistic world view.

What I said in the Goodall meeting was that there are not two different epistemological universes, in which the physical sciences describe one set of laws and the faculty of theology another, but echoes of each with the other, spirituality and creation seamlessly interwoven together. "As above, so below."[31]

When you are meeting an animal's gaze, trying to intuit, understand it, relate to it, then simultaneously (as both Swedenborg and the shamans would say) a spiritual dimension becomes possible. It is a very interesting thing, this "as above, so below": how the nutrients and chemicals of any organic soil turn into plant forms, how they then turn into animal forms as the animals eat the plants, are in turn eaten by human beings, who are, presumably, eaten by the spirits—or at least vexed and tried by them.

Biologists know this. Elements go through chemical transmutations, turn into complex organic compounds, are assimilated and transformed into the neurotransmitters and the cellular substrate of the nervous system. But then they are further transformed into activations of sleeping and waking, into drives and affections, into dreams and good ideas, and then into the life of the soul and its spiritual aspirations.

There are two scientific fundamentalisms. One says, "Well, we don't know that spirit exists, because whatever it is, whatever people say, we only know it through human beings talking about it." The other is the metaphysical fundamentalism, that says, "Ah, this fallen world is corrupt; how far, how low could you fall, so as to become enmeshed in the coils of mere matter!" (This is the gnostic mythos: the child of light falls into the darkness and must win his way back to the light, his birthright.)

Robin: You don't study matter in that model because it is so "fallen"?

Stephen: That's right, the gnostics say that nature is a lower order of manifestation or existence than spirit; and so the two are in a kind of tension. Therefore, we have always to avoid falling back into the swamp, the morass, or the pit of nature because it is always pulling us down through our emotions or inclinations, our greed, our laziness, our fear.

Robin: But I think in a matriarchal or Great Goddess religion both "above" and "below" could be tolerated. It's the relationship that is the primary value; what matters is that things are woven together, the one does not exist without the other. It is a "masculine conceit" (that is to say, exclusively analytic) to say that the one exists without the other, that you can know nature without spirit and spirit without nature. In a certain way, both fundamentalisms are wrong, since they're both one-sided.

I've been thinking for weeks how discernment, the sword of the intellect, develops in the masculine. Now, we're not talking *male* and *female*, but *masculine*, about the masculine mode, this powerful tool to separate one thing from another, so that it can be examined. But in a one-sided culture, in one-sided systems of education, this becomes separateness all down the line, so that, in this, I think we see the masculine mode run mad. This is Mary Shelley's Frankenstein monster.

Stephen: It's the same thing as in the Marduk mythos. Fiery, masculine god cuts things into separate parts and creates the world. But it is a world *fabricated*, a world of appearances, and designed to enact a magical agenda of that god.

Robin: This is one of the things I held myself back from saying in the Goodall symposium. Yes, the Marduk consciousness dismembers and separates.

When a child says, "Oh, but the doggy is a person just like me," and mommy and daddy, say, "No dear, we are human. The dog is different; you may think that the dog is thinking like you, but it really doesn't. It's quite different, and you'll understand when you get older. . . ." we are teaching two disparate lessons. One is the necessary ability to examine our world carefully, to make discriminations, not to project our humanness thoughtlessly onto everything around us. But the other is the destructive lesson of human alienation and arrogance.

Let's say that I'm a little girl, passionately in love with horses, and I'm told, "If you're going to be a good horsewoman, my dear, put away this childish thinking, and let's remember that the horses are animals. They don't really understand, and in fact they don't even love or feel; they don't even feel pain like we do. Now let's be *rational*. . . ." And above all, being a little girl, I don't want to be thought a fool by all the wonderful men around me. So I really do have to put away my feeling side; and little boys who love the animals and want to cuddle with them have to put away their feelings, because if they don't, they won't grow up to be a man.

Now let's look at it differently; let's put it down in our guts and sit with it awhile, and feel how this all works, and feel the wrongs that we've created with this way of going about things, and admit that it's time to start over. And if we really *think* about it—and this is being rational—there are probably more people in the world who would like to change things than those who are satisfied with this mess of inequities and rationalizations.

Stephen: When I was a little boy, I was asked to memorize a poem in which I "put away childish things, and thought like a man." It seems to me the violation—the Mardukian separation—is saying what my father said when I asked whether our beloved Irish setter, Trigger, would go to heaven when he died. He thought awhile and answered, "Er . . . No." (I think he might have been wondering what the official church position on dogs was. They certainly hadn't been baptized or been converted to Christianity, as one did with "natives.") But I pressed the issue—I might have been all of ten—"But they would let them in if they were very 'good' dogs, if they never disobeyed?" (I think I was taught to construe "goodness" and "obedience" as the same thing.)

Dad said, "I don't think so; maybe they have a different heaven for very good dogs; I don't know."

Robin: It's the same question I asked my maternal grandmother, a horsewoman and an original, delightful person. "Grandmother, do they have horses in heaven?"

"Yes, of course, dear, wonderful horses!" she said, "How do you think they pull the fiery chariots?" And then she said, "Besides, what sort of heaven would it be without horses?"

Today I was in the barn with Kevin, the blacksmith, and we were working with our newly arrived albino horse, Silver. Kevin said he had just seen an albino squirrel right near here; and then he said, "You know, there are albino deer here." Now Kevin said he sneaked up close enough to touch the white deer and saw her pink eyes. Then he said, "You know, Native Americans said it was very bad fortune to kill an albino animal. I knew two guys who killed albino deer." Then he started telling us the stories.

Stephen: My hair is standing on end already (that's the authentic, dermal response to the supernatural or the spirit world). You know how I love a ghost story!

Robin: The first one was dragging it out of the woods when he died of a heart attack. The second one had the deer proudly displayed on the roof of his car, was driving home, and was killed in a car accident. I had told Kevin that, in Celtic lore, when the hero meets an albino deer, it ushers him into the magical worlds beyond this.

Stephen: This discussion gives us the segue on to the next section, in which we bridge from the human to the divine.

Robin: Well, that's why the archetypes of the animals are plastered all over the sky and line Black Elk's spirit-tipi, and why there is a "Noah's Ark of the Mind." Animals are spiritual beings, spiritual archetypes, as well as living individual creatures.

Stephen: I am always mindful of the Buddhist story in which a monk has a spiritual practice that isn't so great, but he has a great dog, who goes everywhere with him and is his best buddy. They share their meals and everything. Finally, the monk makes his paranirvana (passes on), and the dog dies of grief. At long last, they come together to the Buddha-lands (the equivalent of heaven). There is a Buddhist Saint Peter at the gate, and the monk presents himself. The guardian inspects his credentials, then looks at the dog and says, "You're admitted, despite your checkered past, but there are no dogs allowed in here."

The monk sighs and turns away. "All my life," he says, " I have yearned for the blessed realm; but this dog and I have been through everything together. If he doesn't go in, I don't go in." The monk turns to leave.

Then the gatekeeper howls with laughter and he's joined by the dog. The monk is embraced, jumped upon and licked, and the gates are opened wide to the both of them.

Robin: He gave the right answer; the dog was the dharma, and the Buddha.

Stephen: "God" spelled backwards.

Psyche and Her Sisters
by Jean de Bosschère

CHAPTER THREE

DIVINE AFFINITIES AND ANTIPATHIES

All was taken away from you; white dresses,
wings, even existence.
Yet I believe you,
Messengers.

There, where the world is turned inside out,
a heavy fabric embroidered with stars and beasts,
you stroll, inspecting the trustworthy seams.

Short is your stay here:
now and then at a matinal hour, if the sky is clear,
in a melody repeated by a bird,
or in the smell of apples at the close of day
when the light makes the orchards magic.
They say somebody has invented you
but to me this does not sound convincing
for humans invented themselves as well.

The voice—no doubt it is a valid proof,
as it can belong only to radiant creatures,
weightless and winged (after all why not?),
girdled with the lightning.

I have heard that voice many a time when asleep
and, what is strange, I understood more or less
an order or an appeal in an unearthly tongue:

day draws near
another one
do what you can.

Czeslaw Milosz, "On the Other Side"[1]

COMPARATIVE ANGELOLOGY

WE BEGIN THE STUDY OF RELATIONSHIP as a spiritual practice by trying to "place" the human experience in its natural context. We can explore human relationships more clearly by seeing them, transparently, as it were, against the backdrop of the web of life (context, weaving, and webs belonging to the archetypal feminine are consciously integrated into our methodology). After having explored the natural world, especially the animal realm, we now open the field of inquiry to include the spiritual, inviting this "larger" context without dismissing the requirements of the biological, social, and psychological levels.

We need to peek up the ray of creation, as it were; after all, isn't that where angels come from? And there seem to be all kinds of relationships between humans and spiritual beings to be explored along the way. These are always interesting and edifying, sometimes electrifying, sometimes unilaterally or mutually destructive.

Most higher forms of mysticism agree with Swedenborg's description: there is a great flooding of the universe by the divine Creator, the source, with a ceaseless, abundant stream of energy. Swedenborg names it *influx*, the divine flow that sustains all things. "A Presence that disturbs me with the joy of elevated thoughts," says William Wordsworth in *Lines Composed a Few Miles above Tintern Abbey*:

> A sense sublime
> Of something far more deeply interfused,
> Whose dwelling is the light of setting suns,
> And the round Ocean and the living air,
> And the blue sky, and in the mind of man;
> A motion and a spirit, that impels
> All thinking things, all objects of all thought,
> And rolls through all things.

The visionary and the poet seem to agree that one transcendent presence "rolls through all things." "All things are God things," in the words of the great Indian saint, Ramakrishna; or as Wordsworth's contemporary, Blake, said: "Everything that lives is Holy." All trembles in incipient "suchness" of being. All things are permeated with influx, or divine energy, but different forms inflect it differently.

Angels have an important role in this cosmology. They are "messengers" carrying information up and down the ladder or ray of creation. They announce and convey divine intentions, and yet also may take an interest in human plights and predicaments, conveying human petitions to heaven. "Angels," so named specifically, seem attached to the Judeo-Christian-Islamic complex; but equivalent figures permeate world mythology, although their names may be different. These beings can be named:

> *Gods and goddesses*: Winged Hermes, but also winged Eros, Morphos (Sleep) and Thanatos (Death), divine errand-girl Hebe, rainbow-messenger Iris; or Rainbow-God of the Navaho, the griffon-like Garuda of Vishnu, and the hummingbird messenger of many shamanic traditions;
>
> *Celestial musicians*: Both Raphael and Gabriel appear in this way, chief among heaven's vast choirs, as do the *apsaras* of India, also often shown with wings;

Guardian spirits: The *Gung-Po* of Tibet, who are Powers of the Directions, and likewise the Four Thunderbirds with their many-jointed wings of the Sioux, or Greek Athena when she appears—sometimes also shown winged—as the companion of heroes;

Soul guides: Those who lead to the mysteries or the land of the dead, the Hindu-Tibetan *yidam*, Egyptian Osiris or Anubis, or Isis as Queen of Magic with her multicolored wings, the Greek *psychopompos*—Hermes again, Islamic Izrafil who is angel of the day of judgment, and veiled Azrael, Angel of Death;

Ancestral guardians: Or "higher spirits," the shen of Chinese shamanism, the "grandfathers" and "grandmothers" of Native America, and many deities in their aspects as ancestors of the people, as in the Yoruba tradition;

Nature spirits: The *oi'ra* or *oironu* of the Iroquois, India's *devis* and *devas*, assimilated into European lore as vegetation *devas*, Arcadian Pan, Cernunnos/Dionysus/Shiva as Lord of Beasts and vegetation divinity.

Although our discussion begins with the Judeo-Christian biblical lore, we consider all of these beings from different mythological systems to be essentially "angelic" presences. In effect, referring back to the Hebrew *Mal'kut'*, angels are the "shadow," or more exquisitely, the diffracted rainbow image, or in modern terms, the slightly blurry hologram, of the unfathomable divine source.

Nor, in our subject, can we neglect the genuine "shadow" of God; for in the fabric of manifested creation, as we experience it, there are always weaknesses, or flaws, it seems, that date back to the "great dissociation," a separation of human intelligence and ego from divine source. If, in the design of things, angels move up and down that ray of creation, carrying messages, then they are prone to (incandescent, spectacular) falls, such as that enacted by Lucifer, Star of the Morning, one of the brightest of the heavenly host. It is said in the apocryphal lore that he refused to bow down before "man," God's latest creation, and in his pride was cast from heaven, and many cohorts with him. Thus arises this idea of hell's being the inverted simulacrum of heaven, the inverse of all things good, harmonious, and "wholesome." "Fallen" angels are thus often equated with devils or demons, "shadows" of God who have chosen to live in the shadow, setting up their own pride in opposition to the divine will.

Useful instruction can also be gained, however, by studying the less polarized *daemones* of Greek religion, or the *devas* of the Hindu–Buddhist complex, because these figures often include both good and evil in their makeup (just like us). Such formulations can become a healing balm on the wounds inflicted by the literalistic fallacy (good versus evil, and I know exactly what they are!) to which the Zoroastrian or Manichean as well as naive Judeo-Christian models are prone. In this way, we try to envision a continuum of angel–daemon energies that are unknowable except through (flawed) human experience. Therefore, it pays, as Jesus said, to "test the spirits" to know their nature, not assume from the beginning that something is evil, lest, as Nietzsche said, "In casting out our devils we cast out the best that is in us," blinded by our preconceptions and failing to recognize or "see" our own blindness.

Nor should we fail to recognize good, because it sometimes wears strange disguises.

We normally think of human beings as susceptible to "guidance" from angelic beings, but to "possession or obsession" by demons. This raises some very interesting issues for the methodology we are articulating here. In relating to other human beings, we also must glimpse our angelodaemonic affiliations and those of our partners. The plot thickens when we do this. We may get a case of metaphysical vertigo, and life is not ever again so simple as it might seem to fundamentalist materialists.

Swedenborg proposes a different cosmology from that of the materialist, who thinks of inspiration, creativity, even the highest spiritual aspirations of humankind, as organic chemistry in action. For Swedenborg, spirit is not an epiphenomenon (outcome) of matter, or mere nature, flailing about chaotically; rather, it is just the reverse: matter is the outcome of the ray of creation that passes through celestial to spiritual to natural. However, the hells of Swedenborg's vision are filled, as are the Buddhist hells, with those who *choose* to be there—the self-absorbed, the greedy, the cruel. There are infernal spirits from this group who vie for the human soul with the angelic forces. In this regard, to be human is to be caught between hierarchies of celestial and infernal beings. Our essence, as recipients of divine influx, is to be receptive to spiritual energies. Unfortunately, this includes "the Dark side of the Force, Luke," as Obi Wan Kenobi instructs Luke Skywalker in the ever-popular *Star Wars* mythic saga. To be truly awake to partnership as a spiritual practice, we need to be aware of this tenebrous inversion of all that is light and good. One Hindu monk could not reconcile the mystical rhapsodies on the Divine Mother he was hearing from the nineteenth-century Bengali saint Ramakrishna, with the condition of life in the world as he found it. "But why, master," he asked the "God-intoxicated" saint, "if the Divine Mother loves us so much, and cradles us in her arms, always, does she permit the existence of evil?" Ramakrishna, without missing a beat, replied, "Because it thickens the plot."

Notice the saint did not fall into the fundamental fallacies of either denying that evil exists or engaging in a diatribe against it—encouraging us to "stomp it out," as if it were wholly "other." Rather, he acknowledged that it exists, and it "thickens the plot," increases the texture, of our experience. If the divine source itself casts a shadow, we ourselves, like the angels, move and live among light and shadows, ambassadors, pilgrim journeyers of the same path angelic messengers must take in each nanosecond, flying faster than the speed of light. But the human journey takes much longer—and encompasses the liminal boundaries of birth and death.

Clinical psychologist Wilson Van Dusen, inspired by Swedenborg's writings, used the eighteenth-century visionary's prototypic spiritual psychology to analyze his contemporary patients in mental hospitals.[2] Van Dusen found, just as we outlined, that human beings are "open within" to spiritual forces. The "lower-order" (we will also use "demonic" to show the negative inflection, whereas "daemonic" will refer to the more ambivalent concept of an activating energic being, or power) will try to obsess, possess, dominate, and control. These are the nasty voices heard by schizophrenics, the sexually perverted or asocial obsessions or compulsive behaviors acted out by some personality disorders, even the black scenarios entertained by the depressed. The key ingredient with the lower order is that it works against one's will and seeks to undermine the effort to evolve psychologically or spiritually.

The higher order, "angelic" forces never infringe on the subject's will. Their interventions, if such there be, are whispered hints or intuitions. (There seems to be respect for the fumbling human attempt at autonomy, chancy enterprise though it be. This is what theologians call "free will," the God-given opportunity to make our own mistakes, as well as to enjoy success, even moments of God-like creativity.) The higher order forces never interfere or try to turn the psyche into a spiritual battlefield; but Van Dusen found them accessible when called upon and willing to give some hints, sometimes, like the Delphic Oracle, ambiguous, so as to cherish the infantile, budding freedom the human ego is trying to exercise.

Van Dusen told a case of a working-class man, a plumber, who developed, in the course of therapy, a feminine "guiding spirit" who was far more creative and knowledgeable than the waking "ego" personality. This figure, a kind of Jungian "anima" figure, or alternatively a "guardian angel," was so intelligent and engaging that Van Dusen became lost in a fascinating discussion with it. Finally, the man whose inner figure she was asked Dr. Van Dusen for just a clue as to what the two of them might be talking about.

In this respect, angels are not only guides, but conduits to a transpersonal wisdom. Our practice should be to seek them out (since they are shy about intruding) and listen carefully, with discernment, to what they say. Many of our spiritually uplifting rituals could be seen as efforts to access an angelic wisdom that is beyond our ordinary reach.

Obsessing, demeaning, or nattering voices, however, that do not respect the wishes of your (poor beleaguered) ego, should be treated with equal discernment; but also with willingness, if they show themselves to be of the lower order (as Swedenborg described in his *Spiritual Diary*, when the lower order really tried to obsess him), to "withdraw the thoughts." This is like the yogic or Zen Buddhist practice of treating the major dynamics of thinking as illusory, and attaching only limited significance to them—or withdrawing into states of inner quietude or rapture, where the nattering voices cannot reach.

On the other hand, with the daemonic, or what we are calling the angelo-daemonic/daemongelic, a sifting, wise discernment is especially necessary. From some of these manifestations—like the devas, ancestral or nature spirits, archetypal powers in the depth psychology sense—our personal myths, our story (our "karma" in Eastern metaphysics) is to be learned and brought forth. The angelodaemonic movement uplifts and refines energies with dark instinctual or karmic roots, and brings them up into the air and light. The daemongelic movement pulls things downward, seeks to shadow and occlude the light; and there is a mystery hidden here, but referred to in Goethe's *Faust*, part 2, where Mephistopheles is depicted as he who intends evil—but ends up serving the good!

An example of this is Sauron's ring-lust in Tolkein's *Lord of the Rings*. The daemonic obsession of the warped demiurge-magician is the secret galvanizing force of the whole epic and provokes grand destinies to be enacted, personal struggles with inertia, pride, power, even, it seems, temptation itself. This is the "thickening of the plot" that leads to great personal revelations and to spiritual evolution. It's not always fun getting there, and the problem with evil is that it is usually mean and stupid; but its obdurate shadow initiates us beautifully into the texture of light.

When we open the human–divine amphitheater to mythology, the plot thickens indeed! Here we have the gods playing favorites above the battlefields of the *Iliad*; Celtic fairytale creatures who abduct human children; even marriages— and children—conceived in love between gods and humans. The Greeks have many versions of that which Christians believe to have happened only once, the interruption by the Divine in the stream of history, the fertilization of a human woman by God (or god, depending on your theology). And what a wealth of lore for our subject, exploited by two-and-a-half millennia of poetic redactions: gods and goddesses of love, goddesses and gods in love. Especially when love—but also sex or children—occurs between angels, gods, or spirits on the one hand and humans on the other, we have what historian of religions Mircea Eliade called, "the rupture of plane." In it, the energy of the universe leaks a little, from level to level. We have said that the "perennial philosophy," or the mystically transcendent view held by Swedenborg, shows a streaming from the divine source—"the Lord"—through the angelic realms through the human and down into biological vegetal and mineral creation. This is an "orderly" progression of energy (through influx and at the same time through symbolic correspondences), so that a person has animals within the soul as well as visible in the world. To do this, the energy flows properly across "discrete degrees," or semipermeable membranes of existence, always from "higher" to "lower" level of manifestation. But the processes we are addressing are not always orderly, as for example when angels fall in love with human beings or gods have love affairs with mortals.

Shamanism is the prototypic study of relationships between the realms: spirit–human, human–spirit. When, for example, taboos have been broken that endanger the primordial harmony, it is serious; illness or catastrophe will result unless the shaman enacts a ritual that restores the balance, propitiates the spiritual powers, and realigns the community with the sacred. In the individual case, the sickness of a person is usually the result of a personal or a family misalignment, and realignment brings healing or cure. Spirituality here is indistinguishable from health: the shaman cures and rebalances the world at the same time. In this regard, Martín Prechtel says, the shaman is like "a plumber" repairing the broken pipeline between the worlds, fixing "leaks" between the divine and the human. The practice is, basically, at this level, something like "damage control."[3]

Where the misalignments are on the level of the whole tribe or culture, the role of the shaman shades into that of the priest—performing rituals of propitiation and realignment for the whole community, rituals that evolve into sacred ceremony. The shaman-priest is also a lawyer, say the Mayan shamans, an *avogado*, an advocate, presenting the needs of the human community to the spirits and relaying their response.

In Chinese shamanism, the spirit-helper is often female, and sometimes the shaman is depicted as married to his guardian spirit and must cohabit with it, despite its often terrifying appearance. To fit him or her for the shamanic role, the shaman-in-training must be initiated and learn ceremonial magic: how to prepare a space for ceremonies and how to align between the spiritual and the human worlds.

From these encounters, we form the idea of a psychospiritual symbiosis between the realms. The spirits need the humans as much as the humans need the spirits. Harmony moves vertically on the ray of creation; when one level is out of alignment, the rest is affected. There is a compassionate reflective awareness from higher to lower. And the human level seems pivotal. When it is out of order, the spiritual world is unhappy, and the nature-world is somehow blighted. What an awesome responsibility—and what an awesome opportunity, this idea that we are somehow related to all of creation. There is no time for indulging in the Sartrean no-exit fantasy; that is an imagination of alienation that, fortunately, bears no relationship to reality. The reality is that we are interdependent, and accountable, all the way up and down the ladder of creation.

SCRIPTURAL ANGELOLOGY

THE RUSTLE OF WINGS IS HEARD THROUGHOUT the Hebrew Scriptures, also called the Christian Old Testament, through the Apocrypha, into the New Testament of the Christian dispensation, and thereafter throughout Neoplatonism and later Christian and Islamic lore.

After the expulsion, in which biblical human history begins, the Lord sets at the gate of the garden cherubim and a flaming sword that turns every way, to keep the sanctity of the Tree of Life, we are told in Genesis 3:24. But then angels participate in another fall and purging. In Genesis 6:1–6, it is written:

> When people began to multiply on the face of the ground, and daughters were born to them, the sons of God saw that they were fair; and they took wives for themselves of all that they chose. . . . The Nephilim [giants] were on the earth in those days —and also afterward—when the sons of God went in to the daughters of humans, who bore children to them. These were the heroes that were of old, warriors of renown.
>
> The Lord saw that the wickedness of humankind was great in the earth, and that every inclination of the thoughts of their hearts was only evil continually. And the Lord was sorry that he had made humankind on the earth, and it grieved him to his heart.

Some say the custom of women's wearing hats in church dates from this passage—that they not be looked upon by the angels and found fair, leading to *liaisons dangereuses*. The biblical flood, that great purging, followed this improper union.

Angels seem to have appeared often to Abraham and Sarah and stayed Abraham's hand when he was about to sacrifice Isaac on God's command. The marvelous ladder on which Jacob saw angels ascending and descending the corridor from the heavens to earth is matched in millennia of poetic inspiration and metaphor only by Jacob's demonstration that not only is it permissible to wrestle with angels, but, in the process, to exact a blessing.

In the Book of Numbers 22, there is an instructive story that hovers close to our subject, the story of Balaam's ass:

Balak of Moab asked the help of Balaam to defend against the Israelites. God appeared to Balaam and warned him that the Israelites were a blessed people.

Balaam went anyway with the princes of Moab; but, on the road, his ass balked "because an angel of the Lord stood in the way for an adversary against him." Balaam beat and rebuked the animal and tried to go forward; this time the ass balked again at the angel, who stood in the way with a drawn sword. Her sudden stop crushed Balaam's foot against the wall; once again, he beat her and urged her on. The third time she went down on her knees; Balaam once again grew angry and beat her:

> Then the Lord opened the mouth of the ass, and it said to Balaam, "What have I done to you, that you have struck me these three times?" Balaam said to the ass, "Because you have made a fool of me! I wish I had a sword in my hand! I would kill you right now!" But the ass said to Balaam, "Am I not your ass, which you have ridden all your life to this day? Have I been in the habit of treating you this way?" And he said, "No."
>
> Then the Lord opened the eyes of Balaam, and he saw the angel of the Lord standing in the road, with his drawn sword in his hand; and he bowed down, falling on his face. The angel of the Lord said to him, "Why have you struck your ass these three times? I have come out as an adversary, because your way is perverse before me. The ass saw me, and turned away from me these three times. If it had not turned away from me, surely just now I would have killed you and let it live." Then Balaam said to the angel of the Lord, "I have sinned, for I did not know that you were standing in the road to oppose me. Now therefore, if it is displeasing to you, I will return home."
>
> Numbers 22:28–34

In this parable, the human ego (Balaam) is the blind one, while the animal and the angel are, as it were, in connection. This reminds us of one of the truths articulated by shamanism, where the divine messenger is usually an animal: in the shamanic universe, natural and spirit worlds are inherently interconnected. It is the human world that needs ritual to keep the energy flowing between the realms. In this story, from the Bible of a people determined to make no "graven images" and especially to allow no theriomorphic images of divinity, the animal merely *senses* the divine messenger. What this means psychospiritually is that we have an instinctive recognition of divine guidance. Here, the instincts perceive what the rational mind refuses to accept: that the way Balaam is going is "perverse" to the divine will.

The visionary and prophet Ezekiel, who lived in the troubled time of the Babylonian captivity, saw some of the most penetrating and visionary glimpses of angels ever recorded:

> Then I looked, and above the dome that was over the heads of the cherubim there appeared above them something like a sapphire, in form resembling a throne. He said to the man clothed in linen, "Go within the wheelwork underneath the cherubim: fill your hands with burning coals from among the cherubim, and scatter them over the city." He went in as I looked on.
>
> Ezekiel 10:1–2

Originally, and before the Hebrew mentions of cherubim, the same name belonged to fierce Assyrian gate guardians, mythological hybrid beasts like winged lions or gryphons with the heads of fierce warrior-kings (and that is truly a different image from the naked little boys with wings, also called "cherubs,"—or, more correctly, *putti*—in Renaissance art). But Ezekiel's vision is extraordinary. First the cherubim appear with fiery wheels (*ophanim*). God tells "a man clothed with linen" to take fire from between the wheels and the cherubim:

> the cherubim appeared to have the form of a human hand under their wings.
>
> I looked, and there were four wheels beside the cherubim, one beside each cherub; and the appearance of the wheels was like gleaming beryl. . . .Their entire body, their rims, their spokes, their wings, and the wheels—the wheels of the four of them—were full of eyes all around. . . . Each one had four faces: the first face was that of the cherub, the second face was that of a human being, the third that of a lion, and the fourth that of an eagle.

Ezekiel 10:8–14

Ezekiel has given us a visionary blueprint that inspired the art of the Middle Ages, anticipated the Book of Revelation, and is said, in the latter recitation of faces of the cherubim, to anticipate the four evangelists of the New Testament.

What a wonderful and telling description, in terms of symbolic forms, of something not easily described in words: The rustling of the wings that can be heard to the ends of the earth; the likeness of human hands beneath them (speaking of doing as well as flying); the eyes to see all, before, behind, and all around; the symbolic faces of royal lion and farseeing eagle, the human and the androgynous mythological creatures combined. The wild-eyed visionary prophet incants it repeatedly—the voice of the pain of the Jewish captivity: "And the cherubims were lifted up, this is the living creature that I saw by the river of Che-bar."

It is a living creature, this angel; and it moves between the worlds, an eye for here, a hand for there, and multifoliate, marvelously rustling wings to soar in the space between the worlds! When we talk about the angels in the discussions and chapters that follow, let Ezekiel's angel come, with its exquisite ambiguous texture, its visionary's fiery mandalic wheels, and its ability to instill awe in the human soul.

The Book of Daniel describes how King Nebuchadnezzar became angry because three Jews to whom he had given high office—Shadrach, Meshach and Abednego—refused to fall down before a golden image set up by the king. Nebuchadnezzar told them to worship before it or be cast into a "fiery furnace," for "who is that god that will deliver you out of my hands?" (Daniel 3:14).

So the king had the furnace heated to seven times its usual heat, the heat being so great it claimed the soldiers who cast the three Jews into the furnace. But, in a little while, Nebuchadnezzar was very astonished, for he saw "four men unbound, walking in the middle of the fire, and they are not hurt; and the fourth has the appearance of a son of the gods [an angel]" (Daniel 3:25).

The event must have profoundly impressed Nebuchadnezzar, for his conversion seems instantaneous: "Blessed be the God of Shadrach, Meshach, and

Abednego, who hath sent his angel and delivered his servants who trusted in him. They disobeyed the king's command and yielded up their bodies rather than serve and worship any god except their own God" (Daniel 3:28). The miracle brought a new religion to Nebuchadnezzar, but his style of religiosity (and cast of mind) remained the same: anyone who now speaks anything against the God of the Jews "shall be torn limb from limb, and their houses laid in ruins; for there is no other god who is able to deliver in this way."

Shortly in the same book, Daniel was invited in to help the king interpret a dream, in which,

> there was a tree at the center of the earth,
> and its height was great.
> The tree grew great and strong,
>> its top reached to heaven,
>> and it was visible to the ends of the whole earth. . . .
> I continued looking, in the visions of my head as I lay in bed, and there
> was a watcher and a holy one, coming down from heaven. He cried aloud
> and said:
> Cut down the tree and chop off its branches,
>> strip off its foliage and scatter its fruit.
> Let the animals flee from beneath it
>> and the birds from its branches.

Daniel 4:10–14

Daniel, at his peril, told the king that the angel (the "watcher and holy one") was prophesying the king's own collapse, and the destruction of his kingdom, which would be divided between the Medes and the Persians.

In the Book of Enoch, an apocryphal book, under the leadership of one "Semjaza," himself already a "fallen angel," the angels descend to earth without divine permission. As in the earlier rupture spoken of in Genesis, they fall in love with the beautiful "daughters of men" and cohabit with them physically. Thus, the angels "defile" the women, who bear giants and monsters (as the Genesis passage implies, but does not say outright. This seems to happen to human women who invite fallen angels into themselves in this inappropriate way). The fallen angel Azazel teaches men the arts of war and women the vanity of cosmetics, and fornication and lawlessness spread over the earth.

Sexuality between angels and humans, just as with animals and humans, across species or "races" is taboo because it inverts and takes to a lower level of vibration the "inspiration," the carrying of divine breath (literally called *spermatikos* or *pneumatikos*, hermetic designations for the "seed" of spiritual fertilization). By upending and sullying the symbol of divine inspiration, angelic lust for human women initiates a daemongelic movement.

Furthermore, for Christianity, that kind of blessed event is the *droit de seigneur*, the Lord's right only, in the form of the Holy Spirit's begetting of the Christ Child upon the earth. (In the apocryphal mythologies that surround Christianity, Islam, and Judaism, the "defilement" of human women, especially celibate nuns or "brides of Christ," by demons or fallen angels thus represents Lucifer's revenge upon humans.)

Moving to the New Testament, we find the annunciation of the birth of the Christ Child to Mary by the angel Gabriel, confirming the status of this archangel as the messenger of messengers. Angels appear in the sky to the shepherds, announcing the holy birth. They appear at the beginning of Jesus' life and at the end, rolling away the stone from the tomb and greeting Mary and Mary Magdalene and John the Beloved Disciple.

And the final book of the evangelists, Revelation, has seven angels dressed in white linen with golden girdles, yet bearing seven plagues, pouring out pestilence, blood and the terrible "mark of the beast." When the seventh angel comes, he pours his vial into the air, "and there came a great voice out of the temple of heaven, from the throne, saying, 'It is done.' "

APOCRYPHAL ANGELOLOGY

A GREAT CONTRIBUTION TO ANGELOLOGY OCCURRED in the sixth century of the present era, with the writings of Pseudo-Dionysius the Areopagite. His definitive angelology is entitled *Celestial Hierarchies*.[4]

In order fully to display Pseudo-Dionysius' view of the angels in their hierarchies, extending down from the divine source, we must first mention that there are nine "choirs" of angels, (choirs being the collective of angels, even as an "exaltation" is the collective of larks or a "pride" the collective of lions). Each choir is further divided into "spheres," which are arranged concentrically around God: the innermost sphere's attention is entirely directed "upward" or toward God at the center; the middle sphere's attention is upon the ordering of creation, its principles and maintenance; the outermost or third sphere's attention is directed "downward" toward the human and what Swedenborg would later call the "natural" worlds. The names of particular angels of the different choirs have been gathered into Pseudo-Dionysius's cosmology over the years by Christian writers drawing upon kabbalist, Islamic, and other visionary sources.

The angels of the first sphere are divided into seraphim, cherubim, and ophanim or "thrones." The *seraphim* are beings of pure love, a light so bright that a mortal beholding their faces made of lightning and their raiment bright and scintillant as new snow would die of fright. The name *seraph* can be translated from Hebrew as "burning" and also appears in the Bible as the name of a fiery serpent, or perhaps a fiery flying serpent; hence, seraphim are sometimes thought of as spirits of lightning. The seraphim are described as "burning" with love and are those angels who inspire the human heart to burn with love of God. The ruler of the seraphim is a luminous being called "Metatron," or, alternately, "Michael"; he is also identified with the prophet Enoch, who was "taken up by God" and transformed in some mysterious way transcending time, into this primal celestial being. Lucifer, paradoxically, is sometimes said to have been a seraph, even the Prince of Seraphim.

The *cherubim* are said to be intermediaries between the human and the Divine—"intercessors." They are the guardians of stars, familiar with the interstellar deeps; their province or nature is knowledge. Their names include Cherubiel, Gabriel (the well-known messenger), Raphael, Uriel, and Zophiel. Samael, the Angel of Evil, also known as Satan or Lucifer, is also ranked high among the cherubim. These classes do not seem to be exclusive; you will notice that the better-known archangels appear several times at different stages of the hierarchy. Also, the angels of the first sphere are described as being completely focused on the Divine, as distinct from the lower spheres, which are concerned with the struggles and development of humankind. The paradoxical nature of cherubim and the fluidity of the distinctions between the different orders remind us that we are applying categories and qualities to a realm of being that is essentially subtle and dynamic. (The name "cherub, cherubim" is itself mysterious, being of an uncertain origin and meaning.)

The *ophanim* are the "fiery wheels" of Ezekiel, also called *thrones*, either because they circle the divine throne or because they represent a feminine enclosing and supportive function for the Divine. The ophanim are also called "many-eyed" and are said to be covered with eyes; their province is universal justice and the ordering or maintenance of the cosmos. Their description reminds us of the mandalic visions of pure light experienced by ecstatics in many times and cultures.

The angels of the second sphere are usually referred to in English as the *dominions, powers,* and *virtues.* The *dominions* (*kyriotetis*), as their name suggests, are in charge of rulership, leadership, and authority; but they are also mediators and arbiters. The *powers* are concerned with birth and death, warnings and premonitions, and are considered warrior-angels who will help protect home and hearth. The *virtues* (*dynamis*) are the angels of movement, accomplishment: miracles, ethics, and achievement. On the planet Earth they regulate the elementals and devas of nature.

The angels of the third sphere are the principalities, archangels, and angels. *Principalities* (*archai*) rule collectives and political bodies, and make decisions that affect whole civilizations; they are the informing energies of *place* and the tribe or nation shaped in that place. When we encounter them by name, they sometimes appear as the great archangels, especially the warrior Michael, the guardian of Israel or Saint Michel of France. *Archangels* are perilous and austere powers that administer the larger issues that affect the times. Michael, Gabriel, and Raphael are named as the greatest archangels: Michael the warrior is chief of the heavenly hosts and God's champion in the battle with evil; Gabriel is the angel of wisdom, foremost of angelic messengers, horn-player among divine musicians; and Raphael is the angel of healing, master of the heavenly harp and patron of all the arts, as well as patron of travelers. The mysterious fourth of their company is variously named, among them Uriel, the angel of dream and secret knowledge, or Izrafel, sometimes listed among the fallen ones (but more often identified with Islamic Israfil). But they are also counted as six in Kaballah, including Zaphkiel, Samael (Satan), and Sandalphon; and sometimes seven or eight. A single archangel may quell legions of ordinary demons, battling and overcoming great demons such as Azazel, Asmodeus, or Beelzeebub. The nature of archangels, like that of cherubim, appears to us as paradoxical, as we find their names throughout both the "lower" and "higher" spheres, suggesting not separate beings but vast, many-layered creatures who fulfill related functions on what we perceive as different levels or planes of existence. Gabriel often is pictured as a graceful youth, but with Sophia and the Shekkinah also appears as feminine. Raphael is the most likely of the great archangels to join a traveler—perhaps an itinerant musician or physician—on some lonely and perilous journey, or to be glimpsed sitting in on a late night jam session in Florence or Avignon or Harlem or New Orleans.

The archangel Sandalphon is the chief of guardians and oversees the work of all the third order of the third sphere. *Angels*, of the common variety, are personal guides or guardians; they resemble the "higher order" of Van Dusen, the watchers and protectors of our destinies. We traditionally meet them standing at the crossroads, comforting in times of woe, pointing out a new way. Advising but never insisting, standing always closest to errant humankind, these angels are most vulnerable to "falling" in love, to becoming involved in the human realm and living at times as mortals.

Swedenborg, never having read Pseudo-Dionysius, gives us a remarkably congruent angelology based on his own forays into heaven, hell, and the world of spirits (the italics in the following are ours):

> There are three heavens quite distinct from each other—an inmost or third heaven, an intermediate or second, and an outmost or first. The Divine which flows in from the Lord and is accepted in the third or inmost heaven is called *celestial*. So the angels there are called celestial angels. The Divine which flows in from the Lord and is accepted in the second or intermediate heaven is called *spiritual*, so the angels there are called spiritual angels. But the Divine which flows in from the Lord and is accepted in the outmost or first heaven is called *natural*.
>
> *Heaven and Hell 50*

The angelic "citizens" of those three heavens— *natural* the outermost, *spiritual* "within" (closer to the divine source), and finally *celestial* at the center— are described by Swedenborg as profoundly identified with their own particular heaven by their level or degree of "perfection." "All perfection increases as one moves inwards, and decreases as one moves outwards." If they try to go to another level, they become acutely uncomfortable and may experience a pain around the heart, we are told in *Heaven and Hell 36* and *37*. Swedenborg says we can also experience such levels in ourselves—as above, so below; as without, so within. We have natural, spiritual, and celestial levels in ourselves, just as heaven does, and "heaven is in the shape of a man," just as in the marvelous cosmology of the Jains (Swedenborg's image of the *Maximus Homo*, or the universe as a vast person, appears in the mystical insights of all the world religions and is found everywhere in shamanic visions).

Swedenborg's angels of the natural heaven resemble Dionysius's ordinary angels: messengers, guides, guardians. The spiritual angels have some things in common with the cherubim, including heavenly wisdom and discernment. The celestial angels resemble the seraphim, transparently receiving and burning with divine love so brightly that one cannot behold them directly. Nor can the Lord, or the divine source, be seen directly; he most often is seen clothed with the sun. He is not the sun but wears its form, burning most brightly, as an appearance: "Divine love is far more fiery [than the sun]" says Swedenborg in *Heaven and Hell* 120, and "therefore does not flow directly into the heavens, but the warmth of his love is tempered bit by bit in transit. The tempering agents look like gleaming bands around the sun. Besides this, the angels are shielded by a cloud, appropriately thin, so as not to be hurt by the inflow." Sometimes, however, the Lord sends out an appearance, as of one of the celestial angels, and moves around the heavens "but distinguished from angels by something Divine shining from his face."

St Augustine puts it, "the Lord (as God) is 'in' the Angel, who is therefore rightly called 'Lord.' 'It is the name of the indweller, not the temple.' But in truth, as Gabriel told Mohammed, God is veiled by 70,000 veils of light and darkness, and if these were suddenly swept aside, 'even I would be utterly consumed.'"[5]

Only poetry or visionary art can capture the multiplicity and symbolic radiance of such beings, and some of the Islamic descriptions of the great angels are marvels:

> Mika'il [Michael] was created by Allah 5,000 years after Israfil [Angel of Judgment]. He has hairs of saffron from his head to his feet, and his wings are of green topaz. On each hair he has a million faces and in each face a million eyes and a million tongues. Each tongue speaks a million languages and from each eye fall 70,000 tears. These become the Kerubim who lean down over the rain and the flowers and the trees and the fruit.[6]

The poet Rainer Maria Rilke writes,

> Every Angel is terrifying. And yet,
> Oh welcome, deadly soul-birds,
> I know all about you. Where are the days of Tobias,
> when one of you bright folk stood at a humble doorstep,
> a little disguised for traveling, hence not so frightening
> (a youth among the young, peering curiously)?
> But if that first angel from behind the stars came down
> we could slay ourselves with the beating of our own hearts!
> Who's there?[7]

Ah yes, angels among us, as in the days of Tobias—that's enough to keep us awake! Do we recognize them when they peek in as a young man at the door? It is not unlike the times in Greek or Norse mythology when gods or goddesses walk the earth—disguised, perhaps, by a cloak and an old slouch hat, such as Odin might wear, or Zeus (Jupiter) when he appears to the Phrygian couple, Philemon and Baucis. Do we offer them hospitality? There is always a blessing if we do, and sometimes the reverse if we do not, or are cruel to them; angels help bring forth and reveal our character.

The story of Tobias is told in the apocryphal Book of Tobit. Tobit is an old, blind, impoverished man, trying to exist under the cruel Assyrian captivity in Nineveh, giving charity to other Hebrews in need and burying the dead slain by bloodthirsty King Sennacherib—at great peril to himself, for there are laws that forbid it.

Tobit is owed ten talents, a large sum of money in those days, by a man in Media (the land of the Medes). He wishes to send his beloved son Tobias to Media to collect the debt; but, as it is a dangerous world, Tobit advises Tobias to hire a man to go with him. Tobias hires a man, who calls himself "Azariah"; unknown to Tobias, Azariah is actually the archangel Raphael.

After they leave, Anna, Tobias' mother and Tobit's wife, rebukes the old man. Their son's life, she says, is not worth the dangerous trip, the object of which is only money. But pious Tobit, without knowing the literal truth of what he himself is saying, replies, "Do not worry; our child will leave in good health and return to us in good health. . . . For a good angel will accompany him; his journey will be successful, and he will come back" (Tobit 5:20–22).

Along the journey, in the city of Ecbatane, in Media, lives Tobit's cousin, Raguel, whose family is under a curse. Raguel's daughter Sarah has been promised, and then married, to seven husbands; but, before the marriage can be consummated, each husband is killed by the great demon Asmodeus (it seems he wants Sarah for himself, an improper rupture of plane). Sarah is disconsolate so to be cursed and wishes now to die.

Then "Azariah" tells Tobias that, under Hebrew Law and by the relationship between Tobias and Sarah, he himself is the right husband and she the wife for him. Tobias is understandably terrified, based on the fate of his seven predecessors.

Now along the way, "Azariah" instructs Tobias to catch a fish, open it up, and extract its heart, liver, and gall. Tobias does so, and the two men eat the flesh of the fish together. The angel tells him that Sarah will be offered to him for a wife, and he should accept:

> When you enter the bridal chamber, take some of the fish's liver and heart, and put them on the embers of the incense. An odor will be given off; the demon will smell it and flee, and will never be seen near her any more. Now when you are about to go bed with her, both of you must first stand up and pray, imploring the Lord of heaven that mercy and safety may be granted to you. Do not be afraid, for she was set apart for you before the world was made
>
> Tobit 6:17

Sarah herself, as it turns out, is the one to greet the young men and bring them into the house. She is demure and beautiful. As they sit at a welcoming meal, Raguel tells the young men about Sarah and is honest about the problem she has endured. Tobias is emboldened, asks his companion, "Brother Azariah, speak of those things of which you spoke on the way," and the angel does so. Raguel and his wife Edna are happy and take Sarah's hand and put it in Tobias'; the marriage is sealed. But Sarah weeps, half, it seems, for joy and half for fear that Tobias will suffer the grisly death the others have suffered.

On the wedding night, Tobias makes the strange fishy incense, as he had been instructed by the angel; and the demon Asmodeus flees "into the utmost parts of Egypt, and the angel bound him."

"Grow old along with me, the best is yet to be, the last of life for which the first was made. . . ," in the words of Robert Browning. Tobias, of a generous heart, lets his new bride know that his intentions are honorable and that he understands that the kind of relationship he intends is the kind sanctioned from ancient times by God and intended for humankind.

Poor Raguel has been digging Tobias' grave all this while, as previous circumstances had conditioned him so to do. But when he goes in and finds Tobias alive and the couple sleeping peacefully, he praises God. Then he begs Tobias to tarry for awhile; and so Tobias asks his resourceful friend "Azariah" to go to Media, collect the debt from the man Gabael, and bring him back to the wedding, which the angel faithfully does.

Meanwhile, at home, Tobit and Anna are besides themselves with apprehension that something terrible has happened. But when the triumphant party returns, with the ten talents, and Tobias married to an appropriate bride, the joy is great. "Raphael said to Tobias, before he had approached his father, 'I know that his eyes will be opened. Smear the gall of the fish on his eyes; the medicine will make the white films shrink and peel off from his eyes, and your father will regain his sight and see the light'" (Tobit 10:7–8). And Tobias did so, and Tobit was healed of his blindness.

Great is the rejoicing then, when Tobit sees his new daughter-in-law. Tobit offers to Tobias' companion half of all that he has, but the angel now reveals himself and says to Tobit:

> It was I who brought and read the record of your prayer before the glory of the Lord, and likewise whenever you would bury the dead. And that time when you did not hesitate to get up and leave your dinner to go and bury the dead, I was sent to you to test you. And at the same time God sent me to heal you and Sarah your daughter-in-law. I am Raphael, one of the seven angels who stand ready and enter before the glory of the Lord.
>
> Tobit 12:12–15

This story leads us to the conclusion of our discussion of the biblical lore, and in it are many of the themes we have been introducing so far: angels as messengers, guides, and companions; their knowledge of divine providence; and here, their help in a situation involving marriage—and demons. It is an interesting variation of the movement that Swedenborg describes, of a happy couple's forming an angel: here the angel helps in the making of a happy—divinely intended—couple: soul mates.

Sarah's situation is completely untenable, with an uninvited "demon-lover" (or in Jungian terms, "toxic animus") holding her back from life. An angel is needed and something from the animal realm as well, the (symbolic) parts of the fish being translatable as "heart, stamina, and discrimination"—exactly what each partner of the couple will need to have for the partnership to work.

Both the angelic wisdom and its power are necessary to combat the improper hegemony of the demon. We could say that a woman in the grip of a demon (a negatively inflected daemon) is a perilous partner indeed; certainly neither mere lust nor misguided love is a match for the demon. We need the more refined pledge of Tobias, namely, the intention of lifelong love, through thick and thin, strengthened with angelic help, to bind the demon and break the spell.

Asmodeus was said to be "the king of devils," who achieved an improper love for Sarah and who killed without mercy. (Be warned then, when you say to your beloved, in anger or jest, "I will kill you!" Asmodeus may be present: he is the demon of murderous rages and the desire to obliterate healthy relationships.) Raphael was also called "Labbiel," in Chaldean lore; the Hebrew word *rapha* means healer or doctor, and *El* was a bright sky-god of Babylon. "Raphael," then, means "shining healer," a figure suggestive of Apollo, and not unlike the ancient god of healing Asclepius—hence his knowledge of fishy medicines for what is wrong. But Raphael is also the wayfaring pilgrim in disguise, the guide and companion, as in the Tobias story. He guides young people, especially young couples, as in the tale, to find their way. He is said to have a sense of humor and a playful love of companionship. But he watches also and knows what we do. According to the lore of ritual magic, he gave King Solomon the pentacle, and rules hidden wisdom.[8]

Having such an angel as a companion means opening playfully, in a friendly but discerning way, to providence, to a divine destiny hidden within the events. Even on the dangerous path of life, with corrupt and violent people in power, the story shows that there are luminous tracks and song lines crisscrossing the desert, the demon-inhabited wastelands. Wonderful old Tobit, in the midst of such soul-stultifying bleakness, still goes about his business, doing acts of kindness and burying the dead (a proper way to "put to rest" our unsuccessful and outworn experiences, rather than leaving them around to putrefy).

Surely the Book of Tobit contains one of the most magical love stories of all time and deserves to be read and learned by young couples of whatever faith, as they approach the marriage covenant.[9]

EROS AND PSYCHE: A DIVINE MADNESS

GREEK MYTHOLOGY DEVOTES MUCH ATTENTION to divine–human interactions, favoritisms, and love affairs. One of the most famous of the Greek stories is the ancient love story of Eros and Psyche, which shows just how fully ambivalent, complex, and yet full of learning, such mythogems may be.

In the Psyche story as it appears in *The Golden Ass of Lucius Apulius*, the moving event is divine/human jealousy.[10] Psyche, a human girl, is so beautiful that everyone says that she is as beautiful as Aphrodite herself. The goddess becomes resentful. This is the theme of this section, the proclivity for gods and goddesses divinely to reflect the worst failings of mortals and to impose at the same time, inhuman tasks and requirements.

Aphrodite sends her son Eros to "shoot" Psyche with one of his arrows, to make her fall in love with "the most miserabilist creature living, the most poor, the most crooked, and the most vile, and that there may be none found in all the world, of like wretchedness."

Psyche's father went to the oracle of Apollo, and the oracle said she would not be married to any mortal man but a dragon, a "Serpent dire and fierce . . . who flies with wings above in starry skies . . . " She must be dressed in mourning clothes, as if for a funeral, and placed on a high rock, to be pounced upon by the fearsome worm.

Instead of a greedy reptile of the upper airs, though, it was Eros (Cupid), Aphrodite's son, who sent the Zephyrs, magical winds, to bring Psyche, all weeping and trembling upon her crag, to him. (Love itself, beholding Psyche, the human soul, in her vulnerable, feminine inflection, had fallen in love with *anima*.)

The Zephyrs brought her into a deep valley and laid her gently on the softest bed of flowers, where she slept. When she awakened, "with a more quiet and pacified mind . . ."

> [She] fortuned to espy a pleasant wood environed with great and mighty trees. She espied likewise a running river as cleare as crystall: in the midst of the wood well nigh at the fall of the river was a princely Edifice, wrought and builded not by the art or hand of man, but by the mighty power of God: and you would judge at the first entry therin, that it were some pleasant and worthy mansion for the powers of heaven. For the embowings above were of Citron and Ivory, propped and undermined with pillars of gold, the walls covered and seeled with silver, divers sorts of beasts were graven and carved, that seemed to encounter with such as entered in. All things were so curiously and finely wrought, that it seemed either to be the worke of some Demy-god or God himselfe . . . and she heard a voice without any body, that sayd, Why doe you marvell Madame at so great riches? Behold all that you see is at your commandement, wherefore go you into the chamber, and repose your selfe upon the bed, and desire what bath you will have, and we whose voyces you heare be your servants, and ready to minister unto you according to your desire. In the meane season, royall meats and dainty dishes shall be prepared for you.[11]

Psyche was apprehensive for her virginity, as she lay down to sleep in the sumptuous bed. "Then came her unknown husband and lay with her: and after that he had made a perfect consummation of the marriage, he rose in the morning before day, and departed."[12] So sweet were her invisible husband's attentions that "soon after came the invisible servants, and presented to her such things as were necessary for her defloration," amenities of the most luxurious kind and beautiful sights and sounds, especially the perpetual music coming out of nowhere, that kept Psyche entertained. But as time passed, she pined for her family—even her sisters, who had been particularly mean to her.

Psyche repeatedly begged her divine lover's leave to have her sisters visit. Such was her obvious distress, for she wished to see them out of love—although the sisters were motivated by curiosity and jealousy—that the God of Love consented, but not without an admonition: "Beware that ye covet not (being moved by the pernicious counsel of your sisters) to see the shape of my person, lest by your curiosity you deprive your self of so great and worthy estate." Psyche replied that she would rather die than be separated from her beloved husband, but she did also love her sisters.

The sisters came to the same rock from which Psyche had been taken and cried out loudly, so that she heard them; then she commanded the Zephyrs, by her husband's leave, to bear them up to her. When the sisters saw the wealth and luxury in which Psyche lived, the twin worms of jealousy and envy began to grow in their hearts. Although richly served and loved by Psyche, when they departed they could think of nothing else but her good fortune, bewailing their own husbands as louts, their estates as paltry. "Verily I live not, nor am a woman," said the one to the other, "but I will deprive her of all her bliss. And if you my sister be so far bent as I, let us consult together."

Psyche's sisters had always been jealous by disposition and cruel, resenting the very sweetness in Psyche that made Love himself fall in love with her. On their next visit, calling out, and leaping down from the rock, caught up by the Zephyrs, they immediately planted an evil doubt. "Surely this lover must be an evil serpent-demon or sorcerer," they said, "using Psyche for his own malign purposes, why else would he be afraid to show himself?"

"Take a razor, and a lamp," they said to Psyche, "and when you shine the light upon your 'husband,' you will see a horrible serpent. When you have seen him, you must cut off his head!" Psyche frowned dubiously, for it went against the grain so to describe the sweetness of him she held, invisibly, in the night. But her nature was to trust, and her sisters were her own kin and certainly more clever than she. After all, what did she truly know? The sisters were, in fact, devilish clever: They told the innocent Psyche that she was pregnant. Then, reminding her of the Oracle of Apollo, they further frightened her for the safety of the child she would bear, for that same "great serpent full of deadly poyson . . . will devoure both thee and thy child!"

That night her husband returned, and she experienced the same delight with him that she always did. Her sensations and feelings told her truly, but still her mind was tormented; one moment she would do the deed, the next, she would not:

> And when he had kissed and embraced her, he fell asleep. Then Psyche (somewhat feeble in body and mind, yet moved by cruelty of fate) . . . brought forth the lamp, and took the razor. . . . But when . . . she came to the bedside, she saw the most meek and sweetest of all beasts, even fair Cupid couched fairly, at whose sight the very lamp increased his light for joy, and the razor turned his edge.[13]

Distracted, Psyche dropped the razor and, overcome by erotic feelings, fell upon the god and kissed him repeatedly. But a drop of hot oil from the lamp fell on his right shoulder and awakened him. "Oh rash and bold lamp, the vile ministry of love, how darest thou be so bold, as to burn the god of all fire?" the text says.

Eros awakened, began to fly away, but Psyche caught hold of him by the right thigh and held on. He flew from the palace, and she with him, clinging for life and love. Lighting in a cypress tree, her husband disentangled himself from her grasp, rebuked her for her faithlessness, and flew away. Then, despairing, Psyche threw herself into a river; but the river, honoring Eros, refused to drown her.

Fortunately nearby sat Pan, the god of shepherds. "Hearken to me, go not about to slay thyself, nor weep not at all," he advised her, "but rather adore and worship the great god Cupid (Eros), and win him unto you by your gentle promise of service." And so Psyche set off upon her famous journey of wanderings—Soul in search of her own Soul.

Something must have hardened in Psyche at being so used by her sisters. She made her way to the first one's house, who was amazed to see her there—probably thinking her weak little sister was by now driven mad or dead of grief, if not truly eaten by the "dragon." When her sister asked her for the story, Psyche told it as it happened, that her husband was the God of Love himself. But she added a twist of her own: As Eros rejected her, Psyche reported him as saying, "Goodbye faithless Psyche, your sister would be a better wife for me!"

The sister quickly rushed off, as Psyche certainly knew she would, leaving behind her husband, property, and children, and went to the rock. "Oh Cupid," she cried, "take me, a more worthy wife!" and leaped. But the Zephyrs were feeling contrary, and did not bear her up "and all the members and parts of her body were torne amongst the rockes, whereby she was made a prey unto the birds and the wild beasts, as she worthily deserved." And the same exact ruse worked with the second sister, and she met the same fate. Thus, evil dreams of selfish bliss worked their sinister magic.

Eros, meanwhile, was suffering from his burn as if it were not from a mere drop of oil, but a dreadful scalding. Perhaps the god of love is especially vulnerable to a wound of love—Apuleius' text gives us no explanation but describes the young god's agony, even saying that he was in danger of death. So great was his distress that Eros hid himself away in his divine mother's chamber.

When Aphrodite heard, some say from the seagull, of the wounding of her son, she was furious. Her resolve to punish this upstart Psyche redoubled.

In her disconsolate wanderings, Psyche found and worshiped humbly at a temple to Demeter (Ceres): the temple was neglected, so Psyche set to work cleaning and putting all in order. The goddess was so moved that she took pity on Psyche; taking her into her confidence, she told her that it was Aphrodite who was angry with her—but Demeter could offer no protection. Even more frightened now, Psyche fled for succor to a temple of the queen of the gods. But Hera (Juno) told her the same: Aphrodite is angry; I can't help you.

Aphrodite sent out Hermes with instructions to find this runaway king's daughter and bring her back, for a reward of seven kisses from the goddess of love. Hermes (he, who when Hephaistos caught Aphrodite in bed with Ares, the god of war, and bound them up in a great net, said, "I would swap places with Ares!" turning the laughter of the gods on Hephaistos) brought in Psyche.

The attendants of the goddess, Sorrow and Sadness, scourged Psyche, (like Inanna scourged before her cruel sister Ereshkigal in the underworld) and brought her before the goddess, whereupon it was also discovered that the goddess was to be a grandmother: Psyche was, indeed, pregnant!

This revelation made Aphrodite even more furious. Now Psyche had to fulfill impossible-seeming tasks, laid on her by the imperious goddess:

> First she took a great quantity of wheat, barley, poppyseed, peason, lentils and beans mingled together on a heap saying, "Thou evil-favored girl, thou seemest unable to get the grace of thy lover, by no other means, but only by diligent and painful service, wherefore I will prove what thou can'st do—see that thou separate all these grains, one from another . . . and let it be done before night."[14]

Psyche felt enormous despair as she contemplated the job, but then as she sat there, an ant hailed her and asked the cause of her misery. He determined to help her and gathered all his brothers and sisters and cousins and second-cousins. They toiled awhile, as ants are known to do, and soon the job was done.

Aphrodite returned just before dawn, from yet another divine party, "tipsy and with garlands in her hair." But she was astonished, then fell into a terrible wrath, when she saw the grains sorted into neat piles.

The next task laid on Psyche by the goddess would be even more impossible-seeming and far more dangerous. There were fierce, dangerous rams, colored like the sun, like the famous "golden fleece" of Jason, some of whose wool the goddess now demanded. It was impossible to approach these rams, who had been known to devour men. Psyche despaired again (such was her nature) when she contemplated the task, and she again determined to cast herself in the water. But one of the reeds of the riverbank, miraculously addressing the poor girl, admonished her to desist. "Wait," said the magical reed, "until the rams, in the course of the day, go to and fro, and come to drink and play in the river. They will leave some of their wool on the brambles; bright as it is, you should have no trouble finding and gathering some!" Psyche did as the reed bade her, and brought back to the goddess a fine bundle.

Now the goddess let herself into a dark fury indeed. Narrowing her eyes, she took out an empty crystal bottle, which she gave to Psyche. Aphrodite told the human girl to go to the source of the black river Styx, the river that begins in the daylight world and flows to the nether regions, and bring back to her a flask of those darkness-intending waters.

The source of the Styx is said to be in a shadowed declivity in the high mountains, where its narrow passage is guarded by sleepless dragons with vigilant eyes that roam ceaselessly. Now Psyche sank yet deeper into despair than ever before. But, as she thought again, "Woe is me, I shall end my life," a farsighted eagle spied the beautiful girl by the river source and swooped down.

"Thinkest thou to dip this water? The gods themselves fear it," the bird said. But taking compassion on her, for he saw her heart was good, the eagle snatched the crystal bottle from her, flew easily past the dragons and dipped it in the stream. Then she gave it to the astonished Psyche, who brought it to the goddess.

The terrible scowl once again darkened that beautiful, imperious countenance, and Aphrodite laid the most terrible of ordeals on Psyche: to cross that river Styx and descend to the underworld, to dark Hades' realm, there to retrieve some of the beauty of the underworld goddess, Queen Proserpina (Persephone). This costly vial of beauty, the goddess said "will serve me the space of one day, for such that I had was diminished by the sickness of my son." Thus, she couched her challenge as a further rebuke to poor Psyche.

Overwhelmed again, Psyche went to a high tower, determined to throw herself off. But to her amazement, the tower itself, even the dumb stones, spoke to her: "Carry two sops sodden in the flour of barley and honey in the hands, and two half-pence in the mouth—and when thou hast passed that way . . . come to the river of hell, pay Charon his fare." The tower told her of the terrible three-headed dog, which she should pacify with a sop. Then,

Thou maist have access to Proserpina without all danger: shee will make thee good cheere, and entertaine thee with delicate meate and drinke, but sit thou upon the grounde and desire browne bread, and then declare thy message unto her, and when thou hast received such beauty as she giveth, in thy returne appease the rage of the dogge with thy other sop, and give thy other halfe penny to covetous Charaon, and come the same way again into the world as thou wentest: but above all things have a regard that thou looke not in the boxe, neither be too curious about the treasure of the divine beauty.[15]

And Psyche did so, following the directions, even to Persphone's throne room; but, on the return, she was "ravished with great desire" to see what was in the box and maybe to partake of divine beauty—a mistake, for she already partook of it, and that was her grace and her woe. But the magic of "Proserpina's beauty" was too powerful for the mortal girl; overcome by it, she swooned.

Eros, finally healed of his wound, could not bear to be without Psyche. He found her lying in the swoon and pricked her awake with one of his arrows. He rebuked her for her perpetual curiosity, which had already caused her woe, and sent her to his mother. But fearing Aphrodite's further wrath and enmity, he himself flew to father Zeus (Jupiter).

Zeus, although he himself had been pricked by Eros, and more than one time, loved the boy. He saw the situation as it presented itself, saw also that Aphrodite's true wish was for Eros to commit to one woman, mortal though she be. Therefore, he gave Psyche the cup of immortality, so she could be a proper and perpetual consort to the god of love.

STEPHEN AND ROBIN IN DIALOGUE

Robin: We've been examining various stories about affinities and antipathies between higher beings, such as angels and gods, and human beings. I am particularly fascinated by the levels of angels. There is an esoteric or hidden association to the *ophanim*, or "thrones," who surround God. They strike me as a feminine symbol because they cradle the holy being. In medieval and Renaissance Christian iconography, Christ sits in Mary's lap, and Mary becomes his throne, so the feminine element is the enclosing, embracing, nuturing quality of the mortal that comes closest to the holy being.

In a sense, God himself sits in the lap of the Great Mother of the universe, something that shows up in Hindu mythology. There, the Great Goddess includes and encloses the male divinities and displays more power than any one or two of them— sometimes more than all of the gods—in the stories of conflicts between them.

Stephen: I like the idea that the ophanim are wheels; like mandalas, they enclose things in that way too—often they are depicted with many eyes, watching the antics of humankind, the awful injustices, and feeling sad.

Robin: There is also much Christian iconography showing the Virgin Mary as the queen of the angels, so that angels are, in a sense, also from the realm of the Mother. In the Tantric sense, whenever we have a manifesting, multiplicitous aspect of the divine, we are experiencing the energy of the divine feminine, the Goddess. Angels are intermediaries; they move on practical missions between heaven and earth, between the unmanifest and the manifest. They "mother" humans in a very practical everyday sense, nursing us along until we can stand up on our own, spiritually.

Sophia is a figure from the Hebrew Bible who also embodies wisdom. She is often depicted as a winged being sitting on a throne and is sometimes, in hermetic writings, ranked among the greater angels.

Stephen: Some of the purist traditions, though, make Sophia "fallen" wisdom, as if the feminine principle is not the equal of the masculine. Greek philosophy also does this thing about *physis* and *nous*, the embrace of matter drowning pure consciousness.

Gabriel is the angel of the "sublunar" realm, the human realm, standing in the ray of creation beneath the moon. Gabriel is in charge of the "terrestrial angels," human beings.

Robin: Yes, the Basque people and, I think, the Gypsies, the Romany, refer to human beings as "walking stars," angels in becoming. I love that idea. And Gabriel is sometimes described as the most "feminine" in energy of the archangels.

Stephen: It's the gnostic idea of the fallen sparks of soul-substance, down into matter; they must remember that they "come from God who is their home."

Robin: By this journey, this descent into matter, space-time, the human being really accomplishes the *hieros gamos*, the sacred marriage of spirit and nature, male and female, wisdom and love. Human beings are permitted the raw materials of love and wisdom to make their own synthesis; this is a truly godly task.

Stephen: Made possible in that human beings are symmetrically apportioned carriers of love and wisdom in different ways. The man has his affections deep inside and intelligence outside, while the woman is the reverse, in Swedenborg's model. I think that the angelic presences guide marriages because they are the earthly simulacrum, the correspondence, of this inner heavenly process.

Robin: I think people have to get to know each other's angel. Then we can truly relate to each other.

But we have also looked at the Eros–Psyche myth. Who are the central characters here? We have a human woman, the "heroine" who is also the *psyche*; Aphrodite, the goddess who afflicts Psyche; and Eros, Aphrodite's son the divine lover. So who or what is Eros? Don't these figures in fact refer to powers, creative energies in a human psyche?

Stephen: What strikes me is the intertwining of a number of motifs: the goddess Aphrodite first hears rumors that there is a human woman whose beauty is so great that it rivals hers. So we begin with the interesting notion that a divine being, from a different realm, is imperiled by something, someone human; this is a fascinating concept, that the divine is dependant upon or can be imperiled by the human.

Robin: It's an extraordinary idea; but I think it's been much woven through Joseph Campbell's work as well. There's a love-hate relationship going on: Aphrodite comes to hate the rumors of Psyche first, and then she sends her son to wound Psyche and make her fall in love with a monster. Thus, she wishes to use the power of Eros amorally, using her son's power to guard her own fragile vanity.

Stephen: Then Love itself falls in love; Love falls into his own nature; the wounder becomes the wounded. It's like the angels falling in love with human women, or one of Campbell's favorite phrases, "Eternity in love with the productions of time."

The descriptions all elaborate on Psyche's amazing beauty, but also her psycho-emotional and spiritual frailty. In the story, when anything bad happens, she is always overcome, she freaks out at the impossibility of everything; and she's easy to hypnotize or give suggestions to—witness her sisters. Yet she is elementally simple and beautiful by her very nature, so this story achieves an eternal poignancy by the fact that it is an allegory or a parable of the development of the human psyche.

Robin: One of the things that strikes me about this story is that it is also a woman's story of transformation, and that the tasks that are given Psyche are the everyday tasks that are important traditionally for women: the tasks of sorting grains, collecting wool, carrying water—these are woman's work.

Stephen: Certainly, the last is one that men seldom do: putting on Proserpina's beauty.

Robin: Yes, that's the fourth one that moves the whole thing *up*, or *on*. I see the three preceding things as being the endless tasks of woman's work, which are never really done, and the fourth one as a shift in dimension. The first three tasks occupy women in ordinary life—sometimes to tedium, although they may also be pleasant and very much enjoyed.

Marion Woodman makes some interesting points about this, in that, in women's transformational stories, the heroine is often required to do some kind of tedious and repetitive work, which gives her a time to grow quietly. In this way, it has a sort of protective quality, while she's doing it. Psyche has experienced this terrible loss, which is—despite her sisters' part—largely the result of her own action, her own gullibility, indecisiveness, lack of faith. Now, in this time of loss and grief, the work creates a space in which she is doing a meditation, a piece of simple daily work, sorting seeds, gathering wool, carrying water.

Stephen: But what about the the anger of the goddess; the jealousy, the viciousness, of the goddess of love? Why is the goddess of love behaving like all of the wicked witches and nasty stepmothers in fairy tales?

Robin: It seems to me that, first of all, she's actually an angry mother-in-law, a figure that is recognized worldwide. In Japanese stories, for instance, we often have a tremendously harsh mother-in-law who is very cool to her son's wife or potential wife; so why do we have that situation, and why is the goddess of love doing this kind of thing?

Well, from one point of view, if Aphrodite did not torment Psyche in several of these tasks, there would be no transformation. This is "psyche," the soul, and she needs to grow and experience these hard tasks, loss, suffering, of ordinary life. She needs to grow through living, and then she needs to encounter death. She needs to go into the realm of Persephone and look into the face of Persephone's terrible beauty.

Stephen: This is another kind of beauty than Psyche's human beauty, or Aphrodite's Olympian beauty, that never dies; it is precisely the beauty of a goddess who has been transformed in the encounter with death.

Robin: It is more then any mortal can bear, and yet every mortal must bear it; so when Psyche opens up the box, she drops immediately into a sleep from which she's not supposed to be awaken. It's the sleep of death.

Stephen: The soul sleeps the sleep of death, but she is awakened by the pricking of Eros' arrows; and at the moment he awakens her, he rebukes her (lovingly, for his nature is all love), for her curiosity, which has been her bane.

Robin: Ultimately, her failure to pass the test, as she was supposed to do—on the surface of things—actually brings about the real transformation and the growth and the final union with the beloved.

Stephen: Earlier, Psyche accepts everything her sisters tell her, even though she knows better. But after the encounter with evil through the lying of her sisters and really "getting" the malicious intent beneath it, she turns ruthless herself. In the beginning, just like Cinderella, whose story is probably based on this one, Psyche's love for her sisters is unconditional, despite their manifestation of continual ill will. They have an envy, spite, and jealousy equally proportioned to her love. So Psyche does already have love, and this makes her in turn, again like Cinderella, lovable.

Earlier in the story she's like most of us at times in life: when an obstacle or an ordeal comes along, she gives up and says, "This is horrible; how did I deserve this fate?" This is the human psyche, and we don't like to think of it as a melodramatic fool, running around in small circles and lamenting, but it often is.

Robin: I think many fairytales are spun out of this story, and possibly "Beauty and the Beast" has some reference back to this, as well as "Cinderella," and "Furskin," and others. Though even Apuleius's version is really literary; somewhere beyond it lies the old, old story.

Stephen: Yes, the Psyche story is probably earlier than all those variants; the very landscape of the dream, the living landscape, speaks to her. The ants speak to her, a reed speaks to her, even a tower speaks to her; an eagle flies down and accomplishes a terrifying task for her. All things conspire to help Psyche, and I think in this there's a profound parable of the soul—namely, Psyche's eternal tendency is to feel alone and afraid in a world she never made, and yet, as in the Tobias story, "everything conspires to help us," this is a kind of relatedness to the universe itself.

Robin: I think this is really key, and this is why we were saying earlier that, on the surface, Psyche fails in all of her tasks; that is to say, she does not really carry out any of them. It's the universe that carries out the tasks for her, and it's the little creatures who come and help her.

Stephen: This shows us the human soul, both helpless and beautiful in its existence, carrying a great fear of life in the three-dimensional world. And unlike the existentialists' first truth, that the universe does not care one whit about us, we have in both the biblical and the Greek stories the idea that the universe participates very nicely in the soul's journey. In the land of the materialist fundamentalists, our feeling may well be that we are essentially abandoned; and so we experience a primal terror. But, as Joe Campbell said, look to the materials: The ancient tales say that the helpers are there. The ants, reeds, the eagle and tower, in a sense, represent different domains.

Psyche was also given very precise instructions in how to encounter the world of the dead. She was told to put two half-pence into her mouth and carry the sops to feed terrible Cerberus, and exactly how to return. The "tower" instructs very well.

The amazing thing about this story is that it's about love and soul-evolution, but includes the negative side, which is also the daemongelic movement. Back to the question you began with, Robin: why does the goddess of love get so mean-spirited and become a horrible taskmistress? And why does the divine get pitted against the human in this way?

Robin: Well, I believe there are four tasks that have to do with life growth, but the fourth one is extraordinary; it takes Psyche down to the deep layers of the psyche, into the underworld and into the realm of the discovery of the deeper self.

Stephen: There is something extraordinary in this story, which has made it a perennial favorite for two-thousand years or thereabouts. It is a love story and a story of divine-human interaction. And it begins to outline a human response to the divine, and the divine to the human, that moves between these vertical layers that we've been talking about. Then it includes the idea of the ordeals to be gone through, as stages of initiation in life's processes. All of this is happening, as you were speaking about before, as the psyche tries to relate to an archetypal power.

The love goddess herself becomes like a witch, like Ereshkigal in the Inanna story. And Psyche is very much like Inanna, the wounded, vulnerable goddess of growth and vegetation, in the deep underworld tortured and crucified by her cruel older sister—as Psyche is betrayed by her sisters and tortured by her mother-in-law. So the archetypal witch energy runs throughout the tale.

Robin: The idea is that, even behind a power like the witch, a power that can't be tamed and can't be controlled—it's an autonomous power—behind that lies a reservoir of hidden, untapped energy and human potential. And that is what the goddess reveals. The goddess of love reveals her toxic other side.

Stephen: Sometimes, with the controversies of the gods, you can't win. So Psyche is a victim of love, Aphrodite is a victim of love, Eros is a victim of love, and all in a variety of different ways. Human smitten with god, god smitten with human, goddess angry at human woman, human woman fearful of and having to abase herself before goddess—traps and snares laid all along the way, but hints and helpers arising. It's amazing.

Back to Psyche's sisters and the witch energy. They do play a rather extraordinary part in the whole process. Does one trust what one is told, or the evidences of one's senses and the testimony of one's heart? Psyche lets herself be led into a delusion by the evil counselors when the evidence of her (so-called inferior) senses, like sound, touch, and smell, and bodily energy, would tell her that her lover is a fine and wonderful, very agreeable lover. This is often Psyche's dilemma and that of the human psyche too—when soul listens to paranoid, invidious mind (the sisters) instead of valuing what heart, body, and intuition tell her.

Robin: But Psyche couldn't have truly grown if she didn't participate. If she didn't pass through the adventure and take the whole thing to the next level, she couldn't ever have actually become her husband's divine wife, live with him openly, and see and know him—a bad mother-in-law notwithstanding—if she hadn't first loved, then questioned, then loved again. Only after going through all of the trials could she be accepted by Aphrodite, and her marriage with Eros finally be immortalized.

Stephen: Yes, now there's also the fact that Eros could not expect Psyche to stay forever in the unreal status quo of a castle with invisible servants, because there is something unfinished about it all. That left the place for the sisters to come in and insinuate these doubtful things; and Psyche's trustfulness is part of her virtue and her foolishness—instead of listening to what she knows she feels at night.

Robin: Yes, she shows herself to be timid, changeable, and easily influenced; but on the other hand, she's existing in a condition of enchantment, an enchanted palace. A spell has to be broken. An enchantment is an unstable condition, a frozen condition in which growth can't take place. So you can't have a real love or relationship while there's a condition of enchantment; it is the very condition itself that has to change.

Stephen: It's also quite evident that, in that initial condition, it's like a fantasy world—that's the enchantment part. It's as if Eros is the ideal lover, but really is only present in a kind of dream. That's why he's invisible, and that's why the castle provides instantaneous gratification. It's really a vision of what's possible, but unreal; and there has to be this loss of innocence and a breaking of the naive relationship between the principle or power of love and the human psyche. We can never be fully satisfied by our fantasy lives, yet simultaneously we can never really do without them: those fantasies, illusions, and dreams are part of the imaginal body. There has to be some admixture of them into reality.

Robin: I think what you are saying is important. The servants around Psyche are invisible, and she can't really see Eros himself, can't see her lover-husband. So as long as the spell holds everyone in thrall, there's this invisibility. She can't see him as he truly is, and she can't see things around her as they truly are, so that principle of true love that Guiraut de Borneilh emphasizes—those eyes that are the "scouts of the heart"—really are not able to operate.[16] There is no discernment.

Thus, the sisters' voices say, "Isn't there something that's happening, more than can be seen? What is the reality here?" It's an unreal condition, ultimately leading the soul to ask the hard questions.

Stephen: Questions that the timid soul might be afraid to ask. It's the questioning elements in Psyche's family that cause her to look further. But the other aspect of these questioning elements is that that's all they know how to do, they needle and question, they never trust; they are essentially untrusting. So we need a certain questioning energy, and we need to make use of it in the appropriate time, but we also need to have a trusting heart.

Robin: Yes, Psyche does have a trusting heart, and that's ultimately what saves her, the reason that she is so deeply loved; there's an innate goodness there. Eros loves her, and all the creatures in nature want to help her. Her essence—beneath the insecurity—is a deep and innocent place, where she is connected to all those beings, those loving and helping parts of herself.

Stephen: Questioning is necessary to a process of growing up. Now it's a poignant predicament that Psyche has two sisters, who gang up, form a kind of collective. It's like teenagers who listen to their mean-spirited peer group, and it twists them, it warps them.

Robin: It's amazing how that works in life: treat some people charitably, and they may sneer and call you "a girl scout." The sister who is innate goodness, kindness, and beauty vexes and disturbs the ones who are not.

Stephen: The sisters' "ruling loves," to use Swedenborg's terms, are different from Psyche's; theirs are primarily jealousy and envy. For them, reality is hierarchical—one must rise to the top—and judgmental: "Mine's better than yours is!" The sisters say to each other: "She's not going to get anything that we don't get."

Psyche does not have that ruling love; she is in love with the god of love himself, and envy is far from her. She never even thought of the invidious comparisons that obsess her sisters (Van Dusen's "lower order" or demonic obsession). Her gentleness, which seems interwoven with her beauty, will certainly take her far in the spiritual universe of the Greeks.

Robin: In *The Witch and the Clown*, Ann Belford Ulanov and Barry Ulanov explore in detail how that nasty, grasping, greedy, power-hungry character of the witch is a powerful and important aspect of the psyche.[17] We don't like that, and it's destructive when it's out of control and when it runs everything; but like the greedy, graspy sisters in both the Cinderella and Psyche stories, these are elements in the psyche that complete the individual and the whole complex of the person. You can't be all gentle and accepting, like Psyche, or all greedy and grasping, like the sisters. There needs to be a threesome, or a foursome, in some way that works together. We have to have the energy and decisiveness to step forth to meet our life, as well as the openness to accept—and to live creatively with—what comes to us.

Stephen: In engineering the deaths of the sisters, Psyche shows herself an adept learner at guile. After the sisters have perpetrated this horrible, twisted lie, for their own purposes, that eventuates in her burning Eros and losing him, she realizes that they have tricked her, and it was her own naive willingness to listen to them that got her in trouble.

She goes to each of them and tells the story, almost completely truthfully. The power of the truth thus carries her trick. Psyche rises to, even exceeds, the deceptiveness of her sisters, which ends in their destruction. But Psyche seemed to understand the principle of ruling love innately, all along. If they had good hearts and simply listened to what Psyche said, they would be morally tormented but still alive. But because the sisters are impetuous and inflated, they run, each in turn, to the crag from which Psyche originally brought them to the castle, via the magical Zephyrs. They cast themselves off, saying, "Catch me!" This shows that they have some fantasy of entitlement. In this respect, the sisters are literally the agents of their own destruction, literally go running toward it, as do the souls in Swedenborg's hell.

Robin: Although the ultimate aim in the interior work of soul growth is to integrate the elements in the psyche, there are things that have to be excised; here Psyche does this work of excision. At last, matured by suffering, she takes responsibility for this hard work required in soul growth.

Stephen: During this time that Psyche is going through her exile, wandering and ordeals, the god of love lies seriously burned. It says in the text that he almost died from the burn received. So love itself was injured by the mistrust and suspicion; they almost kill love. Eros rebukes Psyche, but still his heart belongs to her. Along with other kinds of love, he seems to know the unconditional kind. His critical self is in a sense displaced to his mother, to that overarching principle that is Aphrodite; she's the one who exacts the revenge on Psyche for her misdeed, challenging her to grow. When a couple marry, the critical ghost of the mother-in-law may hover about, and the wife feel compelled to live up to her demands.

Robin: This is an answer to the question of how the goddess of love can be so hateful. On the one hand is the suggestion that she is ultimately fulfilling her role as the initiatrix, in the way that there has to be a Judas for a Christ to be betrayed—that Judas is the "twin" of Christ, the twin who sees that the action is carried out. From that point of view, Aphrodite and Psyche are a pair, light and dark sister, here, as in the Inanna/Ereshkigal story.

And when Aphrodite has to do those spiteful things in order for Psyche to go through her initiation, we see that Psyche really was suspicious and mistrustful. After all, it was not love, but fear, that forced her to take the next, necessary step toward a real relationship. Looking at it another way, if Aphrodite is love itself rather than the mother of love, and when this kind of an assault is done within love—this kind of mistrust and not giving one's self to it in the full and generous way—then love degenerates into anger, jealousy, and spite. It goes through a negative transformation.

Stephen: We're getting close to the issue of the daemongelic, or the transformation of love that happens sometimes into something imperious, vengeful, exacting. So, in addition to being the matrix of many later fairytales, including these perennial themes of fantasy, imagination, and true love, the story of Eros and Psyche seems to be rich in understanding of the valences of love: how love may turn this way and that, how love is volatile, like the oil in Psyche's lamp. Ignited in suspicion, it can burn and hurt. But it also allows a true-seeing to take place; and by this, the story is moved ahead.

Robin: There are representations of Eros from the Hellenistic period, where he is not depicted as a beautiful youth, but as a slightly travel-worn, older man. The imprint of experience is on his face; he's extraordinarily persistent: love that will not die.

Stephen: This is a beautifully inflected, enduring story, which seems to reflect a high culture zone; and yet in the European cultures, it breaks up into fragments, disperses out into Cinderella and other stories. That's a fascinating process—the mythogems that continue to work on the human spirit don't disappear but worm their way into the fabric of culture and continue to instruct us. I think that is why this is a truly big story: it's the story of psyche in relationship to the world, to love, and to its own growth.

Part Two

LITTLE PEOPLE, GHOSTS, AND DAEMONS

Time is a child—playing like a child—a board game—the kingdom of the child.

C.G. Jung, *Word and Image*[1]

A child dreaming in a garden
sees animals in clouds
imagines the King of Frogs
sees little faces peering from the folds
in drapes.
Our mind arranges patterns into pictures
ink blots into cunning demons
frightens itself with all the things
the night holds.
And yet this is its play:
unfettered from the tyranny of sense
mind weaves its selfsame living substance
with the edge of shadow
and peoples the perpetual unknown
with beings from its own being.
Is this a secret glimpse of God's own beginnings?
A child dreaming in a garden . . .

Stephen Larsen

THE WORLD
OF LITTLE PEOPLE

THE WORLD LOVES LITTLE PEOPLE. Our traditional societies have them populat-
ing the woods and hedgerows, wells and waterfalls, grottoes beneath the earth, even
the realms of air and light. Anthropology has dubbed this ubiquitous tendency *animism*—to personify or invest what postscientific thought calls "inanimate" or "sub-
human" things with humanlike purposes and intentions. Psychology uses the term
anthropomorphism, which, placed critically on a term paper, could bring a shiver to
a college student, but does not affect the millions of people around the world who
believe in ghosts and little people. Moreover, children, little people themselves,
keep inventing more little people, animating their toy soldiers into armies and their
Barbies into families, and sitting in secret glades and speaking in hushed whispers
with imaginary companions. We dwell among little people.

Made of psychic energy, the little people seem alive; they appear and disappear magically. Folktales have them often active at night, when the lights of the
daytime ego have shut down, and the forests begin to glow with haunting presences:
there they are, the fairies dancing in rings, the wild hunt that breaks from under the
hollow hills, the will o'the wisp, the marsh haunt (or "moss ha'nt"). When we sleep
and are "dead to the world," they sit up in our imaginations, rub their eyes, and vex
and enchant the night with their antics. The figures of our dreams glow in the dark,
probably a reason we don't need flashlights to see our dreams. They move by themselves; our dreams are populated with characters that lead us into all sorts of interactions with them—our dream dramas, ourselves as players and audience, us and our
ghosts.

To convince ourselves of the universality of these figures, we merely have to
recite the ethnically flavored names of their races, who haunt the margins of the
human imagination: *kabirii, leprechauns, trolls*, all the fey or fair folk both *seelie* and
unseelie; *alfar* or elves of all tribes including *svartalfar* who keep close to the earth,
and *josalfar*, the Norse elves of light who cross the rainbow bridge between heaven
and earth. Cousins to the latter tribe, spirits of air both light and dark make up the
aristocracy of the faery realms: the Celtic *de danaan sidhe* ride the roads of land, sea,
and air on their magic steeds, and the courtly and dangerous *peris* rule the wild and

shadowed regions of what was once Persia. *Brownies* and *hobs* by different names in every land share human homes and byres, while *dwarves*, *gnomes*, and *knockers* live in grottoes and tunnel in the earth beneath our very feet. Hawaiian *menehunes* build weirs far out into the Pacific Ocean; *naïads* disport themselves in diaphanous beauty beneath their cascades, sisters to *dryads*, graceful in their leafy bowers, and to *hamadryads* on their mountain slopes. Shapeshifters are found among all kinds of faerie folk, but specialists include *selkies* who put off their sealskins for human lovers; *púcas* who may appear as horses, dogs, or other beasts; swan-maidens of the northern skies; the worldwide family of werewolves (by many names, among them *bisclavret* and *loup-garou*); the leopard-, jaguar-, and tiger-people who also wed with humans; the *inari-jin* or fox-fairies of Japan; and the mysterious *vampires*. Also, like the elfin tribes, numbered among the races of *sylphs*, sprites, and daimons or elementals of the air are the *apsarases* and *gandharvas*, celestial musicians and dancers, flying entwined like heavenly Hell's Angels; wild *djinns* who ride the desert winds; Japanese *tengu* and occidental *harpies*, quasihuman, fierce and implacable, sitting on the selfsame cosmic tree; even the *gremlins* invented during World War I to explain inexplicable aeronautical flukes and accidents in the very early days of that technology—the "ghost in the machine."[2]

When little people get tangled up with humans, the fun—that is, mischief, problems, and inflations—begins. In medieval times, male and female celibate monks and nuns were titillated and tormented by *succubi* and *incubi*, respectively, male and female daimons (generally thought of as spirits of the air, but sometimes considered to be infernal spirits, *demons*) who sought sexual unions with them, leading the soul itself to relationship or to orgasm, even if the body were denied human contact. As we recall, in the biblical Apocrypha, it is written that the angels, beings of light (spiritual princes of the realm of the *alfar*, elves, who are sometimes named fallen angels), fell in love with the fair daughters of men, but from this improper union, ultimately, came demigods and monsters.

In the nineteenth century, imaginative play of all sorts was discouraged in children. Later psychological studies, however, showed how important it is for children to play, to personify the world, to role-take, to imagine. How else could they understand someone else's position? How else could they learn abstract thinking, which carries us beyond the egocentric—and the anthropomorphic, for that matter! These processes are described in the writings of developmental psychologists Jean Piaget, Heinz Werner, and others.

For children, then, little people bring the world to life and may be the cognitive and affective precursors for the ability to take different perspectives; they aid us in developing the kind of awareness that social scientists feel to be indispensable for participation in any kind of communal life. Thus personifying and imbuing their creations with soul, children may develop the sensibility indispensable to the planetary citizen of the future: a veneration and regard for human life no matter what its gender, race, or ethnic inflection—indeed, for all life, not just the human—and the ultimate attainment of what might be called "universal ethical principles."

People who haven't been allowed to play imaginatively as children—nor been affirmed emotionally by adults who remember what it was like to be a child—act out infantile dramas long into adulthood. We have all witnessed lives that seemed scarcely beyond one long wail or giant tantrum. The psychopathology increases, Carl Jung says, in proportion to the "unconsciousness" of the root fantasy or "complex." "Projection" is the mechanism or culprit in this psychomythic magic-lantern show, as we all try to recreate the world over and again in our image—and over and again fail. The problem grows increasingly acute when the screen of the projection is not a sandbox or the inside of our eyelids in a daydream, but another living being. The clinical term "transference" simply means that we *transfer* our infantile (Freud says, narcissistic, sadistic, or devouring) selves upon the *other*. In Jung's system, one projects one's own shadow—the undeveloped, neglected or feared—onto one's partner. Not infrequently, this comes up immediately in couples who live together for the first time and separate over such issues as who squeezes the toothpaste tube from the bottom or top or who is a "slob" in the living space.

To the little people involved in contrasexual dynamics, Jung accorded the Latin names *anima* and *animus*, meaning female and male "soul" or animating principle. Sometimes the soul (anima/us) appears in dreams as a projectionist in a booth, putting on the magic-lantern show of life, lighting up the world for us; or as a director, putting on a play; even as a witch with an illusion-producing brew. This is a mythogem equivalent to the Eastern goddess Maya, who creates the illusion of the world as we know it, and her sister Lila, divine play. In this peculiar way, the little people help us to people and animate the world around us.

How do you know when you are projecting? As Jungian analyst E. C. Whitmont would say, "It looks like reality, only more so!" This is because the glamour (in the archaic sense of the word) arises from deep within the willing and creative vital self; there is a potent energy behind our illusions. As we have seen, when one is caught, psychologically, in mythic identity, the entire world becomes an extension of our "mask."[3] Self-knowledge or reflection is simply inaccessible: the world is our oyster; but, really, we are oyster-like in our lack of differentiation, at the bottom of the cognitive ladder. Here dwell, at the primordial level, autocrats, dictators, the narcissistic, and the self-absorbed. Enacted, this world becomes identical with the madman's psyche: Hitler reigns, mad bombers visit their apocalyptic fantasies on the rest of us, the "trenchcoat Mafia" stalks. Relationship is drowned in solipsism.

The Nixie of the Millpond
by H.F. Ford

CHAPTER FOUR

GHOSTS AND LITTLE PEOPLE

Ye elves of hills, brooks, standing lakes, and groves,
And ye that on the sands with printless foot
Do chase the ebbing Neptune, and do fly him
When he comes back; you demi-puppets that
By moonshine do the green sour ringlets make,
Whereof the ewe not bites; and you whose pastime
Is to make midnight mushrumps that rejoice
To hear the solemn curfew.

William Shakespeare, The Tempest 5.1.33–40

LITTLE PEOPLE'S LITTLE PEOPLE: IMAGINARY COMPANIONS

THE WAY IN WHICH WE BRIDGE THE ISOLATION and separation from mother, inevitable upon being born, say the object-relations theorists (Winnicott, Kohut), is by "transitional objects." Everyone is aware of Linus' blanket and those strange and threadbare objects clutched or carried by many children, which form a kind of locus in their lives, an ineluctable companion, an emotional sea-anchor that makes the child's "safe space" seem peopled, connected. Often there is no rhyme or reason for the significance attached to this object. Children may be presented with plush wonders from F.A.O. Schwartz, or Toys 'R Us, yet still they cling to that old, unsanitary-looking bear. Even when mechanical wonders, such as marvelous come-apart robots, have been presented and caught a young boy's attention, still, when emotionally distraught or tired, he goes back to good old bear. This issue in the relationship is not curiosity or excitement, but something like projected love; this is the reason the simple, inanimate thing wears an aura of soul. The little person projects psychic energy into its own little person.

A woman client of Stephen's, whom we shall call "Tina," had suffered much acquaintance with death in her young life (grandparents, aunts, uncle, in a close-knit rural family); she lived with her mother, father, and a developmentally disabled younger brother in a remote country area. In her loneliness, Tina would go to a maple grove with a cliff by a babbling brook. This became her magical hideaway, for she would meet here an old, wise, and funny Indian man. She called him "Standing Wolf." He would tell her stories and console her in various ways. He was there whenever she needed him; she could tell him anything.

In school, finally, the shy girl made a friend among her classmates. Once, while playing with her friend in the maple grove, Tina told her about Standing Wolf. The two girls developed a wonderful play-world in the fragrant, sheltered maple grove.

But then the other little girl's mother found out about the imaginary companion, and we will leave the reader to evaluate the quality—or the success—of her response. She took little Tina, about nine years old at the time, aside and inquired of the "reality" of this figure, saying he was "not real." When Tina said, "But he *is* real," the woman became angry and rebuked her for lying. Then she called Tina's mother and said Tina was "making things up" and that she didn't want her daughter to play with such a liar.

Tina was shocked, confused, and traumatized; she had lost, all at once, it seemed, everyone. Soon after, her brother, whom she loved deeply, also died. An awful time had begun for her back then: it brought on her first serious depression, which was to recur many times afterwards. In one subsequent dream, instead of her imaginal companion, small dark figures were coming out of caves in the maple grove. She began to have violent fantasies.

Years later, she was in therapy, a young woman in her twenties, whose recent loss of her mother had thrown her, again, into a profound depression. Stephen guided Tina to establish contact in "active imagination" with the figure she had lost so long ago. Standing Wolf came forth immediately, as if he had been "waiting" all these years. Tina began to weep when she "saw" him, because she had feared he was gone forever. He very gently and humorously told her that he had been watching over her all these years. He understood why she had not gone back to the maple grove, their special place, and why her adaptation to the adult world had been so rocky. It had been too harsh, sudden, and wrenching. The earlier death of grandmothers and grandfathers had convinced Tina that life was a series of losses, and this became a negative personal mythogem for her. After the death of her brother, with whom she had been very close, she became hardened and cynical.

Now Standing Wolf told her that he would help her with the recent death of her mother, the event that had thrown her into the bottomless-seeming depression that brought her to therapy—but she must go back to the maple grove and perform a ritual. Stephen advised her to do exactly as the imaginal figure counseled; and she did—instructing us both in the power of ritual. Once more in her grove, that place made sacred by the imagination of her childhood, Tina reconnected strongly with this archaic figure. Standing Wolf told her many things about her life, and said that he was fulfilling an assignment as a "spirit guide" when he first appeared to her in a form to which she could relate, to help her with her loneliness and her losses. He assured her that he would continue to be with her, in whatever way she wished, sometimes even as an invisible hunch or feeling.

Tina has gone on to fulfill herself as a greenwitch, herbalist, and a powerful healer. Several years later, she developed an interest in sacred sites in South America, working with indigenous shamans in the Amazon forest. She found herself working easily with the shamanic "journeying" metaphor and comfortable in the world of shamanic encounters. Her most recent interest, now, twenty years later, is in environmental activism and grassroots politics, in which she operates in an obviously "adult" and highly functional way.

Imaginary companions often exhibit an important characteristic that gives us a clue to the true nature and function of this type of inner figure. Such a companion might be an animal, a human (a boy or girl "like me," or a wise old man or woman), or a fey, composite creature (a unicorn, a sprite, an angel). He or she should have a childlike quality, perhaps a visible eccentricity, flaw, or weakness, because children often feel weak, and a *peer* quality is very important in these relationships. Sometimes these figures project a wisdom that is beyond what we normally think of as possible for the child to have at such a young age. In this way, the imaginary—or *imaginal*—companion becomes a projecting screen for the capital "S" Self in the Jungian sense.[1] Thus, Standing Wolf reveals himself as *psychopompos* or the inner guide figure. Not all projection is bad; the projection of the wisdom figure that inflects or prefigures the divine source manifests a positive, guiding, or *anagogic* dynamic.

In the naive psychology of the other little girl's mother, *imaginal* equals *imaginary* equals hallucination/delusion equals mental health crisis—or even worse, theological crisis, where folk of the fundamentalist sort feel that anything less than the canonical apparitions are suspect and "of the devil." But in Tina's case, a child found a way of inflecting a spiritual wisdom figure in a way to which she could relate. The demonism is in the literalism, not in the imaginative play process. What the mother and many adults who misunderstand the imaginal world of childhood miss is the exquisite and profound playfulness by which the soul grows itself up through "little people."

―――――――― DEATH AMONG THE LITTLE PEOPLE ――――――――

WE HAVE SEEN HOW DESTRUCTIVE IT CAN BE to slay the imagination. Imaginal companions can be mirrors of the Self and are conducive to healing and to finding a wisdom path, rather than degenerating into withdrawal and schizophrenia, which is the naive mental-health view. The human imagination is our most characteristic faculty: it is that which most truly makes us human. A sophisticated computer can proceed through very complex multiple steps of systematic logic, but it cannot make a leap of the imagination. It is important that adults who have the care of children, as parents, teachers, counselors and healers, interact with this most fragile and profound organ of consciousness in a way that is sensitive, attentive, respectful, and nurturing.

A high degree of skill and intuition is necessary in differentiating between imaginal figures that protect and guide a young soul, and those that are potentially destructive, pathological figures. As we enter upon the great work before our species—that of relearning how to raise and nurture human beings—this may prove to be one of the crucial riddles we must address.

Deborah Blau, the protagonist in *I Never Promised You a Rose Garden*, a book by Joanne Greenberg, is a gifted and tormented young person who retreats to a world of her own, peopled with little people she calls the "gods" of her world, complete with magical powers—flaming and falling beings out of the imagination. But Deborah, a young Jewish girl sent away to a camp where there is rampant anti-Semitism, is surrounded by hate rather than love. As she retreats inward to escape her external situation, her "divine" companions appear at first to be friendly, then crazy, and her inner world itself turns to madness. Deborah is eventually retrieved by a kindly psychiatrist who enters empathically into her world. This imaginative and courageous doctor—like a shaman descending psychically into the depths of the underworld, encountering its powerful and dangerous denizens in order to retrieve a stolen soul fragment—is willing to make that perilous journey. Through the doctor's serious engagement with the patient's personal daemons, Deborah is finally brought back to the "real" world—which is promised to be no "rose garden" for any of us.

There is a clue, in Deborah's story, to our riddle: it is found in the twilight realm between creative imagination and madness. As we observed in our earlier discussion of Wilson Van Dusen's dialogues with the spirit-presences in his patients' troubled psyches, one can test the nature of an imaginal entity by examining the quality of its influence: "lower order" spirits (or, if you will, autonomous elements in the psyche showing a negative valence) manipulate, even intimidate and coerce; "higher order" spirits (those with a positive valence) scrupulously leave the individual's will in freedom.[2] Informed by this insight, we can begin to formulate skillful means of making the necessary discriminations.

Ultimately, what young humans need to grow in soul is genuine connection with caring adults; genuine experiences of courage and compassion; and an affirmation of life. Children recognize indifference and fakery, and they suffer cruelly from it.

Retreat to an inner world of the imagination when the social environment—family or neighborhood—is toxic can indeed become the stuff of "mental illness." It is this very lack of relatedness with which the imagination must now work and a deep inner insecurity which accompanies it. Further, there is danger in the child psyche wounded by negative adult projections, bored by indifference, and exposed to the violence and inherent schizophrenic elements in the culture itself.

The mass-murder of children by other children taking place in our time is not only a tragedy, but the key symptom of a deep illness in our culture. It is the mythos of the evil of the wasteland, a theme that T. S. Eliot brought to our attention so poignantly. In the vast impersonality visited upon us by our institutions of education, government, and entertainment, it is easily possible for children to "slip through the (impersonal) cracks."

In the massacre at Columbine High School, Eric Harris and Dylan Klebold have been portrayed as exiles whose relationships both to the adult world and to peers were impaired. To each other, in a kind of *folie à deux*, there was a primitive relatedness: we two share the same rage, the same grisly fantasy. In this case and others like it, the peer effect becomes enormously powerful, but in the pathological direction. In the cracks in our culture, toxic imagery breeds. The imagination festers with the imagery of hell; and the mythic androgyne (appearing in the guise of rock musician Marilyn Manson) instead of initiating the soul in a positive way to its own androgyny, as in the sophisticated Jungian alchemical model, seems to provoke it to an externalization of childish rage. Television and video games provide a glitzy and hypnotic modeling, guns come all-too readily to hand in our culture, and the rest is history—a mythogem of our time.[3]

Moreover, the wasteland culture's reaction to these tragedies of youthful violence now shows itself to be equally pathological: school staff, teachers, and counselors, justly frightened by the terrible consequences of not paying sufficient attention to distress signals from disturbed young persons in their charge, now rush to persecute all the "oddballs." Throughout the country, students are suddenly being singled out, accused, and labeled—and sometimes summarily dismissed from school. Under the damning rubric of "disaffiliated, antisocial, *different*," creative and imaginative youth are being swept up in the net of fear, even though they may be seriously questing, in the same troubled imagery of our contemporary culture, for a mythology to save and guide their own evolution.

This reaction is not unlike the misunderstanding of fantasy role-play games, such as the original *Dungeons and Dragons*, by some religious fundamentalists. These critics, beginning with simplistic assumptions, think that because such a game may involve overtly evil or demonic figures, include "magic" in its cosmology, and involve the slaying of characters—even the possibility of being "slain" oneself or being reincarnated in another form—it somehow teaches perversion, satanism, and a crooked path through life. Far from it!

In the liminal zone of adolescent world-modeling and building, lots of "little people" are needed, as well as role-playing. At our not-for-profit Center for Symbolic Studies, year after year, we have witnessed the unfolding of a live adventure fantasy game for adolescents entitled "Adventure Game Theater."[4] The archetypal world pictured is not so different from that of *Dungeons and Dragons*; but, in this model, thirty young people from ages twelve to eighteen create a character—"become" a wizard, enchantress, knight-errant, pickpocket, thief, mercenary, elf, dwarf, healer, or shapechanger. Moreover, they get to play their character off against all the other characters so invented and now portrayed. The adult guides and leaders usually plan in advance a structure not so tight as to strangle the creative, nor so loose as to invite anarchy. Older teenagers who have played the game for several years are encouraged to continue in increasingly creative and guiding capacities. Staff and young assistants offer gentle and skillful overseeing as the up-to-seven-day event unfolds. The use of violence or magical power is constrained by the game rules, and players are often encouraged to find subtle or humanistic solutions to problems that otherwise might only invite force. Force, however, is sometimes enacted, with foam-rubber weapons, armor, and headgear. Players lose and mourn comrades, succumb at times to superior force themselves, sometimes die and hover thinly as spirits watching the sad drama of human life continuing to unfold.

The important thing is that they get to experience a dynamic, playful enactment of a self—even a fictitious self—encountering a world of wonders and terrors. Team-building is a major part of the game, and lasting bonds of friendship are formed. It is preparation for life.

Evil has to have a place in the world of the imaginative encounter, of course; how else can our young learn about it? Imaginative play does not teach evil; it teaches about evil—how to encounter it, what its affects are. Whether, in the role-play, they fight against evil or are ensorcelled by it, still, young humans somehow need to learn about darkness as well as light. In a game, they have the chance to experience it "as-if," before they meet the three-dimensional, historical reality. So too, they may learn what spiritual powers must be invoked to enlighten the recesses of the darkness.

You may have seen the odd bumper sticker: "Kids who hunt, trap, and fish don't mug little old ladies." It contains an awkwardly phrased truism that, somehow, initiation into nature and responsible outdoor activities inoculates the soul against violence. We as authors endorse the position that youth tutored in rich imaginative and interactive play (also best done in nature) are not apt to "mug little old ladies" nor shoot their schoolmates. In the bumper-sticker model, we believe it is not merely exposure to hunting and fishing, guns, traps, and boats that fortifies and inoculates the young psyche (the naive view), but exposure to the spiritual beauty and mystery of nature and the process of being mentored by a thoughtful adult in that setting. Likewise with the adventure game. Growing psyches need playing room, room for encounter somewhere between the video game and the massacre.

At our summer games, although the young people have often slain, betrayed, loved, imprisoned, ensorcelled, revived, and saved their comrades all week long, at the end they are bonded as brothers and sisters. They hold each other and weep when the fellowship must be broken; and their friendships continue to support them through the school year. In the same way as social psychology has shown people who pass through an ordeal together are bonded, so the youth are bonded through these kinds of imaginative play.

We have a paradox here: for human beings to live without illusions, without "little people," dries us up. Take away the "juice" of our illusions, and the well of our motivation parches. Yet psychic energy turned back bluntly from the world, as in social isolation, becomes toxic and breeds, as Blake calls them, "reptiles of the mind"—pathology and sadism.

Do we encourage or discourage illusions, celebrate or endure them, make great art from them or analyze them on the couch? What is certain is that in a male–female relationship especially, but probably in any kind of relationship, each one must learn to endure the projection, the psychic magic-lantern show, of the other person, with all attendant misunderstandings, expectations, and even extreme Pygmalion-like attempts to mold the other into a prearranged image.

Seen in this light, even our failed relationships, tragic melodramas, and silly flings as adults take on significance: we are learning through play—live adventure fantasy indeed! Although tears stream down our cheeks and our heart breaks, life at its best has elements of play, and good living is learned through play, through personification and imagination, through drama. When we realize that all our brothers and sisters are involved in the same lantern-show, life gets *very* interesting. Here is the rejuvenation of the wasteland—people it with our dreams!

ANIMA AND ANIMUS

HERE NOW ARE THE LITTLE PEOPLE both Swedenborg and Jung called the *anima* and *animus*. Understanding them in some rudimentary way seems indispensable to conducting a psychologically healthy relationship, which is also the precursor to being able to practice partnership as a spiritual discipline. Since Jung's formulation is better known, we will begin with a critical examination of his idea as it metamorphosed over the years. (Even the little people go through their maturations). In a fascinating way, Jung—aided by his female followers and colleagues—finally ended up with something close to Swedenborg's more gender-symmetrical eighteenth-century formulation.

Jung early showed a fascination with imagination, recording his own dreams and fantasies. His autobiographical description of his mother pictures her as psychic and, to the young boy, magical, dangerous and unfathomable-seeming—especially when compared to his existentially tormented Swiss Protestant minister father, a man who had lost the faith he was obliged to proclaim in the pulpit. The rational, masculine world led to despair, while the fruitful, feminine unconscious, to rebirth and creativity.

But this was not to be Jung's only problem with the patriarchal domain. In his development as a psychiatrist, Jung first embraced Freud's model of the psyche with its cast of little people firmly established: the desirous, primitive *id*, the rule-bound and judgmental *superego*, and the beleaguered *ego*, the mediator. (Although theoretically gender-free, they all seem like bad, pompous, or tormented boys). Jung's own researches on mediumship and his theory of "complexes" were in agreement. The psyche personifies itself into little people who act "as-if" they had an independent existence.

Freud, for all his intuitive brilliance, stopped short in his vision of the human unconscious. He failed to look beyond the details of personal history and the "family romance." Based on the Oedipal dilemma, this model was unconsciously masculine from the beginning, although Freud's female followers Helene Deutsch and Karen Horney tried to compensate for the asymmetry in their master's model.

Jung believed in the fertile, generative realm of "the Mothers" (in Goethe's metaphor), of his own mother, of a deeper knowing, a "collective unconscious"—as large and as deep as the roots of all humankind. Jung's own early dreams, as reported in *Memories, Dreams, Reflections*, and his vast, rambling readings in mythology and esotericism were showing him a richer world of possibility.[5] There they were the hero, the wise old man, the witch, and the trickster. His own favorites, a challenge pantheon to Freud's, were the *persona* (mask or social presentation), the *shadow* (neglected or rejected aspects of the self), the *wise old man* (the wisdom principle, or Self, that guides our development), and those intriguing "contrasexual" figures, the *anima* and *animus* (*anima* being a man's internal, imaginal woman, while *animus* is a woman's internal, imaginal man).

Animus and anima, in particular, were a bold and brilliant addition, enthusiastically developed in the publication of Jung's *Symbols of Transformation*, the book he said he knew would cost him his friendship with Freud (1913).[6] Freud by this time resented what felt to him like an overpopulation of the psyche with little people and the addition of other archetypal figures and forms to his perfectly cozy little trinity.

It was the female students, analysands, wives and mistresses of both men, in fact, who got them to open their male-oriented psychologies to more gender-symmetrical models. Freud had to add an Electra wing to the mansion of the Oedipus complex, to enable women to explore psychoanalytically their relation to their fathers and rivalry with their mothers.[7] (The Oedipus model had centered the psychological predicament only on the son–mother–father triangle.) And Jung was asked, by his female analysands, students, lovers (the latter categories not always so easy to separate—a group lightly referred to as the "Jungfrauen"—to begin symbolizing the *individuation* process from the viewpoint of the woman experiencer—not only as the angelodaemonic *anima,* which is the man's psychological projection.

Jung seems to have had a lifelong fascination with the anima. He early writes of her that she "comes upon us as a nixie might; she sits on top of us like a succubus; she changes into all sorts of shapes like a witch, and in general displays an unbearable independence that does not at all seem proper in a psychic content."[8]

The anima is the factor that lures us into life:

> She makes us believe incredible things, that life may be lived. She is full
> of snares and traps in order that man should fall, should reach the earth,
> entangle himself there, and stay caught, so that life should be lived. . . .
> Were it not for the leaping and twinkling of the soul, man would rot away
> in his greatest passion: idleness.[9]

In effect, the anima is the greater soul of the man, his connection to his vital nature and to the unconscious. In relation to our inner figures, Jung said, "the apprentice-piece" is the work with the shadow, the neglected and unacceptable aspects of the self; and the relation to the anima is the "masterwork" of the individuation process.

The feminist critique of Jung says that he himself was "magicked" by the anima and that the soul-bearing equivalent for women, the animus, is given short shrift in his writing. The animus is often depicted unfavorably—without reference to its transformative power in the individuation process—as a crowd of males, or even animals or dwarves. The animus often marches into a woman's dreams as goose-stepping gestapo or crowds or juries: it inclines a woman to fixed opinions and "inferior thinking." Such examples are certainly valid, even as *anima*-fascination can be faulted in notable instances of male hysteria (the witch trials, for instance). We might even propose that these appearances of the animus as ominous "mob" could have been especially prominent in women's dreams in the years of the rise of fascism in Europe. But such atavistic configurations are certainly not the whole picture for either animus or anima. On this level, it could almost be said that Jung's model gives a negative answer to the question that used to amuse medieval (male) theologians: *Habet mulier animam*? Does woman have a soul?

In "Marriage as a Psychological Relationship," an important essay, Jung says that a relation between a man and a woman—and this probably also extends to gay couples—separates into a "contained" and a "container."[10] The container is "larger," more engulfing. The contained, in effect, operates within the "field" generated by the container, and the container initiates most things. Jung was probably describing aspects of his own marriage, and his relationships with the other women who shared his bed and his heart. His wife Emma Rauschenbach Jung's major contribution to Analytical Psychology (the formal name for Jung's system) was entitled *Animus and Anima* (perhaps she felt she had to affirm her own soul in the face of her husband's many "animas"). Certainly, Emma Jung's work brought a needed depth and expansion to the subject and did much toward opening the way for a more symmetrical view.

But Jung was faced with a number of problems that he seems to have taken seriously: the Jungfrauen insisting on a psychology of women; his own desire for greater symmetry in his model; his recognition that men's animuses can be every bit as collective or shallow as women's; the fact that women are also bewitched and exploited by beautiful women and may idealize them; and the evidence that female artists call on the muses no less than male artists.[11] A great journeyer in the imaginal, Jung put himself inside the animus and realized that, being a male figure, it must have an anima too; likewise, animas must also have animuses. (So men, like women, *mirabile dictu*, can be both "bitchy" and opinionated.)

Stephen has tried for years to find if Jung ever credits Swedenborg for first discovering the concepts of anima and animus, but has not found it yet. We know that Jung read and commented on Swedenborg's writings fairly early in his career. We also know that Swedenborg used the terms *animus* and *anima* in a psychological and spiritual sense two centuries before Jung. But Swedenborg not only anticipated Jung, his model is closest to Jung's *later* formulation. It is something so elementally simple, Swedenborg saw, with his beautiful visionary's naivete, that surely it hovers close to the truth: Each human person, whether biologically male or female, has both an anima and an animus, a masculine and a feminine soul within. The figures are equal: they refer, broadly, to categories of affection and will or discernment and understanding.

Swedenborg conceives the *hieros gamos* to take place both within—and then, beautiful echo—without. An approximation of heaven is reached, he says, when the love and wisdom principles come together in each partner and then flow in a marvelously interactive circuit from one to the other. He writes in *Conjugial Love* 213:

> Those who have real married love . . . love each other with every sense. The wife does not see anyone more lovable than the man, and the man likewise. In fact, no one is more lovable to hear, smell, or touch. This is the source of their happiness in living together in house, bedroom, and bed.

And in an earlier work, *Arcana Coelestia* 10173, he states:

> That which is done from love truly conjugial is done from freedom on both sides, because all freedom is from love, and both have freedom when one loves that which the other thinks and . . . wills. From this it is that the

wish to command in marriage destroys genuine love, for it takes away from its freedom, thus also its delight. The delight of commanding . . . brings forth disagreements, and sets the minds at enmity, and causes evils to take root according to the nature of the domination on the one side and the nature of the servitude on the other.

The couple is not identical but symmetrical, equal and balanced in Swedenborg's model. When his love falls in love with her wisdom, as it were, and her wisdom with his love, it is like a *yin-yang* or *yabyum* mandala. The masculine and feminine principles, equal in value and echoing each other on subtle levels, perform a multidimensional dance, and creation flowers.

There is no exact equivalent to this in Jung's psychology. Jung stresses the entanglement of shadow issues with anima and animus, and emphasizes the endlessness of the disentangling process, as we work through the essential neurosis of our natures. But Jung's animus is far more than just a derivative principle: it is the quest for values and for the wisdom principle in either gender. His model *does* equate the animus with wisdom as does Swedenborg's:

"It is the figure of the 'wise old man,' who symbolizes the spiritual factor," Jung wrote,

> Sometimes the part is played by a 'real' spirit, namely the ghost of one dead, or more rarely, by grotesque gnomelike figures or talking animals. The dwarf forms are found, at least in my experience, mainly in women . . . In both sexes the spirit can also take the form of a boy or a youth. In women he corresponds to the so-called "positive" animus who indicates the possibility of conscious spiritual effort . . . Graybeard and boy belong together. The pair of them play a considerable role in alchemy as symbols of Mercurius."[12]

Freud's and Jung's younger colleague Roberto Assagioli felt the "analytical" or surgical qualities of psychoanalysis were destructive: dismembering and dividing rather than harmonizing and integrating. Assagioli also identified the importance of "little people," but he felt that the task of psychotherapy was "psychosynthesis," rather than just analysis. He, like Jung, felt that it was not enough to diagnose and to face the grim truth about the multiple self; but the real work was to learn a way to integrate those many selves or subpersonalities. As did Jung, Assagioli found himself saying that this integration could only be accomplished in the service of the highest coordinating function—the higher "Self" with capitals, for it is nothing less than the divine Image in the soul. (Historically, Freud dismissed Assagioli out of hand—as he had Jung—for suggesting that there was an *anagogic* [guiding] function in the psyche.) Here Assagioli, Jung, and Swedenborg are firmly aligned: the real meaning of the little people, the inner figures in the soul, is that we must learn, in a thousand encounters, the proper relationship to the divine.

Jung said the integration of the anima was the masterwork of the individuation process. We become more completely ourselves by working through our relationship with the phantom and the real partner at the same time, anima and woman, animus and man. A female student of Jung, Irene Claremont de Castillejo (an American woman whose marriage to a Spanish nobleman must have made the subject of male-female psychology very lively for her) really opened the spiritual depths and implications of the subject. In her *Knowing Woman: A Feminine Psychology*, de Castillejo helps to bring the animus into a symmetrical parity with the *anima*.[13] For the evolving woman, the animus is a soul-guide, a psychopomp, a torchbearer; not only that, but the animus has a distinctly ethical function that helps a woman counterbalance the yielding and accommodating tendency (*la donna e mobile*) that some men call the "changeability" of woman. This is the truly redemptive element that opens this ghost to the transpersonal, that, like the anima, makes it partake of the angelodaemonic, the primordial divinity of being.

Several women interpreters of Jung have argued that the reason Jung's anima/animus treatments are so uneven is that his own two personalities, "Number One," a locally conditioned, sometimes prejudiced Swiss Peasant, and "Number Two," a timeless portion of the soul whose only business is wisdom, were not integrated.[14]

The animus can be seen, then, as anchored in the spiritual, the transpersonal realm, no less than the anima. Its essential nature as ethical principle is to prepare and guide the soul into an encounter with the Divine, and to, when necessary, give a form or an identity—Merlin, Krishna, Christ—to the formless unfathomable source. In this model, women's wisdom is not merely derivative from collective experiences, thus inferior, but plugged into the same source at the heart of the great mystery as the man's anima. The wonderful thing about a hall of mirrors is that you really do get to see yourself from all sides.

Moreover, in the completely symmetrical model, women have access to the creative psyche through the anima and get to do a standard Jungian individuation by integrating their own anima, while men have the opportunity to sort through their own multiple animuses to find ones that are truly wisdom figures and to access their guidance for a process of inner development.

In an interesting twist in which it seems we ever and again need to expand our mirrors of the Divine, many women (and not a few men) prefer to worship the Great Goddess, the Magna Mater, the Virgin Mary, in preference to a male imago, in whose name so many unpleasant things have been done (to women, and to us all). This figure then embodies or mediates a feminine filter through which the unfathomable creative divine source pours out its energy (this is very close to Swedenborg's model). The anima here is not unpredictable, seductive, "bitchy" (male images derived from coquettish, shallow women, or, as Jung points out, from the results of men's own inappropriate projections), but guiding and nurturing, embodying *Sophia*, feminine wisdom, for women or men.[15] Indeed, for men, a feminine divinity can help them be less prone to jump to animus-like projections that God must be wrathful, judgmental, opinionated, and mean-spirited, and so perhaps less prone to go out and do horrible things in God's name.

Swedenborg has an archaic but uncannily truthful-feeling view to account for the dark and stressful elements in relationship between a man and a woman. He conceives of the human being as hollow, filled with a never-ceasing divine influx, the actual and underlying cause of our lives. When we turn away from the divine source, however, lacunae of sorts open up in our energy bodies. In such hollows (equivalent to the *privatio boni*, deprivation of the Divine) each human being is capable of being infected by what Swedenborg calls "evil spirits" and Jung, "daemones," or complexes. In Swedenborg's theologically toned inflection, this duality, hovering between heaven and hell, is allowed by divine providence so that the human being may be left in freedom to make her/his own choices. Under the influence of negative forces which "insinuate" themselves into our vulnerable consciousness, the ego and its fallen anima (soul image) preen and sink into narcissism, egocentricity, or unwitting cruelty. Blame arises easily. Where is all this sudden discord coming from? Naturally, the narcissistic, egocentric members of our inner cast of characters are the first to succumb, therefore the urgency in most spiritual traditions to engage in ceaseless self-examination: whom does this thought, image, fantasy, serve? Am I being tricked by spirits?

The gender-biased biblical version of Genesis has led to such contemporary bumper stickers as "Eve was framed!"[16] But seen symbolically "Eve" is an inner receptivity to an instinctive (serpent) something associated with the underworld, the unconscious, the world of spirits, Goethe's Mothers. And for better or worse, this faculty of the inner feminine principle of listening to the instinct, "knowing it" for the first time, leads to the "expulsion from the garden" and to coming into the world as we know it, flaws and all.

For literalistic thinkers, the biblical version gives men the right to mistrust women, denigrate their reliability, and trample on all serpents—including the entire natural world (the world of instinct). For the symbolic thinker, the inner receptivity of the soul to the wisdom of the serpent leads to eating the apple of knowledge and emerging from the garden of childhood innocence into the world of conscious engagement with life—hence, of suffering and soul-growth. In esoteric lore, Eve and the serpent are, of course, old buddies and had been hanging out since before the dawn of Minoan civilization. "Eve" is a primordial inner receptivity to the serpent wisdom, including healing, knowledge of good and evil, and rebirth (shedding the skin), thus adapting to life in a more "feminine" or organic way. Jungian analyst Marion Woodman equates Eve with sacred sexuality, with acceptance of the spirituality of the body and the natural world and therefore with the development of a "conscious feminine."[17] When Psyche and Eros truly join in matrimony—in the marriage-bed of matter—then one enters fully into life, and the work of becoming an individuated human being can begin.

Woodman says:

> Conscious femininity is living the redeemed body of Eve, regardless of the gender of the human being. This body is conscious of itself as an intelligent instrument, a living system that actively participates in the divine unfoldment of planetary life. While finding the harmony of its own natural laws of being, it is at the same time finding the harmonic with all forms of life on Earth.[18]

So why, again, do we need "little people" at all, these mysterious complex figures we call "anima" and "animus"? Ann and Barry Ulanov, a wife–husband team who often create together and share an interview with us later in this book, have a cogent discussion of this subject in their recent book *Transforming Sexuality*. They argue in favor of the concepts of anima and animus as "bridge" figures to the unconscious. These figures mediate between the ego or sense of self and the awesome heights of the spiritual journey that await in the encounter with the Self, or Other, the divine presence in the psyche. This is the inner play and the play in the theater of the world for mature people that complements the imaginative play of children and adolescents. We dream ourselves forward.[19]

Left unconscious, that is, held in the fantasies of the mythic imagination or projected autistically onto the world, the archetypal figures take on stereotypic imprecision, and deform the world unrealistically (as when John Hinkley's reason for shooting President Reagan was to get the attention of actress Jodie Foster whom he had never met, an anima with no relation to reality; or in the fantasies of most stalkers). Brought into relationship to real people, in an open, playful, and respectful way, these same archetypal images become muses and guides, and there can be no question of the learning and the growth potential awaiting us all.

Some critics have denigrated the Jungian approach without recognizing the difference between stereotypes and archetypes. Archetypes are truly unknowable in and of themselves; they must be allowed a blurred image and a paradoxical twist. This is probably why Jung said, "Thank God I am Jung and not a Jungian." For "fundamentalist" Jungian thought, anima and animus could be said to recapitulate two-dimensional simulacra of true archetypes.

The Ulanovs caution us, however:

> We must avoid all the facile sexual oppositions that flatten men and women into dimensionless categories, such as the maddening granting of intuition to women in contrast to men's intellectual skills, or the appropriation of aggression to the male and an opposing peacemaking quality to the female. Such readings are no more acceptable here than those ancient famous assignments of fickleness to women and dependability to men, of a body-centered preoccupation on the part of women and a matching lack of interest and clumsiness of body on men's part, or of a feebleness amounting to helplessness in women that is compensated for by the physical strength and resourcefulness of men. The best we can say about this sort of generality is that it offers a statistical summation of the roles in which economic, social, and sexist surfaces have replaced archetypal truths.[20]

We can learn much here that enables us to use the little people idea without being victimized by it. "Ideas," writes archetypal psychologist James Hillman, "are eyes for the soul." So are images, myths and stories: they allow for a rich, textured, creatively provocative encounter with life. To be a complete human being is to have an adequate "library of scripts," in the language of cognitive psychologist Jerome Bruner, from which to choose our responses. Bruner says we do not fully understand our experience unless we can make stories about it, a *narratizing* function.[21]

Here again, we need to stress the difference between biologically male and female human beings and the mythologizing or archetypal thinking we do in relation to them, which we are calling *masculine* and *feminine*. "Neither men nor women are ever any one single thing," write the Ulanovs,

> But if they are anything, even a bundle of things, it is never their stereotyped roles. Women have been hunters and fighters; men have been feeders. Men have been ornamental, gentle, intuitive, fickle, passive.

Women have been crude, clumsy, inattentive to their bodies, violent, intellectist, confident and dependable in filling those supposedly customary roles. They are as they always have been, more and less than they
have been thought to be, both men and women, and far more interesting in their complex archetypal identities than in their simple stereotyped reductions.[22]

Anima and animus must be, then, as Swedenborg saw them: dynamic faculties rather than set images, magical reflections whereby we learn about ourselves,
about others, and about the spiritual quest. As with anything else, reify them into
literalistic images, and they blind us and undermine our self-concept and our self-
understanding. Opened to vision, however, "transparent to the transcendent" (in
Campbell's frequent quote from von Durckheim), they become marvelous seeing
devices for the soul. "We find ourselves," wrote Goethe, midway between Swedenborg and Jung (influenced by the former and influential on the latter), "amidst colorful reflections (*farbigen abglanz*)."

STEPHEN AND ROBIN IN DIALOGUE

Stephen: We are discussing how we become demythologized and allow ourselves to
be persuaded that the mythic or the sacred does not exist. The prototype for this is
the child's belief in the tooth-fairy or Santa Claus; the demythologization is usually
delivered by mocking peer groups that rebuke us for allowing ourselves foolishly to
believe that the world is peopled in a certain kind of magical way.

Robin: Then we sink into the opposite that is exactly a mirror image of childlike
belief: disillusioned, jaded, really "grown up." But there is a third way. The third response to either the mythologized or the demythologized state is a thoughtful response to reality itself. It is based neither on a false illusioning nor on the rejection
of that false illusioning. This is what Joseph Campbell often said—that the experience of life itself is the teacher. When we open to that, we find that life is full of the
most extraordinary synchronicities. It is true that we usually have to wait to get the
goodies that are coming to us.

Stephen: Psychologists call that "deferred gratification," as opposed to the instant
kind. Now in the history of our planet, there is a nightmare of the catastrophic and
spasmodic convulsing of a world which has ceased to believe in itself. That is the
fundamental dissociation; so disillusionment follows dissociation. We say to ourselves, on a more subtle level, "I won't be taken in by the idea of even a faint echo
of miracle, of perfection, that we're trying to make up." No more fairy stories, no
more pleasure-principle of wish fulfillment.

Robin: This sort of disillusionment is a cheap initiation, a shallow rite of passage.
It's what our society has substituted for coming into adulthood, but it is just a simplistic seeing through of the "childish pretending" of childhood, the childish

imagining, the childish optimism or fantasy based on wish-fulfillment. So, substituted for this, then, is a shallow cynicism that has no life-wisdom. We've just cut away the meaningful thing and left nothing in its place.

This is a gift my father gave me: I remember being about eight years old, and he was cuddling me and telling me bedtime stories. We were talking, and I think I had asked him some questions about stars and universes, and we talked about relativity, about Einstein—he loved all the great ideas, the heroes of the mind, and he loved to tell me stories about them.

He was my daddy, he was magic, he was the center of the universe, he could do anything, and he knew everything; but he said to me, "You are going to go places that I cannot even conceive of!" It was very scary to think that I might go places my wonderful, amazing daddy couldn't conceive of, but it was also tremendously empowering. He said this to me several times, at really special times—he knew I needed to hear it more then once—and the time when I was eight was one of the earliest times.

He gave me the future. This is the really precious gift we have to give to all of our children—we have to give them their future.

Stephen: That is truly empowering—the correct use of authority to empower. He gave you something to grow toward. That's the positive aspect of anima and animus.

Robin: Regarding Jung's perspective, we're going to follow his lead, and identify masculine and feminine, and animus and anima as archetypes that have a historical dimension and also biological and psychological dimensions; but we are endeavoring not to confuse them with *men* and *women*. That's a literalistic fallacy that has permeated male–female relationships and has also infected, sometimes, a psuedo-Jungian way of interpreting these: "Oh, you are a man, therefore you must be thinking *this*—" or "you are a woman, therefore you must be feeling *this*—"

Stephen: The naive model misses the subtleties and overlays of feeling and identity possible with a symmetrical anima–animus model, like that developed by Swedenborg: anima and animus as exactly equivalent; ideas of men, ideas of women; what women think men think of them; what men think women think of them.

Robin: By the time that I was fifteen years old I was a thoroughgoing little Cartesian, very well trained in it, not yet fully awakened to life. I think I had started out, like most children, as an animist, but had scrupulously learned how not to be one, so that I could be a "good thinker." As I fell in love, married, and had children, I believe the cloak of Cartesianism just fell away from me—it wasn't essential. It was an "animus" thing I had been trained in. But I have never allowed myself to lose the ability to switch into that Cartesian/rational mode when I need it—and to wield Occam's "razor" when appropriate!

I realize now that that kind of discernment is a wonderful tool, but it's just a tool: It's not really an adequate worldview; it's not something you should clothe yourself in totally, as in a suit of armor and then habitually encounter life in that guise. It may be just something you need at certain times. That's all.

Stephen: The metaphor of the sword and carrying it into life is far more wonderful in the symbolic world than it is in the physical world. In the physical world, you have to hack something apart; and if your sword is very sharp, then it hacks apart easily; if it's very dull, you have to whack repeatedly and maybe make a fool of yourself. Intellectually, a sword is something that is used to get rid of unnecessary kinds of thinking, or it can become that razor that peels away empty rationalizations and tries to cut to the bone.

Robin: If you're too rational, you flail with your sword, use it inappropriately, and inadvertently cut off your horse's head. This is the danger of an out-of-control swordsman on a galloping horse. We rush into life, and we cut off the head of the animal that carries us, and then we have no more connection with our feelings or much of anything else. In fact, using the sword of the intellect compulsively (and therefore irrationally), we really cut off our whole body; now we are without any kind of grounding, or body, or connection to life.

When I met you, Stephen, and fell in love, all this stuff welled up inside of me. I remember a particular week in which I found myself grieving for my lost young warrior, because that part of me had died. Or at that point, I thought it had died; I just didn't have access to him anymore, because I realized that I was entering into a place of the feminine and the receptive. I didn't really want to be in that new place (I was a typical "father's daughter"), because I was going to have to sit on the sidelines and let all those young men do their stuff in front of me, and I—myself—wouldn't be able to do it anymore.[23]

I cried. I was very happy, and very much in love, but I cried because I felt I didn't really want to be *just* feminine and receptive, even though I didn't really feel that I had any other choice. I mourned bitterly for the young male inside me, with his beautiful bright sword. It has been a long process, since that time, learning that woman has to be both maiden and warrior: the soul has to be fully peopled. You cannot let that young warrior die. But I didn't know that at the time.

A man's body may not correct him. He can just go headlong into existence and will probably be overtaken by his rational side (that's not the same thing as *being* rational: our cultural bias supports a man's notion that he is rational even when he is totally driven by feelings like rage and frustration). But a woman's body trips her up, subverts her into a whole other way of being. For me, first falling in love and all the body changes that came with that, becoming a woman, and then several years later, being pregnant for the first time—all of these life experiences carried me, whether I would or no, into another way of being.

I thought I was losing my mind, but I was gaining a whole other part of me that I just never was in contact with before. I was sinking into my body, sinking into matter, and learning to be here. My body made me be in a whole different place, in its own deep rightness. And that's the real truth. It's a real biological as well as spiritual and mythological truth.

Stephen: I was not as aware as I might have been of the loss or slaying of your inner warrior, but you shared a dream with me sometime later. I was a young psychotherapist at the Green Street Center in Kingston. You shared a dream of me accoutered as a kind of a knight-errant on a horse. And I remember realizing in that moment that there was a projection that you had on me; and I told myself, be careful of that kind of a projection. Because, in the same way a woman can never be all anima, all love goddess, so to speak, a man can never be all hero.

Robin: Yes. And just as a man must learn to take back his own anima projections from the women in his life, so that he can access his own soul-wisdom and vitality; just so a woman must not give away her inner masculine. She needs its strength and focus. I was about to sacrifice my own hero-nature on the mistaken altar of our relationship, and then wrap you up so totally in my projections that I wouldn't be able to find you anymore.

Stephen: It's an amazing thing to give and receive projections, and work them through as a couple. We're on our own and each other's journey. In this way, a knowledge of myths and archetypes can be very helpful, as in understanding that dream. In that way, personal myths, revealed through dreams and imagery, can clue us to certain social, cultural, and archetypal dominants that are surfacing for us. The key is to keep it all in awareness.

There was a dream I had, not long after we had gotten married, that taught me a lot about my anima:

> I was in a shadowy kind of valley somewhere, with my new bride Robin. All around us were these semidemonic puppet presences, which have occurred in my dreams and fantasies since I was a little child. They seem to exemplify my part-personalities: They're kind of subhuman and obsessive. Here they were very unruly and in a mean mood, that I hadn't experienced since childhood. They all started clutching at Robin and saying, "She's mine, she's mine!" In the dream I am horrified and overwhelmed that I am going to have to somehow protect her against them all.

I awoke in an unquiet, anxious state, and you were nestled alongside me, peacefully; so I suppose this was an early introduction to the difference between a dream figure and the real person who loaned her form, so to speak.

Now, I had been in situations where male friends (or enemies) had tried to hit on my girlfriend, and it felt a little bit like that. But there was a deeper anxiety as well. Just having entered Jungian analysis, it seemed ripe material. I associated immediately to the fact that the previous evening I had been studying and fascinated by the case of a probably "schizophrenic" (by diagnosis) man who was a patient at the clinic where I worked. But I had first seen him as a street performer, electrifying upper Broadway (in Manhattan) with his antics. I called him "The Fleegle-eyed Floogle" after a character invented by cartoonist Al Capp. This patient would appear on the street wearing a ten-gallon hat and a bandanna over his lower face, wraparound sunglasses, and a large cloak which he used to conceal and suddenly manifest strange objects.

I had become fascinated by the life-story of this amazing man to the point of reading the case record far into the night. I thought: You can make up a life and live it; you can be a character that you invent as you go along! What a fascinating idea.

What it did was evoke the plurality of my own psyche—the demonic puppets, just a little taste of my poor "Floogle's" tragic schizophrenia. Each subpersonality wanted to claim my soul (Robin). But any one of them "getting" her would be a catastrophe, I realized. I would be condemned to a one-sidedness or incompleteness that would not reflect my whole self. I realized after that dream that I had to keep my soul for myself, not give her away to anyone outside or any fragmented self within. The role of the ego, "myself" in the dream, was to endure the many voices of the self and stand fast like Odysseus chained to the mast. Nor were dreams about "Robin" literally about Robin: they were messages about the state of my soul.

Robin: I also dream in "Stephens."

Stephen: I've been reading *The Eden Project*, by Jungian analyst James Hollis, on the search for the "magical other."[24] Hollis calls it, along with immortality, one of the two great illusions or errors into which people fall. He connects it to the initial experience of paradise.

Robin: It's the idea that we have nothing but projections on the other.

Stephen: In that way, I find it quite clinical, and quite depressing; it turns the magic, the sense of high destiny, into mere psychodynamics. To be sure, we need to know about each other in some of those ways—what makes each of us tick? Hollis does say that, much as may be brought to consciousness through the examination of behavior patterns, symptomology, and dreams, this encounter is sometimes shocking, occasionally depressing, and always humbling.

Robin: *Psychology Today* once compared the two phenomena of friendship and love. There are characteristics in common: Enjoyment of the other, mutual assistance, respect, spontaneity, acceptance, trust, understanding and confidence. Love carried a higher charge than friendship, though the two things are akin. Physical love and desire leads into obsession with the other as object.

Stephen: It brings up the indissociation that one projects onto the magical other, the idea that one cannot live without that person and so on. This is a common belief in certain cultures where jealousy is used as a measure of how much one is loved, rather than an index of the jealous person's insecurity. In this model, some people believe that, if I am not jealous over you or jealous about you, I don't love you. And conversely, the growth of jealousy symbolizes commitment.

Hollis also says, as did Campbell, that traditionally love and marriage do not go together. This is only a relatively recent thing, in modern times. Usually the love story was enacted among social rules and structures that forbade it, as in *Romeo and Juliet* or the recent film, *Shakespeare in Love*. The tragedy is that there really is love there—or at least the possibility of its growth through the mulch of projections—but the world doesn't permit it.

Robin: Marriage was often arranged as a form of perpetuating social connections and values and wasn't about love at all; it was about procreation, often about bonding one dynasty or one family to another, for some kind of mutual gain. Nevertheless, we know that husbands and wives in these formal situations have often come to love each other deeply. Robert Johnson argues convincingly for the traditional, even arranged, marriage as a vessel for the growth of mature love.[25] But it is true that only in modern times have many people had the experience of having voluntarily chosen their partner—theoretically for love—and then seeing how it all plays out.

Stephen: It seems hard to have a deep relationship with our own self, and yet also a respectful and growing one with the other. Consider how difficult it is to have any relationship at all: I come bearing the wounds derived from my culture and family of origin, and these I am now imposing on you. All of the complexes I have acquired in my life on this earth, you will have to suffer from me.

Jungians and Psychosynthesis theorists feel the psyche is not so much a monarchy, as the ego would have it, nor even as a central intelligence agency, running all the satellites, but rather is a multifaceted, polymorphus, polysemous, polytheistic being. So there are many voices, many intimations, many directives—some heard, some only intuited, but all persuasive. Which voice is mine, the ego asks?

Robin: All and yet none. This the real value in studying the little people—to have a way to name our own ghosts.

Vision of the Empyrean
by Gustave Doré

CHAPTER FIVE

SOUL MATES

So, through the eyes love attains the heart;
for the eyes are the scouts of the heart,
and the eyes go reconnoitering
For what it would please the heart to possess.
And when they are in full accord
      And firm, all three, in the one resolve
At that time perfect Love is born
From what the eyes have made welcome to the heart.
Not otherwise can love either be born or have commencement
Than by this birth and commencement moved by inclination

Guiraut de Borneilh[1]

— MYTHIC SOUL MATES —

ONE OF THE GHOSTS THAT AFFECTS enough people to be called a modern *mythogem*—or a unit embedded in a myth—is the idea of "soul mates." It is explored daily in the classifieds, on the Internet, and in singles clubs, not to mention in literature and the media, where it becomes the *prima materia* of fantasy, novels, and films. The theme is very ancient; and since it is entangled with the mythology of the soul, it brings with it spiritual-sounding concepts like "destiny" and "eternity." Thus, this mythogem calls into question our participation in the universe and in a story greater than our individual lives.

In fairytales, for example, there may be a starting situation that affects the whole country: a dragon lays waste to the land unless a princess is given as sacrifice (a daemongelic scenario, because, as Joseph Campbell points out, although dragons seem to lust after beautiful princesses, they don't know what to with them except hoard or eat them). But even as the horrible ritual is being enacted, destiny produces a hero, appoints helpers or guides, and even concocts magical coincidences to further the dramatic action. Ultimately, a rescue and love story are enacted, the hero and princess found to be "just right" for each other, the land saved, a treasure restored or awarded.

So what is going on here, that we never tire of this elementally simple story? In the baleful solitude of the wasteland of our lives, our lonely souls, in exile from the divine oneness, seek the *other*, the lost "One" of the Platonic myth.

There are two dimensions to this spiritual reunion. The first, as already sketched above, might be called reconciliation to the universe through a home-coming or belonging, the conspiracy of destiny in our fate, a kind of "positive para-noia" (defined as the outrageous belief that the universe conspires in our favor). Thus, simply through the conspiracy of destiny (or divine providence), we become somehow reconciled both to life and the Divine. Our faith in divinity is renewed through the universe's gifting us with a soul mate, either vicariously through the myths and tales or actually in our lives (not always so easy to attain). As we shall see, this is a game fraught with hidden perils, but it may very well be the best game in town.

In the second, one attains the divine beloved through the soul mate, the little, the earthly beloved. The ecstasy of Shakespeare's Juliet and St. Teresa are in-distinguishable. Love of the person becomes the stepping stone to the Divine, and the Divine is indistinguishable from the person. The flowering forth of the soul in the presence of the earthly beloved is a revelation of its own secret nature and its spiritual love affair with the Divine. Bent to this end is the fanaticism of the quest for the soul mate, its obsessional qualities and single-minded, sometimes other-worldly, devotion in the service of an ideal image or form. Both forms will be touched on in this chapter and the next and lead into our own angelodaemonic in-terpretation of it.

As Arthur Schopenhauer points out in his extraordinary essay "On an Ap-parent Intention in the Fate of the Individual," which is often used by Joseph Campbell in his analysis of the tradition of courtly love:

> Everyone, during the course of his lifetime, becomes aware of certain events that, on the one hand, bear the mark of a moral or inner necessity, because of their especially decisive importance to him, and yet, on the other hand, have clearly the character of outward, wholly accidental chance.[2]

James Hillman, Thomas Moore, and other contemporary writers have brought to our attention the importance of seeing life as a journey. We move through the river valleys of experience, acquiring soul depth and knowledge as we do so. We should not be in such a "god-awful" rush to reach the empyrean heights of the spiritual experience, as much in our religious traditions tells us to do, repudi-ating the flesh and embracing the spirit. Rather we should savor the experiences as they come, treating them as intelligible revelations of ourselves, our souls, journey-ing through time. Our life-affirming mythologies are the stories we tell ourselves along the way. These clearly serve a purpose for a frail biological creature whose ul-timate destiny, on the physical level, is guaranteed. We need to remind ourselves often of the romance and the adventure of life, along with its perils. One of the sweetest and most exquisite tales is this one of the soul mate. If Swedenborg has told us truly, we are the stuff angels are "made on." Our lives, with all their stumbling vicissitudes, are the biographies of angels.

Since myths empower behavior and are sources of energy, the image of the soul mate can exert a powerful positive effect on one's life. The idea of this exquisite fulfillment of oneself encourages the ego to change in the service of soul, to grow to meet the challenges posed by the idealized image of the other, who inhabits a condition one can never inhabit, the "otherness" of gender. As in the love portrayed so hauntingly in the literature of the "courts of love" of twelfth- and thirteenth-century Europe, of which the poetry of the troubadour Guiraut de Borneilh is a superb exemplar, the self is stretched by service to an ultimate ideal. The lover perfects his virtue in the service of a contrasexual ideal of perfection.

Rilke speaks of the ineluctable sea-change the soul undergoes in its encounter with a potential soul mate:

> . . . And when you have endured
> the terror of the first glance, the yearning at the window
> and the first walk in companionship, just one time through the garden:
> Lovers, can you remain the same? And when you lift yourself up
> and pour yourself into the other's mouth, drink to drink,
> oh how strangely you disappear in the act.[3]

"And when you have endured the terror of the first glance. . . ."—the poet's essential phrase captures, as does the formula of a calculus equation, a precise spiritual movement and its trajectory. When I with all my daemons meet you with all your daemons, universes intersect. Of course, the moment is numinous, terrifying, fraught with destinies, descendants, genealogies, opportunities, karmas, and the great unknown. It is as if two universes peered into each other and saw stars, nebulae, black holes. If we are truly present, why shouldn't it be terrifying? And why shouldn't it be beautiful?

In the process of this encounter with the human beloved on whom one projects the divine beloved, says the poet, something in us changes. Every sensory experience—the garden trellis strung with roses as certain words were spoken, the hummingbird who appeared at the right moment, the fat, puffy clouds in the sky— all are suffused with the nectar of angelic invitation. In such moments, the world is transformed forever, and only a poet could attempt to capture even a trace of its essence.

In the love encounter, one faces, as in Buddhist meditation, the insubstantiality of the self:

> For in our feelings, we evanesce,
> breathing out and away; from the embers of every moment
> we dwindle. But there are those who say:
> Yes, you have gotten into my blood, so that the room, the springtime
> is so full of you . . . But never mind. They can't keep us that way.
> We slip right past and around. And the beautiful ones?

Who can hold them? Incessantly, appearance arises
in their faces and vanishes again. Like dew from the morning grass
what we think is ours escapes, like the warm fragrance
above a dish of food. Oh smile, whither goest? Oh upward look
New warm returning sea-wave of the heart . . . [4]

The poet takes us here close to the cusp of the intersection of passion and spirit, the sweet zone where each tells of the other; the place where we meet and melt and confirm our insubstantiality. So sweet is it to receive the magic of spirit's projection, so hard to hold on to—is this the "insubstantial fabric" from which soul mates are fashioned? Is the quest really to see ourselves only as reflected in the soul-mirror of another psyche? Or is the "appearance" that rises ceaselessly in the faces of the beautiful, a unique window on the divine essence, its "multicolored reflection" refracted in the prism of the world? Swedenborg says, yes: "The wisdom of the angels of the inmost heaven consists of seeing divine and heavenly matters in individual objects, and marvels in sequences of several," he tells us in *Heaven and Hell* 270:5. Beneath the "appearances" of the world (Swedenborg's word, though identical with the concept in Eastern metaphysics) lies the radiance of the Divine. This is a truly revolutionary idea for a European man of the eighteenth century, and it is still one for a child of the new millennium. Can our spirituality become intertwined, like a Celtic knot, with our lives? Is there a spirituality to be found in living and relating to usher in Swedenborg and Blake's "New Jerusalem"? "And we must love, man woman and child," said Yeats, "dedicating all things as they pass, or else we come to God with empty hands."

SOUL MATES ON THE KARMIC NET

THE RENOWNED "SLEEPING PROPHET" EDGAR CAYCE (1877–1945) had much to say on the subject of relationships. Cayce was one of the best-documented clairvoyants of all time; he did thousands of "life-readings" for people and counseled many hundreds of couples about to embark upon marriage. He regarded his own marriage as central to his life and his spiritual evolution, and counseled others towards marriage as a spiritual work with real substance. Kevin Todeschi, a Cayce scholar, writes:

> One of the undergirding premises in the Cayce information is that we most often come to know ourselves through our relationships to other people. Whether it is through learning about love in the face of someone we hold dear or growing in patience through a lifetime of challenges, it is through our interactions with others that we become aware of our shortcomings and our abilities. It is through our personal encounters that we come to realize what we need to work on, as well as what it is we have with which to

work. Cayce believed that it was also through the dynamics of our relationships that we grow in our awareness of our true identity and our ultimate connection with God.[5]

When people impressed by the specificity and accuracy of his knowledge would ask if "I should marry this person or that one," Cayce would say, "Yes, you could, with the following admonitions," or even "Not such a good idea!" Generally what the prophet seemed to be referring to, in the negative instances, was that there would be spiritual obstacles and frustrations too great to be overcome; in the positive instances, there were challenges that could be encountered and resolved—hence, opportunities for personal and spiritual growth:

> A soul mate is someone with whom you can work through life's challenges and difficulties, even when that individual may appear to be the source of them. In other words, a soul mate is an individual who often reflects or lets us encounter our own strengths and weaknesses.[6]

Cayce believed many people attracted to each other in this lifetime had been together in "other lives" and had already laid down patterns, which, if still unresolved, would have to be dealt with "this time 'round."

Cayce's own meeting with his life-partner Gertrude was preceded (appropriately enough for a "sleeping prophet") by a big dream:

> Edgar was walking through a glade with a woman standing next to him, holding his arm. The woman was wearing a veil so that he could not see her face, but they seemed very much in love. While walking they arrived at a little stream filled with clear, sparkling water. They stepped over the stream and began walking up a hill where a man stopped to meet them. Dressed only in a loincloth, he was the color of bronze. On the man's feet and shoulders there were wings. He appeared to be Mercury [Hermes] the messenger.
>
> Mercury told the couple to join their hands, which they did. Across their united hands, the man placed a long piece of golden cloth and stated, "together all can be accomplished, alone nothing may be accomplished."[7]

In the concluding events of the dream, Cayce and his partner together overcame a sea of mud and climbed a steep precipice, by uniting their efforts. Although it came several years before his actual meeting and marriage to Gertrude, Cayce believed it was a premonition of this life partnership and a kind of initiation into how marriage amplified the powers of each partner. Later, he was reluctant to do readings without Gertrude present, watching over him as he "slept," receptive to the spirits and the guidance that was being given him.

Cayce's approach is that the soul mate is the partner or would-be partner who offers us the most opportunity for growth in this lifetime. Like Joseph Campbell, Cayce believed that each partner should give sixty percent, instead of "just half"; then the relationship would flourish. Because of Cayce's inclusion of the concept of other lives, not found in Swedenborg, there is the idea that many soul mates may arise in this lifetime and others, and that the phenomenon may even happen between people of the same gender, since genders are sometimes exchanged in the process of reincarnation.

The approach of a soul mate might be announced through a dream as Cayce's was, sometimes simply through a "knowing" when one first meets the other person. In order to be prepared for such meetings and such unusual psychological upheavals and confirmations, it is probably desirable to keep an open mind that there are more undercurrents between people than conventional wisdom accepts. If we do not keep open in this way, we may literalize the feelings and act out wildly. We seem to need a sense of transparency and depth to avoid being swept up in our own psychic processes, whether of authentic "past lives" or simply of unconscious mythological fantasies that rise to the surface. In our next chapter on the daemon-lover, we explore the negative instances of such states of possession.

Suffice it to say, whether we prefer to have a single model, the this-life/afterlife model of the Christian/Swedenborgian tradition, or the many-life model of Hinduism/Buddhism, the Theosophists, and Cayce, there are many factors that are brought together in a human nuptial rite. And what about not just past, but future lives, of generations unborn? Are there "teleological" influences, where our potential, unborn descendants may wish this particular union—of what will one day be a patriarch and matriarch of a family dynasty—so they all can be born together in a family milieu?

In general, the Cayce approach is based on the psychological and spiritual growth of the soul, and there is no hard and fast "destiny" to which one is bound. Usually at each point of decision, there are possibilities and options, and free will may never be left out. Here the question asked by both Swedenborg (also known for his clairvoyant abilities) and Cayce would be, "What do you wish?" In this way, the "ruling love" steers us through a tangle of (perhaps past) affiliations or "karmic connections," by which we are not bound but which naturally attract—and repel—us.

Sometimes in the Cayce material there are instances of the finger of destiny pointing strongly that "this is the one." In one instance, there was a Japanese man and woman who knew each other, but were in no way committed, each one having reasons that the relationship "probably just wouldn't work." It is a custom in Japan to pay attention to the first dream of the new year. On January 1, Tobe, the man, phoned to tell Asako, the woman, that he had dreamed about her. But she had had the identical dream—she was being shown around Tobe's house (modest in actuality) as if it were a mansion.[8]

There are many instances in the Cayce material—and in the work of psychiatrist Brian Weiss and Jungian analyst Roger Woolger—where couples come together again and again, down the corridors of destiny, to work through the many vicissitudes of soul evolution.[9] In the past-life material, as the stories proliferate, so do the potential dramas for encounter. Woolger, in his workshops, is fond of quoting Sophocles: "Who is the victim, who the slayer? Speak!" In stories woven longitudinally through the net of time, there are often dramatic symmetries being worked through for the soul's advancement: the aggressor in this life was the victim in the last, and vice versa. And under the direction of a skilled past-life therapist, people relive "being" the other gender, in other times, places, and social situations. This also frequently happened in the LSD research of Stanislav Grof, in which Stephen was a professional volunteer and trainee in the 1970s. It can be very "mind-opening" to experience "being" the other gender, and this kind of work probably has real therapeutic possibilities for helping to heal the wounds of gender.

Both Cayce and Swedenborg agree that there are soul mates: for Cayce there is past life affiliation, for Swedenborg, a future destiny as an angel. And both would agree that spiritual work—exercises in overcoming egocentrism and personal pathology in the service of something greater—are what soul mates are all about.

SOUL MATES ON THE INTERNET

SOMETIME IN 1989, VUSUMAZULU CREDO MUTWA, a Zulu shaman, asked Stephen about a curious item among his prophetic visions: "Sir, I have seen in my visions this strange thing: that people are or will be using the computers for sexual purposes and for making love. I am a poor man in a faraway land, sir, and I do not know how this could be, only that I have seen it."[10] At the time, Stephen was bemused but had no answer for him: now, some ten years later, the answer is abundantly clear. People are looking for any way to connect with that mythical other. Beyond the porn sites and the crude sexual opportunism everywhere visible on the Internet, there is something else happening, and it invites our inquiry in this section. It is an extension of the soul-mate motif, which has opened the channels of possible connection between people through the medium of the computer, language, and fantasy.

This kind of occurrence raises many interesting questions. Are there still to be found, now on-line, those spiritualized and bodiless loves like the ones that characterized the Middle Ages? What happens when the requirements of the physical conflict with the mental and spiritual? Are the sentiments evoked real or artificial? We explore herein on-line romances with two kinds of outcomes: one that ended in an impasse and one that led to an ongoing relationship.

Our first example is actually derived from numerous instances that have come to our attention. For the sake of meaningful comparison with our second example, we have fictionalized the material into one coherent "story."

So, let's say that, once upon a time, a woman named "Miranda" began a passionate on-line romance that consumed her night and day for the better part of a year. The first thing in the morning Miranda went to the computer, and again immediately after returning from work. As she spoke of the intimacies and the meeting of the minds that had occurred between herself and her on-line lover, it was perceptible that this was a soul affair, without the two people ever having met in person. Mind met mind, through the medium of poetry and meanings.

This was not just a fling to Miranda, who had had many lovers but was still unmarried; to her, this was the relationship of a lifetime. Her on-line lover, however, had a wife he could not leave. Miranda even loved him for this steadfast loyalty—while his romantic heart belonged to her. The poignancy of the predicament, as such irreconcilable social constraints have been throughout the ages, was enormously fertile for the mythopoetic imagination. The affair generated hundreds of pages of beautiful, intricate, passionate literature.

Eventually, though, an impasse was reached. Miranda knew she was well into midlife, and the chances of a "real relationship" grew ever more remote. Eventually, she found herself feeling that if she could not expect that, in the foreseeable future, the on-line affair would lead to a physical affair and a growing old together, she would have to abandon it. For her beloved, too, the bonds of physical loyalty and daily affection prevailed over the romantic ecstasy the meeting of the minds had promised. The on-line affair itself, however, still had a sacred and courtly-love quality about it that influenced both for a long time afterwards.

In a second instance Stephen was able to interview and speak with a couple, now living together, who had met on the Internet. The man, whom we shall call "Jeremy," was married, unhappily, he thought in retrospect, to a professional woman; they had one child. The woman, whom we shall call "Cerise," was already divorced and had custody of two children ages three and four. Both Jeremy and Cerise were very literate and had first started exchanging wild mind-monologues in a chat room. Each came to "fall in love" with two things about a person they had never met: the mind of the other and the ability of the other to understand the more "far-out" things about one's own mind. Each said, as did Miranda, that they had been able to tell the other things that they had never been able to share with anyone. The "Net" offered each permission to be both creative and self-disclosing at a rate that was simply breathtaking and seemed, with each exchange, to rise to new heights of intensity. (Each was an aspiring writer, but put all other writing aside once the intensity of this process began. The rewarding side of writing now was addressed to the muse, the anima/animus, the beloved inspirer of the soul.)

Stephen asked Cerise, who had moved across the country with her two small children to be with her "Internet beloved," how she felt she could really trust this person and this novel situation. "Because I felt I knew his mind," she said. "With the intensity that we shared, I felt there was a real knowledge of who he was; the words were like a net or cradle in which our relationship was suspended; in the exchanges, we had incited a deep feeling of trust; and I haven't been disappointed."

It was possible to persuade Jeremy, still in a writing mood, to write about his experience in response to questions: The first pertained, of course, to how everything came to be:

> I had been involved and comfortable with computers since my college days, and used various online content providers for a number of years, but had really written very little. At some point I had stepped over the line; I had begun a more active communication that involved writing to other people. I had to write in order to establish and maintain an identity. That identity came out of me, but was not who I had been. In its constellation, I became deeply involved with another person. We opened up channels of communication, the force of which had surprised us both. (I should mention that I had always been disdainful of online social opportunities, dating services,

etc.) But how could I have become so involved with a person whom I had never seen or talked to?

It was the way she moved.

I had never seen her, not even a picture. It was the way her thoughts moved, and moved in response to mine. It was an essence. As a skeptic and an analytic sort, I quail at the above vocabulary, but it is unavoidable. Neither she nor I were real to the other, at least in so far as reality is customarily measured—we had no mass, could not be empirically verified, and appeared suddenly and unpredictably. We might as well have been angels or daemons.

We were words. This is not semiotics; we existed in the language. We were the words chosen and the words combined, and how they were chosen and combined. Who chose, and why, and how? Thought, emotion, soul, psyche, spirit? The point is this: It was ethereal and unverifiable, but incredibly direct, as if the life force were stripped of its physical habits in both senses of that word: the veils of Maya and the cloaking devices of the Romulans around us. It was . . . spiritual. Which brings to mind the old line: "The spirits have begun to speak." There we were in the flickering crystal ball of the monitor.

This says it, doesn't it? We are talking illusion, magic. In a way, it rivals the astral or the bardo plane, in which souls move on mysterious pathways, the songlines of the spirit realm, to find the beloved other, the soul mate. Here the sense used for the search is the mythopoetic imagination; it brings everything of immediate concern to the soul: mask, meaning, creative mind, the spontaneous, the narrative story, a net of words that mimic the lineaments of the soul. *Physis cryptesthiae philei*, Nature loves to hide from itself—and find itself, and, in fact, play "hide and seek" with itself. This is part of the cosmic game in which we are enmeshed.

Jeremy wrote a poem to Cerise, without ever having met her in person. He entitled the poem "Harrier":

> The harrier up through snow
> wing on edge of white air,
> the laden wind keening
> and he so the wind.
>
> I have freed the harrier
> to ravel the winter gyre
> and spiral the winding star
> binding her to there.
> Tarry here no more.
>
> The hooded hawk
> that was my heart
> and bode inside
> and came to my cincture,
> with unrepentant talon
> and glint of eye,
> Thee I bid goodbye

Falling breath of snow,
heart, wing, or windbeat on my cheek;
hooded hawk, harry me not,
nor heed my call,
for thee I have set free,
go now, go to Shee.

The poet explained that "Shee," another name for "Sidhe," the race of the fey, was inextricably associated with his beloved, and this "fey" encounter that began over the Internet. "Shee" was part of his beloved's on-line address.

The mythological association to the Internet, is, of course, "Indra's Net," a net of gems, spread throughout the cosmos, in which each gem, each node, is a person, his or her immediate nexus stretching out around them, and ultimately tied in with every other, since "each reflects each." Now, we have suddenly a cybernetic "net of gems," woven on keyboards, manifested in the "flickering crystal ball" of the screen. It is as if each of us has been given a metaphysical "crying bowl" or portal of access to another world, in which we may see our own reflection—or that of the beloved.

But what of the corporealization of this representation? Surely much is left out if the romance remains electronic only, and merely literary:

> We have since met, and now see each other every day; and have explored
> the customary manifestations of corporeal beings. And I wonder at times
> if both of us rue the added responsibility. Spirits and Wordsprites run
> lightly over the unfettered word, and the world we create together. Trudg-
> ing through the quotidian and keeping that lightness alive, is what re-
> quires spiritual practice. The first step, though, is to find the spirit.

There is obviously a deflation, a "bringing down" into the zone of incarnation from the rarified zones of the Net, where people meet as spirits, as mythopoetic energy fields. Now there are "quotidian" chores of everyday life, the care and nurture of children, day-to-day tasks, such unromantic things as garbage, diapers, and checkbooks. Under these circumstances, the new human relationship that is struggling to make all the parts work might long for just a little time with each other—on the Net. And maybe couples who do share the realities of family life and raising children should still make time for such things as mythopoetic e-mails on a regular basis or some way of validating the spiritual and romantic dimensions of relationship, lest those more vitalizing aspects drown in dishwater and diapers.

The alchemist says, "As above, so below." In essence, this would mean the Internet is the electronic manifestation of a spiritual "Indra's Net," through Swedenborg's "correspondences." The Internet mimics something the traditional peoples have always said: Grandmother Spider Woman's web unites us: we are all "relations."[11] There are networks of interconnection between us all.

If there seems to be much heavy breathing over the Internet, so be it: at least it is as legitimate a context for exploring the perennial attraction between the genders as bars or laundromats and gives a much-needed forum to the symbolic and spiritual dimensions of relationship, as well as the physical. This method of relating to each other clearly seems to be something with a future, and the angels of synchronicity will probably have an easier medium to play with than in the restricted physical and social opportunities that have constituted most of our patterns of movement in the world.

There will, of course, have to be measures taken to help people avoid encounters with sociopaths who have kissed the (electronic) Blarney Stone, but use words to gain their own twisted ends. There is also always a danger of people's living through their words more fully than they can ever dare to in "reality." Here the same discernment is required that Swedenborg advocates for relationship to spirits: watch for "complexes," places where your on-line partner seems to be stuck, defensive, or paranoid. Pushing the limits of intimacy, here in a discernment-requiring way, can be used as a test, or projective technique, inviting the other's psyche to disclose itself.

The quickness with which intimacy takes place on-line shows how desperate many modern people are for this experience. It is not unlike the intimacies that spring up on airplanes or at business conferences; the transience of these situations provides temporal boundaries, allowing a sense of safety, perhaps illusory, but nonetheless conducive to opening. One longs to know and be known by another. We need to disclose ourselves at ever deeper levels and witness the other doing the same. When it is done together or in an alternating *pas de deux*, it leads to ever deeper self-revelations, the soul's learning about itself and another at the same time, through mutual disclosures. Souls, it seems, love hiding, peeping, and popping out at each other, showing layers, complexity, surprise, creativity.

But here again, as the electronic media open the scale of our possible contacts, discernment is required; for intimacy, by definition, is not something we can do with everyone. We have to sift and work through the many to find the one or the few with whom we can truly be intimate: our soul mate(s).

─────── ROBIN AND STEPHEN IN DIALOGUE ───────

Stephen: What I'm fascinated by is the relationship between word and image in Internet varieties of soul disclosure. This brings up the whole idea of oral tradition and how the mind is free to image and embroider around the word-magic of the story. So as the left hemisphere hears the words, the right hemisphere conjures images—it's incredibly evocative. One can make love with words, as poets throughout the ages have convinced us, on many levels, from the most primitive and unctuous to the most sublime psychomental love-makings. Now there are a million budding Shakespeares and Sapphos out there, at their computer terminals.

Robin: It seems that the Web is an ideal place for romantic love to reappear because on it people are able to present themselves through projections, of a cybernetic sort. You don't really see the person you are communicating with, in any of their physical manifestations—scratching themselves, sneezing, or dropping cigarette ashes on the floor. The amazing thing, though, is that we are able to intuit the presence of the other person.

Stephen: Yes, that's the holographic illusion, that from the words on the computer screen, you can reconstruct the semblance of a live person.

Robin: This brings to mind the world of Lady Murasaki, in medieval Japan, where courtly love was practiced through literature, through poetry.[12] The courtly scene involved extreme formality; yet through word and poetic image, all kinds of subtle nuances could be made. Highly educated women courtesans, the *geishas*, were very adept at this kind of language, and the more refined men, like troubadours in the West, responded in the same way. It is also like the world of the Greek courtesans, who were extremely verbal, literate women exempt from the ordinary lives of Greek women; the courtesans kept salons for the philosophers and poets.

     Also, in all of the above instances, the use of fanciful, semiconcealing masks was a part of certain highly formal yet permissive occasions. These are aspects shared with the Internet: Like a courtly *masque*, its interactions take place within a virtual theater existing only inside its own explicitly defined *temenos* or container, in which participants' everyday appearances are *concealed*, and the medium of exchange is *words*. This is a particularly seductive environment for a woman, because her body is not in the picture; and she may be fearful that it is merely her body that is an object. On the Web, she is invisible, and so this is all mind play. It gives her an entry into a world where she can interact with men in a way that hasn't often been allowed to women. And there's a possibility that this soul magic may be released through poetic language.

Stephen: Yes, I think of *The Pillow-book* of Sei Shonagon: within the magic circle of the courtly love affair, one can intuit the entire edifice of Japanese culture.[13] The love story becomes a kind of magic nexus around which the world moves—the still point—and so the love story reveals the texture of the world. It reveals what the men do, reveals what the women do, reveals the interactions between them, reveals the affiliations and the powers that work in the lives of the couple: for example, economics or feudal codes, involving protocols of behavior, involving the sense of honor, involving the delicate textures of a culture, whether it be of medieval Japan or the (roughly contemporary) world of the so-called courts of love in southern France of Marie de France and Eleanor of Aquitaine.

Robin: Language is its own special magic: the magic of breath, of inspiration and expiration, of silence and vibration. It existed for thousands of years before we ever tried to snare its power in the spirit-trap of a visual symbol-system—rune, pictogram, alphabet. The spoken word is powered by the Holy Spirit, so it is properly the medium of spirit communication: Hence, communication between souls, between anima and animus. The anima is a muse: she loves poetry and inspirited language. The animus is a wordmaster (Jung says an animus-man must be a "master of fine words"), a magician of the element of air, spinning forth marvels from his magic wand, like Prospero. Even as the eyes are the scouts of the soul, so do the soul's messengers ride forth on steeds of speech. Animus and anima communicate through spirited language.

Stephen: I like that, the soul riding on the words, the words are like the spirited horses of the Internet, carrying the soul to its destination. The Net, something that some people think is primarily for commercial or informational purposes, is being used to carry soul messages. I also like what you said about animus and anima; most people experience these little people only through projection, the flickering soul-ghosts that land on and enchant the world, including of course, other people. But in the Internet line of romance, people get to experience being the inspiratrix, and then alternately, the poet. The disembodied condition gives you practice in being a ghost.

Robin: Perhaps that is one reason we are so fascinated by the bright, misty images of the courtly feys, the *sidhe*, the *peris*, the elves of light: they call to our own inner "flickering soul-ghosts." We not only long for them because they are rare, strange and other, but because they are akin to our own phantom-selves within.

Stephen: As I think of it now, I am amazed by the depth of Credo Mutwa's premonition. This Internet love is a much bigger thing than pornography and on-line dating services, those crass exploitations of the beautiful thing that happens naturally and spontaneously between people. The original intent of the Net was that it was for people and by people.[14] Perhaps the true Internet love affairs, which we'll probably hear much more about in the next century, are the redemption of the sleazy and the tawdry elements that inevitably arise. Why shouldn't angels be born on the Internet?

I think what happened with both couples we discussed here was that they were monogamous. And so being, they started to have "soul children"—I think of William and Catherine Blake's "children with bright fiery wings."

Robin: Yes, wings! Perhaps it is through language—the power of the word—that angels find their wings: think of the actinic blue realm of the element of cyber-essence, all a-shimmer and a-blur with transparent spirit wings—fierce, complex cherubim; whirling, multiwinged ophanim; seraphim, the inmost inhabitants of the empyrean, ablaze with love: Indra's net of gems spread out across the mind's sky.

Stephen: Wow! But I think angels have wings mainly for the purposes of flight. Minds, imaginations, take wings and fly. I think that's why people who meet on the Internet, and "fly together," can trust each other, in some peculiar way; it is as if, as Jeremy said, "We were the words chosen and the words combined, and how they were chosen and combined." Thus also the idea of the hawk, the "harrier." Soul flight together. People need to meet each other in a nexus where they are free to dress and undress psychospiritually, imaginatively.

Robin: There are many situations in ordinary life where only the men are talking or only the women, or the women are over here talking together and the men over there talking together. These kinds of dialogues between men and women that we have been looking at are wonderful; for better or for worse, the Internet has offered men and women a substantial forum for dialogue.

Youth: Sarah and Jonathan

(Sarah and Jonathan—she is in her twenties, he in his thirties—were to be married in one month, when this interview took place. As we are talking, first Sarah and then Jonathan are pointing out to us and explaining the symbols and phrases each has included in a symbolic drawing or diagram they have created of what they see as most important in life and how each thinks about relationship. Their drawings are reproduced in the appendix, pages 342 and 343.)

Stephen: You already know we're writing a book on partnership as a spiritual practice; we're particularly interested in the idea of soul mates and whether that idea has played a role in your partnership and in getting to this point. We're fascinated by some of the tools you have developed to aid the process of partnering, among them these drawings.

Sarah: To me it's very important to be connected to the spirit or to the universe, that which is unconditional, that which is ultimately sacred, that which offers spontaneous grace to flow into your life, the ultimate source of love and the transcendent sense of spirit. You need to open to and bring that into your heart or your soul.

This (*pointing to a form providing a base for the drawing*) grounds me; this is sort of the Earth Mom's hips. My spirituality includes transcendence, immanence, and omnipresence. The earth to me represents that which is sacred is omnipresent. Since beauty may be witnessed at any moment in nature, you need to stay grounded and open to omnipresent beauty. Immanence is a spark from the transcendent flame that dwells within each of us—the divinity within, the unconditional piece of our souls. By opening from that centered place to the transcendent (*pointing to an image of a flame*), your center burns like a fire—then you can say "Yes!" to light, "Yes!" to passion, to your dreams, to your heart's longing, those things you ache for. I guess that's the preamble to starting a relationship for me; then it will naturally have a spiritual dimension.

Robin: I like that; that sounds like the kind of spirituality that doesn't alienate relationship, but rather encourages or paves the way for it.

Sarah: My definition of spirituality includes how much *love* can you possibly hold in each cell of your body at any one time. Often times I think of myself as a "grace catcher." Grace is like the rain, falling on everyone; but unless you have a proper vessel to catch it, it will slide off. So part of my soul I try to keep open, like a vessel, to catch the grace from the transcendent.

Stephen: What a wonderful way to think of it, "transparent to the transcendent."[15] What you said about grace was very interesting; and I think it may be a major part of the equation: if people entering into partnership can achieve that transparency, the Divine will support the relationship.

Sarah (*again pointing to elements in her drawing*): Yes, and it's a pulsing, moving vibration that allows you to radiate out to your family and your community: joy, creativity, adventure. You take risks, experience failure, fear, and sorrow, happiness and pain; but you can move through those. Ultimately, you want to radiate awareness, beauty, happiness, freedom, passion, openness, trustworthiness, connectedness, and consciousness.

If you meet someone for the first time, they typically want to know where you live, what religion you are, with whom you studied, which degrees you have, how much money you make, what's your occupation, how old you are . . . To me, those are such superficial ingredients. What I am most interested in is what you say "yes" to and what "no" to. What are your passions, what are your dreams, what do you pursue, and are you even open to questions of this kind?

Sometimes you might be a very small flame, and if that's so, you might need to rejuvenate your energy. But other times, if your heart really opens up, you can find your source and radiate out beautiful qualities of bliss, compassion, and awareness. In my relationship with Jonathan, I spend a lot of time doing soul work, trying to be a grace catcher if you will, but also remaining grounded. When I do that, I am able to be more healthy in relationships, not just with Jonathan but with my family and my community and in my work, because I have more energy and more love that I can extend out.

Photo: Maureen DeFries

Sarah and Jonathan at their wedding.

Robin (*pointing to the flames which appear in both their drawings*): You both have this little bit of fire there: it could pull you together, or it could push you apart. Wasn't there an exercise that you did, fairly early on, to help you understand the dynamic dimensions of your relationship?

Sarah: We were having trouble communicating one evening about whether we had a healthy or unhealthy relationship, and we got stuck in this cognitive, verbal dialogue. So I said, "Why don't we just stop talking!" and got out this big set of Crayola crayons. I said, "Why don't we just draw our relationship?" So, we sat, side by side, both drawing. After about an hour and a half, we each went over our drawing with the other person—and we found out so much about how our models of reality, of relationship, were different, in ways that were hard to qualify verbally.

Robin: So these drawings were the result of that exercise.

Stephen: How did it turn out for you, Jonathan?

Jonathan: Well, first of all, the journey was an interesting one for me. I feel challenged by Sarah's vision of real passion that requires spirituality and community in addition to success. I started to really look at her perspective; and then she was doing the same, trying to understand my perspective. Undoubtedly, you will come to a point where you either do or don't accept the other's point of view. First you have to understand it, then accept it for what it is, and then learn how to mold it into the life where the two of you overlap.

Sarah: I think it was more difficult for me to accept our differences on the verbal level, but to see his picture and have him explain it to me it was—well, I was just amazed by it. I was so thrilled to have this insight into what he was about. And to tell the truth, it defused the disagreement; it put out that fire a little bit, and instead of arguing, we were thoughtfully engaged.

Stephen: Maybe it was the left hemisphere that was stuck, and the right had the answer. That is to say, the ego often defines itself by words, while the soul by images. I would recommend the exercise you did to every young couple approaching a binding covenant. If it's soul partnership you're interested in, you have to evoke the soul—rather both souls—and see how they relate on this level.

Jonathan: On my diagram, I have here what I call, "an enlightenment path." I'm very interested in the velocity and the flow of aliveness along this path. Each way has its own truth: You can go up, to the sides of, or past the peaks. But the main thing is heading in a clear direction of soul work with the other: (*Jonathan is pointing out elements in his drawing*) you go from dreams, to passion and joy, to riches and charity; and the farther you travel from the heart of the core, that's really taking more risk; and the closer you stay, there is more safety here.

Sarah: Jonathan thinks that life and relationships require a lot of risk-taking; if you're trying too hard to be safe, you run out of energy and sag.

Jonathan: If you stagnate, you are surely going toward failure. Along with the safety, you can end up in self-pity and depression, finally in despair. However, if you keep your energy and take risks, even if you fail, all is not lost (*Jonathan points out further movements through his symbols*)—if, through the tempering of pride and going into sorrow, we find humility and eventually nobility and depth. There is also a kind of psychological valve here; and I think communication is key; communication, recognition of beauty and openness, is what makes this valve wide. The velocity, that is, the speed of the communication of the mutual disclosure between the two people, is very important.

It's a constant flow: The velocity has to do with how open the valve is. That would be my ultimate goal, to always have the solid core, to be passing through these encounters at the speed of light, and always be arriving with understanding. You could go down the same path that leads to self-pity, depression and despair, but if you're going in with awareness and communication, there's the possibility of enlightenment.

Robin: I think I get it: in your diagram, maybe there are more dimensions, implied rather than shown, like the consciousness and communication that can open up the ordinary ups and downs of a relationship to something like spiritual awakening.

Jonathan: I think Sarah and I have two symmetrical views of the same terrain. I'm not sure whether it's a male–female difference, but it's certainly one that we have come to recognize between us. I think Sarah, by preparing herself for happiness, is able to reach fulfillment; and for me, by reaching fulfillment, I'm able to find happiness. It could turn into a semantic problem, because, if one is perceived as looking only for success or attaining wealth, that seems simplistic and two-dimensional. For me, those kind of successes enable me to reach for charity and fulfillment through them. I can't put happiness in front of that sequence in my map. Doing the diagram allowed us to see our situation in greater depth and dimensionality. We're looking for essentially the same things, but mapped out differently on the journey.

Robin: The differences might seem extremely important at the time; but, if you are aware of the other stages of the journey and the later destinations on the map, your different paths seem much more compatible. Didn't you also do journal writing?

Jonathan: I tend to be very semantically precise. I have an easier time reaching an understanding through analysis and semantics; often Sarah has an easier time through intuition, even something tactile. So, when we've done these exercises, they help us to bridge communication gaps and to achieve clarity. We started keeping a book of these exercises.

Sarah: The first time that I said, "I love you," he wanted to define what I meant by love. He needs a definition for everything, which is why we have to keep the book so we have definitions of all these times.

Jonathan: It's very easy to misunderstand things: one person might come at it with one disposition, hence definition, and the other another one. So the more clarity, the more help you can have in bridging that gap. We asked the same question: "When we met, how were you attracted to me or how did you grow to love me—in what order: mind, body, soul, heart, or spirit?" We each did it separately, on a piece of paper, and ranked in what order we fell in love with the other person, along each of those criteria.

   Before looking at it, I also asked, and wrote down, "Sarah, what order do you think that I fell in love with you?" And likewise I wrote down what I thought most attracted her to me. Of course, you find that what you think it was about your-self that was attracted to the other person is different in the order in which they were attracted to you and vice versa.

Sarah: Then we went a step farther, and said, "Show me with a kiss how you love me."

Jonathan: Yes, we then brought it to the present, and said, "Okay, right now, at this moment, in what order do you love me?"

Sarah: Because how you initially fall in love with someone obviously changes and evolves; so we took it to the present. When in the present, you can say, "I see you, and you are beautiful."

Jonathan: The present was one of the most important things in Sarah's definition of love, which was naturally very important to me. For me—and some of this I do believe is male–female stuff and probably some is my personal stuff—when I hear, "I love you," I hear, "I promise you." When Sarah says it, though, she's speaking very much at this very moment.

   She was saying one thing, and I was hearing another, which is why it is harder for me to always say, "I love you." Also it's not something I heard from my parents, growing up (although I think they loved each other). But for me saying, "I love you" would be more of a statement of "I promise."

Sarah: So I had to change mediums. I said, "Show me how you love me in these different categories of body, heart, and soul. Show me, please, with a kiss, how you love each of these parts of me."

I think this is really important to our relationship: constantly changing mediums. We need to keep the dialogue open at all costs; but I get very bored with verbal dialogue, and sometimes it gets stuck. It was a fascinating experiment. How do you show Jonathan that you love his body, through a painting? That you love his mind, through a sculpture? It's a very powerful way of communicating.

Jonathan: As long as we could use these things to clarify what was going on—our intentions, our feelings—in the here and now, I'm all for it. It's how we keep that valve between us open and keep stagnation from setting in.

Stephen: Thank you so much; this has been wonderful. The principle that I most love is this idea of the openness of the "valve" between you, the keeping transparent to Grace, and the willingness to look at each other from different perspectives, through the different media.

Maturity: Deborah and Carl

(Carl and Deborah, both in their late forties, were married, by Stephen and Robin as couple, just about a year ago. Carl and Deborah had each had several long-term previous relationships, but they never felt "right" until this one, so there was some way they knew they were already soul mates. They were so certain of this that they wanted to be married by a couple [us], and we had a wonderful collaborative experience helping design and enact the ceremony.)

Stephen: We were thinking about the ceremony that we participated in together a year ago, and how it's been going, since then.

Robin: We were discussing, earlier, our own marriage in our mid-twenties and our dawning recognition that we had done an act of high magic without exactly being prepared for it. We had some inkling perhaps; but you have done all that exploration, and then as mature people, having lived together for two years, came into this union very consciously and created a magical vessel for your marriage.

Carl: Deb and I have had virtually no overt conflicts since we got together, and so I guess we must be on a long honeymoon. There have been uncertainties and issues to resolve, but fighting per se hasn't been a part of our relationship. We tried early on to create safe structures for communication that would ease conflict or the possibility of conflict. We lived together for two years before we decided to get married.

Stephen: Do you recommend that for others?

Carl: I don't know how else you could start to be together and find out if you were in it for the long haul.

Deborah: One of the useful structures that Carl is talking about is based on the vows that you helped us shape. Since we were married a year ago, we have renewed the vows each month. We've revised and talked about them.

Carl: We don't always do it on the first of the month; occasionally, it has been as late as the 17th. It's been very useful; and, as we've done it more and more, we've found that some of the vows don't really mean much to us. But others really come into focus, so we have a spectrum of them to use. And I think they could come in and out of usefulness as we live our lives. We have found things to add, and to cut.

Deborah: Last weekend we were in Florida, and we decided that one of the things we will do on an annual basis is to update them, see what we might want to add and so forth.

Stephen: What would you say to couples or would-be couples who in midlife choose to be together? Would you suggest anything for them or ask anything of them?

Carl: These are good and difficult questions. I feel personally blessed that it's so easy for us to get along with each other. There is none of those little burrs that stick under your saddle—we sort of made sure of that. We really are very close and very respectful of each other.

Robin: In other words, for you it's important that your lover be your friend.

Carl: Not just that. Sometimes there's a natural communion or understanding so that you don't have to go through some sort of formal ritual to make yourself understood. You don't need self-conscious, empathetic listening, and so on. Ideally, communicating effectively is easy; it comes naturally. I am constitutionally a bit of a skeptic about the institution of marriage, so I'm feeling especially blessed by this one, because I think it is really quite rare to be able to communicate as easily as this. People are very different and often going in very different directions, especially in current life, so it's very common to have large zones where communication is not there.

Stephen: Wouldn't you say "permanent human values" (a favorite phrase of Joseph Campbell's) are present here? I mean, you have to have something substantial that you share between you and probably something spiritual as well.

Carl: As you know, I write a lot about sustainability, in regard to the environment, economics, and social justice. The more I've thought about it, the more I realize two things are implicated in sustainability: security and quality. What makes us insecure in our lives and how can we become more secure? And how's the Quality with a capital "Q?" If you think of the Maslovian hierarchy of needs, security is at the bottom, and the transcendent—Quality—is at the top. This model can be applied anywhere to any ecology, including that of the human relationship.

So the really critical questions to me are: to what extent are your security needs being met, and to what extent are your Quality needs being met in the relationship? To what extent do you feel safe and to what extent does the magic of the sacred blossom inside the relationship? If either is lacking, you're probably in some sort of trouble. But where you enjoy a high level of success in both dimensions, you'll find at an emotional level that this is a person that you can open to and be with and really have confidence in. If I thought that Deb made me feel safe but did not have the capacity to reach these magical heights that happen in our communion—bliss, love, ecstasy, sharing, creativity—then I would feel unfulfilled in some way in this relationship. On the other hand, if she were a woman I had these magical encounters with, but I thought might be lying to or betraying me in some way, then that would mean that my security needs were not being met. I feel blessed at both levels, and I think you need that for a truly happy marriage.

Stephen: I think that latter instance, the Dionysian wild intoxication without the security, fuels or drives three-quarters of the world's tragic love fiction.

Deborah: I had decided when I was about thirty years old that I wouldn't get married. I felt it would conflict with the freedom and flexibility I desired for my life. Carl thought that it might enhance our relationship and make it richer. But I thought of all the reasons I'd felt uncomfortable about marriage before.

Stephen: So you had made a resolution earlier, but without all the information you have now, and that resolution might well have kept you from the new opportunity you didn't know about when you made it.

Deborah: Yes, and the reason I was able to call my resolution into question was because of the transcendent quality—because it felt so magical for me. I think of this relationship as "a gift from God," because it covers everything I could possibly want, including the freedom and flexibility. I feel that our lives' purposes are truly aligned and that Carl is willing to support me totally in the things that feel meaningful to me. He is so open, generous, and encouraging about anything I want to do—much more generous to me then I am to myself in many ways. For all these reasons, it just seemed as if I were meant to reconsider my decision. And it has been magical; it feels so right on an intuitive level, on all levels.

Robin: I am really fascinated with that, because I had decided when I was a teenager that I couldn't be a woman and an artist, and also marry. I was convinced about this until I met Stephen, and the thing that drew me in was this sudden return of true magic, deep magic, in my world. That was something that I had thought I had to give up and felt wasn't going to be there. But along with Stephen came this totally unexpected, inner transformative energy.

Stephen: I think this is where, as John Lennon said, "Life is something that happens to you while you're making other plans." But also, it's where we sort of get to make up our own story as we go along, but not really. . . . Because there is this world, and there are these ancestors looking for fulfillment and these souls, as in the Tibetan Book of the Dead, crowding around the lovers, waiting to be born. Further, there's a shortage of angels in the lower heaven, the one Swedenborg calls "the natural heaven." Robin and I both want to go there because we think that's where all the animals will be.

Deborah: The term *angelodaemonic*—is that relevant here?

Stephen: Angelodaemonic means to me that a couple of persons have opened, by their relationship—physical, social, and spiritual—a kind of portal of access, something deep and primordial, and out come rushing demons and angels. You must understand and master the demons, and be open to and empower the angels. I believe that these are present in any relationship. When a couple becomes sexual, for example, they start releasing these creatures. And whether they know it or not, they are creating these creatures of psychological and spiritual potential—that's why they feel so connected to each other—as well as the mingling of biological juices and ecologies (as above so below); and now they have to cope with what they've opened up. If they are unprepared to do that, then those psychospiritual "creatures" can thrust them out of balance or push them over certain thresholds where they're not prepared to go. The relationship grows volatile, obsessive, distorted.

The nature of the angelodaemonic is that male–female relationships provoke the depths as well as the heights. It offers to open the deepest and darkest secrets in our lives, and it can, as romantic literature attests, provoke the greatest and highest possibilities available to us. So, in our lives, it really is an act of magic. You draw a mandalic enclosure around the space, and you get this joining together on all these different levels. It's a very powerful thing to do.

Carl: So far for us, I'm not aware of a lot of devils or negative power. I am aware of a lot of creative power. I'm really aware that somehow there's some transformative process happening; but its true that there do seem to be other spirits emerging.

Robin: William Blake reveres everything. For him the daemonic contains the creative, just because it is chaotic, disrespectful, and energetic. He sees the angelic as harmonious and peaceful. But if you're too peaceful and harmonious, nothing can happen. You get this dynamism inflected in the Hindu Tantric image, where the goddess Shakti is active and Shiva is passive. Shiva sits in yogic bliss, and he's completely harmonious and quietly himself until Shakti dances. The Hindu language is like the Hebrew language, in that the inflection is the energy. So "Shava" [pronounced Sh'-Va] the corpse, becomes Shiva, the dancing god, and suddenly there's energy and he's alive, passionate; he's fire and he's energy joining with her energy. And the universe comes into being. This is in Blake's terminology "daemonic." It's not that sultry, negative inertia that we think of in relationship with the "demonic," plain and simple.

Stephen: Let me add to that. In traditional cultures' mythologies, if the female becomes too active, she is depicted as *demonic*, but really she is *daemonic*. The witch trials were about women who were too smart, too knowledgeable, too energetic, too forward-thinking, too creative-thinking, too sexual. Thus, they were depicted as "an enemy of the state" of existing knowledge and the status quo, which is sleeping. Therefore, they miss the positive inflection of Shakti dancing upon Shiva. Allowing the feminine to awaken the masculine principle becomes a pivotal issue.

Carl: There is something that I have been working on and that came into me in a moment of insight. It is a tripartite model; it proposes that there are three domains of activity where people put their energy: The first is mentation or analysis; the second is society, where there are rules of social interaction and the domain of culture; then there is the third part I call the depth dimension. This one is free of and beyond all mentation and all social rules.

Robin: Blake creates his own personal world in which there is "Urizen," "your reason," who is the god of the Old Testament and the god who measures out the universe, who says, "This is the way it's all laid out." But he gets cold and frigid and stuffy, if he's got the whole thing to worry about. And then there is "Los," this Blakeian "blakesmith"—a daemonic figure who is the poet and the artist; Los is passionate, and he breaks all the bounds. Los arises out of the depths of hell, which is the only term Blake's world had for the underworld and the unconscious. But it is also a smithy, where, in the hellfires, art and passion are forged. Ultimately, Los and Urizen come together, and there is a new birth out of them: a beautiful shining child born out of their interaction. This is the *hieros gamos* for Blake, the marriage of heaven and hell.

Carl: Urizen sounds like "mentation," Los like the "depth dimension.

Stephen: Very much so! Actually, the original theme that Deborah brought up is that, in the connectedness between my lover and me, the angelodaemonic includes the dark and light combinations of cultures, genealogies, maybe family dynasties, imaginal and mythic; and when this is coming together, it raises the deeps, and potentially brings up everything. Blake asks, "What is the price of wisdom, shall it be bought for a dance, or a song in the street? Nay," the poet answers, "it requires all that a man (and a woman) hath." Thus, everything that you have pours into the cauldron of your togetherness. It's an act of high magic, which is why it's often depicted that way in the alchemical images. I suppose this is the reason a lot of magic involves sex, and sex should be nothing less than magical, that "Quality" in your system.

       There's an immense amount of power that's gathered, and the daemonic is the primordial, unevolved part of that energy spectrum. But it's still included; it takes everything. A woman thinks she is happily married, but finds that she can't respond to her husband because she was abused by her grandfather when she was a little child. That skeleton now has to come out of the family closet, because the current relationship is afflicted or wounded by it.

Robin: The issues of respect come up constantly in relationships, respect for the other, a very poignant and dangerous issue in many relationships.

Carl: Our historical patterning plays a big role here.

Deborah: The challenge is to be self-aware, to articulate when issues are there and bring them to the surface.

Stephen: You put them on the table, raise them to consciousness, and look at them. That is crucially important. It's like interrogating the little demons instead of simply being plagued by them, by pretending they're invisible.

Deborah: One of the things in our vows that has been especially relevant is the commitment to talk about difficult things. I think this is the real reason we haven't had any major conflicts; any potential tension is dissipated way before it grows into anything noticeable.

Stephen: This is exactly it: little brushfires are better than the big ones that are ignited accidentally when everything is tinder dry. When I work with couples in marital counseling, one of my most frequently given pieces of advice is to take time to talk the difficult stuff over. You have to do this even if you have busy lives. And try to do it when feelings are not aroused. Any topic that usually is accompanied by an emotional storm has to be brought up at calmer times and worked through, possibly in symbolic form, like Sarah and Jonathan's exercises.

Robin: It's important when you are talking about difficult issues to remember the emotionally loaded gender differences in the way men and women are taught to communicate. It is as if we were raised in different cultures. Women's communication tends to seek a place of connection. Men's is task-oriented or problem-solving, and may be highly sensitized to dominance issues. Individual differences add to this mix, so all too often, when a woman is thinking she makes a connection, a man may resent it as a violation of his status or his personal space. When a man thinks that he's making a peace offering to a woman in a touchy situation, she may experience it as his thinking of her as something he can "buy."

Stephen: When we were little children we used to want to have ducks and battleships and other kinds of things in the tub with us, but now we have a real life partner, a playmate. And that is the right kind of thing for an adult to have in the tub, in the vessel of the marriage, because when that happens you are in the alchemical process—you're assimilating two points of view.

Robin: It seems as if we are standing at the portal of a magical country that we can only enter together.

Deliver Us from Evil
by John Flaxman

Chapter Six

THE DAEMON LOVER

She had not sailed a league, a league,
    A league but barely three,
When dismal grew his countenance,
    And drumlie grew his ee.

They had not sailed a league, a league,
    A league but barely three,
Until she espied his cloven foot,
    And she wept right bitterlie.

"O hold your tongue of your weeping," says he,
    "Of your weeping now let me be;
I will shew you how the lilies grow
    On the banks of italy."

"O what hills are yon, yon pleasant hills,
    That the sun shines so sweetly on?"
"O yon are the hills of heaven," he said,
    "Where you will never win."

"O whaten a mountain is yon," she said,
    All so dreary wi frost and snow?"
"O yon is the mountain of hell," he cried,
    "Where you and I will go."

"The Daemon Lover"[1]

—— THE DAEMONGELIC ROOT OF THE SOUL MATE ——

As WITH ANY ARCHETYPAL IMAGE OR MYTHOGEM, the soul-mate idea is a two-edged sword that can be turned this way and that. It can be used in wounding and slaying, perhaps more easily than in visioning and relating; it is as terrible as it can be wonderful. This is the daemongelic turn, when passion breaks covenants, families, lifestyles, even the Zeitgeist of an era. The same intensity of soul can become the mad obsession of Lancelot and Guinevere, of Tristan and Isolt, or of Paolo and Francesca—whirling in a solipsistic orbit, inaccessible to the outside world, bliss and torment wedded together with the couple's passionate soul-bodies.

Imagine, now, a continuum from devilish to angelic, beginning with the downside, exploring the theme through mythology. It is a knowledge of the psychospiritual terrain we seek, shadowed valleys as well as lofty mountains, beginning in the darkness and spiraling slowly toward the light.

The myth is like a universal traveler, like old Odin in his cloak and slouch hat, a god in disguise, walking the world. He comes to mansions and to hovels, to the dens of thieves and murderers as well as to the hearths of hospitable folk. The myth visits Son of Sam, so that his fascination with young women leads to repeated, compulsive violence directed toward them. John Hinkley shoots President Reagan to get the attention of a film star he has never even met. The serial killer keeps his beloved, whom he never really knew, except at a distance, in a trunk as she slowly putrefies, because that way, at least, "no one else can have her." In this model, the pure and simple *image* of the beloved overshadows the actual person's own wishes or anything he or she may do or say. The stalker laughs when his ex-wife asks him not to show up unexpectedly and terrify her any more. Life and common sense drown in myth.

The same pattern shows up in stories such as Thomas Mann's *Death in Venice*, where the inappropriate, mythic object of the obsession is the beautiful young boy Tadzio or in Vladimir Nabokov's *Lolita*, where the beloved object is a young girl (and step-daughter) and the lover a mature, intellectually sophisticated man. For the obsessed, the mythic image of the soul mate invests the object with numinous fascination and sometimes excites a literal wish to act out the pedophilia, rather than understand it psychologically as a need to find one's "inner child."

Whether the image is projected on child or adult, Depth Psychology has spelled out the dangers of such projections of the anima or animus and of obsessive fantasies about an impossible ideal. Sometimes the very phrase used becomes "demon lover," the daemongelic movement.

A man with a successful family business, a seemingly happy marriage, and young children, came to Stephen for counseling. Awkwardly, he asked if Stephen "believed in soul mates?" (a question that Stephen dodged artfully.) Then he told his story, as recounted in Stephen's notes:

> In the course of work the client had encountered an attractive young woman. They would seem to run into each other by accident, as he went around to different locations for his job. They would talk, and she seemed able to talk with him about anything. She seemed to share all his passions—animals, hunting, car-racing. When he was burning with the

obsession, he came for therapy on an emergency basis. Should he make love to this alluring creature, and thus be unfaithful to his wife and jeopardize his family?

We tried to work with the anima concept, and he was able to grasp it intellectually. Nonetheless, the glamour was already on him, and I could tell from the glazed condition of his eyes as he half-listened that he was already ensorcelled. In parting, I cautioned him with pedestrian ideas about "getting references"—look into the character of his beloved as seen in others' eyes—and to be careful in all departments. (Naturally, I wanted to help him save his marriage and the family business, in which his wife was his partner.) Unsurprisingly, he did not return for two months.

When he returned for therapy, his energy was vastly different—but there was a new glaze and a new predicament. He had been unable to hold himself back from the exquisitely proffered lovemaking. When it began to happen it seemed almost beyond his wildest dreams, sheer ecstasy compared to the "more ordinary" version he had with his wife. It went on for hours. His nixie seemed to anticipate his every need and to know what he was going to say before he said it; he was deliriously happy, and at the same time troubled by misgivings.

As the situation unfolded his "soul mate" began to seem fey and insatiable; she wanted more of him, more time. She began to say derogatory things about his wife and show a fascination about the children—she had none of her own. The *enantiodromia*—the "dance in the opposite direction"—came when my client began to realize that his nixie was also stalking him: she seemed to know where he was all the time. She became jealous of his family life and wanted him to leave right away rather than later, as they had planned. Now he was "in the soup." But his passion was becoming mingled with something like terror.

Then began midnight phone calls to his home and love notes. They were turning daemongelic, from romantic paeans of passion, through fantasies of what their life could be together—ignoring his highly "attached" relations—through secret innuendos (she would adopt his children), finally to overt threats: "If you don't do as I wish, I'll destroy your life!" The daemongelic movement had become complete: his life, like that of the husband in the movie *Fatal Attraction*, had become a living hell.

I encouraged him to go back and do something that he wouldn't do in the beginning—check her "references." When he did so, now in depth, he found that this woman had enacted the same pattern many times before—like the ghosts or demons in Japanese supernatural stories who repeat the same adventure again and again with hapless passersby. (A trap of enticement there in that sand dune, that ancient temple.)

Now the irresistible allure sparkling in the eyes of "soul mate" seemed metamorphosed to an obsessive, daemonic glare. Able to bewitch, this woman was also herself bewitched. Her obsessive acts seemed "out of control," my client said, and so they were! Standing behind this woman was the negative inflection of the archetype of the witch, with its baleful glamour.

As the extent of my client's "bewitchment" became evident to him, he became a far more conscious, somewhat chastened, but wiser man than he had ever been before. He returned to his wife and family with new vigor and a humbler attitude. His wife forgave him for his "madness" as it now seemed, and his life went on. Now some ten years later, he continues to do well personally and professionally. The soul-mate adventure had been an initiation that shook him to his roots, but grew him up in remarkable ways.

In its negative inflection, the idealized and projected mythogem of the soul mate can blind us to the (seemingly flawed) beauties of the actual and put our energies at the service of a kind of "pipe dream" that now pulls energy totally away from the real. It is so easy to prefer the impossible to the actual, especially when it sparkles with our own projected energy.

There is also a deceit offered; and our possibilities for love, spiritual in origin though they be, are stunted and bent to the service of a dark purpose: since the *summum bonum* is projected into a fantasy image, one's actual partner, a biological human being, receives a compensating "shadow." He or she can't do anything right; his or her lamentable actuality, including physical attributes, human limitations, and habits seem to embody everything unacceptable, even horrible. Small flaws, in this catastrophic psychological process, emerge as crippling monstrosities, humps, and blemishes as bad as the worst of the partner's own self-projections seen in the mirror on a bad day. This is the entanglement of the shadow, which Jung explored so extensively, with the anima/animus; it is a dark and troubling incest among the "little people."

Still worse, as in the principle of mythic identity, discussed in the previous chapter, if one believes the other is truly "the other half of oneself," one may treat the other half exactly as one treats oneself (which may be none too good, as John Welwood has pointed out).[2] Our own self-destructive or self-punitive urges may now apply by extension to the soul mate or would-be soul mate. We drive the beloved provocatively until we get a rise out of him or her, or inadvertently manipulate, in the same way as we do with our own internal cast of characters. The ensuing dynamics, be they aggressive fight or sullen withdrawal, become the melodrama within the orbit of which this couple now moves. These dramas can be quite destructive and time consuming.

While myths galvanize and move us, giving purposes to larger dimensions of life, they can limit us severely as well; this is the destructive side of mythologizing. Such an elemental mythogem as the soul mate galvanizes other energies and images around it like iron filings to a magnet. One's innate restless creativity may become engaged and projected. One now engages in a Pygmalion-like effort to reconstruct one's actual partner or treats the other as a kind of art work in progress. One becomes involved in the soul mate as an extension of one's own not fully understood creativity.

In general, these attempts at transformation occur at a lower stage of the soul-mate process. The attempt is merely to "deform" the world to our expectation, our bright, mythic image. In essence, the goal is praiseworthy: transformation of the beloved into something ethereal, something better, something spiritualized. But the actuality is painful, because people are not so easy to transform, although they can put on a pretty good act. The depths often remain untouched or even wax resentful.

Although ultimately we do transform each other, it is seldom in the ways we expect or that match the results of the conscious agenda. Generally, the object must always transform more slowly than the subject, and ultimately projections are mostly our own business. Pygmalion, transform thyself.

——— FURSKIN: SURVIVING THE DAEMONGELIC ———

CONCERNING THE ISSUE OF THE BELOVED or soul mate being perceived as the bridegroom: Marion Woodman has done a lot of work on this theme in *Leaving My Father's House* and *The Ravaged Bridegroom*.[3] In the former book, she works with the fairy tale of "Furskin," in which we have first the spurious bridegroom and then later the true bridegroom. It is a story of how healing can come out of a deep depression. The name "Furskin" is a rendering of *Allerleirauh*, the title of the story as found in the Brothers Grimm; it means something made of many kinds of fur—in this case, a cloak.[4] There is also a beautiful and poignant modern retelling of this in a book by Robin McKinley, where Furskin's time in the forest and her entry into the world of animals is described in a very moving way.[5]

Before proceeding further, it is important to remember that as we speak of the daemongelic movement, we do not mean a movement from heaven toward earth; nor does angelodaemonic describe a movement from earth toward heaven. The psychological vector or impetus in the case of the *daemongelic* is from a relatively static (if perhaps fragile) condition toward *disintegration*, dismemberment, disturbing—but potentially fruitful—chaos. The opposite, *angelodaemonic* impetus is out of chaos toward *integration*, Jungian *individuation*, or in Swedenborg's language, toward *regeneration*.[6]

Furskin is the daughter of a king and queen who have a completely self-obsessed, mutually narcissistic marriage. Queen Goldenhair is so extraordinarily beautiful that her royal husband can see nothing but her, and the child is quite neglected. The mother dies young; the kingdom is then without the feminine element, the queen, and slides into this sterile, wasteland place that both Marie-Louise von Franz and Woodman discuss in several contexts.[7] Then, the daughter begins to grow up, and her mother's beauty begins to be apparent in her. The father is being urged, of course, by all his councilors to remarry: the kingdom must have a queen! He decides to marry his daughter, because she is the only person who is enough like her mother to be worthy of him.

The princess is horrified and very frightened because she knows she can't effectively refuse him. She tells her father the king that she will give him her answer when he can get four things for her: a dress that is golden and shining like the sun, a dress that is silvery like the moon, a dress that is like the stars at night, and a garment that is made of one piece of skin from each of the animals in his own kingdom. She's stalling; she doesn't think her father can get these things for her. But he does.

The princess takes the three beautiful dresses and conceals them—like magic—in an "acorn." She puts on the fur-skin cloak, carries the magic dresses hidden away, and runs off into the forest. In the forest, she hides and lives like a wild animal, becoming wilder and wilder.

One day she is captured by huntsmen who serve a young king in a neighboring kingdom. They bring her back to their king's palace, where Furskin lives in a little closet under the stairs and works in the palace kitchen. She has blackened her face with soot, and she keeps herself entirely covered with the cloak of many skins, so everyone thinks she is some kind of wild person or half animal.[8]

The young king is looking for a wife—his kingdom also has need of the feminine element—but he is more conscious of this process than Furskin's father had been. Instead of fixating narcissistically on his own image of what his bride must be (his anima obsession) like the father, this monarch holds a series of balls, an appropriate social context for a well-placed young man to meet actual young women. Various princesses come, and Furskin does a "Cinderella" thing.

On the first night of the ball, she asks for a little time off from the kitchen to watch the ball. Then, she runs down to her closet, wipes the dirt off her face, takes off her fur-skin cloak, and puts on the gown of gold like the sun. (This refers to the golden sun/father aspect.) She goes to the ball and dances with the handsome young king, who becomes completely enamored of her. Of course, she has been allowed only a short time away from her kitchen duties, so she runs away, darts back under the stairway, and hides her dress. She repeats this act at the next two balls, wearing one of the other two dresses.

On the night of the last ball, she puts on the dress like the stars; but she has even less time at this ball than previously because the head cook needs her help in the kitchen. So, this time she dances with the young king, then rushes back to her room to change. But she doesn't have time to take off the dress of stars, so she throws her fur-skin cloak over it, smears her face with soot, and goes back to the kitchen.

There's more to this story. In the kitchen, Furskin has been cooking a special food for the king. She has been dropping little magical things in his soup—in effect, giving him signs that she is there. The young king calls for the cook who has been preparing this very special food. Furskin is brought before him, and the king sees the dress of stars under her dirty cloak. She is revealed. The king marries the mystery lady, who provides such good nourishment but also splendid stolen moments of romance. Of course, they live "happily ever after."

This is a complex story, as Woodman has so beautifully shown. But we are going to look particularly at the "spurious bridegroom," the king who demands that his daughter marry him. This royal family is haunted by a demon-lover. The king is possessed by the ghost of his dead queen, whose incomparable spectral radiance blinds him to his daughter's humanity, and compels him to make her a captive to his obsession. The princess, on the other hand, reacts with appropriate revulsion to his incestuous demands. She recognizes the demonic visage behind the mask of paternal authority, and rejects the spurious bridegroom. She flees into the forest, into the protective isolation of her own inner *nature*.

Woodman makes it clear that the psychological experience depicted in Furskin's story need not necessarily be read as a literal father-incest event—although it could be—it can also describe a relationship of the feminine to a powerful masculine, to an animus, that is overwhelming. In fairytales, as von Franz's work demonstrates, these elements of the psyche are personified; so in Furskin, we find the overwhelming animus personified as the "spurious bridegroom," the predatory, possessive demon-lover. What interests us here is how the princess survives her encounter with the demon-lover.

In the Brothers Grimm, we are not told how long the princess remains in the forest—fairytale time, like time in the psyche, knows its own seasons. But Woodman sees this as a significant period of incubation. In Robin McKinley's telling, Furskin hides out in the forest for a winter. Her depression is a place like the winter; in the winter, seeds are deep in the earth, germinating. Winter is hard but necessary. None of us likes it when "winter" hits us in our psyche—it's a terrible, desperate time. It feels like the end, like death; and this is where some young people do take their own lives.

This kind of suicide of the young, when they are caught in the place of endless winter, is like a failure of the future. They have no hope of a future to sustain them. We—standing outside their world—know that winter will end and the future will come. But they are separated from us by an enchanted glass wall, so they can't really hear our words of hope. They only see our mouths moving, and they are alone. But if someone in this winter place can hold out—perhaps just curl up and hibernate like an animal or become dormant like a tree—the seeds and bulbs will germinate and send up spring growth through the snow, and new life will come.

It is interesting that Furskin's cloak is made of many animals, because we find a notion in some traditional societies of an animal mother or animal master who may appear as a multiple being. Remember our fantastic composite shaman-beasts pictured on the cavern walls of the Paleolithic? This is a figure who has been with us for a very long time. Furskin is like a disempowered echo of that ancient being. By putting on the cloak of the animal master, she invokes his healthy, natural protection against the unnatural assault of the demon-lover.

Animal-like, she doesn't talk properly. So the castle people, the staff and the courtiers, don't think she's human. The young king is looking for a way to bring the feminine into his life in a very honest way and is searching throughout the kingdom for an appropriate wife. While this is going on, Furskin is in disguise, invisible as it were, living in a masculine world where she can't be seen easily.

Furskin, then, is living in a dark closet under the stairs where everybody else goes up and down; the life of the palace goes back and forth above her. She hides in this dark closet and continues the growing within her, stirring soup or porridge or "witch's brew" and sprouting the seeds of her soul: this is the work of depression. When a woman must go down into her darkness, alone and miserable, she needs a friend, spouse, or lover that she can talk to—because talking about it is very important for a woman. John Gray also recognizes that, at such times, the woman isn't looking for solutions; she's looking for a listener.[9] But Furskin has no listener. In the original Grimms' version of the fairytale, she has no listener at all; she is utterly alone under the stairs.

In Robin McKinley's sensitive novel, we have a variation on the folk version: Furskin talks to the king's dogs, and they understand her. This continues the motif of the animal-skin cloak and the season in the forest. The woman has gone down into her wild place, her animal nature, where the natural goodness of the earth and her own instinctual connectedness to life can heal her. This is "theriotherapy," healing through warm, doggy love—damp noses, silky ears, eyes that regard with no blame, no doubt, communicating unqualified acceptance.

We have spoken in earlier chapters about our work with alienated and distressed teenagers, much of which is done with the aid of horses, dogs, cats, grassy fields and forest. Although we cannot always have access to the natural world, yet we carry our own "nature" within us; we are only as alienated as we *think* ourselves.

Finally, the young king recognizes the princess within Furskin by the glimmer of starlight under her animal-skin robe. He sees the *light* in her. He also has begun to suspect that she is the one who has been nourishing him with the simple soup. In his complex life, she has given him something nourishing and hardy, prepared by loving human hands, not by his official cook (this point is made strongly by Woodman). Both of these things reveal her to him: in other words, he is sensitive to the signals, he is being attentive. He then draws her out of herself. Of course, they marry: as Woodman points out, when the depression is gone through, then it is the appropriate time for the true bridegroom to come.

When the work of the depression and the winter of pain has not been fully gone through, it is too early for the bridegroom; and the woman may be vulnerable to the wrong one, or a spurious bridegroom may come. For the princess, the father was a spurious bridegroom. If she had married him, she would have been the queen and lived in his wonderful, wealthy kingdom, but it would have been a wasteland within because it was not the right call, the calling of the soul. In the fairytale, the princess knows that and runs away; but she doesn't know where she's running to. You don't have to know where you're running to at the moment of rejecting the wrong choice; you just have to know that it's wrong. You have to leave, and you have to go *down in*.

This is also Persephone's work, going down in.[10] And there is no coming up until the time is right. The time is not going to be social time or business time or academic time; that can be hard because it cuts across our human commitments. It is not even really human time: it is earth time—winter.

This also introduces the topic of wildness we're interweaving throughout this whole book. Does the young woman become a wild thing because of the incestuous situation—the unhealthy family context? There is no doubt that incest, even the psychological kind, makes a strange kind of haunted animal out of the victim. But the father's problem is an anima image—a two-dimensional glimpse of someone golden and nice but without a personality per se. The old king is hypnotized by an image. If he had seen his wife as an actual woman, he could mourn her as a person and let her go. Then he could go on with his life and allow his daughter hers.

TRISTAN AND ISOLT
AND THE SOUL-MATE THEME

This is bread to all noble hearts.
With this their death lives on.
We read their life, we read their death,
And to us it is sweet as bread . . .
And whoever now desires to be told of their life,
their death, their joy, their sorrow,
let him lend me his heart and ears—
he shall find all that he desires! [11]

THE SON OF RIVALIN AND BLANCHEFLOR, themselves star-struck lovers, as Gott-fried von Strassburg tells the story, was named Tristan ("sorrow") because his father was killed in battle a few days before his birth and his mother died in childbirth, of grief. [12]

Raised by the loyal steward, Rual il Foitenant, with his true identity con-cealed even from himself, Tristan was tutored by a scholar named Curneval, who taught him to read, to speak several languages, and to play the harp and sing. Not less important in this violent time were his growing accomplishments in sword and lance, to which, for all his poetic nature, he had a ready hand.

As a youth, Tristan was kidnapped and taken to sea by merchantmen, when a great storm struck the ship. After eight days, in a Jonah-like sequence, Tris-tan was set ashore near Tintagel Castle in Cornwall. There he so charmed King Mark by his accomplishments that he was almost adopted by the king, whose nephew he actually was.

But there was a blight upon the land of Cornwall. King Gurmun of Ireland had levied upon King Mark a terrible tribute: sixty young men from the court must be sent to Ireland periodically. (Gurmun is the Minos of the epic, says Campbell, also casting Tristan in the role of Theseus, the hero who will slay the minotaur and abduct Princess Ariadne, here represented by Isolt). [13] The Morhault, or Morold the Mighty, sent to exact the tribute, was a ferocious warrior who had defeated the best of King Mark's court. When Tristan learned of his royal host's plight, he vowed to meet Morold in single combat.

Morold first gave Tristan a wound in the thigh, then shouted for Tristan to yield because his sword was poisoned and only his sister Isolt, holding the secret to the cure for the poison, could now save the young warrior from death. Tristan's re-sponse to this peculiar and cowardly declaration was to cleave Morold's skull, leav-ing a piece of his sword in the bone. Morold's body and severed head were returned to Ireland, where the lamentation was great, the most grievously afflicted being Mo-rold's sister Isolt the queen and her daughter, also named Isolt.

Now Tristan, like the wounded Fisher-King of the Parzival story, developed a wound in his thigh that would not heal, but festered and began to stink, so that none could be near him. Finally, Tristan asked to be put in a rudderless boat with his harp. [14] After forty days (and nights) the boat arrived, magically, in Ireland. The people marveled at the sight—and smell—of the wounded young man. He told them his name was Tantris (an anagram of Tristan) and that he had been ship-wrecked while coming from Spain.

The queen, the elder Isolt, bent her considerable healing arts to the young man—still unknown as her enemy, her brother's killer—while her daughter was his constant nurse. Within twenty days, the two Isolts had so healed Tristan that he could be in social company. When it was learned that he had musical skills and was recovered enough to teach them, the younger Isolt was put in his care. He taught her to sing and play so sweetly that, within six months, the fame of her music had spread throughout the land.

Tristan returned to Cornwall, where, in telling the story of his recovery, he praised the beauty of young Isolt so highly that King Mark became interested (see-ing this as a pleasant way to make peace between the two kingdoms) and sent a pro-posal of marriage—to be conveyed, of course, by Tristan.

Arriving back in Ireland, Tristan learned that an evil dragon had beset the land "with harmful harm so harmfully" (as the poet Gottfried puts it) that King Gur-mun the Gay would give his daughter Isolt to any knight who would deliver the land from the monster. Although thousands had already perished, Tristan made his assay. He galloped at the beast's flaming open jaws and drove his lance deep inside. The dragon bit off the entire front part of his mount to the saddle, but then, wounded, headed for its lair. Tristan followed on foot and delivered its death-blow with his sword. Scorched and battered, Tristan then did a curious thing: he cut off the hideous tongue and thrust it into his bosom. Suddenly afflicted by the burning poi-son in the nasty thing, he jumped into a pond to cool, breathing with just his nose and mouth sticking out of the water.

In a strange twist to the story, enter a cowardly steward, who used to follow the heroes out to see how they fared with the dragon—and maybe pick up any armor or sword they left behind. When he saw the slain dragon, he cut off its head and brought it to the court, saying he had slain it and claiming the hand of Princess Isolt.

Queen Isolt, however, suspicious of his story and reluctant to give her daughter to a churl, went with Isolt the younger to the pond, where they found the half-dead Tristan. Once again, they nursed him to health; and when the steward presented his false claim, Tristan produced the tongue, exposing the churl to all.

Not long afterwards, while Tristan was bathing in a tub, the younger Isolt by "chance" withdrew his sword to look at and, again by chance, noticed the miss-ing piece (which had been left in her uncle Morold's head). A terrible suspicion now arising within her, she matched it to the fragment now kept in a reliquary, after having been extracted from her uncle Morold's skull. Suddenly, she also put to-gether the Tantris=Tristan anagram. Filled with wrath, she threatened to slay him right there in the tub. But Tristan's silver tongue now came into play, and she was persuaded to spare him. Two powerful forces were to come into conflict in the young Isolt: a natural affection for the man she had healed (and for her sensitive teacher who had helped her find her own skill) versus honor and the medieval vow of vengeance on behalf of a slain relative. It is a potent, daemongelic brew, a "bitter-sweet" tincture that can stress the soul (as Freud says of ambivalence, love and hate for the same person at the same time). It can drive us mad or cause us to stretch and enlarge within.

But Tristan had his own character flaw. Having fulfilled the dragon quest, he was entitled to ask for Isolt's hand. He did so, but not for himself, foolish man, but rather for King Mark. (He put his trained deference to the king and to social form above his own feelings.) It was a dolorous mistake for Tristan, one that would render him ever more sorrowful as the tragedy unfolds. Tristan, of course, escorted Princess Isolt (and her lady's maid Brangaene, a cousin) back to Tintagel to marry Mark.

Here enters the love potion, cunningly prepared by Isolt's mother, Isolt the Wise, to be given to Mark and Isolt on their wedding night, so that their love would be passionate and irreversible: "A love-drink so subtly devised and prepared, and endowed with such powers, that with whomsoever any man drank it he had to love her above all things, whether he wished it or no, and she love him alone. They would share one death and one life, one sorrow and one joy."[15] This potion, as we shall see, is the subtle fluid, the vital intoxicant in the soul-mate alchemy.

By "chance" (and we may here read *chance* as the Anglo-Saxon *wyrd*, the ambush of a destiny still unknown), Tristan and Isolt drank from the flask containing the potion. Whether this was done consciously or unconsciously varies with the story; but the moment they drank it, they knew they had entered upon an irreversible fate—that they had "drunk their death"—and the *liebestod* as a theme enters Western literature. This is the poignancy of the soul-mate moment, the recognition that their love is so intense, so pure, so otherworldly, that surely it must wreak havoc with the ordinary. There is a further, metaphysical dimension brought forward by Campbell: being Christians, the love potion and its intoxicating delirium, with the breaking of sacred vows, would place them in danger of hellfire and eternal damnation, all too literal for the mind of the time. This takes the lovers' mutual pledge from the realm of a personal to a spiritual covenant, made equal, by their gesture, to the authority of the church. "If I have drunk disgrace, death, I say 'yes' to it, if I have drunk my death, I say 'yes,' and even if hellfire, 'yes'." So pledge the lovers, and thus create, Campbell says, "a new sacrament."

When Brangaene, Ysolt's kinswoman and companion, who had been entrusted with the potion, saw what had happened, she fainted; and now became, perhaps through guilt, complicit in the lovers' strange madness. "May God have pity on it," said Brangaene, "that the Devil has mocked us in this fashion! Now I clearly see that I have no choice but to act to my own sorrow and your shame for your own sakes. . . ."

> From now on do not abstain on my account from what you will not forgo
> for your own good names. But if you can master yourselves and refrain
> from this, refrain! [Then she goes on to say,] dearest mistress, lovely Isolde,
> let me entrust to you now, into your own keeping, your life and your death:
> deal with them as you please. Henceforward have no fear as far as I am
> concerned: do whatever you like![16]

Of course, they did not "refrain." Tristan and Isolt now became lovers on the boat, while Brangaene sighed and "looked the other way."

There was now the problem of Isolt's ruptured virginity. Brangaene, however, still was a virgin. Here she showed her loyalty indeed—substituting for Isolt on the wedding night with King Mark (and Mark did not notice!).[17]

Now began a vexing, peculiar time in which Mark alternately suspected, then dismissed his fears. Tristan and Isolt danced in and out of stolen moments and glances, always eluding the efforts of Mark to catch them, both of whom he dearly loved (like Arthur with Lancelot and Guinevere). Finally, he condemned the lovers both to leave his court.

At this point, Tristan and Isolt began a time of wandering in the forest; altogether, it would last three years.[18] They slept in a mystical love grotto with a crystalline bed, with which, Campbell notes with interest, Gottfried equates the holy altar of the sacrament. One time, hearing Mark's party hunting in the forest, they retired to the grotto and the crystal bed, but slept demurely, with Tristan's sword between them. Mark found them in this condition, believed he had been mistaken all along, and invited them back to court; whereupon the whole debacle started all over again. The game of hide-and-seek was to continue through a series of deceits, near discoveries, and finally to its strange climax in a trial by "ordeal" for Isolt: she would have to submit to a terrifying test of taking hot irons in her hands to prove her honor. Again, through a complex deceit, the lovers were saved. Isolt was not burned by the irons, and God himself seemingly supported the deception—or the mystery of love was supported by the *secret cause*.

But after this extraordinary moment of validation before all eyes, the strain of continued duplicity began to take its toll on Tristan. He remembered the three years in the forest with longing, observed his lady daily with her royal husband, and doubt grew in him. "Almighty God," he cried, "how utterly astray I am because of love!"

> If I direct my thoughts to more than one love I might easily become a carefree Tristan!
>
> I shall now put it to the test. If Fortune is to smile on me, it is time that I began. For the loyal love I have for my lady has no power to help me. I am consuming my life for her and can offer myself no consolation by which to go on living. . . . Ah, sweet mistress, dearest Isolde, . . . things are not as they were when we two endured one good, one ill, one joy, one sorrow together. Alas, it is not so now! Now I am wretched, but you are happy. My thoughts are full of longing for your love, while yours, I imagine, long but little for me. . . . Your master, Mark, and you are at home, you are inseparable companions; but I am abroad and alone.[19]

Self-pity, common sense, and neglected knightly honor were tugging at Tristan, so he went off warring. His travels took him across the channel from Cornwall to Brittany, where he became companion in arms and champion to a young Lord Caerdin, whose lands Tristan saved in combat. Caerdin had a beautiful sister, curiously also named Isolt—"Isolt of the White Hands." In the course of things and through courtly arrangements, a marriage was arranged for Tristan. An unspoken hope was that it might keep him out of King Mark's bed.[20]

Despite the fact that Isolt of the White Hands was a beautiful young woman, Tristan would not consummate the marriage, for his heart pined for his soul mate beyond the sea. His new wife then became disconsolate and sought counsel with her brother. Caerdin was outraged and demanded of Tristan whether they needed to come to combat over this apparent insult.

In a way that speaks of the power and the esteem held by such loves in those times, when Tristan had bared his soul to his wife's brother, Caerdin then agreed to help in the cause. Many adventures now befell these two—Caerdin even helped Tristan carry off a tryst with Isolt the Fair, while his own sister, Isolt of the White Hands, sat at home in despair. To conclude the story, a strange being named "Dwarf Tristan," who had lost his wife through abduction, came to Tristan for help, and Tristan agreed to help get her back. In the process, Dwarf Tristan was slain, Great Tristan was wounded again, in the loins, by a poisoned spear. And, *mirabile dictu*, the only one who could heal him was Isolt the Fair of Ireland, trained in lore by her witch mother.

Tristan made an arrangement with Caerdin: his brother-in-law and companion-in-arms would go to Cornwall, bearing Tristan's ring, there to persuade Queen Isolt to return with him for the sake of Tristan's life (and in secret, once more after so many years had passed, to deceive King Mark). Tristan and Caerdin agreed that, if the returning boat showed a white sail, Tristan would know that Isolt was aboard; if a black sail flew, she was not (shades again of the Theseus story, pertaining to Theseus' return to Athens after the minotaur adventure).

Tristan, lying wounded, asked Isolt of the White Hands, who could see the ship, if the sail be black or white. Aggrieved by the years of her husband's inattention and neglect (according to Thomas of Britain), she said, "Let me tell you, the sail is all black!" although she could clearly see that it was white. Then it was said, Tristan turned to the wall, "Three times did he say, 'dearest Ysolt.' At the fourth he rendered up his spirit."[21]

When Isolt of the White Hands saw the result of her lie, she was stricken and said, "Oh my God, what have I done?" When Isolt the Fair came off the ship and saw what had happened, she rent her clothing and tore her hair. She lay down beside Tristan, "then straining body to body, mouth to mouth," she joined him in the love-death they had pledged on the boat to Cornwall, so long before. Thomas says:

> Tristan died of his longing, Ysolt because she could not come in time. Tristan died for his love; fair Ysolt because of tender pity.[22]

———————— STEPHEN AND ROBIN IN DIALOGUE ————————

Robin: In this chapter, we've examined the soul-mate theme from different perspectives. How do you know your soul mate? What happens when there's a premature fixation on somebody? There's a lot of pain around that kind of experience.

Stephen: When there is a divine seizure—as in the case of the man who was happily married but then what seemed to be his soul mate, his ideal woman, came into his life—that state of enchantment will not hold. Everything seemed perfect for him, but then the situation deteriorated; it was not mutual anymore. He realized to his mounting horror that he was the quarry, the object of a predator. Jung asks the question, "Who is the container, and who is the contained?" Who has the larger agenda, that the other one fits into? An equal relationship seems to happen more rarely because people bring such an asymmetrical concentration of powers to the encounter.

Robin: The notion of the phantasm of the soul mate is often used as a device of the fairy world to entrap a human being. There is a kind of shapeshifting fairy or demonic being who wears a guise, which is drawn out of the desires of the soul of the human prey, so that this magical creature looks into the human and becomes what that human most desires.

Stephen: Where does the anima woman get her divine cocktail of mischievous, alluring, and entrapping qualities? She must be a brilliant intuitive at modeling the male fantasy in this regard. We could even say that the male fantasy is a ghost wandering abroad in the world and can be seized upon by somebody with a magical proclivity. Then the woman is acting not herself but is acting exactly what the energy tells her the man expects and desires. This is where the ensorcellment takes place.

Robin: In the case of an actual woman who enacts this male anima projection, not a creature in a fairytale, she is trapped by this ghost. There are movie stars who have carried this ghost, such as Marilyn Monroe, who fit themselves to the anima projection beautifully. Some of them become possessed and sucked dry of their own spiritual vitality by this projection, while others seem to manage it in more creative ways. It's a troubling aspect.

Stephen: I'm thinking a story I heard of a woman with a serious delusional disorder, who, at one point in her life, prepared herself to meet the mystical bridegroom, who said he was Jehovah. He was going to meet her at a hotel and take her away. She should dress herself as a bride and wait for the divine beloved. She was committed to a residential treatment facility.

In another instance, a woman had fallen in love with her spiritual teacher, a Zen master with whom she had studied. She thought he was going to marry her. Nothing could dissuade her from this belief—including the teacher himself. I've seen other situations involving stalking, where a man is obsessed with a woman who wants to have nothing to do with him, but he insists on following her around and leaving strange messages for her, intervening in the stream of her life, terrifying herself and her family.

Robin: It's not unlike Robert Johnson's and also Marie-Louise von Franz's discussion of the anima of the Western man.[23] The creative, vital energy and the transformative energy in a man's life can become displaced onto a real or imagined woman, so that, instead of living out his own life transformation, he is demanding that this woman be all things to him: always beautiful, loving, present. She is supposed to supply him somehow with the erotic passionate energy for his life. This energy is actually his own deep life vitality, and it is evoked not only by sexual fascination but also by the call to spiritual transformation. Johnson discusses the Tristan and Isolt story and talks about the displaced or misunderstood anima obsession of contemporary Western man, who has become fascinated with the unobtainable Isolt, rejecting the more obtainable actual woman in his life; he also neglects his own creative life development.

Then we have the female side of this, where we have the image of the spiritual bridegroom. Christ appeared as the bridegroom to a number of great woman mystics in the Middle Ages, St. Teresa and Hildegarde of Bingen among them. In the Hindu tradition, you have the image of Krishna and Radha, where the soul is Radha and Krishna is God as the lover, the bridegroom. In the Song of Solomon, you have a call of the beloved to the bridegroom who is coming—wonderful love poetry that is a call to and from the Divine, summoning the human psyche to transformation.

At a more mundane level, we fairly often see women friends who are at a crossroad in their lives. There's a lot of creative energy bubbling around, and they immediately find a new man. It's almost as if they interpret the call to transformation as the need for a relationship with a man. It may not even be a real relationship, a really deep relationship that can aid both partners in transformation. Rather it's often an inappropriate one that can just dribble away spiritual energy. I'm looking at this image, then, of the bridegroom that as a divine summons can lift us to new heights, or else end us up in a mental institution waiting for an illusory "beloved" in a white robe. What a "loaded" area this is.

Stephen: Obsessive love is the negative aspect of the soul-mate theme. The Tristan and Isolt story is a microcosm of the history of romantic love since the Middle Ages.

Robin: It has captured the imagination of the West since then, particularly that of the emerging middle classes, who were enamored of the minnesingers and were moved by the story of tragic love. The middle class was coming slowly into literacy, but could appreciate a good story told at dinner or at an entertainment, and could afford to pay for the services of bards and minnesingers. They could identify, for the duration of a tale, with the great lords and ladies whose society they could not quite enter.

Stephen: The message is that love triumphs over all—although it leaves social propriety in wreckage, overcomes the religious conventions of the time—and opens to an unknown, completely mystical future of something so fragile and ephemeral, a human, a personal covenant.

Robin: This is what Joseph Campbell has established, and Robert Johnson brings out in his book *We*. This is an essential issue, this paradoxical, dangerous moment is where the Western psyche begins to find its soul life, its soul growth. We can't pretend that this doesn't happen; we can't *not* pass through this moment.

It is like the moment when Launcelot walks across the sword bridge to rescue Guinevere from one of her several kidnappings. You have to take this perilous step out over the abyss, where all your social props fall away; and now the next question is, "Do I simply become an outlaw thrashing about destructively, or does this experience become a wellspring for the renewing of soul life?"

If you take the story of Tristan and Isolt as a metaphor, you have it as a parable of the growth of soul life; but if you take it as a literal history, personal and biographical, what you see is a failure, a tragedy, because Tristan never separates his own soul growth from the projection onto Isolt.

Stephen: Because he keeps "acting out?"

Robin: Yes, he gives her back to king Mark, but he keeps cheating, always going back to her, compromising her further and further. If he loves her in a mature way, why do it? First of all, they are always deceiving King Mark. They always seem to be his "loyal knight and lady" and yet they're always lying.

Stephen: It seems like lying—which is the true sign of trying to "make up your own reality" (understood psychologically) and of a discontent with ordinary reality. This almost always pursues the soul-mate love, especially when it is on the fanatical or obsessive side.

Robin: It's not fair; every time Isolt almost gets her life in order with King Mark and things are comfortable for her, Tristan shows up again and they cheat again. What kind of a love is this? Does Tristan really love her? He keeps saying he wants her to suffer as much as he suffers! This is the extent of his love: he wants to know that his lady is also suffering.

What is going on here, if this is a metaphor for soul growth? It is a way of testing to see that you're out on the edge, that your soul is alive, that you're not just sinking into the commonplaces of life. You are constantly putting yourself out there in life, walking the tightrope, in order not to become a couch potato of the soul.

Stephen: I like that. Psychologically, it's a key to soul aliveness, acted out literally between individuals; it's like compulsive pathology. I think those Renaissance audiences liked the vicarious thrill of being almost caught again and again, of living dangerously.

Robin: Living dangerously. Tristan and Isolt perfected it. Tristan is projecting his soul life onto this woman, basically harassing her, stalking her, screwing her up, coming back every time she gets things together, and making a mess of his own life, betraying Isolt of the Fair Hands, who ultimately does him in. And so here we have a picture of what happens when you don't own your own soul, and you lay it on someone else.

And there's another piece: it sometimes seems as if no one is holding Isolt herself responsible for her ethical failings, as if all she need be is a beautiful woman and a royal by birth: nothing more required. Even God seems to excuse her, in the ordeal by fire. But quite aside from her perhaps understandable confusion about her marriage to Mark, there is this nasty little detail about Brangaene. Isolt's lady's maid, who is also her cousin (blood kin!), has been loyal to her from the beginning, even to taking her place in Mark's bed on the wedding night—a dangerous deception. Yet Isolt became afraid that Brangaene would betray her, and actually sent men to kill her cousin. Only their unexpected mercy saved the young woman's life and prevented Isolt from murdering her closest friend. Gottfried seems to be saying that true love—*amor*—transcends all moral concerns, precisely because it transports the lovers beyond the merely human into a divine rapture. It takes them out of their minds.

This reminds me of the explanation in the ancient classical world, and in many indigenous societies, for the execution of a murderer: one who has taken a life has assumed a divine prerogative, thereby removing him- or herself from the realm of mortal judgment into that of the Divine. Only the gods can pass judgment on a god-like act.

It seems to me that at the moment when Isolt did *not* kill Tristan in the bath—that is, she did not carry out her human obligation, according to the only laws she knew, to enact vengeance for her kinsman's death—she stepped out of her place in society and began her own ultimately lonely journey into the nonhuman realm of spirit. In her case, this could well be seen *not* as soul growth, but as its failure, a negative devolution into obsession and paranoid isolation. The stories give us an inconsistent and perplexing picture of Isolt. We can see her as the victim of royal marriage custom and Tristan's untrammeled anima projection; or we can also see that she might have brought her own troubled soul-stuff to the brew.

Stephen: So we have both things implicated: personal biography and a lesson for all humanity. But we also have the other Isolt. What do you feel about Tristan's wife?

Robin: The third Isolt, she of the White Hands, is the beautiful wife who nonetheless doesn't capture Tristan's anima, the woman who doesn't excite him. She's evidently an attractive, socially desirable—that is, aristocratic—woman about whom we never learn very much: a young girl betrayed by her husband's inability to separate his own soul need, his own soul life, from its projection onto Isolt the Fair, who's always away in the distance somewhere. This is the unconscious, unexamined projection of the anima out into the world. Robert Johnson says it is at the genesis of the Wasteland in the Western world.

Stephen: What of the *folie à deux* aspect of this story, how Tristan and Isolt egg each other on, each becoming the stalker of the other?

Robin: This is the paradoxical thing about this story: they are living a lie. They are passionate and physical lovers, yet telling everybody they are not. But every time they're almost caught, everything in nature conspires to help them, to prove their innocence. In other words, they *are* innocent—in the romance tradition of the twelfth century they were innocent. Their devotion to romantic love was a purification. This is also what the Church got so upset about, in this mystical interpretation of love. All the lying and dissembling were completely absolved by the purity and intensity of their passion, it was a cleansing fire.

Stephen: Do you think there is an equivalent element in modern soul-mate situations of the more fanatical sort? Are we absolved of lying when we are possessed, like my client with the nixie?

Robin: There's not much that can justify lying to and hurting everybody who cares about you, deceiving your closest friends. I don't really think any of us would condone that. We would say "Something's wrong here; this is obsession!"

In the Tristan and Isolt story, when King Mark exiles them, they go off into the Wood of Morois; and every time he almost catches them, they have Tristan's sword between them or some equivalent. This says something: we are not talking about a literal love of a man and a woman for each other. We're talking about the way in which the life of the soul breaks through into life in the external world of society, and it has demands beyond the demands of ordinary life. So what ultimately has to happen is the response to soul demands within the soul, in the interior. And we are told that the great poets of the romances understood their material in just this way; they knew the difference between divine seizure, and ordinary adultery. Both von Franz and Johnson discuss this at some length; and both point out that the real problem is that *we* don't know the difference.[24] Literalism, as Campbell reminds us, has been the bane of the West: in this vital matter of soul life, we have again forgotten the inner reading of the images; we have forgotten symbol and metaphor, and bogged down in the soap opera.

To be sure, there are times for "acting it all out" crazily as a young person. Maybe that is allowed because we learn from it; but after we've bounced off the walls of society and friends and family a little bit, we're supposed to begin to grow up— that means taking back our projections, among other things.

Stephen: That is where Aschenbach, the character in Mann's *Death in Venice*, and Nabokov's protagonist in *Lolita* are in the pathological, the daemongelic mode. The old man, the *senex*, is supposed to open the doorway to the inner child, not molest the outer one.

Robin: That's right. There must be a place in the psyche, in the soul-world, where we check in on what is deeply right or wrong. Being both true to our natural sense of goodness (our helping animal within) and true to our quest for the divine beloved—this kind of both/and dilemma is just where we are stretched to become most human.

After three years in the forest, one day Tristan wakes up from the initial enchantment, and says, "What have I done?" He turns Isolt back over to Mark and goes off on his journeys through many lands to be alone, to suffer and so forth.

Now Robert Johnson, along with other thoughtful Jungians who have written on this same theme, mentions that we have three years of bliss in the forest (dirty, disheveled, out of touch with the "real world" of other people—but this is a romance, and they have no mirrors in the forest; that's the point). In magic, the fourth is always *something else*, so the fourth year is the year that Tristan and Isolt have a chance to take back the projections and move them to a new stage, in which they can acknowledge their love for each other as human beings—a normal human relationship beyond the divine seizure.

There is quite a bit to be said about this, so I would like to do a little diversion here. The basic law of the fairytale, of enchantment, is a variation of waltz-time: one, two, three, four. A work of magic completes itself and steps up to the next level (or down) on the fourth beat. In a Russian fairytale, you will have three Baba Yagas, and the feminine fourth is the enterprising young woman who either breaks the spell or directs the hero as to how to outwit the witch. Furskin has three exquisite princess costumes and one animal-skin cloak. There are three Isolt's—mother, mistress, and wife—and one Tristan.

Robert Johnson points out that the three years in the forest meet this magical requirement: the spell of the love potion, the divine madness of being in love, needs this period to run its course. During this time, Johnson says, the man lives only with the projection of the anima, in the fogs of his projections.[25]

Then the fourth year comes, and the spell of the forest falls away. Tristan's king calls him back to the kingdom, the human world; the queen's husband calls her back to their court. They take a look at where they are in society, they make a clear and honest decision, including Mark in it. It seems like a good compromise with reality.

Stephen: But compulsion is stronger than life, the epic tells.

Robin: Yes. They fall back into the old scene, sneaking and cheating again. Then Tristan goes off to Brittany and marries Isolt of the White Hands. But he won't consummate the marriage, he's obsessed with the image of Isolt the Fair, across the sea in Tintagel.

Stephen: The male is most vulnerable when his imagination—and other parts— won't cooperate.

Robin: He freezes, goes into paralysis; he can't touch her. He remembers that he is being unfaithful to the other Isolt and that he has to suffer. He turns away from his wondering young wife. She says, "Husband, what have I done wrong, have I offended you? Please tell me." He lies to her, tells her that he has taken a religious oath; he and his wife have to be celibate for a year. She accepts it because she's a very trusting child.

Stephen: Doesn't that begin the whole cheating thing again?

Robin: Yes, it does. He actually persuades his brother-in-law to accompany him on his next foray to Cornwall, to Mark's court; there he is, popping up in Isolt's life again, and they fall back into bed together. She gives him a ring of jasper—the exchange of love tokens—and they're back in the enchantment.

Stephen: So that's the denouement; the irresistability of the intelligible destiny that Schopenhauer talks about. Each one is who he or she is, life is what it is, and so the story is told.

Robin: Apropos of the peculiar arrangement with the sails, the younger Isolt must have finally gotten furious that she couldn't have her husband even in deathwound. That's why she says the boat has a black sail. Her own life has been a blackness of oblivion and depression, of feeling unlovable and worthless, because her husband carries a ghost.

Stephen: It's a very human story, one that teaches through its wounds. Joseph Campbell is right: this story proposes a new stage of development for humankind, based on its psychological implications. We are instructed in love and the daemonic at the very same time: passion and obsession, the noble and the base. Maybe we should put it on the required reading list for couples about to get married.

Part Three

THE WILDNESS OF THE HEART

They [rebels and wild men] are still in touch with the instinctual energies that give them the courage to defy the collective chains that would maim their imaginations. If we lose touch with those rebels and wild men in our dreams we are lost because the old models are dead. . . . When our imagination fails, we stand traumatized, unable to step back, unable to step ahead. We feel our terror silent as a stone.

Marion Woodman, *The Ravaged Bridegroom*[1]

In God's wildness lies the hope of the world & the great fresh unblighted, unredeemed wilderness.

John Muir, *John of the Mountains*[2]

THE WILD CHILD

THERE IS SOMETHING BEAUTIFUL AND TERRIBLE to be found in running with the wolves—the wildness, the keen air, the hunt, the kill, and the red feast. The imagination of Europe and the Americas has long been prey to the idea of "wolf-children," the most well-known of which was Victor, the "Wolf Boy of Aveyron," studied by Itard, and the subject of a later film, *The Wild Child*. These instances have fascinated the "civilized" mind; they speak of what is wild and what is tame-in humanity.

It seems to be a perennial open question how much of "the wild child" still resides in each one of us. How much did our elders "tame" or "train" the wildness out of us? (We seem to be beings who cannot afford to be truly wild, and yet are never fully tamed.) What are the mythologies, the soul-instructive stories, of the theme of the wild child? How does this theme relate to the overall subject of this book? What happens when we cannot abide, or underestimate, the wildness in each other? Are there ways of mutual taming and wilding that work better than others? Is there a gender politics of wildness?

The wild child—the eternal child, the *puer aeternus*, the Peter Pan of the imagination—intrigues, vexes, and transforms civilization ever and again, appearing most recently in "inner-child" workshops. It seems a creature of magical and manifold potential. It is also where we all began, so in the archetype of the wild child, which we return to later through mythology, there is a promise of return to beginnings, of innocence, and of endless potential.

But ever and again, we meet wildness in the form of the restless hyperactivity of children; self-absorption; a vivid cartoon-like fantasy life that interferes with learning; "primary-process" or mythic thinking, even oppositional-defiant disorder, especially when we adults up the ante and demand more compliance with our taming. This is called—regardless of the society in which the effort is enacted, and for better or worse—the "socialization" process.

The task is to graft onto this restless little hairless primate, this strange, unruly being with its manifold potential, the impress of all that society, propriety, and even mythology deem appropriate. The creature, be it male or female, will (it is hoped) come to value communication, social relationships, shared culture sentiments, ethical and religious systems, a sense of humanity, aesthetic canons, and philosophical ideals. And now we are faced with a learning task evidently quite difficult for the entire species: to add to this list the skill of environmental understanding, the idea that we exist in a web of interdependence with other life forms. The very task itself reminds us that our species itself is still childlike, in an awkward adolescence.

The frustration of the process is witnessed by every schoolteacher of almost any level. Who is really able to take in what? And what can the student do with it once assimilated? Will he or she give back a crude parroting or a subtle recapitulation? Can later stages be accomplished if earlier ones are bypassed or blighted by negative experiences?

Fortunately, several generations of developmental and cognitive psychologists have now mapped and charted the terrain, addressing the questions of what kinds of developmental patterns, what kinds of myths, what kinds of relationships are going to characterize a certain age bracket. School psychologists and, later, social workers, clinical psychologists and psychiatrists will study the failures, giving the disorders that are endemic to our society names like Attention Deficit Disorder (ADD), antisocial behavior, narcissistic personality disorder, and many others. Estimates have ranged as high as three-quarters of the population of prisons and juvenile reformatories having ADD. The cost of ignoring this problem is costing society billions of dollars in correctional, therapeutic, and remedial programs, not to mention destruction of property and costs of insurance. And how does all this begin?

First of all, we know from Spitz's pioneering studies in the 1930s on institutionalized infants and the "failure-to-thrive" syndrome that mere biological satisfaction and physical safety are not enough. An emotional bond is required and a human relatedness. Every study showed that children fed and diapered but not related to were weaker, smaller, less robust, and less intelligent than their peers; many died of inexplicable causes.

During the 1960s, Harry and Margaret Harlow, a couple who did animal research, found that monkeys without adequate mothering never became adequate mothers themselves. Infant monkeys reared in isolation never learned to play the monkey games so instrumental to primate socialization. When as adolescents they were introduced into a group, they did not know how to socialize and remained aloof or interacted stiffly with other isolates. When the monkeys became sexually mature, they did not know how to approach each other or how to signal for matings.

> Both males and females were abnormally aggressive. They attacked and bit
> young monkeys, which normally reared animals almost never do. They
> also launched attacks against the largest and most dominant adult males,
> an extraordinarily maladaptive action for an adolescent.[3]

About ten or eleven years of ferality, wildness, had elapsed, when Victor, the "wild-child," was captured in southern France and brought back to "civilization." (Aveyron is a forested hill and deep-vallied region roughly between Provence and the Dordogne.) Although called a "wolf"child, Victor's main companions had been squirrels, deer, and birds. He had no human language, except squeaks, whistles, and body signals. Victor was so thoroughly feral in his ways that he seemed ineducable. (When shown a book, he tried to eat the letters off the page, as if they were bugs.) Victor was far more interested in the squirrels outside than in his lessons, and often scurried up the draperies, to the consternation of his tutors. He never learned human language, let alone writing. The poor lad died in captivity, and was deemed, indeed, to have been ineducable.

Lha-Mo, the black goddess of Tibet

CHAPTER SEVEN

THE WILD CHILD

The anaconda lifted its head toward me and opened its huge mouth. There were images inside. I peered in. People. I was delighted to see them: my mother and father, a junior high school science teacher who had taught a course on hygiene, a nurse, several medical doctors. They were all gibbering away, instructing me not to get my feet wet, not to eat foods unless I was sure they were properly prepared, to always wash my hands. In unison, they warned me that if I didn't follow the rules of hygiene I would get very sick. "You could die," they admonished in a single voice.

"No," I shouted and tried to run from the anaconda. I stumbled and fell to the ground.

An arm helped me sit up. It was the old man. "Change the dream," he advised.

John Perkins, *Shapeshifting*[1]

NATURAL WILDNESS

THE SAD STORY OF VICTOR THE WILD BOY raises a flurry of questions: was he "wild"? Is "wild" the same thing as "feral" or "unsocialized"? Was Victor's condition in any way like that of a natural wild animal, or was he merely a tragically unfinished human being? What, after all, does it mean, in human terms, to be "wild"?

The last question alone could fill a book and has filled several; of recent writers to address this question, Clarissa Pinkola Estes' evocative examination of wildness, wolves, and women's psyches is particularly cogent.[2] Her work suggests that at the core of a healthy and natural wildness is the freedom to be, to become, oneself. Wildness is necessary for the soul's vitality.

At its simplest, wildness is not being "owned," even as the "virgin" goddesses of the ancient world represented the divine feminine, unowned by any man or god. Aslan, the divine lion of C. S. Lewis's Narnia tales, is "not a tame lion."[3] For the

Sufi poet Rumi, the experience of the Divine is utterly beyond all limits, all caution, all control: it is wild.[4] God is not tame. An angel, surely, is not tame. Nor should the human soul be tame.

Wildness, then, is very much more than lack of socialization. The young of wild animals, in fact, are socialized in the normal course of their upbringing, even as are human children. And like human children—but to differing degrees depending upon the complexity of each species' developmental processes—young wild animals suffer and can fail to thrive or to grow into adequate adults of their kind, when they are isolated during the "sensitive periods" of their infancy.

Nor is wildness merely a failure to relate, although as we shall see, relationships can suffer from inappropriate or asymmetrical wildness. It is not just a glimpse of "un-relatedness" that makes our heart leap up at the sight of a fox drifting across our path in the mist of morning. In wildness, we sense the presence of all that is *not-us*, but to which we are, in some mysterious and potent way, profoundly connected. In the myth of the wild child, we catch that glimpse—as if in the mists of morning—of original, innocent wildness. Once we were a part of that natural wildness. It still lives in the Old Forest of our souls.

But how, then, do we relate to wildness? How do we integrate it into our lives and loves as human beings? Victor was, in fact, neither Tarzan of the Apes nor Mowgli of Kipling's *The Jungle Book*. But his story does have lessons for us about some of the many aspects of wildness.

The literature on social isolation is, in fact, quite unromantic; it describes how badly children fare if raised without human contact. (If unrelated to, wildness remains wild, and we are reminded how much relationship means at every step of the developmental ladder.) Moreover, the story of Victor raises the idea of sensitive periods in the development of the psyche: certain specific periods of time during which the imprints of external experience find a receptive psyche. (The most famous biological example is the "imprinting" period of geese and other wildfowl, which must take place during very specific windows of time, or the goslings will not learn to follow the mother.) With this principle, if you deliver the stimulus or education at the wrong time, then the innate wildness throws off the civilization; the graft does not take. Pass that time for language learning, as in Victor's case, and, try as you might, very little learning seems to take place.[5] This principle shows that, in human as in animal development, inner processes must match the outer.

Swedenborg avers that there are indeed such sensitive periods in the maturation of children, during which time primal imprints from the social environment must be made on the soul. Children shown unconditional love, nurtured, protected, but also encouraged to find their own sense of autonomy, grow spiritually; these positive "remains" stand them in good stead later in the adult world with its own midlife stresses and crises. Those with no such embracing or modeling are prey to their own biological impulses and, because they lack a developed sense of self, fall prey to selfish or egocentric impulses (the artless narcissism of the sociopath and the dictator).

On the spiritual level, having closed the door to positive spiritual intuitions or guidance, such people can easily be manipulated by evil or "lower order" spirits, says Swedenborg. They remain open only to the "natural" and cannot develop spiritually. In fact, for them, it is as if the spiritual did not exist. However,

Swedenborg asserts most earnestly that it *does* exist and that the Divine is the source of all inflowing life and energy. Here receptivity (rather than narcissistic oblivion) to the Divine opens the way toward an exquisitely regulated developmental process of the soul that continues from infancy through maturity, old age, and even beyond, into the spiritual world, and later into the realms called the heavens and the hells. This Swedenborg calls the process of "regeneration." But shut off from the spiritual influx by their own inattention or disbelief, people become prey to their baser impulses, anxieties, and conflicts. They thirst for something valuable, yet the quest is enacted in materialistic terms, the quest to acquire possessions, prestige, status. Other people become objects to be used, abused, or exploited.

Here, Swedenborg and Freud are not very far apart. Freud says the instinctive self is naturally selfish, acquisitive, grasping, cruel, and sadistic (giving to any psychology modeled on the psychoanalytic value scheme, a kind of denigrated value for modeling the self). In Freud's view, only the rules and structures of society—and social sanctions—keep people from acting out all sorts of horrors on their fellows. This does indeed seem true when we look at the inventory of nastiness that may take place in lawless societies. Both Swedenborg and Freud see the human being as caught between two principles: good and evil, heaven or hell on the one hand; and Freud's superego and id, rules versus instinct, on the other. Swedenborg agrees fully that the human being without divine or angelic intervention may well be "selfish, acquisitive, grasping," etc. This is true of the "natural" self or *proprium*. At this level, the person is drowned in self-love and hypnotized by the attractive surfaces of the world.

After death, says Swedenborg, everyone travels to, or in a sense awakens to, a world of spirits. Stripped of the fleshly envelope, the person's authentic nature is visible to other spirits.

> So at that time people can tell, when their eyes see him [the newly arrived spirit], what he is like, not just from his face but even from his body, and especially from his speech and behavior. And since at this point he is "in himself," the only place he can be is where there are people like himself.

> *Heaven and Hell 552*

That is to say, he "finds himself" in one of the communities of the world of spirits, ultimately heaven or hell. The hellish nature that is in people, now unconstrained by social propriety, blossoms forth as evilly as does the good in those who operated out of charity or compassion for others.

> Broadly speaking, they are forms of contempt for other people and of kinds of menace for people who do not do them homage. There are various distinct kinds of hatred; there are various distinct kinds of vengefulness. Viciousness and cruelty show through them from their more inward parts; yet when other people praise them or do them homage or revere them, their faces compose themselves and something is visible, like a happiness arising from pleasure.

> *Heaven and Hell 553*

This sounds like a textbook description of egocentricity or narcissism.

There is a little joke, or mini-parable around and about, which addresses the difference between heaven and hell, and may help us understand Swedenborg's perspective: what is the difference between heaven and hell? Well, they're exactly the same place (a very Buddhist paradox). In hell, people sit in long rows on both sides of a table on which the most luscious banquet is spread. They are starving, and their mouths are watering. There is only one problem: the only utensils are forks three feet long, and the food must be eaten with forks. (Try it! You can't get any food in your mouth!) Heaven is exactly the same place, down to the last detail. The only difference is that people help each other, across the table, to the food. (The banquet is savored in an atmosphere of helpful exchange, and all are fed to satisfaction.)

For Swedenborg, love of one's fellow human beings ("the neighbor") ensures a continuity of the divine influx by passing on the love, passing on "uses," his term for practical behavior with good consequences for someone else. Therefore, the easiest way out of personal hell is to forget about yourself and see what you can do for someone else. (This is also the basis of the Japanese *Naikan* therapy—psychological healing through selfless, even menial, social acts, as a cure for neuroticism and its attendant self-preoccupations.) The Lord, the divine source, seeks to turn the individual from the hell of self-preoccupation and self-aggrandizement toward an endless process of passing on the love and wisdom that abound everywhere once one looks beyond the *proprium*, the self or lower ego.

The implications of this for practicing relationship as a spiritual discipline are profound. Being in a relationship with a significant other gives one an adequate chance to observe the interplay of self-gratification versus altruism—generosity of spirit to the other. The community of our families and friends gives us a varied and challenging workshop for practicing heroic challenges to the giants and demons of self-gratification, self-absorption, and all kinds of unexamined and primitive power trips. Caring for children and helping the aged develops patience and compassion. It gives us a chance to grow up.

Monkeys who were raised around other monkeys, and with plenty of maternal affection—as well as permissiveness—develop social and mating abilities much more easily. They communicate their meanings effectively with gestures, looks, sounds; ask for what they need; and find their place in the social stratification. They exchange affection, support and help out their friends, and may protect the helpless or infants (in the case of chimpanzees, who are much closer to humans on the primate family tree, these helping, sharing, and nurturing behaviors are common and central to their social organization.[6]

The key seems to be a mixture of protectiveness (especially in the early stages), yielding gradually to a related permissiveness. (Heinz Kohut referred to this as the "rapprochement sub-phase," where the mother is attentive and connected to the child, but permissive in allowing its exploratory movements.)[7] At first, the child remains nearby, then explores farther and farther from its mother's influence, thus actually demonstrating a processing of learning how to be independent.

For human children who are well nurtured, the unconditionality of the love given them "remains" as a tangible psychoemotional legacy, affects the process of intellectual, emotional, and spiritual maturity, and furthers a neverending process Swedenborg calls regeneration: a process of being built from within by spiritual energies, while modeling a thoughtful, loving life without. Outer and inner do mirror each other in Swedenborg's model, emphasizing the esoteric notion that human beings are bridges between the worlds—wild and tame, natural and spiritual, angelic and demonic. One who learns love at the breast, in the cradle, the home, or the community gives it freely and easily. Altruism is, in fact, known in very young children, as is empathy—they are concerned when other children are sad or have been punished for something; and they will hand over their toys to appease another child who is crying and manifest concern for the emotional well-being of another child. In their innocence, Swedenborg said, infants resemble the angels themselves, "trailing clouds of glory"in Wordsworth's felicitous language—so recently parted from the divine essence that they bring a luminous mantle of it innately forward with them. (Can you see it in their smiles or hear it in their merrily bubbling laughter?)

Here, it seems to us that Freud fell flat on his face (along with much current social-scientific thought), in ascribing the presence of any positive social traits or altruism in children only to social learning or imitation. Swedenborg's view is closer to, and anticipates, Jung's perspective that there is a kind of "spiritual instinct," something in the psyche that is not really happy or fulfilled without some kind of spiritual meaning. If one accepts this idea, that there is something of the Divine within, immediately a greater valuing of the self is possible. True, we are only sparks, splinters of the divine plenitude, but there is a sense that we have everything we need: "We are matched to the Universe, and it to us," Joseph Campbell would say, and there is a developmental journey of the mature psyche (*regeneration* or *individuation*) that is accomplished by a gradual unfolding of the individual encountering her or his destiny—as if divine providence comes out to meet us, to fan our soul-spark to full blaze.

The transpersonal position, beginning with Swedenborg and the New England Transcendentalists, moving on through William James and Carl Jung, and then modern theorists, of whom the most well-known are Stanislav Grof and Ken Wilber, posits that there is always a gateway to the transpersonal available in our inventory of psychological experiences. As Swedenborg said, the divine influence, mediated by angelic presences, is always there to offset the hell that also lies within us (and to which we are never denied access, if we choose it). "We are always in a balance" between the celestial and the infernal forces.

As we shall see in the next section, where children are treated "hellishly" (neglect, emotional abandonment, various forms of abuse), it invokes the hells within. Treated with earthly love—and spiritual wisdom—the child grows in the same qualities, as the energy of heaven flows in. But it is also true, as Kohut's theory suggests, that, at certain phases, we need to withdraw parental influence and supervision to allow the teenager or young adult enough space to try their own wings, their own approaches to living, and the invaluable permission to make their own mistakes! The wildness here needs room to make its own explorations. Wildness curtailed by rules never learns to be self-limiting.

Joseph Campbell was fond of quoting Jesus from the gnostic Gospel of St. Thomas: "The Kingdom of God is spread upon the Earth and Men do not see it." What does it take to see it? This simple idea is that the other must be accorded the same attention or love as the self. This then opens the way to the Divine, as one sees that "thou art that" (Sanskrit: *tat tvam asi*). The other is also the vessel or the vehicle of the Divine, and God bows to God, as one does in India, saying, *Namaste!*

THE SHADOWSIDE OF WILDNESS:
CRUELTY, TYRANNY, AND PERVERSION

VICTOR THE WILD CHILD WAS ANIMAL-LIKE, more like a squirrel than a human in some ways; but he did not seem to be cruel, perverse, or neurotic, thus supporting the idea that these negative traits may well be the "shadow" of the civilizing process, twisted arts taught by humans to other humans. Most people feel that nature is cruel, but "cruelty" in nature is usually impartial, based on strength or dominance, biological privilege, or even seditious invasion or mass reproduction of organisms, as in plagues or epidemics. Human cruelty, however, is often gratuitous, directed at individuals or groups, sometimes sadistic and deliberately demeaning of its object—psychological cruelty.

In her long-term study of the wild chimpanzees in the Gombe Preserve in Tanzania, Jane Goodall has observed close-up and repeated demonstrations of the likeness of chimpanzee and human minds: chimpanzees in the wild live highly socialized lives in which they show the capacity to plan ahead, make a variety of tools in advance of their use, and cooperate in complex ways; like humans, they both weep and laugh.[8] Females and males, mature and immature individuals will care for injured or ill relatives or friends, and may adopt and successfully nurture orphaned infants. Adult primates in the wild, Goodall observes, rarely share food with other adults; but, "in chimpanzee society . . . even non-related adults frequently share with each other, although they are more likely to do so with kin and close friends."[9] They will defend a family member or friend at risk of their own life. And—to continue the comparison into its dark side—they will join forces to do battle, alas, even to, in one observed instance, carrying on a prolonged *war* (Goodall's term) between related groups. Over a four-year period, one band of chimpanzees systematically killed, one by one, every member of a neighboring band, which had once belonged to their larger group.[10]

> Chimpanzees, as a result of an unusually hostile and violently aggressive attitude towards non-group individuals, have clearly reached a stage where they stand at the very threshold of human achievement in destruction, cruelty and planned inter-group conflict. . . . But while chimpanzees have, to some extent, an awareness of the pain which they may inflict on their victims, only we, I believe, are capable of real cruelty—the deliberate infliction of physical or mental pain on living creatures despite, or even because of, our precise understanding of the suffering involved. Only we are capable of torture. Only we, surely, are capable of evil.

"Yet let us not forget," Goodall goes on to say,

> . . . that human love and compassion are equally deeply rooted in our primate heritage. . . . And while chimpanzees will, indeed, respond to the immediate need of a companion in distress, even when this involves risk to themselves, only humans are capable of performing acts of self-sacrifice with full knowledge of the costs that may have to be borne.[11]

"Full knowledge"—there lies the distinction between the innocent altruism of animals and of young children, and the conscious acts of self-sacrifice and intentional cruelty of the human psyche in its full maturity. But what is the source of this cruelty, and what—if any—is its ultimate purpose?

There can be no doubt that cruelty runs rampant on playgrounds. Children routinely torment other children because of their handicaps, to elicit an emotional display, such as tears when being attacked, or even for simple "difference," or for not being "one of group." They taunt and call names, subject each other to nasty little rituals of exclusion, or may even lock the "outsider" in a basement. We cannot pretend that these are not microcosmic versions of what adults, at their worst, also do to other adults—or to children. So many of them seem learned behaviors. William Golding's novel *Lord of the Flies* shows the apotheosis of this world, where children lacking adult supervision of any sort, form a vicious, fragmented hierarchical society. But the question remains open, answered by theorists in ways consistent with their own ideas: nature or nurture? Are nature's cruelty and human cruelty comparable? Or is the wound between nature and the human socialization process itself ("human nature"), as Freud avers in *Civilization and Its Discontents*. For him, the ego always is a battleground between instinct and appetite on the one hand (id), and the prohibition or regulation of urges on the other (superego). Or is Alice Miller's paradigm the more accurate? Her clinical and psychobiographical studies show just how dictators and sociopaths emerge almost entirely from cruelly-treated children.[12] The abuse she and many other therapists have chronicled may be physical, sexual, or emotional (and usually concomitant verbal), or several of them together. Physical abuse of children by adults has been almost commonplace in many cultures up to the mid-twentieth century, and it has too often been portrayed as indispensable to the development of character to sustain a certain critical number of beatings.

But increase the use of the rod in the "spare-the-rod-and-spoil-the-child" model and you get not obedient children, but sullen, resentful, or repressed ones. They become people who have conjured a "false self" into existence merely to survive in the punitive atmosphere, people who seethe with inner rage. At the worst end of this spectrum are the dictators who inflict the same punitive model they endured on everybody else. At the "better" end, there are the passive obedient and those who knuckle under too easily to unjust authority. The simplest forms of behaviorism show us that punishment teaches the recipient to fear the punisher and, where the punishment is cruel or inconsistent, generalizes into a kind of "learned helplessness" that characterizes the entire subsequent approach to life.

Early sexual initiations by adults seem to spawn often untold, and usually pathological, consequences in their wake and blight the unfoldment of a mature Eros. It is a psychological truism that, as an adult, a person who has been so abused will carry the wound into each subsequent relationship. Extreme sensitivity is needed on the part of the other partner to handle these distortions, and it is certainly a domain where skillful therapeutic disentanglement of issues can make an enormous difference.

Sigmund Freud did us the service of showing how pathology festers in the bosom of the nuclear family, especially where patriarchal autocracy rules the family environment. Where such an authority structure exists, female "penis envy" is undoubtedly provoked, but probably for political rather than biological reasons—the little girl wants the power, the sovereignty, not the penis that is its emblem. And castration anxiety is very easy to imagine, especially where Zeus- or Chronos-like dominant males run the show. But fear of unjust or inconsistent punishment—and the idea that one must submit—is the psychological heart of the anxiety, not removal of the physical organs. Nonetheless, the dynamics that Freud pointed out are largely valid, although needing to be flexibly interpreted in new cultural and social contexts.

But Freud's gift was immediately followed by a mean trick. In the very next historical moment, the good doctor proposed the "seduction theory," in which he said that most women who have memories of sexual molestation by older male family members were merely engaging in a kind of "wishful thinking," creating "screen memories" in the service of the ego's attempt to protect itself and the primitive desires of the id. According to Freud, there was, in effect, no abuse, only in the delusion-prone mind of the (female) experiencer.

Jeffrey Masson, Alice Miller, and many other post-Freudians have taken the master to task for this patriarchy-serving gambit. Epidemiological studies in the last couple of decades have shown just how wrong Freud was. Not only is sexual seduction of little girls (and boys) by adults enormously widespread, it is mostly done by older males, fathers and stepfathers, uncles and grandfathers, older brothers, and cousins. Often, the victim is further sworn or threatened into a deadly, covertly destructive secrecy that may be perpetuated for decades.

Masson was the Freud Library director who occasioned one of the greatest scandals ever to afflict the field of psychoanalysis when he revealed that the master himself had indicated in various ways that he had very good reason to suspect that many of these reports that his (mostly female) patients told of sexual abuse were legitimate; still, Freud held to his pet theory and suppressed his suspicions, thus doing a disservice to all women. And he practiced clinically what he preached, in a number of cases—subjecting confused women patients to his "good idea." Judged in the cold light of history, it seems the master himself preferred to protect the integrity of his theory against an unpalatable truth. (Whether done in the name of science or psychoanalysis—Freud sometimes had them confused—this was reprehensible and ultimately a disservice to both fields. Nor was Masson able to keep his post, for the Freud family did not relish the disclosure.)

Early in his psychotherapeutic practice, Stephen worked with a woman whom we shall call "Claire." Her story bears witness to the consequences of the wrong kind of therapeutic mythologizing. Claire is now, we recently learned, deceased; and so her story had to be constructed from Stephen's thirty-year-old memories:

> In early adolescence, Claire had been sexually abused by a man she called "uncle," although he was really a more-distance relative and a so-called friend of the family. The abuse had gone on for some time; she found out later—one of her ways of verifying the truth of her experiences—that it had also happened to a sister and a cousin.
>
> When she first entered analysis, Claire was already in her late-twenties, prone to fits of anxiety and depression, and sexually dysfunctional. She found a traditional psychoanalyst and poured out the sordid secrets she had carried for more than a decade. He should understand; after, he was a specialist in sexual aspects of neuroses, right?

After listening to her story, the analyst made the following interpretation: "You realized the man was giving your older sister attention and felt jealous. You wanted his attention for yourself, so you imagined that he was in love with you and vividly fantasized this love affair you really wanted to have with him."

After this interpretation, Claire left the session mute. She fell alternately into rage and depression. She would not go back to the analyst—or to any other therapist, for that matter, for a number of years.

Now another decade had passed, stormy and difficult years. Claire knew she still needed help, but this kind of help had betrayed her before! An attractive brunette in her mid-thirties, sedate without, but roiling within, Claire now sat in my office. She wondered how she could trust me and why she should even try.

She told the story of her sessions with the first psychoanalyst. I noticed that she was gritting her teeth, her hands were knotted into fists, her eyes flashed fire. It was very hard to be in the role of a male therapist at that moment. I knew my task was to convince her that I was really listening to her. I asked probing questions that plunged her back into the memories; at times, the fire flashed in my direction. She was a woman with a critical and penetrating intelligence. I had come to believe her story, although not uncritically. But the moment did arrive when I was honestly able to tell her that I believed her story completely.

In subsequent sessions, as we did guided imagery and psychodrama, I had Claire "talk back" to her first psychoanalyst. Her feelings erupted like a volcano: "How dare you tell me my own experience was not true, making me doubt myself!" She roared. "How dare you do that, know better than everyone! All you know are your stinking theories!" (I wondered if, in whatever office he sat, his ears were burning at that moment!)

As I had her line up all the males that had wronged her, from the perpetrator, to her father who blindly "threw her to the wolf," to various manipulative boyfriends who also had tried to own her, use her, or tell her what she thought and felt, I had an early glimpse of Jung's *animus* and understood why this figure shows up in dreams sometimes as phalanxes of goose-stepping soldiers. An accumulation of negative experiences, all from the same gender, creates a collectivized image of that gender: archetype becomes stereotype. Every male who now meets that woman must either wear that mantle or prove that it is misplaced.

Fortunately, Claire was a resourceful and courageous woman. Patient work with the layers of trauma and misunderstanding freed her from much of the confusion. She was subsequently able to enjoy a stable and happy relationship with a man—whom she nonetheless tested thoroughly before taking into her life.

Thus, to the earlier abuse and the conspiracy of silence to which Claire was sworn by her abuser had been added another conspiracy of silence by the therapist, with a toxic negative implication about the psyche of the woman herself. The implication: "You are weak and perverse enough (as a woman) to make these things up and try to perpetrate a lying hoax, deceiving everyone else, as well as yourself." These practices on the part of professionals add a vicious and gender-inflected psychological abuse to the physical. (It differs very little from the courtroom situation faced by many female victims, in which they are accused by defense attorneys, and even judges, of having incited or attracted the rapist to themselves—basically of having "asked for it.")

If we accept an important aspect of female wildness as being that which is "not tame, not domesticated, not *belonging to* anyone," we are confronted with the crucial truth that there is something in each woman that can never belong to any man. This is in the essential nature of wildness. No matter how much the woman herself may fear and mistrust it, no matter how hard she tries to give it away, it remains free, or it dies. This is not a concept that is acceptable within our prevailing system of familial ownership. We can see how, extending back to the biblical story of Eve's weakness and deceit, female wildness is mistrusted in the service of a corrupt male myth.

To be sure, the opposite scenario is equally reprehensible, where therapists, casting about for a cause for the patient's obvious neurosis, suggest that the patient must have been sexually abused—and probably by so-and-so—and thus unintentionally *create* a "memory." Such a memory is a myth in the sense of "attractive fiction." (Some men, claiming they were falsely accused, have created a coalition to scrutinize therapists who instill or encourage such false memories in daughters or nieces.) The deceit here is double: you must be as (defective) as you are simply because of some single traumatic event; and someone else is probably to blame for your problems.

In response to such distortions, the advice for therapists (or ministers, counselors, or simply balanced people who have been confided in) seems inescapable: your head and your heart together are required. Have compassion, first of all, for the person, and the hard road we all must tread from birth to death—and the vicissitudes in-between. If a person is telling you a story, there is probably a reason. Now use your head to sift through what you hear, and your discernment to place it. Did it happen pretty much just as told? Does the teller really believe him or herself? Is the teller's goal merely to blame—and place blame and rage elsewhere—or to understand, to heal and grow, and ultimately to forgive? What is the "feeling" of the feelings (*affect*)? Beyond these internal caveats, the self-aware therapist intrudes no meanings, only helps the client to clarify her or his own.

Nowadays, most mental health professionals are mandated by their associations, and by state guidelines, to report even suspected instances of child sexual abuse to Child Protective Services, usually a branch of Social Services. In one situation in which Stephen had to report such an instance to the state sexual-abuse hotline, it was almost forty-eight hours before he got a clear telephone line because the line was so busy with other calls, a truly sobering indication of the scale of the problem, now that the "conspiracy of silence" has ended. (It would be horrifying even if only half the reports were authentic.) This is the state of society, when the wildness, "ferality," is unconscious in adults, and instincts and secrecy rule. Studies have shown that most adults who commit sexual abuse with children were so abused themselves.[13]

How then to extract the wildness from the perversion? Behind the crude urge seems something resembling love. Pedophiles, in some sense, may love the inner child or need to return to a stage or condition of development which was never fully completed. Also it could be said they have an urge toward initiation—they want to initiate children into one of the mysteries proper to adult life. (Tragically, this is an initiation they themselves have never completed. It must be admitted in all conscience that our society is notoriously deficient in *rites de passage*.) For those who have lived through it, however, early sexual abuse is a wrenching, horrible caricature of tenderness and intimacy, and mixes in a psychological witches' brew of misused authority, lies, threats, and swearings to secrecy. It stretches a child soul with powerful adverse forces that have been known to fragment even adults; it can lead to an immature, but jaded, sardonic attitude in which the victim trusts no one and believes in nothing.

These are negative "remains" in Swedenborg's system, and it is easy to see why they would "open one to the hells." The hells, from Swedenborg's description, are indeed made up of people with similar "dirty little secrets" on their consciences from their lifetimes; when they enter the world of spirits, they continue doing what they always did, only more so. The commonality of their condition attracts them to each other, and they do things to each other that are consistent with their "ruling love." It is easy to imagine how lots of people (spirits) whose ruling loves include manipulation of others, sadism, and perversion could create a hell. Hell is not a place to which you are sent, Swedenborg says, but a condition of the soul.

RECOVERING WILDNESS: THE MYTHOS

IF SOCIALIZATION HAS ITS WOES and civilization its discontents, it would not seem unreasonable that a compensatory mythology would arise; and it is in fact a story that carries us back into an idealization of nature and thus to paradise regained. Being a mythology, it is, of course, more idealized than the actualities of social isolation we have discussed; yet, sharing in the power of myth, it points the way to some new realizations and our understanding of the wildness in our own and in each other's natures.

Of the many stories of the wild child, some of the most influential are Kipling's ever-popular *The Jungle Books*. Mowgli (Mother Wolf's little naked "Frog") is a child who is stolen by a tiger, adopted by wolves, and finds in the world of the jungle his first relationships and—through two sequels—his lifelong loyalties (to the delight of every child who has ever participated in this little mythology). Who of us who learned to read from Kipling's masterpiece can ever forget loving and fierce Wolf Mother, loyal Grey Brother, Mowgli's wise and formidable teachers, Balloo the bear and sleek Bagheera the panther? But then there are ambivalent figures who embody the perilous and changeable power of the forest: the tricksy Bandar-log, the monkey people; Kaa the mighty python, whose primordial devouring power everyone fears; and Shere Khan, the numinous, terrible tiger, incarnation of cruelty, and of all those proud chieftains who believe themselves to be above the Law. And the Law is ever present in Mowgli's jungle world, encoding and supporting the entire, intricate matrix of living creatures, beasts and plants, seasons of greenness and plenty, seasons of drought and fire. It is, by contrast, when Mowgli ventures into the alien human world beyond the forest, that un-Lawfulness becomes the rule. Kipling prepared generations of children for an understanding of connectedness with "all our relations," for an ecological ethic, with his magical verses:

> Now Rann, the Kite, brings home the night
> That Mang, the Bat, sets free—
> The herds are shut in byre and hut,
> And loosed 'til dawn are we.
> This is the hour of pride and power,
> Talon and tusk and claw.
> Oh, hear the call!—Good hunting all
> That keep the Jungle Law![14]

These figures, combining name, personality, and a specific emotion or complex of emotions (Swedenborg's "affections") allow us to meet the creatures as if they were figures in our world, too. As Mowgli comes to know them, we do as well; through Kipling's artistry, we enter the nonhuman world of the jungle through its inhabiting powers, its animal masks.

The Tarzan mythos, to the fascination of some and the scorn of others, seems to resurface ever and again—most recently in the film *Greystoke* and the Disney animated version. Although Edgar Rice Burroughs' fictional treatments bear no relationship to either ethology or ethnology and are packed with his early twentieth-century ethnocentrism, it is the myth that exhales the tang of the jungle, the unfettered arboreal lives of the "great grey apes" who raise the young Tarzan (and who do not actually exist). It is a return of sorts to the Garden of Eden, the dawn of creation, and the recovery of innocence.

The books have been translated into most of the world's languages, and some seventy Tarzan movies were made (the most famous of which feature Olympic swimmer Johnnie Weismuller). Burroughs complained mightily that the movies present Tarzan as a monosyllabic, primitive chap, whereas his original literary rendition of the character is far more interesting and complex. Burroughs' point was that Tarzan's English aristocratic genes came to the fore, enabling him to wear an English Lord persona and circulate in polite society, when not swinging through the middle terraces of the primeval forest, nor engaging in the "Dum-dum" of the "great grey apes." In the novel, the ape-raised child, when he first encounters books in the cabin of his long-dead parents, thought, like Victor, that the black marks on the pages were insects. Tarzan, however, learned (those superior genes) how to read without any tutoring, whereas Victor could not do so even with diligent and patient efforts to educate him. We can learn from Burroughs' veering toward the mythic (and away from reality). The story says, basically, that a child with all potential in him/her (those excellent genes, again) exposed to the merely animal nurture, can, in effect, socialize himself/herself. (Yet Kala, Tarzan's ape-mother, like Mowgli's Wolf Mother, always remained dear to his heart). The almost-truth behind this myth is, then, that early, merely animal nurture counts for very much in the worlds of later development.

When wildness is totally lacking, as in urban lives lived in highly contexted and restrictive societies—for example, people raised with post-Victorian values and among stiff and stuffy social occasions—the secret fantasies begin to emerge. These explain why Burroughs' novels were so popular. Caught in a social wasteland of rules and obligations, our inner wildness cries out for wildness all around. People "break out," do wild things they never, heretofore, considered. The English lord takes an Indian wife and "goes native"; the painter Gauguin, tiring of European salons, flees to Tahiti; or (more of ancient days) the proper Athenian housewife runs off with the maenads and becomes a devotee of Dionysus, running wild on the mountain tops, catching and eating living animals, and enacting sexual orgies with strangers, because these activities are sacred to the god (an extreme example). Where abstraction rules, a kind of death sets in; this is the wasteland motif we explore in the next chapter. Since wildness is energetic, the stuff of instinct, we turn to wildness to find our lives.

It is hard to say where the serious movement to reclaim wildness began in modern times. In the late 1960s and early 1970s, Carlos Castaneda published his *Teachings of Don Juan*, a piece of alleged field ethnology about himself as a young anthropologist who decides decisively to enter the magical world of the *brujo*, the sorcerer.[15] This represented a departure from the usual "objective" stance of scientific anthropology. The anthropologist is dedicated to describing the alien (the term *primitive* used to be applied) culture zone simply from the viewpoint of social science. In effect, Castaneda "went wild" by entering personally into the experiential world of the traditional healer. He experienced all kinds of spontaneous visions and, finally (in one of the later books), a meeting with the *Nagual*, a terrifying personification of the primordial abyss, the "not I." We will return shortly to the importance of this being and this concept.

In 1976 Stephen published *The Shaman's Doorway*, attempting to pave the way for a return to ancient shamanic ways for contemporary people. He was followed shortly in this endeavor by Michael Harner, *The Way of the Shaman*, and Joan Halifax, *Shaman: The Wounded Healer*.[16] Soon *The Shaman's Drum* appeared, a popular but high-quality journal investigating this phenomenon. Suddenly, shamanism was becoming a household word, and people were exploring visionary paths, journeying, working with animals and helping spirits, and carrying medicine bundles. A new era for anthropology had begun, in which the anthropologist personally entered into the magical world of the traditional society.

In the early 1980s, two books by Jungian analysts appeared, on a different but related theme: Sylvia Perera's *Descent to the Goddess* and Edward Whitmont's *Return of the Goddess*, which announced a mythic phenomenon of our time that seemed to be under way—a veritable regendering of the face of God.[17] Along with the announced return of the goddess was the appearance of her consort—the ancient horned one of the pre-Christians: Cernunnos, Pan, Dionysus, the divinity of the shamanic realms—and her retinue, the world of nature embodied: fauns, sprites, and elves. Findhorn announced the return of the vegetation devas. Shamans talked to their "helping animal" spirits. Wiccans (those who feel closest to an ancient tradition with ties uniting the animal and the human realms) felt re-empowered to insist their belief system was a religion, not an aberration, the terms *witch* and *witchcraft* long having been portrayed as evil or regressive.

Throughout the 1980s, poet Robert Bly ran groups for men, who felt their real initiation into adult life had been somehow neglected. A mythopoetic men's movement sprang into existence, which used not only rites of traditional societies, but an overt return to wildness in the form of vision questing, mythmaking, drumming, and reconnecting with the "wild-man" within. In 1990, Bly published *Iron John*, a distillation of his findings, based on a fairytale of a wild man—who becomes the initiatory shaman for every young man on the threshold of evolution. Bly says,

> The moment the boy leaves with Iron John is the moment in ancient Greek life when the priest of Dionysus accepted a young man as a student, or the moment in Eskimo life today when the shaman, sometimes entirely covered with the fur of wild animals, and wearing wolverine claws and snake vertebrae around his neck, and a bear-head cap, appears in the village and takes a boy away for spirit instruction.[18]

The shaman is the "priest of wildness," accountable to a supernatural order, not a social, human hierarchy of any kind. Because shamanism is so ancient, it is possible to assign any kind of visionary activity to the realm of the shaman.[19]

In 1992, Jungian analyst Clarissa Pinkola Estes published her immensely successful, *Women Who Run with the Wolves*. Overnight, it seemed, women resonated with the same call to find the vitality in the heart of wildness. It was as if "civilization"—at least the sort most of us, of both genders, received—left us conspicuously lacking in this vital connection. It was time to reconnect with wildness.

How do we account for this amazing modern movement that has erupted all around us, to help us find our new path through the wilderness of life? There are people who have made it their work to lead vision quests, who study the wounded male, the wounded female, the inner child, the helping animal, spirit guides, animal and plant devas, and intelligences that guide healers, forays into wildness for the sake of our very souls. The following are just a few people to whom I (and many others) feel a debt of inspiration: Brooke Medicine Eagle, Bradford Keeney, Vusumazulu Credo Mutwa, Brant Secunda, Michael Meade, Tom Pinkson, Malidoma Somé, Sam Keen, Riane Eisler, Jean Houston, Gioia Timpanelli, Robert Bly, Marian Woodman, Joan Halifax, James Hillman, Tom Brown . . . the list goes on (with apologies for the many medicine brothers and sisters we have omitted). Natalie Goldberg has shown in *Writing Down the Bones* just how the wild mind hovers close to the real inspiration of the writer.[20]

Bly and Estes show us a paradoxical thing: how wildness is used to initiate the developing soul into its own maturity. We "grow-up," become civilized, through wildness consciously encountered. This was how the Native Americans initiated their young men—send them off on a solo vision quest: nature and the spirits, or the great *Wakan*, would take care of the rest, maturing, incubating the soul in the midst of wildness. (The raw shall become cooked, but not in the vessels of civilization, rather in the campfire of the solo vision quest, in the slow way of nature.) The quester returns with a new power, new connections (helping animals and spirit guides). Once initiated, the brave is now "cosmically instructed," has developed his own relationship to the universe.

Estes has done modern women the equivalent service of helping them recontact their wildness, open that doorway to their deep inner natures. A Jungian analyst and a storyteller, she is helping revalidate women's depth experience on their own, not in male analysts' terms. She writes:

> The old one, The One Who Knows, is within us. She thrives in the deepest soul-psyche of women, the ancient and vital wild Self. Her home is that place in time where the spirit of women and the spirit of wolf meet—the place where mind and instincts mingle, where a woman's deep life funds her mundane life. It is the point where the I and the Thou kiss, the place where, in all spirit, women run with the wolves.[21]

In *The Mythic Imagination*, Stephen analyzed approximately three thousand dreams from clients, collected over twenty years of psychotherapy. People re-dreamed the landscape of faery, encounters with helping animals, spirit guides, underworld journeys, a landscape entirely alive from within, redolent with myth and meaning. In particular, there was the return of an old mad woman, appearing in the dreams of men and (mostly) women.[22] Her dress and circumstances varied, but were almost always humble: living at the bottom of a well, deep under the sea, running the elevators in the Empire State Building; daft and full of raving, potent wisdom, cackling and crackling like Crazy Jane in Yeats's poems: she is the goddess returned as a numinous bag lady. The lowest of the low, she incarnates, nonetheless, the heights of wisdom for the soul's next peregrination. In Celtic lore, this outrageous crone bestows sacred kingship with a kiss. She seems a figure almost analogous, in her lowly estate, to the Christ child in the manger, or Demeter as a beggar-woman, rags thinly concealing divine radiance.

Estes names the personifications of this wild essence of the feminine, Mother of Days, Mother Nyx, Coatlique, Hekate. Add to these Artemis (Diana) the virginal huntress, to whom wild animals are sacred and so to be treated; and Aphrodite (Venus), whose wildness is that of the bedchamber and who loves to break tidy enclosures and vows of marriage or chastity. Go further east, and the wildness gets wilder: Kali, with her necklaces of skulls, drinking the blood of children; Lha-mo who rides her pied mule saddled with the skin of her flayed child; the beautiful and terrible Dakinis who gallop on the wild tempests that lash the Himalayan peaks; and Durga, who also rules the winds and takes on the great buffalo-demon Mahistha, who has defeated all the male gods, finally beheading him. Backtracking the sun to Japan and beyond, we find the terrible wrath of Amaterasu when provoked by the rash act of her younger brother, Susano, the god of war; and still further east (in fact, so far so that it meets West in the midst of the world's greatest ocean), Hawaiian Pele, the volcano goddess, who is to be feared above all other deities, for her terrible and explosive temper, fiery red fury running down verdant mountainsides into the sea.

Not only the goddess' wildness but her wrath concern us next. What happens to the Great Goddess when not only her worship and her image are broken (those images of Ashtoreth and Baal the biblical "Jahwists" were smashing and burning all over Cana), but also her very attributes (the feminine in the psychological sense: receptivity, nurturance, listening, relating, giving "unconditional love") are devalued and demoted?

THE BLACK MADONNA

IN MANY CATHEDRALS, BASILICAS, even small grotto shrines throughout Europe, one finds an astonishing image: a small black woman, usually holding a child, sometimes made of simple materials, sometimes with a corona and robe of pure gold. She is always held in the greatest reverence and enshrined in places of high holiness. The images of men are, of course, everywhere in the same churches, from the ivory statues of bishops and popes to the image of the crucified Christ over the altar or baptismal. Let us remember that, in the theology of Christianity, there was, until the recent Roman Catholic "Assumption of the Virgin," no official feminine presence in heaven.

The authors have made it a point to visit such shrines throughout Europe, just recently returning from Spain and Portugal, where the Black Madonna is everywhere. In Montserrat, above Barcelona, for example, in a dramatic mountain setting amid rugged sandstone spires, is a very fine Black Madonna from the twelfth century. After the noon mass, which features a hauntingly beautiful boy's choir, people line up in a queue that extends through the church and out into the courtyard. Pilgrims and tourists wait expectantly to pass before the Black Madonna in her glass case, to make a petition or ask a blessing. Signs along the wall in the long corridor remind the petitioners: *Silencio!* (The basilica, burned first by Napoleon and then destroyed by political revolutionaries in the twentieth century, has been totally rebuilt through contributions, such is the strength of her worship.)

If one travels down a long winding path below the buildings, pausing frequently to enjoy the breathtaking views, one finds another image tucked away in the *Santa Cova*, the holy cave, said to be where the Black Madonna of Montserrat herself was found (according to tradition, in the ninth century). The shrine reminded us of the older one in Rocamadour, France, also set in a grotto and with an ancient paleolithic cave still deeper within the great cliff-escarpment to which the town of Rocamadour is vertiginously plastered.

Why is the Black Madonna associated with ancient grottoes, and why is she black?

There is an exquisite Black Madonna in Madras, India, at the simple, beautiful basilica dedicated to St. Thomas (who is said to have brought Christianity to India in the years just after the death of Jesus). There, in the culture-zone of India where gods and goddesses alike are venerated, such a figure seems naturally and gracefully at home: a little black goddess, petite like the Dravidians themselves, garlanded with flowers and offerings. She fits right in among the Ganeshas and Lakshmis and dancing Shiva. And the comparison to the Black Lady of India, Kali/Durga, is unavoidable.

Kali makes us uncomfortable because of her wicked-looking weapons and her necklace of skulls, her long, red, blood-drinking tongue. Yet, the high mystics of India have said that her worship is the sweetest, the deepest, the most profound the human soul in quest of the Divine can experience:

> O Wisdom Goddess, your essence alone is present within every life, every event, Your living power flows freely as this universe. Wherever I go and wherever I look, I perceive only you, my blissful Mother, radiating as pure cosmic play.

> Ramprasad[23]

Kali's image, like the statue of the Black Madonna, usually is garlanded with flowers and surrounded by twinkling candles and burning incense. Beneath her image crouch women shrouded or scarved, begging supernatural aid for their children and their loved ones.

To understand this paradoxical image of the feminine, let us take a step back, behind any one representation of the Divine. Joseph Campbell writes that *all* representations of the Divine by human beings fall short, by definition, of that ineffable presence. They are conceived for the sake of human sensibilities, to have some form to hang onto, something the mind can wrap itself around. Campbell would quote the great nineteenth-century Bengali saint Ramakrishna. Whenever he was approached by a Western pundit or philosopher looking for a discourse, the saint would look at them with his piercing, twinkling eyes, and ask, "Would you like to talk about God *with* qualities, or *without* qualities?" (These refer to the two states of spiritual absorption with which the saint was familiar—on a daily basis. *Savikalpa samadhi*, the "lower" form, in which the divine presence manifests some qualities, is beheld wrapped in a nimbus of celestial love or angelic presences, or conveys a message. In the "higher" form, *nirvikalpa samadhi*, the absorption in the Divine is complete—there is nothing to be said.

Once, in a story Campbell was fond of telling, a distraught follower approached the Hindu saint. "You and the other holy ones and all the scriptures tell me to love God. But how, master, can I love this impersonal vastness that is beyond anything I can conceive of?"

"I understand," said the saint, and thought awhile. "What *do* you love?" He finally asked.

"Oh, my little precious niece," the man said. "She is so full of innocence and beauty, like a little *apsaras* (angel)."

"Then worship God through her," the saint replied.

Kali is the fertile, pregnant void out of which we all emerge, as apparitions on the stage of time and space. Her blackness comes the closest to a metaphor (if such is allowable) for the Great Unfathomable Mystery, Rudolf Otto's *Mysterium Tremendum et Fascinans*, the womb and the tomb that bound our coming and going. Of course, she is terrifying; nothingness and the indescribable always is.

The poet Ramprasad, quoted in Lex Hixon's *Mother of the Universe*, a book of praise to Kali, says of her:

> Chariots and drivers, horses and horsemen,
> arrows and archers, she devours whole.
> Elephants of war stampede and are lost in her as moths
>   consumed by the flame.
> The incomparable light of Kali's beauty
>   pervades the universe,
> as she swallows into her dazzling darkness
>   the ferocious array of demonic passions.
>   She has destroyed the narrow hopes
>   of every limited self in creation.
> by consuming the objective and subjective worlds
>   in ecstatic conflagration.

All beings must now renounce
conventional projects and projections
None will survive the fury of her illumination.[24]

The question posed by the symbol of the goddess Kali is this: Can we behold the dimension of undoing, the deconstruction of all forms—including some we hold dear *and* ourselves—the black hole of unbecoming, in this feminine form and still accord her the sacred respect she is due, the love, even? (She isn't pretty; it's like having to give the snaggle-toothed ogress in the Celtic fairytale the kiss.) Maybe only a few saints, like Ramakrishna, have accomplished this, and Jesus, who it is said, "Went to the cross as a bridegroom to his bride," because it takes a being of substantial spiritual accomplishment to say yes to the range of experiences some of us find the most difficult in life: limitation, illness, ugliness, destruction, death. It is easy to see why ordinary folk prefer to not look too closely at Mother Kali.

There is a bumper sticker, not infrequently affixed to the Volkswagen of Wiccans. It says, "The Goddess is coming [or returning] and is she pissed!" If it is true that the last two- to three-thousand years have seen her repression and that of certain archetypal feminine qualities with her and have witnessed the hegemony of male gods and their values elevated, then it is easy to imagine a gender-polarized reversal and a clearcut return of an angry, neglected goddess—that wild woman in the dreams of some of Stephen's clients.[25]

God in our dreams, goddess *with* qualities: shouting bag-ladies, raunchy crones, numinous animals, voluptuous black women dancing in church or giving birth in our own wounded souls—these are the divine forms demanding our attention today. They ignore the mediation of priesthoods and sacred texts. They burst through the walls of our hearts, breaking open the cages we have so carefully constructed around our lives. They remind us that God is wild, that our souls are wild. They belong to that Holy Wildness, and we cannot tame or confine them and retain our vitality. Marion Woodman speaks of the new kind of awareness in feeling and in thinking, which is growing now in women and in men. It is a *human* conscious, offering us new possibilities of relatedness within our own psyches and with one another, male and female:

> Dreams can be interpreted in many ways. The important thing is to experience the essence of the images so that the ego opens to new possibilities. The Black Madonna repeatedly appears in modern dreams, and her presence suggests the possibility of a feminine consciousness as yet unknown to us. Her coming presages a new understanding of light in matter, light in nature, light in our own bodies. As for what her child symbolizes, most of us can only imagine. Our dreams try to guide us with images we do not yet comprehend. They urge us to cross bridges, leap over dangerous chasms, out of the world as we have known it.[26]

The Jungian analyst Edward Whitmont, in his chapter on "The Feminine and its Repression" in *Return of the Goddess*, says that warfare and violence are not the province of men alone (though predominantly):

Among Germanic and early Celtic tribes women fought alongside men. The stories about Valkyries and Amazons testify to this fact. Moreover (quite the opposite of what one would expect) many of the early prehistoric divinities of warfare were female: Sekhmet in Egypt, Inanna in Sumer, Anath in Uruk, the Morrigan in Ireland, Bellona in Rome, to name but a few.[27]

Whitmont offers the most cogent psychological explanation we have encountered for the almost vengeful zeal with which the patriarchal world has suppressed the matriarchal. He quotes the famous classicist Janellen Harrison:

> Matriarchy gave women a *false*, because *magical* [italics Whitmont's] prestige. . . . Man, the [physically] stronger, when he outgrew his belief in the magical potency of women, proceeded by a pardonable practical logic to despise and enslave her as the weaker.[28]

But other scholars, notably those influenced by Marija Gimbutas' work, doubt that there was ever a time of actual female dominance; instead, increasing evidence points to a pre-invasion period in the eastern Mediterranean of a more egalitarian society, based on gender partnership rather than dominance. If these scholars of the Great Goddess are correct, there were five- to ten-thousand years of gynolatric culture—peaceful, largely agrarian, ritualistic. Women priestesses served a goddess in various forms. There was a natural emphasis on women's mysteries, of course, sometimes, undoubtedly, a peripheralizing and devaluing of the masculine.

With the coming of the nomadic Indo-European invaders, tribal societies specialized for war, the less catastrophic blood-mysteries of the Mother world were overwhelmed. The newcomers were devotees of the gods of storm, and they came like a storm themselves in their thundering chariots: Ionians and Dorians into Greece and Macedonia; Vedic Aryans into India, with male deities of thunder and wind, Indra and Varuna; even the very Habiru (the Hebrews) into the Middle East, who stood outside the walled agrarian cities of Cana and blew their trumpets until their sky god Jehovah, full of thunder and lightning, smote the gates of the city asunder (and the idol worshipers therein were put to the sword, and their graven images broken and burned).

Raphael Patai has shown, in his compelling excursus, *The Hebrew Goddess*, just how systematic, determined and violent was the later Hebrew or "Yahwist" movement against the goddess religion:

> For about six centuries [after the Israelites arrived in Cana] . . . down to the destruction of Jerusalem by Nebuchadnezzar in 586 B.C., the Hebrews worshipped Asherah (and next to her also other, originally Canaanite, gods and goddesses) in most places and times. Only intermittently, although with gradually increasing intensity and frequency, did the prophetic demand for the worship of Yahweh as the one and only god make itself be heard and was it heeded by the people and its leaders.[29]

All textual evidence that the Hebrews themselves once worshiped a goddess was as much as possible concealed by the "Yahwist" editors of the scripture. (You would have to work pretty hard not to have a goddess in the Middle East in those days, says Patai: her manifestations were everywhere.) "There is plenty of extant evidence about the Hebrew Goddess from four sources," Patai continues:

> (1) The evidence of the Bible, which in spite of the efforts of its monotheistically oriented authors and/or editors, contains incidental information as to the court ritual and popular religion which a few judges and kings and all the prophets strove to suppress, eliminate and replace by monotheistic Yahwism.

> (2) Local archaeological evidence, admittedly limited, but nevertheless useful, and with the intensive work going on in Israel, daily increasing in volume and variety.

> (3) The considerably more ample data contained in Canaanite, Syrian, Mesopotamian, Iranian, Anatolian, and Egyptian archaeology and mythology, with their detailed information about the deities who, according to biblical evidence, were worshipped by the Hebrews.

> (4) Literary sources of post-Biblical Judaism which flow richly especially in the first few centuries of the Christian era; which, because of their less sacred character were not subjected to the same scrupulous scrutiny as the Holy Book; and in which, therefore, many references and recollections of early Hebrew polytheism were able to pass muster.[30]

The "graven images" against which the biblical revisionists inveigh are probably of the Canaanite Asherah, "Lady Asherah of the Sea," the seas being her favorite resort, and her son Baal, a male deity associated with the sun. (Comparable goddesses are the Sumerian Astarte and the Babylonian Ishtar or Inanna.) Often these images were made of wood, and the biblical texts record the frequent breaking, burning, and defiling of such images, even by trampling the ashes under foot, thus explaining the lack of evidence. (Even if not burned, such images do not last well enough for archaeologists to find.) Clay figurines, however, have survived in abundance and are familiar-seeming, reminding us of many Neolithic and Bronze Age "venuses," with hands on or beneath ample breasts, cylindrical pediment or matronly hips, and sometimes rays or bolts of energy from the head, also called "horns," showing divine status.

Edward Whitmont seems to agree with M. Esther Harding's point that the term *virgin*—when referring to primordial goddesses—means "self-possessed, belonging to no man," not the patriarchy-serving later meaning of sexual innocence. Inanna, for example, the Sumerian goddess, is both *hierodule* (sacred harlot) and *virgin*: "eternally youthful, dynamic, fierce and independent; embodying the playful, self-willed, never-domesticated aspect of the feminine."[31]

Clarissa Estes says of this figure:

> Wild Woman as an archetype is an inimitable and ineffable force which carries a bounty of ideas, images, and particularities for humankind. Archetype exists everywhere and yet is not seeable in the usual sense. What can be seen of it in the dark cannot necessarily be seen in daylight.[32]

What is this root-nourishing darkness of the depths of the feminine experience? Among other things, it does not wish to be routinely tamed and subjugated;

it is virginal in the archaic sense of "her own mystery." The archetypal feminine has been differentiated from biological femaleness; it brings to inner processes the important qualities of enclosing, gestation, patience, and nourishment.

Edward Whitmont's companion in the second half of his life was Dr. Sylvia Brinton Perera, who, in her work *Descent to the Goddess,* used the story of Inanna's descent to the underworld and her meeting with Ereshkigal as the primary and complete mythos of the mystery dimension of the feminine. In this mythos, one of the oldest coherent mythological tales we have, Inanna must descend to the underworld to rescue her lover Dumuzi and confront her dark sister, Ereshkigal. On the way, Inanna is stripped of all of her ornaments, her raiment, her beauty, everything, and finally subjected to the most cruel torture by Ereshkigal. It is an extraordinary inflection of the theme of the underworld journey of the hero/heroine, and the savior motif—Inanna lays down her life for her friend. It is not difficult to see why she was enormously loved and venerated throughout the ancient world.

By herself, Inanna is a little too solar, bright, and sunny. Sometimes a war goddess, like Athena, she also incorporates "masculine" elements. She is called "the heart of the battle," and the "arm of warriors." Jungian analyst Anne Belford Ulanov, writing with her husband Barry Ulanov, in *The Witch and the Clown,* examines this issue of "masculine" qualities in the feminine and in females, as well as "feminine" qualities in the masculine and in men.[33] Jung touched upon it with his suggestion of an "animus of the anima" and vice-versa; and Emma Jung has done an intensive examination in her *Animus and Anima.* Belford and Ulanov's treatment is the most subtle, complete, and useful we have found.

To simplify, the Ulanovs propose that the more assertive of the qualities traditionally ascribed to the masculine and the male psyche appear, properly, in the feminine and in the female psyche also, but differ proportionately as culture and biology affect each individual. The "witch" (the term is carefully distinguished in their use from the Wiccan context; it refers here to the archetypal figure appearing in folklore and dreams in potent and usually negative form) carries the feminine aspect of this dynamic; the "clown" incorporates the equivalent "feminine" qualities for the male. The witch is aggressive, ambitious, powerful, scheming, opportunistic: all qualities described in Machiavelli's *Prince* as appropriate for rulers and regarded in the modern business world as necessary for successful executives. The witch is *not* nurturing, does not have warm cuddly feelings for weaker creatures; in fact, she despises weakness. Her world is competitive and adversarial; she regards anyone who is not "hers" as an opponent, and she does not hesitate to take advantage of one who falters. These qualities are not endearing, but, to be honest, many men who occupy positions of dominance in their fields or societies operate by principles that require or predispose toward this sort of character. Many of these men are openly admired. But there are times when a woman also, for life's varying reasons, needs to be *not* nurturing, needs to be competitive, assertive, strong, ambitious, even combative or fierce. The Ulanovs propose that the energy and power of the witch is a *wild* resource, not to be easily appropriated in the service of the conscious agenda; still, it is a woman's resource. When a woman finds an effective way to bring it into her life, she can draw upon its formidable energies for creative rather than destructive ends. The solar goddesses, who tend also to have warrior aspects (Durga on her lion, Sekhmet as lady of the plague, Isis as witch-mistress of magic and poisons), incorporate this non-motherly witch aspect into their personae. Even gentle Bastet, Sekhmet's little moon-sister (who is said to have no witch aspect) is the warrior-cat who battles the terrible Apophis serpent. Without witch and warrior power, women would be as weak as patriarchal stereotyping pretends. Where then would be our mother-lion, when our children, our lovers, or our souls, need us to defend them?

But Inanna also precedes and embodies Aphrodite and, like her, is the goddess of the "morning and the evening star," the planet Venus. Whitmont writes of Inanna that "she extols the desires and delights of lovemaking, invites her lover, her 'honey-man' (her lover, Dumuzi). . . . She celebrates her body in song. Her receptivity is active."[34]

But what seemed to be required, if this myth were to speak of the feminine in a complete way, was that confrontation with the dark sister, she who negates all of those daylight world virtues—thus showing forth a different, more difficult aspect of the archetypal feminine. Perera writes in this regard of the descent to Ereshkigal:

> This necessity—for those destined to it—forces us to go deep to reclaim modes of consciousness which are different from the intellectual, "secondary process" levels the West has so well refined. It forces us to the affect-laden, magic dimension and archaic depths that are embodied, ecstatic, and transformative; these depths are preverbal, often pre-image, capable of taking us over and shaking us to the core.[35]

Here then, is the old woman who appeared in so many of the dreams cited in *The Mythic Imagination*. She is not only the neglected and despised feminine, asking for a "Return of the Goddess" in our time, but the very principle of feminine initiation itself: the importance of the "descent into darkness" into incarnation, fallibility, vulnerability. The despised, outcast and neglected principle is the initiatrix. Her wildness is the wildness of the instinctual source of life.

Whitmont writes:

> The feminine experiencing is thus given over to, or interconnected with, the process of growth and decay, the natural cycles of living, ripening and dying, and the rhythms and periods of nature, spirit and time. Thus, we designate it moon-attuned. Feminine consciousness experiences time as quality, not as an abstract measure of action. As a result, it is attuned to the mood, meaning, and favorable or unfavorable quality of the given moment. It is able—nay compelled—to wait more patiently than the male for the right moment in which an event or impulse may be given birth.[36]

Whitmont adds in a later paragraph: "We prefer not to look too closely at the awesomely dissolving and destructive, yet also dangerously attractive, abyss of the dark side of the goddess."

Ereshkigal's consort is the old horned god, Cernunnos, the Roman forest-god, who seems to turn into Satan through a strange transmogrification (the cloven-hoofed, antlered god of the old order becoming the devil of the new); he also appears as Dionysus and Pan, Shiva, of course, with his garlands of serpents and tiger-skin loincloth or throne-covering. Alain Danielou, the Indian specialist who has traced the East–West lineage of this god, in his book *Shiva and Dionysus*, says that the two figures are essentially one: it is the archaic lord of desire and death.[37] This god's province is madness, intoxication, violence, refraining from violence (as Shiva does when he meditates), ecstatic sex, and transformative trauma of all sorts, but especially the principle of rebirth through dismemberment and reconstitution (the shamanic journey).

Whitmont writes of her that "Ereshkigal rules over everything that seems opposed to life: death, nonbeing, annihilation, emptiness." She strips solar Inanna of everything that she values: all her graces, adornments, symbols of being someone. In our lives, she does the same thing, constellated as the opposite of all that is patriarchal (reason, progress, law and order); she is annihilation, the abyss, the black hole so vast it can swallow stars.

Whitmont connects Ereshkigal with the Medusa:

> With terrible face and tusks like a boar, head and body girdled with serpents, her sight makes the beholder lose his breath and on the spot turns him to stone. She is slain by Perseus, the solar hero, under the tutelage of Pallas Athena. Still later in the Grail cycle we encounter her as Kundrie the Grail messenger and the Ugly Dame or Goddess who is to be honored and given sovereignty again if the Grail is to be restored. In the Greek version (which is already patriarchal) her cut-off head is given over to Pallas Athena who wears it on her breast and on the *aigis* ("goatskin"), her shield, thus reminding us that the goat god Dionysus is associated to the underworld, indeed is Hades, death. Athena also was addressed as "Gorgon-faced" or "she who petrifies," a goddess of fierce battle as well as a protectress of arts and civilization.[38]

Medusa's story is worth telling. She was a beautiful, virginal priestess in the temple of Pallas Athena, goddess of all justice and righteousness, patroness of the city of Athens. Poseidon, god of the sea, brother of Zeus and Hades, had long lusted after Medusa. Finally, marshaling his divine powers of persuasion, he decided to come to her in a form she could not resist, as a radiant, vibrant stallion. The divine obsession was consummated. Medusa, virgin no more, now carried Poseidon's child.

When Athena learned what had occurred, her fury knew no bounds—and her sense of proportion and fairness withered accordingly. She transformed Medusa into the monstrous form for which she is best known, with baleful features, living serpent locks, and deadly stare. Where else could Medusa go, but to a remote cave, to dwell in misery and disgrace with the other, immortal gorgons who were now her sisters?

Thus the scene that solar hero Perseus stumbled in upon; using the technique of indirect gaze—through his shield—he decapitated poor Medusa.[39] At that moment, several things happened: Poseidon and Medusa's child, the beautiful winged horse Pegasus, sprang forth and soared into the air; and Medusa spurted forth two fluids from her severed neck. One fluid would bring life—a cure for many deathly ills; the other would bring death, but with a sweet peacefulness. We know that Athena is said to have mounted the countenance of Medusa on her shield or escutcheon, a baleful aspect of the goddess of reason and proportion.

Medusa, loyal priestess who sought only to serve the goddess, was the victim of (divine) sexual abuse. Like the figure of Job in the Old Testament, the vicissitudes that were visited upon her were no fault of her own, but the outcome of a conflict between powers greater than herself. This tells us something about the creation of a monster: take something innocent and beautiful and subject it to irreconcilable demands—Gregory Bateson's "double-bind," where you are "damned if you do and damned of you don't"—and sooner or later you evoke Medusa's mask, with its paralyzing pain and hatred. (According to the stress-diathesis theory of schizophrenia, it is the impact of such double-binds on an intrinsically flawed psyche that produces the full-blown psychosis.)

In one of the early experiential mask workshops that we held, a woman felt intuitively drawn to make the mask of Medusa. Magically, it worked to help her "face" (the mask of) her rage, and release it; and then to heal (those two fluids). Then we told her the mythic story, about the winged horse, the redeeming symbol for the decapitated, thrice-wronged gorgon. Every woman in the room lit up at the myth of the winged horse.

Whitmont says of processes like this in which the dark element is confronted and honored, "Brought into the daylight of consciousness through strife and conflict, the forces of the abyss can become elements of creativity." He points out that Eris, discord, is not far from Eros, love; and that discord and the working out of conflicts is just as important to relatedness as attraction, union, and harmony. All relationships have conflict, because neither individual can completely subjugate the wildness in the self to another's program—it needs to be honored, expressed, and integrated in and of itself. Thus, the working through of conflict can take us deep within (Inanna's descent), but yield enormous value (the riches of the underworld, buried treasure, Pluto's wealth).

Our hope is that, at this point in the chapter, we have paved the way for the following discussion of wildness and taming, as they operate between men and women, in our own lives and the lives of the people around us. Ultimately, we feel there are, embedded in this material, messages for how to undertake relationships in the new millennium.

STEPHEN AND ROBIN IN DIALOGUE

Robin: There is a feminine wild and a masculine wild, and both need to be honored. In a really supportive relationship between a man and a woman, each needs to support not only the part of the other that *relates*, that is present and human and loving, but the parts that are wild and contrary.

Stephen: That could be difficult.

Robin: But indispensable. That doesn't mean that we need to inflict our wild contrariness on each other all the time and make excuses for not relating. But those weedy parts of the garden have to exist, and so we need to develop (each couple in their own way) a way of working with those untamed parts in ourselves and with our partner, and to allow the creative energy to bubble out of those wild places into the relationship or into the private creative work of each partner, supported by the other.

Stephen: I can see where there would be one version of this for the new couple and another for the seasoned one. Doesn't wildness have a kind of timetable? Sometimes it's there right in the beginning, you can see it all over the person. But sometimes it erupts later on in life in the most unlikely people—*Lady Chatterley's Lover*, where the respectable woman finds *Eros* with the gardener.

Robin: Speaking as a woman, I think one of the difficult places for the woman is in these situations where the man says, "Well, honey, you stay home and take care of the kids, but I'm the man and I need time to roam in my life." And off he goes, while she's supposed loyally to await his return, in the tameness of the kitchen.

There's already a culturally encoded image of the man as the one who has the wildness, and the woman can't pin him down. But the other side of this is that, when a woman gives herself to a man and has his child, in fact, he *has* captured and pinned her down. Yet she has her own wildness, her own wanting to ramble. And society (supported by biology) puts a lot more onus on a woman to stay put. It's very *bad* if she disappears, and leaves the children with the man—or her mother. If a man does it, he's irresponsible—but in a manly sort of way; but if a woman does it, she's not being womanly, she's a bad mother, a very serious thing. A woman, by nature, should be a good mother. A man by virtue of culture and responsibility and decency *becomes* a good father, but not necessarily by nature. This, of course, is one of those knotty issues the visionary leaders of the men's movement—like Keen, Bly, and Meade—are addressing.

Stephen: You remember, in Portugal, how much prickliness there is among traditional Portuguese women over the freewheeling, insouciant American women. They are seen as a wild and dangerous life form. "In our society we don't tolerate women acting like that!" Portugal is a "high-context" society, so the rules are really enforced. I remember from graduate school, an anthropology course: a man in a rural Spanish town who was married and with a family, began living with a woman with a reputation for "loose morals." (Now infidelity and fooling around was expected, but this was flagrant, immoral *living together*.) The people of the town, mostly women, went out night after night and beat pots and screamed insults, so the peace and privacy of the couple was destroyed, and any romantic atmosphere certainly quelled. The couple tried various ways of coping, but eventually the community succeeded in destroying this little foray into wildness—their relationship. It's much easier to explore wildness of this kind in "low-context" societies like ours where (for the most part) neighbors may not even know or care what's going on in the next house. But even in our own circles of fairly liberal friends, I can remember gossip and eyebrows being raised about people who were thought to be really dangerous to relationships.

Robin: Well, you remember Afghanistan in the late 1970s: if I hadn't been with my husband, I couldn't have been there at all. Even though I dressed very demurely, there was still an attitude toward Western women. If you're alone, you're either a whore or fair prey; a man can carry you off as a slave or put you in a harem.

Teachers, people who work with children, know that little boys tend (I stress *tend*) to act out more roughly and wildly than little girls do. Little girls are more concerned about pleasing and doing things "right." There is more peer pressure within the girls' community to behave in a socially acceptable way, a way socially acceptable to adults. I think that here we have an issue that has to do with fragility.

We need to differentiate *wildness* from *out-of-controlness*. I think that losing control may be one of its manifestations, but they're not the same thing. At its most profound level, wildness is related to the inner journey, the journey into darkness, that night sea journey that is necessary for a human being to become individuated and creative, and to have a strong and deep way of living life. In this sense, there is as much wildness in little girls as there is in little boys. And they, as adults, will need to go down repeatedly into their own darkness, suffer, and transform—but their relationship to their wildness seems more fragile. I don't know whether that is a function of nature, their need to grow up to be nurturing mothers, or whether this is simply a cultural issue. Nevertheless their wildness is, at least at this stage, more easily stamped out, driven underground; and so the nurturing of wildness in little girls becomes psychologically very important.

One of the symbolic themes I've been researching is this one of "the secret garden." You know the story, it has been well rendered in a popular novel: in a big old Victorian manor in England a boy and girl find a secret garden—and each other—and a fantasy life together in which they build worlds. There are many variations, and the theme occurs throughout European literature in more adult and metaphysical permutations. In the East, this theme of the secret garden appears in tantric imagery as the *manipura*, the "jewelled isle" or "city" or "walled garden" at the heart of the mandala.[40]

Stephen: Having just been to the Alhambra, I find that the theme takes on historical and visual dimensions: a sheltered courtyard, protected from the outside world, where a piece of nature is enclosed. It's nice if it's as real as possible, a brook running through it, a fountain, some orange trees and honeysuckle, beauty all around—" and thou," on a marble bench. It is a protected island in a chancy world.

Robin: The garden is not an image of wildness, but of nature, vegetal nature, and also animal nature, if unicorns come there or if there are birds or exotic creatures in cages. There is the sense of a protected place, protected by walls, away from other people's interference, where the child is safe, but still in nature. I think that image is a key to the psyche of a little girl.

When I was a little girl (five or six years old), one Sunday—after my family went off to church without me because I refused to get dressed up—I ran out into the yard to scamper about barefooted and be a wild thing. There was the next-door neighbor's yard, filled with the most luxurious, beautiful tall grass that I had longed to explore. I slipped into the tall grass. Not only did I know that I had escaped from Sunday school and being a little lady, but I was now violating the admonition not to trespass onto my neighbor's property. There I was, standing up to my knees, or maybe even my waist, in this beautiful grass. I looked up at the sky and thought about the very angry God up there who must be thinking that I was extremely sinful and wild and bad, and I had a kind of realization: if that were the nature of God, and if God didn't approve of me being barefooted in this wonderful luscious grass and running about, but wanted me to sit in a pink pinafore and patent leather shoes in Sunday school, then I was not one of God's good sheep and would never be. I would always keep my wildness. That was my decision.

Stephen: Wildness is where the energy and spontaneity is. We dip into it to find our life, to find our energy; and indeed that is where it often is to be found. If, on the other hand, we try to rely totally on wildness and have no balancing functions, pretty soon our lower nature takes over and a desultory self-gratifying lifestyle ensues. Then the wildness is in the beer can and on television.

Robin: In relating to inner wildness, it is important to remember that this is not a license for being undisciplined. In the work with dream and creative self, the wild inner self is not to be ignored or stamped out, but discipline and the tools of discipline are very important in working with it. Marian Woodman shows us ways of doing this.

Stephen: I might have been around the same age as your story about the escape from Sunday school, maybe third grade, when my cousin Peter and I had one of our first big adventures. It was totally mad and quite dangerous, in retrospect, I suppose.

The newspapers had been full of the news of a "maniac" who had escaped from Creedmoor (an institution for the criminally insane) and now was at large in the swamps near College Point (Queens, Long Island). Perhaps we had read too many adventure novels about kids doing amazing exploits; but when we missed the school bus that day, our plan was to explore the swamp and help find this maniac.

The maniac had been described in the paper: he was hunchbacked, red-faced with thick glasses, and balding. He was reputed to have a large knife, and to kill (and eat?) cats. The day was a little overcast, and our hearts were thumping as we walked along the road that went right through the center of the swamp. I remember how every sight and sound became more intense. Then came the heart-stopping event, still clear fifty years later: there, in a little clearing off the dirt track, was a man: stocky, balding, red-faced, and stooped, almost hunchbacked. He had thick glasses; in one hand, he held a large knife and in the other something indescribable—red and grisly. He stared at us, we at him, frozen for about three heartbeats; then we broke all kinds of personal records for a breathtaking sprint, encumbered by our bookbags, back the same way we had come, maybe a half-mile away.

What we had seen was real enough, and we went over the details again and again to make sure we had seen the same thing. But I think what was important for me was the adrenaline-producing quality of the adventure. Peter and I talked about it endlessly, and it, among other experiences, occasioned some of our first mythologizing (written about in *The Mythic Imagination*). I think for me mythologizing was the early exercise of wild mind; it kept me from being paralyzed by public education and churchly propriety. The maniac would be a wild man, living like an animal, and insane as well, so, wild in that sense also. I guess I had a hankering for the wild man before I ever read Robert Bly.

The mythologies that appealed to us boys in those days were of the jungle, the forest, and surviving in a wilderness environment. Cub and boy scouts also emphasized this—wilderness skills so that you could survive in the woods.

Robin: When I became a teen, we lived on the edge of an industrial town, but there were woods nearby. On Saturday morning, I'd get on my horse and ride out to find the other kids, looking for tracks in the dust; and then I'd find tracks that were fresh and follow them. And between my horse sniffing them and me following the signs, I'd catch up with the other young riders. It was a tracking game we'd play through fields and forests. We'd track and find each other, then have a great chase at the last. I learned you could go along at a trot and read the signs. Learning to track, to recognize each friend's horse by their hoofprints, to follow them through changing terrain—this was very magical and exciting.

Stephen: There's a great resurgence of interest in this subject through the work of Tom Brown, Jr. (*The Tracker*). After I read the book, I turned [our son] Merlin, a teenager at the time, on to it, and we began to do some tracking. We loved especially to go out on the farm after a new fallen snow. One winter's morning we were skiing through the back pasture, just under the two-hundred-foot rocky slabs: there were four great odd-looking prints in the snow, bigger than any dog's I had ever seen. There was another set, fifteen feet away, but facing in a slightly different direction. As we reconstructed the events that must have produced such tracks, an amazing scene came into mind—later we were to verify the tracks as those of a mountain lion—of a great cat, gamboling, romping joyfully in the new snow. We tracked it up the steep rocky slabs and into a tumbled grotto of boulders and ice almost impassable in winter, but which had shown other evidence of being a lion's den—the accumulated bones of some fairly large animals—but decided not to go any further. I think tracking something wild is good for the soul. For teenagers, it rises up to meet their own wildness, and there is a match; when young faculties are engaged in reading the book of nature, even youth who have been "at risk" in society seem less so.

To shift our focus a bit, I want to turn to issues of gender and wildness as they affect a young couple, or a partnership to be. I'm going to tell a story that is brutally shocking in its reality; but we need to look at it in this context of power, wildness and relationship. A young woman whom we shall call Wendy was beautiful, talented academically and artistically (music and dance), was socially popular, and on her way to a good college. One balmy evening she accepted a car ride with a charismatic, wildly likeable, but not-so-aware young man whom we shall call Wayne.

Wayne, with a little cocaine and a lot of alcohol in his veins—he was kind of excitable and impulsive anyway—decided to ride the twisty country road at ninety miles per hour, jumping his parents' car off the bumps—called "getting air" just like in skiing—only here with two tons of flying metal. The almost predictable (for most adults) outcome was that the car left the road for good and encountered a large tree. Wendy was killed instantly, Wayne, still drunk and unharmed, got out of the car and wove off down the road, seemingly oblivious to the seriousness of what had happened, until he was apprehended. He was tried and convicted of manslaughter, and sentenced to three years in the state prison—Wendy's parents thought the sentence far too lenient.

Robin: The subtle coding when I was growing up was that we were simply told the boys won't like you if you didn't go along with them. Those of us who were naturally self-directed were having it undermined. My mother was giving me this message, even as she was warning me to be careful—and I think it was there, everywhere, in our environment. When we look at our schools and all the people who help to teach young people now, we have to be very careful about the messages that are being given them; so we don't mindlessly carry this thing on. There is probably something biological here, where the woman is nurturing, and the man protective—hence, possessive. But we need to understand what's going on, not just let it rule us in a destructive way and continue the mindless transmission. Wendy was probably just trying to please Wayne, trying to be acceptable to him.

We have to tell young girls this: it's okay to be strong and assert yourself, especially where the male is off-base. "Hey! you shouldn't be driving! Sorry; don't anybody get in that car with him!" Wouldn't it be wonderful if teenaged girls could say these things to boys? "Wayne, go run around in the woods till your wild attack wears off; then maybe you can drive a car. Go to a Robert Bly workshop! Get a drum!" And we need to support boys and educate them about the other gender, so when they become young men, they aren't frightened or angered by an assertive young woman who speaks the truth to them. There are too many stories like this one.

Stephen: This case became paradigmatic for the entire community around here, and many of us found our consciousness raised. We and other parents began to brief our daughters and the daughters of friends not to be persuaded by intoxicated young men, no matter how charismatic or "cool," and to stand their ground, to choose designated drivers. The empowerment begins here. With subtle or crude power plays where young men are trying to get young women to go along with a program they have in mind and being coercive or manipulative with them, the young women have to be able to say, "Stop! I don't think this is good for either of us." And young men have to have a place in them where they realize that it does not demean or diminish them to swallow hard, and say, "All right, you're right."

Robin: Amen! Maybe the media and the arts can show subtle or interactive situations between the genders where the truth can be told: women really prefer men who honor a woman's sovereignty. Or where each partner has his or her strong position, but they are able to really know and understand each other through their process of conflict and resolution. We need to raise young people who will *prefer* strength and self-awareness in their partners, regardless of gender.

Stephen: It seems that the real strength is being able to stand your ground, know what you really need, and say so. Both partners need "to be on the same page" and have some idea this is okay, and even that it is a sign of real courage and growth not to be unilateral; and that hysteria or bullying or verbally or physically abusive reaction is actually a sign of terror or weakness.

Robin: There is a weakness that really disables or discomforts the woman when she has something that needs to be paid attention to, but she is afraid she'll be seen as resisting or not cooperating.

Stephen: In this regard, a proactive approach toward relating is going to be the most productive for the new millennium. Young couples should experiment, in a variety of ways, with decision making, building trust, and coping in situations where it is really hard to find common ground. I think of a couple that was in so much trouble until I explained to them the simple rules of "fair-fighting." If couples know how to work through those conflicts that rise up from *Eris* (Discord) also as a part of relating, they will then have a tool that can help them provide a nucleus of psychological as well as physical security.

Robin: Things get acrimonious because there is an unequal balance of power invoked again and again. Over and over, one partner, influenced by the other, does something he or she doesn't feel like doing; if it tends too much to be the same partner, this is not all right. And then the consequences have to be faced. And the consequences may be very negative; bitterness and resentment accumulate, and we have trouble. We may have violence, if the male is in the position of being the dominant, decisive one, and "decisive" degenerates into "coercive"—particularly if he doesn't feel really sufficiently self-empowered, and the domination becomes chronic.

Stephen: Then it becomes a problem that could drive the couple apart. On the other hand, if there has been sufficient strength and balance exerted by both partners all the way along the line—a self-rectifying principle sort of like biofeedback— you're never going to get so far out of balance that those toxic guilty and blaming energies become salient.

Robin: When people first start out as a couple, they need to develop some tools to balance and to acknowledge each other, because we carry so much baggage from the way we were raised. If we develop some working tools early on with young couples, they can move, with the aid of those tools, toward a more organic relationship, a mutually supportive one.

Stephen: There is a procedure used by Roman Catholics that seems quite wise. I think they call it a "pre-Cana." It has some elements of a real proactive approach to the kinds of problems that a couple might encounter on the road of life together. (The only problem is that the classes are usually led by a celibate priest. In my book, it would be far better to have an older couple minister in this way to a younger.) Maybe there should also be the psychospiritual equivalent of the "prenuptial agreement," which is usually economic in nature, where the couple says mutually, "Okay, these are the conditions under which we're getting together, our social contract. Let's get it down at the outset, to avoid those projections and delusions we all seem to get about each other. This is who I am and who you are, and we agree to go on together in the following way." To be sure, the arrangement ought to be able to be changed along the way, within creative parameters, as the couple changes, matures and grows. Here is where a skillful marriage counselor or psychotherapeutic contact could be very useful.

Robin: I think it is important to look at this dynamic between men and women which is specifically culturally supported, in which the male is empowered to push and the woman is trained—although many resist this stridently and ineffectually— to submit. This becomes destructive right away with those early teenage relationships; that's where the pattern gets "ironed in" to permanence. Teenage boys push, and the girls don't know how to say no. This includes those horrible car accidents and, of course, sex.

Right in the beginning, in the teenage years, we can learn a dysfunctional style that will, with many couples, turn a meeting place of joy into a battleground. At this sensitive age, girls are often subjected to a lot of shame and guilt because girls are raised to be "good." They want to be good and to be loved, and when they yield to the boys, they are "bad." When the boys succeed in persuading a girl to have sex, they get a double message: "You shouldn't have done this—but now you're a man." That is, the accomplishment makes him a man. What does the girl get? Certainly she doesn't gain any social esteem. She may get a reputation for being "bad," and she may get pregnant.

Working with these deeply ingrained differences is never simple; but we have some very helpful insights and tools available, as more thoughtful and caring people conduct serious and well-designed studies of how men and women, adults and children, communicate and relate or fail to relate. There are three very important books in this regard. Indeed, I think they could be considered "required reading" for all of us who are trying to live together so that our families really work: Alice Miller's *For Your Own Good*, Patricia Evans' *The Verbally Abusive Relationship*, and Deborah Tannen's *You Just Don't Understand*.[41] All propose workable guidelines for relationship, and they all are talking in very related ways, offering perspectives and tools that can be of help to men and women in all kinds of troubled situations, and to those who work to protect children. All three authors are saying that, in the context of our culture, support for the use of strength to govern a relationship puts the man in the dominant position. He may not be a native abuser, but, with the best of intentions, we lack models for egalitarian partnerships. What we are looking for are ways of developing new awareness, honing our sensibilities, nurturing compassion—for both men and women—changing the cultural environment to one which will make for healthier couples.

Stephen: It becomes obvious that solving—or at least seriously addressing—the political, and that means power, issues at an early stage in a relationship predicts very well for a relationship or can support that relationship so that those more primitive dimensions don't come back and ruin things later on. We could say that this is the platform, or the groundwork, so even if a couple, particularly a young couple, don't know each other that well, they can arrive at a number of techniques, say, fair-fighting techniques.

I have a young couple in marital counseling right now, where these techniques are proving very helpful. With one middle-aged couple I worked with a few years ago, fair-fighting techniques saved the marriage. After three sessions, and then trying the techniques out in their daily lives, they said, "We're cured! We're both abiding by those suggestions and techniques; we've really made them part of our daily lives." In their previous model, it was not just the fights, but the resentments from wounds suffered by each in the ruthless free-for-alls they had. It was as if each came out of his or her respective corner punching below the belt, and that was the generic style they had been exposed to in their families of origin. They had never really examined that. Now, with a business and a complex family life together, there were plenty of opportunities for disagreements.

I first took the approach, "You have to be able to *have* these conflicts, to disagree; it's human." Then we looked at how each partner is a carrier, like it or not, of those family values, possibly extending back generations. If the person who is the carrier of the major familial problem can see that, and it can be witnessed by both therapist and partner in a nonjudgmental and supportive way, you pave the way for actual change. Then they can be taught ways to disagree without wounding the soul of the other person.

Robin: This underlines the idea that, if the two people are essentially healthy but operating with the wrong tools, then they have a chance to make a change, provided they have these correct tools. Even where there are deeper problems, the tools can help. Just living in a culture where it is no longer seen as virtuous to beat your child gives us a chance to separate out those people who do it for really sick reasons. Maybe better tools could help them, too. But I think our whole culture needs help in this regard.

We'll wrap this discussion up with the topic of how we bring our wild animas and animuses to a relationship, not "taming" them so much as persuading them, respectfully, in a sense, to be more or less attached to this particular person, this particular limited being. Can we do this?

Each of us offers our wildness up, if you will, on the altar of the relationship, and that's an amazing and important thing: that two people, from love, should want to give each other such a gift. Going back to what we were saying earlier, if that's too easily done by a woman, she loses the most precious thing too easily—not because she does it as a voluntary mature choice, but because society expects it: And that's not right for anyone, woman or man. Nor will such a premature sacrifice make for a vital, healthy relationship. Sacrifice is a powerful act, to be done out of self-awareness and a place of power. Otherwise, there is no truth in it.

But perhaps it is more viable to think of this process as one in which each partner simultaneously is working on her and his inner soul-making. We need to remember that we have to grow both ways at once: from the outside in, teaching the skills of socialization and relationship to the wild thing inside us; introducing this outside other person we have chosen as our mate to the tribe of ancestors and totem animals who live in our psychic forest. But also growing from the inside out, paying careful attention to the messages from our inner world as they come to us in dreams and other intuitive ways; learning to be honest with ourselves about the communications rising up from deep within that may not fit so easily into our day-world expectations. If we cannot learn techniques for looking within honestly, we will get unpleasant surprises, perhaps many years into our marriage. This is part of the life-long work of integration, to which we all are called. However the individual partners respond—whether partially, whole-heartedly, tardily, or negatively—so will their relationship flourish or fail. Every couple goes through some version of this mating of their inner lives, sooner or later; if not, all hell breaks loose in the second half of life, and respectable congressmen go scampering off with young Playboy bunnies, or dutiful wives leave home with cowboys or gurus.

Stephen: When we were first married, I think my anima was pretty woozy, first with repression, then stereotyped images from popular culture, then too much freedom and a consequent anxiety. Was it mature enough for me to really be in a committed relationship?

In my case, it was a dream that helped me out. We had been married about five or six years. But now you were, or had just been, pregnant; and that changed everything. What I thought of as my private preserve had now been entered by another being that took priority—Merlin, our unborn child. I found myself looking at other women again and being attracted. A friend of ours was regularly going to orgies and had invited us (we didn't go, but I sure thought about it).

Then came the dream: in the dream, I was at an orgy. It was sort of like being in Hugh Hefner's mansion: luxurious accoutrements on every side, all these beautiful naked women around. Some were already playing around with partners, and there were men and women doing the most amazing things in combinations, and all that kind of thing. It was amazing scenery, diagram out of the *Satyricon* or something, but I was just sort of disconsolately wandering around looking for you, looking for Robin, in the dream. I had a kind of lonely heartache, of missing and wanting to find Robin. That was it, pretty much. Simple, eh?

When I explored my own associations to "Robin," I found myself thinking of the friendship with you, the warmth, the companionship; effortlessly, I knew they were what I wanted. The sexual part was there too, but was meaningless without those other things that my personal mate, "Robin," meant.

I believe that one dream alone probably did what years of conventionally oriented advice in therapy by a therapist who simply advises you, might have done. It wrought an amazing emotional and psychological change with me; and I will say that it has been easy to be faithful for the almost thirty years since then, because the dream helped me to see that yes, you could sample "the garden of fleshly delights," and achieve many transient pleasures and ecstasies—that option is open to you—but here is what your heart chooses, this personal relationship. I choose you! In the "Chakra" system, this is movement to chakra four (spiritual compassion and empathy), rather than chakra two (lust). It also speaks of the personal, the "thou." I was looking for a specific person, with whom I wanted, on the heart level, to work it out; not a collective (Hugh Hefner's mansion).

Robin: I'm remembering that, maybe even a little earlier in our relationship, I had a series of dreams about Dionysus. What I remember right now is one in which he appeared to me in a hotel, where there was a party going on. What I remember most vividly, in that dream and in several others, is what he looked like—one particular Hellenistic sculpture of Dionysus as an extremely beautiful young man.

One of the dreams was in a cabin deep in the woods. In that dream, Dionysus had curly black hair down to his shoulders; and I think he might have had on a headband. He had clear luminous skin, he was slender and graceful, he had a very sweet sensuous mouth, and the most piercing, wild, exciting and dangerous eyes I think I have ever seen, utterly wild eyes. At that moment, looking into those eyes, what I knew was: this is not just a sexy young man. This is a god.

Now, recalling this, I am struck by something I never thought of before: the other time in my life when I had that same knowledge was when I was just a little kid, and I saw the Divine in the eyes of a horse, the eyes of a mare. In fact, now that I think of it, there was that same quality of depth and endlessness, infinity, darkness. The other qualities were not the same; it was a different divinity, a different energy, a different power. But there was a sameness to it: *this is a god!*

Stephen: I remember feeling kind of shivery when you first told me some of those dreams. I had to realize I had competition; there was a god visiting you. Just telling each other our dreams made a big difference. We didn't always have a neat interpretation, but the dreams gave us a handle on some of the powers that were working through us; something happened that aided the process of maturation.

Robin: It is down there, in the dream depths, that the root growth takes place. The juicy sap has to rise up from there, to nourish this living organism we are growing together—this partnership, this friendship, this love affair, this marriage.

From *The Story of King Arthur and His Knights*
by Howard Pyle

CHAPTER EIGHT

THE MAKING OF THE WASTELAND

Where are the roots that clutch, what branches grow
Out of this stony rubbish? Son of man,
You cannot say, or guess, for you know only
A heap of broken images, where the sun beats,
And the dead tree gives no shelter, the cricket no relief,
And the dry stone no sound of water. Only
There is shadow under this red rock
(Come in under the shadow of this red rock),
And I will show you something different from either
Your shadow at morning striding behind you
Or your shadow at evening rising to meet you;
I will show you fear in a handful of dust.

T.S. Eliot, *The Waste Land*[1]

─────────── ROMANCING THE CHAKRAS ───────────

OUR GOAL IN THIS CHAPTER IS TO EXPLORE the troubled relationship between love and power, as it has emerged historically over the last two millennia. Love and power seem to be antithetical and yet to cohabit with the slight tang of old bedfellows, fighting and loving their way through a million relationships. Like Mars and Venus, they are attractive opposites and yet carry a flavor of the illicit, the opportunistic, the role of domination, and the discordant notes of abuse and subjugation. Why do we fight with those we love? How does love arise even in the midst of power struggles?

To understand their truly complex relationship, we turn first to the Indian *Kundalini* yoga system, first clearly articulated in Tantric texts of about the seventh or eighth centuries. In these, a cogent, powerful map of psychological stages of development is drawn. *Chakras*, or "wheels," centers of psychic energy, are laid out along the human spine, from the "root-base" to the crown of the head. Progress up the chakras represents psychological and spiritual evolution, one center, being successfully grappled with, opening to work on the next. All interact with, feed, and support the others in a living network; and there are both potential harmonies and conflicts between each of them. It is true that love and power are both pivotal human issues, and indeed their chakras occupy center stage in the yogic seven-chakra model.

Joseph Campbell worked with this system extensively and believed it represented one of the most complete extant models for psychospiritual development. Other systems of thought, such as Sufism and Native American shamanism, have similar models of "centers" along the spine. If the system seems unfamiliar or complex to you, follow us as best you can, in the simplified tour we conduct; if on the other hand, the system is familiar to you, bear with us while we explain the chakras and watch how exquisitely chakra theory can be brought to bear on the topic of relationship and spiritual practice. In fact, the theory seems indispensable to understanding both love's shadow and its fulfillment.

Movement through the chakras from the base of the spine toward the top of the head represents psychological and spiritual evolution. We come from humble beginnings—the "reptile brain," sheer instinct, the need to hang on to life at all costs. *Muladhara*, then, the "root-base" at the perineum has a primordial dragon energy; its psychological quality is "holding on" and security. The kundalini serpent, the life force itself, sleeps here while we are alive, coiled around a lingam or phallus. Ordinarily, it will only arise and uncoil at our death—climbing the spine like a ladder and exiting through the "aperture of Brahman" at the top of the head. (The exception to this is when the kundalini is awakened through esoteric practices or experiences a spontaneous "awakening." But the texts offer caution here—you may achieve madness instead of enlightenment if you awaken her prematurely!)

Svadisthana, "her favorite resort," is located behind the genitals. The "her" whose "resort" is this chakra is the *shakti*, the kundalini, the life force itself. Her mood is erotic play, and her psychology is Freudian dynamics (in Freud's words, she is "polymorphously perverse," wanting sexual and erotic contact of whatever level, in whatever way). The mythological figures here are Aphrodite/Venus, and Eros (Kama, male god of love in Hindu mythology). Visualize the pink and plump little naked *putti* of Renaissance painting, aiming their arrows; visualize harems, the orgies of the *Satyricon*, even Hugh Hefner's Playboy Mansion. All is made of sensuous surfaces and drowned in love, allure, dalliance, pleasure.

The third chakra, *Manipura*, "city of jewels," the solar plexus, carries aggressive and assertive energy, and its psychological quality is "Adlerian"—the will to power. Here are "ego trips," collisions of will; here are conflict and warfare. The mythological figure is Ares/Mars, or warlike Sekhmet or Bellona of the Romans on the female side. Dominance hierarchies rule the world when this chakra is activated. Darwin's "survival of the fittest," the "ruling class," "put-downs" and "one-ups" hold sway.

The first three chakras then—security, sex, and power—are the forces that make the world go round. Three-quarters of worldly transactions have something to do with these three, they are what make the news. Think about it: stocks and bonds, "securities," property (chakra one). Love affairs and their vicissitudes, love assayed, love requited, love's labors lost (chakra two). Power—personal, political, economic—and the use of violence to secure it (chakra three). Violence in the service of security, as in "We have to protect our national security" (three acting in the interests of one). Violence in the service of love—lovers' quarrels, domestic violence, violent sex (two and three all mixed up with each other). In this third chakra, we find not relationship, but domination/subjugation patterns of sexuality: bondage, dominatrixes, or masters; and unthinking male domination of women, simply because men are in positions of power. (This confusion is, in fact, the central one with which we are concerned in the making of the Wasteland.)

But a strange and subtle shift, perhaps similar to the one that appears in the musical octave (do-re-mi—then a half-step—fa), that leap from the third to the fourth, takes place here—and changes everything. (In some Tantric diagrams, a smallish chakra, corresponding to the pericardium, is shown between three and four.) It is at this point that spiritual energy first enters the psychic system of the being. Now we have not just the needs of *I*, but the needs of *thou*, as well.

The fourth chakra, *Anahata*, is the compassionate heart, located on the spine just behind the physical heart. Think of images of Christ as the Sacred Heart, with his heart open and visible, sometimes shining forth like the sun. Contemplate likewise the compassionate bodhisattvas, who will not enter the Blessed Realm until all sentient beings are saved. This is a vastly different energy from that of chakra three, and, in some ways, represents its redemption. (Christ blesses the very soldiers who laugh and bang in the nails.) Its psychology is transpersonal or Jungian, and it represents the beginning of the spiritual path.

Vishuddha, in the throat, the fifth chakra, rules sacred song and praise, also language. When the heart is full of joy, song breaks forth in *kirtan*, holy songs, and hymns of praise. Poetry and its divine meaning and bestowing fire are also located here, as is all oratory, charisma, and verbal persuasion. Five is the chakra of communication; the classical deity Hermes or Mercury appears here, as also in chakra six. In five, dialogue unfolds; in effect, it is an inflection of two: love in the form of exchange.

Ajna, the "third eye," at chakra six, rules mentation, clairvoyance, and spiritual wisdom. Its capacity is both visionary "seeing" and cognitive discernment and clarity. The awakening of the Ajna chakra confers the ability to see past and future and things that are hidden from others. It is the seat of the imagination, and of creative insight.

Brahmchakra, at the top of the head, chakra seven, also known as *Sahasrara*, the "thousand-petal lotus," is the portal to divine consciousness, the place where, in esoteric lore, the soul enters the body at the beginning of incarnation, and from which it leaves at death. When the kundalini has climbed through the chakras, without defilement or opposition, to the Brahmchakra, then *samadhi*, enlightenment, is the result. The mind beholding the universe, and the universe itself are filled with radiance. *Atman*, the soul, and *Brahman*, God, are united.

Each chakra, when activated, configures the psychology, the motivation, the perception, even the mythology, of the person with its unique imprint. The human being is thus an overlap, as Abraham Maslow said, of needs for security, affiliation, self-assertion and esteem, love and belonging, and creativity.[2] (Moreover, at the end of his life, and with Anthony Sutich, Maslow opened to recognizing the transcendent needs, thus initiating Transpersonal Psychology—chakras four through seven.) While Behaviorism (chakra one), Psychoanalysis (chakra two), and the Adlerian vicissitudes of the ego in dominance hierarchies and power trips (chakra three) have characterized much of Western psychology in the twentieth century, it is entirely possible that the psychology of the twenty-first, and the new millennium, will be concerned with those top four chakras (we surely hope so). This would be a transpersonal psychology of the soul in evolution, prefigured by Swedenborg's visionary insights and consolidated by the late-twentieth-century depth psychology of soul: Jung, Hillman, Estes, Woodman, Belford Ulanov.

But, the Tantric texts caution: do not be too quick to accomplish the journey. We all see in ourselves and in our neighbors, problems with security, sex, and power. These can occupy us for most of a lifetime—or if the Hindus are correct, many lifetimes. And we even see higher chakra energy bent into twisted form by the lower: compassion subverted into mindless sentimentality, poetry collapsing into charismatic political rhetoric, and the mind's amazing powers run amok with power trips, politics and bureaucracy. Sometimes chakras become tyrannous, dictating the "ruling love" and deforming the world into a caricature of a royal palace, bordello, or an armed fortress. But, balanced and harmonized, chakra energy can make the world a beautiful, perpetually flowering garden of souls with whom to play, work, and delight together.

Next-door neighbors can either cooperate and form friendships, becoming very close—or alternatively get into horrible conflicts. After all, that's who's there. So sex and power, Venus and Mars, chakras two and three, are often tangled up with each other. For better or for worse, lovers fight and struggle for dominance; power issues creep into every relationship; hierarchies intrude, even where we would wish them not to. On the dark side, we have sadism, people who can't get sexually aroused or even merely engaged with life, unless there is some kind of abuse, dominance, or torture present; and masochism, people who require such abuse to be done to themselves to become aroused or feel alive.

Historically, much rape has taken place on battlefields or in wars, as conquerors have their way with the hapless bereaved women, when the men defending them have been killed. These latter produce some of the darkest problems between the genders imaginable; and we have associates who bravely have undertaken the task of counseling and working with the Bosnian and Albanian women, pregnant after being raped by Serb soldiers. (How do you reconcile the emotions of motherhood with the presence of the child of your enemy in your body, and then as a helpless infant?)

The history of relations between Mars and Venus, Ares and Aphrodite, Marduk and Tiamat, Set and Isis has left permanent scars in the relationship between the genders. But is this not also the rift that Banu Kiranmireva and Moromudzi sought to heal in the Zulu myth, as discussed in chapter 1? And we ourselves are looking for mythologies to help heal the wound left by the outdated and unequal mythologies—particularly the hegemony of a patriarchal mythology that denigrates not only the archetypal feminine but also women themselves, their emotional and civil rights in the outer world.

It seems to us, then, that the precise organ of healing for this wounded conflict zone is the fourth chakra, the gentle heart of compassion. Like number two, it is a neighbor of troublesome chakra three, but represents the higher inflection. The precise mission of this chakra seems to be to uplift and "redeem" chakra three, as when the compassionate heart undoes a power conflict. The "open heart" of Christ or the Buddha enters the field of Darwinian struggle with a redeeming principle—the ability to understand the predicament of another. This is also that spontaneous, instinctive altruism we have spoken about in both animals and humans.

We have the raw *Eros* of chakra two, here transmuted into two other possible inflections of love: *agape*, the Greek word for spiritual, selfless love (the kind that is supposed to have characterized the early Christians); and then, *amor*, the power that moves the tradition of courtly love, which is spoken of as the awakening to "the gentle heart" that is supposed to beat in the breast of the courtly knight, the troubadour, and the lady herself, so that she remains open to the communications that come from her beloved. (In this regard, many of the *amores* of the medieval courts of love were never consummated, so unbiological were they. Rather they were literally affairs of the heart. One worshiped the name, an article of clothing such as a scarf or garter, even the very idea of the beloved.) Likewise with the agape, it was conceived of as akin with the love of God or Christ, who "so loved the world" that he enacted the sacrifice of the cross; this same love was to extend to brothers and sisters in Christ.

But what has this to do with love, sex, and relationship? Life tricks and pulls us into the most amazing learning experiences. We start with this inchoate urge to mate, to explore erotically with the other sex (chakra two), which leads us then into other things: relationship, the bearing of children, solving the problems of the domestic environment, raising the children, and then growing old together as mates and companions. The dynamic side of chakra three is that the parents, led by the father, aggressively make their way in the world, acquiring power and money, and making an island of protection and nurturance (security, chakra one). The negative side is power and dominance, abuse, overprotectiveness from men toward women, and the domination of children (one, two, and three); or inertia, resentment or rebellion (one, two, and three) from women toward men; sullen resentment and passive-aggressiveness of children, teenagers especially, toward parents (one and three, inertia and stubborn resistance).

With the differences between men and women—both "embodied" differences (their musculature, hormones, cycles, etc.), and psychosocial (women taught to be "good little girls," men to be "aggressive and assertive"), as well as spiritual (which include the gender of the highest principle, and the role men and women play in the significant stories—that is, myths—of the religion)—compassion is clearly needed at every turn. And this is the domain of the fourth chakra. As Jesus and the compassionate bodhisattvas of the East show us, we must learn to understand the significant other, to forgive, to empathize just when it is needed, and to sacrifice, both for the children and the other. God/Goddess gives us mighty lessons when he/she gives us sexuality, and we are pulled further into the matrix of creation and invited into relationships—which finally grow us spiritually.

The other chakras get involved in the complete package of relationship, too. Chakra five (the throat) for communication, from simplistic "dirty talking" (chakra two) to the love poetry of Shakespeare (two, four, and six, the visionary element). We have already discussed romances that begin "on-line," in which people fall in love with each other through an arabesque of words (chakra five) delivered by computer, but find themselves with an awakened heart (chakra four)—or even loins (chakra two). The knight, who engages in perpetual deeds of force (chakra three), still awakens the fourth (the warrior's "gentle heart") expressed through love poetry (chakra five) but also occasionally gets caught in his lady's bedroom (chakra two).

Chakra six (the third eye) rules clairvoyance and intuition. It is involved whenever people share perspectives, dreams, and visions together. The "third eye" can help us see the other as the luminous being she/he truly is, and whether or not this is the soul-mate, the one with whom to walk the long journey.

Chakra seven (the roof-chakra) brings us to ultimate things: Can we worship together, in whatever way? Does the presence of each add to the other's spiritual journey, instead of distracting from it, as the medieval theologians had it? Can we live with such a complete resonance with the other that we fly out of the tops of our heads one day and make an angel? Ultimately, what is promised through romancing the chakras is a dance of the whole exquisite mind-body-spirit dimensions of each partner. In the process, you can be sure, not a stone is left unturned, in the inventory of psyche, of karma, of personal mythologies. We grow towards wholeness in our significant relationships.

The portal chakra, however, to relationship and all the good things in store for us is the fourth. Our heart opens the way to communication, to the higher faculties of the mind, and to the spiritual. The heart tells me there is someone outside myself (partner, children, in-laws, neighbor). It tells me their needs may be as, or, at times, more important than mine. It shows me the way to empathize with their problems, their human limitations, as they muddle along just like me; we learn the arts of tolerance, patience, and empathy.

Stephen had a dream, which appeared as this book was being conceptualized:

> I was distance swimming in Lake George, a long Adirondack lake that I
> love. The water was fairly calm, and I felt strong and capable, swimming
> along. Suddenly I realized that Robin had unobtrusively joined me, and we
> both swam along easily, side by side, in it for the distance.

The dream provided a simple, but beautiful metaphor to explain what we were doing in our life at that time, our thirty-third year of marriage, kind of pacing each other, but in it for the long haul.

Couples wishing to face the full complexity involved in psychospiritual development might look at the magnificent work of artist Alex Grey (see interview in chapter ten), particularly his series of monumental works reproduced in the book *Sacred Mirrors* (*Kissing* is reproduced on page 262). The visionary artist shows us the layers within layers of which any human being is made: fleshly sheath, emotional sheath, mental sheath, energy-body sheath, angelic or divine sheath—just as in the marvelous Hindu metaphysical system (where the sheaths are called "*mayakosha*").

What a thing it is to bring two human beings together with all these layers, meridians, chakras, vibrating, trembling in (or out) of harmony in a kiss.

Expanding our context matures us, as Swedenborg says. The human man-woman relationship is a nursery for psychospiritual development. Body entices soul into involvement, interdependency, relationship. In *Conjugial Love* 191, also called *Love in Marriage*, Swedenborg says:

> It seems as if the love arises from the body into the soul, because as soon as the body is enticed the enticement goes through your eyes like doors into your mind. This is how it goes through sight as an entrance to your mind and acts in lower things according to their arrangement. So a lascivious mind acts lasciviously, and a chaste mind chastely. The chaste mind arranges the body, and the unchaste mind is arranged by the body.

This passage is a graphic, internal description of the poet de Borncilh's "the eyes are the scouts of the heart" (although certainly Swedenborg was not particularly familiar with the Arthurian romances). There needs to be some kind of arrangement of energies in relating to the other person; of course, one is often in lust while in love, and maybe or maybe not having a mind-romance as well. The mind is no sluggard in the game of attraction, either, as witnessed in the classic story of *Cyrano de Bergerac*, or in the recent film *Shakespeare in Love*.

Moreover, since relationship is archetypal, anima-animus, yin-yang, love and wisdom, there is a beautiful something going on in the very inner soul, a *hieros gamos*, a sacred marriage; the inner, spiritual thing is stimulated by the outer events of being in love. Swedenborg quaintly refers to this process as "heavenly wedding-games." These are the dance of love and wisdom, discernment and intention in the psyche. He says:

> These wedding games of love and wisdom in action in your soul continue as they go on toward your chest cavity and stay there, and there they stand out perceptibly in an infinite variety of delights. And on account of the chest's marvelous communication with the genital region, the delights there become the delights of married love, which rise above all delights that there are in heaven and earth. They rise above them because the activity of married love is much higher than all other activities, since it is where the continuation of the human race comes from, and from the human race the angelic heaven.

Conjugial Love 183

Here we have the music of the chakras, the fourth communing, singing in harmony with the second, to produce delights of body, mind and spirit. The heart, love, uplifts the sexual drive, lust, and uses its energy to touch and awaken the higher centers. It is Swedenborg's Tantrism, the easy movement between the lower and the higher in a spiritually attuned couple: love and wisdom mingling on levels both natural and spiritual, and producing this positive angelic being.

The unevolved human being, on the other hand, has built-in wars, conflicts guaranteed, as lust, power, insecurity, and vanity vie for center stage. Particularly where there is a lack of compassion, we have the inherent differences between the genders and the inevitable conflicts occasioned by the first three chakras to guarantee the mischief—energy sparking and ricocheting off each psyche, awakening the reptilian and lower mammalian brains: sex, violence, possessiveness, jealousy, stalking, abuse in many varieties, and finally segregation of men and women into different camps, who basically hate each other. The relationship seems demonically plagued, the opposite of the positively inflected love story that seems so close, in Swedenborg, to an experience of heaven. This is the Wasteland.

Let us go back now to the beginnings of the story, and see how that negative inflection gets created, so that by the end we have considered all the textures, light and shadow both, in the many-dimensional display that is life.

THE GENDER WARS

IN HER COMPELLING BOOK, *Adam, Eve, and the Serpent*, historian of religions Elaine Pagels says that, throughout the Western Judeo-Christian tradition, there has been a systematic attempt to show that women were untrustworthy, dangerous, and inferior, and ought to be subservient to man.[3] Even in the Hindu tradition (which is also an Indo-European and patriarchal tradition in many of its aspects), the Laws of Manu state that "no matter how wicked, degenerate or devoid of all good qualities a man may be, a good wife must . . . revere him like a god." In that culture also, the rite of *sati* was instituted, in which a wife (no matter how young, talented, or full of promise she be) should, at the demise of her husband (no matter how early or late the demise, and even if self-inflicted through incaution, bellicosity, or dissipation) join him on the funeral pyre.

Of course, there is not much archaeological evidence to document the antiquity and extent of this practice, because of the fate of the evidence, but comparable burials and tombs stretching from India to the Near East show both how old and how widespread the practice was, whether involving burning or burial. On the death of a great lord or noble, he had to be equipped, naturally, for the other world. This often seems to have involved the burial alive of one or even several wives, as well as household servants, horses, and chariots—all to accompany such a god-man on his ultimate journey. The wife in such societies has no value in and of herself, but only in the service of the man to whom she is dedicated. Our language still echoes this attitude: We say, "Man and wife," not "Woman and husband"; and how often do we hear or read, "They came into the land bringing their husbands and children, cattle, and horses"?

From the sixth century BCE, male priesthoods were in the ascendancy, and the religion of the Great Goddess waning. As Robert Graves pointed out, while the Greek myths tell us of gods and goddesses marrying, fighting, and separating, this is really a depiction of what happened when their cults came together, or collided and separated. Hebrews who kept Asherahs (images of the goddess) in their temple or home shrine were persecuted or shunned by the partisans of Yahwism, the patriarchal, monotheistic group. Gnostic Christian sects who believed in individual worship, daily praise, and equality between men and women in the eyes of God, were anathematized, as well as persecuted.[4] Ecumenicism and tolerance themselves became suspect and were subordinated to the patriarchal hegemony. The centuries of peace under the Great Goddess, which some scholars affirm to have endured for millennia, was over.

The reformers sometimes got carried away with their new idea. Raphael Patai writes that Joshua (639–609 BCE) commanded complete destruction of the seven nations that had inhabited Canaan before the Hebrews came:

> Their altars to be broken down, their pillars to be dashed to pieces, their Asherahs (statues of the goddess) hewed down, and their graven images burnt. In addition, it is warned: "You shall not plant for yourself an Asherah, any tree, beside the altar of Yahweh your god which you shall make for yourself. Neither shall you set up a pillar, which Yahweh your god hates."[5]

The "witch mania" begins in Hebrew times: "Thou shalt not suffer a witch to live" (Exodus 22:18). Women with powers that the men did not understand were deemed dangerous and to be taken firmly in hand–or else put to death. If some historians of religion see this as an inevitable and necessary effort to consolidate patriarchal monotheism, it also must be seen as a war on women–and a war on shamans, clairvoyants, diviners. In effect it removed from women, and from the people in general, the right to "go inside" to find the answers to life's serious questions. It forced the *polis*, the people, to be reliant on a book, the Torah, or the Bible, hence on its (primarily male) priestly interpreters. These prototypes paved the way for twenty centuries of patriarchal patterns in religion.

There is debate among scholars about the medieval "religion" of the witches and its persecution. In the early nineteenth century, no less an authority than the German folklorist Jacob Grimm had thought that folk-beliefs dating from pre-Christian times helped form the witch mythogem in German culture. In 1828, Karl Ernst Jarcke, a law professor at the University of Berlin, commented in a legal brief about a witch trial that what the witches believed in was the nature religion of the ancient Germans.[6] Roman Catholic historian Franz Joseph Mone, archivist at Baden, proposed that the religion of the witches was clearly a return to the worship of Dionysus. In *La Sorcière* (1862), Jules Michelet proposed that witchcraft was a justified, if hopeless, revolt of the lowest classes of society against the aristocracy and corrupt ecclesiastical authority that was oppressing them.

Michelet proposes an amazing image at the center of "The Black Mass," who sounds like the rejected goddess:

> . . . not the Devil, nor a man impersonating the Devil, but a woman—a female serf in her thirties "with a face like Medea, a beauty born of sufferings, a deep, tragic, feverish gaze, with a torrent of black, untamable hair falling as chance takes it, like the waves of serpents. Perhaps, on top, a crown of vervain, like ivy from tombs, like violets of death."[7]

Note the iconography of Medusa and the mention of Medea, the tortured and spurned feminine element.

In two monographs published in 1917 and 1920, ethnologist Margaret

Murray tried to show that the religion of the witches was the descendant of a much older folk-religion extending back into antiquity and full of shamanic remnants: witches were said to change into animals (theriomorphism, or "shapechanging"), to be able to fly (shamanic flight, or "journeying)," to associate with spirits, to use magical powers, and to scry or divine, predicting future events.[8] For Murray, the religion was primarily oriented toward fertility and earth-renewing magic. At the center of the religion was a two-faced horned god, who was called "Dianus or Janus" (also Cernunnos). This figure gave rise to the well-known stereotyped image of the horned and hoofed Satan.

The countervailing view is well developed by Norman Cohn in *Europe's Inner Demons*—that there was no "religion," no organized society of women; rather a systematic delusion, elaborated over time, was gradually assembled by various clerical extremists, for their own reasons. After a while, the believers could no longer distinguish fact from fiction. Most of the unpleasant elements of this vividly and darkly imagined ritual are from the core symbolic elements of a vestigial shamanism, but much is inverted Christianity: the mysterious flight to the place of the "synagogue" or "sabbat" (the supposed connection with Judaism); the horned god (the ancient "Lord of the Animals" or Cernunnos); the cannibalistic feast on infants (a literalization of the internal, symbolic, shamanic feast); a dark version of the Eucharist, involving unnamable substances; the swearing of fealty to the Dark Lord (a mirror image of the Christian *credos* addressed to the Lord of Light); ecstatic dancing (present in traditions from the shamanic to the Pentecostal); the kissing of the horned god or beasts or toads "under the taile," on the anus or genitals (probably mirroring kissing the cross, chalice or host); wild promiscuous sexuality (the return of the neglected element, since Christianity equates the sexual with evil); and various pacts with the devil (equivalent to declaring one's faithfulness to Christianity, a capitulation based on belief).

Cohn says the witchcraft so invented and contrived by the paranoid and self-serving clergy was a "blasphemous parody of Christianity."[9] The Inquisition and others served by witch-hunting added the extra twist that transforms an earth-centered, animal inclusive and related, women's rights affirming, visionary and healing tradition into the specter of the satanic cult. As was done with the persecution of the Jews, the early Christians, the Albigensians, the Waldensians, and many other minorities, the imaginative inquisitors added the dramatic exaggeration that speaks the lie: women who came to these sabbats brought their own infants for sacrifice, dashed them against stones, roasted them, smeared themselves with baby fat, and joined in a cannibalistic feast with the flesh and blood of the children.[10] Further, they gave obscene kisses to goats and other animals, and coupled indiscriminately with the animals, humans, and demons in the forms of incubi and succubi, including members of their own families (incest being the oldest taboo in town) and the Dark Lord himself.

These "abominable practices" recorded by the Inquisition fly in the face of the life-affirmative dimensions of archaic religion. The purpose of the slaying of the year king at Nemi, the core of Fraser's *The Golden Bough*, was to renew and refresh the land, the crops, and the kingdom. The old must die, so the new can come in. (Fraser's scholarship was very influential on Margaret Murray's thesis.) It is also not clear how common actual king sacrifice was in the older strata of pre-Christian Europe; some scholars suggest it may not have been as widespread in its literal practice as previously thought. There is also little evidence of extensive human sacrifice before the nomadic warrior peoples entered the region of the early agricultural societies; the great chieftain burials belong to the period of conquest and cross-fertilization after the sixth to fourth millennia. In any case, there is no real evidence of any significant survival of these practices into post-Roman Europe. If desecration of traditional Christian symbols, the cross and the host, was actually practiced, there is a fairly good chance the desecration was done by people who felt upset at their own maltreatment by the powers who used these symbols. Cohn insists the women who were killed by the millions over several centuries were easy prey, not only because they were women, but precisely that they *weren't* organized—they were sometimes wise women or simply very pretty women, but often eccentrics and misfits from all walks of life.

The heinous acts of the Black Mass are not only a grotesque parody of shamanism, the Dionysian religion, and paganism generally (Diana or Artemis was thought to be present at some of these rites), but a negation of the most basic feminine instincts—the care and nurture of children and sexual modesty (not for moralistic reasons, but a kind of innate fear of infection with sexually transmitted diseases, or unsupported pregnancy). The women who were attacked were often greenwitches, herbalists and midwives. Some of the women were probably holders of secrets, "women's mysteries"—those of gynecology and obstetrics, herbal lore related to same, and also contraception, and abortion. (They also might be the one you would go to if your husband were being unfeeling or violent.) They often interpreted dreams, read portents, and gave counsel. (Do we really wonder why the patriarchal establishment regarded them as the enemy and proscribed all divinatory and shamanic activity!)

Estimates vary, but in a documentary film based on this gender war, called *The Burning Times*, it is suggested that the number of witches burned during the persecution may be double the number of World War II Holocaust victims (six million).[11] This is "gendacide" indeed, an unremitting war of one gender on another, extending over centuries—just as the Zulu myth of Moromudzi and Banu Kiranmireva tells. There was a time when men made war on women. . . .

It seems odd, then, that both Jews and Christians have persecuted witches, when their own religions have also been targeted by inimical and paranoid fanatics. They too have been accused of incest, infanticide, cannibalism, and other abominations. We also see that, psychologically, that which is deemed abominable is found in the eye of the beholder. That is, to say, it is more frequent for people to imagine that others do awful things than to find people actually doing them. Another way of saying this is that people easily "devilify" others as a magical way of divesting the self of the negativity and as a prelude to persecuting or trying to exterminate them. ("What's the ugliest part of your body?" maverick musician Frank Zappa would inquire raspingly: "Some say your nose, some say your toes, I think it's your mind!") This is Norman Cohn's point precisely: the fantastic, inverted, impossibly evil acts of the "witches' sabbat" seem more like delusions of the mind (twisted minds to be sure) than practical weekly rituals for believers. And more evil has probably been done by people who imagined they were doing "good" than by people who set out on a deliberate course of mischief. Think of your average crusade, ethnic cleansing, or *jihad*.

It was believed in the Middle Ages that no less than a tenth of the angels of heaven fell to earth with Lucifer. They entered the sublunar realm (beneath the moon), hovered on the night airs and embarked upon a ruthless campaign to ensnare human souls. Therefore, there were more than enough to go around. (Remember, in this tradition, nature is corrupt, so demons could lurk in nature as copiously as spirits or devas abound in animistic religions.) For the most part, following the lead of St. Augustine, demons were indeed held to be inverted angels, insubstantial like angels, but eminently capable, as were their luminous counterparts, of affecting or influencing people. St. Thomas Aquinas believed, as did Swedenborg, that demons and angels vie for control of human consciousness.

In the war against women, those most persecuted were particularly two kinds of women: old, deformed, hag-like (therefore not good for much in the man's world), on the one hand; or irresistibly beautiful and alluring on the other (possibly enough so to make your average man lose his control, his wits, his invaluable rationality). These represent two kinds of witches, in common parlance, but notice the definition of the witch is determined not by who they are, but how the man reacts to them. In this sense, men manufacture witches.[12]

The infamous *Malleus Mallificarum* of the sixteenth century, says,

> For though the devil tempted Eve to sin, yet Eve seduced Adam. And the sin of Eve would not have brought death to our soul and body unless this sin had afterwards passed onto Adam, to which he was tempted by Eve, not by the devil. Therefore she is more bitter than death. More bitter than death again because death is natural and destroys only the body; but the sin which arose from woman destroys the soul by depriving it of grace, and delivers the body up to judgment for its sins.[13]

There can be no doubt that, if the masculine spirit felt eclipsed by the "magical advantage" of the feminine during the millennia of goddess worship and gyneolatry, it took its revenge in the two-and-a-half patriarchal millennia leading up to the present. Until the nineteenth century in most, even "advanced," cultures, women could not vote and enjoyed no political power.[14] Men freely projected their shadows on women and thought that just half of the human race was moody, fickle, subject to biological tides, imaginative, delusion-prone, and manipulative. It is the simple "otherness" of the genders that allows us to do this—the fact that, when we have never inhabited their condition, we can think the most amazing things about our companions and helpmeets in this grand human enterprise: the other gender.

Failing to honor the angels, we face a world of demons. Judging from this period of history, it seemed that demons, misunderstood "fallen" angels, abounded on every side. But the zealots who were most concerned about eradicating demons themselves behaved demonically and set our world all topsy-turvy. In the name of the gentlest of redeemers, they enacted the cruelest of persecutions. Jesus had already said, at the would-be stoning of Mary Magdalene, a prostitute, "Let him who is without guilt cast the first stone," but organized Christianity has been dyslexic, and not only the judgmentalism of which Jesus spoke but also intolerance and violence have dogged its history. Whether the millions of women (or even a small portion) perse-cuted by male inquisitors and judges were practicing an ancient religion or not; and whether some of them were guilty even of subversive or rebellious attitudes towards the popes and bishops who accused them of committing horrendous acts, still for all time, what is historically evident is that men in positions of power made war on helpless women and tortured them physically, psychologically, and, yes, spiritually, in large measure for the condition of being born female.

We move next to a condition of the world in which the masculine princi-ple has pretty much accomplished its goal. It is a world of social hierarchies and rules, of high expectations and judgmentalism about those who do not meet them; punishment and cruelty are regularly enacted, and social and class discrimination is rampant. It is a world in which all important controversies are settled by violence (third chakra). Warriorcraft rules the day and is just barely tempered by a chivalric code (one of sixth-century St. Columba's contributions was an early version of this, in which he put out the radical idea that women and children should be spared, by both sides, rather than slaughtered wantonly in most battle situations). The chival-ric code promulgated by Arthur's "Round Table" was another version of this. In it, a "gentle knight" or a "gentleman" was not someone who was nonviolent, but who held it part of his honor to spare or protect the weak (chakra four).

Our next section explores a story of how the masculine principle, run ram-pant, creates the "Wasteland."

THE ORIGIN OF THE WASTELAND

Joseph Campbell's Master's thesis at Columbia University was on the subject of "The Dolorous Stroke." No one except a few Arthurian scholars in the romance traditions even knew the story existed. But the story now emerges as enormously im-portant, because its symbolic themes indeed usher in the Wasteland, still character-ize it wherever it is found, and invite the feminine mystery of the Grail to enter the stream of Western history as a redemptive element. The story begins, appropriately, with a sword, the fey sword that would one day become Launcelot's:

> There had come a damosel to King Arthur's Court, and she had been girt with this selfsame sword; and that was the first world had ever seen of it. She had been "sent on message from the great lady Lile of Avelion." And the king had had great marvel, and he said: "Damosel, for what cause are ye girt with that sword? It beseemeth you not."
>
> "Now I shall tell you," said the damosel. "This sword that I am girt withal doth me gret sorrow and cumbrance; for I may not be delivered of this sword but by a knight. But he must be a passing good man of his hands and deeds and without villainy or treachery, and without treason. And if I may find such a knight that hath all these virtues, he may draw out this sword out of the sheath."[15]

You know the kind of story, if not the story itself. There is a destiny in the sword, and only the right man may pull it forth. Arthur assays, but this is not for him. In sequence all of Arthur's men try, until the lady says, "I weened in this court had been the best knights, without treachery or treason."

There was with King Arthur, however, one Balin, a prisoner in the court for the slaying of a knight that was the king's cousin; despite his poor raiment and low station in the court, Balin asked if he might try. The other knights murmured, for they deemed that many a better knight had tried, but the lady said, "Ye shall not know a man by his `tatches!'" (clothes); and so the king gave him leave.

Then Balin took the sword by its hilt and drew it out easily. The young woman said,

> "Certes, this is a passing good knight, and the best that ever I found, and most of worship without treason, treachery, or villainy. . . . Now gentle and courteous knight, give me the sword again."
>
> "Nay," said Balin, "for this sword will I keep, but it be taken from me with force."
>
> "Well," said the damosel, "ye are not wise to keep the sword from me; for ye shall slay with the sword the best friend that ye have, and the man that ye most love in the world, and the sword shall be your destruction."
>
> "I shall take the adventure," said Balin, "that God will ordain me."[16]

Now with these words, smacking of spiritual wisdom when combined with a sincere inner attitude, but here equivalent to a wisecrack—mocking the very power it lightly invokes—Balin has set the stage for the adventure which follows and for the fashioning of the Wasteland.

Now came the Lady of the Lake, "richly bysene," and stood before the court asking for a gift which King Arthur owed her (in exchange for the gift of the sword Excalibur, which she had given him). But the lady made a strange bloodthirsty request: "The head of the knight that hath won the sword or else the damosel's head that brought it; for he slew my brother, and that gentlewoman was causer of my father's death."

Arthur demurred, but, while he pondered, Balin heard what had transpired and saw the Lady of the Lake, who he believed had slain his mother and whom he had been seeking for three years. Balin approached and addressed the lady: "'Evil be you found. Ye would have my head, and therefore ye shall lose yours!' And with his sword lightly he smote off her head before King Arthur."[17]

Now King Arthur went into a towering rage, for the act was a violation of all court protocol and a grievous insult to the king. With this offence added to the knight's previous crime, Arthur could have ordered his execution; but being true king, he did not wish to expiate death with death. So he banished the impetuous youth forthwith from his court; and Balin rode off in high disgrace and feeling much aggrieved, but pleased to have kept the fairy sword.

Balin proceeded through a series of violent adventures, in which he also caused the death of an innocent young lady—the first of a series. Then appeared to Balin the wizard Merlin:

"Thou has done thyself great hurt," [the wizard] said, "Because of the death of this lady thou shalt strike a stroke most dolorous that ever man struck, except the stroke of our Lord; for thou shalt hurt the truest knight and the man of most worship that now liveth, and through that stroke three kingdoms shall be in great poverty, misery, and wretchedness twelve years, and the knight shall not be whole of that wound for many years."

And Balin said: "If I wist it were sooth that ye say I should do such a perilous deed as that, I would slay myself to make the a liar." And therewith Merlin suddenly vanished away.[18]

Now that we have set the stage, we can visit the gory details that comprise the rest of the story with some alacrity. Balin rode forth, like knights were wont to do in those days, on errand. And "whatever enemy he met he dealt a deadly blow . . . but at the same time caused some disaster."[19]

Many adventures unfolded, but in the pivotal one that concerns us, Balin was employed to give safe conduct to a young lover. He was doing so, when someone invisible rode by and smote the young man to the death. As he died, he told Balin the name of the invisible knight, and asked him to carry the tidings of his death to his damosel; now Balin became her protectress, and they were joined by another knight. But once again came riding the invisible, lethal horseman and smote this man through the body.

Then Balin and the lady came to the castle of King Pellam ("the man of most worship who now liveth"). The couple was made welcome, but as they sat to feast, Balin espied the man he believed to be the invisible slayer and stared at him. Then Garlon, for it was indeed he, came over and confronted Balin, and smote him in the face for rudely staring, saying, "Do what thou camest to do!" At this Balin leaped up and clove Garlon's head with the fairy sword. Whereupon a pandemonium ensued that led to the Great Catastrophe: King Pellam was outraged, for Garlon was his brother (nor as we have already been reminded, was it perishable to kill anyone within the bounds of a king's feasting-hall). He caught up a weapon and went for Balin. In defending Balin's head from Pellam's blow, the fairy sword was shattered, and Balin fled weaponless with Pellam in hot pursuit.

They ran on through the corridors of the palace, and at the last,

> Balin entered into a chamber that was marvellously well dight and richly, and a bed arrayed with cloth of gold the richest that might be thought . . . and thereby stood a table of clene gold with four pillars of silver that bare up the table, and upon the table stood a marvelous spear strangely wrought. And when Balin saw that spear, he gat it in his hand and turned him to King Pellam, and smote him passing sore with that spear, so that King Pellam fell down in a swoon and therewith the castle roof and walls brake and fell down so that he might not stir foot nor hand. And so the most part of the castle, that was fallen through that dolorous stroke, lay upon Pellam and Balin three days.[20]

Merlin appeared again, and was there as Balin awoke. "I would have my damosel," Balin said. "Lo," said Merlin, "where she lieth dead." And Balin rode forth, but on every side were people dead and slain, and those who lived cried out: "O Balin, thou hast caused great damage in these countries; for the dolorous stroke thou gavest unto King Pellam, these three countries are destroyed, and doubt not but the vengeance will fall upon thee at last."[21]

Thus, we see the making of the Wasteland, the scene into which Parzival will come years later, finding Pellam still wounded and now called "the Fisher King." (And Parzival, himself a child of the Wasteland, will fail the first time to ask the redeeming question.)

Many adventures—or should we say "misadventures," for every one of them went awry—now were encountered by Balin; and they were not much different from what we have learned to expect from him (here clearly "character is destiny"): despite the fact that the fairy sword had given its initial approval of him as a knight "most of worship, without treason, treachery, or villainy," he showed himself consistently to be heedless and violent. Balin finally entered his ultimate "misadventure." It took place in a fairy castle on an island, full of ladies (a scenario in which the Arthurian landscape seems to abound). The Indologist Heinrich Zimmer, whose version of this story we are using, says, "It is like the *Château Merveil* of Sir Gawain." (Also "full of ladies," and where Gawain must encounter various magical ordeals— a place of initiation and transformation, in the realm of the Feminine.) Balin had finally come to the Land of No Return.

On entering this zone of marvels Balin changed his shield (by which he might be identified)—even after meeting a damosel who warned him not to go on without his own shield; but Balin (he has identified himself now as "the man who doesn't listen") went on. Finally, he met a knight, all arrayed in red, and they came together, first on horseback, then on foot. Equally matched in strength, they exchanged blow for blow, until both lay in a pool of blood, exhausted and dying. Then finally they recognized each other: The Red Knight was Balin's twin brother, Balan. Balin, coming to his senses, said: "O Balan, my brother, thou has slain me and I thee. . . . Alas, that I ever saw this day." And they died. Having sprung from one womb, the brothers were now buried in one tomb; and all the ladies wept for the sadness of it.

THE WASTELAND MOTIF

HEINRICH ZIMMER SAYS OF THIS STORY, that there was an "enchantment" on Sir Balin from the beginning. And that the fairy sword represents Balin's style of masculinity: a thoughtless aggressiveness. In the first place, Balin is in the court under a sentence for a violent action—killing the cousin of the king. In the story, it says that only a knight "without villainy or treachery" can draw the sword, so those must not be Balin's flaws. He has, rather, an impetuous and willful leaping into action, without thinking things through. The fairy sword corresponds to Balin's nature— that is why they are meant for each other. The surface of the story says the knight who draws it forth must be "of worship" in addition to being "without treachery and villany." The deeper or concealed meaning of the magical sword is that it is a bearer of destiny (*wyrd*, the Anglo-Saxon term). King Arthur cannot draw this sword forth (unlike the one in the fable *The Sword in the Stone*, for which he is famous), not because he is not a better man—he proves that by his forbearance in this (and many another) matter. Rather it is because the bloody destiny in the sword is not calling to him. It calls only to Balin. He is, indeed, the "perfect knight" to carry the "karma" of his age and culture to its crucial moment, its moment of truth. Moreover, Balin easily can relate to the idea that it is a magical sword, every little boy's dream. Now he can "waste," as they say, every enemy, frustration, or obstacle that gets in his way. But he fails to grasp that he, and it, are subject to a larger magic, a *wyrd*, a destiny that is bringing in the Wasteland.

The Wasteland symbolically comes into being, then, half through the sword's action and half through the fulfillment of Balin's character. Note that the first act that occurs when the sword slithers easily into Balin's hand is that he refuses to release it back to the lady when she asks for it. Here he fails to recognize her as the feminine guardian spirit of the deadly weapon, the anima or wisdom that could instruct him in its proper use. It is interesting to speculate upon the initiation that might have followed, and a true gifting, if Balin had shown humility and subtlety at that moment. But it is, most specifically, the feminine initiation that Balin rejects.

Next, as the Lady of the Lake stood before the king, in a place traditionally associated with respect and honor, "lightly he smote off her head." With female blood then, the curse of the sword is activated: Balin and his sword have become one. This act was especially vicious, no matter what Balin believed his personal vendetta was, because the Round Table stood for an emerging ethic: protection of the weak, women and children. ("Weak," in this social context, means primarily one whose life is not dedicated to taking life.) Here personal revenge eclipses the code of honor.

The wisdom principle of the psyche appears to Balin many times, in the form of Merlin, to warn him. And he responds with the one attitude that the divine and spiritual powers usually treat quite harshly: careless mockery. This is the dangerous quality Jungian analyst Marie-Louise von Franz calls "frevel," which leads to the undoing of many a hero (or antihero) in the making.[22] The psyche forgives us a lot on the way to becoming, but this attitude is particularly problematical.

It is certainly true that the world in which Balin lives is violent: "Garlons," invisible smiters, abound. There are people who take advantage and who love to kill. In the story, the ghostly figure keeps attacking not just any knights, but in particular ones pledged to ladies, that is, relationships in the making. So "Garlon" is this principle of sudden violence and impetuosity that invisibly dogs Balin and surprises him time and again. We see that, psychologically, this quality destroys relationships, as the story specifically mentions couples being broken, and leaves women—or the creative feminine—bereaved, unprotected, and, as the anima, exposed and isolated, with no means of actualization.

Among Balin's earlier misadventures was one in which he agreed to help a knight who had lost his lady; and while searching, Balin found the lady in the arms of "the foulest knight that ever he saw," and the two sleeping. His (psychologically disastrous) response was to lead the distraught lover to the scene. The knight went mad, smiting off both their heads (people are always "losing their heads" around Balin) and then when he saw the consequences, and that he had killed what he loved, he reaved himself on his own sword.

The killing of Garlon also occurs in the hall of a king (an insult to the king because it calls into question his ability to maintain a civil court). Balin could have accused Garlon before the king and court; and Pellam might have proposed some adjudication or trial by combat, even though the evil Garlon was his (dark) brother. But Balin rises to meet violence with (once again) instant violence. Now the fairy sword itself is destroyed (fairy weapons have a way of abandoning a hero who is not attuned to his inner guide—as represented by magical ladies or wizards; this one will later be reforged) under the onslaught of Pellam.

Finally, Balin finds himself in a holy place, where a spear hovers magically in the air above a beautiful golden vessel (the Grail) and a table. (The spear is associated with the spear of Longinus, which pierced the side of Christ, the table with the Last Supper, and the Grail with the chalice of that event.) At this stage of the game, Balin does not recognize a holy symbol when he sees it, nor pause at the magical state of suspension in which everything is frozen. This is the pivotal moment, when yet one more (habitual, unconscious) act of violence "wastes" the king, the castle, and the entire countryside.

What a statement. And no wonder Joseph Campbell was fascinated by this story; for it shows clearly that a masculine, macho attitude, out of control to the point of compulsion, lays waste to the world and sets up the psychological wasteland that spreads wherever creative magic and love are absent. Campbell interpreted the spear as associated with ancient male fertility rites, possibly connected with the God of Thunder.[23] It is certainly a masculine symbol, but enshrined in this way it signifies the inner, mystical dimension of the principle. It is not to be used as a weapon as Balin uses it. He wounds "the man of most worship in the world" in the thigh (or probably the genitals), the procreative power; in other words, his violent male attitude damages the symbolic masculine procreative power, the creative thrust, that is held in mystical relationship to a feminine symbol: the bowl, baptismal vessel, or Grail that holds the waters of life. The Grail also evokes the pre-Christian symbol of the cauldron or feminine vessel of transformation (the cauldron of the wizard-queen Ceridwen that appears in the story of Taliesin). It contains the precise waters that must be released, but in the proper way, to nourish the Wasteland.

Zimmer and Campbell point out astutely that Balin/Balan are complementary principles. We don't know much about Balan, but we do know that he was equal to Balin in strength and courage, and we are told that the ladies in the castle loved him. Perhaps they were a pair of opposites, like the twins in mythology often are. Certainly, Pellam, the man of most worship, and Garlon, the sneaky smiter and cock of the court, were opposites, and Pellam's kingdom really was brought down by the impetuosity of his dark brother.

Chakra three, then, the principle of unbridled masculine assertiveness, threatens the worlds of all the others. When it is unrelated, it disrespects everything else in the psyche and in other people. It wounds love and security, chakras two and one, blights communication, chakra five, and blinds spiritual perspective, chakra six. This is how the Wasteland enters the psyche as well as the outer landscape. The mythology itself tells us of the healing: the redemption of the Wasteland and the healing of the Fisher King will come through the asking of compassionate questions: Why is the King wounded? What is the meaning of the Spear, the Grail? How may one serve the Grail? (This is chakra four, compassion, concern for the other.) We will return to this theme of the Grail knight and the asking of the question in a little while.

Campbell said the Wasteland motif emerged in Western culture history because people were living inauthentic lives—following social roles, rather than living authentically from within. T. S. Eliot saw this condition still very much present in our time—the inauthentic life:

> The desert is not remote in southern tropics,
> The desert is not only around the corner,
> The desert is squeezed in the tube-train next to you
> The desert is in the heart of your brother. [24]

In the story we have just reviewed, we see how an excess of the male principle contributes its share to the devastation. There is no receptivity, hence no fertilization; the land is dry and desolate, the desert "in the heart of your brother."

Contemporary culture has inherited the Wasteland, and you don't have to go very far to see it. It is there in the chaos and carelessness of every urban sprawl, in the asphalt of the parking lot, and the layout of the strip mall. It is there in the convenience store, offering the same malnourishing things, day after day, in the piles of garbage that accumulate, in the vacuous gaze of the family in front of the electronic eye of the television, and in the empty and violent phantasmagoria that we see in that eye. The Wasteland is present in institutions, bureaucracies, and the media, but it also exists in the psyche.

One of Stephen's clients in the early years of his practice dreamed week after week, month after month, of the same environment, seedy run-down buildings, parking lots, convenience stores; and he was all the while searching, searching for something, a drink of water, a crust of bread, any kind of affirmation, in the Wasteland. The adventures sometimes varied, but the backdrop was the same, an underlying, endogenous depression. When the client finally moved, changed his job, and took on a new hobby, folk music, that livened up his life, his dream environments became more natural with parks and forests, amid which the dream adventures took place. But whenever he went back to that same slummy place, he knew depression was in the offing.

A suggestion, then, to therapists and interpreters of dreams: watch for the Wasteland, and look for its redeeming events: rain, thunderstorms, new growth.[25]

——————— STEPHEN AND ROBIN IN DIALOGUE ———————

Stephen: We could say that the shadow of Western civilization first appears mythologically in the symbolism of the Wasteland; it is the place in need of redemption. T. S. Eliot picked it up and called modern literature's attention to it. It is the backdrop against which the Grail story emerges as the redemptive mythos.

Robin: Perhaps most tragically and most horrifyingly, the Wasteland exists in the passionless gaze of far too many young people, teenagers and people early in their lives, whose eyes are not afire with hope and expectation and passion. Here is where contemporary culture shows its rootlessness and exhibits its failure to provide either experience or meaning. It is in this wasteland soil that the seeds of violence and evil are sown.

Stephen: I remember a professor at an academic conference recently asking, "How do you teach passion?" It seems to me that passion flows from the unfettered heart; that passion flows from deep wellsprings within. It rises up in greeting for the world: the "Oh brave new world that hath such creatures in it," of Miranda (in *The Tempest*). But circumstances show you again and again that the things that you desire in life are not available to you; then you are constantly frustrated, and something that psychologists call "learned helplessness" ensues.

Robin: Also, if you are given the message continually that the things you desire are really only surface glitter, there is nothing that is really worth giving everything for. You don't really expect happiness or fulfillment; this is the message of our culture at this time. And we find so many people are now delving back into this problem of the masculine and the feminine, and asking where it all went wrong.

I was between eight and nine years old—I remember the particular evening—I was in my bedroom; we lived in Chicago. And I had this horrible thought; I said to myself, "Don't go there, don't think that. I will not remember this." I wanted to go to sleep and just be a kid again. But, in fact, the thought would not let me go. It kept coming back, and actually when I met you, Stephen, we shared and shuddered. We had both had it. I had to give it a name: "the gas station reality!"

When you look at a gas station when you're a little kid—I remember the magic of them—I'd see the red winged horse (of the Mobil sign) flying overhead, and the bright lights, and the banners. It looked like an amusement park, the most wonderful thing; and we would just drive toward it, and it would just be a gas station, nothing more, no magic, no entrance into another world, nothing for your mythic child's mind to grapple with.

All of that stuff was a sham, the red winged horse, the banners, the whole thing, the bright lights. That was my disillusionment as a little kid, and so I became a leader in guerilla warfare. Whenever the local vacant lots would suddenly blossom with heavy equipment and cement or asphalt-laying machinery, my friends and I would try to harass them in every way we could, because they were cutting down the trees, bushes, and shrubbery and paving the vacant lots that we played in that were the wilderness of my urban childhood.

Stephen: In the movie *The Emerald Forest*, the shy "Invisible People" of the deep Amazonian rain forest call the civil engineers "The Termite People," because they see them digging the earth all the time, building their dams. But I remember the same thing. It is very easy as a kid to be outraged by the gratuitous onslaught of civilization.

Robin: I discovered years later, when I first worked for a construction company as a designer, that they had special insurance for this kind of thing; every construction company has insurance that pays off a certain percentage, writes off a certain percentage of the "kid" damage every year.

Stephen: This is tied in with the great dissociation, or maybe the "great unmasking." Every child has a version of this, where they demythologize the scenario their parents have presented to them: They say, "What Santa Claus? What Easter Bunny? What virgin birth?" There's a demythologizing principle, an unmasking. The tooth fairy goes, and when this happens, we deform the world into a caricature, or the opposite of what we once believed to be true. The correct posture is now sardonic and sarcastic, nothing is true, nothing is believable, and this also paves the wasteland. Merlin appears to Balan and makes a prediction and Balan jokes crudely, "If I believed you I would slay myself and make you out a liar."

Robin: In the Balin story, women appear everywhere, as messengers, prophetesses, witnesses of violence. There is that castle right at the end there, where all the women look on, and weep at the demise of Balin and Balan. Women are no strangers to the Wasteland!

How would you have liked to have been lady Macbeth—fourteen years old and married to this grim Macbeth guy? You were just told by your father: "Here is your husband!" But you're smart, passionate, and ambitious. You really don't want to have your whole life circumscribed, laid down and controlled by this ass, this bore, this brute, this guy with no imagination and no personal ambition. You're passionate; what do you do in that situation?

What if you were Medea, and you were married to a narcissistic hero like Jason, who just thinks of you as spoils of war. All of your intelligence, your skill, your knowledge of herbal lore are merely tools to be used for his power trip. He doesn't even notice that you gave up your whole family, your culture, everything you knew for him—and then he leaves you for another woman. What would it have been like to suddenly find yourself in a culture that doesn't really respect you as a wise woman and a lore mistress, just "there's that doxie that Jason brought home," that's all you are; and he can just toss you aside if he wants to. What would it have been like to be Medea?

Stephen: Medea is not one of my favorite characters, but you're right about her predicament. Anyway it is clear that social and political disempowerment creates wasteland lives.

Robin: I think the answer will be found in the place deep inside us that's accessed by dream work and by art. It is the wellspring of passion, and it's like the magic fountains in so much of the Arthurian material. The problem is to clear away the debris from the mouth of the spring and let the waters flow again. And the Grail itself is the source of these, of the vessel through which flow these waters of spirit and inspiration.

Stephen: So we're talking about a moistening principle and an archetype, probably a feminine energy that provides the basis for nourishment and growth. In the symbolism we then have the water to revive the parched landscape, the elixir of immortal life, the wellsprings in the soul. It is the visionary capacity that warms the blood to love and adventure, the juice of life.

Robin: Our dreams and visions are the waters of life. Contact with them provides both hints and answers. That's what redeems the Wasteland.

Stephen: I think you are right; how many dreams, visionary experiences or images have tried to bring this home to women? It's uncanny, but all the themes we are working with in this chapter come up in imaginal form.

There are many similar stories, but I'm thinking of one very creative and imaginative woman in particular. She was recently and happily married, and liked to climb into the hot tub in the evening with her beloved and share a glass of wine. Then, these overwhelming feelings would come up; and in that most romantic and erotic of occasions, she would seem to have fallen into a dark pit. Horrible images would flit through her mind, and she would freeze up inside.

In the therapy session, I made sure she felt secure and comfortable, and then I asked her to go into that pit, and see what was there. Immediately she fell into a medieval dungeon: all around were the paraphernalia of torture and two men. They were torturing her, probably to death. We didn't stop to establish whether this was a "past life," a collective memory belonging to all women, or simply an imaginative excursus triggered by the revelation of rapes in Kosovo. Generally, with some exceptions, the best therapeutic wisdom says, "go through the experience." I invited her to go back to the beginning of the story that was occurring to her.

In her vision, she saw herself as an herbalist. The setting was very detailed: the rolling green countryside, the little cottage, the rafters hung with sweet herbs and grasses. She saw herself making little dolls and talismans of the herbs and other natural objects, and creating stories that included the magic of their healing powers. She started to cry as she thought of her patients, mostly children, and of how she would heal them with the stories and herbs she had packed into her basket.

In the town, some miles away, there were anxious rumors, but the woman just went about her business, healing others. Then came men who took her away. When they interrogated her, she didn't know what to say; she kept having the awful feeling that nothing she could say would make any difference. Then began the torture, which we went through, detail by horrific detail. (During this part of the imagery, her body was shaking like a leaf in a storm.) It involved the most intimate and loathsome violations. The goal seemed to be to keep her alive so she could experience more pain. Finally, she was burned alive, which seemed almost merciful compared to what she had been through. I asked her to accompany the soul to the spirit world, and she grew much calmer, and many beautiful and healing events then unfolded. She left the session weak and shaken, but relieved.

Robin: I can imagine, but it must have been very hard to do that session as a male therapist.

Stephen: Very hard indeed. More than once I found myself apologizing for my gender.

Robin: Well, how did these strange events affect her partner?

Stephen: Fortunately he was a very gentle and sensitive man. He was more concerned with her well-being than being disappointed at the evening being blighted.

Several times after that, the same romantic setting—including the hot tub—produced the same results, she fell into a black pit, and felt frozen all week until the therapy session. The scene changed, though almost invariably it seemed to involve herself as a woman, at some previous period of history experiencing some violation from a man. I had her live through whatever imagery came up.

All this time, I should say, the news was full of the horrors of the war in Yugoslavia, and new revelations of what had been done to women in particular. I think these events were priming the pump.

Robin: Sometimes when we've been arguing, I have a feeling that it's not just us. Whole genders, whole generations are crying and struggling inside us, trying to come forth and be heard, to tell their stories and be healed. Our fight is everyone's fight, and our drama, theirs.

Stephen: One session came along where my client had just a simple core fear, of being a female and having a stronger male violate her—something that, as we have said, was not even an issue in her current relationship. It was not a personal, but a collective issue, as if she were feeling the fear of all women. She said she felt too weak and shaky to go into the imagery in the cathartic way we had been doing. I wondered how best to help her, and then remembered that the one common denominator in all these experiences was the victim role—where the woman is helpless before the male aggressor.

I asked her to visualize the generic situation, from above, as it were, with all the elements in place, asking the question, "If there were one thing you could change, what would it be?" (The dialogue is paraphrased from my memory of the session.) She speaks first:

> Client: Ugh! The figure who is me, is B., is helpless, paralyzed, frozen. What can I do ?
>
> Therapist: Talk to him, take some power, try to look into his soul.
>
> C: Well, he's the one in spiritual peril
>
> T: Aha! Look deeper, How did he get to be the way he is?
>
> C: Uh . . . I think he's being mistreated and abused in his childhood. He doesn't have a chance. He's scared and mean at the same time.
>
> T: Good! If he had not been abused in childhood, what would he have been like?
>
> C: Oh, he has a nice smile, now that I'm looking at him in this way, and he has a gentle side, a little more complicated.
>
> T: See if you can juxtapose him on the other one, the one who's about to do the raping.

C: That's what my words are for. I have to believe that my words can reach this one, the gentle one, and he'll come out. He's actually stronger than the mean one.

T: You're doing very well. (I'm happy with the way the session is going now, and I try something else, with this adept visualizer). I want you to imagine that, in this moment, you have great power, magical power to affect the world. What happened in your vision, when you brought out the gentle man within the rapist?

C: I felt lighter, and as if there was light all around.

T: Yes. Now I want you to let that light—ask gently within for it—to multiply, and get very bright.

C: Oh yes, it feels bright (she smiles). It's like little rainbow sparkles everywhere that cleans and heals and makes happy what it touches.

T: I want you to take some of that and help me fly around the world and spill it into dark pockets of abuse, sadism, and unconscious dominance.

C: Oh, they're everywhere.

T: Yes, but off you go now! (Now the inner child is beaming through my client and off she goes into the imaginal realm, on a magical flight to heal the world!) She returns a little while later and opens her eyes, smiling softly.

"Anyway I can help to do that?" I ask.

"You already are," she beams. "I think I might have resented you if you made me go somewhere I didn't want to."

Robin: I think you did pretty well in empowering her to find her own way. And we need to remember that in this Wasteland material, we are also talking about redeeming the nurturing creative within the man, his feminine: Those healing waters are trying to come welling up within both genders. Knowing that gives us a little fertile ground to work with, even in a very parched, wasted psyche. I have several stories that come to mind here, but I'd like to tell one.

Remember the symposium on "Women Coming of Age" in California at the ITA conference? Gwyneth (our daughter) was a teenager and invited to be on this symposium with some pretty powerful women: Jean Shinoda Bolen, Gloria Steinem, and Brooke Medicine Eagle.

The story Brooke told was of being alone in Mexico, walking down a street, and suddenly she realized she'd gotten herself into a bad place. It was near dusk, and she could see a group of slightly drunk young Mexican men walking toward her. They saw her, and they saw her as a lone woman walking, which you just don't do in a little Mexican town, and they began to joke among themselves, and they were preparing to come up to her to be really aggressive.

There was a moment, I suppose, of absolute panic, which any woman would feel, and then, wonderful medicine woman that she is, Brooke said she just suddenly looked at these young men walking toward her and she said, "Wait a minute—they are my brothers; those young men are just like my brothers. They're a little drunk, they're a little callous toward women, they're all the things my brothers were, you know." She just said that in her mind.

Then she walked toward them, rather than trying to turn around and walk away, she walked toward them, as she would walk toward her brothers when they were being rowdy, and a bit out of control, she just looked at them, as if to say, "Hello brother, I'm your sister, remember me?" They looked at her, and she looked at them, and she walked right through them, right past them, and they saw her as their sister.

Stephen: That's a wonderful story, and I can easily see Brooke doing that, with her wise-woman energy, just like an act of magic. Whose reality are we in, mine or yours? If I project that reality with medicine power, it really does affect those guys. They're in a kind of shiftless dream anyway, looking for trouble, letting the alcohol work on them.

She really changed the mythology of the situation, from a scenario of "this is happening in outer space; I'm the victim, and these are the predators," to a sibling family construct, which was exactly the right thing to do. To say or do exactly the right thing at that critical moment you did not plan on, and yet there you are—this is the "heroic" dimension in life, for a person of either gender. This is the "gentle warrior."

Robin: Sam Keen says in *Faces of the Enemy* that it is the truly "unknown" quality that makes for enemies.[26] What is unknown, is separated, is over there. This is what allows the enemy to be essentially faceless, and then to receive the projection of hatred and hostility and dangerousness. Whenever we are projecting, we need this distance of the other, to depersonalize them. They don't have feelings like we do, they don't suffer like we do, they don't have the same basic rights to their lives like we do.

Stephen: And that's the peculiar thing about the other gender: they are, in an existential sense, *other*. It's a situation that's both intensely dangerous and intensely interesting. It invites projection, big time, and it even invites the *nagual*, the unknown, to which we now have to relate.

That's what came to the woman in the hot tub, that black pit is the *nagual*. If you keep it at bay, you are haunted by a shadowy well of demons. But go into it, and it also turns into a well of story. That's how my client was healed, by telling her stories, or the stories that wanted to come through her. She's doing very well, by the way, exploring art, making things, writing. She identifies very much with the greenwitch in the first story she experienced. We went back and found that little magic lady under a black heavy rock.

Robin: I think you did a nice piece of soul-retrieval there. The piece of soul broken off by trauma is recaptured through an encounter with the darkness within, and brought back through story and image. This is exactly what I was talking about before in regard to the redemption of the wasteland. The therapist has to bring the compassionate heart to the painful wound in the soul and clear away the debris from the old well—then the water can come bubbling forth that heals the Wasteland.

From *The Story of King Arthur and His Knights*
by Howard Pyle

CHAPTER NINE

THE REDEMPTION
OF THE WASTELAND

But the view of humans as separate and superior to the rest of Nature is only part of larger cultural patterns. For thousands of years, Western culture has become increasingly obsessed with the idea of dominance: with dominance of humans over nonhuman Nature, masculine over the feminine, wealthy and powerful over the poor, with the dominance of the West over non-Western cultures. Deep ecological consciousness allows us to see through these erroneous and dangerous illusions.

Bill Deval and George Sessions, *Deep Ecology*[1]

SPIRITUALITY AND CREATIVE MYTHOLOGY

IF THE DOMINANT CULTURE OF EUROPE had devalued the feminine through the Middle Ages, it seems astonishing to contemplate the renaissance of the feminine ideal in the tradition of courtly love and the celebrations of the troubadours. We have said that the redemption of the power urge is its encounter with compassion, chakra four. In the language of the troubadours, this is called the "gentle heart," and its cultivation is truly the awakening of a psychic organ—the organ of refined and empathic feeling.

We remember de Borneih's "The eyes are the Scouts of the Heart." The heart is thus, without question, first smitten by the physical beauty of its object. Beauty should convey qualities beyond itself, however. Sweetness of temperament, loyalty, strength of character, depth of understanding, compassion (especially for those weaker than oneself), and tenderness for children—these are the province of the heart for a person of either gender. And these qualities of heart in sufficient measure bode well for the long-term relationship—in short, for the creation of an angel. If the heart is sound, the other faculties circle around it, like the planets around the sun. Each little "world" within the soul, then, develops an ecology of its own. The psyche is fruitful, energetic, centered; there is a warmth to the personality that overflows to "all our relations." The wasteland is revivified. But night and dew also play their part in the making of a fruitful world, as well as clouds, rain, and crackling thunder. "As above, so below." These phenomena of nature also hold a place in our souls.

Swedenborg's view of the texture of reality is that it is self-reflective. At every stage of the Ray of Creation, it manifests its divine radiance in symbolic forms he called "correspondences." His insights are not much different from those of the ancient Taoist metaphysicians or the medieval alchemists: of course, the human heart "corresponds" to the sun. But Swedenborg goes further. Every time you take a breath, and your heart beats, synchronously or not (and there are various psychophysiological implications of cardiac-respiratory arrhythmias) a *mysterium coniunctionis* takes place, a heavenly marriage. In effect, while your heart beats and your lungs breathe, they support one another's activities, and even beget spiritual children in the mind. (That is why many spiritual disciplines involve control of the breath, something which Swedenborg also practiced, as revealed in his *Spiritual Diaries*.)[2]

> In order to learn not just the fact that there is a correspondence of heavenly things (matters of love) with heart motions and of spiritual things (matters of faith from love) with lung motions, but to learn also how this happens, I was allowed on one extraordinary occasion to be for some time among angels who presented this vividly.
>
> By a marvelous flowing into circles, quite beyond the power of words to describe, they formed a likeness of a heart and a likeness of lungs, with all their inner and outer fibers. They were then following the flow of heaven freely, since heaven strives toward this kind of form because of the inflow of love from the Lord. In that way they presented the details within the heart and then a oneness between heart and lungs, which they also pictured by a marriage of the good and the true.[3]

You don't have to join an ashram to do this (but you may choose to). Every breath and heartbeat celebrates a mystic marriage. The beneficiaries of this *coniunctio* are the brain, well nourished by blood and oxygen, and the soul well nourished by contemplating heartfully and understandingly. Slow your breath—or do rapid "rebirthing" breathing—and your consciousness will definitely alter; new kinds of understandings will be precipitated. Hold these rather poetic ideas in mind as you add, next, the layer of the inspired (spiritually breathed-into) images and words of the medieval courts of love.

The eminent mythologist Joseph Campbell is thought by many to have articulated a new direction of psychospiritual development for the West in the coming age. From over twenty years of studying with him, we feel that this is so. In this chapter, we explore his ideas in some depth, using the material that was the core of his vision for humankind and the core of his magnum opus *The Masks of God*.[4] The tetralogy at first inspection would seem to be a kind of tour de force of erudition and scholarship, leading from "primitive" to oriental and occidental mythologies. By the fourth volume, *Creative Mythology*, it was as if Campbell had paid his dues intellectually to the major culture zones of the planet. Now it was time for his own creative mind to take off into the zone of possibility, the mind of the heart to follow the eyes of his spirit into new territory. (The authors feel just that way at this point in this book; we've laid the groundwork and paid the dues to the shadow; now it is time to envision what partnership might be like in the new millennium.)

Since his earliest scholarship at Columbia University, Campbell was fascinated by tales of the Grail, that mysterious vessel that seems to contain something nourishing for the Wasteland, the setting in which it appears. His Proudfit Fellowship (a Guggenheim or Rhodes-like award) was to take him to France in his midtwenties to research the Grail literature from the south of France, the Vulgate Latin and Provençal texts. At Columbia, Campbell studied with Roger Loomis, the noted Arthurian scholar, and encountered there the writings of Geoffrey of Monmouth, Robert de Boron, and, of course, Thomas Mallory. Now he was to go into the zone of some of the more mysterious sources of the Arthurian material: Guiraut de Borneilh, Chrétien de Troyes, and their own, older sources. Campbell spent a year, with the aid of a special tutor, H. K. Stone, an American scholar who had long dwelt in Paris, attacking the more difficult texts.[5]

But by the end of that year, 1927–1928, Campbell's mind was already straying north, to a zone that ignited his metaphysical as well as romantic imagination. Here the Arthurian authority was Wolfram von Eschenbach, in his great high-Gothic work *Parzival*. Campbell later was to say that, through this work, Wolfram announced the new path, at once spiritual and secular, for the West. It is this *Parzival* we shall use herein, as well as some of Campbell's insightful recountings and interpretations of this story—which redeems the broken hearts of Abélard and Héloise, Tristan and Isolt, and undoes the curse of Balin.

Campbell also began reading James Joyce, Freud, and Jung that year. He leaped out of the culture zone of France and Spain, and into German and Sanskrit studies. Work of these cultures added, he felt, the psychospiritual dimension lacking in the French Romance tradition. He spent the year before the Great Depression (1928–1929) in Munich, at its great university, the Proudfit having been extended, after a request from Campbell, for another year. A new depth and breadth had also been extended to Campbell's medieval studies, never reached by those who stayed obediently in their separate scholarly provinces.

Those of us who heard Campbell lecture in person on this subject over and over remember how he lit up when he came to the story of Parzival. His eyes would glitter, and he would seem to begin to channel Taliesin, or Wolfram, for that matter. Robin remembers that, before he ever used slides in his lecturing, Campbell would vividly describe some mythological figure such as Cundrie, that repulsive, magical hag all dressed in satin, sitting saucily on her piebald mule, with her "snout and tushes like a boar." Campbell, as he told her story and described her, would "place" her by gestures somewhere on the stage of the lecture hall. Then he would go on to other matters—no less vividly evoked; but sometime later he would return to the subject of Cundrie, and as he gestured to that spot on the stage, precisely where he had placed her, members of the audience could be seen to turn their heads in that direction: there she would remain, an "eidetic image," just as he had fashioned her; or so it seemed to those of us truly enraptured. This, we thought, was the power of Gwydion, spell weaver of the *Mabinogion*, to make the listener see what the bard says.

This is the same way audiences throughout Europe, from the Renaissance onward, heard these tales, well told by minnesingers and bards. Through the ambience of countless courts and theaters, a mythology was born of the soul in the service of a gentle heart. It was to change the world. *Courtoisie*, knightly speech, deeds of valour in the service of a lady—these captivated the heart of Europe, from the courts of Castile and Aragon to Avignon and Carcasonne. Everywhere, too, the growing middle-class of townspeople—merchants and craftsmen and their ladies—demonstrated their new wealth by the presence at the dinner table of poets who could recite the irresistible romances. The Arthurian tradition involves about as many historically and dramatically interesting women as men; and it was the women who inspired the deeds of the men, the women to whom Balin would not listen, the magical castle full of women that shows up in Gawain's adventures.

The tradition spread so rapidly and enthusiastically that it seemed eleventh-, twelfth-, and thirteenth-century Europe had found its soul. But the Catholic Church became alarmed. This business of souls was, after all, their business. And this poetic, secular tradition was much too passionate, popular, and attractive. Their patriarchal Wasteland was being greened by a grassroots tradition. Something had to be done!

Marie-Louise von Franz says,

> In the love courts men began to develop a relationship to women, and women to men; that was the start of individual love relationships with the other sex. . . . The Church fought courtly love, because things began to slip out of its hands. And at the moment of the abolishing of courtly love and the rise of the cult of the Virgin Mary to replace it, the witch hunts began. . . . So by replacing the individual choice with a collective archetypal symbol of the Virgin Mary, the personal element was lost. Only the collective feminine element was preserved.[6]

The theological landscape of Europe had been in danger of becoming the desert of the patriarchs. The little Black Madonnas had survived in their shrines and grottoes throughout the landscape and continued to inspire and work their miracles. But in the twelfth century began the "highest concentration of moral fervor" ever in the West, as Henry Adams put it in *Mont-Saint-Michel and Chartres*, the building of the "lady" churches of Europe.[7] The great cathedral at Chartres, still one of the wonders of the world, was later to be followed by greater and lesser *Notre-Dame* churches everywhere.

The outlay of time, effort, and capital has never been equaled in the service of any single cause short of war, says Adams. Conservative estimates, in the nineteenth century when buildings cost far less than today, are of over five billion dollars expended during a single century, not to mention the volunteer work and loving artisanry given *pro bono* for the Virgin that is impossible to estimate.[8]

It was an enormous countermovement to the "Goddess defamation league" for whom Eve, Lilith, "the Witch Venus," and the Scarlet Woman of the Apocalypse, steeped in sexuality and sensuality, were all next to the devil in wickedness. Here we had an etherialized counterpart, the Lady believed to have carried our Lord in her womb. (We have mentioned those delightful little statues and *pietas* through-out Europe, where Christ is seen as a luminous babe, or a mature slain savior, in the lap of his mother—the divine-human spiritual principle clearly shown supported, nourished, held in the "lap" of a larger feminine principle, the "Great Goddess," the Ground of all Being. This theme will emerge in a different form in some of our tales.

Churches and *places* are dedicated to her because she is environment, con-text, and sacred enclosure. Against her velvety nourishing darkness, Christ, the an-gels, the succession of saints are luminous apparitions whose comings and goings mark our calendars (BCE, AD, etc.) Historically, it seems the cult of the Virgin was offered as a sacralized, acceptable version of the "Lady" cult, offering a legitimate ec-clesiastical alternative to those who longed for a way to celebrate the feminine face of the Spirit. (From this historical perspective, it may have slightly wooed devotees from their courtly-love enterprises; but in other ways, it enriched that mythology with a celestialization of the feminine principle, and, suddenly, women had some-thing positive in their archetypal *imagos* again.)

Campbell was enamored of von Eschenbach's treatment because it was a secular, humanistic awakening that was prophesied and a mythology of the coming together of the genders. The *hieros gamos* was to be discovered and revealed in the biographics and adventures of human characters. To be sure, divine guidance and providence appear everywhere in *Parzival*, and the whole adventure is permeated by spiritual themes. But Campbell loved the Grail material so much probably because it pertained, on the whole, to a feminine symbol, the Grail itself. In another way of saying it, driven, phallic men, acting out a deadly charade of machismo kept stum-bling into the feminine: mysterious women who arrive girt with deadly swords, damask-wrapped feminine arms that extend them from lakes; damsels who offer apocalyptic words at crossroads; others who need rescue, but also ones who impose formidable ordeals; and those who dwell in mysterious castles together, as in the *Chateaux Merveilleuse* in Gawain's story. Mysterious and beautiful women announce quests, and then become the prize, like the Grail, at the end. The real hero in Campbell's definition is not a "Rambo," who smashes all obstacles by dint of natu-ral endowment or special mission. The deeper *mythos* is that of the hero who has gone to the depths, encountered the unknown, been wounded, even died, like the shamanic initiate, and returned with "the power to bestow boons on (his) fellow men." The authentic hero learns not by exerting *force majeure*, but by submitting and learning from experience.

In the early 1970s, the authors were traveling with Joseph. In the car were also Lenni Schwarz and Joan Halifax, women who loved Joe deeply. He started to tell a story that obviously left him piqued, probably about one of his Sarah Lawrence students. He told how she kept wanting to play the male role in the hero adventure. "But darling," he had said to her (Joseph was never archly patronizing, only sweetly so), "You initiate the hero's quest, inspire and guide him, await at the end of his journey, and make love to him. What more do you want?" The young woman had-n't missed a beat: "I want to be the hero." Joseph implied that this was a bit much.

Then, it got lively. Joseph tried to hold his ground, but also laughed and ob-viously admired the fire in the three women's minds. "I am not the Great Goddess," said Joan. "I do not wait in towers to be rescued," said Robin. "I need to be more than symbolic," said Lenni. (Stephen wisely shut up.) The gist of their very worthy argument was that, indeed, the hero journey is not for men alone. It is the story of the psyche on its road of adventure, valid for human men and for women. Call it a rather lovely atavism, but Joe held on to his courtly love position. That gallant tradition allowed him to put women just a little higher up and closer in to the Throne of Love than men, and that's probably just fine. (He never would change the masculine gender pronoun in his writing, either!) Joseph also, despite what he said, played the traditional role of "mother's brother," providing weapons of scholarship for many an aspiring young female knight-errant. Robin remembers, "He cheered us on as we rode forth to adventure, and he supported and comforted us when we sometimes took a hard fall."

But let us peek, now, at both the original material from which Campbell learned so much, and his own grappling with it, while remaining mindful of our overall intent: what can the Parzival story tell us about the fashioning of angels?

PARZIVAL'S JOURNEY

"BRAVE, AND SLOWLY WISE: thus I hail my hero," says Wolfram von Eschenbach.[9] Thus, we also know that the spiritual task being modeled is the art of learning wisdom from experience. This is something quite different from the blinding flash of Eastern traditions. It is a gradual revelation, as the "intelligible character" (Schopenhauer's term) of the hero meets her/his destiny, spread out over both geography and history. (Please now consider the word "hero" to be gender-free, in the sense we have introduced, pertaining to the soul growth of either gendered individual.)

Parzival's father, Gahmuret, was a knightly hero who ultimately would meet his death on the battlefield. But the story really begins before Parzival was even "a twinkle in Gahmuret's knightly eye" when he visited the mysterious African kingdom of Zazamanc and fell in love with a beautiful black princess, Belakane. The princess confessed she had been "hesitant in love," and her beloved, Isenhart, a noble and worthy youth, to get her attention rode into battle without a helmet and was killed. Now two armies besieged her, one to avenge Isenhart, the other for herself and/or kingdom. Gahmuret rode forth and defeated the champions of both sides, whereupon the grateful Belakane bestowed upon him, the poet says, "both her kingdom and herself." But alas, so great was the queen's love that she tried to restrain Gahmuret from knightly deeds, for therein resided, she sensed, his death and her loss. But his *wyrd*, his destiny, drew him on to that deadly game that was his chosen medium of self-expression. Gahmuret would not be contained.

And so Belakane had even more reason to mourn the knightly path, as did many a damsel in that age, for she was pregnant with Gahmuret's child; but now alone and in sorrow, she bore their son, Parzival's older brother, Feirefiz Angevin, due to enter this story later; and whether this is the poet's naivete or a marvelous dramatic touch, "he was said to be piebald, like a magpie's plumage," black and white, reflecting his ancestry; and we are told that Belakane kissed all the white spots on her son and mourned her lost love.

Riding far to the west, Gahmuret came upon a tournament declared by Herzeloyde of Wales: the victor was to wed her. Present were the formidable Morholt of Ireland (whom we have met in Tristan and Isolt as Morold); Arthur's and Gawain's fathers, King Uther and King Lot, respectively; Rivalin, who would sire Tristan; and many another noble knight and lady. Onto this scene, with his beautifully caparisoned horses, came the "Rich King of Zazamanc" (Gahmuret), to set up his lavish tents and pavilions. In the fray Gahmuret unhorsed many and many a mighty man, until he alone ruled the field; thus came to him Herzeloyde, who offered herself as the rightful purse of the victor.

Gahmuret explained about his African wife, but Herzeloyde insisted on the primacy of Christian baptism over his Moorish marriage and on her right to his hand and love. He finally accepted her when she had sworn she would not try to keep him from knighthood, as had Belakane. Then he did an amazing thing, such was the generosity of his spirit. He gave gold to all the men he had defeated on the battlefield, and set them free (though by law he could have laid any *geis* on them he wished). The halls were full of praise of the rich King of Zazamanc that day.

Soon Herzeloyde was with child and Gahmuret at war, helping his old patron, the caliph. In that war, mighty though he was, Gahmuret was slain, and two women widowed at once.

The child of Herzeloyde, like his half-brother, was also large and strong. His mother now, by choice, lived simply in a cottage, in a place apart from all normal social commerce, courts or knighthood. Herzeloyde called him, "*bon fils, cher fils, beau fils*" ("good boy, dear boy, handsome boy) and was the boy's only companion for many years. Gradually he grew older—and more inquisitive, this strange social isolate. But his mother told him "not to ask too many questions." When he asked her about God, she told him that God was "brighter than day, yet assumed the form of a man." So it was that one day while wandering out in the woods, he encountered two mounted knights in their bright, polished armor. The youth thought they must be "God's angels" and fell to his knees. The knights assured him of who and what they actually were, and he listened wide-eyed, his attention riveted.

When the young man returned home, he told his mother what he had seen, how wonderful these creatures called "knights" were, and what they said; she promptly fainted. He now resolved to go forth and find more knights. Herzeloyde did not want to lose another man she loved. She dressed young Parzival in fool's clothing, and gave him four pieces of advice: cross streams where they are the most shallow; greet people with the words, "God protect you!"; ask advice of those with grey hair; and, finally, win a good lady's ring and then kiss and embrace her. She also sent him off in the opposite direction of King Arthur's court—which path he went along bobbing and saying "God save you!" to everyone he met. (When he left, his mother, gazing down the road where he had gone, fell over and died.)

The young man proceeded blithely along until he came to a wood, where a tent was to be seen. There a lovely woman lay asleep. Parzival pounced on her, took her ring, stole a kiss, ate some food—wasn't he hungry?—took another kiss by force, and went his way. When the lady's knight, Duke Orilus de Lalander, returned, he was furious at the violation, but took it out on the lady. He announced that he would now curb her pride: she would be obliged to wear rags and to ride upon a broken saddle (which he wrecked), and her horse would be starved. This noble knight then rode off in search of the youth who had insulted his honor, while his lady trailed wretchedly behind him.

Then Parzival found a lady beneath a forest cliff, holding a dead knight and weeping. When she asked him his name he said the only thing he remembered his mother calling him, "*bon fils, cher fils, beau fils.*" It was Sigune, his mother's sister's child, and she recognized him. "Your name," she told him is Parzival—'through the middle'—for the furrow of grief that love cut through your mother's faithful heart,"and she made sure he knew that his father had been the cause of it. The knight in her lap had died defending his heritage against Lähelin, who had also wronged Parzival's mother, and Orilus, the man Parzival had just insulted. Now Parzival knew his name, at least. He continued on his muddled way.

But a fisherman (take note) took pity on him, and brought him back in another direction to King Arthur's court. On the way into the hall, he passed a red knight riding, with a cup, out of the hall. The knight sent the ragged fool inside with a message. He apologized for spilling wine on the queen as he had seized the cup, a way of asserting his claim to part of Arthur's kingdom. And now he waited outside for his challenge to be met. His name was King Kukumerlant. Parzival did as he was bade. He went inside and stood before the snickering court. He asked if he could be made a knight and how to get armor, as the great knight outside had. The company laughed at Parzival, and Keie the seneschal told him to, "Get it yourself!"

Now there was in the court a young woman, one Cunneware, about whom it had been prophesied that she would never laugh in her life, until she saw the "flower of knighthood." But she laughed at Parzival. And crude rude Keie, so used to seeing her taciturn, beat her with his staff.

So Parzival trotted outside, got on his pony, went to the armed knight, and asked for his suit of armor. The knight, already in a fighting mood, scornfully reversed his lance and sent Parzival and his pony flying, whereupon Parzival got to his feet and flung a dart (a small spear he had practiced with, day after day in the woods) right through the grill of the Red Knight's vizor. The mighty warrior fell to the earth, dead.

With the help of a little squire, Parzival got the armor off the dead man and onto himself. He put his rough (but effective) darts down; picked up the lance, shield, and sword (the squire giving him quick coaching in how to use them); mounted his new charger; and rode away, sending the squire back in with the cup and a message to tell the beaten maid, Cunneware, that he would avenge her.

Parzival rode his horse at a gallop all day, and by nightfall had arrived at the towers of Prince Gurnemanz de Graharz. The gray-haired man sat, with his falcon beneath a tree; Parzival, as he had been told to do of gray-haired men, asked advice of him. The old knight had noticed that Parzival spoke, artlessly and ceaselessly, of his mother. He was moved to help the callow youth, and so gave him hospitality for a season and, during that time, much training in the arts of knighthood. The old man told him never to lose his sense of shame, for such a man has no worth; to have compassion for the needy; to be moderate, neither squandering nor hoarding; not to ask too many questions; to be merciful as well as brave—to accept the oath and grant the life of a fallen foe; to be manly and cheerful; to treat women with honor; and to understand that husband and wife are as one, blossoming from a single seed.

Old Gurnemanz wanted Parzival to marry one of his daughters, but the young man said he must first prove himself in the field. (Note that, through all his foolishness, there is wisdom beginning to show in this youth. Obtuse and literalistic from his social isolation and neurotic mother, still he has incredible strength and good reflexes, and he listens to wise counsel.)

Parzival then left on quest. At this time, he began a practice, noted by Campbell as highly significant, of laying the reins of his horse on its neck and letting the animal take him whither it would. In this way, Parzival came to a strange castle, under siege. It was heavily defended, but a woman leaned out of a window and asked if he were friend or foe. He replied that he was eager to do her service, and his answer gained his admittance.

Parzival was led through the defenses of the castle, past ranks of fighters and other folk, all lean and sickly from the privation of the siege. Nevertheless, he was treated with royal courtesy, relieved of his armor, bathed, and clothed in a mantle of sable fur, which had (the poet tells us) "a fresh, wild smell." He was then taken to the maiden queen Condwiramurs, whose radiance outshone even the two Isolts. He sat mute beside her, obedient to old Gurnemanz's teaching, as he thought, until the queen—who was becoming increasingly self-conscious—at last broke the silence. Then Parzival told of his training by Gurnemanz, and she identified herself as the old lord's niece.

At last, the young knight was escorted to his bed, where he fell asleep. But in the deep of the night, he was awakened by Condwiramurs, weeping by his bed. Wolfram says that she was dressed for combat: she wore a nightgown of white silk and a mantle of samite.

When Parzival saw the maiden kneeling there, he asked if she was mocking him: "Lady, one kneels like that only to God." But she begged him to promise to behave honorably and not to wrestle with her.

And so there they lay, the youth and the maid, side by side, and she opened her heart. There was a powerful king, one Clamide, with his seneschal, Kingrun, a fierce warrior, who had taken every castle of her land, killed the elder son of Gurnemanz, and now wanted Condwiramurs for his wife. "But I am ready," she said, "to kill myself before I will surrender my maidenhood and body to Clamide. You have seen the high walls of my palace; I will cast myself down into the moat before he shall have me by force."

As she wept bitterly, Parzival's heart was moved: "Lady," he said, " you shall be defended by my hand so far as it is in my power."

So the following day Parzival rode out of the gate into the army of Kingrun and singled out its leader. They came together so hard that the girths of both saddles broke. Their swords flashed and presently Kingrun lay on his back, and had to surrender. Parzival remembered his mentor's advice, and said the defeated man must go to Gurnemanz.

"You would be kinder to kill me; I slew his son, Schentaflurs," said the knight.

"Then you must surrender to Queen Condwiramurs."

"Were I to enter her town, her people would hack me in pieces," Kingrun said.

Parzival got an idea: "Go to King Arthur's court and submit yourself to the maiden who suffered pain there because of me."

Parzival was proving apt at his father's skill, the winning of kingdoms belonging to beautiful women, without ever having been tutored by him.

So Condwiramurs embraced her deliverer before all the citizens, and declared him to be her *ami*, her lord and theirs. Peculiarly, the couple lay chastely in the same bed for three days, before finally they entwined legs and arms and Parzival found the closeness sweet; and that custom, old yet ever new, was theirs thereafter.

Then arrived Clamide himself, with all the engines of war. When he learned of the marriage of the woman he had come to force, he declared a challenge for single combat to her new husband. Parzival rode forth and, in front of the assembled army, vanquished Clamide. He was about to do him in, when the latter begged for mercy; again, Parzival sent him to Arthur's Court, to the Lady Cunneware, to present himself for service. Thus began an amazing series of arrivals, for that court, of knights that Parzival had overcome and spared.

Now there were fifteen months of "love and jubilation," and the newlyweds found happiness and fulfillment in that time. But there came a day when Parzival longed for news of his mother and said to Lady Condwiramurs that he must seek her out. Although she was sad, the young wife let him go. Parzival was not long gone when suddenly he entered the zone of mystery.

His horse carried him through forest and marsh as it would, for the reins lay loose on its neck as before. But now the Red Knight rode through the changing foliage of September into October, until one evening he arrived at a lake where two fishermen sat in a boat at anchor. One was dressed as richly as a king, wearing a hat plumed with peacock feathers. Parzival inquired of this gentleman where lodging might be found. The fisherman—a man of sorrowful mien—gave him directions to the one nearby house, a castle on a hill surrounded by a moat. "But ride with care," the fisherman warned. "The roads here can lead you astray on the slopes. If you arrive safely, I myself will be your host tonight."

Parzival proceeded as instructed and finally arrived at a castle, saying "the fisherman sent me." He was admitted, and his armor removed. When they saw his boyish form and innocent face, they rejoiced. They clad him in a silk cloak and brought him into a vast hall, lighted by a hundred chandeliers and more candles upon the walls. There were as many couches, placed well apart, and upon each were seated four knights. They had no need to count costs in that wealthy house: in three grand marble fireplaces blazed fires of fragrant aloewood. The lord of the castle was carried in and positioned before the centermost of these. It was indeed the Fisher King, who now bade Parzival sit beside him. Wolfram tells us elsewhere that this lord's injury was such that it gave him incessant pain, and he could not sit, lie, or stand. His great household was ruled by sorrow.

Suddenly, a squire came rushing into the hall, bearing a lance; by this rite, the sorrow sharpened. Blood gushed from its point and ran down its length to the bearer's hand, where it reddened his sleeve. The squire bore the bleeding lance once around the hall while all the company wept and wailed. When he reached the door again, he ran out.

Twelve maidens then entered by twos and fours, some princesses among them; all were gowned exquisitely. These were followed by six more, two bearing on cloths two sharp silver knives that gleamed in the light of the candles borne by the other four. These ladies' gowns were of two kinds of silk, one dark, the other shot with gold. Approaching the lord's table, they all courteously bowed. They placed their two knives upon the table, and all six withdrew and joined the earlier twelve. Now entered six more noble maidens in similarly particolored gowns; these carried glass vessels containing lights of costliest balsam. After them entered the queen, Repanse de Schoye, radiant as the rising sun. She was dressed in Arabian silk; and on a deep green silken cloth shot through with threads of gold, she bore the Joy of Paradise, both root and branch.

This was the Grail. No earthly joy was equal to it. Its bearer was required to preserve her purity and spurn all falseness. This queen, with her six maidens bearing the lights of balsam, bowed courteously as she placed the Grail before the host—while Parzival, watching, could only think, "The robe I have on is hers."

A hundred tables now were brought in and set before the couches and white cloths spread upon them. The host washed his hands from a vessel, which was then offered to Parzival so that he could wash from the same. Costly golden vessels were likewise carried to every knight in the hall, and a hundred squires, bearing white napkins, gathered from the Grail a marvelous feast that they served to all the seated company.

Wolfram tells us that whatever one reached one's hand to take, it was found there before the Grail: warm and cold food, both cultivated and wild, for abundance flowed from the holy vessel as from heaven. And Parzival beheld all this wonder and stayed numb and frozen inside. Had not Gurnemanz, his tutor, told him not to ask too many questions? Even when his host gifted him with his own sword, young Parzival—too well tutored now in the ways of the courtly manners—merely thanked the lord but otherwise kept silent. Then dinner ended, and everyone politely, if perhaps sadly, filed out from the great hall.

And so Parzival retired for the night, politely treated, and well hosteled, but with terrible threatening dreams. In the morning, he awoke in a silent, empty-seeming castle. He found his steed nearby; as he left, he heard a squire at the drawbridge—the only living soul in sight—call out, "Ride on, you goose, and bear the hatred of the Sun." Further on he again met a woman with a dead knight, and again recognized Sigune, his cousin. When she ascertained he had indeed visited Munsalvaesche, she said breathlessly, "I see that you wear the sword. Did you ask the question?"

Parzival replied, "I asked no question."

Then she grew angry: "Alas that I must look upon you! How could you witness such marvels—such suffering—did you not feel pity? You are cursed! At Munsalvaesche, you forfeited both honor and fame. I will say no more." Then Parzival was saddened and despondent, and he went on his way.

Along the way, Parzival met Jeschute, the "lady of the tent" still treated with disgrace and cruelty by her husband, Duke Orilus; wearing rags and forced to ride upon a poor nag with no saddle, she must trail along behind her husband's warhorse. When the woman saw Parzival, she said, "I have seen you before. . . . And may God give you more honor and joy than from your treatment of me you deserve!" Now Orilus, hearing the whinny of Parzival's stallion, came galloping back, spear at the ready. They fought fiercely, but Parzival finally vanquished the other, and commended him to King Arthur's court, and to the Lady Cunneware (whose brother, strange to say, Duke Orilus was). The knight Orilus, humbled, kissed his wife for the first time in a long while. Parzival swore on a sacred relic that she had been blameless in the earlier matter and that he was indeed a fool in those days, who had forced himself on her out of ignorance. The couple was reconciled, and rode off to Arthur's court, in joy.

Now ensued a dream-like sequence. Arthur and the court of Karidoel were out hawking and hunting in pavilions. The time was early winter. Parzival, riding, unbeknownst, nearby, saw three drops of blood in the snow, where hawks from the party had struck at geese. He became lost in a trance, thinking of his wife's complexion: white like the snow, her cheeks and lips as red as blood. The Lady Cunneware's squire saw the strange knight, lost in his trance, and alerted the court knights. One after the other, Sagramors and Keie attacked the strange knight, while he, dreamlike, unhorsed them, and went back to his contemplation. It was Gawain, that thoughtful man, who tried to grasp the nature of the trance. "What if it be love that holds that man enthralled?" he mused (this is important), and rode out more curious than warlike. He threw a yellow scarf over the drops of blood, and Parzival "came back to himself." When he was recognized as the Red Knight who was sending all of his conquests back to King Arthur's court, he was cheered, and Lady Cunneware emerged to welcome him with a kiss.

A feast was celebrated. But then, not much time for merriment had elapsed, when Cundrie the hag, beautifully dressed in silk and satin and riding on her piebald mule, came to the court.

She had a dog's big nose with two wicked boar's tusks protruding from her unappealing lips; her eyebrows were so long she had them braided to her hair ribbon; her ears were like a bear's, and her face was alarmingly hairy; her fingernails were like a lion's claws, and her hands as charming as a monkey's. Her tongue was also not lacking in sharpness.

"Cursed be your beautiful face!" she said to Parzival. "I am less a monster than are you. Sir Parzival, speak! Tell us why, when you sat at table with the sorrowful Fisherman, you did not relieve his suffering?"

She continued in this vein until Parzival was thoroughly humiliated. Then she broke off weeping and wringing her be-ringed hands. Regaining her composure at last, she addressed the entire court with a new challenge.

"Is there here no noble knight who longs to win fame and noble love? I know of a Castle of Wonders where four queens and four-hundred maidens are captive. All other adventure is mere wind compared to what might be won there. The journey is difficult, and yet I shall be in that castle this very night."

Then Cundrie la Sorcière rode off abruptly, crying out, "O Munsalvaesche, sorrow's home! To comfort you, alas, there now is none!"

Parzival learned on this occasion much about his ancestry and birth, and heard of the noble man, his half-brother Feirefiz. A knight arrived at the court and gave to all polite greetings, save Gawain, whom he denounced as murderous and dishonorable, and challenged to meet him forty days hence in a place called

"Schanpfanzun." Gawain, always cheerful and optimistic, accepted the challenge courteously. Then he came to Parzival and kissed him.

"My friend, God give you good fortune in battle," he said, "and may his power help me to serve you one day as I would like."

"Alas," replied Parzival, "what is God? If he were great, he would not have heaped undeserved disgrace on us both. I was in his service, hoping to receive his grace. But now I renounce his service. If he hates me, I shall bear it. Friend, when it is your time for battle, may a woman's love be your guard! I do not know when I will see you again, but my good wishes go with you."

At this point, in *Creative Mythology* and often in his lectures, Campbell declares an "intermezzo" and so should we, lest the details of the story overwhelm us, and we lose its sense. We will sift through a few themes and issues, before returning to the stories of both Parzival and Gawain; and we will see how they are interwoven and related, before this tale's completion.

THE FIRST FAILURE OF THE GRAIL TASK

THERE IS SOMETHING AMAZING ABOUT Wolfram von Eschenbach's story. Although Parzival has failed the Grail quest, been rebuked, and cursed God, still he seems to be on the right track. There is something favoring the *wyrd* of this holy fool. He has done lots of things wrong, but a few right. But his heart seems to be good (remember how important this is in von Franz's formulation). He does not suffer the awful curse of Balin, where everything that he touches really does go awry. Parzival has muffed quite a few things so far, but in ways clearly traceable to his upbringing. He rode forth into the world as a naive fool, because of his mother's anxiety. What is Herzeloyde's fear? That she will lose what she greatly loves, as she loved and lost fierce, noble Gahmuret. She knows, with her mother's heart, she must lose Parzival sooner or later. She develops a neurosis, fears everything associated with knighthood, which, truth be told, is a Dance of Death that separates many tender hearts.

The story, like any good myth, explains the problem that is its deeper subject, and it is related to our theme: The tableaux Parzival keeps stumbling into is a kind of *pieta*, a woman with a dead knight in her lap. The anguish of women in this crazy, violent medieval world must have been palpable—a grief wound in the morphogenetic field. Women who sent their sons to battle in the twentieth century know the same anguish: "Did I conceive in love, carry, birth and cherish this beautiful young man, to go into this unmitigated horror of a world at war?" Herzeloyde's neurosis was a kind of cultural mental illness engendered by the masculine principle totally out of control.

Parzival is receptive to maternal instruction, and this is good. However, we know that no amount of mother's love can keep him from life, from an encounter with the world in which he lives. But that love, given to a child, can imbue him with an overflowing heart, a generosity of spirit, and an essential security that, matched with good genes, carry him far (Swedenborg's "remains"). Unlike Balin, Parzival does not suffer from an inattentive, explosive, oppositional-defiant learning disorder (mingled with hyperactivity), rather the opposite: "Yes mother, tell me what to do and I will do it." This approach will carry Parzival much farther and in an opposite spiritual direction than Balin, but still he has to become conscious of his fundamentalistic obedience.

We remember that social psychologist Stanley Milgram, developmental psychologist Lawrence Kohlberg, and many others have shown that unquestioning obedience to authority is at the bottom of the ladder of cognitive development. (It might be fine for a six- or seven-year-old, a little regressive for a ten- or eleven-year-old; but it is "uncool" for a teenager and a truly dangerous quality of mind for an adult.)

Youthful, naive, and full of juice, Parzival obeys his mother—to the peril of Jeschute, the woman in the tent. He doesn't think to imagine the consequences of his action for the woman, nor consider the paranoid and violent overprotectiveness of the man.[10] Then emerges a horrible charade of wronged manly honor, when Orilus subjects his wife to unremitting humiliation for something that could be no fault of her own. Orilus should have known how perilous a woody bower, off in nowhere, could be, yet he rode off, leaving her there, vulnerable. This is not unlike Medusa's humiliation by the combined deities Poseidon and Athena. The sexual attractiveness of the woman (one of the things that makes her a witch) provokes a god in the Medusa story; in the Parzival story, a fool. Jeschute had to bear humiliation, simply because she was a sexually attractive woman.

What is telling is that, in the later meeting, Parzival has learned enough to know why Jeschute rebukes him. He is beginning to face, unlike Balin, the consequences of his actions *before* they snowball. He sets out to make restitution. First, he undoes violent Orilus—the only way to bring this proud cock to a receptive attitude—and puts him at the service of a lady, even as he has exerted his unquestioned right over one. Then, Parzival explains his earlier foolishness, apologizes, making specifically sure he swears on a holy relic that Jeschute is innocent, and sends them both on to Cunneware.

Now this lady, Cunneware, is one of the most fascinating characters in the tale. Her name means "holder, or knower, of the feminine organ." Thus, knight after knight must learn, at the hands of the holy fool, to submit to the feminine. One learns, through defeat, to be the deeper kind of hero Campbell is proposing. This is one of the ways that a violent, headstrong warrior can be transformed into "a knight of gentle heart," a gentle-man. It is the opposite of what naive male warriors tell themselves, that they can only become a hero by winning. Cunneware is a lady under a curse, that she may not laugh until she sees "the flower of knighthood," which means she may not show genuine feeling, spontaneous mirth, until the holy fool—who is also "the flower"—appears. She suffers, in his presence, the unthinking, crude violence of Keie. The restitution is that she thereafter receives male after macho male, to submit themselves to her insruction. (In effect, Cunneware becomes a kind of social worker who works with spousal abusers and violent, impulsive men.)

Parzival meets Condwiramurs, literally, she who "leads to love," in a veritable battlefield, a battlefield of and for love. Here we see the third chakra taking the second, like spoils of war—Clamide trying to win his lady by "taking her lands" and leaving her no choice. Violence is his path to love, and the lady will have none of it.

Now the lady does come "dressed for war," the text says, in a diaphanous silk nightgown, to Parzival's bed. This is like the later "tests of character" that Gawain endures, when the beautiful wife of his host tries, in several situations, to seduce him (the most famous is in the medieval, "Sir Gawain and the Green Knight"). After Parzival's victory, and their marriage, he and Condwiramurs lie demurely for three nights, probably a significant number, before they "entwine arms and legs." That is to say, they are a couple who discover love mutually, not the unilateral thing Clamide and Kingrun have in mind. These violent impulses must be defeated by the "gentle way" of mutual finding of love. Thereafter, and Campbell credits von Eschenbach for this, they are truly and mutually married, a model, a paradigm for the future.

Parzival's father, Gahmuret, twice won ladies in the same way, by over-throwing knights that were vying for the lady's hand or besieging the kingdom, and twice won kingdoms in which he would not stay. Nor will Parzival, at least the first time around, for suddenly a qualm of conscience about his mother—of whom he seems not to have thought this entire time—surfaces. But this is the call to the next stage of his adventure.

Parzival fails the test of the Grail because he is now caught in the world—several steps beyond where he started, to be sure of social anxiety. Like Balin, he fails to realize that a different logic from one's habitual thinking pertains to the sacred. Balin snatches at the holy mystery and uses it violently. Parzival, contrastingly, is paralyzed, ineffectual and mute.

We should look at Joseph Campbell's analysis of why he fails the Grail Quest the first time around:

> Parzival's mind on that occasion was on himself and his social reputation. The Round Table stands in Wolfram's work for the social order of the period of which it was the summit and consummation. The young knight's concern for his reputation as one worthy of that circle was his motive for holding his tongue when his own better nature was actually pressing him to speak; and in the light of his conscious notion of himself as a knight worthy of the name, just hailed as the greatest in the world, one can understand his shock and resentment at the sharp judgments of the Loathly Damsel and Sigune. However, those two were the messengers of a deeper sphere of values and possibilities than was yet known, or even sensed, by his socially conscious mind; they were of the sphere not of the Round Table but of the Castle of the Grail, which had not been a feature of the normal daylight world, visible to all, but dreamlike, visionary, mythic—and yet to the questing knight not an unsubstantial mirage. It had appeared to him as the first sign and challenge of a kingdom yet to be earned, beyond the sphere of the world's flattery, proper to his own unfolding life: a kingdom hidden from the known world and screened from even himself by his fascination with the glamour of knighthood; a kingdom the vision of which had opened to him—significantly—only *after* his series of great victories, not as a retreat from failure but as his guerdon of fulfillment. His

decision to act in that intelligible sphere, not according to the dictates of his nature but in terms of what people would think, broke the line of his integrity, and the result to his soul was shown to him alone by the bald-ness of his cousin, but then to all the world, and to his utmost shock and shame, by that Loathly Damsel, richly arrayed, as ugly as a hog.[11]

Sigune, Parzival's cousin, is the sharp-tongued truth "related" to one, that harsh inner voice that would instill "the sense of shame," that Gurnemanz had counseled him to develop. Parzival usually encounters her when he is alone, in the company only of a dead knight she is mourning. What is the truth with which she confronts him? The truth that haunted his mother's unconscious: that this is a seri-ous, lethal business these great boy-men are playing at, as if on holiday, and women are the perennial victims—their murderous games wound women. But taken still further in, to the psychospiritual level: If you insist on blundering around in the world as a jousting field, seeing it as a series of contests, you will strew behind your-self a series of tragedies that will make the soul (the women) mourn and create a wasteland of the world in which you live.

But Cundrie is a still further inflection of this apparition, the "ugly truth" dressed as royalty, in satins, with *panache*, a great feather in her broad-brimmed hat. She is the greatest fear of the socially conscious youth: public humiliation. Here "that which you greatly fear" comes upon you (Job's predicament), and you must weather the ordeal. (What do you do if you are the admittedly youthful president of the country and a would-be Grail King, and your closet sexual peccadilloes are re-vealed to the world and chewed on publicly by the press and by your cruellest crit-ics? Well, if you, and they, have the courage to learn from the experience and see it as an initiation, that is what it will be. In our time, Dame "Ugly Truth" needs to ride into Washington, into Moscow and Peking, Kosovo and Baghdad.) We learn that Cundrie is a secret messenger of the Grail Castle, she rides her long-legged mule out on the business of the Grail—the symbolically feminine inflection of the highest spiritual principle, the Self.

Parzival needs to meet this Loathly Damsel in an episode of public humili-ation; the men are thunderstruck, the women empathic toward the excoriated knight. Now Parzival goes into a black depression with theological overtones. Feel-ing sorry for himself, he renounces his service to God.

These would seem dangerous words, but perhaps they are more acceptable to the spiritual powers than Balin's scornful disregard. Gallant Gawain (the other side of the hero) says, "May God's power help me to serve you one day as I would like." Gawain is all heart, friendship, and devotion, qualities that reside in Parzi-val as well. Going down into darkness' heart, into existential depression—espe-cially about things we ourselves have wrought, but even about things that happen to us—seems indispensable to the soul-making process and is, in fact, a definable stage of the process. To be angry at God is still to be connected to God, and those of us who are therapists have again and again faced the task of helping someone who is estranged from God. (Stephen has found some of the most extreme exam-ples of this in helping parents through the death of a child; the heart is wounded toward the universe or toward "any kind of God that would allow this"—the hor-ror—to happen.)

We return to the Loathly Damsel later in this chapter and the story of Sir Gawain. Suffice it to say at this point that she is also a sow-goddess, with the secret of the underworld as well as of the Grail Castle, keeper of a Mystery and the initiatrix of heroes.

Parzival's "love-trance" speaks of his bond to Condwiramurs, and of what he later says to Gawain, that he must carry (the idea of) his lady into battle, to be victorious. Parzival demonstrates this principle, as well as the Zen of the enraptured mind, by knocking some of Arthur's finest off their horses without seeming even to notice what he is doing. Here we have the opposite of intentionality: unconscious spontaneity winning out, even in the game of the phallic thrust, which seems to be about intention. It takes sophisticated and thoughtful Gawain to realize it is a love trance and to bring Parzival peacefully into the gathering.

In the next series of adventures, Campbell points out, Parzival and Gawain quest on parallel yet related journeys. Parzival is the introvert, Gawain the extrovert; Parzival the naive, Gawain the worldly; yet both men's major adventures involve relating to the ladies. "Could the exploits of Gawain be a disguise for Parzival's initiatory experience?" asks Edward Whitmont penetratingly. He notes that there is also an association of Parzival with Pryderi, of the *Mabinogion*, whose earlier name was "Gwri Gwalt Adwyn," meaning "bright hair." This later is contracted to "Gawain."[12]

Follow us a little further on these parallel tracks, and you will see how both heroes fare with the feminine. While depressed Parzival wanders in the Wasteland of the world, determined never to experience joy until he achieves the Grail, his counterpart, Sir Gawain, optimistic and cheerful as ever, with no such agenda, is heading toward the castle of Schanpfanzun, in a telling adventure.

─────── PARZIVAL AND GAWAIN: TWIN INITIATIONS ───────

VISUALIZE GAWAIN NOW, A YOUNG MAN a little older than Parzival, but a seasoned warrior, and of such a mien that ladies never could resist him, riding his white fairy horse Gringuljete, prancing for joy, and eager to begin the adventure.

Gawain immediately encountered one of those situations with which we are becoming familiar: A castle under siege. King Meljanz had asked for a lady's hand in marriage, Obie, the daughter of his own vassal, Duke Lyppaut of Bearusche. The old duke was eager to grant the king's request, but his daughter said, "No!" and the father would not force her (would that there were more fathers like this). So now Lyppaut had to defend himself against Meljanz. Lyppaut begged Gawain to help him, but Gawain demurred. That is, until little Obilot, about ten years old, Lyppaut's younger daughter and the difficult Obie's little sister, in the most eloquent and courtly of speeches, introduced herself to Gawain and, with charm and young female magic, swore him to be her knight. He would ride against the champions of the other side on the following day.

"What a gallant and good man," said the duchess, Lyppaut's wife; and immediately had a little girl's golden silk dress made, and sent the sleeve to Obilot's knight. Gawain placed it on his shield and wore it onto the jousting field. By the end of the day, he had struck down King Meljanz and sworn him to the service of little Obilot. *Mirabile dictu*, the now-humbled Meljanz in the service of the little maid, behaved in such a courtly manner that love awakened in Obie, and they were married after all. (What a learning for him, when all that he could not gain by force was given freely, and Love itself demonstrated its wildness—and its divinity. Love does not abide coercion, which bestows the very kiss of death on its lips, but gives itself away freely to those who humble themselves before it.)

Next, Gawain entered one of the "temptation scenes" for which he became rightly famous. Vergulaht of Ascalun (which Campbell says is the same as Avalon and connected with the world of faery) pursuing a falcon, had fallen in a pond, and Gawain found him in that condition, dripping with algae and embarrassment. Gawain asked the way to Schanpfanzun, and Vergulaht gestured at a castle visible in the distance. "My sister is at home," he said, "who will care for you until I am done here."

Gawain rode on to the castle and found it both huge and splendid. There he was greeted by the maiden queen herself, who was, of course, beautiful.

"Since my brother has recommended you to me so warmly," she said, "I shall kiss you, if you wish. But you must instruct me how I shall entertain you, according to your sense of what is proper."

She was standing before him most graciously, and Gawain was never slow to appreciate a lady. Wolfram says her mouth was plump, hot, and red: upon it, Gawain placed his own, and the kiss they shared was not the usual kind for greeting guests. (In our time, we would say those two felt some special magnetism from that first moment.) The lady and her guest then sat down to converse.

The servants brought delicious food and drink, then discretely withdrew, leaving the couple making sweet talk. Things then progressed so that "something very nearly happened," when an old white-haired man came into the room and bellowed that there was an intruder. A battle royal then ensued, in which the swordless Gawain and the lady defended themselves against all comers, using a chessboard for shield, while the lady threw what we are told were very heavy chessmen and Gawain wielded a door bar. Quite a crowd assailed them, including King Vergulaht who arrived to discover and join the fray; until Prince Kingrimursel, who had originally challenged Gawain, came into the scene of the unequal contest, and stopped it. He lectured Vergulaht for his inhospitality and failure to honor the immunity Gawain should enjoy until they met in single combat on the battlefield.

Kingrimursel, actually, had just been unhorsed in the forest by Parzival, told that he must go in search of the Grail, and if he failed to find it, present himself to Condwiramurs for service. Now it was agreed by all concerned, that the Grail task should be turned over to Gawain. Kingrimursel would forgive him for his father's death if he would get the Grail for Vergulaht of Ascalun. With the hot adieu kiss of Vergulaht's sister on his lips, Gawain rode Gringuljete into the forest.

He would encounter many adventures. One day, as he rode through the forest, he happened on "the tableaux" (as we might now refer to it): a lady beneath a tree with a bloody knight in her lap. Sir Gawain, no stranger to wounds, made a tube and showed the lady how to suck off the bad blood and ease the wound, and learned the name of the man who had given her knight the wound: Lischoys Gwelljus. Now, following the bloody trail back to where the battle must have taken place, Gawain entered at once a realm of enchantment.

It was the demesne of the magician Clinschor (Wagner's Klingsor) whose hilltop castle was said to spin like a top. There at a spring, where it welled from the rock, Gawain met a beautiful damsel—with an acid tongue—the Lady Orgeluse. At each courtly, self-humbling assay Gawain made, Orgeluse mocked it and insulted him. Yet, strangely, he persisted, saying "Who wants love unearned?" swearing his undying fealty to her. And so they went along together, with her saying "Who cares."

At one point, Gawain, ever the healer as well as the hurter, saw a plant he knew would benefit the wounded knight and went to pluck it. "Oh good," Orgeluse mocked, "I am going to learn something." The plant indeed had miraculous healing powers, for soon the wounded man was better, saying it was the Lady Orgeluse on whose behalf he had been wounded. He asked Gawain to lift his own lady onto her horse, and while the gentle knight did that, suddenly the man leaped onto Gawain's horse and galloped off.

But then, back rode the knight for a passing jibe at Gawain. "Now I have paid you back for that beating you gave me when you took me to your uncle's house, and he kept me four weeks eating with the dogs."

"Urians!" Gawain recognized him. "But I saved your life."

Urians laughed. "Have you never heard the old saying about saving someone's life? He will be your enemy forever." Urians, the Prince of Punturtoys, had ravished a lady of her maidenhood. Gawain followed after and overthrew him, remanding him to the justice of King Arthur. The king ordered him hanged; but Urians begged for his life, and Gawain pleaded with both the offended lady and the king on his behalf. They granted this only on the king's condition that he eat for a month from the trough with the palace dogs. Urians was unable to appreciate the gravity of his crime, the clemency offered him through Gawain's intercession, or the symbolic appropriateness of his punishment. Now once again Gawain had saved him. But Urians mocked his savior and rode off laughing.

Now a "strange squire, Malcriatiure" by name, and of relation to Cundrie, with pig-like face and tusks such as hers, had come to join Gawain and Orgeluse, and begun to travel with them. He had a rickety nag. Gawain was afraid it was too frail to carry him, so he walked, leading the horse, carrying his own spear and shield (in those days, a very humiliating condition indeed for a knight).

They came to a castle of ladies. Then suddenly, approaching at a full gallop, appeared the knight Lischoys Gwelljus, who had just beaten Urians and thus won the fairy horse from him. Gawain had only the rickety nag, so he fought on foot and soon wrestled Gwelljus to the ground. Gawain spared his opponent's life, but the other would not yield. Suddenly Gawain recognized Gringuljete, his white fairy horse that had been taken by the ungrateful Urians. He took possession of Gringuljete, but something was new: Gringuljete was now branded with the dove, the sign of Munsalvaesche.

A ferryman came to the river and told Gawain it was the custom of the place for the loser to forfeit his horse to the ferryman, but Gawain—who wanted to keep his own Gringuljete—gave the ferryman instead the nag and the knight. The amused ferryman accepted the swap and had his daughter Bene care for Gawain at their little inn by the waterside. Gawain looked out the window that night to the lighted castle across the way and saw ladies moving about.

When he awakened in the pleasant, fragrant room, Gawain rose to enjoy the birdsong at dawn. He was astonished to see the ladies continuing to move around in the castle, just as they had when he retired. (And now, Campbell comments, he had reason to know he was in an enchanted realm, a timeless realm, that of The Mothers.) In that place were, in fact, Gawain's mother, grandmother, and two sisters, all caught in the same enchantment. None could recognize him, nor he them. It was "a strange twilight compulsion," in Campbell's words. The two enchantments, this one and the one of the Grail Castle, were both different and symmetrically equivalent.

Gawain slept again, and woke, and there stood little Bene, daughter of the ferryman-innkeeper. He greeted her courteously and asked just what those ladies were doing. "Oh, sir, do not ask me!" Bene pleaded, and broke down weeping. When the ferryman heard the question, he too became emotional, but finally answered, "You are in the Land of Marvels, at the Castle of Marvels, about to encounter the Bed of Marvels, where your fate will certainly be death."

The ferryman assured him it would be no dishonor to abandon the quest now, but very dangerous to continue. When Gawain stood firm, the ferryman offered his own shield. "And never let go of this shield or of your sword," the man told him, "for the moment you think your troubles are ended they will have just begun. Whatever adventures you have known, they will seem child's play to what you will now face."

When Gawain entered the castle, all the ladies had withdrawn, but there was the bed. The floor was so smooth that he could scarcely keep his feet. As he approached the bed, it darted away over the slippery floor. He chased it until finally in desperation he achieved it in one great leap, with shield, sword, and all, and lay uneasily on his back in its center, "whereupon, with the greatest speed anyone has ever seen, that irritating article of furniture began dashing, bumping back and forth, slamming into all four walls with such force the entire castle shook."[13] All the time there was a mighty racket. Gawain got little rest in that bed. He covered himself with the ferryman's stout shield and gave himself into God's keeping. Now all at once the din ceased and the bed stood quietly. But the wise warrior remembered the ferryman's warning and held firmly to shield and sword.

Suddenly, stones began to fly at him from all sides, rattling off his shield—five-hundred slings were firing all at once; then as many crossbows shot at him, and their bolts struck quivering in his shield. Even beneath its cover and through his chainmail, Gawain was bruised all over his body. Now a stout, hideous oaf appeared, garbed in surcoat, trousers and cap all of fishskin, who menaced Gawain with a massive bludgeon.[14] But when the knight sat up, weapons in hand, the fellow saw that he was outmatched and backed out, cursing and threatening worse to come.

It came. Immediately there leaped into the chamber a raging lion as tall as a horse. Gawain sprang from the bed with his shield raised; the lion struck at it so fiercely that its claws stuck, and Gawain sliced off its leg. The lion continued to battle on three legs, while the already slippery marble floor became so wet with blood that the knight could hardly keep his feet. He was also hampered by the severed foreleg, which hung from his shield. All at once the desperate beast flung itself upon Gawain, who thrust his sword through its chest. The lion fell dead, and Gawain, dazed and bleeding, collapsed unconscious across its back.

So badly wounded that he was barely alive, Gawain revived, apologizing repeatedly for his wounded, unseemly condition. The castle ladies set about to restore him, their leader being Queen Arnive, his own grandmother and the mother of King Arthur. She still did not know him—neither did his mother nor his two sisters, Itonje and (a different) Cundrie; and he did not know them, such was Clinschor's spell on that place. Arnive healed Gawain with balm from the Castle of Munsalvaesche. Yet, even surrounded by all those beautiful ladies, he still longed for Orgeluse.

He was in no wise fully recovered when he saw outside a lady, the Duchess of Logroys, leading a knight, Florant the Turkoyte. His grandmother warned Gawain that Florant was a valiant knight and that he was in no shape to joust; but Gawain, in much pain, nonetheless called for his armor and Gringuljete. Soon the Turkoyte lay on his back, and the ladies rejoiced.

Orgeluse was as scornful as ever, "That lion's paw on your shield is quite a sight," she mocked (it was still stuck there), and "Those ladies up there think you wonderful. Well, go back to them! You would never dare what I have in store for you now—if you still have heart for my love."

Now, writes Campbell, this was to be the final test and the revelation of who Orgeluse really was, for she asked him to bring a wreath that hung on the branch of a certain tree. It was in a wood of tamarisk trees, called "Clinschor's" wood. To get to it, Gawain would have to leap a perilous chasm and fight a knight, "the man that robbed my of my joy," Orgeluse said as she led him to the ordeal. And the ladies, looking on, wept, for they loved Gawain for his gentle, manly heart, and they knew how few made it through this enchanted gauntlet.

Orgeluse showed the first sign of a tender heart, weeping when Gawain and Gringuljete fell just short of the leap, the horse's front hooves scrabbling at the far bank. Knight and steed plunged down into the roaring water in the chasm, where Gringuljete was swept away. Gawain, encumbered by his armor, nonetheless made it to shore and ran downstream, where he was able to pull his struggling horse to safety. He mounted, rode to the tree, and plucked the bough; and when he had wreathed his helmet, he saw a knight riding toward him unarmed. He was a handsome man, splendidly attired in a cloak of grass-green samite trimmed with white ermine, so luxurious that it trailed the ground on both sides of his horse; he wore also a hat bedecked with peacock plumes.

This gentlemen announced, "Sir, I have not yielded my claim to that wreath!" He was its guardian, King Gramoflanz of Rosche Sabins: so proud was he that he had sworn never to fight fewer than two knights at one time. "I see by the battered condition of your shield that you have survived the Bed of Marvels. That adventure, also, I should have achieved, were I not friend to the magician Clinschor; much of this region is under is rule. He and I are enemies of the Lady Orgeluse, whose husband, Duke Cidegast of Logroys, I killed. I held the lady captive for a year and offered her my name and lands, but she repaid my service with hate. I must tell you this, for I know well that she has promised you her love and sent you to seek my death."

Gramoflanz told him that, alas, he could not fight him alone, because of his oath, and gave him a ring to deliver to a lady named "Itonje" (Gawain's own sister, whom he has by now recognized, although he seems to remain unknown to her). The only man he would fight alone, he said, "would be Gawain"—the man he hated above all others because Gawain's father, Lot, had killed his own father.

The gentle knight responded, "I am Gawain."

At last, Gramoflanz would get to avenge his father, but on a man he now perceived was noble of spirit.

A date was set for the combat, and Gramoflanz, in the grandiose and mythic spirit of *carpe diem*, said "And since our fame will be increased if ladies are invited, I shall bring along fifteen hundred. You have those of the Castle of Marvels—the four hundred. Arthur's whole court should also be invited."

Now when Gawain returned, with a bound over the water, bearing the bough, Orgeluse's disposition was vastly different. She threw herself at his feet and said, "Sir, I am not worthy of the risks I have demanded of you."

Now Gawain in turn became stern and said "If I am still to be mocked, I can do without your love."

Orgeluse wept more and told the story of her husband, Cidegast. "How could I give myself to anyone less the knight than he? These have been my tests, and you have proved gallant, golden." Gawain, of course, understood very well the nature of a lady's "tests." He reminded her that soon, again, he would risk his life for her, saying, "There is no one about, grant me your favor." To which she responded, "At the castle I shall not resist." But Gawain kissed her. As they rode back, she wept again, and told Gawain: "You are not the first I have tried to use to kill Gramoflanz." The other was that good King Anfortas, who was meant to be in service only to the Grail; because of me, he now is king to pain and sorrow, and my grief for his misfortune has been even greater than for Cidegast."

The lady continued, "I have sent out companies of knights to bring down that arrogant Gramoflanz, yet he survives. Although none has succeeded, no man has ever refused my service, save one: that one was armed all in red. He fought with my knights and felled five. I offered him my land and myself in return for his aid, but he refused me, saying that he already had a wife beyond compare and that he had grief enough from the Grail and needed no more."

Upon hearing this tale, Gawain said to himself, "That could only be Parzival," but he kept the secret of the Red Knight's name.

Gawain and his lady returned via the ferryman and his daughter Bene, to the castle of ladies where suddenly there were four hundred knights Gawain had not seen before, jousting colorfully on the lawn. That night a festival was declared, and even Lischoys Gwelljus and the Turkoyte were set free without condition. Queen Arnive made a point of asking that Orgeluse accompany Gawain to his chamber to salve his wounds and make sure that "he was covered," which she gladly did. And so Gawain and his beloved were together at last.

Soon the new master of the Castle of Marvels received word back from Arthur that the king and all his court would attend Gawain's fight with Gramoflanz. He asked his grandmother about the mysterious Clinschor, whose spells sustained the whole apparatus, and Arnive explained that Clinschor's magic was beyond measure. "These marvels you see here are lesser ones," she said, "compared with those in many other lands under his sway. He has power over spirits both good and evil. At one time, he was a noble of Capua, but he won the love of Queen Iblis of Sicily. When the king found Clinschor in his wife's arms, one cut of the king's knife made him a capon."

Gawain learned how the eunuch Clinschor (the shadowed echo of the Grail King) now filled with hatred for all, learned magic in a land called Persidia. This hate-filled mage now found no joy greater than robbing those who were happiest of their joy. Campbell writes, "For not the passion of love, but a castrate's revenge against it, was for him the source of the pall of death over both the palace of life (the Castle of Marvels) and the palace of awe (the Castle of the Grail)."[15]

Here we move from Gawain's story to Parzival's again—only to bring them together presently, at the end of their quests. Visualize the two knights executing a kind of *pas de deux*, as in the riding art of *dressage*, two horsemen weaving a figure-eight, not in physical, but in mythological space. Campbell likens the "parallel stories" to Joyce's Leopold Bloom and Stephen Dedalus, social man and inner man, woven through *Ulysses*—the twins who appear in so many mythologies.

Riding one day in the forest, Parzival encountered a hermitess, wearing a hair shirt beneath her gown and crouching beside a coffin. She invited him to eat, saying that the food was from the Grail Castle, and that Cundrie brought it by on her missions. The woman spoke of her mourning for a dead knight, her husband in the coffin, yet mysteriously preserved. Curiously, the marriage was never consummated. Of course, it was his cousin, Sigune.

"How fare you now in your search for the Grail?" she immediately asked.

Parzival chided her back for the ill will she seemed to bear him. "Because of the Grail, I have lost all joy. I behaved at that time as one bound to be a loser. We are kin, dear cousin. Give me counsel."

Sigune answered him more kindly. "May help come to you now from God's hand, who knows all sorrow. You may yet find a path that will take you to Munsalvaesche, for Cundrie has just now gone that way. She leaves her mule over there whenever she comes, standing where the spring flows from the rock. I advise you to follow quickly; she may not be far ahead."

As he rode into the forest, Parzival for the third time (the magic number three) let his horse's reins free, thinking, "Let God show this steed the way that is best for me." And so he came to the place where Trevrizent, the brother of the Grail King, dwelt.

Parzival's initial words to the hermit showed that a *metanoia*, a change of mind and heart, was already under way in him: "Sir, give me counsel. I am a man who has sinned." The hermit led him to his cave, and Parzival saw books and an altar with a cask of holy relics (he recognized the selfsame ones on which he had sworn Jeschute's innocence to Orilus). Asking Trevrizent the date, he reckoned that he had passed that way four-and-a-half years and three days before; and he sighed.

"How long! Unguided and in grief! Toward God I hold great hatred," he said. "He is the Lord, they say, of all help. Why then, did he not help me?"

The holy man was quietly regarding him. "May God help us both!" he prayed. "Young sir, explain to me, calmly and soberly, how this wrath of God occured, by which he earned your hate."

Trevrizent was a good psychotherapist. He invited Parzival to tell his story, and he listened carefully. A therapeutic dialogue unfolded between the two men, an *anamnesis*, as psychoanalysis has it, a remembering. But Trevrizent also lectured Parzival on God's nature, more directively: "God is loyalty. Be loyal! He is truth. He abhors what is false. Anyone seeing you defy Him with hate would take you for insane. With such anger you get nowhere. Remember the fall of Lucifer and his host—how they lost heaven through their rancor."

Finally Trevrizent spoke of the failed Grail knight (Parzival himself, still unrecognized) "a foolish man, who rode away in sin, because he spoke not one word of sympathy to the king, although he saw his anguish." Then he asked Parzival's identity. When he heard, he said, "Alas O world! You have slain your own flesh and blood. The Red Knight, Iter, was your kinsman; and my sister Herzeloyde—your mother—because you abandoned her, died of grief." This was the first Parzival had heard of his mother's fate; it seemed to take all of Parzival's courage, then, to master his sense of shame and reveal that he was also the failed Grail knight.

The hermit, the man he now knew as his uncle, was not sanguine about Parzival's chances of achieving the Grail or having a second chance. It had never happened before. It was contrary to everything that he, the brother of the Grail King, knew. But Parzival was not dissuaded. He resolved to go on. (We should note here that life has taught Parzival to learn from experience and from experienced teachers; but he has kept his native perseverance of soul. He doesn't know when to quit. It is the virtue of a holy fool.)

We now re-enter Gawain's story, where the ladies, their escorts, and King Arthur's court had been assembling to see the great death match between Gramoflanz and Gawain.

On the appointed day, Gawain saw a solitary knight approaching in red armor. He wore a wreath from the tree Gramoflanz guarded. Gawain recognized the wreath; and immediately they went at it, unhorsing each other, and finally fighting with swords, alone on the plain. Gawain found himself hard pressed and realized that he might lose this fight, and his life. As the two were fighting, King Arthur's court arrived; and two messengers of Arthur rode near enough to recognize Gawain: fearing for his life, they cried out his name, at which the other knight flung down his sword and said, "I am fighting myself!" It was Parzival. On his way to battle Gramoflanz himself, Parzival had seen the unguarded tree and knew enough about the ritual (more on this later) to pluck the bough in anticipation. He mistook Gawain for Gramoflanz and determined to do him in, hence his ferocity.

Gawain had been badly battered in the fight; and when the real Gramoflanz shortly appeared, that haughty king, seeing his opponent's exhausted state, refused to fight until the morrow, as there would be no honor in combat with a man in Gawain's condition. Parzival offered to appear in Gawain's stead, but that Gramoflanz refused. When Parzival repeated his offer to Gawain, Gawain also refused him. "God bless you friend, for your offer," he said, "but I believe in my own cause. With good fortune, I shall win."

The following day, nonetheless, when Gramoflanz arrived early on the scene, Parzival slipped ahead of Gawain, fought Gramoflanz, and prevailed. Gramoflanz yielded. Now Gawain said courteously, "Sir King, I shall do for you today what you did yesterday for me: we shall meet tomorrow."

Now came to fruition something that been brewing in the background concerning Bene, the ferryman's very bright little daughter. We remember Gramoflanz's sending a ring by Bene to the Lady Itonje, who was his beloved, and (unknown to herself) Gawain's sister. Bene, it seems, was present this day in Itonje's entourage and, having discovered all these separate strands of kinship and courtship, revealed all to the lady. When Itonje learned the truth, she was stricken: "Shall the hand of my own brother cut down my heart's beloved?" When Arthur came to know the situation, he took pity on Itonje and arranged a truce. The text mentions that all hearts, at this point, were softening: Orgeluse's need for revenge against Gramoflanz was being softened by the attentions of Gawain; King Gramoflanz himself, now becoming alarmed that he might lose Itonje's favor, was further softened by seeing his enemy, Gawain, in her company, also with a younger brother—so like the two of them—who moved the knight's heart with his grace and vulnerability. And then there came to his mind the fact that Parzival, who had plucked the bough, as well, had overcome both Gramoflanz and Gawain, thereby fulfilling the magic of the ritual. Arthur took Gramoflanz to a tent of ladies and bade him kiss the one he loved. He chose Itonje.

In this "festive chapter" as Campbell puts it, everyone marries everyone, in the kind of finale that modern audiences still love. After all their trials, the somewhat less haughty Gramoflanz finally wed his proud Itonje. Then Gawain's younger sister was given in marriage to Lischoys Gwelljus; and their widowed mother, the Lady Sangive, wedded Florant the Turkoyte. Gawain and Orgeluse were also romancing in those pleasant meadows, finding much deserved pleasure in each other's company. With so many fair ladies and noble knights gathered together by the riverside, love and joy among the pavilions were the order of the day.

Only Parzival was left out of the general pairing and partnering. Quietly, he rode off, thinking of his Condwiramurs. He had not traveled far when he met a "pagan knight" more richly accoutred than any he had seen. They clashed together and seemed virtually evenly matched; but, when the other knight called out "Thabronit," he prevailed. (Thabronit was where this knight's lady, Secundille, lived). Then Parzival thought of his lovely wife and his two little boys, Kardeiz and Loherangrin (Lohengrin); he shouted, "Pelrapeire," (the city of Condwiramurs), and Wolfram von Eschenbach says, telling us of the battle-worthiness of courtly love, the spirit of Condwiramurs came across four kingdoms and gathered her knight with the power of her love. Chips flaked and flew from the Moor's gem-encrusted shield. Then, with a fierce crack down upon the heathen's ornamented helmet, the sword of the Christian broke—that blade he had taken so long ago from Ither, the Red Knight, forsook him at last.

"I see, brave sir," said the noble Moor, speaking French, "you will now have to fight without a sword. That will gain me no fame. Desist now, and tell me who you are. Believe me, I have never in my life before encountered such a fighter as you."

"Shall I name myself out of fear?" asked Herzeloyde's son.

"Not at all!" said the courteous stranger, "I shall give you my own name first. I am Fierefiz the Angevin, and many countries pay tribute to my rule."

"How Angevin?" asked Parzival. "Anjou is mine by inheritance from my father. I am told that I do have a brother, living in heathendom, who has won great love and praise. If you would so trust me as to bare your face, I could tell, sir, if you are that one."

The other knight threw down his sword and asked, "What does your brother look like?"

Parzival replied, "He is black and white, they say, like written parchment. "I am the one."

When they recognized each other, there was weeping and embracing, and Fierefiz said these things, which now heal and salve the death wound of the Balin-Balan battle, so comparable, but so tragic: "My father, you, and I were one; but this one manifested in three parts. I rode against myself and would gladly have killed myself. O Jupiter, write this miracle down! Your power saved us from tragedy." He laughed and wept, and tried to conceal his tears.[16]

When Fierefiz learned that there were many ladies back at Arthur's pavilions, he came willingly, and wonder and excitement followed wherever he was seen. Once again, a great picnic was declared, a great round silk spread out, and the feast prepared. And once again, to everyone's astonishment, there appeared Cundrie, the Grail messenger, with an unexpected message of joy:

"O crown of man's salvation, Parzival: in youth, you kept company with sorrow; joy will now be your companion. You have striven for the soul's peace, waiting in sorrow for the body's joy. You are now lord of the Grail. Condwiramurs and your son Loherangrin have also been named to that high service. Kardeiz, your other son, will be crowned king of Pelrapeire. Greetings I bring, also, from the noble King Anfortas. It is time now for your truthful lips to ask that question that will at last relieve that sweet man from misery."

Tears of joy flowed from Parzival's eyes. "Tell me, lady," he asked, "how I am to go forward to my duty and my joy?"

"Dear my lord," Cundrie answered, "you must choose one man to be your companion. It is now my honor to lead you home to Munsalvaesche." At this, all the company gathered there began to murmur, passing on the tidings.

Parzival chose Fierefiz, and the brothers rode away with Cundrie. (Notice that there is no problem in Wolfram's tale, that the Muslim Fierefiz should enter the Grail Castle, unachievable by many Christian knights: it is Fierefiz's good heart that qualifies him.)

Now all the time that Gawain and Parzival were questing, Anfortas, the Grail King, dwelt in excruciating pain, unable to stand, sit, or lie, for long. He might have asked for death, but it was his service to the Grail, and to the promised heir, that kept him alive. When Parzival arrived, he came to the couch of the maimed king. He asked, in tears, "My lord, tell me where the Grail is kept. If God's goodness triumphs in me, this company shall witness."

He was shown. He turned his face to the Grail, genuflected three times to the Trinity, and prayed that this sorrowful man might know health and joy. When he rose to his feet, he turned again to Anfortas and asked the long-awaited question: "*Oeheim, was wirret dier?*"[17]

It says in the text that a beautiful luster came over Anfortas' flesh, in that moment, called *fleur*, the bloom in maiden's cheeks, the rosy complexion of healthy children. But it was more than that: an unearthly beauty spread over the old man, that put all present, even Parzival, to shame. This healing, and the fact that the writing on the Grail proclaimed the name "Parzival," made him now the Grail King, the king of Munsalvaesche.

Parzival rode out from the castle to meet Condwiramurs, who was riding toward the Grail Castle. On the way, he visited Trevrizent, and the old man said, "Greater marvel has seldom come to pass: you have forced God by defiance to make His infinite Trinity grant your will."[18]

Condwiramurs had arrived in the company of old Kyot, father of Sigune. It is said that they met on the exact spot, where, years before, Parzival had become arrested by the vision of his beloved. Now they went to visit Sigune at her hermitage. Sadly, they found the hermitess still kneeling, but dead. They placed her into the coffin with her beloved, prayed and wept over them, finally burying them properly. Then they returned to Munsalvaesche.

When presented with the Grail, the story tells us, Fierefiz could not see it, until he would be baptized. But he could not take his eyes off the Grail Maiden, Repanse de Schoye. Unfortunately, both to win her and see the Grail, he had to renounce the religion of his upbringing, Islam, and embrace Christianity.

Fierefiz was not one to quibble theologically: "Whatever I have to do for that girl, I will do," he said.

Then the Grail was uncovered in his sight and there was a new writing:

ANY TEMPLAR APPOINTED BY GOD'S HAND TO BE MASTER OVER A FOREIGN FOLK MUST FORBID THE ASKING OF HIS NAME OR RACE AND HELP THEM TO THEIR RIGHTS, BUT IF THE QUESTION IS ASKED OF HIM THEY SHALL NO LONGER HAVE HIS HELP.[19]

The sad news was received shortly that Fierefiz' wife, Secundille, had died. Subsequently, in India, the story tells, the Grail Maiden, Repanse de Schoye, gave birth to their son, and his name was Prester John. (But his is another story.)

THE GOLDEN BOUGH
AND THE UNDERWORLD

AS THIS TIMELESS STORY COMES TO ITS CRESCENDO and finale, the wisdom contained in it becomes ever denser and juicier, especially for the sake of our subject. If this is a story of "fertility magic," as Joseph Campbell, Heinrich Zimmer, and Margaret Murray all believe, then we are asked to look into the nature of the fertilizing and receptive powers, their flowing, parching, renewing and recovery. This is the symbolic *hieros gamos*. The story tells us what two human souls might need to begin the successful development of an angel—and the perils they might encounter along the way.

We have already seen one history and etiology of the Wasteland in the Balin story. Clinschor's story tells the parallel one: Clinschor, like Abelard, was castrated in the service of courtly love. He and the maimed Anfortas (wounded in the thigh, sometimes construed as the genitals) echo each other. The spring from which male vitality flows is ruthlessly cut off. (And yet we notice how many times springs appear in the healing story.) The magician-eunuch who holds the land in its spell,

Wolfram implies and Campbell states flatly, was the pope (Innocent III, the most politically powerful pope ever), emblematic of a powerful, controlling secular state erected upon a platform of spirituality. Prior to his wounding, Anfortas, also, although his heart was good, behaved in a manner inappropriately worldly for the Grail King.[20] In the numbing trance, no one recognizes even their closest kin, there is a pervasive blighting of spontaneity and the authentic individual life—all is drowned in dogma and political enforcement of theological ideals.

Men, encased in iron and carrying long, sharp tools, attack each other again and again, simply because the other is there, it seems, and because they need to act out a Darwinian dream of dominance. So clad—we find this in almost every story—the men don't even have a clue who the other is, as if they are smothered in their armor and in their role. "Armoring" is interesting in the psychological sense, for body analysts speak of "character armor," carried in the attitudes, musculature, and tone of the body. Held rigidly, it can be used to suppress every emotion except those associated with crude sex and power: lust and the towering rages that break through, all emotions channeled into this one violent mode. The armored figure is recognizable whether in medieval iron or modern gabardines.

Women behold these spectacles, as if from the sidelines or grandstands. They are literally wounded when the knights are wounded, but in their imaginal bodies. They see the "flowers of knighthood" maiming and killing each other with a fairly insane code of honor: force meets force, or trial by combat, or ordeal.

Chakra theory says the third (power), a male chakra, does its violent dance, while the feminine, in the second (passionate) and fourth (compassionate) chakras watches on, in love and empathy. It's odd, but when violent knights seize or besiege a lady they do so in a tower (the first chakra). They exhibit this protectionism and possessiveness, some sociobiologists have proposed, as a way of securing their line of descent, the genes that must be passed on: chakra one. But when chakra three, the power chakra, gets its objective—the woman—it doesn't know what to do with her. Towers, guards, and chastity belts pertain to chakra one, while chakra three is the arena of violent security and secure violence.

When power's objective is denied, then, it degenerates into Balin's role and uses *force majeure* to obtain it—the naive hero seen in Hercules, Achilles, Samson. This was happening all over the world shown us by the Parzival story. The worst of these offenders was Urians, the rapist. He not only raped the woman, but, in the values of their world, he deprived her of her "maidenhead," that is, her psychospiritual virginity, supposed to be bestowed, as a symbolic and magical prize, on her husband. Thus, he committed a double theft, physical and spiritual, a crime worthy of Gawain's retribution. Is Urians' guilt mitigated by the fact that sexual abuse was not identified as social malfeasance or crime for eight-hundred years, until the late twentieth century?

Why wasn't it? The woman was conceived of as booty, the spoils of war, in this violent world, and she was supposed to cooperate when you took her as spoils. But this story shows the women to be far from passive recipients of all this autistic treatment, and that is why the Grail story is a feminine story. Throughout the tale, zipping in and out, causing consternation and dismay, yet keeping things moving, they come: ugly but cogent Cundrie; Sigune the unremitting truth teller; Condwiramurs and Obie, who say "no" to the knights of the aggressive mode; little Obilot who won't take "no" from Gawain; Orgeluse, whose angry mind won't forgive the violent man who killed her husband, "a unicorn of a man," basically a pure and dear heart (how do you embrace the man who kills your love, fairly or not?), who courageously takes to horse, riding constantly in search of a champion; little Bene ("Good") whose form of empathy is to see horror in the making for Itonje, if her brother and her lover fight to the death; Arnive, the grandmother, advising and healing the wounded men of their battering world; and last of all, the simple presence, the witnessing of all these events, collectively, by the women—from the sidelines, the grandstands, the besieged centers (and the hospitals)—and to the number of four hundred, or fifteen hundred, for that matter. These "castles of women" are, in fact, the Greek chorus of the Arthurian play, who stands, witnesses, and comments on the futility of most of what men do, especially when they are full of themselves.

But what of these mysterious doings in the "Tamarisk Wood," involving boughs and garlands? Joseph Campbell, on his return from Europe in 1929, resolved to read Sir James Frazer's *The Golden Bough*, in its entirety. This was no mean feat, since the book comprised twelve volumes, but Campbell had done so by at least 1934, probably for the most part in a small cabin near Woodstock, New York. For him, it confirmed the "fertility magic" thesis of his Master's thesis at Columbia on "The Dolorous Stroke." Thereafter, in Campbell's writing, there is a strain of interpretation based on Frazer's thesis.

What Frazer had pursued, *ad infinitum*, was the vestige of a matriarchal society in which the perennial personage was the Priestess-Queen, Diana of the Sacred Grove, always virginal, because always self-possessed, while her consort, the "Year-King," was renewed periodically, replaced with a new one via a trial by combat in a sacred grove, with only one victor emerging, the new king. The land was believed to be fructified and renewed by the rite.

The tamarisk is a peculiar hybrid tree, evergreen-like, but also deciduous, the needles turning golden and falling not long after the leaves of the deciduous trees. The "golden bough" Frazer associates with the mistletoe, "ever green," blooming in winter—the symbol of the dying, perpetually renewing principle of life. The mistletoe was said to turn gold at the solstices, part of its solar magic, hence "The Golden Bough." There was also its association with "beautiful Baldur," the Norse "golden"god slain by Loki the Trickster, evocative of dying and reviving gods wherever they be found.

Frazer introduces the reader to the shores of Lake Nemi, and the grove and cove called Aricia:

> In that grove grew a certain tree round which, at any hour of the day and probably far into the night, a grim figure might be seen to prowl. In his hand he carried a drawn sword, and he kept peering warily about him as if at every instant he expected to be set upon. He was at once a priest and a murderer; and the man for whom he was watching was sooner or later to murder him and hold the priesthood in his stead. For such was the rule of the sanctuary: a candidate for the priesthood could succeed to office only by slaying the incumbent priest in single combat, and could himself retain office only until he was in turn slain by a stronger or a craftier. Moreover—

and this is especially significant—he could fling his challenge only if he had first succeeded in plucking a golden bough from the tree which the priest was guarding.[21]

So this is the ancient game Clinschor and Gramoflanz were playing. Orgeluse was the (dispossessed) priestess, held against her will by Gramoflanz. Her personal choice for the Year King was her kind husband, not this harsh braggart (won't fight less than two men); but in this situation, personal needs must be subordinated to the collective—the ritual of renewal involving the passing of certain tests, the plucking of the bough, and the ritual combat. (That doesn't mean that Orgeluse was a happy camper!) What Cundrie is on the physical level, an ugly, ungainly incarnation of the feminine—the minnesingers, medieval authors, never tired of reciting her loathly attributes—Orgeluse presents on the psychological level, the sharp-tongued woman.

In Eskimo and Native American stories, we find the figure of *Sedna*, who dwells in deep lakes and rivers of British Columbia and the Yukon, virtually the same figure who is called the "Mother of the Sea Creatures" by the coastal-dwelling Inuit. This figure becomes angry at human disrespect for nature or for the spiritual realm and gets ugly. She pouts and sits in a corner of her undersea home. She witholds the game, causes drought, or rises in wrath in the form of storms. The shaman becomes the one who propitiates her, combs her tangled hair, speaks sweetly to her, and asks her to restore the game.[22] (So we are looking here at a clear mythological message, emerging five hundred years before the ecological crisis we now face. When we abuse Mother Nature she turns ugly.)

Moreover, we find in Frazer an explanation of Cundrie. The pig was the sacred animal associated with the *thesmorphia*, the ritual to Demeter and Persephone, commemorating Persephone's abduction by Hades, Demeter's ensuing grief, the turning of the earth into a Wasteland, and its periodic renewal through the Eleusinian mysteries. In the myth, when Hades broke forth from the underworld and stole Persephone, who was plucking flowers with her maidens in an asphodel field, a herd of swine fell into the chasm created as he returned to his domain. And when Demeter went to find her daughter, the hoofprints of pigs descending into the earth obliterated Persephone's tracks. At the yearly ritual in ancient Greece, pigs, pine branches, and cakes of dough were thrown into chasms in the earth in mythic remembrance. The pig-goddess, then, is associated with Demeter in her role as Mother Nature, angry when her daughter is dishonored (abducted and raped), and with Persephone herself. Frazer connected the ritual with the corn, or the ear of wheat, and the renewal of the agricultural cycle (the pig being the animal form of the corn or wheat, and its flesh being consumed ceremonially with the cakes).

In Melanesian ceremonies, Campbell notes, a sacrificed pig is often substituted for a person for the underworld journey. The pig is taken to represent the fleshy, mortal part of the person that must be sacrificed and sent as an emissary to the underworld, while the human being "buys a little time" in the daylight world. Pig-flesh is traditionally said to resemble that of humans; and pigs eat everything that humans eat, thereby also sharing some of our intestinal parasites. Some ancient traditions have the pig eaten as part of the sacrificial feast; for some (the ancient Hebrews among them), the flesh was considered "unclean" or taboo. Both approaches, ritual eating and ritual abstinence, may be considered equivalent as acts of acknowledgment of the animal's numinous status. The boar bears the image of the changing moon in the curling tusks of his formidable jaw, thus marking the pig as a beast of the Goddess, especially in her aspect as the dark mother of death. In Celtic tales that begin with a hunting scene, it is well to note of what animal the hero rides in pursuit: a white hind may take the hunter into one sort of realm, a stag having his magical destination, but a fierce boar or a great old sow will generally take the hero *down* into the realm of mystery, dismemberment, and perhaps transformation. Attis was said to be killed by a Boar, as was Diarmuid; so the pig, and particularly the boar, may be dangerous to heroes.

Frazer writes,

> the animal was looked on, not simply as a filthy and disgusting creature, but as a being endowed with high supernatural powers, and that as such it was regarded with that primitive sentiment of religious awe and fear in which feelings of reverence and abhorrence are almost equally blended.[23]

Cundrie, then, is the theriomorphic (animal-shaped) aspect of the Goddess, associated with the underworld, capable of bestowing fertility or of withholding it, of blessing or cursing, she who presides over the deepest mysteries of initiation and transformation. She shows up in the tale of "The Loathly Bride" in which Gawain, again, is the protagonist. We recount it briefly to shed additional light on our theme of the greening of the Wasteland.

King Arthur was out hunting one day when he wounded a white stag and tracked it further and further into the forest, until he did not know exactly where he was anymore. He finally came upon his quarry, exhausted in a thicket, and dismounted to dispatch it, at which vulnerable moment a huge mounted knight, in some accounts dressed in green, came upon him. The knight announced himself as Sir Gromer Somer Joure, the owner of the demesne onto which Arthur had tracked the deer. The restitution for his trespass, the huge man declared, was that Arthur must present himself in the same spot in a year and a day with the answer to a riddle: "What does a woman want?" Failing the test, his head was forfeit. (Freud needed such a knight, threatening to cut off his head if he couldn't answer the same question, after thirty years of psychoanalysis on women patients.)

As Arthur emerged from the wood his nephew, Gawain, observed the king's fallen countenance, and asked, "What troubles you, uncle?" (Notice, Gawain effortlessly solved the riddle with which Parzival struggled so hard.) Arthur told him of the encounter and the *geis* the knight had laid on him. But Gawain said, "That shouldn't be so hard. We'll ask lots of women. I'll help you."[24]

So, for a year, they asked women, old, young, about to be married, already married, even widowed. And the answers came: "security," "a handsome, gentle husband," "wealth," "lots of children," "a fine home," "a secure old age," etc. Gawain, diligent scribe of the female heart, put them all in a great book. But when the year was accomplished, and he and Arthur rode toward the appointment with the book, they felt hollow inside; both knew they had not gotten the right answer. Then all at once a mysterious, pig-faced woman with long snout and tushes (the medieval authors all elaborate with delight upon the details of her grotesqueness), yet elegantly dressed, like Cundrie, accosted them at a crossroad. Her name was "Dame Ragnell."

"I know what you're looking for," she said. (The knights exchanged startled glances).

"You don't have it," she said, gesturing at the book, "And Arthur's going to lose his head," (more discomfort), "unless I tell you *the* answer."

"Madam," they responded, courteous gentlemen that they were, "Please tell us!"

"Not so fast!" said the hag, "There's a price!"

This, of course, further discomforted the two, but King Arthur asked, "Well, Madam, what is your price?"

"Oh, not so much," the outrageous hag answered, "but I've been kind of wanting to get married, and young Gawain here would do just fine."

"But I can't do that to him!" Arthur sputtered, then, perhaps recovering himself a bit, he explained, "Sir Gawain is his own man; it is not for me to so dispose of him." (Now we know that, in feudal times, it was precisely the authority of a king to so dispose of his nephews, nieces, wards, as with his own children, and in certain cases the children of less closely related vassals. What Arthur is doing here is making a significant statement of Sir Gawain's right of *sovereignty*.)

Gawain, however, always gallant, took Arthur aside, and said, "I want to do it for you uncle, and that's that!" The bargain was struck, and Ragnell whispered the riddle's answer in Arthur's ear.

Arthur rode on alone to the trysting spot, and was not long there when the monstrous knight came crashing through the woods. "Well!" he roared, "what's the answer?" Arthur took out the book, desperate to save Gawain, and tried one after the other of the answers they had collected. But the Green Knight only laughed louder with each attempt. "So, Arthur, King of the Britains, prepare to die!"

Finally Arthur pulled out his trump card—the Loathly Lady's answer. He gave it: "sovereignty."

The knight bellowed his rage, and said, "You must have been talking to my sister, that treacherous Dame Ragnell!" and stormed away.

Arthur's head was saved, and he and Gawain were relieved—until they were all too soon joined by the lady herself. "Now you must introduce me to the court, and we must have a wedding, husband!" she said, batting the long lashes gracing her pig-like eyes, at Gawain.

When Arthur suggested Gawain and he should ride ahead to the city to prepare properly for her, Dame Ragnell insisted on riding home with them, immediately; she made quite the grand entrance of it, being sure she had the attention of all as she progressed with her two royal knights through the streets of Camelot.

When Dame Ragnell was introduced to the startled Guinevere, the queen managed to receive her graciously, and immediately perceived the situation (she and Arthur were attuned in this matter): "Perhaps, madam, a small, intimate wedding, in the little chapel?"

"Oh no, I want a big wedding!" the grotesque creature insisted, "And all the court shall attend!"

And so it was that a castle full of ladies—more than the lords—grieved for Gawain, as he publicly married the ugliest creature anyone had ever seen: Sir Gawain, above all knights so handsome, so brave, so sweet of manner. . . .

The wedding dinner was an ordeal: The lady ate like the great sow she resembled. She crunched up meat and bones with her frightful teeth, splashing drool on the table and her groom's finery. There were those of the court who truly feared for Sir Gawain's life, when he should be alone with the monster. Arthur and Guinevere kept the party going as long as they were able, to put off the dire moment.

When at last the couple retired to the nuptial chamber, Gawain found himself frozen, unable quite to face his bride. But, ever aware of courtesy, he forced himself to look at her. Ragnell lifted her rheumy eyes to Gawain's, and said "Aren't you going to kiss me, husband?" There was no coyness in her voice.

As he looked into those eyes, Gawain saw a deep sadness, and he felt pity. "Not only will I kiss thee, Lady, but hug thee as well, and do for thee all that a husband should," he said, embracing her warmly. Suddenly, he held in his arms the most beautiful of women.

Properly married they were already, and they looked on each other with desire. So those two made much joy that night. But in the wee hours, Ragnell told him. "Alas, husband, I am under an enchantment. You can have me beautiful, as you see me now, by night; yet ugly as when we first met, by day; or the reverse, beautiful by day before all men's eyes, and a monster in your arms at night. Choose now, my lord." She stared at him, with exquisite pain.

Gawain pondered long, while the lady looked down, but held her breath in suspense. Finally he said, "Your burden is the greater, Lady, yours the suffering. The choice must be yours."

(His heart, not his head or his loins, had the right answer, the compassionate one.)

"Ahhh!" she cried, "Now you shall have me beautiful, by night and day; by your courteous answer, you have broken the spell all the way! You have restored to me my *sovereignty*!"

They emerged in the morning from the bridal chamber and everyone was astonished at Ragnell's beauty. And she and Gawain lived happily together for seven years.

Now this story amplifies the depth and texture of two of our characters from the Parzival story, Sir Gawain and Cundrie, also called the "Loathly Lady." Gawain is as developed a practitioner of courtesy, as Parzival is ignorant of it. Moreover, Gawain's heart seems to be in the right place, as in both stories he defuses some potentially lethal situation, or asks, artlessly, "What ails you, uncle?"

Furthermore, he follows through: "Oh, a crazy magical riddle? With your head forfeit if you fail? I'll help!" And he does so for a year, cheerfully interviewing the ladies, no doubt to the enjoyment of both, and no doubt learning much about human nature in the meantime. (Gawain both attends and learns well.) But his *courtesie* goes deeper. He reads the suffering in Ragnell's eyes and lets the presence of soul outweigh physical ugliness or beauty (clearly he is open in his heart chakra). Thus, he not only kisses but hugs her, and affirms that he will consummate his marriage vow. This was no small matter; in feudal Europe, consummation implied not only braving her ugliness (and we are also told that her odor was unbearable), but was essential to the legality of the marriage contract, which disposed of extensive estates and any heirs their union should produce. Gawain was granting her, already, a significant portion of *his* sovereignty. Then, with her enchantment only half-broken, and her "piggyness" still an undoubtedly vivid memory, he makes exquisite love to her, confirming her beauty. This must have been enormously reassuring—healing, indeed—to one so recently suffering from and still under the cloud of an enchantment-imposed ugliness.

In the service of the king, he marries Ragnell, putting his own needs to one side. Then, in the service of Ragnell, all over again, puts her needs above his own and instinctively, through the compassionate heart, grants her the "sovereignty" of choice. Women's right to make their own life decisions was clearly at stake in this medieval world—one of those rights we now regard as inalienable and God-given in today's democratic societies. It was women's rights, generically, that the series of brutes we have been reading about seemed to ignore, crudely pursuing their romantic and materialistic goals with force. This primitive old game of the dominant male seems to begin in primate groups. Those who defeat all the other males get to the top of the dominance hierarchy and thus have access to, or "ownership" of the females.[25]

This is, in fact, the mythological formula of the priesthood at Nemi, whose roots, Frazer tells us, are buried in darkest antiquity, perhaps in that primal horde Freud wrote about so compellingly—and inaccurately. The male "priest-king" has killed his predecessor and will probably be killed by his successor. By the time of Arthur, and the stories that followed his mythical reign, the scene from Nemi was being acted out all over the landscape, as knights fought knights for the favor of ladies—or rather to possess them and their lands. But the origin of the ritual in a matriarchal era, had been forgotten.[26] Here the magical idea was to renew the land, and the ritual of the *hieros gamos*, through a sacrifice, and that is why the "king must die." The priestess-queen of the grove, who was identical with the land, and her matrilineal line endured. Her male lovers, however, under the principle of *carpe diem*, came and went in their season, enjoying their day in the sun, probably dying violently, but sacredly, at their appointed time, causing a regeneration of the secret mythic powers that sustain the entire enterprise.

In the patriarchal age, however, the sense of the feminine had disappeared under the onslaught of a Middle-Eastern religion and its priestly administrators. Males ruled not only by their greater strength, along with social customs and values that supported that dominance, but male priests celebrated a male triune god, and used male gender pronouns to speak of that which was holy. Culturally, the skeletal arrangement was there: the land and the lady remained associated, as is magically proper, but now the male owned the land, owned the lady, owned the children, and everything else, leading to enormous abuses of power. Joseph Campbell has documented the time, in the Middle Dynasties of Egypt, when the wily pharaohs, instead of allowing themselves to be sacrificed in the interests of the common weal, elected a surrogate who was "king for a day," and then sacrificed in his stead—so the pharaoh could go on ruling. This was a clever idea, but it defeated the earth-wisdom of the original formula: new blood perpetually brought into the highest office in the land. It also allowed pharaohs with rather serious personality problems (delusions of grandeur being the least of them) to reign for a long time, thus causing difficulties for the priesthood (who retaliated in their own ways) and for the populace.

In the naive version of this patriarchal scenario, as in our Arthurian stories, the female, once the sacred priestess and the secret power behind the scene, is not asked whether she likes the arrangement. If she quibbles, she could be abused, humiliated, even killed. This power of male *force majeure* was used routinely, ruthlessly and unconsciously. That is why all the ladies of the castle look on, with extreme interest, at Gawain in his exercise of courtesy, the contribution of the fourth chakra that undoes the violent sexual tyrannizing of the third.

Ragnell, like the ladies of the Castle of Marvels, has been placed under an enchantment by an evil magician, in some versions her brother Sir Gromer Somer Joure, or a henchman of her brother, for his own purposes. The answer that freed her, "sovereignty, you choose" was the very thing that had been denied women—in the arranged marriages, in the trophy or booty mentality, and in the use of greater male physical strength.

Clinschor's enchantment is precisely the world where these brutalities are allowed, ruled by a eunuch priesthood, out of touch with nature and the feminine, a powerful but bankrupt dynasty. In this world, no one really knows anyone else (i.e., constant mistaken identity as the knights charge about wearing steel buckets over their faces), as in our urban wastelands. The eunuch sorcerer's *raison d'être* seems to be, "I'm fanatical, ascetic, and celibate, and I'm not having any fun—so neither should you!" Gawain, warm, life-affirming—perhaps soulful more than spiritual, and certainly not religiously pious—sensitive, courtly, suave but never discourteous toward women or men who might be thought his social inferiors, and above all, compassionate—is the right man to undo the awful curse of the eunuch-magician. This is also the figure—the other side of Parzival, the Grail Knight—to relieve the Goddess of her pig mask. Who can fail to understand the source of her anger?

And there, lonely, floating on the lake, in his own painful enchantment, his "thigh" (his masculine vitality, if you will) wounded, able to find no rest, is the Fisher King of the Wasteland. We have seen how his predicament is the result of Balin's impulsive style and failure to pause in the presence of a sacred mystery: we recall that it was in a chamber in the castle of Pelleam, or Pelinore, where the mystery itself dwelt in magical suspense, the spear hovering in the air, the Grail upon the royal table. Balin seized the masculine element in this beautifully balanced, symbolic *tableaux*, and used it ruthlessly, as a thousand of his compatriots were doing all over Europe. And now the feminine element is carried in and out of the Great Hall of the Grail Castle in a trance-like ritual, endlessly repeated, because still unresolved, a beautiful cauldron of transformative mystery, waiting for a *knight* (a male committed to a violent profession) to ask the compassionate question. This mystery perpetuates itself and could be said to be still waiting, in exactly the same way, for the question to be asked, again and again and again, in the lives of millions of men and in the *animus* zone of millions of (enchanted) women, as our world seeks increasingly desperately for redemption.

But this is not only a matter of sexual politics, wherein biologically male and female individuals struggle for their rightful places in society, and in turn, struggle to mend the torn fabric of society itself. Here are implications for the whole web of the world's life—all our relations, as we have been saying—and for the integrity of our inmost region of soul.

Gawain's compassionate heart reveals that he is connected profoundly to his own intuitive, original nature and, through that, to the greater world of nature.

His empathy transcends the limitations of gender, social position, even of race and species (he is facing not merely an uncomely woman, but a monstrous being who may not be human); he opens himself to the *other*. At this moment, he opens his life's possibilities to the hugeness of the imagination—the imaginal—and of the spirit.

Who, after all, and what, is Dame Ragnell? Seven years, we are told, this woman of unearthly beauty remained with Gawain in blissful marriage. Then (according to the version) she died or disappeared. This, we recognize, is the sure sign of a fairy bride. They grace our lives for seven years (or three, or thirteen); they bless us with their gifts of wealth, beautiful children, secret lore, creativity; and they return into the mists, or the forest, or under the mountain, or beneath the waters, or beyond the sky.

Like the shaman, Gawain renews the compact of the human with the worlds of nature and of the spirit. Thus, he begins his journey toward individuation, in Jung's language, or toward regeneration, in Swedenborg's language. Such an act of compassion springs from an experience of unity with life, in a universe informed by a vision of wholeness, like that of Swedenborg's *Maximus Homo*. Such an act, in an integrated universe, propels us all—all relations—together toward renewal.

The Wasteland, the adventure, the achievement of the Grail and the union with the Beloved—all take place within our own soul. It is our soul—for each of us—that is to be renewed by the healing waters of the lady's fountain, fertilized by the potency of the divine king. And through each of us—and only through us—the Wasteland of our relationships, of our culture, of our wounded world is redeemed and rededicated.

With the usual timeliness of synchronicity, a woman came to Stephen for counseling, in bereavement for her father, who had died some six months before. Although he was a leading public servant, no one in the whole world seemed to love him, no one but his daughter (the client, whom we shall call Anya). She spoke of the cold shoulders from relatives as he lay dying and the stiff faces at the funeral. It seemed like a bleak and mournful scene. Stephen asked Anya if she had any dreams in the last few weeks or month, and she could remember only one, a fragment it seemed, with one odd twist.

She had dreamed of her father, standing there, stern and alone, lost and pale, in an endless-seeming tunnel. In a strangely trance-like state, she found herself bowing down to him, deeply. That was the dream.

Stephen asked the dreamer to go back to the dream and see where the imagery led her. As she closed her eyes to visualize, a different scene emerged, as she remembered him from an earlier, happier period of their lives. It was an early morning, near the family home on Martha's Vineyard. Anya's father loved fishing, and there he was in a fishing outfit, about to go out on an early New England morning. Stephen suggested she "just let the imagery take over." Off he went, alone in a little boat; the morning was misty, and soon he was lost in the mist—it was a little like the tunnel in the dream, now. At this point, Stephen made a suggestion (the "guided" part of "guided affective imagery"): Ask your father to *look up*. Anya mimicked the action she wanted him to do by tilting her own head upward. Suddenly, a bird appeared (in her imagery), and Stephen suggested she and her father follow it. Now it turned into a seagull flying ahead strongly, the boat following.

Stephen suggested at this point that she imagine herself in the boat with her father and having a conversation with him—it would emerge as the one she never had, but had so wanted to, before he died. The dialogue triggered a profound release of feeling, and some things that had needed to be said by each to each. Anya's father affirmed, as it were, the special place she had always held in his heart.

We both knew her father had to be "released" from his stuck place in the tunnel, and to go on—he now seemed willing to go and bade a moving farewell to his daughter. Off he went, standing tall and almost kingly, now, in the boat, following the seagull—off, off, into the bright hollow mist.

The impasse Anya had felt since his death was broken in tears and renewed understanding of the man. Her father was no longer a ghost in the Wasteland. Stephen then brought up the story of the Fisher King, and the client was thunderstruck: "Yes, that's it, that royal aloofness that separated him from everyone." There was something that he embodied that was spiritual, even in the Wasteland of city government where he worked. The myth brought life itself to life for her; she could see many correspondences. Moreover, she understood her own role. She was always the one who would ask, "Are you all right?" ("What ails you, uncle?") Now she had not only a renewed appreciation for her role, but a sense of having given her father the send-off he deserved.

Somewhere, in the Wasteland, a Fisher King is fishing, going into the depths of the watery element to find the living thing, the sparkling, nourishing thing of the depths that will help to heal a perennial wound. The wound is at its worst where people cannot see or hear each other, and act out mythic charades in the daylight world—taking each other as dispensable players in their own solipsistic dramas.

But there is a new greening to the Wasteland, the story of the individual journey and the compassionate heart. No longer do we have to be spiritual only in churches or synagogues, but in our lives. "For according to this mythology there is no fixed law, no established knowledge of God, set up by prophet or by priest, that can stand against the revelation of a life lived with integrity in the spirit of its own brave truth," writes Campbell in the concluding volume of *The Masks of God*:

> Every so-called "fall," or departure from the "law," is then itself a creative act in which God (to use a mythological term) participates . . . God's initiative is represented in the inborn, sealed-in soul or "intelligible character" of the individual at birth; and the initiative, the freedom to act, must thereafter be one's own, guided not by what other people say, have done, or may tell one is God's will, but by one's own interior voice; for indeed (continuing to speak mythologically) it is in one's sealed-in soul, its hidden God-given difference from all others, that "God's will" has been secreted, to be found and shown, like an Easter egg: and not by retreat to a bed of rapture either in darkness or in light, but through action here in this mixed world (why, otherwise, be born?), where nothing is foul, nothing pure, but all, like a magpie's plumage, mixed.[27]

"And though life is bittersweet," Campbell would twinkle at us, sadly joyful at the end of a long weekend of Grail lore, doing some of his most brilliant teaching in his seventies and eighties, and at times painfully aware of his own losses, frustrations and tragedies: "we must say 'yes' to it!"—to the universe, the *Mysterium Tremendum et Fascinans* in which we all are apparitions, ceaselessly arising, ceaselessly falling back into the mystery. Recognizing this is the deeper meaning of the hero-journey.

STEPHEN AND ROBIN IN DIALOGUE

Stephen: I'm intrigued by what you've been telling me about in your readings, having to do with a suppression of the individual experience in courtly love, and a substitution of the collective, such as the cult of the Virgin.

Robin: What von Franz is pointing out is that a war was specifically enacted against the individual path for women. It was a reaction to courtly love—against the nature of love as expressed in the dramas most beloved in the courts—and it was this idea of a personal fate which one follows for good or ill, and of two people living it together (Campbell's favorites, Tristan to Isold: "If this is my death I drink, I do so gladly." Héloise to Abelard: "Even if this means eternal damnation, I accept it for the sake of my beloved.")

 The conflict occurs when the individual element is not allowed to flourish. In the fairytales of the "proud princess" or the "black princess," a young woman falls into the rejecting or the daemonic posture. It often happens at sixteen, when the girl is going to be married, when her individual self is going to be bulldozed into the collective. At this point, this violent aspect of the feminine rears its head. It is the death throes of personal individuation set against the traditional pattern: now you will fulfill this social role of mother, housewife, whatever.

Stephen: Therapists often see this kind of thing. A typical situation could be of a young woman just graduated from college and bound for graduate school, who decides to break off with the young man from the neighborhood she has been with since forever and ever. Perhaps her parents and those of the young man have become very good friends, and the whole thing seems very *gemütlich*—then she changes her mind about the relationship. She wants to play the field a little more. Her parents suddenly become outraged, forbid her to use the car to go out with other young men, and give her the cold shoulder.

 The situation would escalate: "Ok," she decides, "that's the way it is." She gets pretty angry in turn, and restricts her own affectionate display. The parents then accuse her of being cold and trying to punish them: "Whatever has come over you?" I think when they see this cold, harsh face coming back at them, they have a hard time facing it. Now if we can have this age-old conflict playing itself out in these relatively "enlightened" times, think of what it must have been like when the parents knew they had the right to make any kind of arranged marriage for their daughter that suited their purposes.

Do you think this is the problem of Orgeluse? That sharp tongue has to come from somewhere.

Robin: Shakespeare's *Taming of the Shrew* takes its source from a folktale, a princess for whom no suitor is good enough ("King Thrushbeard" is the permutation that appears in the Brothers Grimm): they are too fat or too skinny, or they have buck teeth. There is one particular prince who has a scraggly beard, and she puts him down with all the others. Her exasperated father proposes a riddle contest. The prince (who will turn out to be her true love) first comes in as a poor potter and solves the riddles. Now she has this hard life living in a hovel and going to town to sell pots; then a horseman rides by and breaks them all. In the end, the potter, the horseman, and the prince are one man, her true love; he had to appear in these guises to humble her.

Stephen: Interesting. So here we have the social level of the sharp-tongued, truth-telling woman. She has to meet genuine kindness and persistence in a lover, someone willing to see behind her corrosive mask. Orgeluse is "tamed" by Gawain's essential kindness and generosity of spirit. What about the psychodynamic and the mythic levels?

Robin: The *Taming of the Shrew* is a story told at a time when everyone believed that a man should dominate and a woman be submissive. Therefore, a woman who was outspoken, and trying to determine her own life—to have sovereignty—was an out-of-place shrew. Psychodynamically, the reason for her shrewishness is that she sees all the hypocrisy and deception of the social world, is aware of the social constraints she is supposed to labor under, knows she's most likely to have to spend her life saying "yes, my lord" to some bully who hasn't half her brains—and so she develops a keen sense of irony. She is conscious of all of these nuances and lets us know about it.

At a deeper mythic level though, the "princess" is a quality of soul that wants more perfection than is allowed in this life. She has an illusion of "royalty," she's too good for it all. . . . There has to come a humbling; it can't all go her way. Yet deeper still, the soul is "royal," and its destiny is union with the "kingly Beloved."

Stephen: So all the time that Gawain is undergoing the acid bath of Orgeluse's tongue, they're both transforming. It's a very touching moment when she tells her story to Gawain—she gives the history, the reason for the acerbic temperament and the sense of irony. The acid tongue and the cold shoulder both belong to sovereignty impaired, diminished, and wounded. The reason given in the story for Gawain's willingness or ability to stand the excoriation is that he is so much in love that he seems oblivious of the continued abuse. But only when he has survived ordeal after ordeal on her behalf, and she has suddenly become vulnerable and honest, has actually apologized, does he address how the abuse makes him feel. His own tongue gets a little sharp, a little ironic; basically, he says, "If I am to be mocked, I can do without your love!"

Robin: In the *Taming of the Shrew*, or in its fairytale predecessors, if you see the princess as a woman, Katherina, and the prince as a man, Petruchio, you can find another way of reading it. Here's a man who really sees her and values her not only for her looks or her father's wealth, but for her courage and self-determination. (Yeats said it: "But one man loved the pilgrim soul in you.") In the culture they live in, he can't get to her: she's rejecting him along with all the guys who are too fat, skinny, old, and—most essentially—don't really see her. So the one who is truly right for her can't get to her either, because her defenses are so strong. So here is Gawain's seeming oblivion—or the clever King Thrushbeard in the Brothers Grimm, or Petruchio in *The Shrew*—who wins her in all these tricky ways, but what he offers her is one who loves her for who she is and perhaps for what they may be able to be together; if she gets that, she doesn't have to fight him off. These are different ways—mythic, social, psychological—of looking at one folk tale.[28]

Stephen: Orgeluse is doing her archetypal thing on Gawain, but he's a sly one. He seems to be doing this, "Oh, I'm so much in love with you that I'll ignore your wicked temper and black outlook on life." But actually he has used her acid tongue to inspire his deeds of valor. With these, he breaks through the prickly exterior and wins her vulnerable heart, which craves all the things she seems to mock: loyalty, cheerfulness, goodness of heart, courage.

Robin: It seems to me that, in this tradition, the knight and the lady used each other and their love as a kind of a vaulting pole for spiritual experience. Romantic love is necessary as an understanding of partnership as a spiritual process. Failing to understand, we always project anima and animus onto each other, a piece of our soul out in front. The troubadours, Robert Johnson says in *We*, were more conscious of this process. They were using the idealization of the other as an impetus to soul movement, soul growth.

Stephen: When this isn't understood, though, it's quite dangerous, because the projection of the male soul-life onto the woman is also giving it away, and the woman then becomes responsible for fascinating the man. She carries his vitality, his creativity; and she's responsible for all of this.

Robin: And he carries her courage, resourcefulness, and loyalty. Of course, in this type of fascination, neither the man nor the woman sees the other. They are looking beyond and through the living person to a spiritual vision. I think the Sufis do the best job with this—the beloved is the visible image of God. We must give our soul to the beloved and then take it back, ultimately separating our image of the Divine and the power in it from the other person, and owning it.

This is my emphasis, now: I think that the real work of the loving partnership begins when you have both the ecstatic path of romantic love and the love of a *real* man for a *real* woman— and the partnership, when you can use both of these things in your journey together. I think this is a very very powerful and really a new way of looking at this. In the Middle Ages, in courtly love, the two individuals were never supposed to live together and struggle with the ordinary things of everyday life; they did that in their separate marriages. The only time—this is quite interesting—the only time that I can think of, when the lovers came together and lived together, would be in the "Forest Idyll." This is one of those motifs that appears in many stories; but the prototype is that of Tristan and Isolt. Tristan and Isolt were actual lovers; but while they were in the forest—I believe it was a period of four years—they always managed intuitively to sleep with the sword between them just when King Mark was about to find them. In any case, the forest years were eventually so hard on Isolt that for her health they had to give up and come back to Mark. So even in the quintessential romance, living together was hard on the lovers.

Stephen: It seems to be the actual living together that Gahmuret, for example, can't abide. The moment it gets peaceful and content, he scrams back into the Great Deadly Game, what Freud identified in *Beyond the Pleasure Principle* as *thanatos*, the death instinct, of perennial fascination for males since whenever. Even Parzival, who has what he wants in Condwiramurs, goes in search of his mother—first time he has even thought of her—but it's really adventure, soul development, that something in him knows he can't get at home.

Robin: It's always struck me that for all the bad rap that clings to Hades for abducting Persephone, they are one of the most stable couples in the entire Olympian pantheon. He does, after all, marry her, make her his queen—and he makes an arrangement for her need for sunlight, beaches, a separate vacation. He comes to accept the times when they're away from each other, he lavishes gifts on her, takes good care of her—shows her cool places in the underworld.

Stephen: Hades, or Pluto, depending on whether you're in Greece or Rome, is said to be the possessor of great wealth. Sometimes he's even shown with a cornucopia, which is a related symbol to the Grail. There is richness there in the deep unconscious, and maybe some of the moisture and dark that would help to bring fruitfulness to the Wasteland. Perhaps that is why Persephone, Kore, goddess of all spring flowering, needs to descend to the depths periodically for darkness and moisture.

Robin: This is certainly a myth that is central for modern women to explore. To go into their own depths is the offset for the surface receptivity and compliance, the social accommodation that is thrust on women much more than on men. You know, it's almost as if there is a real, literalistic version of this religion being acted out in the world. I'm thinking of girls and young women with a lot going for them, intelligent, beautiful, who take up with the seediest characters—real underworld dudes with serious Plutonian problems: addictions, crime, violence. And these women keep coming back for more.

　　If such women are capable of seeing the archetypal level, rather than acting it out, there would be a lot less grief and destruction for them.

Stephen: We're back to the problem of the literalistic acting out of symbols and energies in the psyche. There has to be a certain amount of it; and, yes, it almost makes the world go round; but it does take its toll on life, limb, and happiness.

Robin: There was a particular point where the real audience of the great tales of courtly love—Tristan and Isolt, Arthur and Guinevere (and Lancelot), the Gawain cycles, Parzival—were the middle classes, the merchant classes, that came to hear these stories told by the minnesingers and troubadours. Later, there were the plays of Shakespeare and Marlowe, which are very rich in soul-projection, anima/animus stuff.

　　Robert Johnson points out in his book *We* that romantic love has existed throughout history and in many cultures. We find it in the literature of ancient Greece, the Roman Empire, ancient Persia, and feudal Japan. However, our modern Western society is the only culture in history that has experienced romantic love as a mass phenomenon; we are the only society that makes romance the basis of our marriages and love relationships, and has posited the cultural ideal of a "true love" for everyman. The romantic movement, which is different from the courtly love tradition, really begins with this, though, with Tristan and Isolt and the love poems and songs of the troubadours.

Stephen: Which means we're also free to make our own mistakes; in fact, they're guaranteed, as two naive psyches project their contents—some from the surface and social conditioning, the stereotypes and caricatures from popular culture—doomed to shatter on the actualities of living together, balancing checkbooks, and raising children. Then there is the other stuff, the deep unconscious material that might erupt periodically, but certainly is bound to come more to the surface once the honeymoon phase is over, and as the couple ages. The children leave, and there they sit, familiar strangers.

Robin: Now we get this maze, this labyrinth of powerful projections between people. Marian Woodman has excellent material on what the woman is projecting onto the man, and Robert Johnson does a good job on what the man is projecting onto the woman; so it is interesting to consider this material together. There are idealizations that hurt the actuality, and yet what is projected also tells of the soul and leads each gender forward toward a deeper maturity.

Here we are confronted with a paradox that baffles us, yet we should not be surprised to discover that romantic love is connected with spiritual aspiration, even with our religious instinct. It was a way that spiritualized a knight and his lady and raised them to the experience of another world, an experience of soul and spirit. Johnson says this is the greatest paradox and deepest mystery in our modern Western lives. We seem to be seeking a human relationship, and that's an important part of it. But we are simultaneously seeking a religious experience, a vision of wholeness.[29]

Stephen: This is where Swedenborg comes in and, as far as I am concerned, outreaches all the depth psychologies in his vision of what is possible for a human couple to achieve. It is a new alchemy between the genders, to fashion something transcendent. It goes beyond Gurdjieff, who says that, unless you work on yourself, you are only "food for the moon," subject to the sublunar realm of life, decay and death. And why do all this spiritual work unless you feel that it's going somewhere, that you are fashioning something truly spiritual, that indeed transcends biological and social life? In the alchemy of coming together, something new begins, a being that incorporates your two souls in synergy.

The era of courtly love really accompanied a great cultural renaissance culminating a little over five-hundred years ago, leading to the Enlightenment and the development of modern civilization. If we have learned anything at all about the relationship between men and women, we have learned that they are different, yet the same, passengers on Spaceship Earth who need each other, not only for reproduction of the species, but for psychological growth and for spiritual evolution. And it seems that whenever this primary relationship fails, it is either a sign or a precipitant of a "Wasteland" mythology. When either enjoys undisputed hegemony, the situation seems unbalanced, asymmetrical. These imbalances may be studied in physical relationships, language, social, economic or political inequities, mythologies, religions and spirituality. They have been shown to be all-too-visible in the world of the Middle Ages and the Renaissance; but, in the same stories that chronicle violence, abuse between the sexes, political inequities, dark lingering resentments, and belief systems that tolerate these things, there is abundant redemptive hope in such symbols as the Grail, and in the adventures and discoveries of the many characters, male and female both, on a path of spiritual evolution.

Kissing
by Alex Grey

CHAPTER TEN

ANGELIC DIALOGUES

Mature men and women of the new age will be bound together less by the attraction of opposites than by their shared humanity. This shared humanity does not neutralize sexual attraction. Differentiated masculinity in a woman attracts strong men. Differentiated femininity in men attracts strong women. The energy at work in a male body functions differently from the energy at work in a female body. . . . The unity of the human race dictated by the global village we anxiously inhabit—while still looking for a safer place to settle—is a unity that far transcends the sexual attraction of the opposites. It is rather a unity that issues from a profound identity that needs urgently to be understood.

Marion Woodman, *The Ravaged Bridegroom*[1]

When our two souls stand up erect and strong,
Face to face, silent, drawing nigh and nigher,
Until the lengthening wings break into fire
At either curved point—What bitter wrong
Can the earth do to us, that we should not long
be here contented?

Elizabeth Barrett Browning, *Sonnets from the Portuguese, 22*[2]

SPEAKING AQUARIAN

JOSEPH CAMPBELL ALWAYS INSISTED THAT a "living mythology" must keep abreast of its culture, including its social, scientific, and technological developments. One of his biggest complaints about the organized Judeo-Christian tradition was that it seemed to hold to symbols generated two-thousand years ago, whereas now we have very different conditions of living and require mythologies that address them. Emanuel Swedenborg probably would have agreed, from his eighteenth-century perspective: Christianity was in need of an updating, and the "New Church" was the name that adhered to the religion founded on his teachings, a new way of Christianity more attuned to spiritual realities and the inner life. Swedenborg believed the literal or "natural" sense of the Scriptures was outdated, and a new dispensation, with a "spiritual" but really very psychological way of interpreting them, was necessary.[3]

We do not have to look far to find mythologies of "the New Age." They are all around us. But those who will not learn from history are doomed to repeat it, says the old saw, and there is no way to build a new world, a new mythos, or found a New Age without a careful appraisal of the old. That is just what we have been doing throughout this book—looking to our old patterns to find the indications and contraindications of the future—especially in this field of gender relationships.

So far, many of our sources, from Zulu shamans to the Apocrypha, to the Arthurian stories, Swedenborg, Jung, von Franz, and finally Campbell, Woodman, Welwood and other contemporaries have been saying that the key to our next stage of psychological development is through relationships. We have been largely addressing male/female relationships and the masculine/feminine *imagos* that go with them. Moreover, we have seen how mythologies impact on this process, from the antifeminist elements in the book of Genesis, to its later interpreters who continued for centuries to blame woman for "the fall of man." But Campbell has said that "the next mythology cannot be predicted any more than tonight's dream, for a mythology is not . . . something projected from the brain, but experienced from the heart."[4] So this leaves us in a kind of impasse—but with the reassurance that, if we stay close to the revelations of the heart, we shall not go so far amiss in apprehending the mythology of the New Age.

Astrologically, the age that is about to start is the Age of Aquarius, following the two-thousand years of the Piscean era (the fish, the symbol of Christ). Aquarius belongs with the air signs (with Libra and Gemini), not water, though the symbol of Aquarius is a starry man pouring water from a vase. As an air sign, Aquarius is regarded as intellectual but also intuitive and innovative, and is co-ruled by the planets Saturn and Uranus. Saturn moves slowly, solidifies, densifies, and brings things down; it represents learning through limitation and practical, skeptical knowing. Uranus, on the other hand, is wild, limit-breaking, risk-taking, innovative, communicative, truth-discovering. It seems that any sign with these two planets ruling would have a kind of built-in paradoxicality: a conservative radicalism, a Confucian Taoism, a skeptical and visionary quality.

It was in 1967 when we heard that Edward Whitmont was due to give a series of six lectures at the C.G. Jung Foundation in New York on the theme of the Aquarian Age. We were graduate students in New York, Stephen at Columbia and Robin at New York University, and we had been coming to an amazing lecture series at the Jung Foundation for three years. It was where we first had heard Joseph Campbell and pivotal Jungian thinkers like Joseph Henderson, M. Esther Harding, June Singer, James Hillman, and Arnie Mindell. Upon occasion, the renowned scholar Marie-Louise von Franz would show up and dazzle us with her insights into fairytales and their mythic structure. The lectures were presented in a lecture hall on East 46th Street, right across from the United Nations, so there was something of the feeling of a psychological summit in those early days.

Now we were due to hear Edward Whitmont. He was a small man of an amazing, precise mind and indeterminate age. Sometimes he seemed indeed to incarnate the wise old man, with his bald head and unruly tufts of white hair sprouting from either side. At other times, certainly in his quickness and unexpected novelty of mind and youthful flexibility of movement, he seemed much younger. (He was actually, we calculated later, in his late fifties.) Whitmont was already famous for his unique combining of homeopathy (he was a medical doctor, trained in Austria) and Jungian psychology. Whitmont had cured Stephen of an intractable-seeming tropical fever he had contracted in Mexico, with a single dose of one of his magical potions. He was also versed in astrology and a formidable classical scholar, as well as a musician.

Stephen had entered Jungian analysis with Whitmont about a year-and-a-half prior, and Robin was with Ann Belford Ulanov, a recently trained analyst who had an office in the same complex as Whitmont. It would be very interesting for us to hear what this man, with his scholar's erudition and yet wild mind, would do with the topic of the Aquarian Age. When we signed up, the Jung Foundation drafted Stephen to do a chronicling of the lecture series for the *Analytical Psychology Newsletter*. So we listened very carefully, and took copious notes.

The time was the genesis of the Rainbow Gatherings and the "Summer of Love." It was "the dawning of the Age of Aquarius," and the culture was alive with a visionary fervor of transformation. If we could just stop Vietnam, the last great unjust war . . . Let's protest war, poverty, social discrimination—they're so stupid anyway. We participated in the first "Human Be-in" in Central Park, launched a Yellow Submarine in the East River, marched (the first of many) on Washington. On the lower East Side where we lived, we would frequently see Louis Abolafia, the "Naked Candidate for President." He would attend a party wearing an overcoat and nothing else but a big "I've got nothing to hide" written in magic marker on his chest; since in those years we felt every politician did have something to hide—Nixon, Ford, Johnson—Abolafia's seemed an appealing platform. Maybe we could change society by electing a hippie and "liberating" the universities and the legislatures. After all, if people "made love, not war," wouldn't the world be a better place soon?

Dr. Whitmont dispelled that myth fairly quickly—"nice, but terribly naive and evanescent," was his assessment. The real work of Aquarius was to be a work of reconciliation between the symbolic energies of Saturn and Aquarius, he cautioned us, between conservativism and radicalism, the *senex* (unyielding old man) and the *puer aeternus* (eternal insouciant youth). It was not going to be an easy job and could stretch well into the next millennium or two (the duration of Aquarius).

The "water-bearer" contains the only completely human figure in the zodiac, and thus it pertains to the human world. Aquarius features two snakes (the "waters") undulating next to each other but not touching (in contrast to Pisces, which has two fish turned away from each other). In Pisces we have had opposites constellated and polarized with relation to each other: good versus evil; spiritual versus natural; male versus female (we remember Suzuki's comment on Western religion, with its polarities of man against God, God against man, God against nature, etc.). In Aquarius, those dynamisms are to be brought out of opposition and placed next to each other in an oscillatory movement; waves "entraining" each other. No

THE FASHIONING OF ANGELS

longer opposites in opposition, but opposing or parallel dynamisms influencing each other, like electrical sinewaves, like brainwaves.

Thus, there was going to be a lot of "hard relating" going on; that is to say, intensive dialogues would have to be enacted between all of the above pairs of opposites: nature and spirit, conservative versus radical, male versus female or their archetypal qualities, masculinity and femininity, these latter being the most of interest to us here. Each must exist independent from, yet *related* to the other. Swedenborg described the "wiggling" as accomplished through correspondences: a problem in the daylight, "material" world also is dreamt about, thus represented in the "spiritual" world. Further, if you are mindful of the dream and bring a creative insight to the physical situation, you are continuing the dialogue, the process Jung called "the transcendent function," which Stephen discusses in *The Shaman's Doorway* as "creative shamanism," or Stage Five in his "Stages of Mythic Engagement." We can learn to balance inspiration and perspiration, ideal and real, word and image.

Between a man and a woman, there needs to be lots of "wiggling," and this is certainly true on the natural, erotic plane, but is even more true on the physical plane. The facts are in: men and women speak different languages.[5] We have to first interpret then re-understand each other, going in and out of the other's meanings many times, before an adequate picture of each other's inner world or motives really becomes apparent to each—and for this we need a good deal of patience, courtesy that flows both ways, and a willingness to arrive at some understanding or empathy. On the mythic or archetypal level we need myths that not only equate in the simplistic sense: a "Goddess" figure to match every image of "God" that is distinctly male, but a gender parity in the stories and lore of the gods and goddesses themselves, or the human heroes and heroines, in which the attributes of gentleness, waiting, and receptivity are as much lauded and rewarded as assertiveness, directness, or impetuous violence. This includes a new hero lore in which heroines abound, and their capacity for relatedness or receptivity, along with the aggressive assertion, wins the day (this actually seems to be happening in the popular media as many more women play the roles of active, warlike heroines such as TV's *Zena, Warrior Princess*, but also model feelingful personal relationships. In another TV series, we have a *Hercules*, who between feats of preternatural strength, is tormented by existential angst and bouts of empathy.) Thus, popular media are coming to represent, and favorably depict, the development of strength in women and receptivity in men. These are symmetrical "wigglings" of the snakes of relationship.

Deeper still, on a spiritual level, men and women need constantly to support and partner each other—in moral choices, self-development and individuation, and, most importantly, in relationship to the divine behind and beyond all forms.

"And we must love, man, woman, and child, dedicating all things as they pass, or else we come to God with empty hands," says the poet Yeats.

The Age of Aquarius should be a time for men to find a way of being more congruent with their higher potential, and for women to help them move that way, while doing equivalent work in their own animus development. Aquarius does model a positive masculine *imago*:

Aquarius involves creativity, humanitarianism, brotherhoods, intellectual abstraction (science) and drama. There is a tendency towards rebellion against fixed ideas and concepts. There is a striving towards consciousness, initiative, inventiveness. There is little or no respect for orthodoxy. Since Leo and the Sun are opposite, there is a struggle constellated between individual and group. Leo involves individual, egoistic motivation and Aquarius group oriented motivation.[6]

So we see radicalism tweaking the bounds of propriety in many forms as the twentieth century winds to a close, and the New Age begins in actual, not ideal form. We are stumbling and lurching into the new millennium as a species, with all the problems we now have and many new ones as well, as population increases, resources dwindle, and industrial pollutants blight the ecosystem. For the most part, a sexual libertinism and openness exist as at no time in history, with the possible exception of the Roman Empire or on Polynesian Islands. Most modern cities abound in sex shops, porno theaters, and "red light" districts, not to mention media and Internet uses of sexuality. (Chakra two has been liberated in a way Dr. Freud might never have thought possible.)

At the same time, there is a horrified response from the "moral majority" and a clearcut political lashback, to return to older codes of morality and biblical attitudes toward sex and the body. In addition to the social response, the biological world makes its own inarticulate rejoinder to sexual promiscuity through sexually transmitted diseases (which some members of the religious right hold to be the scourge of God for libertinism). Here the physical world shows a "morality" or rather a prudence of its own, free of socially originated codes. Suffice it to say that this area represents one of these zones of potential dialogue, if not conflict. Dialogue, and a dialectic that continues moving forward, is clearly preferable to stonewalling or an impasse that goes nowhere.

Intellectual life, literature, the media, the arts all become sparring grounds for these polarities represented by Saturn and Uranus. In addition to religious fundamentalism, we now have scientific fundamentalism, so that the revelations of science become a new secular religion. The skeptical inquirer and the scientific establishment pooh-pooh the idea that the universe is a seamless whole, with mystical interconnections from part to part, so that such things as ESP and mental telepathy are *not* anomalies—and yet at the same time the crème de la crème of science, the New Physics, says it *is* just that—a seamless, interrelated whole, each feature of the visible universe carrying a model of "the implicate order" of things. The brain, documented as a machine, shows its holographic potential and refuses to act simply "mechanical" (Karl Pribram is known for his groundbreaking work in this area).[7]

On one occasion, we brought together astronomers and astrologers to have a dialogue we thought would be interesting. After all, both study the stars and use complex tables to predict their movements; but, evidently, that is all: the mythological clash that unfolded was worthy of a medieval heresy trial, with names called and acid-dripping invective employed throughout (we remember the clash between the university scientists and the animal rehabilitators in the Jane Goodall seminar). In many university settings, the social science department barely communicates with the humanities department, even where their subjects overlap, as in psychological dimensions in literature. These are clearly places where the simple principle of dialogue is necessary. It can be polite: "Pardon me, but you don't really believe that planets, chunks of rock and minerals millions of miles away from us, have effects on personality or embody psychological characteristics, do you?" "Pardon me (in return) but you don't really believe this vast, exquisitely regulated phantasmagoria, the *mysterium tremendum et fascinans*, is entirely meaningless—aren't you, with all your meanings, a part of it?" And so on. It can be a very exciting thing to meet an intelligent opponent on a relatively level and civil playing field. This would be dialogue.

Whitmont made some rather trenchant points about conflict, citing animal ethologists, such as Konrad Lorenz and Robert Ardrey, who find aggression involved in all animal behavior, including primate social interactions. (Ardrey believes that the "T" is the "mark of Cain," the sign of a type of feral protohuman going back as far as maybe a million years, who used a tool as weapon to slay another of his own kind—"Abel.") Aggression (chakra three) is as widespread, over the earth, as are sexuality (chakra two) and territoriality (chakra one). There is a serious question open about whether attempts to control aggression by legislation or religious morality have been successful at all, Whitmont pointed out. "All conditioning, all training, when and if it is to take a real hold, cannot in the long range pit itself directly against the will of the instincts. . . . We can only accomplish something with our will where it aligns itself somehow or somewhere with an instinct."[8] Therefore, ways of controlled release or a display of aggression in ritualized contexts becomes important, as is done in games such as football or the martial arts. Here Whitmont agreed with Freud, saying "The instincts may not be legislated away"—it is probably better to contain, or sublimate them:

> The surrounding world must offer us both satisfaction (reward) and resistance, to be really interesting for us. If there is too much resistance by the environment, and not enough satisfaction, of course one loses interest, and stagnation results. Conversely, if there were instant satisfaction of every wish and desire, and no initial resistance from the world, the result would be identical, boredom and then stagnation. The result of this is that man [gender pronouns left as is in original] *must* have an enemy, of just about equal strength to himself. Further he must make sure this enemy *doesn't leave him*. This introduces the relationship, then that really exists between love and enmity (*Eros* and *Eris*). One must have some strife in order to be able to love. Conflict itself then must be seen ideally as a play in which one seeks only to pit oneself against the other for mutual benefit, not to completely destroy him.[9]

Thus, we have William Blake's "Opposition is true Friendship." We have to be willing to engage in conflict as a precondition to love—fight, it seems, in order to be able to "make up." The aggression of the third chakra seems necessary if we are to find a place in the world; but the warrior must be tamed, in both men and women. Whitmont points out that most species of animals have the "I yield" or "uncle" posture, in which the victorious aggressor recognizes the submission and stops the conflict. Remember that Parzival is told "not to kill those he has vanquished," which he remembers pretty well throughout the story. (And then he adds a delightful creative touch in sending them to Cunneware, the wronged lady.) Compassion mitigates the lethality that inheres in conflicts. After this Parzival might be able find the trail of the Grail again.

Thus, in the Aquarian Age, we have to be able to tolerate controlled aggression, or aggression contained in a ceremonial context, as in the martial arts, or in psychodramatic enactment, without quitting the playing field. We dance our separate dances but in simultaneous relationship, each mimicking the other.

Aquarius, the symbolic image, a man in the stars pouring water—from whence? Since he is doing it interminably, clearly the water flows from a inexhaustible source. Is this also the Grail, the cornucopia, the perpetual moistening, to green the Wasteland? The Aquarian impulse is ethical and socially minded, but it loves philosophy, and perhaps most of all, it seeks an understanding of the cosmos and the mind of God. Receiving this elixir, as does the visionary, direct from the source, the revelator, the gift-bringer pours it out for humankind: "Come and drink!"

Emanuel Swedenborg's date of birth—January 29—placed his sun in Aquarius. From what source did those almost fifty volumes flow? Inspiration, "divine influx," a flow that never abates. But more than this, he was motivated by a desire to pour out the revealed "truth" (the spiritual correspondence of water) to humankind, endlessly receiving from the invisible source, endlessly pouring forth a new dispensation of spirit. Swedenborg, in effect, modeled the new Aquarian male, philosopher of the spirit, pouring water into the cultural wasteland of the eighteenth century, which was increasingly divided between the burgeoning science and religion. (King Charles XII was to rule, an effect of Descartes' having come to Sweden, that the new sciences, mathematics, philosophies might be taught in their own faculties, but were to have no say on matters of religious faith or biblical veracity.)

Swedenborg was known to be honest, kindly to people, respectful even to those who served him, a "gentle man" indeed; and with this, he also possessed a voracious intellectual appetite. He learned languages, sciences, and technologies, invented submarines and prototypic airplanes, became an authority in geology, metallurgy and copper smelting, and put forth pioneering propositions in physics. Aquarius is introverted, the opposite of Leo—across the horoscope—which is extraverted and dramatic. Swedenborg spoke with a slight stutter for much of his life, but was a respected member of the Swedish Board of Mines for many years and was praised for his practical sagacity. One of his recurrent obsessions was creating safer and more humane conditions for the miners (he made numerous inventions and procedural innovations to this end).

Swedenborg understood the principle of dialogue implicitly. The natural and the spiritual; the *proprium*, the self, and the Lord (the Divine Principle); good and evil (in a dialogue indispensable to spiritual freedom); will and understanding (translated by George Dole as "intention" and "discernment"). The discernment must be married to the intention. In another way of saying it, it is easy to learn something that you love, and not so easy to learn something that you don't. Or in Whitmont's early example, cognitive activity must be grafted to an "instinct," a drive or emotional state that fuels activity connected with it. Thus, what you love, or whom you love, becomes an endless source of interest and delight. The highest form of this love would be the love of "spiritual things," which Swedenborg developed in the second half of his life and which entrains the psyche to things that sometimes might seem strange to the Freudian fundamentalist: spontaneous acts of altruism (and we have noted the altruism that happens between species), charity, empathy, compassion, communication of intellectually and spiritually "juicy" ideas, creative synergy, cognitive cross-fertilization, mutual empowerment, and other wonderful manifestations that Swedenborg says characterize "heaven" (remembering also that, for him, "heaven" is a condition of the soul, in which we are already more or less present, in the here and now).

Jung and Assagioli affirmed what Freud didn't, that there are spiritual "instincts," something built into us that finds meaning and fulfillment in these aforementioned activities. This is also why Joseph Campbell said, "Follow your bliss!" The bliss of which he speaks is that associated with the spiritual quest (the vibration that allowed Parzival to find his way to Munsalvaesche, the Grail Castle). When we are tuned in at this level, no external coercion, no laws, are necessary to stimulate the altruistic and spiritual activities; they emerge spontaneously, greening the Wasteland.

Dialogue involves the "wiggling," waves entraining and disentraining each other, in blissful or ecstatic lovemaking, in discussion, even in arguing, coming together and going apart. The legalistic attitude, on the other hand, produces the Wasteland by its deadly legislation, by rigidity and lifeless adherence to law over all. An attitude prohibiting all conflict and strife breeds resentment. Frustrated enmity leads to and becomes hate. Thus, it becomes out of proportion. The enemy is no longer playfully vied with, but destroyed. Rules in moderation increase the dynamism of the life play, but too many of them frustrate dynamism and interplay. Further, attempts to legislate away all aggressiveness are simply unworkable. A loving, deadly peace ensues. Applied excessively, legislation does away with real love and creativity.[10]

Compare Swedenborg: "It is worth knowing that the fear of penalties is the only means of controlling the ferocity and rages of the people in the hells. No other means exist" (*Heaven and Hell* 542). But, he also tells us, those who are in heaven do that which is good and think and feel that which is true, without laws to compel them to do so. By participation in the dance of divine energy, the "way of bliss," their beingness radiates and expresses love. As he states in *Heaven and Hell* 38, "All the evidence in heaven bears witness to the fact that the Divine which . . . influences angels, and makes heaven, is love. All the people who are there are actual models of love and charity. They look bewilderingly beautiful; love radiates from their faces, their speech, and every detail of their lives."

For Swedenborg, the marriage goes on all the time in our human, that is, physical/spiritual bodies—in the interplay of heart and lungs, in between the two hemispheres of the brain (he had very advanced knowledge of our cognitive lives as made of the interplay between the processing styles of the left and right hemispheres):

> [S]omething of marriage is in every substantial thing—even the smallest.
> . . . as that there are two eyes, two ears, two nostrils, two cheeks, two lips,
> two arms and hands, two sides, and two feet. And inside the person are the
> brain's two hemispheres, the heart's two ventricles, the lungs' two lobes,

two kidneys, two testicles, and where there are not two of things, still they are divided in two . . . because one belongs to will and the other to intellect, which act marvelously together to make a unit. So two eyes make one vision, two ears one hearing, two nostrils one smell, two lips one speech, two hands one work, two feet one walk, two hemispheres of the brain one habitation of the mind, the heart's two chambers one bodily life through blood, the lungs' two lobes one respiration, and so on. And masculine and feminine united through the real love in marriage make one fully human life.

Conjugial Love 316

This is a remarkably premonitory idea of the holographic theory of the brain, first articulated by Pribram, in which, like binocular vision or binaural hearing, the world takes on dimensionality and "reality" through two different sampling loci and ways of processing information. (Likewise to produce an auditory stereo image, or a 3-D movie, we need two imaging sources to create the illusion of something real between them.) Our experiencing itself is thus a marriage.

And so it is an interesting thing, that the signature of DNA, the symbolic form underlying all life as we know it, is an intertwined helix, two energies wrapped around one another. Swedenborg, in an early attempt to formulate the atom (before Bohr, of course) said it was two vortices of energy going in and out of each other. For Yeats, the human soul was an interface of two cones, combining four "faculties" (Will/Mask, Creative Mind/Body of Fate). And in the East, we have the *Shri Yantra*, made up of intersecting cones, and the kundalini system's twin channels of the *ida* and *pingala* twining about the *sushumna*, the central channel of the spine.

These then, are the snakes of Aquarius, the wavelike energies of life, neither turned away from nor locked into each other, but in a parallel dance: a choosing to manifest the elemental energy of life in this way, symbol of itself, manifesting forth from its self-induced resonances and radiating perpetual energy in the form of waves. And this is a key ingredient in the fashioning of angels, their dance together. If they learn to dance well in this world, why shouldn't the dance go on through transitions to another realm? After all, the door between the worlds seems to be DNA-shaped, intertwining spirals of this realm and that, taking the form of birth canals, tunnels of light, and panoramas of vision opening, as it were, from within.

———————— STEPHEN AND ROBIN IN DIALOGUE ————————

IN THIS SECTION, WE REFLECT upon the relationship between Joseph Campbell and Jean Erdman as one paradigmatic for our time. After some deliberation we decided to do this section as a dialogue rather than a prose essay—this approach offered to reflect the couple in stereo, through both our psyches, hence more dimensionally, and we hope dynamically.

We began writing *A Fire in the Mind: The Life of Joseph Campbell*, in 1989, two years after Joseph died. We had known him since 1964 and had many adventures and long, richly rewarding conversations together. Less often, we would socialize with Joseph and Jean as a couple, because each of them was so deeply involved in their own work. These occasions, though, always held a special kind of delight, because of the way Joe and Jean sparkled and radiated warmth in each other's presence.

As we did the research phase of the biography, we found ourselves spending much more time with Jean, including traveling together. During this time, we became closer friends, coming also to appreciate her stature as an artist and innovator in the discipline of dance and theater. Her work with Martha Graham, beginning at Sarah Lawrence, was only a launching pad for a brilliant career of her own in modern dance, where she is acknowledged as being one of the most distinctive and significant choreographers among the many fine ones to come out of the Graham company. Much of the material we gathered during our travels and conversations is covered in the biography, particularly chapters 12 and 13, on Joseph and Jean's courtship, and chapters 24 and 25, on their last days together.

In this dialogue, we would like to build on what we already know, focusing specifically on how these two brilliant and creative people forged a relationship that lasted forty-nine years, while simultaneously self-actualizing. This is the part that we feel becomes paradigmatic for the New Age, as to how two creative artists of high caliber weave their dance of solo performances, dedicated scholarship, mutual support, and a beautiful loyalty and love.

Stephen: I want to open this by saying that Joseph Campbell and Jean Erdman were two independently creative people very different from each other in temperament, style and background, yet who remained in love for almost fifty years. Also, we know that around them was this wonderful, flowering creative environment, the Theater for the Open Eye, which put on Jean's plays and dance performances, and Joseph's lectures, during the 1970s and 1980s in New York.

There was this incredible cross-fertilization going on as myth inspired drama, and theater gave embodiment to abstract symbol.

Robin: All around were Joe and Jean's creative "children," as we thought of them. Some came to the couple from Jean's orbit, like Chungliang Al Huang (dancer and tai chi master). Others from Joseph's areas of concern, like Sam Keen or Jean Houston, both exploring the possible human and the new mythology. Each was a creative original person in his or her own, important innovators, who yet felt some sense of legacy or special mentoring from Joseph or Jean or both.

Stephen: Yes, and as I wrote to Joseph and Jean one time, they had another kind of children. Those "with bright fiery wings" (in the words of William and Catherine Blake), their creative endeavors and influence touching all these lives—soul children of all kinds.

Robin: They decided, at a fairly early stage in their relationship, probably before they consummated the marriage, that they were not going to have any earthly children. This came out as we were writing *A Fire in the Mind*; and Jean said it was a very conscious decision. Not many couples make this kind of decision so deliberately, with the agreement of both. It's more common that one doesn't want the responsibilities of child care and all that kind of thing, and the other may feel that this is really where their fulfillment lies. But here the choice was made consciously, and

Photo: John Lenz

Authors Robin and Stephen Larsen.

they never went back. They actively re-confirmed their compact about ten years later, as we were told by their close friend Gert Robinson. And this then paved the way to all kinds of other things that they did together.

Stephen: Joseph really had dedicated parents, as did Jean. And I think he had a truly ethical sense of what it took to raise children. If he had them, he wasn't going to skimp on them; he'd do every-thing he could, and that was an agenda inconsistent with the creative and schol-arly depth he wanted to attain. And that was also why he wanted to marry a pro-fessional artist.

I want to say a few things about where they started in the beginning. Their generation began at the beginning of the twentieth century: Joe, born in 1904, was thirteen years older then Jean, but surely the culture of the nineteenth century in-fluenced them—through their parents and environment as they were growing up, reinforced by the fact that he was the older. He was established in his profession; she had, in fact, been his student at Sarah Lawrence: So we have the makings here of a thoroughly conventional nineteenth-century-style marriage, in which the man is the "teacher," rather than a relationship of creative partners. The woman is to be in some way subservient, in that she should minister to his needs and celebrate the great man.

Robin: Instead of this, Joseph used his "authority" to influence her to use her cre-ative working time as he used his creative working time. She was not to putter around the house while he was doing his creative work, but go to her studio and do her own work. In our interviews as we were doing the biography, Jean affirmed that, as young as she was, and open to Joe's influence, this was tremendously important for her.

They developed some practical ways of maintaining this equilibrium. When Jean cooked, she did so with artistry; but Joseph thought it would be best if they ate out frequently, to keep Jean from expending her creative energy on shopping and preparing meals. This was an investment they made in her life as an artist.

Stephen: This may be helpful for those people who have started out with the sense of a kind of an asymmetrical relationship: "I'm the professor and you're the student . . ." Those kinds of patterns, it seems to me, could haunt a relationship all the way through. Once initialized, they could be very hard to undo. But Joseph used whatever patriarchal authority he might have had to empower Jean's own self-actu-alization—really to get her to expect nothing less of herself than he expected of himself.

Robin: Both of these people had a commitment to their art. This was a high call-ing that brought them together. Each saw in the other, I think, a kind of guide, a highly creative individual with a great deal of potential and an equivalent dedication. So that's one of the messages they impart for this coming New Age—that a man and woman, or committed partners of whatever kind, can self actualize in parallel tracks.

There's another little piece here that I want to add. They were artists in a time when art was perhaps more groundbreaking than it has ever been. And a kind of radicalism was at the heart of the great notion of the artist as the one who steps out into the unknown, who breaks the boundaries. It began right around the turn of the century (actually it was probably initiated by the Romantics, and particularly fueled by Keats's concept of "soul-making"), and I think it's something that each one has carried right into their later years. I think Jean still carries that sense, and I know it was equally important to Joseph.

Stephen: I think the sharing of such a value and a vision was equivalent to what sharing a religion or a philosophy or a deep connection to a cause is for some couples. And the incredible thing is that each of them had enough self-knowledge—right there at the outset—to know what the contract was; and because of that, I think they were on solid ground. As we talked about earlier, in chapter seven, the power issues should be addressed beforehand, so power doesn't need to be exerted in the wrong places. And in some ways it has to be recognized that there are inequalities: Joseph always was superior in the verbal domain, Jean in the artistically creative domain.

It was very interesting in their courtship correspondence: he would wax professorial in his letters, as we all knew that he could do, and had become fond of doing with other creative women—to lay out a kind of a map or model of the underlying method of their art. He had begun the process earlier with Angela Gregory in their correspondence, and with his sister Alice (both sculptors). In a way, it was kind of presumptuous, but he was very busy trying to help both them and himself, to articulate the canons of abstract art.

Robin: But Jean didn't just kowtow to the great theorist; she had her own ideas about her art, and she spoke them right back clearly to Joe. So she constantly corrected his theoretical oversimplifications or called his attention to the places where he drew from theory rather than experience.

Stephen: He really questioned the most fundamental things when he was trying to see if he would be really compatible with a woman. I think he did this with Adelle Davis (with whom he had a youthful romance); he saw they were interested in different domains; and then with Carol Steinbeck, where he realized that he had really been so moved by Carol and John as a couple, and now he was in a position to destroy their marriage (this is related in chapter six of A Fire in the Mind, where Campbell found himself in a love triangle with John and Carol Steinbeck).

First of all, Joseph was concerned for the couple; then he wondered if Carol left John for him, and moved from California to the East Coast, what would her life in New York be like? Would she support him as she did John—helpmate to creative genius, but now trying to adapt out of her own element? Would that be fair to her? For Joe, it seemed ethics prevailed in the formulation of these things, all the way along the line.

Robin: In his journals apropos of the John and Carol episode, Joe says, "The marriage itself is maybe the thing that I love the most about these two people, and here I am about to destroy it." I think even back then (1930, age twenty-six) he had that notion of a relationship as a thing in itself with its own integrity. That seems to have come from deep in his own nature.

Joe Campbell and Jean Erdman in Hawaii.

Photo: Joseph Campbell Foundation

Later, when he did marry Jean—his first and last—he did really regard it as a kind of death for his single self, because he took it so seriously. He knew—unlike many who enter the same covenant—that he really was saying goodbye to a lot of his independent habits. And he meant it. It would have been less of a sacrifice if he hadn't taken it so deeply. In the same way, he put away music as a serious occupation when he became a full time writer and scholar—because he did things with that kind of integrity and intensity. If he had decided to have children, he would have been a very dedicated father. Even the way he treated Gwyneth (our daughter and his goddaughter), helping pay her tuition at school and staying in touch all the way. And Jean has done the same thing. They really did not do these things casually.

Stephen: So for paradigmatic qualities in this couple that model the relationship for the New Age, I would emphasize, in the first place, their self-knowledge, based on a serious, not casual assessment of self—and of the other. Secondly, the ethical sense of integrity that considers the other seriously enough to take the time, both on one's own behalf and the other's behalf, to say "yes, this is right for both"—that serious way he imagined what kind of life he would make with Adelle, or Carol, or Jean.

Once made, that commitment lasted a lifetime, with the vicissitudes of attention and separate professional and even social lives pulling in opposite directions. The "third thing" requires holding to the decision thus seriously made.

Robin: I think there was also a kind of mature self-knowledge. Self-reflection was a very consistent thing with Joseph. We know from his dream journal and his diaries that he was carefully examining his relationship to Jean, so that he would catch himself being "the professor," for example. He would dream, and examine it, and maybe ask himself: "Okay, now do I want my relationship with my beautiful and gifted young wife to be just this? How can I open it up so that we don't get stuck at this point?" He noted at one point that he had a tendency to sort of fall into relationships with a woman, where he was her guide and she was his muse. He was very subtle in his thinking and constantly examining himself.

Stephen: I wanted to say a few more things about their courtship, because this was such a fascinating thing, when Joseph tried to lay out the canons of Jean's art, and

Jean said, "Yes, but you left out this and this." She had to make her own statements about the way that it worked for her, and she did that. I think it gave their interchange a kind of a wonderful tension in a positive sense, a kind of a muscularity in the exchange between the two of them, each individually questing for truth and meaning.

Robin: A lot of what really developed his ability to talk to artists so eloquently, so sensitively, were the dialogues that he had in his formative years with very creative people—the artists of Woodstock, his own sister Alice, the sculptor Angela Gregory, as well as other writers—and Jean. He was always bringing his very highly conceptual mode to this meeting place with artists and getting their feedback—and this continued throughout his life with Jean.

Jean Houston has pointed out how Joe thinks with his body, an early feeling he developed as an athlete and a musician, which helped him really to understand dance. So the letters that he exchanged with Jean are interesting because you see this bright young dancer affecting the way a developed intellectual thinks and speaks about art. Between them, I believe they shaped a language that Joseph was to take to a high level of refinement, in his career as a writer and thinker about art.

Stephen: Remember the conversation we had with Gert Robinson [wife of Henry Morton Robinson, a Columbia professor with whom Campbell wrote *A Skeleton Key to Finnegans Wake*]—she was still able to summon fifty-year-old memories vividly at ninety-four. She spoke of her husband "Rondo" as "a ladies man." When she reminisced about Joe, she said he was not "a ladies man" in the same sense. Women adored Joseph Campbell and flocked around him, and he did indeed bask in their refulgent attention. But he did not see them as erotic conquests, but as wondrous creatures whose minds and sense of aesthetics he wished to plumb and—if the relationship developed—nourish. And he loved having their attention on him as he danced with their minds—I guess that's why the job at Sarah Lawrence (a women's college in those days) was so appropriate.

Once he had set his course, it seemed pretty well established. There were so many times, where we saw repeated in his later life what must have begun in his earlier life: Attractive women tried to come on to him, or tried to ensnare him, and he was simply unavailable or invulnerable; but he would also detach himself in a very elegant and lovely way that did not make the person feel rejected.

Robin: I saw it many times over the years, but I really appreciated it the time I watched a very troubled young woman, very intelligent, quite attractive, trying to get Joseph's attention, and perhaps start something with him. Jean wasn't around. We were all off at this retreat center for a week or so. He could have been quite vulnerable in that situation. We were a locked-up, intensely questing community, in search of the mysteries. But what I really saw was his "gentleness," as in the tradition of courtly love. He saw this woman's neediness, her brightness, her potential creativity, and he focused on that; and so he kept their conversations going into the areas where he could really empower her. And he very skillfully did this kind of *tai chi* around her physical come-on and just redirected that. I feel he did a very great service for women who had those things confused. Because women in our culture all too often confuse their own creative inspiration with attraction to a highly interesting, creative man; and then they miss their own calling.

Joseph understood that. He wrote about it in his journals, especially in his relationship to Jean and to other young women he mentored. He understood it very well and demonstrated it repeatedly—invariably to their advantage.

Stephen: Remember that their marriage was performed by Jean's father, who was a pastor. It had to be on the fifth day of the fifth month, and there were all kinds of numerological and astrological considerations that Joseph had taken into account, with his detailed mind. But there was also the simple fact that Jean's father was in town.

Their honeymoon was a very simple one in a little cottage near Woodstock, New York. They drove up from New York City; as they went, Joe was driving faster and faster, rushing along, and then suddenly there it was, something they were almost expecting without knowing what it would be: a funeral procession winding its way along the country roads near Woodstock. They both just sort of took a deep breath, and Joe said, "Well there it is!" They were acknowledging the old association of funerals with weddings. Something in each is dying in order to be born anew—into the relationship—and so it was conceived by both as an auspicious, rather then a negative omen.

Robin: Yes, and they both continued, very consciously, to cultivate the "new-ness" of their marriage. I remember how—right into their last years—Joe would invite Jean out to dinner as if they were young sweethearts, courting. And Jean always sparkled with delight at those dates—even when they were eating out daily!

Stephen: Some contemporary women might snort at Joseph's door-opening, courtly deference, use of "my dear" and other mannerisms that remind us that, no matter how radical his mind was, still it was born in a body in 1904 and raised in a culture still dominated by nineteenth-century social conventions. But this respectfulness and gentility for women made it possible for most of those who really understood it, to feel very safe with him. They knew that their wishes were respected in helping define the relationship. It would be a wonderful thing for this jaded age to have relationships in which an older man does that for a younger woman—maybe her father never did it. . . . I think of Jean Houston's wonderful encounter and subsequent friendship—as a teenager—with Teilhard de Chardin. What a lot of power can come out of a relationship like that!

Robin: Rebecca Armstrong (another one of Joseph's "god-daughters," the daughter of George and Gerry Armstrong, singers and performers, and Joe's really good friends) describes what a wonderful experience it was to have Joseph Campbell as a godfather, because he really did take seriously his role of being her father in things of the spirit, imagination, and creative mind. So he told her lots of stories, especially about goddesses and heroines, and he really inspired her—even incited her—in that way to grow up to be a strong, creative woman. Rebecca describes being about fourteen years old and talking with Joseph one morning—of course, whenever he came to visit, she wanted to stay out of school and be there all day long, hearing the stories. She said, when he told her the mythological stories, when he talked to her about the central place of the feminine and the goddess in those great adventures, he'd make her feel, "YES! I'm a WOMAN!" Rebecca says this with her powerful, singer's voice, and her tremendous gusto, and you feel it with her, like a deep belly-shout.

Stephen: In Joseph's private journals, it was revealed later on that he was aware of many attractions, and he knew he had an Achilles' heel, which was a kind of vulnerability to people who did something for him. He would feel grateful, and this would sometimes possibly take him more dangerously close to women. There was one who was his assistant for many years, and because of the service she gave him, he began to feel very close to her. I'm sure at times Jean may have felt polarized, a little left out, because there they were, sitting there working together every day, while Jean went off to her studio. The assistant and Joe were both intellectuals, working in the same sphere, sharing time, a language—the assistant was certainly intelligent and attractive enough, and they sat working knee-to-knee. That could have been very uncomfortable for Jean.

But simultaneously Joseph was analyzing all this in his journal, with this same meticulous kind of attention he brought to most things.[11] Campbell knew that psychological self-examination could be one of the major keys to successful relating. He analyzed it just as he did his attraction to and romanticization of Carol Steinbeck.

Robin: It is important to notice that these are two people who were often separate in their work: Jean traveling with her dance performances, later with her whole company, and teaching master classes. Joseph was teaching all day long, surrounded by young women—he once likened one of his classes at Sarah Lawrence to a field of multihued flowers, brunette, redhead, and blonde. But there were also other intellectually compatible female professors, one of whom was very influential, and probably shaped a lot of Joseph's political perspectives. I'm sure that Jean must have felt anxiety or uncertainty at times.

On the other hand, remember when Jean told us of a time she was often in the company of this one male dancer, who paid visible attention to her. Joe could not have cared less. But one time a peer of his, a serious scholar and a witty, intellectual fellow, paid attention to Jean at a prestigious international conference. That really got his attention, and he was quite anxious in his turn.

Stephen: But you know, that's so appropriate in terms of anima-animus theory. Probably any of us is most likely to get jealous about someone we esteem—they carry or seem to carry a magic that maybe we haven't actualized ourselves. So naturally we expect them to be scintillating to our partner. This is one of these Jungian "animus of the anima" or "anima of the animus" funhouse mirrors. Our anima or animus is the one who does the deciding whether this particular one is dangerous or not. Joe's compensation for this uneasy feeling was to analyze it as thoroughly as he could.

Robin: I think they were actually one of the most non-jealous couples I ever saw, but they did come to it gradually, through self-analysis and mutual growth. This is a sign that serious dedication to your art is mentally healthy. It was a sea-anchor for each of them, and from that solitude, they treasured the comings together that they did have. They were continually coming back to a place of looking at what the other needed and what the other was really asking for, and grounding themselves in their own integrity. These were both people with a high level of integrity; and so, over the years, trust grew, and they came to know beyond all doubt that the other was honest, loyal, and trustworthy. These are very important things to know about your partner.

It is possible to love someone, and even have a lifelong partnership, with someone that you don't feel is entirely trustworthy. But it may not be possible to have a really deep, growing relationship under those terms. I think that, with Joe and Jean, there was a high degree of security developed; it wasn't all there from the beginning. Joe and Jean really worked on developing this trust with each other. This is important, because it is one of the ways I think they broke ground for the rest of us: their marriage means so much as a model, precisely because they had to work at it. And so can we.

Stephen: Yes, Campbell would always say that to make a relationship succeed was "hard work." He would emphasize this as if he knew what he was talking about, and I believe he did. It seems quite clear that he was practicing that himself. He did not ever take the relationship for granted, or allow himself to slide in that way. And he really gave it a high priority in the inventory of things that require our daily attention, and I think that's another way in which he remained ethical in his marriage

In the concluding section of this chapter, we share with the reader some of our most wonderful experiences in its preparation: sitting down with other couples we know and love, and letting the energy flow all around.

───────── THE MAGIC OF ANGEL MAKING ─────────

SUPPOSE THAT WE LIVED ON AN EMERALD-BLUE phosphorescent sphere floating through black nothingness around a warmly glowing yellowish sun, at the edge of history. Suppose we lived on a warm marble in space, surrounded by a gaseous envelope that sustains life—oh so delicately—within its fraying periphery, held together by a mysterious nothing we call the ozone layer. Suppose we were in a "free-fall into globalism," with all of the old categories outworn, and the new yet unbirthed and even barely a twinkle in the eye of ourselves, an angelodaemonic being in the womb of the collective unconscious of the species. . . .

Joseph Campbell sometimes would channel a little wizened Taoist. He would become mischievous, hermetic, impossible to catch, dancing down paths in a forest of possibilities, where the manifest and the unmanifest dissolve in and out of each other, and the world is hospitable to the impossible: "If you follow your bliss, . . . doorways will open that you didn't know were there." (Bliss is the rocket fuel your angel will fly with—the same fuel as Swedenborg's "ruling love.") Or Jean Erdman: "The mystic and the artist are one; only the artist has a craft." These are people whose dialogues point the new direction for our new age.

We have interviewed a number of couples living creative lives, at what feels like an extremely poignant moment in history—fashioning angels. They are dancing an amazing, luminous yin-yang dance in the mandala of being. The human couple looks into each other's eyes and sees stars.

We sit with these couples, from many walks of life, in a crystal dome, at the edge of history, in dialogue. Picture it like the Rainbow Room at the summit of Rockefeller Center, an improbable lucid bauble of glass above the teeming city, under the sky. The restaurant is dimly lit, with the sparkle of 1930s stardust all around. The Art-Deco elevator opens, like a vessel from another dimension, and a couple emerges. We introduce them briefly in turn, below; then they join us in a comfortable, upholstered enclave looking out on the luminous night. The city below represents the vast, teeming civilization all around us. You who would be lovers, we sense all of you there, too, trying to achieve an alchemy of your souls and a new level of healing, as our adolescent civilization careens into a new millennium. We feel our words reaching you somehow, as we talk with these representative couples—talk about angels, about souls in becoming, about the bittersweet essence of relating.

May their journey, and our journey, empower your own.

The Magic of Commitment: Becky Bear and Eric Jackson

The bell rings and the elevator doors recede. Our first couple, of mixed races, steps forth. Eric Jackson and Becky Bear reside in Juneau, Alaska. Eric is white, midwestern, college-educated and articulate, tall and dark-haired. Becky is eight inches shorter, *zaftig*, energetic, equally articulate, and very jolly—an African-American woman with a Ph.D.—and a great storyteller. In addition to her African genes, and her outsider credentials as an avant-garde media artist in the 1960s, she became a convert to Judaism, which she practiced for over a decade. At one point, her significant other was another woman. During a trance-dance at Esalen, the bear came to her as her totem, and she adopted the name "Bear"; this was significant in helping her get in touch with the Native-American part of her heritage (her paternal grandmother is Cherokee). Now Becky works with special needs children in the Juneau school system.

Eric and Becky have been together for more than twenty years, still in a committed ever-deepening relationship. Their story is especially interesting because this couple has allowed love and loyalty to win through many vicissitudes. Some years after they met, Eric began to suffer from a bipolar disorder mostly characterized by crippling depressions, leading several times to stays in a residential treatment facility, leaving Becky home as the primary wage earner and parent of two energetic boys. Eric has shown incredible courage and determination in overcoming his illness and is more functional today than ever before. Theirs is a story of love warming and penetrating the valley of shadows, and reversing a (probably inherited) daemongelic pull—the depression and the consequent economic privation endured by the family.

Stephen: We're very interested in how you weathered racial and social differences between you, all the adversities that came your way, and the stress of raising two boys (now grown).

Eric: I think that, in spite of the obvious differences in our backgrounds, we really came together with an amazing degree of similarity. The main places where we differed and had real friction were mostly housekeeping details; but, when it came right down to the nitty-gritty of the way we view the world and the way we think the universe hangs together, we were remarkably in tune with each other and have remained so.

Stephen: So would you say that spirituality was an important factor?

Eric: I would say that was perhaps *the* most important factor. Being able to share a basic spirituality of life was probably the key to our relationship, and everything else flowed outward from that. I have a hard time imagining marriages in which there is a strong difference of opinion in that regard, and yet there are many of them. But I think each of us felt the need to find a mate that shared the same basic outlook.

The point at which I realized there was a true similarity was a night we spent back in Illinois. Becky was living in Crete, outside Chicago, and I visited her for a weekend. We sat up all night, until dawn, just talking because we were in tune. It was an act of discovery of each other. What we kept discovering through the whole conversation was that, at the core, we shared the same values.

Educators/entrepreneurs Becky Bear and Eric Jackson.

Becky: The bond that really holds us together is a shared spiritual space and, yes, even though I'm not a WASP, a shared intellectual space. It really is important to find someone that is on your wavelength. I often describe my relationship to Eric as being that our minds like to play with each other. And I think a sense of humor might have to be there. Why did Jessica Rabbit marry Roger Rabbit? He made her laugh.

I really enjoy Eric's sense of humor and the way we're able to play. So I think there are three elements: spiritual, intellectual, and playful. But I do think the spiritual space is most important, because I really can't really imagine being married to someone who doesn't have spirituality as a large part of their life and a path they can walk together.

Let's start back at the drawing board, the questions that preoccupy us during our twenties: do I believe in God, do I believe that there is a written "Word of God," and if so, what is it? I did a lot of reading at that time, asking these questions; but what was truly amazing to me is that Eric and I had developed the same understandings of how the universe is held together, and what was expected from us as souls in the universe. I *read* it, but Eric had *reached* it intuitively. That night in Crete was very fateful, I will tell you. At the same time that we came to a meeting of minds and found we really shared the same questioning, but deep spirituality, we also conceived our elder son, David, who is now finishing college.

Robin: That makes sense from things I've experienced. You get the premonition of the angel, and your body and the unborn beings just say "Yes!" It's like Molly Bloom's soliloquy in Joyce's *Ulysses*, where she says, "Yes—yes—yes!"

Becky: That night was really the start of our getting together. What was probably the most amazing thing about this was doctors had told me that I couldn't conceive. But it was just like a total opening that had happened at that point. So our sons David and Michael are very special young men who are the children of love and our feelings, and they seem to know that.

Eric: I think we also both felt that we had had past-life history together, and maybe some unfinished karma to work out. Since sooner or later you have to work out that stuff, we thought we might as well get it all taken care of sooner—this go 'round. Early in the relationship, we worked pretty hard on trying to make each other over, and that was kind of futile. But since then, we have sort of knocked all the rough edges off each other, and now that we have done that, we've polished the relationship, and it seems worth continuing.

Stephen: I really like that, "knocked the rough edges off." We all do seem to come with corners! Things may be a little smoother now. But what about trying to have a biracial marriage in a rural setting?

Eric: The people who were on the bottom rung of the ladder in Juneau were traditionally the native Alaskans. Seems wrong, but that's the way it was. There really was very little antiblack feeling in the community. In fact, Juneau became known as a place that was relatively free of prejudice, and a number of black families had moved into town for that very reason. This was particularly true in the early years. African-American Coast Guard personnel would come to be stationed in Juneau, and after their tour was over, they would elect to stay because it was an open community.

Becky: Regarding the differences in cultural backgrounds between Eric and me, there are those ones that are obvious: he comes from a frugal, rural midwestern background unlike my urban, inner-city multiethnic background. But, despite our differences of origin, I think of these things as surface differences. Of things a little deeper: Eric's mom was a teacher; my mother and grandmother were teachers. So then there are values you share—providing education to young people, something that will color their whole life. Teachers also share the same socioeconomics.

When David was first born and Eric came down from Alaska to see his son (I was still living in Chicago), one of the first things we did was go up to see his mom and introduce her first grandchild. You know his mom was kind of freaked out: not only was he tied up with a black woman, but now he had an illegitimate child—and no one was saying the "M" (marriage) word. We were headed out to see her, and I remember saying to Eric, "What does your mom do?" And he said, "She's a teacher." And I said, "Well that's a piece of cake; I can do teachers. I've grown up with teachers."

When Mrs. Jackson finally spent the weekend with my parents, they immediately fell into "shop-talk." There was the shared experience of twenty-some-odd years of meeting the needs of first-grade students. There the commonality of the milieu of teaching transcends the ethnic and cultural differences.

Stephen: Eric, if you feel comfortable, could you speak a little of your hard times, when you kind of went "under"?

Eric: When my whole worldview was being turned upside down or inside out (the depression), Becky was still the person that I felt the safest with. There were times when I trusted no one and nothing. And maybe I even questioned whether I could trust her. But there was still an element of that bond between us that wasn't severed. I don't know how to describe it.

Stephen: How did you know it was there?

Eric: Through the patience that she displayed. She would listen to me when I was trying to explain my nightmarish view of things; and even though she would never agree with me and would do her best to dissuade me—surely what I was experiencing couldn't be right—she was asserting that the God as I was experiencing him (in the pit of depression) was not like her experience. Still she would listen—and it was not just a single instance. It was day-in and day-out patience, over years and years of difficulties. That's irreplaceable.

Becky: The soul of our marriage has always stayed good, even through Eric's difficulties, even when it didn't look so good to people outside.

We live in a house that requires a lot of upkeep [an innovative owner-built home in a rural area of Juneau]. While Eric was away in treatment, the refrigerator failed and the available replacement was an inch too wide for the space. I ended up changing the kitchen all by myself, in the middle of winter, feeling pretty proud of myself for having accomplished these things. But I wanted the recognition from my mate; I really wanted him to say, "Attagirl! Girl, you did a great job!" When he returned to the family, I would start a conversation, talking about all these things I took care of while he was gone, and all I really wanted was a pat on the back.

But all he seemed able to hear was "Look what happened because you failed to take care of your family!" as if I were blaming him. We were getting into some nasty fights; and at one point, we were attending a Presbyterian church and we went to counseling with the minister. We assured him from the beginning that the soul of our marriage was fine, but we had some things to work out. Well, in his office—a safe space with, it felt like, a mediator present—we began to really argue: that was what we came for, I guess. We were able to say things we had previously been unable to say. We really got into it.

When we got to the end of the counseling session, the minister looked at us and shook his head and said, "I am not sure that the soul of your marriage is in good shape!" We were stunned. We said goodbye, went downstairs and ended up standing in the kitchen, hugging, crying, and talking to each other. For the first time I clearly understood why Eric was freaked—he really felt I was reproaching him; and for the first time he understood that I wasn't reproaching him, or at least I wasn't trying to reproach him. All I was asking for was a pat on the back.

So there we were, crying and hugging, and that minister walked by about ten minutes later. And I know that, to this day, he does not understand what possibly happened; but what happened was—the soul of our marriage, that place where we connected, was still fine.

Stephen: Sounds just fine to me. Your minister might not have been trained enough in therapy to tolerate the discord that can lead to harmony, or the principle of just "lettin' 'er rip" for a while, to then spell out and articulate the issues—and come to reconciliation.

Becky: Yeah, he allowed himself to go with the surface when we had told him the depths were okay. He really just had to witness our process.

When I first met Eric, I was struck by this strong sense of trust—it was virtually overpowering, I can't say why. It was a feeling that I could trust this person. That feeling was immediate and impossible to ignore, so that has always been there to sustain me. When Eric talks about how patient I was, I have a hard time imagining myself as patient, because I think that many times my mind would be raging inside about things that were happening, even though I was sitting there quietly listening and being supportive.

When he wasn't in the throes of depression, we really bonded, with genuine understanding; I think I had to have glimpses of that to feel really comfortable. He would ask me to wait until he had overcome the depression and really felt like he was free as a soul.

I think the last part of what kept us together was his willingness to work on the problems that were happening. I said to him early on, "I'm willing to support you in your reach for wholeness, but I'm not willing to support you if you simply slide into illness." Eric has been incredibly meticulous about doing what his doctors and therapists have asked him to do, and I admire him so much for that. I'm going to hang with him, that's all.

Stephen: Were there times that were crucial or critical?

Becky: When we got married, David was five months old. We were in a social circle of people most of whom had never had children. Our relationship must have looked chancy, so a lot of people were saying to us, "What happens if you two divorce? Have you figured out what you are going to do with the kid? Do you have a plan? Maybe you should put all this down in writing, in a prenuptial agreement."

But we said, "Divorce is not an option!" I strongly believe that words have power. Neither of us had any desire to give the coming apart of the relationship any power. So we were saying, "We're not doing this; we're getting married for the duration." When we were courting, we used to sing the Beatles' song *When I'm Sixty-four*. . . .

Creative Magic: Alex and Allyson Grey

The elevator dings and opens again. Alex and Allyson Grey emerge, slim and elegant, seeming to step from one dimension to another, with their petite, elfin daughter, Zena with them. Zena is nine and already an accomplished film star. She will sit wisely and quietly with the adults, taking in everything. Alex is the artist who brought the shamanic x-ray style to a new perfection in his monumental series of paintings and in his book *Sacred Mirrors*.[12] Allyson is also a recognized and exhibiting artist, who collaborates with Alex in their performance pieces. The Greys' world is anything but gray—transparent, layered, breathing color and meaning.

Stephen: You are both visual artists. I wonder how you've worked cooperatively rather than competitively. How do you get the ego out of the way in your kind of relationship?

Alex: Together we create a mind that's larger than either of us singly, her aesthetic seen through my eyes, my aesthetic seen through her eyes, through which the greater being that is the angelic one from the *mundus imaginalis* comes forth.

(To Allyson) I have a great respect for your vision, your design capability, and for your intuition, so I almost count on it. In this respect, I feel incomplete without having asked your opinion—on practically anything.

I have worked on a vision many times, seeing it from a particular angle. Allyson will come over and say, "Oh Alex, its just got to be in the center. You have to move this thing over there!" Her clarity of understanding, reframing my vision through her eyes—the greater us—will change a piece for the better. It will change a piece that might have been merely interesting into a piece that's fabulous and iconic.

Allyson: You're giving me that power. It means so much to you, and it is so important to the work. You give me an incredible amount of power, which allows me to allow you to be the source—of our life, really. I think of you as the "power source" and of me as the "power feeder." For our engine to work effectively, that seems what's needed. Now turn that around—when the emphasis is on my work, it comes from me and you feed that. Your opinion is also important to me. I feel like a powerful equal: equal power, different job.

Stephen: I like the nonhierarchical model and the power metaphor for turning out creativity.

Allyson: I couldn't love a person who didn't need me in that way. My opinion has to count and matter to be involved, enmeshed in his work. Our favorite time is working near each other, sitting down and working at adjoining tables, the earmarks of a perfect day.

So I'll be sitting there and wondering what he's thinking about. And I'll ask him, "What are you thinking about?" and he'll say, "I was just thinking about

Photo: Jim Schwartz

Artists Allyson and Alex Grey.

the Neoplatonic influence on the Florentine idea of the soul, and this particular quote from Plotinus." "Oh," I reply, "I was just thinking of what my Mother said when we were talking on the phone yesterday, and what's for dinner." It takes me outside of myself to have a person who thinks so differently from me.

Alex: Allyson helps me to stay grounded. In *The Mission of Art,* I would go off on some philosophical blather, and Allyson would start to nod, or her "bull" meter would go off: "Hey, wait, give me an example! Lets get to an experience or story, flesh it out or ground it." We tend to work like that. The thing that is run through the meat grinder of both of our intelligences is a superior product.[13]

Allyson: And I think that, if your relationship is really a powerful thing, how can that loving energy that you generate be brought into vision or affect the relationship you have with other people—even groups and schools and organizations, even governments and worlds, and the way people interact with each other on a wider scale? That's as tricky as it is to work it out with each other.

Cynicism and postmodern fragmentation have led to the inability of people to have relationships where they do trust each other, and this has led to a kind of nihilistic sense of the possibilities of life. If you don't have that with good friends or your spouse—who should be your best friend—if you don't have that kind of trust developed, then how can you ever sense that life in general can be trusted?

Alex: We've been through our dark spaces and our cathartic healings. Purifying negativities is an ongoing task. Each of us had specific pathologies to manifest—complementary pathologies, if you will. In the positive instance these can reinforce each other toward healing. Noncomplementary pathologies accelerate confrontation with both pathologies.

In the complementary way, each wound can be focused on by the couple to be expressed and healed in a context of love and support. We are not talking new-agey, dolphiney spin. My wound is depression, not exactly catatonic despair, but a hopeless despair which can really blacken an atmosphere of loving, like a black hole, affect everything around it.

Allyson: And I come from the captain-of-the-cheerleaders tradition—I'm always trying to put a positive spin on things, make it so that Alex can see things in a different way. I have my stuff, an angry Russian Jewish background. I believe there really is an anger that can be inherited. Alex never gets angry at me, although I do at him, or really at the world sometimes.

Stephen: I once asked Edward Whitmont, "Why do we always take it out on our nearest and dearest?" He replied: "But who else are you going to fight with?"

Allyson: And who will always forgive you in the end?

Stephen: Jung has this concept that, in a relationship, there is always a "container" and a "contained."

Alex: Is it like Russian dolls or Chinese boxes, one the container, one the contained?

Stephen: Sort of; but I like the more androgynous idea of being inside and outside of each other, in a nonhierarchical way that you two seem to exemplify.

Alex: It boils down to an atmosphere of trust, as long as you can access that and regard it as way beyond the body. Regard it as the boundless Buddha-field that is our primordial nature, or that love is the fundamental foundation of the universe. It's not that love is an aberration or brief coming together of meaningless molecules, bumping up against each other and enjoying the sensation. Love is the fabric and foundation of every manifest thing. This is all the ornament of what is ultimately a seething light of love. These condense into weird little colorful packets [people] that we can encounter in this way.

Underlying it all, beyond time and space and matter and all the limits of the known universe, there is the boundlessness of love. It floods the firmament, the body of God, the universe that is the field of the *hieros gamos*, the sacred marriage of being. From that field of energy are precipitated all these angels who form the dyads. The purest are the ones who recognize themselves as emanating from the divine source.

Stephen: I love that: couples are perturbations in this seamless net of love that extends out from the unmanifest source. It is as Swedenborg says: because God is made of love, we also are made of it. But love's nature is to love another, so a relationship of some kind is implied in the way the whole thing is set up; the angels-in-becoming are free to circulate that love within their dyad-sphere, a concentration of divine love and wisdom. And that is how they become self-enclosed little "heavens," as Swedenborg puts it.

Alex: The couples become temporal expressions of a trans-temporal field—I feel the Tibetan Buddhists put it nicely—with emptiness, clarity, and great compassion. Just the emptiness and clarity has some ring of intellectualism, but if infinite compassion is coextensive with emptiness and clarity then that is the great primordial field that is fundamental to all loving relationships and all expressions of love. It is beyond sex, beyond the curl of the DNA. It is the superimposition of one force upon the other, and so it is that dynamism that plays out in the field.

Robin: South Indian poetry describes the lovemaking of Shiva and Shakti, and the beads of perspiration from their lovemaking. These diamond-like beads fly out from them: each one is a multifaceted universe, containing worlds within worlds of life, because it is created by the force of their love.

Alex: So that myth contains the primordial archetype of all those little angels that Swedenborg was seeing, doesn't it?

Stephen: They are little two-part answers to the Platonic myth of the dividing of the original beings: little dewdrops of love with a portion of the original divinity in them.

Robin: The way Swedenborg saw angels as two human beings together is echoed in the Tibetan *yab-yum* figures; any deity or Bodhisattva expressing *yabyum* [locked in a sexual embrace] is really the metaphor for a spiritual dynamism.

Alex: That's also the archetype for the *Dzogchen* teachings: Samantabadhra/Samantabadhri, the naked, embracing-tantrically, male/female Buddha. The premier symbols for the high *Dzogchen* teachings are the loving, embracing, peaceful Buddha, the king who creates everything, Samantabhadra, the Adi Buddha or highest naked blue Buddha of space; and Samantabhadri, a white or red dakini-like goddess form. If the blue Buddha is the *Dharmakaya;* then the white Shakti energy is the world of form, the *Rupakaya*, that is the visionary realm of the *Sambhogakaya*—the luminous forms; but also the *Nirmanakaya*—the physical realm, the *Rupakaya*.

The form realm is always in love-embrace with the formless, the relationship that creates everything: in their loving dynamism, they are basically kissing.

Stephen: Campbell's way of paraphrasing it, from Joyce is "Eternity is in love with the productions of time." There we are again, and the symbol is the women, the beautiful "daughters of men" wearing veils or hats in church, so that the angels not see them and conceive an improper love. If humans love angels, they are likely to love in return.

Alex: That kiss and interpenetration, they don't exactly go all the way to the hermaphrodite image as you see in the alchemical stuff; they have a loving king/queen energy in the alchemical sense, *yab-yum*, continuous.

Robin: The distinction between the androgyne and the king and queen embracing is significant. Those differences are recognized as different moments in the process: the king and queen both preface the androgyne and carry it to the next, more refined stage. It's that same visionary place of the opposites coming together, in order to perform a loving dance in the moment.

Stephen: Allyson, you said you felt like the nourisher of the dyad, this primordial force that comes through everything. I think that you are more than a "main squeeze" for each other: lovers, partners, critics, inspirers. How did all that change with the arrival of a magical munchkin, Zena?

Allyson: For many years of our marriage, we would never go places without each other: grocery shopping, errands. With Zena, all that changed. For awhile we developed separate interests. Alex was particularly interested in the *Dzogchen* community, and Zena and I trailed along to some retreats. But I didn't feel I could make the same commitment he had made to it. I was now more preoccupied with Zena and her needs and, as she aged, her friends—picking the children up. And I also became involved in teaching aerobics. For three years it was a different type of lifestyle. But it was really good for us. We learned from that that we could operate in separate worlds, and then come back together and work on our life, to make the Chapel of Sacred Mirrors [their extraordinary series of life-sized paintings].[14]

Alex: We recognized that we needed to develop those aspects of ourselves. Zena brought a new independence, a new aspect of our training to become whole people, as well as lovers. Each one helped the other. Allyson's fitness helped remind me about the needs of the body. And there were elements of the Tibetan Buddhist retreats, practices, and readings from which we all, Zena included, benefitted. It all became part of our lives.

Stephen: As modern people between spiritual epochs, how do you handle the spiritual aspect of Zena's education?

Alex: I was doing Tibetan Buddhist retreats. Zena noticed that I had had a Christian upbringing and that her mom is of Jewish background, yet we practice Buddhism. When Chanukah comes around, we light the candles—and she gets "geld." We also celebrate the Christian Nativity and tell the stories. She has gotten an idea of the sacredness of all these traditions.

Stephen: When Gwyneth was small, she had a very hard time in public school, not with the curriculum, but the abrasiveness and intrusiveness of the other kids. We found a private school, called High Meadows, where the atmosphere was much more loving. We first went to the school in mid-December and noticed the celebrations of the holidays: Chanukah, Christmas, but also two or three other religions from around the world that had simultaneous holidays. I told Joseph Campbell about it; he said, "That's where you want to be!"—and sent a check for her tuition.

Alex: We try to do, or participate in, many ceremonies. We also adapted ceremony to Zena's personal life. She had something that used to come to her in liminal moments, when she was anxious, or would wake up in the night. She would call them "the scary features." We invented a ritual for the scary features. She would go on a walk down the road, where she would meet Krishna, beautiful and blue, and they would play together. She would go on, open a door, and there would be Buddha, radiating light. Spiritual archetypes from all over the world started to pop up in her mythic pantheon. She loves every high holy day: Christmas Eve, spiritual child born ever new, pagan rituals of renewal like Beltane. She loves to dance around the bonfire.

Allyson: She has all these rituals. She told us this morning that she prays every night and talks to God about how she's taken good care of herself during the day. Since she was ill at seven, she has reported in like that.

Children love God, if you're not cynical and don't discourage it. But you also have to be open about your own relationship, and not practice one thing and preach another—send the kids off to Sunday—or Saturday—school, and don't go yourself. A lot of people have done that. Thank God Zena isn't learning some of the things that I learned.

Here I would say to parents, Be honest! be honest! be honest! We can't choose a religion for our children, but we can expose them to what we find meaningful. Zena is just as much Alex's as she is mine, just as much Christian as Jewish, Buddhist, Hindu, pagan as we are. We just keep sharing and loving all the stories of all the faiths.

Alex: Dogmas and the myths. The more dogmatic the religious practice, the more they try to indoctrinate you and get you to parrot back all the things that you are supposed to believe without having experienced them. I think this is a turnoff to people; it engenders resentment after a while. Myths are the interesting part. More open-ended, wise through implication, not statement. And I think we could do more ceremony; just provide a basic structure, and let the experience flow.

Allyson: The natural knowing we have about the existence of a force, a love energy that permeates the universe, comes through. It's not just telling yourself to be good because God's watching you; it's an experience. If you have a mystical experience, you're just not questioning any more. That comes through. I think in that way Zena doesn't feel us as hypocritical. If you're true to what you're about, you pass these things along.

Alex: In a conversation I had with Ken Wilber, he was quoting an Asian proverb: "Chase many birds, catch none!" I guess that's valid in a way, but I tend toward a salad-bar spirituality. If spirit is Spirit, you should be able to access it at every moment, not rely on something having happened in the past, or someone to interpret it for you. It *is*!

Allyson: If you lived in a closed Tibetan community, or in a *stetl*, or the ghetto, the closed Christian village, that monism is okay. But if you live in the "salad-bar" community that we *do* live in, and you don't recognize the presence of these others, that's a problem. Here they are, right here. But you're putting blinders on and keeping everybody away, because it seems alien to your own indoctrinated tradition. I believe that spirituality is all around me, and I embrace it. There are things to be learned from all.

Stephen: I once was riding along with Joseph Campbell and deploring the "cafeteria-style spirituality" of the late-twentieth century, where you could be a Sufi one week, a Taoist the next, and a born-again-something the following week. It seemed to me an affront to the dignity of the traditions. Campbell looked over at me quite seriously, and said "I think each of these traditions has something to teach us." And I knew, suddenly, he was right. Maybe that's what we need to be doing, sampling deeply.

Alex: As long as it adds up to a whole that is greater than the sum of a heap of broken images—the finding of the one in the many, and the many in the one.

Stephen: Joseph liked to go to the great teachers in any tradition, listening for the voice behind the surface wisdom—the Taos Pueblo man, Mountain Lake, who befriended Jung, the Inuit shaman who found cosmic instruction out in the Arctic wastes—and then he would compare that knowledge to the Upanishads and Meister Eckhardt. He got criticized a lot for that—you're not supposed to compare, in some circles—but it was his business. You should go behind the surfaces of all traditions to the one truth, and never mistake the symbolic surface of the religion for its depth, the finger that points to the Great Mystery instead of that to which it points.

Alex: As long as you point to the Mystery. If the system ultimately points to the Mystery, you can rely on it. If it has it all figured out, you start to wonder.

"X-ray vision" [in *Sacred Mirrors*. See *Kissing*, page 262, for an example.] presents both metaphorically and visually the ability to penetrate to the depths of things or to see beyond the surface—the dualistic dynamism of the physical realm. By creating this transparency, we were able to see the unity through the polarity that ultimately comes together in the sacred marriage, the underlying mystic primordium of love, the background to the foreground of the surface realm.

Stephen: A person unfolding in a relationship stirs the archetypes, racial and cultural warring tribes, male and female genotypes. The love bower becomes a meeting of historical forces, things that can't come together any other way—ancestral dynasties, culturally separated elements; they're all there in that tiny, exquisite enclosure.

Alex: It's like the karmic cleaners, the rustling in the DNA—the things that are brought together in the *hieros gamos*—the games of conflict resolution. All these disparate things to be brought together in love, symbolically and literally.

Stephen: No wonder it needs a boundary drawn around it—sacred space indeed.

Archetypal Magic: Ann Belford Ulanov and Barry Ulanov

The elevator door rolls back and a mature man with a scholar's look about him, but an impish twinkle in his eyes, steps forth; on his arm is a handsome woman with a keen gaze, in her early sixties. Ann Belford Ulanov and Barry Ulanov sparkle together; Barry's professorial erudition and Ann's steady analyst's wisdom give their work uncommon depth. Their aura swirls with classical myths, philosophical insights, and a wise compassion for humanity.

Stephen: I'm interested in how you folks, with your "myth and symbol" orientation, manage to hold high faculty positions in prestigious institutions. (Barry is McIntosh Professor of English Emeritus at Barnard College, and lecturer in psychiatry and religion at Union Theological Seminary. Ann is Johnson Professor of psychiatry and religion at Union Theological Seminary, a position she maintains along with her private practice.) My experience is that Jung is frowned upon or dismissed in most academic circles.

Barry: Well, our intellectual purview is very broad, and my special interest is St. Augustine, and his influence. And Jung can be placed in a larger intellectual and cultural framework. His influence is perhaps more accepted in theological than philosophical circles and, of course, in depth psychology.

Your friend Campbell was so devoted—and in an almost religious sense, because I think he heard voices proclaiming the need for relationship with nature and with the mythic, the spiritual realm—to a sacramental meeting with the world. That's what he proposed.

Stephen: I agree, and that's what Campbell and Jung had in common. And that's why we feel that Campbell's work relates very much to the subject of our book. We're exploring all different levels of partnerships and relationships from nature, to animals and children, and—at the pinnacle of challenge and joy—to the significant other.

Robin: Ann, we were just talking about your marvelous work in helping Jungian scholars decode the difference between "female" and "feminine," and "male" and "masculine," and all the associated stereotypes that are so hard to sort out. In fact, your work, along with that of Christopher [Edward C.] Whitmont [whom the Ulanovs knew well], goes a long way toward overcoming that horrible specter of Jungian fundamentalism—the reason Jung said "Thank god I am Jung and not a Jungian."

Ann: Let's start with archetypes and stereotypes. I have long maintained that people fall into stereotypes because they cannot connnect personally with the archetypes, a

Scholar and professor Barry Ulanov and Jungian analyst Ann Belford Ulanov.

much more inward, self-reflective process, requiring a degree of psychological subtlety hard to find where people's attention is directed outward. Their soul images are then drawn from cultural dominants like the macho man or the movie love goddess, and then they try to fit their far more complex, deeper psyche into a simplistic kind of role or image.

Barry: It's quite clear that it's the amount of consciousness that you have that determines whether the archetype works psychologically or literalistically.

Ann: In fact, literalism and fanaticism increase exponentially with the unconsciousness, and the unlived-throughness of the archetypal energy behind or within the projection. Collective stereotypes leave out huge chunks of the masculine and feminine identities inside each of us.

Stephen: The definition of fanaticism that I like is "Redoubling your effort, when you've forgotten your aim." But I think I can remember that as a teenager. Here came the heroes, the cultural icons—who were you going to identify with? Well there was Elvis: nope, not him. Jimmy Dean: not really. Now, Jack Keroac came closer, but still . . . Joseph Campbell combined the scholar and the athlete, though. And he himself had his youthful heroes: he wanted to be a combination of Leonardo da Vinci and Douglas Fairbanks Jr.

Ann: When all you have is a stereotype, then the more inchoate, indeterminate quality of the archetype is lost, drowned in the stereotype. There's no "third thing"; it's all reduced to what fits or what soothes or causes the least discomfort. In the theories of cultural conditioning and object relations, you have your history: "That's real; these things happened in my family, and I guess I am who I am because of that." That's the literalistic historical fallacy. But go to this other level: "These are the cards that have been dealt to me, now why have they been dealt to me? And what can I do with them? What are the possibilities I've been imagining in these cards?"—a more inward, self-responsible psychological approach.

Stephen: This would be the opposite of the persistent behavioristic, materialistic fallacy where you are simply the outcome of your history of conditionings. That totally bypasses your ability to say "yes" to this, "no" to that, and chart your own eccentric course of behavior from within. Thus, you are reduced simply to a responding bit of protoplasm, not an autonomous, self-directed force.

Ann: But there are also the needs posed by the archetypal world within, which may not be turned down. I'm thinking of this young friend of ours. It suddenly hit Barry and me that she was at the crossroads of her life, and there were these tremendous announcements welling up from the unconscious through dreams, and from outside too:

"Stop being such a good mothering presence to everybody. This is not enough for you, you can't just be everyone's Great Mother. You have to develop in these other ways." She ignored these warnings, and then her entire reproductive system had to be taken out because of incipient cancers. She didn't get it symbolically, so it was literally taken out of her. You know it was there all the time, because as we were talking later, she said that she admired people tremendously who followed their dream; but she had a dream she'd never followed—and so that was the crossroad opportunity.

Afterward we were talking, and I asked, "So now what of this ravaging of seemingly unknown origin? Maybe these horrible operations are to say, 'This is not the route for you. You'd better follow your route, follow your dream now, or you're going to be dead.' Are you going to do it or not?" As we pursued it, though, you could just see a whole world open up for her.

Stephen: As a psychotherapist, I couldn't agree more. But I think that this kind of perception—it's kind of teleological—is not respected in ordinary psychological or therapeutic circles, because they are so busy tracing things as an outcome of the past that they miss the daimon of the future, the "god trying to be born in you" as Rilke put it.

Barry: Absolutely; there is a great bogging down in material causality.

Ann: Now I am in full agreement that there are social and historical forces that wield great power, and discrimination against women is a political and cultural fact; but it's also possible to see something that's mostly missed, by feminists and social theorists alike. Maybe the whole revolution about the feminine is not triggered by the political, but maybe the political itself is a response to the psychological attitude toward the feminine archetype.

There is surely this powerful rising of the feminine in the late twentieth century. But if your soul isn't deepened or enriched, if you see it only politically, there's no growth from within, no addressing of the archetypal feminine within people of both genders. And I think of the dangers of reductionism and literalism, because you can burn out to a cause. I have known some of these women. They are eaten by the collective, like a ripe fruit, and don't even know it is happening.

Stephen: 'Til they're drained and empty! Is it when the archetype is not recognized that it becomes predatory? I think of the Northwest coast totem pole where a human figure, the shaman maybe, is in the clutches of a great Bear or Eagle. Is that what Jung meant by possession by the archetype?

Barry: Going back to our friend, I think that the point Ann is making is that the woman was trying to enact a drama from her own childhood: the loss of the mother. Where you lose the physical experience of a mother as a child, you may try to regain it, at a terrible price. Then you get drowned in the maternal—in the largest sense of the word. Meanwhile, there's a greater destiny calling this woman—she's really been dreaming about that. But while she's been dreaming about seizing something, something is seized from her.

Ann: She's a very generous, complex woman; she's also a very good person who gives to everybody, goes everywhere. There's an overflowing that's the first thing to be addressed. But then again there's the issue of how the ego is positioned in relation to the reality the symbol points to. Then if there's a collapse between the reality and the symbol, so the symbol becomes the end in itself—that's another problem.

Stephen: Possession by the archetype here?

Ann: Well, that would be the total result, and then you would be fanatical in one way or another. Either you would be bullying everybody else to perform, or inwardly bullying all the other parts of you to perform whatever you have fallen into. But there's an unreal or collective quality about the adaptation. That's where the stereotype comes in; but it's lifeless, a departure from the way real vitality needs to be actualized, unfolding to everybody else—and that's what's ruthless about it.

Stephen: I think I get it. The archetype is ruthless. It's like the things that happen to Gaia or Rhea, in Hesiod's *Theogony*: they start to give birth, and then that's all they can do—after the gods come the titans, then monsters and grotesques, things to inhabit the deep noisome layers of the Earth. Mothering runs mad—"in loco parentis" [laughter].

Ann: It's like an encounter with the sphinx. You have to answer it or it will tear you apart. Archetypes in their raw power are like this.

Now back to the question about Jungian fundamentalism. When we first learn about animus and anima, we bring in all our culturally conditioned stereotypes, images from childhood, and whatnot. But the anima/animus is meant to be more than a hodgepodge of such images or attributes; it is also a connection to the creative, and to the Divine, that transcends such categories.

Neither gender is just one thing alone. Women can be aggressive, men fickle; women intellectist, men passive and intuitive. Real people are more complex and interesting than any constellation of stereotypes. The real anima is beyond any figure of movie or fiction, the animus more complex than any reductive image— warrior, king, lover. In fact, when the animus stays as any one thing too long, watch out! It is unhealthily frozen.

Stephen: Isn't the danger really that, if you're a Jungian fundamentalist, you will try to label that which is within you with something from without, as if it all came from there, or as if you can't understand the mind without reference to something that came through the senses?

Ann: Exactly, the anima/animus is to be a bridge to the unknown but authentic relationship to the Self.

Robin: I assume you mean a kind of bridge to the Divine, or the Divine within.

Ann: Yes, they are not meant to be static, but a dynamic function, leading us somewhere—into our own individuality, or our own entelechal becoming.

Stephen: Would you say this was like Swedenborg's "divine providence?"

Barry: Swedenborg's definitive virtue for me is in his extraordinary and elegant use of the imagination; he has a very richly cultivated imagination. Whereas some people might dislike this or that exaggerated little metaphor, or performance, it seems to me not to take away from the great achievement of his use of the imagination. For me, the peak is his concept of divine providence and its accompanying range of understanding. It's much richer than most of the theological words written by people in the more formal tradition of the theologies.

Stephen: Yes, Swedenborg was essentially untutored philosophically or scholastically in any theology. Some consider him a diamond in the rough in that sense.

Barry: It's not all that rough, either—the natural feeling he has, the way the imaginal can take you all the way up into the supernatural—I like the way he weaves these things together.

Stephen: Robin and I believe that we have woven our own kind of astral net that includes natural, spiritual, and celestial. And I would say it's either done consciously or unconsciously. When you are lovers with someone, when you are lovers and partners, these things get all entangled together. One of the questions that we're working with throughout this work—and we understand the value of questions as opposed to answers—is about the *angelodaemonic* or *daemongelic* movements that begin to happen. The movement either takes one down into worse and worse conflicts and conflagrations, and into hell; or the other possible movement takes one into heaven, not a simplistic two-dimensional heaven but a heaven that's woven from all the textures that one encounters on the way up to the higher realms in that sense.

Ann: Yes, it does seem that there is a movement like that, and which direction makes a difference.

Stephen: One of the phrases that I found so compelling in your work on this was that it was as if there were an overflowing "reservoir of love" which was transpersonal, available to couples, or other relationships in the human sphere. I wonder, can this be diffused or misspent, or is it an inexhaustible reservoir?

Barry: We go into this in *Transforming Sexuality*.[15] My problem here is "parts of speech." What is love? It's a noun, it's a verb, it's an adverb, it's an adjective, it's a preposition. Love is each of these things, and it's all those things, and at each level, it's both subject and the object, the modifier of the adjective, the noun, and the verb. It's love playing on love playing on love, increasing, enlarging, deepening. When we talk about the demonic and the angelic, the subject is so large that we have no measurement for it. That's why the parts of speech are in such trouble here, why we have so much trouble; we are not used to doing this.

Ann: It's clearly transpersonal, love, both goal and process.

Robin: It's interwoven. I have been drawing angels for twenty-five years, but I've seen it in a lot of traditional art too. It's there in traditional oriental and Native American rugs and carpets, in weaving of all sorts, in pottery patterns in many cultures—so there is something going on here: love, woven of wings and eyes and energy.

We had some angel-sightings a couple of years ago in our area, around Christmastime, and we interviewed a woman who was reported as having seen an angel. Steve can tell you more about this because he interviewed her.

Stephen: The woman, who had an eighth-grade education, said she was coming back from a prayer meeting kind of disappointed, because it hadn't lived up to her expectations. On the drive back, she was praying for something more satisfying, I guess, from God. As she was driving down a secondary road, through a rather beautiful cemetery, this angel appeared to her. He was big and strong and muscular, and she saw every detail, she said, not only the wings, but the dewdrops on them, and he looked to her "as if he had traveled a great distance on those wings."

The apparition became a life-transforming event for her, and when it hit the newspapers, it affected a lot of the people around her. They were either scornful or curiously respectful, like we were, and touched by the experience. At least we convinced ourselves, Robin and I, that she was absolutely sincere.

Barry: This is the issue: do you believe in it?

Stephen: The gooseflesh I get around them, even the lore about the way they appear, and the places of their apparition, says yes.

Robin: I think for me, on a gut level, yes.

Barry: I am uneasy with people who talk about angels as if they were the playthings of very little children and have no real significance for us as we grow older, because clearly such creatures could not exist. People who think this way have done very little living in the imagination. Over thousands of years, we have been graced with such rich material on angels, all the different kinds of angels, all the extraordinary uses of the imagination to conjure up ways of feeling, knowing, understanding angels.

Ann: I think it depends, though, on your tradition, your background, because you're more Catholic then I am, so the idea of the intermediary is very familiar. I am hopelessly Protestant, where you are just supposed to go right to God.

Barry: Except that the angel is only the intermediary, or more precisely, the messenger of God. The angel is not to be confused with God.

Robin: But in some traditions it's called "the shadow of God," which is fascinating.

Barry: But the angel is not supposed to be a break away from God; it's a bringing closer to God. That is the angelic path.

Ann: We were just in London, and we were looking at one of Barry's favorite paintings, Carlo Crivelli's *Annunciation*, a wonderful architectural painting, full of buildings and rooms and balconies. The angel comes and speaks to Mary, who's in the kitchen: he has got these enormous, tough muscles.

Barry: The announcement's being made through the window, so to speak. And there hearing it is a little girl, who's peeking around the corner at the event. She's astonished. It is revealing; it is so poignant.

Stephen: There is Rilke's beautiful poem, *Duino Elgies*, which begins "Every angel is terrifying," where he asks, "Where are the days of Tobias?" [quoted on page 66].

Barry: Do you know James Bridie's play *Tobias and the Angel*? It's a dramatization of the apocryphal book. Bridie makes the whole story so present, now. I walked out of that theater—I swear I did—in London, onto the street, and I expected to find the angel I had just seen on the stage. Because clearly that angel wouldn't have to worry about getting a ticket or getting through the doors; it could get through without any struggle. It's a very great story, and I resent those who try to relegate it to some kind of lower level canonically, because it comes from the Apocrypha.

In any case, I share—I think we both share—what you are saying about angels. There is a realm that is fundamental to spiritual understanding, getting beyond what we see on surfaces and allowing ourselves to be pulled into the spaces between the worlds, between the material and the spiritual.

Stephen: The question Rilke asks, "Where are the days of Tobias?" is our question too. Can we structure and texture our lives so that there is a place for angels, even in the guise of the ordinary, peeking around a corner or through a window at a reality of which Swedenborg was so very certain—that we live in the spiritual and the physical world, at the same time.

Ann: Do you think that it's rather rare for there to be committed couples, growing together in this way you are talking about, now?

Stephen: We are told sometimes we are "an endangered species" and that, for the most part, the question is not whether a relationship goes on, but whether it goes on with life in it. There are many couples who have stayed together, "until death do us part," but they do not really know each other, and they do not really love each other, nor communicate with each other on soul levels. So I guess the question is whether an unexamined relationship is worth having.

Ann: *Unexamined* is the principal word here. Because the archetype merely hints at the potential. It can manifest tremendous energy that will just amaze you, or it can leave you with a shell of what could be. I think you have to be willing to be stretched in the encounter with it—then it leads you further into the growth that is your own fulfillment.

Stephen: I think of Christopher [Edward] Whitmont's favorite quote, "He who is willing, the fates lead. He who is unwilling, they drag!" The angelodaemonic energy is so powerful that it does not let us go lax or unconscious. If it does, some tempestuous or emotional scenario comes along to wake you up.

I do want to believe, and that's our reason for writing this book, that there will be many more of us in the new millennium, making a new world by enriching our relationships and our ways of expressing love. I know when you meet the children of loving relationships, raised in loving families, there's a beauty and a health, an abundance really, about them.

Ann: That's true, and there is another side to this: we wrote in *Transforming Sexuality* a little section on having children, in which what we say is, "This child is so wondrous, not even just 'something out of nothing' but a real someone." This magical being is luminous, and it attracts the projection of the Self, and we're drowned in its radiance. It deserves everything. But then it's so much work that parents are completely exhausted. So the child gets everything, and the two people, who were they?

Stephen: Absolutely, that's when they project all of their unlived life onto the child and never live it. They've missed their own luminosity.

Ann: And then they become "Ma" and "Pa" and kind of fade.

Robin: My father, bless him, said that very strongly. The child is not you and its not yours.

Ann: That's one of the basic meanings around rituals like baptism. The child belongs to God and to all the people. It's not just yours. It's born again, in the water, you see.

Barry: It's because we think we know what a child is supposed to be. We're talking about the archetype-stereotype problem again. Stereotypes are often frozen archetypes. We do that with children all the time. We've murdered the education of very young children in this country, and in response, the children have murdered each other. I wrote a piece called, "Dead Children, Dead Imaginations," which spells all this out.[16] We're allowing them to kill each other, as we have allowed the whole inner world of the imagination to be ripped away from children. They have no fairytales, their imaginations are peopled by the stereotypes they see on TV. Children's souls are sick because we have not allowed them enough of fairytale creatures, of angels. They're beset instead with their own inner demons.

Robin: I've been struggling with the angelodaemonic construct. A *demon* is one thing, probably to be resisted, to get strong by resisting it. But a *daemon*, this is what brings us into life—away from heaven and into creation. At the same time, this force often gets created more unconsciously than consciously for a couple. It is created as much out of our hassles with each other as out of our successes. Perhaps too much out of our struggles and our failures—you know, "Wait a minute, you are not a part of me, you are somebody else and you're putting your thing on me!" Our "third thing" can become very dark and needy.

Barry: It's ruthless.

Ann: The archetype is never to be taken for granted.

Robin: "It's not a tame lion"—as C.S. Lewis says of Aslan in the Narnia stories.

Ann: No, it's not a tame lion.

Barry: It seems to me the large lesson we must learn from all of this is to open up and out our contexts of relationship. The greatest stories go on and on. We think—this is very important—we think it's all for ourselves, but we are forgetting that we're still here, in the larger context; and because we are still here, the story must go on.

The Magic of Ideas: Denise Breton and Christopher Largent

The door opens once again, and a substantial, intelligent-looking bearded man and a striking woman emerge. Denise Breton and Christopher Largent also come from "the academy," to the soul of partnering. They bring classical philosophical training and brilliant intuition to tasks involving growth; but they walk their path together.

The enterprise they run together is called "Idea House," and they do bring new ideas to us through the really committed and intelligent ways they have worked on their relationship.

Stephen: You each brought so much to your relationship and were already well-defined adult people at the time you got together. How did this work for you?

Christopher: I'd like to answer this one first, because marriage, as I've come to discover it through being married to Denise, has two distinguishing qualities, one that needs to be embraced and one that needs to be avoided.

The bad news first: when two people get married, their subconscious minds go rummaging around the memory banks looking for a role model ("now, let's see—marriage, marriage, there must be a marriage manual here somewhere"). What almost always emerges is the parents' marriage, so that each partner is tempted to react—again, usually unconsciously—like one or both of the parents.

If either or both partners give in to the temptation, they find themselves married to their parents. And in our generation, our parents' views of marriage were muddied by idiotic notions: women and children as property, men as aggressive breadwinners, women and children as vulnerable, men as insensitive, etc.—things we now need to outgrow. Later generations may have better marriage role models, but in the end, we must each forge our own model.

Photo: Elizabeth Oberdorf

Educators and authors Denise Breton and Christopher Largent.

Stephen: Yes, that's exactly what we're after, this new model, and we're interested in the cutting edge of where that happens, where the old changes to the new; and that's what we feel we can learn from you.

Christopher: In marrying Denise, I was reminded early and often that this behaving like the parents would not do. The first time we had to move, for instance (as Denise was off to graduate school), I began "taking charge," telling her what should go where. This, after all, was what my father had done in most of the half-dozen moves I'd made as a child. Denise, however, just sat down in the middle of our apartment floor on a pile of clothes we were packing and said, "What is this?"

Her reaction was so unexpected that I found myself telling the simple truth: I was doing what my father had done; I was telling her what to do. Denise smiled one of—well, what P. G. Wodehouse would describe as "a smile intended to sting"— and said, "I don't need to be told what to do."

From that moment, I began the long road to realizing that we had to work out our own relationship, one that was true to us and so inevitably different from our parents' relationship. And I had to ask myself why I picked that charming little piece of behavior to mimic—could it possibly have been because she was off to a prestigious graduate program on a full scholarship, and I wasn't? The other part of the long road was continuous self-examination.

Denise: I did not want to marry and was adamant, even militant, about it. I wasn't drawn to living the traditional roles for women, and most of the men I dated seemed full of role expectations. This was sufficiently off-putting to me that I didn't date much after high school and even wore a wedding ring on my right ring finger all through college to indicate that I wasn't available: "Nothing personal to you, it's the category of life I'm not interested in!" Of course, this reflected to a great extent my observations of my parents' relationship, which seemed to me to be heavier with role expectations than with genuine intimacy.

My undergraduate degree was in philosophy, and Chris had been a teaching assistant in one of my logic classes, though I never attended his sections. I didn't think I needed them. He graded my papers, though, and so knew my name. Some time later my sister spotted him at a basketball game and assured me he was married and not interested in a relationship, so I went over to chat. He seemed safe.

I was trying to sort out going to graduate school in religion, and soon found out that Chris' undergraduate degree was in comparative religions. Starved for someone to share ideas with about philosophy and spirituality (our philosophy department was dry-as-dust analytic), Chris and I had the first of decades of genuinely soul-satisfying conversations about everything. This was February 6, 1976—Chris's twenty-seventh birthday.

During the course of the evening, he told me he had been separated from his wife for several months and was getting a divorce. That threw me. We were friends now, and I couldn't push him away in my usual perfunctory manner. When he asked me out, I accepted; but after I got home, I came to my senses and sent a note to him via my sister saying I couldn't go out after all. Whereupon he, a student of symbol systems, analyzed my handwriting.

That got me riled up—for the presumption—but also curious, and the curiosity won out. Our first date was to see the movie *2001*, and one question I remember putting to him was, "What exactly are the philosophical foundations of numerology and astrology?"—fightin' words, philosophically speaking. Of course, he laughed and off we went on another philosophical-spiritual-and-anything-else dialogue. Thanks to David Bohm's distinction between discussion and dialogue (discussion being a contest to win, dialogue being a shared exploration and learning), I now understand that it was his capacity to engage in real dialogue that won my heart.

Robin: I think you are a kindred spirit. I had decided I wouldn't get married, too. My goal was to become a career artist, and I didn't see marriage and children as part of that.

Denise: When I realized that the relationship was growing serious, I got scared. I could talk to him as I never could with anyone. And yet I was frightened—frightened of being stuck in women's roles but also frightened that Chris might have another side that would emerge after we were married. This latter fear proved valid, for we both had many original family issues to deal with. He in particular had serious healing from trauma to do, for he had been beaten and abused growing up.

A couple weeks before the date we had set to be married, I experienced several days of intense crying. At the time, I couldn't put into words exactly why I was crying, but I also couldn't stop. In a few months, my life had turned one hundred eighty degrees from what I had imagined it to be, for I had been fully reconciled to going it alone. Two days before the wedding, I went to Chris while he was on a break from teaching tennis camp to say I couldn't marry him. Chris put his tennis cap over his face and said, "Well, whatever you want." I wondered why he didn't argue with me more; so, like a cat, as long as I wasn't being pushed, I was willing to give it a shot. I knew I loved him, and I loved the life of talking philosophy and spirituality to my heart's content. No one I had ever met shared my passion for ideas and possessed his intellect and dead-on intuition for pursuing it. We were married July 2, 1976, by a justice of the peace.

Robin: There is a lot of lore that explains about the "little death" that marriage is for each of us, what we're giving up.

Christopher: Marriage differs from friendship or other affiliations in that it leads to ever deepening intimacy, and that means that each person is going to change. Of course, such intimacy is built on friendship, and many people will go to friendships for intimacy and avoid it in their marriages. But for a marriage to be the genuine spiritual discipline I've found it to be, each person must take a journey of profound self-discovery. An apparently harmless "I do" really means questioning who I am, who she is, what the higher purpose of the relationship is, and even what humanity is and what it's here for.

Stephen: I think you've got it here, just what you said about involving so much more than the simple-seeming thing itself.

Christopher: In this context, marriage can be one of the most demanding and rewarding spiritual disciplines humans engage in. I was a fairly good meditator when I met Denise, for instance—and our lives remain contemplative to this day—but I've learned as much in marriage as in meditation or contemplation. In fact, my contemplative life and my married life support each other all the time, naturally.

Denise: An astrologer had told Chris before we were married (he began studying astrology at that time) that, should we marry, our marriage would most likely break up after ten years. Now an astrologer himself all these years later, Chris finds that a highly irresponsible comment. Nonetheless, it hung over us, and I swore that we'd stay married eleven years or else. Actually, the astrologer was onto something, for our mutual inner healing issues started coming to a crisis around the mid-1980s. Chris experienced bouts of raging. Fortunately, I knew him well enough by then to know that what was coming out of his mouth didn't sound like him.

John Bradshaw was appearing on PBS fund-raisers at that time, so we soon had the tools to identify the other "voices." At that time, it seemed easier for women than for men to embrace the recovery process, so I was grateful that he was willing and open to embark on the recovery path, fully by his choice and pursuit, not by my urgings. Healing from our original issues has been a long process that continues. Had we not engaged so fully in recovery with each other as our primary support group (we neither did therapy nor attended support groups), I do not see how we could have remained married. It would have been too painful for both of us. Now those experiences have given us an in-the-trenches understanding of what's at stake and what's involved with healing that has become so central to our professional work together.

Stephen: Chris, would you say a little more about how you met Denise?

Christopher: Yes. After a trip to Europe, I had decided my life was too small. And my marriage had gone stale. Because I'd studied ancient and Oriental religions and noticed, as most students do, that mythic themes repeat themselves universally, I went looking for some universal symbol system—a symbolic language in which all those repeating themes come together. To that end, I began studying every symbol system I could get my hands on: graphology, astrology, numerology, palmistry, the *I Ching*, tarot symbolism—the fields the academic community considered less than respectable. Then Denise entered my life. I'd already met her, oddly enough. But it wasn't actually a meeting. She'd been in some classes during my graduate work, so I knew who she was. Her youngest sister was in one of my classes at a private school (where I was teaching religion and philosophy), and she'd mentioned Denise.

What surprised me, though, was that her sister described Denise as "single." Denise had always seemed cheerful but aloof around the Philosophy Department, and she dressed well in an era when the rest of us were casual (read "sloppy"). But she wore a wedding ring. On the wrong hand. Since I knew she wasn't a professor and yet commanded respect from everyone in the department, I assumed she was an older student and maybe a professor's wife—older because she always seemed more mature than everyone else, and married because of the ring (you can see how astutely my mind worked in those days). Maybe this wrong-hand business was some European custom I didn't know about. Besides, Denise always spoke in an English so clear and articulate that people hearing her thought she was foreign.

I would learn later she was exactly the right age for an undergraduate (five years younger than I was), and she was respected because of her unusual intellect. It was this intellect that would grab me when I met her again. As for the ring, Denise wore it to keep men at bay. A nice reflection for me is that the sister who reintroduced us later said to Denise, "If you don't want to get married, don't go out with Mr. Largent, because if you do, you'll marry him; he's exactly like you."

Stephen: So you would say your marriage in part draws its stability from compatibility, similarities.

Denise: They are certainly there in our intellectual lives. We both know the field: philosophy and spirituality—but how to make a living at it has been a challenge. For nearly twenty years, we team-taught philosophy and the world's religions at the University of Delaware's Philosophy Department. We loved working together in the classroom, and students enjoyed seeing our interaction. Thinking through subjects together before a class became an easy and exciting experience, one of shared discovery. We did not work for the Philosophy Department full time, though, because we did not want to become part of the institution with its politics and pressures. Of course, that meant we had no guaranteed income and no benefits.

Whenever we team-teach—one of our favorite things to do—people say they notice or like the way we interact with each other.

In 1994, we taught our last class at the University of Delaware, for we found the structure of education contrary to our principles. Specifically, our research in recovery opened our eyes to how damaging the practice of grading—and worse, grading on the bell curve—is to learning and self-esteem. Alfie Kohn's works on this subject are quite compelling, documenting the extensive research done in recent decades on the deleterious effects of rewards and punishments.[17] This is a long story, one that we've attempted to explore in our book *The Paradigm Conspiracy.*[18] Suffice it to say, we no longer could participate in a system that we believe is as damaging to people's inner lives as the current system of education is.

Robin: Having taught at colleges for a number of years, I can really appreciate that. We're freelancing these days too.

Christopher: There's one factor about our relationship I don't want to leave out. It's that Denise is beautiful. Even the chairman of the department, who was an admirer of her intellectual prowess and usually understated about everything, commented to me that "Unlike the rest of us, she'll always look great doing whatever she does in a classroom. I think she's the most beautiful woman I've ever met."

The night we met, my astrology teacher and her husband were in the stands above us at the basketball game, and the astrologer said, "Who's that down there with Chris?" And the husband replied, "I don't know, but I wish someone with those looks would stare at me the way she's staring at him." The blows he received for that comment, by the way, are a testimony to the ups and downs of marriage.

But I discovered that Denise did not seem to be aware—either of her good looks or the intensity of her intellect. To my astonishment, I found myself talking to an intelligent, beautiful, and humble person. Where had she been all my life?

Stephen: That's a good example of "the eyes recommending to the heart" concerning the beloved. It doesn't hurt to have the people we love be beautiful, so we can watch them—and enjoy it.

Christopher: I can't dismiss it in this case, but more to the point of my spiritual quest, she seemed to discuss things from a consistent background that I couldn't identify. She hadn't studied any of the crowd that was getting popular in those days—Mircea Eliade, Joseph Campbell, Rudolf Bultmann, D. T. Suzuki, *et al.*—so I couldn't figure out where the consistency came from. But I could smell a system behind it. And I loved the consistency and the integrity.

Denise: Our individual spiritual paths, our individual passions, for philosophy, spirituality, and how they impact our lives and culture, brought us together. That's why we have a partnership in the first place; and when we have troubles, that shared orientation and the understanding we get from it helps us through. How we've come to understand things together is very different from how we imagine we would have done alone. Our interactions are completely synergetic, for we discover things and push the envelope together in ways I couldn't have done alone.

Before I met Chris, I used to joke that I could only marry a traveling salesman who was never home. Now Chris and I work together all day every day. We're seldom farther than one hundred yards from each other. I would have thought this horribly claustrophobic or unhealthy, but now I experience this as a constant spur to stay on the path, to deal with my own issues, to keep developing, to keep questioning. And I wonder how people who do not see each other for most of their waking hours are able to sustain a relationship, especially given all the chores that occupy off-work times. Chris' one complaint is that we don't spend enough time together. I don't think he's being insatiable or co-dependent, to use those terms. He's acknowledging the time relationships require and the riches that relationships hold for personal and spiritual development. And those things take time. Perhaps the cultural "norm," whatever that is, takes what's involved in relationship too lightly.

Christopher: After our meeting, my spiritual quest took a turn that wouldn't be completed for years. Having come from a violently abusive family, my personality was fragmented, and I knew it. Because I had a talent for religion and philosophy, though, I used them to keep myself together as best I could. It didn't always work (religious disciplines cannot of themselves always heal fragmentation, especially if the shattering happened consistently in the family of origin and if both parents participated in the abuse). But because of this, few people noticed the fragmentation. (It did, of course, come out. One of the hard things about recalling compulsive behavior is how many people think you're a jerk when you're giving in to the behavior.) I didn't know how to articulate the fragmentation or how to deal with the compulsive behavior it created. But in Denise I saw a philosophical consistency that was matched by an inner integrity. Here, I thought, is the light at the end of my tunnel. If I can work with this person, I can figure out how to be whole again.

Stephen: I'm so moved by your candor about that. Most people don't have either the integrity or the courage to take it on consciously like that.

Christopher: As Denise and I spent hours on the telephone—our three-hour chats got to be a joke in her family—and hours walking at the beach and driving who-cared-where, I began to feel that healing was possible. The heavy work would come later, after we discovered *recovery*—John Bradshaw, Alice Miller, Anne Wilson Schaef, Charles Whitfield, John and Linda Friel, Patrick Carnes, and all those other wonderful writers and counselors who intend to heal old wounds and give methods for each individual to engage in his or her own healing.[19] But for now, I was allowing much of the confusion created by ego-shattering to be dispelled.

Denise: Earlier in our marriage, I did not realize this so clearly as I do now, and sometimes it took a crisis for me to see that we weren't giving enough time to our relationship. Plus I had my own issues of workaholism that got in the way—the low self-esteem that says you're not worth much if you're not working or outwardly doing some good. Having been raised with two workaholic parents, it's no surprise this became an issue that, unaddressed, could have done serious damage to our relationship. Since my work was always about spiritual ideas, it sometimes seemed that the relationship was in competition with my work, though I must also say that Chris has always been hugely supportive of my work and worked hard to make sure I had time for writing. Once I dealt with the recovery issues involved, my sense of there being a conflict disappeared. I conclude from this that it wasn't the relationship but a compulsive response within me that caused my perception of a conflict.

Stephen: What about things you've really had to work hard at?

Denise: One area of conflict that we've had to work out is the sexual side. Like everyone else, we've grown up in a culture conflicted about sexuality and spirituality: sex is not spiritual, and "spiritual" people are not sexual. So we had to consciously confront this programming and get it out of our relationship. Pat Carnes' books, especially *Sexual Anorexia*,[20] were most helpful in developing more healthy views of sexuality and spirituality.

Christopher: I had my emotional conflicts. I had begun to rage over things that even I thought weren't important. Even if they were, who I thought I was wouldn't have handled them that way. I tried to pass this off as just the consequences of professional pressures. After all, hadn't my father justified all of his ragings? And if he could justify his, which were physically violent, surely I could justify mine, which weren't. And wasn't justifying behavior what any adult male did? But even I didn't believe the justifications and rationalizations. And the pain I caused Denise—who had never failed to support me—caused me great grief and anxiety.

Fortunately, after each raging period, Denise said exactly the right thing: "This is not you, and we're going to find a way to get you back." We developed an ad-hoc support group of friends and therapists and discovered very helpful writers associated with the recovery movement. And I began to heal.

Stephen: It seems hard to get past those rationalizations, especially if you have seen a "godlike" parent use them.

Christopher: As it turned out, this was the missing piece in our work. Denise and I had already written one book, *The Soul of Economics*. Our idea was typical of philosophers: if all of us just clear up what we're confused about, everything will be okay—right? Well, not quite.

As we taught the world's religions (for over twenty years), we had come to wonder: what's the twentieth century equivalent of the analysis of evil? Religions had always been good at spotting the roots of destruction in their own cultures and eras. So what was ours? What did we in the twentieth century have that would equal the Buddhist analysis of evil as ignorance, the Taoist analysis of evil as over-aggressiveness or lack of balance, or the Hindu analysis as attachment (allowing for the fact that these analyses are more sophisticated than I've made them sound here)?

We found the answer in those writers I've mentioned above. They see destructive and self-destructive behavior as the result of trauma, therefore something that could be healed. Humans weren't infected with evil (as some schools of religion and psychology have it); they're wounded. Heal them, and they become wonderfully creative.

Denise continued to be a perfect support-group partner for me, and we realized that ongoing healing was a crucial component in marriage. Having already been married for ten years, we engaged on a new journey that reached significant turning points again and again.

Stephen: Alex Grey put this beautifully in his interview, and I think he and Allyson have done the same thing, really—you have to address the "pathologies" each of you carry together.

Christopher: This work had an unexpected result for me. Everything I'd ever read about enlightenment from great teachers had made sense to me—but head-sense. I knew the teachings, I could teach them to students, and I understood them. But I knew they were largely in my head or artificially tacked onto my behavior; I tried to be nice and pleasant and helpful and upbeat and placid and anything-else-that-seemed-enlightened. After all, everyone I'd done spiritual work with wanted to be enlightened, and all of us worked hard at it.

After the first decade of adding recovery to our spiritual work and our marriage, however, I realized that I'd stopped working at enlightenment. Without my working at it, though, it nonetheless had come to make heart-sense to me. And I didn't try to force any behaviors; my process was (and is) my process; that was all. Teachings about enlightenment didn't seem like teachings about enlightenment anymore. They simply seemed the way normal folks live.

Stephen: Campbell would say that we are adequate to life, just adequate, and it to us. It seems to me, and the Japanese tradition seems to have grasped this more than the world-abnegating Hindu version, I think, that one of the human goals of enlightenment is to have a better life.

But I'd like to move to the crux of our dialogue, which is partnership as a spiritual practice. I think you two have practiced this at a depth that most couples never reach.

Denise: We do not belong to a church or any other spiritual group or organization; neither do we consider ourselves ascribing to one tradition or another. We genuinely value what good we see in all of them, although we also see blemishes and dark spots, especially when it comes to the institutionalized side of religions.

As a result, we very much take our partnership to be our spiritual practice. Our relationship provides the forum, the space, and the constant reminder to focus on what's most important, to wrestle with core spiritual ideas, and to be transformed in our whole way of being, as a result. Naturally, our development together draws on the inner work and research that we do on our own. Chris is an avid scholar, often staying up to the wee hours of the morning reading astrology or Buddhism or Plato or some obscure who-knows-who-from-when. He continually feeds my spiritual life with the ideas he discovers, although I do my own reading and contemplation too.

Christopher: My family-of-origin abuse especially encouraged (along with raging) lying, sexual compulsivity, relationship addiction, abuse of food, hypervigilance, and a host of other endearing responses. But after I settled down and rethought what had just happened, I'd find deeper issues, which I could trace back, Buddhist-style, to the original trauma. Then I could process it. Taking this tracing-back and processing as a method, Denise and I could more and more spot a trauma before it bloomed into some perfectly stupid behavior.

Stephen: So your *sadhana* (spiritual practice) emerged from the wounds themselves; they became the guides.

Christopher: Over time, as more and more wounds were healed, the interaction became easier and more creative, and we found even deeper intimacy, which led to deeper understanding, and to more healing—the spiral of healing, intimacy, and spiritual development that we came to see as typical of marriage at its best.

Denise: In the last ten years, Chris has found he has an ability to connect on inner levels, to do shamanic journeys to other dimensions. This is a private practice for our own learning and development. He has not pushed it to levels that shamans traditionally do or that Swedenborg did. As it has developed, he relaxes and connects, and I ask questions about anything. This part of our life together has been profoundly supportive and affirming of our spiritual path. For years it kept us going, especially with the writing when it didn't seem as if it would ever see the light of print. The perspectives he gets puts everything back into the big picture, and that's so helpful.

We also walk in a beautiful public garden every day that we can, which is nearly every day. It is a profoundly restoring time, being in nature and being alone with each other to talk, without phones ringing. If we have a run of bad weather and we don't get out, we notice it. I would say this is an important part of our relationship as a spiritual practice too.

Stephen: It sounds like the "sacred stations" exercise that Robin and I developed. Preferring the cathedral of nature to most churches, we would run up Mohonk mountain, stopping at each gazebo to have a deep and meaningful conversation about our process, a new project in becoming, or something we didn't have time to process any other way. So I support your walks in the park; let nature do its steady healing work.

Denise: Because of the nature of our professional work, we experience that as part of our spiritual practice as well. Whatever we write about or study, we find coming up in our personal processes—so much so that we're thinking of writing next about "Trips to Vermont" or "French Cooking" instead of philosophy and culture. Each in our different spheres of expression, we feel pushed to a place of not-knowing that makes us open to what is beyond us—and we regularly support each other in this process, since it comes up all the time.

Of course, sharing our experiences of inner, emotional healing and soul-connecting forms a big part of our spiritual practice. Those are the times, for instance, when we stay up much later than we intended talking about where we are and what's going on with us—stuff that didn't have a chance to surface during the hubbub of the day. It's easy to get caught up in busy-ness so that this part gets short shrift, but whenever that happens, something comes up to get our notice, and then we both automatically give top priority to our time together. Nothing is more important to us than having our relationship move with us in our development, no matter how much time it takes. Again, working for ourselves and not having to answer to a boss, corporation, or institution makes this vastly easier. Whenever we need relationship time, we take it.

Christopher: We also realized that while some issues needed attention and could create frustrations—especially finances and time demands—these were merely doorways to some deeper process. If we took the time to engage in that process, we'd again find ourselves in the spiral of healing, spiritual evolution, and deepening intimacy.

Denise: Marriage is a special relationship, as I see it, because it engages my whole being in a way no other relationship does. There's a totality of participation about marriage that's singular. There's also an unconditional quality of support and love. Naturally, there are parts of me that Chris doesn't fully know or access, but that's true for me about myself as well. If we're not fixed quantities but beings in process, then uncertainties and unknowns are inevitable. That's where the unconditional support comes in.

Marriage for me means a commitment to work through things together, no matter what comes up. True, there have been times when we had to question whether we could continue in that commitment. Then the marriage was in question. But as long as we're both committed to the marriage, then we're committed to working things through. Other relationships don't have that quality of commitment. And because of marriage's commitment, I feel an intensity to the relationship as well as a trust that is singular. Because of all that we've been through together, I feel no one understands me as easily or as readily as Chris does, even though sometimes we have to work to maintain that level of mutual understanding. Sometimes it comes more easily than others. But the commitment to have it—and to work until we get it—remains constant.

Christopher: It's clear that every couple needs to make the time to process issues and get in the spiral of healing and intimacy. Professional demands tend to be against marriages here, but this is a trend each couple needs to reverse. When Stephen Covey in the mid-1990s came out in favor of spending more time at home with spouse and children, he sounded a note that the whole culture needs to hear. We must get away from what was called in the 1800s "wage slavery" and reclaim our lives. That's my soapbox pitch.

Stephen: Any advice for other couples trying to achieve their version of what you and Denise do?

Christopher: I'd look at what I wish I'd known when Denise and I first got together. I would have liked at the beginning of our relationship to know as much about recovery as I knew about religion and philosophy. I wish I'd experienced the works of John Bradshaw, Patrick Carnes, Wendy Maltz, Alice Miller, Stephen Wolinsky, Anne Wilson Schaef, John and Linda Friel, Abraham Twerski, Terence Gorski, and Alfie Kohn. I'd like to have known about Dudley Weeks' book on conflict resolution, *The Eight Essential Steps to Conflict Resolution*, which turns conflicts into conflict partnerships. And I'd like to have had under my belt Douglas Stone, Bruce Patton and Sheila Heen's wonderful book *Difficult Conversations*,[21] which shows people how to turn nightmare misunderstandings into learning conversations.

And I think I'd like to have encountered Coleman Barks' translations of Rumi earlier, to help offset some of the dualistic confusions around the relationship between spirituality and everyday life.[22] And I'd love to have had a good counseling astrologer help me claim parts of my personality that I kept trying to deny. Finally, I wish we'd had the support team that we have around us now—the great therapists, shamanic practitioners, multidimensional healers, and friends who represent our extended family.

Stephen: We've shared with you our angel concept. What do you think?

Denise: The sort of angelic being our relationship might create would blend philosophy and spirituality, understanding and healing. It might be a prophetic sort of angel, Jeremiah style, in that we are always looking behind the appearance of things to see what's going on in consciousness and beneath the surface. This is often the subject of our dialogues. Sometimes what we find is inspiring, and other times it calls for some waking up. I have a feeling that our angel would also be the type that's here to do a job, for that's how we feel. I just hope the angel has a clearer sense of what that is and how to do it than we've often had.

Christopher: The image of a relationship's creating an angel is a wonderful one, I think, and one that can help all kinds of relationships in the future (even if the legal institution of marriage doesn't survive, which it may not). And the kind of angel our marriage creates is one that I've identified earlier as a spiral—of ever deepening intimacy, greater creativity, more profound healing, and spiritual evolution. The one phrase for this angel might be transformational love, while my experience of it with Denise is soul-satisfying play. After all the pain and work has been considered and confronted, this is an angel of fun.

Synchronistic Magic: Ron Lavin and Penny Price

The Art-Deco doors open once again, and another couple steps confidently into the room. Ron Lavin is tall, dark, and broad-shouldered; Penny Price, medium-sized, blonde, curious, and sparkly. They love each other in a way that is palpable. Each has come to this soul-mating in mid-life in full awareness. Ron brings his clairvoyant vision and healing hands; he is a spiritual healer and the founder and director of the international healing schools, A Healing Touch. Penny brings her bright clarity and visual artistry, and is an award-winning producer, director, and writer whose work includes *The Mike Douglas Show*; *Good Morning, America*; and *NBC Magazine*, and now runs her own company, Penny Price Media. They live in Rhinebeck, New York, with a glorious view of the Catskill Mountains, and manage to create warmth and beauty wherever they go.

Stephen: I know there's a wonderful love story here, or a myth, or both, about how your relationship came to be.

Penny: A number of years ago we met a very well-known psychic named Dr. Alex Tanous. He was a lovely man, and one of the few people who were studied by the American Society of Psychical Research.

Ron: He would sit in a room wired with an electrocardiogram and project his spirit into a steel coffin in another room down the hall. He would enter the coffin in his spirit form, climb a little ladder that was about six inches tall, ring a bell, and look through a hole at the end of the coffin into a randomizer and repeat the number, letter, and color displayed there. He was one of the very, very few who could do that

Clairvoyant and healer Ron Lavin and media consultant Penny Price.

quite consistently. He was also hooked up to a biofeedback machine measuring his vital signs and, in this way, scientifically demonstrated the ability of being in two places simultaneously.

Penny: I met Alex through my work. I have always had two major motivations throughout my media career—one was to use the light of media to focus on dark, problem areas, trying to correct wrongs and to help change the world; and the other, to use the light to bring in inspiring and empowering ideas. I was a producer with Geraldo for seven years and had the good fortune to be able to do both (one of my investigative programs won a Maggie Award). Geraldo's hard-news sense wasn't initially open to "body, mind and spirit," human potential programming, but once management saw that these topics delivered ratings (which I intuitively knew they would), I was given permission to produce many more of these kinds of programs. I felt that Spirit put me in just the right place and that I was being well used. It was during one of these programs that I booked and met Dr. Tanous. After the taping, Ron and I had dinner with him, and the instant he saw us, he had a precognitive vision of our relationship.

Ron: Yes, he said it was the first time he stood in the presence of a couple that represented the relationship of the future.

Penny: I said, taken a little aback, "What do you mean? What a lovely thing to say." Then we talked about it. We had been students of the Alice Bailey teachings, channeled by the living master, Djwal Khul, and the Bailey teachings state that there are three kinds of relationships.

In the first, people are together because of Karma, a debt from the past that must now be paid.

In the second, people are opposites and come together to learn by trial and error, the qualities their mates have come to teach them.

And the third kind of relationship is called "the relationship of tomorrow." In this relationship the energy or attention that a couple gives each other is equal to the amount of energy that they give to something idealistic that they both support in the world. In other words, giving energy to some kind of heartfelt mission helps to hold the relationship in balance. A relationship may get out of balance when they give too much to each other or to this "other thing." So the dance of the "future couple" is really about learning perfect balance between the individual and the collective, and then all is right with the world. When I described this to him, he said, "Yes, that is exactly what I am talking about."

Stephen: What an interesting way of portraying it. Campbell would say that the couple needs "a third thing" that is neither you nor I, but this something we create between us. Now if you add Swedenborg's concept of "uses" to that, we see that there is a socially useful or world-benefitting dimension to the relationship, which almost guarantees that "third thing," and stops the couple from floating into solipsism, like Paolo and Francesca in the *Divine Comedy*. Perhaps this is the fulfillment or redemption of the simplistic "soul-mates" idea.

Ron: I must say that, when Penny and I came together, it was complete magic. There was none of the pedestrian attempts to make something fit. What she offered was to hold my spiritual focus as the centerpiece of our relationship and join with it. And this was the first relationship that I had ever had where my core was so honored.

Robin: I think for a couple to "make an angel," it needs to be that way. You have to respect, deeply, each other's spiritual path, or better yet, join it, to meld together this third thing.

Ron: Penny took charge, in a sense, of our outer worlds, helping to bring my spiritual work to the outside; and my work was focused on our inner worlds. I worked to nourish and nurture her inner world, because she was in the world of media, a distracting and destructive force for many people. But ultimately our work together has been to raise one another up, by continuing to kindle and rekindle the spiritual fire within us. And with this fire we continue to build our love and the work that springs from it.

Penny: Now, thirteen and a half years later, our vision remains consistent. We met at a Native American *Quodoshka* seminar and we knew we were to be together. Although it took me about ten days, it was an immediate knowing for Ron.

Ron: It took me about three seconds. She walked into the kitchen at the workshop seminar, into this huge, gorgeous, private home above Pepperdine University in Malibu, California. Something compelled me to turn around and as I saw her, a voice inside me said, "You're going to marry that woman!"

Stephen: Would you say something about Quodoshka?

Ron: It's based on Cherokee and other indigenous Native-American teachings, and it concerns sexual spirituality, in some ways like Tantra. Some of the exercises resemble kundalini yoga, regarding chakra breathing techniques and teaching how to direct pranic energy up through the spinal column.

Stephen: I'm once again impressed by the angel of synchronicity. What a perfect place to meet!

Ron: We were taught that every human being is responsible for his or her own sexuality. Our teacher, a shaman named Harley Swiftdeer (who is part Cherokee and part Irish), showed us how to awaken and move the sacred energies through our bodies, creating an incredibly beautiful and harmonious space and experience. In the early 1980s, I spent about eighteen months at the Berkeley Psychic Institute in California, working with many forms of psychic and healing energies, including kundalini, and I saw that Harley's teachings identified the same energies, with a slightly different emphasis in the systems.

Penny: I think that, so often, the initial energies that arise in the relationship are also what endure through the years; and while most of the people who came to that workshop were there for personal reasons, I (and I later learned, Ron also) attended because I was interested in trying to bring the information to others. I was interested in doing a video, and Ron was exploring the viability of bringing Harley to a center that Ron was affiliated with in northern California.

Stephen: That is such a needed thing. The Western tradition has exiled sexuality and placed it in opposition to the sacred, whereas they each clearly need each other. Modern sexuality has gotten very secular, as a consequence, and promiscuous for the sake of promiscuity. Along with that, then, it loses this exquisite zone of pleasure entered into as a sacrament.

Penny: So Ron and I both went to the workshop, ostensibly to serve a larger purpose, that being to bring this work to the world; and yet this intensely personal and wonderful thing happened to us! Over the years, we have continued to draw from this seemingly endless well to nourish and enhance the energetics in our relationship. We are both very supportive of each other personally, and we both help to nourish whatever the other is working on, whether it's new knowledge, a workshop, or media program, so that others may benefit. So it's still the same initial agenda that we signed on for. We do go through our changes, but there is a really wonderful collaborative thing we do together.

Robin: I can feel that. It's really true. You both support each other's work, love each other, and generate something extra between you.

I'm a hopeless romantic, and hence greedy for more about that moment of witnessing, and how you really knew that there was a soul-mate thing occurring. It has to be the most pivotal thing imaginable for our subject—and our readers.

Ron: I was in a relationship when I went to that fateful seminar. There were many beautiful aspects to that relationship, but the spiritual side was lacking; but when I met Penny, I realized that here was someone who was seeing me in my spiritual fullness, for who I was as a man, and in a sacred manner.

Stephen: She was doing that exquisitely dangerous thing men and women sometimes do to each other, called "really listening."

Ron: Not only was she listening, she was really there. She met me in a place where I have never been met before. I was struck by a thunderbolt! I came out of that five-day intensive seminar already having proclaimed my love; soon after I returned home and ended the relationship with my girlfriend.

Penny: Ron, being psychic, told me that whenever he was attracted to a woman, or she to him, he would clairvoyantly "see" how long his relationship would endure and what kind of relationship it was. But I know with me a very different kind of thing happened.

Ron: When I'd meet a woman, I'd tune in to my guidance and get a response of "ninety days" or "a great weekend" or even "two years." And so I was always living in a relationship that I knew had a clock ticking. But with Penny, I didn't get that at all. I got this image of a huge mansion, with all the windows on all the floors brightly lighted. I knew immediately that this relationship would take a lifetime of exploration. And in some ways, still, I feel we've just started.

Penny: My awakening to my inner voice and intuition began when when I was eight years old. It was an unforgettable experience. I asked what my life purpose was and was told that I was here to help communicate "unusual and God-ideas to large numbers of people." And as I grew older, I still felt very aligned with that. After I met Ron, we studied the Alice Bailey material with teachers Corinne McLaughlin and Gordon Davidson. When we learned about the purpose of the future New-Age couple, we both felt a deep harmony with this concept. I hadn't heard it expressed like that before. We still have problems and challenges, like other couples, but these deeper strands of commitment help us to maintain perspective.

When Ron and I met, we felt like we had deep old-soul connections. I saw at least two past-life experiences. One was Egyptian, and one was Native American. The Native American vision came to me when I was in meditation. I experienced the Egyptian vision as we left a Native American gallery in Sausalito, and I was so emotionally moved by seeing original R.C. Gorman paintings that I energetically slipped into the *Nagual* [a shamanic term for a state between the worlds]. Exiting the gallery, I looked into their window and to my amazement, I saw my own reflection, but I was dressed like an Egyptian! I turned and looked at Ron, and sure enough, he too, was dressed in Egyptian attire! The visionary experience lasted a few minutes and then left as quickly as it came. It was and still is one of the most remarkable experiences of my life. I didn't say anything about it for several hours, since I wanted to feel it fully, before discussing it; but when I began talking about it, much to my ecstatic surprise, Ron, being psychic, saw the energy move, moved with it, and saw the same thing! We each described each other to a tee. Here we were walking down a beautiful Sausalito street, arm in arm, energetically dressed in our Egyptian past lives, feeling like we had walked that way, arm and arm, centuries earlier.

Stephen: Interesting. At the very least, it's an imaginal identity, rising up and supplanting this one. As a therapist of some thirty years or so experience, I have heard of many instances like that; there might be a very interesting metaphysical explanation for it.

Ron: It felt very real to us, very tangible, and it also felt very old. Neither of us got wrapped up in the drama of that past life, since we didn't feel any sense of trauma or anything unfinished about it; but rather, the experience was a feeling of confirmation, that we had a very deep connection that was guiding us to trust and honor this present time together. Both of us live very much in the here and now.

Penny: Several days later, during meditation, I got the first and last syllable of an Egyptian name for Ron, which helped explain why it had been strangely difficult for me to remember and say his name.

In another vision during meditation, I saw our Native American lifetime, which was eerily verified. In my vision, Ron and I were shamans in the same tribe, and I was assisting him in a ceremony. We were high on a hill, on a star-filled night and the tipis below mirrored the stars, with their campfires sparkling. Ron was dancing around the fire, praying to the Great Spirit and asking for some protection and a blessing, and he was dressed in this incredible costume with feathers coming out all over his arms and head. I felt like I really saw it. (And I'm seeing it now, again, as I am telling you.) And when I told Ron about this, he said, "Do you want to see the feather costume?"

Penny: He told me that several years before some Native Americans serendipitously arrived at his home, knocked on his door, and said they were guided there by Spirit, to give him these spiritual gifts.

Ron: Three sacks full of fifty-year-old Ghost Dancer eagle feathers, all strung together, to be worn on the wrists and ankles; and two eagle feather hats.

Penny: And then he showed them to me, and they were like the ones I saw in my vision. In that vision, while he prayed and danced for the tribe, I was feeding the fire and helping to hold the energy of the ceremony. Contacting this past life material was a very momentous experience for us.

Stephen: When we have such experiences, we increase the texture of the relationship—out into the imaginal world. These are sheaths, layers, connections for the soul. And why shouldn't it be multidimensional and translucent?

Penny: As we began our relationship, I saw that our interaction was unlike any of my former models, unlike family and other experiences I've had. I began to wonder where it came from. It felt as though it were from my dream of what was possible in a relationship, from somewhere long ago. I know that sounds very mystical, but it actually felt like that.

Stephen: Such experiences seem to say that relationships in and of themselves are something so powerful that they transcend the normal bounds of time and space, and that we may do them over even, in new disguises.

Therapeutically, I know of many therapists whose work I respect, who do not hang out shingles as "past-life therapists," who take these things quite seriously when they come up: Edward C. Whitmont among them.

Penny: The Theosophists took transmigration for granted. True, they were inspired by Hindu and Buddhist metaphysics, but it's also there in Western esoteric lore.

Stephen: Once I asked Don Alberto Tacxo, a South American shaman, about whether he referred to past lives in his work. He said, "You don't need to go back and relive it, just watch how you're driving the car now. It's all there." It was an odd metaphor for him to use, since he comes from a zone without cars in the Andes of Ecuador, and I was mentally translating his Spanish, but I think I got it right. I think he meant "vehicle"—as in your body, and how you treat it.

Ron: That's exactly it. When I first psychically "read" somebody, I'd go inside and ask my Higher Self what that man or woman needs; and I often sense issues or lessons that a person is carrying with him or her from another life. But I don't go into that life, per se; I think that it is often a distraction—people get into the story and ignore the work they need to do in the now. The point of power is always in the present moment. I think that, when people go into the past, they are experiencing a story, and they often get caught up in the drama of that story. But I feel that the only place that one can heal is the present moment.

Stephen: I'm glad to hear you say that, because I believe it is largely true, although I have seen some very powerful "past-life" catharses with Roger Woolger, Morris Netherton, and Brian Weiss, and they feel very real. But I've also sometimes wondered if the high drama of the session was a distraction away from here and now.

Ron: Exactly. If you can come into the present, with everything that's here—this is the pivotal point where it's all happening.

Robin: There is something about relationship here that's very important. When I—with all my ghosts, little people, and stories—meet you with yours, it's quite a show. There's a lot going on. It is easy to get distracted, though, and to focus on this or that little dramatic sideshow, which isn't really the center-stage event. We bring such a lot to our encounters with the other.

Stephen: Which is why these ceremonies, these rituals we do, are helpful; because when we set aside time and make sacred space, those ghosts can dance, rather than just mill around—or even get in the way. The ritual lays the ground rules for the energy to move, to dance in.

Now the formal part of our discussion has come to an end, and the group drifts into side conversations that blend into the murmur of sounds in the Rainbow Room. The stardust in the decor twinkles with reflected light from the city far below. Soon food will arrive, and the guests' main business will move to earthly nourishment.

But we feel that in their words, and in these conversations with them—mutually invoking images and visions of relationship—a banquet has been served. We hope you enjoy it in the reading as much as we have in the partaking.

Shiva Ardhanari

EPILOGUE

AT THE INCEPTION OF THIS PROJECT, we looked at each other a little askance. What would this project do to our relationship? This was to prove a question with many parts, to which we now have some of the answers:

Would it bring out flaws in our own relationship? Yes.

Would it sensitize us to already sensitive issues between men and women? Yes.

Would it give us new ideas for working on our relationship? Yes!

Would it offer an occasion for healing—not all, but some of the wounds we carry? Decidedly, yes!

The fashioning of angels may be, above all other things, a work in progress; of course, so is life. The myths and models that serve us best are ones that allow for dynamic interplay, not a static "take" on this or that feature of life. To be sure, we need deep abiding values and stable underpinnings to our approaches to living and relating. We have tried to impart some sense of these, as we have followed our trail of story through different cultures and periods, although we are aware that these values also reside in the perennial philosophy, as well as in some deeply human common sense we carry: the ones closest to the bone, for this book, are respect for nature (our own *human nature* included); for children as well as animals, insects, plants; for the very elements of which our earth is made—all analogues of spiritual realities as well; and respect for the images and ideas that have nourished and sustained human beings for millennia—our symbolic apprehensions of the Divine—from Great Spirit to the little gods of landscape and hearth.

We affirm Joseph Campbell's dictum: a mythology should expand with the knowledge of the folk who hold it. So, let's move our mythic sensibilities beyond Descartes and Newton, and beyond the rigid orthodoxies that have plagued organized religion of whatever flavor for the last twenty or thirty centuries, at least. Among these, the first to go must be religious ethnocentrism, which insists that if your god does not look and feel like my god, yours is a false god. This is not to claim that all concepts of "god" are equivalent, but that, if more violence and intolerance has been enacted in the name of religion than any other single factor, then the new millennium requires a religious sensibility that is ecumenical, at the least, and broadly informed mythologically, at best. With this in mind, we can begin to grasp why *these* particular people, from *this* geographical and ethnic sector, worship the ineffable godhead in *this* way. This would be the opposite of the iconoclastic urge that has marked the last twenty centuries of "stony sleep," in Yeats' words, the need to break other people's religious forms to establish the primacy of our own.

Further, we see that neither gender may dictate rules or values to the other, but each has profound wisdom to receive from the other. (Religious traditions that denigrate either gender could be regarded as retrogressive and in need of education or evolution.) It seems to us, from our travels to sacred sites all over the world, that people need to be able to walk into a mosque or temple, visit a Ganesha shrine in India or a holy spring in Ireland, or even an archaeological site like the Parthenon and open their spirits with respect to the way God(ess) walks here. And, too, in a world that has truly "come of age," they should be received as holy pilgrims.

In these ways, spirituality opens itself to the changing times. Can serious spiritual practice now be brought out of the synagogues, churches, and temples, and into daily life, so those who "walk the walk" are as witnessed and respected as those who "talk the talk"? We are not suggesting that we should disband the collective forms of worship, but rather that we need to recognize how individuals—and couples, for that matter—who may profess very little orthodox belief, nonetheless are at labor in the vineyards of the Lord and gardening the Lady's own Earth. They express their spirituality through Swedenborg's "uses," by passing on the fire and the energy of life. Atheists too are sometimes profound humanitarians and carriers of a deep existential courage.

In our time, we are prone to a dangerous illusion: not that matter is reality, but that reality is not real. A consequence of this illusion is that we have littered our "unreal" environment with "unreal" garbage, and we are now facing the problem of cleaning up. Sam Keen, asked to name one of the most pressing issues of our time, replied simply: "Garbage!"[1] Garbage is discarded stuff, undifferentiated, unprocessed, unrecycled, untransformed. Like our arboreal primate relatives, we proceed through life casting behind us our leavings—unsorted trash, unfinished projects, unresolved life issues, abandoned relationships, worn-out loves, out-grown people. Contemporary world culture is founded upon the notion that, when we are through with something—when it no longer works for us—we can simply throw it away.

One of the valuable—indeed precious—lessons of our time is that we have begun to acknowledge that, for the preservation of life, there are times when a person needs support in leaving an abusive or inappropriate relationship. And there are times when a relationship simply does not continue: its work is done, its time is over. We need to develop our discrimination, to examine our associations carefully, to make considered judgments about when to leave and when to confirm a true commitment. How well does your angel fly?

Abusive marriages, codependent partners, obsessive and violent lovers, former spouses, partners, or friends whose life course has diverged from ours—these fall into our own long shadows, where they trail behind us like tin cans tied to the tail of a fleeing dog or to the rear bumper of the newlyweds' car—a noisy reminder of the karma, the legacy of the past, each has brought to the relationship and has worked out—or failed to work out. Every relationship creates an "angel"—but some may not be brought full-term. The question then is, "What happens to abandoned angels?" Are there cosmic singles clubs where holographic angelic potentials hover—or maybe descend on people like the ghost of an androgynous Eros, compelling them to unpremeditated acts in the name of love? Or does the idea of all true loves, whether actualizable by humans or not, endure, shining and archetypal?

We believe the principle of "recycling" works on psychospiritual as well as ecosocial levels. Old garbage is whatever we have not fully sorted out, recycled, and eventually transformed into new stuff for our lives. Still it stays with us—our wounds, our losses, our regrets. But these can also become the recycled material with which we build our futures, the gifts we bring to our renewed lives, shadow as well as light to give texture. As so many of our courageous interviewees—lovers all—have shown, it is not *despite* but *with* the shadow that we become real.

You who would become angel makers—our exploration has prompted us to urge one more thing of you: visualize your angel. Let him/her be colorful, and yet translucent—transmitting light, but also wearing a garment of shadow, with all those earthly ancestors, and totem animals, *genii loci*, little people. Don't deny your angel her beautiful tissue of scars, the wise council of his wounds. Don't neglect to add to this mix a flavor of feeling in all its hues and tones, history, stories, myths, areas of creative concern, art and music; and call upon the highest aspirations of which your soul is capable—those angels already formed whose energy you love and respect: Raphael, Michael, Gabriel, Uriel, and the lesser angels who watch over our little terrestrial causes. And above all, invite the Great Spirit to bless your union and watch over your steps.

If we all do this, pledging always our openness to more and more—whether we meet you here, or in that fragrant garden that lies just the other side of this world—we will hear in your presence a marvelous rustling of wings and see many winking eyes; see memory and feel music all about you; learn stories, exchange wise and merry laughter. For our angel will have met yours, where it was sitting alone, in Billy Collins' words, "in little gardens changing colors" or swinging "like children from the hinges of the spirit world, saying their name backwards and forwards" or flying "through God's body and com[ing] out singing." When that happens, we will have, as Swedenborg was fond of saying to the cleric who attended him before he died, "much to talk about"; and boredom, in the spirit of all its past transgressions, will have gone straight to hell.

But, fortunately, we don't have to wait until then, for already, angelhood beckons. In your daily life, the way is being paved. Nourish it with some of the exercises we recommend in the following section, and follow the suggestions of some of our interviewees in the preceding chapter: Help each other to work on the shadow, make your relationship the measuring stick for your successes in other departments, and allow it to nourish and inspire those other aspects. So now, working together or in your separate domains, bring in and strengthen the sense of your partnership as a spiritual path. As you do this, you will create an indefinable but sweet atmosphere around you that others will feel—especially animals, children, and other lovers—and to be in your presence will undoubtedly cause pleasure. So if we were to visit each others' home or to sit in the same hot tub, stories, laughter, mutual appreciation, and an increasing depth of connectedness would develop, and we would all come away richer in some sense—having inspired and been inspired, having stretched others and been stretched ourselves, and grown spiritually in the process. In this way, the work of eternity begins here and now.

i.
Your silence curves
around my words
like folded wings
My silence fits itself
within the spaces
of your speaking.

ii.
In our green times
we know ourselves to be a brimming bowl
But in a guarded season
we walk chill halls
Lips that have often kissed
beak-sharpened now, and menacing. . . .

iii.
At last that scintillant veil
of sweet illusion
what you wished me to be
what I so needed you to be
has frayed, torn,
blown loose in living wind.

Groping toward ourselves
through those last shrouded phantoms
we recognize each other again
for the first time:
a seam unraveling
the velvet plush worn thin in places
One brilliant button eye now lost
reveals what it concealed: the merely human eye
a bit crinkled about the lids,
needing glasses and learning to see in the heart.

So we start again
honoring one another's tattered humanity
foolhardy courage
outrageous humor
impossible persistence of vision

Is it possible that from our patchwork lives
we birth one radiant winged being?

iv.
A storm of rising
drums our unique and double-helixed hearts
Now we fall out at last into earth
beyond sun and moon and shouting stars
our multifoliate wings breasting space with one rhythm
as heaven inbreathes us.

How long, love, and how often—
May I have this dance?[2]

EXPERIENTIAL EXERCISES[1]

THIS SECTION CONTAINS "EXPERIENTIAL" EXERCISES developed from the themes of this book. For these exercises, we suggest that you set apart a separate time and space in which to do them; make a special or "sacred" boundary around them, to contain fully the elements that invite powerful self-encounter. While the exercises are for the most part designed for two participants, many can be done by one person at a time. Be sure that you and your partner understand the nature of experiential exercises, and both are ready to do them. Here we caution you and warmly encourage you: these exercises, like homeopathy, can "aggravate" on the way to healing. Some issues once raised may need to be worked through with professional help or with a neutral third presence, a "fair witness" who helps you keep things fair and moving along.

What is important is that you enter these exercises with the expectation that you could achieve something new, a genuine transformation, and work towards an outcome characterized by both greater love and greater understanding between you. Both are required.

Some exercises evoke images of "gods," "goddesses," "angels," or "demons." If thinking in these terms is discomforting for you, feel free to conceptualize these figures in some way that is more acceptable. Perhaps you prefer to think of them as energy complexes, or poetic metaphors that can help mobilize your imagination. Approach this work with an attitude of serious playfulness; remember to bring along your sense of adventure.

Like riddles or koans that change you in the answering, experiential exercises invite you into a self-learning experience. They are not unlike real-life situations—adventures or travels undertaken together or projects such as marriage and raising children—they help to show us who we are. And the good side is that self-knowledge gained in such exercises models real-life situations, and those, if the mystic speaks truly, model a life in the spirit as yet unimaginable to us. In effect, all these experiences, integrated in the service of the Spirit, lead one up a developmental ladder toward angel-making.

These exercises may be done neatly integrated between the readings of chapters and are labeled accordingly (with the number of the chapter they best go *after*). They require mostly two people and that "sacred space" where you are not likely to be interrupted. Some of the exercises would benefit from the following tools: a tape recorder and fresh tapes, as much as you might need; pen or pencil, paper, journals, notebooks, unlined paper and magic markers, and, for some, where suggested, modeling clay. Some exercises invite you to bring or construct personal talismans or shrines. For these, it is good to bring symbolic objects that have meaning—a pebble from a particular idyllic beach, a feather from an auspicious raven who squawked warning that day—you get the idea. In more complex exercises, such as making a family shrine, suggestions for materials are put into the exercises.

Some of the exercises require you to divide yourselves into "journeyer" and "helper." That means you decide who would like to be the experiencer, and thus cared for, protected, encouraged; or a helper, whose role is to see that the journeyer is both protected and encouraged to explore the suggested exercise to its limits. Here we encourage noncoercive directing and a simple witnessing of the other person's process, or just gentle, intelligent, and positive suggestions that move the process along. The helper may be asked to do things such as control the environment—control or provide the heat, light, seclusion, or handle the tapes and recorders if desired—or to function as a stenographer for the journeyer. After the process is over, the helper should say something like, "I am so moved and impressed to be the witness of your journey/process." The journeyer may respond with something like: "You were really there for me when I needed you. You are my guide in two worlds. Thank you!"

Remember: throughout these exercises, creative disobedience is fully expected, as part of the formula. Please forgive us for what may seem like unevenness in the exercises; we know that some seem solemn and some silly—just like life in its alternating shadings. We have found, though, that sometimes silly can become solemn, and simple exercises or rituals often precipitate complex and profound insights. Wherever our suggested words seem unsuitable for you, use your own. While many of the exercises are predicated for man-woman couples, we feel they can be enjoyed and beneficial to gay couples; especially those who are in touch with their contrasexual little people within. It can also be useful for these couples to identify archetypal masculine and feminine energies inside each other and use those to role-play or connect with gender-specific instructions.

——————— PRIMORDIAL ONENESS ———————

Chapter One

This exercise requires a large bathtub, hot tub, or flotation tank, privacy, and a battery-operated tape recorder. Each partner will experience the role of the infant being born, as well as that of the "helper" or facilitator. The journeyer should feel free to be like an infant: helpless, needing total attention. The helper handles all details, making sure everything is in place, doing whatever is needed with the tape, and fielding any distractions. The helper also reads, slowly and thoughtfully, the instructions suggested below:

Helper: I am totally devoted to your needs. I will do what I can to satisfy them. Please relax and yield yourself totally to the experience. . . . (generic relaxation instructions if desired). [Room is dimly lit. Candles and incense are appropriate.]

Journeyer: [Gets into the tub, with the water at a temperature that can be comfortably tolerated for a half-hour. The journeyer closes his or her eyes and begins to journey.]

Helper: Take as much time as you need to answer [spaces out questions evenly]. Imagine yourself in the place before you were born, or even in mother's womb. What is it like? Are you comfortable? How do you feel? Under these circumstances, how do you know who you are? Is there anyone with you? What do you need, if anything?

Now you are in mother's womb. [Repeat the questions as above.]

Now you are being born. [Repeat the questions above, but add]: Is your birth easy or hard? How do you feel being out of the womb?

Now you are a tiny infant, just born. [Repeat the questions above, but add]: How does it feel to be separated from mother? Do you still feel connected to her when she is away? Is father there? When does he come in, and what is your connection with him like?

Now you are a child growing up. . . . [Explore this process, especially the landmark I-thou relationships.] Who are your significant others?

Now you are a young adult entering into your first sexual relationships and courtships. Do these nourish you and help you grow, or do they frighten or frustrate you in some way? Why and how? If there are problems, do you get to talk them over with someone or not?

Bring yourself gradually back to the present; come back and open your eyes. Do it at a rate that feels comfortable to you.

Journeyer: [He or she thanks the helper for this loving service and attention, then says to the helper]: "All this I bring to you and to our relationship. . . .

Helper: [He or she responds, and a dialogue ensues that concludes the first session.]

After a break, come back and exchange roles, with the journeyer now being the helper. If you can, after the second person is fully processed, have an open dialogue between the two of you about what you have learned about yourselves and your relationship.

PRIMORDIAL PARTNERS

Chapter Two

This exercise requires a quiet, private space; a tape recorder; magic markers; and animal talismans. The helper reads the following instructions, or a third person may assist, while the journeyer and helper lie down comfortably. After each exercise, emerge, draw or write something that captures the exchange. Go back in. When the process is done, share with your partner what you experienced, drew, or wrote about.

(1) Roots: Of all the minerals on earth, pick one—metal, crystal, stone, even earth—with which you resonate. Explore its qualities. What do you know of the origins of this mineral? What are its uses?

(2) Stem: Of all the vegetable manifestations on earth, pick one—a tree, shrub, or lichen. Imagine the being of this life form: how does it gather sustenance, what is its purpose, how does it reproduce or flower?

(3) Branches: Pick an animal that has been special for you: you may feel it in your body, kinesthetically, hear its sound or voice, or simply "feel" it. What are the habits, what the "ecological niche" of this animal? What are its powers or special appeal?

Decide what chakra this animal might reside in within you and what its effect on you might be. If you have more than one animal that expresses and embodies your power, assign each a different level in your energy field or chakras. Bring together the animals periodically for a sharing or "parliament," or medicine circle of the animals (see Stephen Gallegos, chapter 2).

You may want to continue to explore your relationship with your animal: collect images, lore, or symbols that pertain to this animal or its habitat. Put them in a medicine bundle or shrine (see suggestions for creating a shrine in "Making Images Together," page 335.

Couples Ecology: Share the result of your quest for affiliations in nature with your partner. Learn about the other's ideal habitat, and help him or her create, encounter, and explore it. Help research your partner's totem pole. Can you think of a drawing or a poem that expresses the bringing together of you and your symbolic energies from nature? Work on this, possibly over time. Do you and your partner have allies (mineral, vegetable, animal) in common? Try to make your partner's affiliations your own, like a part of the family.

You may want to develop a family totem pole: this can be described verbally in your journals, become a totem poem, or be simply diagramed or take form as a drawing you do together. The more adventurous may want to try a sculpture in clay or some other material.[2]

---------------- DIVINE AFFILIATIONS ----------------

Chapter Three

Variation One: Think of Greek mythology, the panoply of gods and goddesses; add to it, if you know enough, Hindu mythology, African, North American mythology. From this panoply of gods and goddesses, who especially seems to favor you? Who do you study or venerate for her/his qualities?

Who is your contrasexual god/goddess? Imagine how you might best serve him or her. Think of offerings or ways of pleasing this divine figure. What benefits does she or he bestow on you? Which of the gifts for which this goddess/god is known are you able to receive? Which have you yet not been able to receive?

What about antipathies: is there any god or goddess that seems particularly dangerous or inimical to you? Try to understand why. Is there any ritual of propitiation you could devise?

Share some of this with your partner, and listen to his or her divine affiliations. If your partner has such affiliations, try to understand more about that divine figure. How does it play a part in your partner's life?

Variation Two, A: Who are the angels with whom you most resonate? Michael, the warrior; Raphael, the healer and companion; Gabriel, the messenger and bringer of light; Samael, guide to mysteries; or others? Do you have a personal angel? Look again at the story of Tobias (chapter three). At a difficult crossroad, choice, point, or trauma, how might you have received guidance? Can you think of any instances where an angel might have made a decisive difference in your life?

Make a shrine, and enact a ritual of appreciation for this angel (again, see "Making Images Together"). Think of ways you might honor her or him in your daily life. Express to this angel that you are open to guidance from him or her, and ask for protection in any special endeavors or problems you may face.

Variation Two, B: Now try to get a sense of any demons that may dog your steps. Where do you feel mired or blocked, rageful, paranoid? How do your personal demons undermine you, trick or devalue you? How could you prepare yourself better for encounters with this personal demon? What resources could you draw on? Remember that "demons" often conceal or block sources of energy within you. Does the demon have any redeeming qualities or energy that you could reclaim? Does your demon serve a purpose? If so, what and how does he or she perpetuate that purpose? And lastly, how could your angel make a difference in your ability to integrate, utilize, overcome, counteract, or banish your demon?

IMAGINARY COMPANIONS

Chapter Four

Think back to when you were a child, three to seven years old. Did you have any imaginary companions? If so, what were they like? If you can't identify them at first, think of your stuffed animals or pets. Could a companion be hiding in humble guise for you? Give them some attention now. How would it feel to meet the companion as an adult? Would they still be helpful? Does their role have currency for you, or was it only appropriate at a certain time in your life? If you have a dialogue with your imaginary companion, write it down.

If you feel comfortable and would like to develop your companion further, share him or her with your partner. Listen to your partner's imaginary companion. Now, what would they have to say to each other? Imagine your imaginary companions meeting in a secret garden. What whispered conversations might they have, what secrets would they share? Write these down as if they were actual dialogues. Read them over, together, several days later. What do they tell you about your psyche, about your creative powers?

ANIMA AND ANIMUS

Chapter Four

Imagine yourself as having been born of the other gender. What kind of person would you be? Try to describe or inventory your characteristics as completely as possible. What would you do in this situation or that situation?

Share this image with your partner. Imagine what it would be like to be same-sex friends with your partner. Listen to his or her anima/animus. How well would you get along with this person?

Now imagine that this person has another contrasexual figure—your own gender. What would the anima of your animus or the animus of your anima be like?

Again, share this with your partner. Watch for each other's personal mythology and creative life in this exercise.

SOUL MATES

Chapter Five

Variation One: If you have always had a longing for a soul mate, imagine what that person would be like. What kind of values and attitudes might your soul mate have? What sorts of talents and abilities? What sorts of shortcomings? What would your soul mate do for you, and what would he or she need from you? Who in your life so far has come the closest to this ideal?

Create an ideal adventure or situation that you might encounter with your soul mate. How would you go through it together? What resources and capabilities might each of you bring to the encounter?

Variation Two: If you are in a committed relationship already with a soul mate, how could both of you work to fine-tune the process. Explore your intuitive connection with each other, your communication skills, your ability to share projects, or pool your energies to accomplish things in the world. What similarities to yourself do you require of your soul mate? Where is it acceptable to have differences—even necessary for a kind of leaven to the relationship?

DAEMON LOVER

Chapter Six

Try to get a sense of where you have not tamed your own wildness. Where would you look for ways to gratify this wildness that are not available to you now?

Make an inventory of some of your own "shadow" characteristics: where do you tend to take chances, play fast and loose, forget your commitments? Now imagine a contrasexual version of this figure, filled with energy, alluring; how would you handle him or her?

If you have already had a relationship like this, try to spend some time reflecting upon it. What was the vulnerability in yourself that made you accessible to such a person? What did he or she see in you? What was this person's agenda? What did you see in him or her? If the relationship was hard to terminate, try to analyze why. How is your vision and your perception different now?

WILD THINGS

Chapter Seven

Each person should do this exercise alone, before deciding to share together what you have received.

(1) Think of Maurice Sendak's book *Where the Wild Things Are*. You are Max, the little boy who puts on his wolf suit and goes to a world of wildness. In that world are friends and enemies; chart your encounters with several of each. Construct the world with plenty of unsuspected places and encounters with wildness. Write it down and/or draw it; act it out in a sandbox. Then decide how or whether to share

your worlds with your partner. If you do, play out an adventure in each other's fantasy world. Invent a character (for example, a schoolteacher, cowboy, or a ghost) that fits.

(2) You are going to be initiated by a shaman in the region of the Hudson Bay. Imagine the village, the shaman. The shaman extracts your soul from your body, and you go on a journey. Where do you go? Do you meet any powers of the spirit world? Do some befriend you? Are some inimical? What powers, helping spirits, or animal guides accompany you? What illnesses might you be able to heal thereafter?

(3) Imagine yourself as a character of the opposite sex. You have just taken a "demon-lover." What kind of creature or being might this be? What are its bad sides like, and what are its magical strengths? Now, what would it be like if you met this lover as yourself? Are there parts of you in him or her? Do you conflict? How would you describe your conflict?

—————————— FAIR FIGHTING ——————————

Chapter Seven

All couples need, at times, to be able to disagree, to argue, and to work through differences. Done in a healthy manner, such disagreements can lead to greater understanding, deeper empathy, compassion, and acceptance of the other's position—perhaps some kind of resolution or compromise, a win-win situation. On the other hand, the situation can end with both parties angry and estranged, with no further comprehension of what went on or how future conflagrations could be avoided (lose-lose). This kind of conflict does indeed keep happening until estrangement, separation, or divorce supervenes. Fair fighting provides us with guidelines that can help us break out of "no-exit," repeating loops of destructive behavior and opens up our relationships to broader perspectives and renewed growth together.

Here are some rules of fair fighting:

(1) Generally commit yourself to an attitude of "mindfulness practice," which includes self-monitoring and attending to the environment and the needs of the partner. Decide whether to have a fair witness or mediator, or whether you do this alone. (If the latter, the mindfulness practice must go up several notches, as there are no outside checks on volatility or escalation.)

(2) As part of this practice, monitor your own tone of voice and body language as well as what you are saying. Have a rule that either one can make a "T" (for time out), without question or reproach, to allow you both to withdraw and become calmer when necessary. (On the other hand, try not to break contact with issues unresolved or feelings still wounded.)

(3) Be willing to resume again, as if afresh. But don't come back until you have tried to grasp the other person's perspective or seen some new angle. Share this with your partner, and listen to her or his insight.

(4) Avoid name-calling, threats, ultimatums, or other forms of provocation. These are always counterproductive; not only do they set the dialogue back, but they build resentment and arousal to intolerable levels. Try to not "hit below the belt."

(5) Do not use therapeutic or other insights gained in counseling or personal work to attack the other person. (This is extremely important, because it is a nasty trick of the shadow side to turn against us our genuine insight and healthy self-awareness of our own wounds and our deepest self-reflections.)

(6) Try to begin statements with "I feel" or "It seems to me that. . . ." Be aware that you are offering to the other person a worldview that is not necessarily (!) his or hers. Give your partner a chance to respond to each of your "feeling" statements with his or her own feelings. When the other shows a genuine feeling that now seems more comprehensible to you—perhaps because of the way it is expressed—acknowledge your new insight.

(7) Replies should also be feeling or conditional statements, so as not to place non-negotiable issues on the table. Listen attentively to what the other person says, and then say, "I feel different—let me explain. . . ." or "This is how it has seemed to me. . . ."

(8) Avoid avalanches of such feelings or resentments; try to parse them out into manageable or negotiable units. (Reproaches given in one installment leave the other person feeling attacked and or undermined.) Try to work on one or two resentments at a time.

(9) Realize that the psychology of perception indicates that two people scarcely ever perceive the same event in the same way. (Here is where the subjective factor—our gender, state of emotional arousal, history, complexes, needs and desires, expectations—always configures and bends our experience of reality.)

(10) Beware of hidden complexes. These are like land mines in the relationship. They are often "made" out of your own unexamined problems and complexes in juxtaposition with those of the other's. The alchemy of all this together makes a truly daemongelic mix. Beware of acting-out trance-like dramas or of being stuck or caught in a whirlpool (where you have the feeling of going around and around, but you're sinking instead of rising above it).

(11) If you reach impasse as in (10) above, this might be a time for constructive withdrawal: journal writing, clay modeling, or drawing images of your feelings, and then coming back again. Have either of you had any dreams that might touch on this problem? Be willing to discuss your feelings with your partner in an open and insightful (but nonjudgmental) way.

    If these techniques have not brought you noticeably closer to resolution, consider using a fair witness, such as a therapist or other neutral helper.

(12) Be willing to consider bringing up in a calm situation all of the points raised in a volatile one, and going over them point by point. Try to discuss these problems again, seeing them from as many angles as possible.

If you identify "complexes," typical "push button" situations or areas of controversy, try to avoid raising them where there are other exigencies, such as a social occasion or a schedule crunch, that make you more volatile and "stupid."

Summary of Exercise

Try to imagine what it is like to be "sparring partners" in boxing or wrestling. There must be rules such as "No biting or gouging, no hitting below the belt; we have five rounds," etc. The goal is not to annihilate or "blow away" the other person—then there would be no sparring partner. Done within the rules, this exercise develops strength and skill mutually, by ritual combat and interaction. Kittens and puppies do this effortlessly; and children and adults can also do this, endlessly, with each other. Strangely, to do it as adults we seem to need permission. Consider that permission granted.[3]

THE WASTELAND

Chapter Eight

Try to get a sense of where the Wasteland operates in your life. What tasks or chores do you find yourself neglecting or running away from? Where in you does it feel like the desert lies? What does it need or require to bloom or flower?

Think of activities, people or energy that is the opposite of this Wasteland—that "greens" the Wasteland for you. Where is your access to this energy blocked? How could you bring moisture, warmth, color, flowering to the Wasteland?

On a psychological level, where is there an attitude or emotional state that keeps things dry and wasted? (Look specifically to anger, depression, and skepticism.) What about areas in your relationship? What keeps things dry, frozen, or barren? Where could you bring in the redemptive elements of moisture and energy?

Share with your partner how he or she helps or could help you revitalize the Wasteland. Find projects to do together that could help you green the Wasteland all about.

COURTLY LANGUAGE

Chapter Nine

This exercise requires some basic equipment: a bowl of water, four ceremonial candles, and several tokens that speak of the archetype of the opposite gender for each of you. Put them on a table in front of you.

Sit silently. Each of you dips a hand in the bowl of water and wipes it across your lips. Say, "I cleanse my mouth of the language of the marketplace, of everyday, and vow to speak a language of the heart. I seek to speak my truth in all its essential beauty."

Next, light the ceremonial candles. Say, "These candles witness the language of love that we speak to each other. Let them remind us to keep our hearts warm."

Think of your partner as someone deserving of the utmost respect—as royalty or an ambassador from a foreign country. You are seated ceremonially with this person before an assemblage of peers. You are trying to notice everything about him or her. How now would you address this person? Allow her or him to respond (as if this person were following the same directions). Treat your partner as a living incarnation of the opposite gender, and feel as if all men and women were present witnessing what you say to him or her.

Record your conversations in your own "Book of Courtly Love," and read them to each other from time to time. These may become especially important in moments of adversity or estrangement. Keep the atmosphere free from any sarcasm or rebuke: simply read the words you spoke to each other. (Remember the key technique: issues that arise between you in moments of high emotion—especially anger—should not be allowed to lie until the next blowup, but should be worked on or worked through in times of objectivity and clarity. This exercise can be one of them.)

REDEEMING THE WASTELAND

Chapter Nine

Variation One: [This can be done individually or with the helper/journeyer model described in the first exercise.] Using the instructions for going into a light trance, set yourself on a Grail quest. Begin in the Wasteland (see the previous exercise). What dangers or difficulties might you encounter? What allies or secret helpers could come along to assist you? Imagine the Fisher King and the approach to the Grail Castle. Now direct this question to yourself: "What ails you?"

Next, allow yourself to imagine that you have completed the Grail quest. Yours is the power to restore the kingdom. Imagine how this might go—what problems would you address first? Visualize yourself greening the Wasteland, whatever that would involve in the way your Wasteland is made. When you are done, ask yourself: "Whom does this serve?"

Record the dialogue in a journal, along with the answers you receive.

Variation Two: Sit with your partner, helper to journeyer, and ask him or her to share a Wasteland experience with you. How has this Wasteland operated in your partner's life? Ask your partner, "What ails you?" Make an earnest inquiry into helping him or her deal with the Wasteland/illness in her or his life. Imagine now the symbol of the Grail, and how it might touch and transform these problems. Allow the image of the Grail to talk to you. What does it say?

SACRED SEXUALITY
(FOR CONSENTING ADULTS ONLY)

Chapter Ten

Plan a weekend or other uncluttered time with your beloved. Assemble together personally meaningful things: pictures, talismans, journals to read to each other and write in, tape recorders, if you wish, to record oral tradition—pillow talk, for example, whispered twilit conversations, or storytelling about each of your childhoods—special liqueurs or intoxicants allowed to adults, costumes or sex toys, if such is your proclivity. (In these latter two categories, be sure that *both* of you are comfortable with whatever is brought.)

Beforehand, look through some love poetry of your choice and make selections. Memorize these or photocopy (or hand copy, a good way to memorize) them for use in the love ritual. You could also be prepared to play music for each other or with each other. Bring also massage oils and perfumes, and be prepared to anoint—and be anointed—with skill and languor. It is helpful, but not obligatory, to have a hot tub, or large bathtub on hand, or be in an outdoor setting that is sequestered enough for nudity.

Feeding each other is also a delightful and symbolic practice, so have some tidbits on hand—the grape is associated with Eros—perhaps a little wine, liqueur, or grape juice, if you prefer. Larger ceremonial meals could also be included in such an event, depending upon how long you wish to prolong the delights.

An important preparation might be to study a little Tantra (the sacred sexuality of India) or Qi Gong (the energy system of China) with their skills of "withholding" for the male. An especially important book in this regard is *Earth Honoring: Toward a New Male Sexuality* by Robert Lawlor. Some of the books by Mantak Chia are also useful; and *Our Bodies, Ourselves* (specifically for women) by Ruth Bell and others.[4] These studies help men and women learn to experience sexual excitement as energy in the body, learn to breathe with it; they can help women to learn the art of multiple orgasms while withholding some of the energy, and men to learn the art of control—that is, to allow excitement to build without ejaculation or to have orgasm without ejaculation, a more subtle level of attainment.

Greet each other ceremonially as "beloved," or an equivalent of your choice. Try throughout the weekend to speak in a courtly, polite manner. Begin with a ritualized form of address in which you assure the beloved that you have great love and respect for him or her; and that this ritual, done together over the weekend, is done for each other, for the sake of your angel, the "third thing" in becoming between you, for the world of nature, for the world of humans (with its gender discords and need for healing), and as a sacrament to the spiritual world.

You may also honor your ancestors, telling them that you carry their seed and wish to bring forth earthly (or if not) spiritual children. If your purpose is conception, ask your personal guides for protection and angels to maintain order in the jostle of little souls swarming around the birth couple. (This is just how it is described in the Tibetan Book of the Dead, at the moment of rebirth.) You send forth a prayer that the right child/children will come to you, will be souls who are right for this lineage, this time and place, and that you can learn and love together.

If your goal is decidedly not physical procreation, you can state that preference in the ritual, saying that you are using these precautions and do not wish for the conception of a child to come now; but that you are open to spirit "children" being born between you, new creative ideas, new ways of relationship, or that "third thing" we have been discussing. You wish the biological energy thus to feed the spiritual and the celestial, to be gateways to the Divine. You affirm that you do this by mutual consent before the Great Spirit and to serve the good of all levels. You further invite angelic beings, whose right and proper place in the divine order is to dance with you in lovemaking, the Shiva and Shakti energies, or Krishna and Radha, to dance with you as the physical act is performed. In this way, the physical stokes the soul fire, and it reaches higher toward "heaven" or, in Swedenborg's language, "creates a heaven."

You intersperse journal reading and writing with episodes of sacred sexuality: eating together, reading and discussing, walking, or bathing. If a hot tub or large tub is available, you get in together, bathe and soothe each other, and exchange stories—say, of what it might have been like to be in the womb (see earlier exercies) for each of you.

When the time you have had together is drawing to a close, dedicate all to your angel, and resolve to bring this energy to your "third thing." (See the interviews with Alex and Allyson Grey and with Penny Price and Ron Lavin, in chapter ten, for specific ideas on how a couple does this.)

GENERAL EXERCISES

The Inner Child

Recall an important time in your childhood in as much detail as you can, and write about the child who experienced it. Specify your sensitivities, fears, resentments, but also your secret delights. Now each present your child to each other. Imagine them meeting. Then construct an adventure for them to have together that reveals something about the other to each of you. (You might set your adventure in a tree-house, on a river, on a mountain, or in a foreign country.)

Animals and Your Chakras (after Stephen Gallegos)

"Scan" your chakras: start with one and end at seven.[5] Stay long enough at each chakra for an animal to appear. When you have discovered an animal for each chakra, bring them together in a parliament. Notice where your animals meet, and what each contributes to the meeting. For a second installment, share your animals with your partner, and listen to theirs; now allow the animals to advise, heal, or give information to each other.

Talismans

Stephen and Robin were each given miniature crystal balls at a special conference that involved myth and ceremony. Each dedicated the little talisman to being a light that would shine when they felt the most despairing, the angriest, most cut-off, or just out of sorts with the other. The balls were both placed in the house-hold shrine (in a little bird's nest with other objects in it, symbolic of the home nest). Each gave the little (marble-sized) crystal ball to the other, with an expla-nation of what it meant, and the other put it in the shrine, with acknowledg-ments. You can use any object as your talisman. We used crystal balls to help us see in times of darkness.

The Grail Questions

Ask these questions about a significant activity or issue, even a wound or something painful that concerns both you and your beloved.
> "Whom does it serve?"
> "What ails you?"
> "How can I help?"

Making Music Together

Find two musical instruments, or one musical instrument and use your voice as the second. (If one of you is a musical virtuoso, find an instrument with which you are less familiar.) Sit down together and each declare his or her intention to make something beautiful together that teaches you about the other.

Variation One: Person one sets up a drone, or fairly mechanical beat or repetitive syncopated rhythm for several minutes, keeping relaxed and comfortable. Person two enters the musical space respectfully, mimicing or directly responding to the on-going work of the first, then gradually departing, then returning, taking larger mu-sical risks, and returning.

Variation Two: Person two repeats the steps described above for person one.

Variation Three: This is the same as one and two, but roles of rhythm section and soloist are exchanged.

Variation Four: This is the same as the patterns described above, but it uses a capella singing only.

Variation Five: Combine Variations One through Three above with singing woven in somewhere along the line.

Variation Six: Play with other musicians, but ask permission to introduce a theme with just the two of you. The other musicians will come in improvisationally, as the spirit moves them. But then they drop out, either one by one, or all together, and leave the two of you to finish the theme.

Making Images Together (Chapter Ten)

This involves drawing/painting/sculpting/assembling. Choose media with which both partners feel comfortable—or which are new to both of you, if possible. Embark with a sense of free play: Whatever your final product looks like, you should have fun experimenting together; and you will certainly learn things about yourselves. See a photograph of the Larsen shrine in the appendix.

Assemble your materials: if you already engage in an artistic endeavor, you will have preferences. Otherwise, we suggest you start with poster paints, oil crayons, or any type of modeling clay.[6] You will need drawing paper or illustration board (choose surfaces you like to touch, papers thick enough to survive water or vigorous work); and clean rags or paper towels; water in several containers; brushes, if appropriate; glue (a matte polymer like ModPodge is good); and a collection of fabrics or interesting papers.

Choose a place where the light is pleasant and sufficient, and where messes are not an issue or can be kept under control. A sheet of plastic can protect a table or rug; scraps of thin plywood make good work surfaces. Set aside three-to-four hours of time if possible, and prepare to let yourselves get lost in your creative project.

Drawing or painting, like journaling, can be integrated into most of the exercises we have suggested; so too sculpting in clay, which carries you into the third dimension and allows you to dig in with your hands and fingers, to get really physical. Many people who have never tried to sculp and who are unhappy with their previous experiences in drawing or painting are surprised to discover that they can model quite satisfactory shapes more easily than they can draw them. In any case, remember that this is not a test, but an adventure in exploring your own inner country in company with someone you love!

Collage is a way of using cut-out or torn-out images from many sources, including your own and family photographs, as well as papers (try scraps—or photocopies of scraps—from old letters, recorded dreams, concert programs), fabrics, or natural materials like leaves or grasses, to create evocative images. Collages can combine bits of images and objects that are meaningful to you and to your partner, in the intuitive and surprising way of dreams. The important thing here is that the materials you choose have significance with reference to the work you are doing on your self and your relationship; again, let the exercises work for you, dropping suggestive hints into your creative unconscious.

Assemblages simply carry this process into three dimensions, where you may include your own drawings and sculptures with tokens and memorabilia. These constructions can also be made as personal or family shrines.

A shrine is a device for remembering what is important: your inner life, your journey together, your teachers, guides, family, ancestors. . . . You might create several little shrines with different themes: one for both your childhoods' inner worlds; one for a place you both love, or an imagined place you would love to share; a shrine for your animal guides; a shrine for the angel you are making together.

Shrines can be made in many ways. You might simply set aside a section of a shelf, cabinet surface, or window ledge where you place those special objects and images that help you to center yourself, such as a candle or flowers. The creation of a family shrine can encompass all members, including the children (who will love making their contributions); if a grandparent lives with you, ask for something he or she feels comfortable adding.

Shrines are often made in little boxes. Simple cardboard will do and can be made beautiful with interesting papers and fabrics. If you prefer something more durable, try a drawer from a discarded cabinet: the wood itself is sometimes quite handsome. An old picture frame fitted over a small box works nicely. What you and your partner choose to put into it is what makes your shrine magical.

The Little God of Circumstances

Try to identify unexpected coincidences and the "tricks" of destiny, as they worked in bringing you together with your beloved. Think of how—when you weren't trying at all—things happened. Enumerate the circumstances—share them. Make a statue, drawing, or shrine to honor the "little god of circumstances," the trickster.

The Shadow of the Relationship

Enter this exercise soberly and thoughtfully. Try to see where each of you casts a shadow, by enumerating three qualities you think belong to your shadow. Listen to each other's recitation respectfully and nonjudgmentally.

Then, each of you retires with a notebook or drawing pad. Enumerate three qualities of the shadow you might cast as a couple. For example, you are social luminaries in your community; have you made anyone feel unwanted or ostracized? You are very involved in each other; do your children or other people have trouble getting your attention?

Compare your answers thoughtfully, and then say to your angel: "What ails you, uncle?" "How can I help?"

The Fashioning of Angels

Sit with your partner in a sacred space; each of you has a seat or a cushion, with a third left empty for the angel. Invite the angel to be with you.

Sit for a while in silence. Then ask the following questions: "How is your health?" "What do you need?" "Can we do something together that will make your life better?" and lastly, ask, "What can you tell us that will make our lives better and make your own energy to flourish in the coming times—months, years, decades?"

Variation for Two or More Angels

Do the above exercise simultaneously with two, three, or four couples. Then, after a break or refreshment, come together as a group and share what you discovered about each of your angels in becoming.

Set aside a protected time and place; invite both of your spirit guides, or higher selves, to preside over the exercises so that they are occasions for learning.

(1) Angelodaemonic: Draw a small circle around yourself, outside of which you may not go during this exercise. Allow yourself, within this sacred enclosure, to become daemonic. What vexes, irritates you, sets you off? In what ways do you "gnaw a bone"—stay with a negative state or obsession, refusing to release it? How do you vent your paranoia, blame, rage?

Then, carefully dissociate yourself from that negativity, and imagine your circle washed in a sacred light. Dissolve the boundary and come forth. Write in your journal.

Do the exercise with a partner, witnessing as helper. Then reverse roles.

Now, inquire together, each working as a "co-counselor" for the other. What power or potential resource might lie behind this anger? How could you mine it? What does it serve?

If anything in the situation seems especially intransigent, difficult, or dark, work it through with a therapist or doctor.

APPENDIX

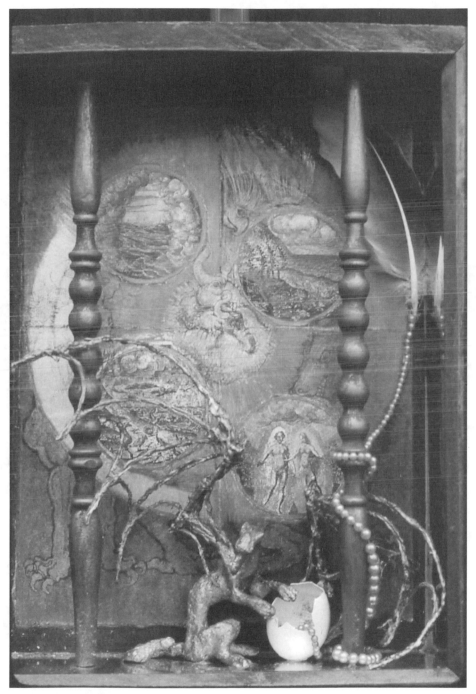

Portal: Alembic I.
Personal shrine of Larsen houshold

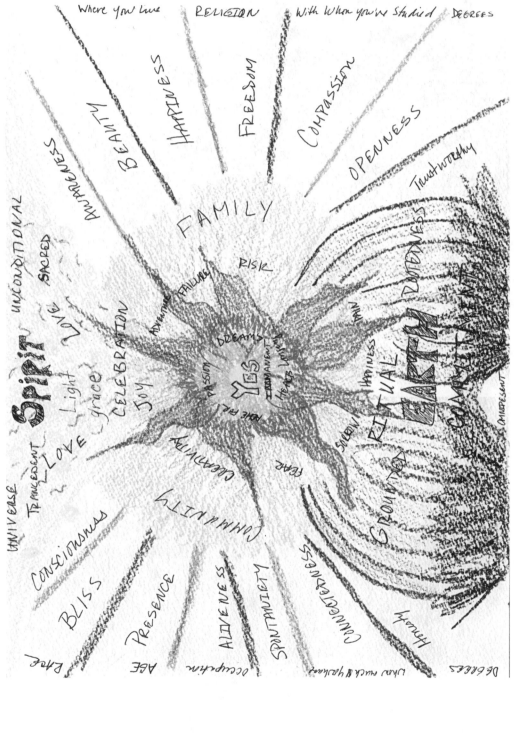

Sarah's image

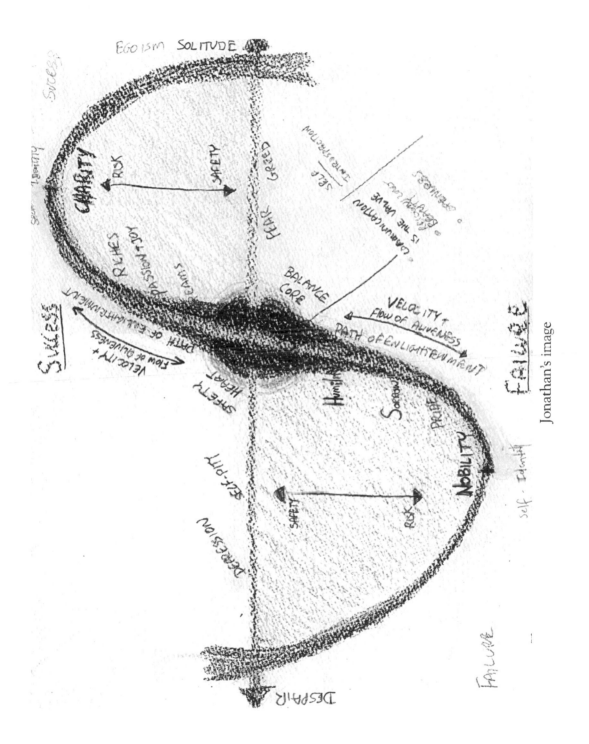

Jonathan's image

NOTES

Introduction

1. Billy Collins, "Questions about Angels," in *Questions about Angels* (Pittsburgh, Penna.: University of Pittsburgh Press, 1991), 25–26.

2. See especially Stephen and Robin Larsen, *A Fire in the Mind: The Life of Joseph Campbell* (New York: Doubleday, 1991); Joseph Campbell, *Baksheesh and Brahman: Indian Journal 1954–1955*, edited by Stephen and Robin Larsen and Antony Van Couveering, in *Collected Works of Joseph Campbell* (New York: HarperCollins, 1995); and Joseph Campbell, *Oriental Mythology*, vol. 2 of *The Masks of God* (New York: The Viking Press, 1962).

3. C. G. Jung and C. Kerényi, *Essays on a Science of Mythology*, translated by R. F. C. Hull, Bollingen Series XX: *The Collected Works of C. G. Jung* (New York: Harper Torchbooks, 1963), 1; also quoted in Stephen Larsen, *The Shaman's Doorway* (New York: Harper and Row; Station Hill Press, 1976), 19.

4. See Campbell's pivotal essay in Joseph Campbell, "The Symbol without Meaning," Eranos-Jahrbuch XXVI (Zurich: Rhein-Verlag, 1958). A greatly amplified version of this paper can be found in section V of *The Flight of the Wild Gander: Explorations in the Mythological Dimension* (New York: The Viking Press, 1951), 120–192.

5. All references to Swedenborg's writings are taken from the redesigned *Standard Edition of the Works of Emanuel Swedenborg*, 2nd edition (West Chester, Penna.: Swedenborg Foundation, 1993–1998), unless otherwise specified. As is customary in Swedenborgian studies, the numbers following titles refer to paragraph or section numbers, which are uniform in all editions, rather than to page numbers.

6. See especially George Dole's "Image of God in a Mirror," Stephen Larsen's "Abyss of Nature," among other articles in Robin Larsen, ed., *Emanuel Swedenborg: A Continuing Vision* (New York: The Swedenborg Foundation, 1988).

Part One: Web of Life

1. Stanislav Grof, *Realms of the Human Unconscious* (Pomona, Calif.: Hunter House Inc. Publishers, 1976).

2. In the novel *Sophie's Choice*, by William Styron, living under the Nazi regime in Poland, the protagonist Sophie is forced to choose between her own two children: who shall live and who shall die. It is a psychological choice for which the actual story is an embodiment. Stephen has noted in his clinical practice over the years that many people have felt this dilemma—the sense that they may have to choose between two people they love. This could be seen as an exquisite torture the mind inflicts on us as if to prepare us for some of the harder choices and pains of life or a sampling of our own loves—which are realer, deeper? Does love bond us to its object in the right or in the wrong way?

3. Erich Neumann's works were first published in Zurich in the 1940s. All of them are now available in English, among them, *The Origins and History of Consciousness*, trans. R. F. C. Hull, Bollingen Series XLII (New York: Pantheon Books, 1954); and *Depth Psychology and a New Ethnic*, trans. Eugene Rolfe (New York: G. P. Putnam's Sons, 1969); and Erich Neumann, *The Great Mother: An Analysis of the Archetype*, trans. Ralph Manheim, Bollingen Series XLVII (Princeton, N.J.: Princeton University Press, 1972).

4. See Alice Miller, *The Drama of the Gifted Child: The Search for the True Self*, trans. Ruth Ward (New York: Basic Books, Inc., Publishers, 1981); and Alice Miller, *For Your Own Good: Hidden Cruelty in Child-Rearing*, trans. Hildegarde Hannum and Hunter Hannum (New York: Farrar, Straus and Giroux, 1985).

Chapter One: The Great Dissociation

1. Marion Woodman, *The Ravaged Bridegroom: Masculinity in Women* (Toronto: Inner City Books, 1990), 17.

2. All quotations from the Bible are taken from *The Holy Bible: New Revised Standard Version* (New York: Oxford University Press, 1977), and will be cited within the text.

3. See Elaine Pagels' excellent book *Adam, Eve and the Serpent* (New York: Random House, 1988); and on the subject of redeeming Eve, see Marion Woodman's

Leaving My Father's House (Boston: Shambhala, 1993).

4. Echoes and variants of this can be found in other African cultures. We will give considerable attention to this concept of the masculine within the woman and the feminine within the man, as it is central to Swedenborg's very subtle psychology of the sexes. Also, the figure of the enigmatic Nommo will appear again, shortly, in our retelling of a Zulu myth. For more African creation stories, see Susan Feldman, *African Myths and Tales* (New York: A Laurel Original, Dell Publishing Co., 1963), 67–69.

5. Max Müller's translation of the *Bri hadaranyaka Upanishad*, quoted in Marie-Louise von Franz, *Patterns of Creativity Mirrored in Creation Myths* (New York: Spring Publications, 1972), 118.

6. From *Primal Myths*, based upon the poetic translation of N. K. Sandar: Barbara C. Sproul, *Primal Myths: Creation Myths Around the World* (San Francisco: Harper SanFrancisco, 1991), 93–94; N. K. Sandar, trans., *Poems of Heaven and Hell from Ancient Mesopotamia* (Baltimore, Md.: Penguin Books, 1971), 73–111. The Babylonian epic of creation known as the *Enuma Elish* was found in the ruins of the royal library at Nineveh. Sproul notes that while the library dates from King Ashurbanipal's reign (668–626 B.C.E.), the epic itself is ascribed to the reign of Hammurabi (ca. 1900 B.C.E.); and some of the deities' names go back to the more ancient Sumerians.

7. Sproul, *Primal Myths*, 95.

8. This description is taken from the summary of the *Enuma Elish* found in the mythological dictionary edited by Maria Leach; the story is well told, in a voice which we feel is appropriate to the material. This is a well-edited volume that provides responsible introductory access to materials not always readily available in English translations from the primary sources. Maria Leach, ed., Jerome Fried, assoc. ed., *Funk & Wagnall's Standard Dictionary of Folklore, Mythology, and Legend* (San Francisco: Harper & Row, 1979), 676. See also the entry on Tiamat, 1112–1113.

9. Leach and Fried, *Dictionary of Folklore*, 677.

10. As we will elaborate later, by "matriarchy," we do not mean a mirror-image of "patriarchy," with women on top and men on the bottom. There is, in fact, no archeological or anthropological evidence that such a society has ever existed. Marija Gimbutas and other scholars of the Neolithic agrarian societies in "Old Europe," the northern and eastern European region, have reconstructed a social order in which women evidently held positions of authority in the political-religious systems; but these scholars describe this as a "balanced" system, with men also being regarded as important. Marija Gimbutas, *The Language of the Goddess*, (New York: Van der Marck Editions, 1988).

11. Sproul, *Primal Myths*, 106; Sandar, *Poems of Heaven and Hell*, 73–111.

12. Leach and Fried, *Dictionary of Folklore*, 677.

13. Gimbutas, *The Language of the Goddess*, xv–xx.

14. Campbell, "Introduction," ibid., iv.

15. In one of the genuine anomalies of modern science, the Dogon of Central Africa seem to have known of the existence of this White Dwarf at least thirty years before there were telescopes capable of seeing it (or really discerning its presence in the wobbling of Sirius, due to its gravitational effects). It was referred to as "the mustard seed," and if a man where to be on it, all his matter would collapse into a cubic centimeter. Later Carl Sagan was to take an interest in the anomaly, and even try to debunk it. See also Marcel Griaule, *Conversations with Ogotemmele: An Introduction to Dogon Religious Ideas*, introduction by Germaine Dieterlen (London: Oxford University Press, 1973).

16. Stephen compiled and edited Credo Mutwa's most recent book, his first to be published in the United States; this was a project of the Archive for Traditional Wisdom, a program of the Center for Symbolic Studies. The archive records, preserves, and assists in the publication (books, audio/videotapes or other media) of the lore of traditional elders, teachers, and healers. Vusumazulu Credo Mutwa is loremaster of the Zulu nation as well as a practicing healer and artist. Vusumazulu Credo Mutwa, *Song of the Stars: The Lore of a Zulu Shaman*, edited by Stephen Larsen, Station

Hill Openings (Barrytown, NY: Barrytown, Ltd., 1996), 129.

17. Mutwa, *Song*, 128.

18. This story was a favorite of Campbell, one we heard him tell on many occasions. It is also recorded in *Myths to Live By* (New York: The Viking Press, 1972), 94.

19. Mutwa, *Song*, 129.

20. Keith Thompson, *Angels and Aliens: UFOs and the Mythic Imagination* (Reading, Mass.: Addison-Wesley, 1991).

21. Ibid., xii.

22. Jane Goodall shows in her thirty years of fieldwork with chimpanzees that they are naturally xenophobic, sometimes to the point of serious aggressiveness, yet able to overcome this in their associations with strange chimpanzees, with other primates such as baboons, and with human beings. Jane Goodall, *Through a Window: My Thirty Years with the Chimpanzees of Gombe* (Boston: Houghton Mifflin Company, 1990).

23. John Mack, *Passport to the Cosmos: Human Transformation and Alien Encounters* (New York: Crown, 1999), 18.

24. Mutwa, *Song*, 171.

25. Ibid., 210.

26. S. Milgram, *Obedience to Authority* (New York: Harper, 1974).

27. Lawrence Kohlberg, *The Psychology of Moral Development*, vol. 2 of *Essays on Moral Development* (San Francisco: Harper and Row, 1984).

28. The work of Jean Piaget is extensive, and all of it can be said in some way to touch upon this crucial area in human development. In this sense, Piaget's psychology is in essence an examination of the developmental details of how we become human. In particular, see *The Origins of Intelligence in Children* (New York: International University Press, 1952); and *The Moral Judgement of the Child*, translated by Marjorie Gabin (New York: Collier, 1962).

29. James Hollis, *The Eden Project: In Search of the Magical Other*, Studies in Jungian Psychology by Jungian Analysts (Toronto: Inner City Books, 1998).

30. Alice Miller, *For Your Own Good*, op. cit.

Chapter Two: The Soul of Human–Animal Relations

1. Edward Field, trans., "Magic Words" in *Magic Words* (New York: Harcourt, Inc., 1998.)

2. John G. Neihardt, *Black Elk Speaks* (Lincoln, Nebraska: University of Nebraska Press, 1961), 25. See also Stephen's discussion of this episode in *The Shaman's Doorway*, pages 103–117.

3. Dr. Samuel B. Ross is founder and director of Green Chimneys Children's Services, Brewster, New York. Horseback-riding programs for youngsters with cerebral palsy and other conditions that limit their physical mobility and ability to play freely have been well established since the early1950s. (The earliest European project, in the Netherlands, was established by a woman athlete who had been stricken with polio, which was virtually epidemic at the time.) A growing body of research and field experience lends credence to the increasing numbers of programs bringing together animals as healers with children, seniors, hospital patients, and teens and adults in residential rehabilitation facilities.

4. Marie-Louise von Franz, *Interpretation of Fairytales: An Introduction to the Psychology of Fairytales*, private limited edition (New York: Spring Publications, 1970); Marie-Louise von Franz, *The Shadow and Evil in Fairytales* (New York: Spring Publications, The Analytical Psychology Club of New York, Inc., 1974); Marie-Louise von Franz, *The Cat: A Tale of Feminine Redemption*, Studies in Jungian Psychology by Jungian Analysts (Toronto: Inner City Books, 1999).This is a posthumous collection of two lectures by von Franz.

5. Von Franz, *Shadow*, 119.

6. Ibid., 119–120.

7. Christopher Bamford and William Parker Marsh, *Celtic Christianity: Ecology and Holiness* (1982; rpt. Edinburgh: Floris Classics, Floris Books, 1991), 19.

8. Ibid.

9. Retold by Joseph Campbell from an Irish manuscript translated from the *Codex Kilkenniensis*. Joseph Campbell, *Occidental Mythology*, in series *The Masks of God* (New York: The Viking Press, 1964), 459.

10. Origen, *Homilies*, in *Leviticum Homiliae*, vol. 2).

11. Eligio Stephen Gallegos, *The Personal Totem Pole: Animal Imagery, the Chakras, and Psychotherapy* (Santa Fe, N.M.: Moon Bear Press, c1985, 1987).

12. Swedenborg's writing on his concepts of "correspondence" and the "universal human" resonate strongly with a shamanic worldview, which Swedenborg himself would possibly have seen as a remnant of his concept of the "Most Ancient Church." However, his was an extremely subtle mind trained to fine discriminations; his ideas are perhaps too easily simplified and misunderstood. With regard to this, we recommend the translations of George Dole as being the most scrupulous and sensitive for the contemporary reader. Two particularly accessible introductory works compiled by Dole are *A Thoughtful Soul* (West Chester, Penna.: Chrysalis Books, 1995), and Emanuel Swedenborg, *The Universal Human and Soul-Body Interaction*, edited and translated by George F. Dole (New York: Paulist Press, 1984).

13. Stephen Larsen, *The Mythic Imagination: Your Quest for Meaning through Personal Mythology* (New York: Bantam Books, 1990).

14. There are many variations and many different stories of the Bear-marriage. See Paul Shepard and Barry Sanders, *The Sacred Paw: The Bear in Nature, Myth, and Literature* (New York: Viking, 1985) for bear-lore from around the world. The "animal bride" or its bridegroom variant is found, literally, worldwide and incorporates many species of animal or bird. Sometimes the shapechangers began as human and ultimately must become fully human again; sometimes they are magical beings from the realm of spirit-animals, who must return to their own place or die in order to return. Of the familiar werewolf kind, one of the most charming is Marie de France's *Le Lai de Bisclavret*, in which the werewolf is a noble baron, possessed of a noble heart; his human wife is the deceiver and betrayer. Marie de France wrote her *Fables* and *Lais* in the latter part of the twelfth century; her work is available in modern French and English. Marie-Louise von Franz's little book, *The Cat: A Tale of Feminine Redemption* (op. cit.), closely examines an animal-bride story and demonstrates valuable principles and techniques for working with these images. Michelle Jamal has collected together many stories of animal/human shapeshifters, including several bear-marriage stories in her evocative and magical book *Deerdancer: The Shapeshifter Archetype in Story and in Trance* (New York: Arkana, Penguin Books, 1995).

15. Alan Herrera, *From the Heart of the World—the Elder Brother's Warning*, video tape recording, documentary, Mystic Fire Direct, 1991

16. Denise Levertov, "Come into Animal Presence," *The Jacob's Ladder* (New York: New Directions Publishing Corp., 1960).

17. Dr. Louis Leakey sent Jane Goodall to Gombe in Tanzania, in 1960, to begin her fieldwork with chimpanzees. Richard Leakey has continued his parents' work, and has made further discoveries of major significance in the study of human evolution. Richard E. Leakey and Roger Lewin, *Origins: What New Discoveries Reveal About the Emergence of Our Species and Its Possible Future* (London: Macdonald and Jane's Publishers, 1977), 10.

18. Ibid., 10.

19. Marija Gimbutas, *Goddesses and Gods of Old Europe, 7000 to 3500 B.C.: Myths, Legends and Cult Images* (Berkeley: University of California Press, 1982).

20. Joseph Campbell notes this especially in his introduction to Gimbutas's *Language of the Goddess*; he also stresses this in the new version of his video lectures put out by the Joseph Campbell Foundation, *Mythos* series, in the lecture on the late neolithic transition from goddess to god orientation. Gimbutas, *Language of the Goddess*, op. cit.

21. One version of this lecture is available from the Joseph Campbell Foundation, in the video on paleolithic beginnings, in the series *Transformations of Myth through Time*.

22. Swedenborg distinguished several layers of ancient "churches"; but through his cousin and friend, the biologist Carolus Linnaeus, he was informed about people like the Sami ("Lapps") of subpolar Scandinavia and others who were still living in shamanic cultures. Fascinated by these people, he asked his young relatives who emigrated to America to send him information about the "Indians," whom he believed must be in more immediate contact with the Divine than Europeans. See the relevant articles in Robin Larsen, ed., *Emanuel Swedenborg: A Continuing Vision* (New York: The Swedenborg Foundation, 1988).

23. Joseph Campbell, *The Way of the Animal*

Powers: Mythologies of the Great Hunt, Historical Atlas of World Mythology, vol. 1 (New York: Perennial Library, Harper & Row Publishers, 1988), 64.

24. Campbell, *Animal Powers*, 2, 60.

25. Ibid., 63.

26. Ibid., 76.

27. The Pawnee chief Letakots-Lesa, in a conversation with Natalie Curtis, *The Indians' Book: An Offering by the American Indians of Indian Lore, Musical and Narrative, to Form a Record of the Songs and Legends of Their Race* (New York: Harper & Brothers, 1907), quoted in Campbell, *Animal Powers*, 2, 25.

28. See Penelope Smith, *Animal Communication*. Dawn Hayman and Bonnie Jones Reynolds of Spring Farm C.A.R.E.S., in Clinton, New York, which is a not-for-profit organization "devoted to the retirement and rehabilitation of abused or unwanted animals, and to the practice and teaching of animal communication," also do a fine job of teaching compassion and responsibility to humans of all ages.

29. Hope Ryden, *America's Last Wild Horses* (New York: Ballantine Books, 1970).

30. Susun Weed is a greenwitch, healer and herbalist, author of numerous books on these subjects and on soul-growth and health in women; among them, see Susun S Weed, *Wise Woman Herbal Healing Wise* (Woodstock, N.Y.: Ash Tree Pub., 1989); and *Menopausal Years: The Wise Woman Way* (Woodstock, N.Y.: Ash Tree Pub., 1992).

31. *As above, so below*: a wisdom utterance frequent to medieval alchemists, based on certain sayings of Hermes Trismegistus, a semimythical wisdom source.

Chapter Three: Divine Affinities and Antipathies

1. Czeslaw Milosz, "On the Other Side," in *The Collected Poems, 1931–1987*, translated by Robert Haas (New York: HarperCollins Publishers, 1988).

2. Wilson Van Dusen, *The Presence of Other Worlds* (1974; reissued New York: The Swedenborg Foundation, 1991).

3. Martín Prechtel, *Secrets of the Talking Jaguar: Memoirs from the Living Heart of a Mayan Village* (New York: Jeremy P. Tarcher/Putnam, 1998).

4. He is called "pseudo" because one so named is said to have been present at the Mars Hill address of St. Paul, which would place him at least five centuries earlier than the writing of his great work. The following distillation of the complex subject of angel hierarchies is derived from some years of interest as mythologists. Among the sources that have been most helpful in this summation are Peter LambornWilson's beautifully illustrated overview of the subject and the research Robin did while illustrating Ravenwolf's book. See Peter Lamborn Wilson, *Angels: Messengers of the Gods* (1980; rpt. London: Thames and Hudson, 1994); and Silver Ravenwolf, *Angels: Companions in Magick*, illustrated by Robin Larsen (St. Paul, Minn.: Llewellyn Publications, 1997).

5. Wilson, *Angels*, op. cit., 331.

6. Ibid., 27.

7. Rainer Maria Rilke, *Duino Elegies*, second elegy, verse 5. All translations of the poetry of Rilke in this book have been done by Stephen Larsen.

8. Ravenwolf, *Angels*, op. cit., 22.

9. Rembrandt has exquisitely illustrated the story of Tobias, with his sensitive image of the angel as the "young man . . . who curiously peeked through the window."

10. Our retelling of Apuleius' tale of Eros and Psyche is based upon the charming and sometimes risqué translation by William Adlington, reprinted from his edition of 1639. We are fortunate to have a well-preserved copy of Bodley Head's elegant limited edition of 1923, noted for its illustrations by Jean de Bosschère. We have tried to retain the flavor of Adlington's Elizabethan language, while somewhat simplifying his archaic spelling. Lucius Apuleius, *The Golden Asse of Lucius Apuleius*, edited and translated by William Adlington, with an introduction by E.B. Osborn, illustrated by Jean de Bosschère (London: John Lane The Bodley Head Limited, 1923 (reprint of edition of 1639), 101–135.

11. Ibid., 106. Does the castle remind you of the one described in *Beauty and the Beast*? Well, Apuleius wrote it first, although who first told the story is a secret hidden in time.

12. Ibid., 108.

13. Ibid., 117–118.

14. Ibid., 129.

15. Ibid., 104.

16. Guiraut de Borneilh (variously, Borneil or Bornelh) was a twelfth-century troubadour, said in his day to have been the "master" of troubadours; he spoke of the "eyes as the scouts of the heart." Joseph Campbell mentions Guiraut in a number of his discussions of courtly love.

17. Ann Belford Ulanov and Barry Ulanov, *The Witch and the Clown* (Wilmette, Ill.: Chiron Publications, 1987).

Part Two: Introduction

1. Carl Gustav Jung and Aniela Jaffé, eds., *C.G. Jung: Word and Image*, Bollingen Series XCVII (Princeton: Princeton University Press, 1979), 198.

2. *Daimon, demon,* and *daemon* are, of course, all the same word; but, since its applications and connotations have varied so greatly over time and among different groups, we are going to assign distinct references for each variant:
   —*daimon* will refer to an elemental being (as of water, air, fire, earth), essentially belonging to the world of nature, without good or evil affiliation;
   —*demon* will be used in the limited sense of the negative or evil spirits who oppose angels, usually in the context of the Judeo-Christian-Islamic traditions;
   —*daemon* will be used when we are speaking of a powerful psychospiritual energy, perhaps equivalent in some sense to an angel, but having an opposite motion or tendency. In the last case, the distinction is more subtle; we may not necessarily be speaking in terms of evil versus good, but of negative and positive vectors in the psyche or in spiritual development.

3. The reference here is to W. B. Yeats' complex system of psychospiritual "tinctures," which underlay much of his poetry, a system set forth in W. B. Yeats, *A Vision* (London: Macmillan, 1969). Yeats continually revised this work; its earliest full publication may have been the Cuala Press edition of 1925. Macmillan published it in 1937; this edition was followed by five revisions, the fifth finalized by Yeats' death.

Chapter Four: Ghosts and Little People

1. *Imaginal* is the more appropriate term here. It was introduced by Henri Corbin to make a distinction between the ordinary sense of imaginary as something "merely imag-ined"—therefore having no "reality"—and those profoundly true experiences of subtle realities, beyond ordinary sensing, accessible through the human imagination. See, among other works of Corbin, the introduction to this concept in Roberts Avens, "The Subtle Realm: Corbin, Sufism, and Swedenborg" in Robin Larsen, ed., *Emanuel Swedenborg: A Continuing Vision* (New York: The Swedenborg Foundation, 1988), 382; and "*Mundus Imaginalis,* or the Imaginary and the Imaginal" in *Swedenborg and Esoteric Islam,* translated by Leonard Fox (West Chester, Penna.: Swedenborg Foundation, 1995), 1–33.

2. Van Dusen, *Presence of Other Worlds,* op. cit.

3. Horrifying statistics tell us that deaths of children by guns have become so common in the United States of the1990s that it may soon surpass the numbers of child deaths in car accidents (in 1997, government figures for children killed by firearms totalled 4,223, mostly in accidents while playing with other children, at home; reported in "The New Age of Anxiety," *Newsweek,* August 23, 1999, p. 39. We have all been aware, for some years, of the escalation in urban violence that takes many young lives. In April of 1999, at Columbine High School in Littleton, Colorado, two seventeen-year-old boys, Eric Harris and Dylan Klebold, killed twelve fellow students, a teacher, and then shot themselves. Since then, it has become all too clear that the problem is not urban but nationwide. While the debate continues on the dangerous accessibility of guns everywhere to everyone in our country, many educators and health-care professionals are also reexamining the issues of alienation and depression in children and adolescents, and strategies for developing stronger, more sensitive support networks.

4. Adventure Game Theater (AGT) is a fantasy role-play game developed by Howard Moody and Brian Allison; the game utilizes skills of character development, theatrical improvisation, and team-building. See the website of the Center for Symbolic Studies (www.mythmind.com), and Adventure Game Theater (www.agt.org). Also see the chapter on adult fantasy role-play and the highly creative group world-building experience originated in 1983 by

Nick and Sue Hogan, Tim Shaw, and Billy Joe Thorpe ("Live Adventure Quest") in Stephen Larsen, *The Mythic Imagination: Your Quest for Meaning through Personal Mythology* (New York: Bantam Books, 1990).

5. In his later writing, Jung preferred the term *objective psyche* to refer to this vast region of the more-than-personal unconscious. For his memoirs, see C. G. Jung, *Memories, Dreams, Reflections*, edited and recorded by Aniela Jaffé, translated by Richard Winston and Clara Winston, reprint, 1961 (New York: Random House, Vintage, 1963).

6. C. G. Jung, *Symbols of Transformation: An Analysis of the Prelude to a Case of Schizophrenia*, 5th ed., translated by R. F. C. Hull, reprint, 1956, Bollingen Series XX: *The Collected Works of C. G. Jung* (Princeton, New Jersey: Princeton University Press, 1967).

7. *Complex* is actually Jung's term; Freud rejected it and was upset when his followers kept using it with his own theory, calling it the "Oedipus complex." In general, *complex* refers to an area of highly emotionally charged contents of the unconscious mind.

8. C. G. Jung, *The Archetypes and the Collective Unconscious*, Bollingen Series XX: *The Collected Works of C. G. Jung* (New York: Pantheon Books, 1959), 25.

9. Ibid., 25.

10. C. G. Jung, "Marriage as a Psychological Relationship," in *The Development of Personality: Papers on Child Psychology, Education, and Related Subjects*, vol. 17, Bollingen Series XX: *The Collected Works of C. G. Jung* (New York: Pantheon Books, 1954 [first published 1925], 188 ff.

11. Some of the finest early work in response to this need was done by M. Esther Harding, Marie-Louise von Franz, Emma Jung, and Irene Chairemont de Castillejo: M. Esther Harding, *Women's Mysteries, Ancient and Modern* (New York: Harper and Row, 1976); M. Esther Harding, *The Way of All Women* (New York: Harper Colophon, 1975); Marie-Louise von Franz, *The Shadow and Evil in Fairytales*, op. cit.; Emma Jung, *Animus and Anima* (New York: Spring Publications, 1969); Irene Claremont de Castillejo, *Knowing Woman: A Feminine Psychology* (New York: Harper & Row, 1973). To learn more about the remarkable women who gathered around Jung, see the carefully researched and discerning book: Maggie Anthony, *Jung's Circle of Women: The Valkyries* (York Beach, Maine: Nicholas-Hays, 1999).

12. Jung, *Archetypes*, 215.

13. de Castillejo, *Knowing Woman*, op. cit.

14. See Ann Belford Ulanov and Barry Ulanov, *Transforming Sexuality: The Archetypal World of Anima and Animus*, C. G. Jung Foundation Book (Boston: Shambhala, 1994), 19; June Singer, *Androgyny: Toward a New Theory of Sexuality* (Garden City, N.Y.: Anchor Books, 1977), 258–326. See also Claire Douglas, *The Woman in the Mirror: Analytical Psychology and the Feminine* (Boston: Sigo Press, 1990).

15. Jung, "Marriage."

16. There is much evidence that, at certain pivotal points in Jewish history, the biblical stories were rewritten to remove all references to the goddess or the feminine element; see, for example, Raphael Patai, *The Hebrew Goddess* (New York: Ktav Publishing House, 1967); and Merlin Stone, *When God Was a Woman* (New York: Harcourt Brace Jovanovich, 1976).

17. Particularly in *Leaving My Father's House*; but all of Woodman's work in some way addresses the issue of the "redemption of Eve," so crucial to our time and arising spontaneously in the dreams of many contemporary women and men. See also the work of Ulanov and Ulanov: Marion Woodman, *Leaving My Father's House*, op. cit.; and Belford Ulanov and Ulanov, *The Witch and the Clown*, op. cit., for example.

18. Woodman, *Leaving*, 195.

19. See Belford Ulanov and Ulanov, *Transforming Sexuality*, op. cit., for details. See also Singer, *Androgyny*, op. cit.

20. Ibid., 18–19.

21. Jerome S. Bruner, *Actual Minds, Possible Worlds* (Cambridge, Mass.: Harvard University Press, 1986).

22. Belford Ulanov and Ulanov, *Transforming*, 19.

23. Marion Woodman does an important examination of the "father's daughter" in our society in several of her books. For example, see *The Ravaged Bridegroom*, op. cit.

24. James Hollis, *The Eden Project*, Studies in Jungian Psychology by Jungian Analysts (Toronto: Inner City Books, 1998).

25. Robert A. Johnson, *We: Understanding the*

Psychology of Romantic Love (Harper San-
Francisco, 1983).

Chapter Five: Soul Mates

1. Guiraut de Borneilh (ca. 1138–1200),
   quoted by Joseph Campbell in his examination of courtly love, Joseph Campbell,
   Creative Mythology (New York: Viking
   Press, 1968), 177.
2. Quoted by Campbell, *Creative Mythology*,
   193.
3. Rilke, *Duino Elegies*, second elegy, verse 2.
4. Ibid., verse 5.
5. Kevin J. Todeschi, *Edgar Cayce on Soul
   Mates: Unlocking the Dynamics of Soul Attraction* (Virginia Beach, Va.: A.R.E. Press,
   1999), xvii.
6. Ibid., 13.
7. Ibid., 18–19.
8. Ibid., 24.
9. Roger J. Woolger, *Other Lives, Other Selves:
   A Jungian Psychotherapist Discovers Past
   Lives*, with a foreword by Ronald W. Jue
   (New York: Doubleday, 1987). Woolger's
   book is the best introduction to past life,
   or as Woolger prefers, "other life" regres-
   sion work. See also Brian L. Weiss,
   Through Time into Healing (New York:
   Simon & Schuster, A Fireside Book,
   1992).
10. Mutwa, *Song of the Stars*, op. cit.
11. Spider Woman, the weaver of the web of
    life for many New World peoples, is also
    echoed by Anansi the Spider in Africa and
    is sister to all the weaving goddesses of the
    ancient Mediterranean world.
12. Shikibu Murasaki (ca. 978–1026) was a
    noble lady and writer in the court of Em-
    press Akiko of Japan. Her *Tale of Genji*
    (*Genji monogatari*) is perhaps Japan's great-
    est literary classic, probably the first full-
    length novel in world literature.
13. Sei Shonagon (966 or 967–1013) was an
    aristocratic diarist who served in the court
    of the Empress Sakado and who has left us
    an account of court life between
    991–1000. Like the work of Lady
    Murasaki, Sei Shonagon's *Pillow-book*
    shows us the highly refined and formalized
    world created by women within the often
    brutal realities of the male hierarchies of
    feudal Japan. She was a skilled observer,
    who recorded the many nuances of diplo-
    matic and social negotiations in the com-
    plex web of both women's and men's
    worlds.
14. Scientists and scholars developed it to slip
    around the skirts of the governmental bu-
    reaucracies that were impeding the free-
    flow of ideas across national boundaries.
15. "Transparent to the transcendent": Karl-
    fried Graf von Durckheim's phrase, often
    quoted by Joseph Campbell. Karlfried Graf
    Von Durckheim, *Hara* (London: Unwin
    Paperbacks, 1977 [originally published
    1962]) .

Chapter Six: The Daemon Lover

1. Anonymous, England and Scotland, per-
   haps Middle Ages or earlier; quoted in
   Robert Bly, ed., *News of the Universe:
   Poems of Twofold Consciousness* (San Fran-
   cisco: Sierra Club Books, 1980), 264–266.
2. See John Welwood, *Love and Awakening*
   (San Francisco: HarperPerennial, 1997).
3. See Woodman, *Ravaged Bridegroom* and
   Leaving My Father's House, op. cit.
4. Jacob Ludwig Carl Grimm and Wilhelm
   Carl Grimm, *The Complete Grimm's Fairy
   Tales*, based on the translation of Margaret
   Hunt, revised and completed by James
   Stern, introduction by Padraic Colum,
   folkloristic commentary by Joseph Campbell, illustrations by Josef Scharl (New
   York: Pantheon Books, a division of Ran-
   dom House, 1944).

   Everyone knows who the Brothers
   Grimm were—but most of us don't know
   much about them. Wilhelm (1786–1859)
   and Jacob (1785–1863) were German
   philologists and folklorists. Jacob was author of *Deutsches Grammatik* (1819–1837),
   considered the foundation of German
   philology, and is known in that field for
   "Grimm's Law." Both were librarians in
   charge of important collections, serving
   under rulers and princes, including a Bona-
   parte. They published their *Kinder- und
   Hausmärchen* in several volumes between
   1812 and 1815.
5. Robin McKinley, *Deerskin* (New York: Ace
   Books, 1995).
6. Swedenborg's term *vastation* is useful in this
   context. Although it more properly describes a purifying or emptying out of the
   soul which occurs in the spirit world (negative elements, qualities, and experiences
   are separated from positive ones), it might
   also be applied to the utter emptiness of

deep despair, that psychic "place" where one hits bottom. There are only two possibilities from that position: to stay stuck and die (and then begin the work of regeneration in the world of spirit) or to start to climb back up into life. In fact, Strindberg uses *vastation* in this latter sense in his work. See the discussion of this by Göran Stockenström, "Strindberg and Swedenborg," in Robin Larsen, editor, *Emanuel Swedenborg: A Continuing Vision* (New York: The Swedenborg Foundation, 1988).

7. See von Franz, *Interpretation of Fairytales* and *Cat*, op. cit.; and Woodman, *Leaving*, op. cit.

8. In the version that Robin McKinley works with, there is more about the dogs: Deerskin—as McKinley calls her—lives, communicates, and sleeps with the dogs while she works in the kitchen.

9 See John Gray, *Men Are from Mars, Women Are from Venus: A Practical Guide for Improving Communication and Getting What You Want in Your Relationships* (New York: HarperCollins Publishers, 1992).

10. In connection with this work of "Persephone," the underworld journey of the feminine or of the contemporary woman, see Jennifer Barker Woolger and Roger J. Woolger, *The Goddess Within: A Guide to the Eternal Myths That Shape Women's Lives* (New York: Fawcett Columbine, 1989).

11. Gottfried von Strassburg, *Tristan*, trans. by A.T. Hatto (with fragments of the *Tristan* of Thomas (Baltimore, Md.: Penguin Books [1960] 1972), prologue, 44.

12. Our retelling of Tristan and Isolt will be drawn from Gottfried von Strassburg's *Tristan*, with reference to Joseph Campbell's discussion of it in lectures that we attended and in *Creative Mythology*, the fourth volume of *The Masks of God* series. Gottfried, whose birth date is not known, lived around the turn of the year 1200. His *Tristan* was fashioned on the earlier work of a Norman French poet known only as Thomas, ca. 1160. Gottfried's lovers were called Tristan and Isolde, sometimes Isôt; Thomas called his Tristran and Ysolt. In other versions, depending upon period and language, we find Drustan, Dristan, Trystan, and the usual English, Tristram; the lady is variously Isolt, Isôt, Iseult, and the familiar Yseult. We have followed Campbell, who uses Tristan and Isolt (and Bran-

gaene, for Isolt's companion, whose name is as variously rendered).

13. Campbell, *Creative Mythology*, 304–307.

14. About this Joseph Campbell says, "So that the same marvelous child who had been carried by storm to Cornwall, now, as a youth, was again borne by the tides" (*Creative Mythology*, 227–228). In regard to being at sea in a coracle, without oars or means of steering, the Tristan story also resembles the much earlier Welsh Taliesin story, where the young boy, Gwion Bach, is abandoned by his sorceress-queen mother, Ceridwen, in a coracle (for forty days or forty years), there to be instructed by three magical species: salmon (masters of sweet and salt), selkie (seal shapeshifters, masters of land and sea, both beast and human), and gray goose (masters of three worlds—earth, sea, sky). Taliesin is the prototypic bard, a tradition into which Tristan falls later.

15. von Strassburg, *Tristan*, 192.

16. Ibid., 201.

17. Brangaene was also, we are told, beautiful; perhaps she bore a cousin's resemblance to Isolt. Gottfried says, "Indeed I would wager my life on it that false coin of such nobility had never been struck since Adam's day, nor had so acceptable a counterfeit ever been laid beside a man" (Ibid., 207).

18. Gottfried does not specify the time, but the earlier *Tristan* of Bēroul, a Norman troubadour, established the tradition of the three-year exile, ending in the fourth. Three years, of course, is a magic time. In the fourth year, the spell is broken or is transformed into something different. We will discuss this further in the following dialogue; also see Johnson, *We*, op. cit.

19. von Strassburg, 296–297.

20. At this point, Gottfried's narrative breaks off, and we turn to other sources, including that of von Strassburg's mentor and source, Thomas of Britain.

21. In the incomplete text of Thomas's *Tristan*, appended to that of Gottfried von Strassburg, *Tristan*, 352.

22. Thomas, in von Strassburg, *Tristan*, 353.

23. Johnson, *We*, op. cit.; and von Franz, *The Cat*, op. cit.

24. Both Johnson and von Franz discuss this in several places, as do Belford-Ulanov, and Woodman.

25. Johnson, *We*, 107.

Part Three: Introduction

1. Woodman, *Bridegroom*, op. cit., 125.
2. John Muir, *John of the Mountains* (personal journals, 1938), 317. From quotations collected by Harold Wood, The Sierra Club website, sierraclub.org.
3. Harry F. Harlow and Margaret K. Harlow, "Learning to Love," *American Scientist* 54 (1966): 244–272; and "Effects of Various Mother–Infant Relationships on Rhesus Monkey Behaviors," in B. M. Foss, ed., *Determinants of Infant Behavior*, vol. 4 (London: Methuen, 1969), 15–36.

Chapter Seven: The Wild Child

1. John Perkins, *Shapeshifting. Shamanic Techniques for Global and Personal Transformation* (Rochester, Vt.: Destiny Books, Inner Traditions International, 1997), 67.
2. Clarissa Pinkola Estes, *Women Who Run with the Wolves: Myths and Stories of the Wild Woman Archetype* (New York: Ballantine Books, 1995).
3. The Narnia stories are comprised of seven, much-loved books "for children," as the title pages state. Aslan is "not tame" because he is God immanent. C. S. Lewis, *The Lion, the Witch, and the Wardrobe* (New York: Collier Books, 1950).
4. Jal ad-Din ar-Rumi (c. 1207–1273), Persian mystic and precursor of the Mawlawiya fraternity of Sufis, or Whirling Dervishes, is considered by many to be Sufism's greatest poet. See the translations of his poems by Coleman Barks and John Moyne, *The Essential Rumi* (San Francisco: HarperSanFrancisco, 1995).
5. For some social scientists, this raises the specter of actual similarities between biological organisms and human beings: sensitive periods in geese being equivalent to maternal bonding in the human infant and the learning of nest building or flight in birds being perhaps equivalent to language learning or other forms of socialization. Proponents who view the analogy as valid include sociobiologists such as Edmund Wilson.
6. See the Goodall material on chimpanzee–human kinship in this chapter, in the section following ("The Shadowside of Wildness"). Dr. Goodall notes that the structure of human and chimpanzee DNA differs by just over one percent—truly, they are our closest relations.
7. Heinz Kohut has published extensively on the formative phases of the sense of self, especially in relation to rage and other strong emotions. See Heinz Kohut, *The Analysis of the Self: A Systematic Approach to the Psychoanalytic Treatment of Narcissistic Personality Disorders*, The Psychoanalytic Study of the Child, no. 4 (New York: International Universities Press, 1971); and Heinz Kohut, *The Restoration of the Self* (New York: International Universities Press, 1977). In addition, Kohut contributed a number of papers to the series *The Search for the Self*, vols. 2 and 3, edited by P. H. Ornstein.
8. Jane Goodall, *Through a Window: My Thirty Years with the Chimpanzees of Gombe* (Boston: Houghton Mifflin Company, 1990).
9. Ibid., 211.
10. Ibid. For a comparative look at the primate mind, see chapters 2 and 18, especially pp. 208–211; for the troubling details of the "war," see chapter 10, and comments on p. 210, chapter 18. Jane Goodall's research project at Gombe Preserve, in Tanzania on the west coast of Africa, has continued since Louis Leaky sponsored her original fieldwork in 1960. Over the years, Goodall's team has continued close-up observation of the wild chimpanzee groups, recording the entire life histories of several generations of numerous individuals. Their work has changed our picture of natural primate society and given us a fuller portrait of our own original mind.
11. Ibid., 215.
12. Alice Miller, *For Your Own Good*, op. cit.
13. See Alice Miler, among others.
14. This is the "Night-song in the Jungle," which old Baloo the Bear teaches Mowgli, along with all the specific, courteous ways to greet the different creatures of the jungle in their own hunting grounds or ranges. The image conveyed is of an elaborate and extensive network of animal cultures with their customs, each in its rightful place in the web of life. Mowgli learns that no beast breaks the "law" of this network—the laws of nature—without severe consequences for all. Humans, of course, are seen as the habitually uncaring because unknowing (not having been properly raised to the law, like any good wolf, deer, or snake) lawbreaker. Animals who become law-

breakers or outlaws, like Shere Khan, the tiger, or the Bandur-log, the monkey folk, do so because they have been corrupted by contact with humans. This view made a profound impression on us when we had these stories read to us as children. When we later encountered the writings of John Muir and some other of the great naturalists, there was a resonance; the ground had been prepared.

15. Carlos Castaneda, *The Teachings of Don Juan: A Yaqui Way of Knowledge* (Berkeley, Calif.: University of California Press, 1968).

16. Joan Halifax, *Shaman: The Wounded Healer* (London: Thames and Hudson, 1988); and Michael J. Harner, *The Way of the Shaman* (San Francisco: Harper & Row, 1990).

17. Sylvia Brinton Perera, *Descent to the Goddess: A Way of Initiation for Women* (Toronto: Inner City Books, 1981); and Edward C. Whitmont, *The Return of the Goddess* (New York: Crossroad, 1982).

18. Robert Bly, *Iron John: A Book about Men* (New York: Addison Wesley, 1990), 14.

19. Swedenborg falls into the shamanic zone, in this regard; see Stephen Larsen, "Swedenborg and the Visionary Tradition," in Robin Larsen, ed. *Emanuel Swedenborg: A Continuing Vision*, 185–206.

20. Natalie Goldberg, *Writing Down the Bones: Freeing the Writer Within* (Boston: Shambala, 1996).

21. Estes, *Women*, 25.

22. See Estes' section on "The Shadow, Magic and the Feminine," 131.

23. N. Lex Hixon, *Mother of the Universe: Visions of the Goddess and Tantric Hymns of Enlightenment* (Wheaton, Ill.: Quest Books, 1994), 1.

24. Ibid., 25.

25. See Larsen, *Mythic Imagination*, op. cit., 132.

26. Woodman, *Ravaged Bridegroom*, op. cit., 124.

27. Whitmont, *Return*, 122.

28. Janellen Harrison, *Prolegomena to the Study of Greek Religion* (New York: Meridian Books, 1922), 285.

29. Raphael Patai, *The Hebrew Goddess* (New York: Ktav Publishing House, 1967), 29.

30. Ibid., 31.

31. Whitmont, *Return*, 134.

32. Estes, *Women*, 26.

33. Belford Ulanov and Ulanov, *The Witch and the Clown*, op. cit.

34. Whitmont, *Return*, 154.

35. Perera, *Descent*, 14.

36. Whitmont, *Return*, 133.

37. Alain Danielou, *Gods of Love and Ecstacy: The Traditions of Shiva and Dionysus*, rpt. 1984 (Rochester, Vt.: Inner Traditions International, 1992).

38. Whitmont, *Return*, 135.

39. The hero knows that a monster/dragon/demon can invade the protective envelope of the hero's self (his shield) through the portals of his own eyes. But, conversely, like Mowgli in *The Jungle Book* or like Max in Maurice Sendak's *Where the Wild Things Are*, and like all children who have read Edgar Rice Burroughs' novels and played Tarzan, the hero can conquer monsters with the skillful use of his focused stare. Is the shield/mirror, here, a kind of pretechnological, gaze-focusing laser?

40. Robin wrote her doctoral dissertation on mandalic imagery in the temple architecture and ritual patterns of dance movements in tantric and shamanic traditions. The *mandala* is a sacred diagram that is at once a map of the cosmos and of the psyche. It is a central form in the religious art of Hindu and Buddhist cultures, but can also be identified everywhere in the arts of agricultural people. While scholars have traditionally ascribed its earliest appearance to the hierarchic, settled societies of the neolithic period, mandalic forms can be recognized in the shamanic art of the earlier hunter-gatherers. Art teachers know that the world of the child is circular; Jungians note that the world of the mind is circular.

41. Miller, *For Your Own Good*, op. cit; Patricia Evans, *The Verbally Abusive Relationship* (Holbrook, Mass.: Adams Media Corporation, 1996; and Deborah Tannen, *You Just Don't Understand: Women and Men in Conversation* (New York: William Morrow and Company, Inc., 1990).

Chapter Eight: The Making of the Wasteland

1. T. S. Eliot, *The Waste Land and Other Poems*, rpt. 1958 (New York: Harcourt, Brace and Company, 1930), 29–30.

2. Abraham H. Maslow was a prolific author whose work spearheaded the Humanistic

Psychology movement. See especially Abraham H. Maslow, *Toward a Psychology of Being* (Rvd. Princeton, N.J.: Van Nostrand, 1968); Abraham H. Maslow, *The Psychology of Science: A Reconnaissance* (New York: Harper & Row, 1966); and a posthumous work, Abraham H. Maslow, *The Farther Reaches of Human Nature* (New York: The Viking Press, 1971).

3. Elaine H. Pagels, *Adam, Eve, and the Serpent*, op. cit.

4. See Pagels, ibid., and *The Gnostic Gospels* (New York: Random House, 1979).

5. Deuteronomy 16: 21–22, cited in Patai, *Hebrew Goddess*, op. cit., 48.

6. Norman Cohn, *Europe's Inner Demons: An Enquiry Inspired by the Great Witch-Hunt* (New York: New American Library, 1975), 103.

7. As quoted in ibid., 105.

8. Margaret Murray was an early president of the Folklore Society, but her work is now controversial. Margaret Alice Murray, *The God of the Witches* (New York: Oxford University Press, 1970).

9. Cohn, op. cit., 117.

10. In fact, as mentioned above, for far too many centuries, "child murder" was the standard accusation levied upon those whose presence was annoying to the church or town authorities. It was the battlecry on more than one occasion when guardsmen or mobs committed bloody mayhem in Europe's Jewish ghettos; it was frequently used to imprison and execute the Gypsies or Romany; it was one of the accusations that justified the torture and execution of the Knights Templar; and, during the religious wars of one of Europe's most acute phases of madness, it was one of the claims that condemned Protestants, Masons, alchemists, early experimental scientists, and miscellaneous intellectuals to the Inquisition's fires.

11. Donna Read, *Women and Spirituality: The Burning Times*, 1989 (first release), video tape recording, documentary, ASIN: 158350026X, produced by The Film Board of Canada, 1999.

12. We have previously mentioned Ann Belford Ulanov and Barry Ulanov's examination of the witch archetype as it appears in folklore from antiquity. In the female psyche, as opposed to the male imagination, this figure represents "masculine" qualities of ambition, assertiveness, rationality, and focused power, which are denied to the woman in male-dominated societies. See *The Witch and the Clown*, op. cit.

13. Quoted in Whitmont, op. cit., 125.

14. Women's suffrage was not instituted in Switzerland until 1971, although the University of Zurich was among the first to accept women as full enfranchised students (1864). Most western European countries granted the vote to women by the 1930s.

15. Henrich Zimmer, *The King and the Corpse: Tales of the Soul's Conquest of Evil*, edited by Joseph Campbell, Bollingen Series XI (Princeton, NJ: Princeton University Press, 1973), 138.

16. Ibid., 138.

17. Ibid., 140.

18. Ibid., 141.

19. Ibid., 140.

20. Ibid., 143.

21. Ibid., 143.

22. Von Franz, *The Shadow and Evil in Fairytales*, op. cit.

23. Thor is the equivalent Norse god; Lugh, the Celtic sun god, bears the all-powerful spear for the people closest to the origin of the Arthurian material. In the Greek pantheon, Zeus and Ares share the required qualities, while Yahweh was a thunder-god in his youth. Indra would be the Hindu equivalent; with his dreadful spear, he slew the dragon of the winds, Vayu. But Babylonian Marduk, of course, is forefather to the lot of them, as he laid waste to the world of Mother Tiamat with his invincible spear.

24. T. S. Eliot, "Two Choruses from 'The Rock,'" *Waste Land*, op. cit., 83, 84.

25. In general, it is a good idea to notice and observe the setting or the context of any dream. See Whitmont's suggestions in this regard in Edward C. Whitmont and Sylvia Brinton Perera, *Dreams: A Portal to the Source* (London Routledge, 1989); and Edward C. Whitmont, *The Alchemy of Healing: Psyche and Soma* (Berkeley, Calif.: North Atlantic Book, Homeopathic Educational Services, 1993).

26. Sam Keen, *Faces of the Enemy: Reflections of the Hostile Imagination* (San Francisco: Harper and Row, Perennial Library, 1986), with accompanying video and study guide.

Chapter Nine: The Redemption of the Wasteland

1. Bill Devall and George Sessions, *Deep Ecology: Living as if Nature Mattered* (Layton, Utah: Peregrine Smith Books, 1985). See the Deep Ecology website also.

2. Swedenborg began keeping his "spiritual diaries" in 1746 and continued them for about twenty years; they are a unique record of the spiritual transformation of a dedicated natural scientist and active diplomat at a crucial moment in the European history of ideas. Swedenborg lived in the time when Europe's intellectuals were engaged in the examination of the relationship of science and religion that would constitute either the "enlightenment" or the "soul loss" of Western civilization (depending on one's position). First published in English in five volumes between 1883–1902, volume one was translated again in 1962: Emanuel Swedenborg, *Spiritual Diary: Records and Notes Made by Emanuel Swedenborg Between 1746 and 1765 from His Experiences in the Spiritual World*, translated by W. H. Acton and A. W. Acton (London: Swedenborg Society, 1962); and volumes two through five have been reprinted, Emanuel Swedenborg, *Spiritual Diary*, translated by G. Bush, J. Smithson, and J. Buss (New York: Swedenborg Foundation, 1978).

3. Emanuel Swedenborg, *The Universal Human and Soul–Body Interaction*, edited and translated by George F. Dole, introduction by Stephen Larsen, with a preface by Robert H. Kirven (New York: Paulist Press, 1984), paragraph 3889.

4. Joseph Campbell, *The Masks of God*, 4 vols. (New York: Viking Press, 1959–1964).

   The four volumes are *Primitive Mythology*, *Oriental Mythology*, *Occidental Mythology*, and *Creative Mythology*.

5. Stone also introduced Campbell to a young American woman, Angela Gregory, a sculptress studying with Antoine Bourdelle, Rodin's most influential student. Campbell's correspondence with Angela Gregory—about art and life—would go on for sixty-five years and compass a mutual friendship with Krishnamurti.

6. Von Franz, *The Cat*, op. cit., 60.

7. Henry Adams, *Mont-Saint-Michel and Chartres*, with an introduction by Ralph Adams Cram (Garden City, New York: Doubleday, Anchor, 1959), 101.

8. Ibid., 100–101.

9. In the recital that follows, we refer often to Joseph Campbell's retelling in many lectures we attended over the years. We draw upon our personal notes, as well as Campbell's taped lectures "The Grail" (1979), "The Medieval Tradition" (1979), "Courtly Love and the Grail" (1981), and "Arthurian Tradition" (1982) (©Joseph Campbell Founation [www.jcf.org.]). We are also relying on our own reading of Wolfram's story in translation, and related stories in Chrétien, the *Mabinogion* (in several translations), and other Arthurian sources. Dialogue in quotations, unless otherwise indicated, is simply a narrative device, using our own paraphasing. For a more complete examination of the Parzival story, see Joseph Campbell, *Creative Mythology*, op. cit., and Wolfram von Eschenbach, *Parzival: A Romance of the Middle Ages*, translated by Helen M. Mustard and Charles E. Passage (New York: Random House and Alfred A. Knopf, Vintage Books, 1961).

10. Such violence was common and even condoned by the social structures of that time. Von Eschenbach, the troubadours and minnesingers, and the ladies great and lesser who presided over the European courts of love were radical in their time for questioning this state of affairs.

11. Campbell, *Creative Mythology*, 455.

12. Whitmont, *Return of the Goddess*, 167. There are several related derivations for the name "Gawain"; Whitmont references the great Roger Sherman Loomis, also Campbell's teacher, as his source in this instance. Roger Sherman Loomis, *Wales and Arthurian Legend* (Cardiff: University of Wales Press, 1956), 35–36, 154. In the Welsh *Mabinogion*, the central story is that of Pryderi or Peredur, the son of Pwyll and the magical lady Rhiannon. She, in turn, is mysteriously both a mortal and a fairy lady, and also the Lady of the Birds and the White Mare—in short, goddess of love and arts, horses, and heroes. It is never explained how Gawain comes to ride upon a fairy steed: Gringuljete is described as white with shining red ears, and sometimes with red mane, tail, and legs. These are fairy markings, also found on the hounds

and horses of the fey lord of Annwn, the under- or otherworld of the Welsh stories.

13. Campbell, *Creative Mythology*, 495; von Eschenback, *Parzival*, book vi, verse 567.

14. "Fishskin" is was a term used for a type of chain mail. However, it may here have an additional sense: Campbell reminds us that both fish and lion are animals belonging to the Goddess.

15. Campbell, *Creative Mythology*, 512.

16. Fierefiz calls upon "Jupiter" because "pagan" and "Muslim" were thought to be the same.

17. Von Eschenbach, *Parzival*, book xvi, verse 795.

18. Campbell, *Creative Mythology*, 562.

19. Ibid., 563.

20. Anfortas's fault is variously described as having been a failure of faith, too much preoccupation with ladies and feats of arms, or an adulterous or in some way improper affair. In the Balin-Balan story, he seems to have been guilty only of failing to curb his nasty brother, Garlon. Wolfram says of Anfortas, "With his adventures the sweet and valiant man won such fame that never in all the lands where chivalry held sway could any one question that his was the greatest of all. *Amor* was his battle cry. But that cry is not quite appropriate for a spirit of humility." And he has Anfortas, after he has been healed and has yielded his crown to Parzival, say that his intention is to return to his first passion, a life of feats of arms! von Eschenbach, *Parzival*, book ix, verse 479.

21. James George Frazer, *The New Golden Bough: A Study in Magic and Religion*, edited by Theodor H. Gaster (New York: Criterion Books, 1959), xv.

22. Stephen Larsen, *Shaman's Doorway*, op. cit., chapter 2, 87.

23. Frazer, *Golden Bough*, 453.

24. In our workshops, we use the version of the Loathly Lady story that follows. This variation is based on several folk versions. Parts in quotations are dialogue we perform in our workshops.

25. Although, as we now know from field studies of primates, including chimpanzees, as well as feral horses, wild dogs, lions, and a number of other species, the females always seem to find a way around the dominant male's monopoly, thereby ensuring genetic diversity. In spite of all the bully-ing, the ladies do sometimes choose. See our discussion of Goodall in previous chapters.

26. Or perhaps more accurately, in an era of "partnership society" or "gylany" (Riane Eisler's useful term) in which women held positions of authority. There is no evidence that there has ever existed a society in which men, by reason of their gender, were subservient. The work of Gimbutas (cited in previous chapters) and others now suggests that full matriarchy may be only another myth born from the patriarchal imagination, with its conditioned suspicion of all things female and feminine, and its tendency to project a patriarchal cast upon whatever it considers, seeing what is not of the patriarchy as being, therefore, structured like it but merely opposite. See the discussion in chapter one. Riane Eisler, *The Chalice and the Blade: Our History, Our Future* (San Francisco: HarperSanFrancisco, 1988).

27. This can be read as a summons to the service of universal human rights—including those of "foreign folk"—in the year 1215! Campbell, *Creative Mythology*, 565.

28. Steinbeck has done a delightful piece of work with this motif in his *Acts of King Arthur*. Sir Marhalt and his Lady are the middle-aged couple on quest; while young Ewain is paired off with the elder, rather sarcastic Lady Lynne. Gawain in this rendition fairs poorly as the self-satisfied professional hero. Sir Ewain apprentices himself to the difficult Lynne because, as he says, he is "the youngest of the three [knights] and not so strong or experienced; therefore let me have the oldest lady. She has seen much and she can best help me when I have need..." John Steinbeck, *The Acts of King Arthur and His Noble Knights* (New York: Ballantine Books, 1976), 166.

29. Johnson, *We*, op. cit., 52–53.

Chapter 10: Angelic Dialogues

1. Woodman, *Ravaged Bridegroom*, op. cit., 16–17.

2. Elizabeth Barrett Browning, *Sonnets from the Portuguese* (London: 1850).

3. This is not unlike the thought of Joachim of Flores (ca.1145–1202), a contemporary of Wolfram von Eschenbach, who said that there were three ages for humankind: the Age of the Father, the Old Testament

Mosaic law and Judaic patriarchy; the Age of the Son, Christianity; and the Age of the Holy Ghost, the "New Age," which he hoped was going to begin in the thirteenth century. One thing you can say about the concept of "The New Age"—it's very old!

4. Joseph Campbell said this in a number of lecture presentations; he also wrote variations on this statement in several books. We quote him here from lectures we attended.

5. See Deborah Tannen, *You Just Don't Understand*, op. cit; and John Gray, *Men Are from Mars*, op. cit.

6. Edward C. Whitmont, "Changing Ethical and Religious Values in This Epoch of Transition," Series of Six Lectures, March 2–April 13 (C. G. Jung Foundation, New York, 1967).

7. See George Dole, "An Image of God in a Mirror," 374–381; and Michael Talbot, "Swedenborg and the Holographic Paradigm," 443–448; and Stephen Larsen's study of Swedenborg's own wrestling with the scientific/spiritual paradox, in "The Soul and the Abyss of Nature," 489–496; in Robin Larsen, editor, *Emanuel Swedenborg: A Continuing Vision* (New York: The Swedenborg Foundation, 1988). Carl Pribram is the author of numerous articles; see in particular Karl Pribram, "The Neurophysiology of Remembering," *Scientific American*, no. 220 (January 1969): 76–78; Karl Pribram, "The Cognitive Revolution and Mind/Brain Issues," *American Psychologist* 5, no. 41 (March 1986): 507–519; Karl Pribram, "Interview," *Psychology Today*, February 1979: 71ff.

8. Whitmont, "Changing . . . Values," 6.

9. Ibid., 6.

10. Ibid., 7

11. Joseph Campbell was not a psychotherapist or a Jungian analyst. Many people who haven't read our biography make that assumption, not knowing that he was a college professor of Comparative Literature, who taught for thirty-eight years at Sarah Lawrence, an avant-garde and very sophisticated women's college. He had read Freud and Jung very closely, as well as a German developmental psychologist, Edouard Spränger.

12. Alex Grey, *Sacred Mirrors: The Visionary Art of Alex Grey*, with essays by Ken Wilbur,

Carlo McCormic, and Alex Grey (Rochester Vt.: Inner Traditions International, 1990).

13. Alex Grey, *The Mission of Art*, with a foreword by Ken Wilbur (Boston, London: Shambhala, 1998).

14. See *Sacred Mirrors*, op. cit.

15. Belford Ulanov and Ulanov, *Transforming Sexuality*, op. cit.

16. Barry Ulanov, "Dead Children, Dead Imaginations," editorial, *Journal of Religion and Health* 37, no. 3 (Fall 1998): 193–194.

17. Alfie Kohn, *The Brighter Side of Human Nature* (New York: Basic Books, 1990); Alfie Kohn, *Punished by Rewards* (Boston, New York: Houghton Mifflin, 1993); Alfie Kohn, *Beyond Discipline* (Alexandria, VA: Association for Supervision and Curriculum Development, 1996).

18. Denise and Christopher are co-authors of a number of books, including the following: Denise Breton and Christopher Largent, *The Soul of Economies: Spiritual Evolution Goes to the Marketplace* (Wilmington, Del.: Idea House Publishing Company, 1991); Denise Breton and Christopher Largent, *The Paradigm Conspiracy: Why Our Systems Violate Our Human Potential and How We Can Change Them* (Center City, Minn.: Hazelden, 1996); Denise Breton and Christopher Largent, *Love, Soul and Freedom: Dancing with Rumi on the Mystic Path* (Center City, Minn.: Hazelden, 1998). *The Mystic Heart of Justice*, a book that they are currently working on together, is scheduled to be published by the Chrysalis Books in 2001.

19. John Bradshaw, *Healing the Shame That Binds You* (Deerfield Beach, Fla.: Health Communications, 1988); Patrick Carnes, *The Betrayal Bond* (Deerfield Beach, Fla.: Health Communications, 1997); John Friel and Linda Friel, *Adult Children* (Deerfield Beach, Fla.: Health Communications, 1988); Anne Wilson Schaef, *Escape from Intimacy* (San Francisco: HarperSanFrancisco, 1989); Dudley Weeks, *The Eight Essential Steps to Conflict Resolution* (New York: Tarcher/Putnam, 1992).

20. Patrick Carnes, *Sexual Anorexia* (Center City, Minn.: Hazelden, 1997).

21. Douglas Stone, Bruce Patton, and Sheila Heen, *Difficult Conversations* (New York: Viking, 1999).

22. Coleman Barks and John Moyne, *The Es-*

sential Rumi (San Francisco: HarperSan-Francisco, 1995).

Epilogue

1. Sam was asked this question about ten years ago at a conference on environmental issues from a transpersonal perspective, at which we were joint presenters, with Thomas Berry and Brian Swimme. See Sam's many provocative and groundbreaking books, among them Sam Keen, *Fire in the Belly: On Being a Man* (New York: Bantam Books, 1991) Sam Keen, *Learning to Fly: Trapeze—Reflections on Fear, Trust, and the Joy of Letting Go* (New York: Broadway Books, 1999).

2. Poem by Robin Larsen © 2000.

Experiential Exercises

1. ©2000, Robin and Stephen Larsen. Please use these only for responsible personal work and work with groups in a workshop setting. If you reproduce the exercises and distribute them in such a setting, you must cite us as authors. Use for publication or any larger distribution or media use is subject to all copyright laws.

2. Stephen and Robin's family totem pole has grown to include the helping animals of our children, also. We have made their masks periodically, and our son carves them in tree trunk sculptures and actual totem poles.

3. Over many years of practice as a psychotherapist, Stephen has developed fair-fighting techniques to help couples. He recounts his impressions from many instances where this tool alone was instrumental in saving the marriage.

> In counseling, couples in mid-life who have wounded each other bitterly in fights face each other in my office with hard and battered glares. I often wonder if I can do anything about so many years of lacerating emotional wounding. I ask them to describe their most recent contretemps to me. As they do so, I hear echoes of families of origin. There are the looked-for dysfunctions: alcoholism, emotional and physical abuse, and other problems. In those atmospheres, separately, each partner had developed patterns of fighting

that were wounding and counterproductive.

> Their arguments are often full of what I call "hitting below the belt"—using name-calling, insults or belittling sarcasm to wound and demolish the other person, exaggerating their defects and making them seem horrible to themselves. In subsequent sessions, I teach them "fair-fighting," and they usually take to it like ducks to water. Their next few arguments are, in fact, almost pleasurable, as they model "I feel" statements and give each other time to respond to each point that is made. The name-calling usually stops.

> This strategy can be so effective that, within three sessions, their major problems are in process of resolution.

4. Robert Lawlor, *Earth Honoring: The New Male Sexuality* (Rochester, Vt.: Inner Traditions International, Ltd., 1989); Boston Women's Health Course Collective, *Our Bodies, Our Selves: A Course by and for Women* (Boston: Boston Women's Health Course Collective, 1971).

5. If you find it helpful, use the helper/journeyer model, and guide each other up the chakra "ladder," as in the "Primordial Partners" exercise, above. With practice, you will be able to do this alone, also.

6. Oil crayons need not be of the more expensive kind you buy in an art store; the "CrayPas" type, by any brand name, is easy to use, has a good assortment of rich colors, and will not smear as easily as chalks or pastels; eventually, the surface will "set up." Clay comes in several types: the familiar water-based ceramic clay is inexpensive, and many people prefer the way it feels. It can be wet and used again; but if you want to preserve your work, it will need to be fired in a kiln. Oil-based modeling clays, such as "Plastilene," will also be familiar from childhood; they do not normally harden and are meant to be re-used. The newer clay-like modeling compounds, such as "Sculpey," can be reworked for varying periods of time; to be kept, your pieces can simply be cooked in an ordinary oven for a few minutes. But many people find these less pleasant in "feel"; they also cost more than the older types. Art and crafts stores carry them all. Experiment!

BIBLIOGRAPHY

Ackerman, Diane. *A Natural History of Love.* New York: Vintage Books, 1995.

Adams, Henry. *Mont-Saint-Michel and Chartres.* Garden City, New York: Doubleday, Anchor, 1959.

Anthony, Maggie. *Jung's Circle of Women: The Valkyries.* York Beach, Maine: Nicholas-Hays, 1999.

Apuleius, Lucius. *The Golden Asse of Lucius Apuleius.* Edited and translated by William Adlington. 1639. Reprint. London: John Lane The Bodley Head Limited, 1923.

Avens, Roberts. *Imaginal Body: Para-Jungian Reflections on Soul, Imagination and Death.* Washington, DC: University Press of America, Inc., 1982.

Bamford, Christopher, and William Parker Marsh. *Celtic Christianity: Ecology and Holiness.* 1982. Edinburgh: Floris Classics, Floris Books, 1991.

Barks, Coleman, and John Moyne. *The Essential Rumi.* San Francisco: HarperSanFrancisco, 1995.

Bell, Ruth, et al. *Changing Bodies, Changing Lives: A Book for Teens on Sex and Relationships.* New York: Vintage Books, 1971.

Bellin, Harvey F., and Darrell Ruhl, comps. and eds. *Blake and Swedenborg: Opposition Is True Friendship.* New York: Swedenborg Foundation, Inc., 1985.

Bly, Robert, editor. *News of the Universe: Poems of Twofold Consciousness.* San Francisco: Sierra Club Books, 1980.

———. *Iron John: A Book about Men.* New York: Addison Wesley, 1990.

Bly, Robert, and Marion Woodman. *The Maiden King: The Reunion of Masculine and Feminine.* New York: Henry Holt and Company, 1998.

Boston Women's Health Course Collective. *Our Bodies, Our Selves: A Course by and for Women.* Boston: Boston Women's Health Course Collective, 1971.

Bradshaw, John. *Bradshaw on the Family.* Deerfield Beach, Fla.: Health Communications, 1988.

———. *Healing the Shame That Binds You.* Deerfield Beach, Fla.: Health Communications, 1988.

Breton, Denise, and Christopher Largent. *The Soul of Economies: Spiritual Evolution Goes to the Marketplace.* Wilmington, Del.: Idea House Publishing Company, 1991.

———. *The Paradigm Conspiracy: Why Our Systems Violate Our Human Potential and How We Can Change Them.* Center City, Minn.: Hazelden, 1996.

———. *Love, Soul and Freedom: Dancing with Rumi on the Mystic Path.* Center City, Minn.: Hazelden, 1998.

Brody, Steve, and Cathy Brody. *Renew Your Marriage at Midlife.* New York: G P. Putnam's Sons, 1999.

Bruner, Jerome S. *Actual Minds, Possible Worlds.* Cambridge, Mass.: Harvard University Press, 1986.

Campbell, Joseph. *The Flight of the Wild Gander: Explorations in the Mythological Dimension.* New York: The Viking Press, Inc., 1951.

———. "The Symbol Without Meaning." *Eranos-Jahrbuch* XXVI. Zurich: Rhein-Verlag, 1958.

———. *Primitive Mythology. The Masks of God,* vol. 1. New York: The Viking Press, 1959.

———. *Oriental Mythology. The Masks of God,* vol. 2. New York: The Viking Press, 1962.

———. *Occidental Mythology. The Masks of God,* vol. 3. New York: The Viking Press, 1964.

———. *Creative Mythology. The Masks of God,* vol. 4. New York: Viking Press, 1968.

———. *Myths to Live By.* New York: The Viking Press, 1972.

———. *The Way of the Animal Powers: Mythologies of the Great Hunt. Historical Atlas of World Mythology,* vol. 1, part 2. New York: Perennial Library, Harper & Row Publishers, 1988.

———. *Baksheesh and Brahman: Indian Journal 1954–1955.* Edited by Stephen and Robin Larsen and Antony Van Couveering. *Collected Works of Joseph Campbell.* New York: HarperCollins, 1995.

Carnes, Patrick. *Out of the Shadows.* Center City, Minn.: Hazelden, 1992.

———. *Sexual Anorexia.* Center City, Minn.: Hazelden, 1997.

———. *The Betrayal Bond.* Deerfield Beach, Fla.: Health Communications, 1997.

Carus Mahdi, Louise; Steven Foster; and Meredith Little. *Betwixt and Between.* La Salle, Ill.: Open Court, 1987.

Castaneda, Carlos. *The Teachings of Don Juan: A Yaqui Way of Knowledge.* Berkeley: University of California Press, 1968.

Collins, Randall, and Scott Coltrane. *The Sociology of Marriage and the Family: Gender, Love and Property*. Nelson Series in Sociology.Chicago: Nelson Hall, 1988.

Daniel, Alma; Timothy Wyllie; and Andrew Ramer. *Ask Your Angels*. New York: Ballantine Books, 1992.

Danielou, Alain. *Gods of Love and Ecstacy: The Traditions of Shiva and Dionysus*. 1984. Rochester, Vt.: Inner Traditions International, 1992.

de Castillejo, Irene Claremont. *Knowing Woman: A Feminine Psychology*. New York: Harper & Row, 1973.

Deldon, Anne McNeely. *Mercury Rising*. Woodstock, Conn.: Spring Publications, Inc., 1996.

de Troyes, Chretien. *Arthurian Romances*. Penguin Books, 1991.

Devall, Bill, and George Sessions. *Deep Ecology: Living as If Nature Mattered*. Layton, Utah: Peregrine Smith Books, 1985.

Dole, George, ed. and trans. *A Thoughtful Soul: Reflections from Swedenborg*. Foreword by Huston Smith. West Chester, Penna.: Chrysalis Books, 1995.

Douglas, Claire. *The Woman in the Mirror: Analytical Psychology and the Feminine*. Boston: Sigo Press, 1990.

Edwards, Lawrence. *The Soul's Journey: Guidance from the Goddess Within*. Putnam Valley, N.Y.: Published by author, 1996.

Eisler, Riane. *The Chalice and the Blade: Our History, Our Future*. San Francisco: HarperSanFrancisco, 1988.

Eliot, T. S. *The Waste Land and Other Poems*. 1930. New York: Harvest Books, Harcourt, Brace and Company, 1958.

Estes, Clarissa Pinkola. *Women Who Run with the Wolves: Myths and Stories of the Wild Woman Archetype*. New York: Ballantine Books, 1995.

Evans, Patricia. *The Verbally Abusive Relationship*. Holbrook, Mass.: Adams Media Corporation, 1996.

Feldman, Susan, ed. *African Myths and Tales*. New York: A Laurel Original, Dell Publishing Co., 1963.

Frazer, Sir James George. *The New Golden Bough: A Study in Magic and Religion*. Abridged and Edited by Theodor H. Gaster. New York: Criterion Books, 1959.

Friel, John, and Linda Friel. *Adult Children*. Deerfield Beach, Fla.: Health Communications, 1988.

Gallegos, Eligio Stephen. *Animals of the Four Windows: Integrating Thinking, Sensing, Feeling and Imagery*. Santa Fe, N.M.: Moon Bear Press, c1991, 1992.

———. *The Personal Totem Pole: Animal Imagery, the Chakras, and Psychotherapy*. Santa Fe, N.M.: Moon Bear Press, c1985, 1987.

Gimbutas, Marija. *Goddesses and Gods of Old Europe, 7000 to 3500 B.C.: Myths, Legends and Cult Images*. Berkeley: University of California Press, 1982.

———. *The Language of the Goddess*. New York: Van der Marck Editions, 1988.

Giovetti, Paola. *Angels: The Role of Celestial Guardians and Beings of Light*. Translated by Toby McCormick. York Beach, Maine: Samuel Weiser, Inc., 1993.

Glick, Robert A., and Steven P. Roose, eds. *Rage, Power, and Aggression. The Role of Affect in Motivation, Development, and Adaptation*. New Haven, Conn.: Yale University Press, 1993.

Goldberg, Natalie. *Writing Down the Bones: Freeing the Writer Within*. Boston: Shambala, 1996.

Goleman, Daniel. *Emotional Intelligence*. New York: Bantam Books, 1995.

Goodall, Jane. *Through a Window: My Thirty Years with the Chimpanzees of Gombe*. Boston: Houghton Mifflin Company, 1990.

Gorski, Terence. *Passages through Recovery*. Center City, Minn.: Hazelden, 1989.

———. *Getting Love Right*. Center City, Minn.: Hazelden, 1993.

Gray, John. *Men Are from Mars Women Are from Venus: A Practical Guide for Improving Communication and Getting What You Want in Your Relationships*. New York: HarperCollins Publishers, 1992.

———. *Mars and Venus on a Date: A Guide for Navigating the 5 Stages of Dating to Create a Loving and Lasting Relationship*. New York: Harper Paperbacks, 1997.

Grey, Alex. *Sacred Mirrors: The Visionary Art of Alex Grey*. With essays by Ken Wilbur, Carlo McCormic, and Alex Grey. Rochester Vt.: Inner Traditions International, 1990.

———. *The Mission of Art*. Foreword by Ken Wilbur. Boston: Shambhala, 1998.

Griaule, Marcel. *Conversations with Ogotemmele: An Introduction to Dogon Religious Ideas*. London: Published for the International African Institute by the Oxford University Press, 1973.

Griffin, Susan. *Woman and Nature: The Roaring inside Her*. San Francisco: Sierra Club Books, 2000.

Grimm, Jacob Ludwig Carl, and Wilhelm Carl Grimm. *The Complete Grimm's Fairy Tales*. Based on the translation of Margaret Hunt. Revised and completed by James Stern. Introduction by Padraic Colum. Folkloristic commentary by Joseph Campbell, illustrations by Josef Scharl. New York: Pantheon Books, 1944.

Grof, Stanislav. *Realms of the Human Unconscious*. Pomona, Calif.: Hunter House Inc. Publishers, 1976.

———. *LSD Psychotherapy*. Pomona, California: Hunter House Inc. Publishers, 1980.

———. *The Cosmic Game: Explorations of the Frontiers of Human Consciousness*. Edited by Richard D. Mann. SUNY Series in Transpersonal and Humanistic Psychology. Albany: State University of New York Press, 1998.

Grof, Stanislav, and Joan Halifax. *The Human Encounter with Death*. Pomona, Calif.: Hunter House Inc. Publishers, 1977.

Grosso, Michael. *The Millennium Myth: Love and Death at the End of Time*. Wheaton Ill.: Quest Books, 1995.

Guggenbuhl-Craig, Adolf. *Marriage Dead or Alive*. Translated by Murray Stein. 1977. Dallas: Spring Publications, 1981.

Halifax, Joan. *Shaman: The Wounded Healer*. London: Thames and Hudson, 1988.

———. *The Fruitful Darkness*. San Francisco: HarperSanFrancisco, 1993.

Hall, Elizabeth; Michael Lamb; and Marion Perlmutter. *Child Psychology Today*. New York: Random House, Inc., 1986.

Harding, M. Esther. *The Way of All Women*. New York: Harper Colophon, 1975.

———. *Women's Mysteries, Ancient and Modern*. New York: Harper and Row, 1976.

Harlow, Harry F., and Margaret K. Harlow. "Learning to Love." *American Scientist* 54 (1966): 244–272.

———. "Effects of Various Mother–Infant Relationships on Rhesus Monkey Behaviors." In *Determinants of Infant Behavior*, vol. 4, edited by B. M. Foss. London: Methuen, 1969.

Harner, Michael J. *The Way of the Shaman*. San Francisco: Harper & Row, 1990.

Harrison, Janellen. *Prolegomena to the Study of Greek Religion*. New York: Meridian Books, 1922.

Hauck, Rex. ed. *Angels: The Mysterious Messengers*. New York: Ballantine Books, 1994.

Hearn, Lafcadio. *Shadowings*. Tokyo: Charles E. Tuttle, Publishers, 1971.

Herrera, Alan. *From the Heart of the World—the Elder Brother's Warning*. Video tape recording, documentary, NTSC format, Color, HiFi Sound. ASIN: 6303504191. Mystic Fire Direct, 1991 (video release date).

Hillman, Anne. *The Dancing Animal Woman: A Celebration of Life*. Norfolk, Conn.: Bramble Books, 1994.

Hillman, James. *Re-Visioning Psychology*. New York: Harper & Row, 1975.

———. *The Dream and the Underworld*. New York: Harper & Row, 1979.

Hixon, Lex. *Mother of the Universe: Visions of the Goddess and Tantric Hymns of Enlightenment*. Wheaton, Ill.: Quest Books, 1994.

Hollis, James. *The Eden Project*. Studies in Jungian Psychology by Jungian Analysts. Toronto: Inner City Books, 1998.

Houston, Jean. *The Search for the Beloved: Journeys in Sacred Psychology*. Los Angeles: Jeremy P. Tarcher, 1987.

———. *The Hero and the Goddess*. New York: Ballantine Books, 1992.

Jamal, Michelle. *Deerdancer: The Shapeshifter Archetype in Story and in Trance*. New York: Arkana, Penguin Books, 1995.

Jastrab, Joseph. *Sacred Manhood: Sacred Earth*. San Francisco: HarperCollins, 1994.

Johnson, Robert A. *She: Understanding the Feminine Psychology*. Harper & Row, 1976.

———. *We: Understanding the Psychology of Romantic Love*. Harper SanFrancisco, 1983.

Jung, C. G. "Marriage as a Psychological Relationship." In *The Development of Personality: Papers on Child Psychology, Education, and Related Subjects*, vol. 17. Bollingen Series XX: *The Collected Works of C. G. Jung*. 1925. New York: Pantheon Books, 1954.

———. *Symbols of Transformation: An Analysis of the Prelude to a Case of Schizophrenia*. 5th ed. Translated by R. F. C. Hull. 1956. Bollingen Series XX: *The Collected Works of C. G. Jung*. Princeton, N. J.: Princeton University Press, 1967.

———. *The Archetypes and the Collective Unconscious*. Bollingen Series XX: *The Collected Works of C. G. Jung*. New York: Pantheon Books, 1959.

———. *The Structure and Dynamics of the Psyche: Including "Synchronicity: An Acausal Connecting Principle."* 92nd ed. Translated by R. F. C. Hull. Bollingen Series XXII: The Collected Works of C. G. Jung. Princeton, N. J.: Princeton University Press, 1960, 1961.

———. *Memories, Dreams, Reflections*. Recorded and edited by Aniela Jaffé, translated by

Richard Winston and Clara Winston. 1961. New York: Random House, Vintage, 1963.

Jung, C. G., and C. Kerényi. *Essays on a Science of Mythology*. Translated by R. F. C. Hull. Bollingen Series XX: *The Collected Works of C. G. Jung*. New York: Harper Torchbooks, 1963.

Jung, Carl Gustav, and Aniela Jaffé, eds. *C.G. Jung: Word and Image*. Bollingen Series XCVII. Princeton, N.J.: Princeton University Press, 1979.

Jung, Emma. *Animus and Anima*. New York: Spring Publications, 1969.

Keen, Sam. *Faces of the Enemy: Reflections of the Hostile Imagination*. San Francisco: Harper and Row, Perennial Library, 1986

———. *Fire in the Belly: On Being a Man*. New York: Bantam Books, 1991.

———. *Learning to Fly: Trapeze—Reflections on Fear, Trust, and the Joy of Letting Go*. New York: Broadway Books, 1999.

Kernberg, Otto F. *Aggression in Personality Disorders and Perversions*. New Haven, Conn.: Yale University Press, 1992.

Klein, Viola. "Women, Status Of." In *Encyclopaedia Britannica, Macropaedia*, vol. 19. 15th ed. Chicago, 1974.

Kohlberg, Lawrence. *The Psychology of Moral Development*. Vol.2 of *Essays on Moral Development*. San Francisco: Harper and Row, 1984.

Kohn, Alfie. *The Brighter Side of Human Nature*. New York: Basic Books, 1990.

———. *Punished by Rewards*. Boston, New York: Houghton Mifflin, 1993.

———. *Beyond Discipline*. Alexandria, Va.: Association for Supervision and Curriculum Development, 1996.

Kohut, Heinz. *The Analysis of the Self: A Systematic Approach to the Psychoanalytic Treatment of Narcissistic Personality Disorders*. The Psychoanalytic Study of the Child, no. 4. New York: International Universities Press, 1971.

———. *The Restoration of the Self*. New York: International Universities Press, 1977.

Lacan, Jacques. *Feminine Sexuality: Jacques Lacan and the École Freudienne*. Edited by Juliet Mitchell and Jacqueline Rose. Translated by Jacqueline Rose. New York: Pantheon Books, 1982.

Larsen, Stephen. *The Mythic Imagination: Your Quest for Meaning through Personal Mythology*. New York: Bantam Books, 1990.

———. *The Shaman's Doorway*. New York: Harper and Row; Station Hill Press, 1976.

Larsen, Robin, ed. *Emanuel Swedenborg: A Continuing Vision*. New York: The Swedenborg Foundation, 1988.

Larsen, Stephen, and Robin Larsen. *A Fire in the Mind: The Life of Joseph Campbell*. New York: Doubleday, 1991.

Lawlor, Robert. *Earth Honoring: The New Male Sexuality*. Rochester, Vt.: Inner Traditions International, Ltd., 1989.

———. *Voices of the First Day: Awakening in the Aboriginal Dreamtime*. Rochester, Vt.: Inner Traditions International, Ltd., 1991.

Leach, Maria, ed., and Jerome Fried, assoc. ed. *Funk & Wagnall's Standard Dictionary of Folklore, Mythology, and Legend*. San Francisco: Harper & Row, 1979.

Leakey, Richard E., and Roger Lewin. *Origins: What New Discoveries Reveal about the Emergence of Our Species and Its Possible Future*. London: Macdonald and Jane's Publishers, 1977.

Levertov, Denise. "Come into Animal Presence." In *The Jacob's Ladder*. New York: New Directions Publishing Corp., 1960.

Lewis, C. S. *The Lion, the Witch, and the Wardrobe*. New York: Collier Books, 1950.

Loomis, Roger Sherman. *Wales and Arthurian Legend*. Cardiff: University of Wales Press, 1956.

Mack, John. *Passport to the Cosmos: Human Transformation and Alien Encounters*. With an introduction by Stephen Larsen. New York: Crown, 1999.

Marashinsky, Amy Sophia, and Hrana Janto, illustrator. *The Goddess Oracle: A Way to Wholeness through the Goddess and Ritual*. Rockport, Mass.: Element Books, Inc., 1997.

Maslow, Abraham H. *Toward a Psychology of Being*. 1962. Rvd. Princeton, N.J.: Van Nostrand, 1968.

———. *The Psychology of Science: A Reconnaissance*. New York: Harper & Row, 1966.

———. *The Farther Reaches of Human Nature*. (Posthumous). An Esalen Book. New York: The Viking Press, 1971.

Massingham, H. J. *The Tree of Life*. London: Chapman & Hall, 1943.

McGuire, William, ed. *The Freud/Jung Letters: The Correspondence between Sigmund Freud and C. G. Jung*. Translated by Ralph Manheim and R. F. C. Hull. Bollingen Series XCIV. Princeton, N.J.: Princeton University Press, 1974.

McKinley, Robin. *Deerskin*. New York: Ace Books, 1995.

Meade, Michael. *Men and the Water of Life*. HarperSanFrancisco, 1993.

Milgram, S. *Obedience to Authority*. New York: Harper, 1974.

Miller, Alice. *The Drama of the Gifted Child: The Search for the True Self*. Translated by Ruth Ward. New York: Basic Books, Inc., Publishers, 1981.

———. *For Your Own Good: Hidden Cruelty in Child-Rearing*. Translated by Hildegarde Hannum and Hunter Hannum. New York: Farrar, Straus and Giroux, 1985.

Milosz, Czeslaw. *The Collected Poems, 1931–1987*. Translated by Robert Haas. HarperCollins Publishers, 1988.

Monick, Eugene. *Phallos: Sacred Image of the Masculine*. Studies in Jungian Psychology by Jungian. Toronto: Inner City Books, 1987.

Montgomery, Pam. *Partner Earth*. Rochester, Vt.: Destiny Books, 1997.

Murdock, Maureen. *The Heroine's Journey*. Boston: Shambhala, 1990.

Murray, Margaret Alice. *The God of the Witches*. New York: Oxford University Press, 1970.

Mutwa, Vusumazulu Credo. *Song of the Stars: The Lore of a Zulu Shaman*. Edited by Stephen Larsen. Station Hill Openings. Barrytown, N.Y.: Barrytown, Ltd., 1996.

Neihardt, John G. *Black Elk Speaks*. Lincoln, Nebr.: University of Nebraska Press, 1961.

Neumann, Erich. *The Origins and History of Consciousness*. Foreword by C. G. Jung. Translated by R. F. C. Hull. Bollingen Series XLII. New York: Pantheon Books, 1954.

———. *Depth Psychology and a New Ethic*. Translated by Eugene Rolfe. New York: G. P. Putnam's Sons, 1969.

———. *The Great Mother: An Analysis of the Archetype*. Foreword by C. G. Jung. Translated by Ralph Manheim. Bollingen Series XLVII. Princeton: Princeton University Press, 1972.

Ovid. *Metamorphoses*. Berkeley: University of California Press, 1954.

Pagels, Elaine H. *Adam, Eve and the Serpent*. New York: Random House, 1988.

———. *The Gnostic Gospels*. New York: Random House, 1979.

Patai, Raphael. *The Hebrew Goddess*. New York: Ktav Publishing House, 1967.

Perera, Sylvia Brinton. *Descent to the Goddess: A Way of Initiation for Women*. Studies in Jungian Psychology by Jungian Analysts. Toronto: Inner City Books, 1981.

Perkins, John. *Shapeshifting: Shamanic Techniques for Global and Personal Transformation*. Rochester, Vt.: Destiny Books, Inner Traditions International, 1997.

Petrak, Joyce. *Angels: Guides and Other Spirits*. N.p.: Curry-Peterson Press, 1996.

Piaget, Jean. *The Psychology of Intelligence*. Translated by Malcolm Piercy and D. E. Berlyne. London: Routledge and Kegan Paul, 1950.

———. *The Origins of Intelligence in Children*. New York: International University Press, 1952.

———. *The Moral Judgment of the Child*. Translated by Marjorie Gabin. New York: Collier, 1962.

Piaget, Jean, and Bärbel Inhelder. *The Psychology of the Child*. Translated by Helen Weaver. New York: Basic, 1969.

Prechtel, Martin. *Secrets of the Talking Jaguar: Memoirs from the Living Heart of a Mayan Village*. New York: Jeremy P. Tarcher/Putnam, 1998.

Pribram, Karl. "The Neurophysiology of Remembering." *Scientific American*, no. 220 (January 1969): 76–78.

———. "Interview." *Psychology Today*, February 1979, 71ff.

———. "The Cognitive Revolution and Mind/Brain Issues." *American Psychologist* 5, no. 41 (March 1986): 507–519. *The Quest of the Holy Grail: La Queste del Saint Graal*. Translated by William Wistar Comfort. London: J. M. Dent and Sons, Ltd., 1926.

Raine, Kathleen. *Collected Poems, 1935–1980: Kathleen Raine*. London, Boston: Allen & Unwin, 1981.

Ravenwolf, Silver. Angels: *Companions in Magick*. Illustrated by Robin Larsen. St. Paul, Minn.: Llewellyn Publications, 1997.

Read, Donna. *Women and Spirituality: The Burning Times*. 1989 (first release), video tape recording, documentary, NTSC format, Color, ASIN: 158350026X. Produced by The Film Board of Canada, 1999.

Rilke, Rainer Maria. *Duino Elegies*. Translated by Stephen Mitchell. Shambhala Pocket Classics. Boston: Shambhala Publications, Inc., 1992.

Rountree, Cathleen. *The Heart of Marriage*. New York: Harper SanFrancisco, 1996.

Rowan, John. *The Horned God*. London and New York: Routledge & Kegan Paul, 1987.

Ryden, Hope. *America's Last Wild Horses*. New York: Ballantine Books, 1970.

Sandar, N. K., trans. *Poems of Heaven and Hell from Ancient Mesopotamia*. Baltimore, Md.: Penguin Books, 1971.

Sardello, Robert. *Love and the Soul: Creating a Future for Earth.* New York: HarperPerennial, 1995.

Schaef, Anne Wilson. *Escape from Intimacy.* San Francisco: HarperSanFrancisco, 1989.

———. *When Society Becomes an Addict.* San Francisco: HarperSanFrancisco, 1989.

Schwartz-Salant, Nathan. *The Mystery of Human Relationship.* New York: Routledge, 1998.

Shepard, Paul, and Barry Sanders. *The Sacred Paw: The Bear in Nature, Myth, and Literature.* New York: Viking, 1985.

Singer, June. *Androgyny: Toward a New Theory of Sexuality.* Garden City, N. Y.: Anchor Books, 1977.

Smith, Robert C. *The Wounded Jung: Effects of Jung's Relationships on His Life and Work.* Evanston, Ill.: Northwestern University Press, 1996.

Sproul, Barbara C. *Primal Myths: Creation Myths around the World.* San Francisco: HarperSanFrancisco, 1991.

Steinbeck, John. *The Acts of King Arthur and His Noble Knights.* New York: Ballantine Books, 1976.

Steinem, Gloria. *Moving beyond Words.* Simon & Schuster, 1994.

Stone, Douglas; Bruce Patton; and Sheila Heen. *Difficult Conversations.* New York: Viking, 1999.

Stone, Merlin. *When God Was a Woman.* New York: Harcourt Brace Jovanovich, 1976.

———. *Ancient Mirrors of Womanhood.* Boston: Beacon Press, 1984.

Swedenborg, Emanuel. *Arcana Coelestia: The Heavenly Arcana Unfolded.* 12 vols. 2nd ed. Translated by John F. Potts. West Chester, Penna.: The Swedenborg Foundation, 1995–1998.

———. *Conjugial Love.* 2nd ed. Translated by Samuel S. Warren, revised by Louis Tafel. West Chester, Penna.: The Swedenborg Foundation, 1998.

———. *Heaven and Hell.* Translated by George F. Dole. New York: Swedenborg Foundation, 1979.

———. *Heaven and Hell.* 2nd ed. Translated by John C. Ager. West Chester, Penna.: The Swedenborg Foundation, 1995

———. *Love in Marriage.* Translated by David F. Gladish. New York: Swedenborg Foundation, Inc., 1992.

———. *Spiritual Diary.* Translated by G. Bush, J. Smithson, and J. Buss. 1883–1902; rpt. New York: Swedenborg Foundation, 1978.

———. *Spiritual Diary: Records and Notes Made by Emanuel Swedenborg between 1746 and 1765 from His Experiences in the Spiritual World.* Translated by W. H. Acton and A. W. Acton. London: Swedenborg Society, 1962.

———. *The Universal Human and Soul-Body Interaction.* Edited and translated by George F. Dole. New York: Paulist Press, 1984.

Tannen, Deborah. *You Just Don't Understand: Women and Men in Conversation.* New York: William Morrow and Company, Inc., 1990.

Thompson, Keith. *Angels and Aliens: UFOs and the Mythic Imagination.* Reading, Mass.: Addison-Wesley, 1991.

Todeschi, Kevin J. *Edgar Cayce on Soul Mates: Unlocking the Dynamics of Soul Attraction.* Virginia Beach, Va.: A.R.E. Press, 1999.

Twerski, Abraham. *Addictive Thinking.* Center City, Minn.: Hazelden, 1997

Ulanov, Ann Belford. *The Feminine.* Evanston, Ill.: Northwestern University Press, 1971.

Ulanov, Ann Belford, and Barry Ulanov. *The Witch and the Clown.* Wilmette, Ill.: Chiron Publications, 1987.

———. *Transforming Sexuality: The Archetypal World of Anima and Animus.* A C. G. Jung Foundation Book. Boston: Shambhala, 1994.

Ulanov, Barry. "Dead Children, Dead Imaginations." Editorial. *Journal of Religion and Health* 37, no. 3 (Fall 1988).

Van Dusen, Wilson. *The Presence of Other Worlds: The Psychological/Spiritual Findings of Emanuel Swedenborg.* 1974. New York: Swedenborg Foundation, Inc., 1991.

———. *A Guide to the Enjoyment of Swedenborg.* New York: The Swedenborg Foundation, 1984.

Veltri, Raylene. *A Garden of Woman's Wisdom: A Secret Haven for Renewal.* San Francisco: Halo Books, 1995.

Von Durckheim, Karlfried Graf. *Hara.* 1962. London: Unwin Paperbacks, 1977.

von Eschenbach, Wolfram. *Parzival: A Romance of the Middle Ages.* Translated by Helen M. Mustard and Charles E. Passage. New York: Random House and Alfred A. Knopf, Vintage Books, 1961.

Von Franz, Marie-Louise. *Interpretation of Fairytales: An Introduction to the Psychology of Fairytales.* New York: Spring Publications, 1970.

———. *Patterns of Creativity Mirrored in Creation Myths.* New York: Spring Publications, 1972.

———. *The Shadow and Evil in Fairytales.* New

York: Spring Publications, 1974.

———. *The Cat: A Tale of Feminine Redemption.* Studies in Jungian Psychology by Jungian Analysts. Toronto: Inner City Books, 1999.

von Strassburg, Gottfried. *Tristan,* with surviving fragment of the *Tristan* of Thomas. Translated by Arthus Thomas Hatto. Harmondsworth, Middlesex, England: The Penguin Classics, Penguin Books, 1972.

Weed, Susun S. *Wise Woman Herbal Healing Wise.* Woodstock, N.Y.: Ash Tree Pub., 1989.

———. *Menopausal Years: The Wise Woman Way.* Woodstock, N.Y.: Ash Tree Pub., 1992.

Weeks, Dudley. *The Eight Essential Steps to Conflict Resolution.* New York: Tarcher/Putnam, 1992.

Weiss, Brian L. *Through Time into Healing.* New York: Simon & Schuster, A Fireside Book, 1992.

Welwood, John. *Love and Awakening.* San Francisco: HarperPerennial, 1997.

Whitmont, Edward C. "Changing Ethical and Religious Values in This Epoch of Transition." Series of Six Lectures, March 2–April 13. C. G. Jung Foundation, New York, 1967.

———. *The Symbolic Quest: Basic Concepts of Analytical Psychology.* New York: G. P. Putnam's Sons, for the C.. G. Jung Foundation for Analytical Psychology, 1969.

———. *The Return of the Goddess.* New York: Crossroad, 1982.

———. *The Alchemy of Healing: Psyche and Soma.* Berkeley, Calif.: North Atlantic Books, Homeopathic Educational Services, 1993.

Whitmont, Edward C., and Sylvia Brinton Perera. *Dreams: A Portal to the Source.* London: Routledge, 1989.

Whone, Herbert. *Church, Monastery, Cathedral: A Guide to the Symbolism of the Christian Tradition.* Compton Russell Element. The Old Brewery, Tisbury, Wiltshire: Compton Russell Ltd., 1977.

Wilber, Ken. *The Marriage of Sense and Soul.* New York: Random House, 1998.

Wilson, Peter Lamborn. *Angels: Messengers of the Gods.* 1980. London: Thames and Hudson, 1994.

Wilson, Peter Lamborn, Jill Purce, picture editor. *Angels.* London; New York: Thames and Hudson Ltd.; Pantheon Books, 1980.

Wolkstein, Diane. *The First Love Stories.* Harper-Perennial, 1992.

Woodman, Marion. *The Pregnant Virgin.* Toronto: Inner City Books, 1985.

———. *The Ravaged Bridegroom: Masculinity in Women.* Toronto: Inner City Books, 1990.

———. *Leaving My Father's House.* Boston: Shambhala, 1993.

Woolger, Jennifer Barker, and Roger J. Woolger. *The Goddess Within: A Guide to the Eternal Myths That Shape Women's Lives.* New York: Fawcett Columbine, 1989.

Woolger, Roger J. *Other Lives, Other Selves: A Jungian Psychotherapist Discovers Past Lives.* New York: Doubleday, 1987.

Yeats, W. B. *Essays and Introductions.* New York: The Macmillan Co., 1961.

———. *A Vision.* 1925 first ed., revised edition 1937. London: Macmillan, 1969.

———. *The Variorum Edition of the Poems of W. B. Yeats.* Edited by Peter Allt and Russel K. Alspack. 3rd printing. New York: Macmillan, 1966.

Zimmer, Heinrich. *The King and the Corpse: Tales of the Soul's Conquest of Evil.* Edited by Joseph Campbell. Bollingen Series XI. Princeton, N.J.: Princeton University Press, 1973.

INDEX